Time Out
Tokyo 東京

Penguin Books

PENGUIN BOOKS

Published by the Penguin Group
Penguin Books Ltd, 27 Wrights Lane, London W8 5TZ, England
Penguin Putnam Inc., 375 Hudson Street, New York, New York 10014, USA
Penguin Books Australia Ltd, Ringwood, Victoria, Australia
Penguin Books Canada Ltd, 10 Alcorn Avenue, Toronto, Ontario, Canada M4V 3B2
Penguin Books (NZ) Ltd, 182-190 Wairau Road, Auckland, New Zealand

Penguin Books Ltd, Registered offices: Harmondsworth, Middlesex, England

First published 1999
10 9 8 7 6 5 4 3 2 1

Copyright © Time Out Group Ltd, 1999
All rights reserved

Colour reprographics by Precise Litho, 34–35 Great Sutton Street, London EC1
Printed and bound by William Clowes Ltd, Beccles, Suffolk NR34 9QE

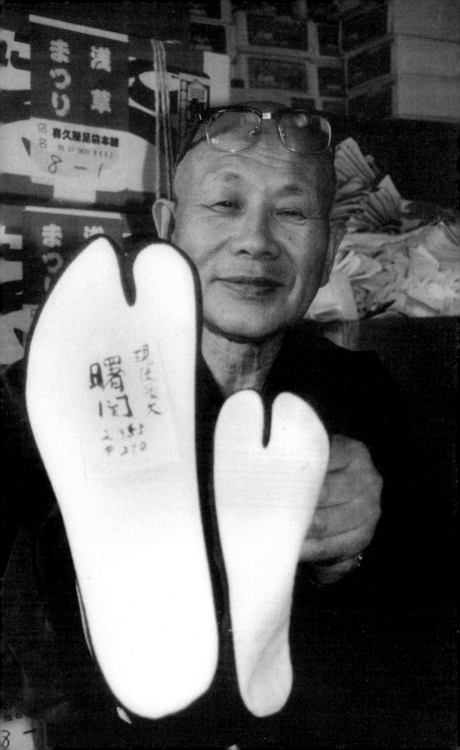

Edited and designed by

Time Out Guides Limited
Universal House
251 Tottenham Court Road
London W1P 0AB
Tel + 44 (0)171 813 3000
Fax + 44 (0)171 813 6001
Email guides@timeout.com
www.timeout.com

Editorial

Editorial Director Peter Fiennes
Editor Nigel Kendall
Deputy Editor Nicholas Royle
Copy Editor Rhonda Carrier
Researcher Amano Jun
Proofreader Tamsin Shelton
Indexer Cathy Heath

Design

Art Director John Oakey
Art Editor Mandy Martin
Senior Designer Scott Moore
Designers Benjamin de Lotz, Lucy Grant,
Thomas Ludewig
Picture Editor Kerri Miles
Deputy Picture Editor Olivia Duncan-jones
Picture Researcher Kit Burnet
Scanning & Imaging Chris Quinn

Advertising

Group Advertisement Director Lesley Gill
Sales Director Mark Phillips
International Sales Manager Mary L Rega
Advertisement Sales (Tokyo) Shinjo Takako
Advertising Assistant Ingrid Sigerson

Administration

Publisher Tony Elliott
Managing Director Mike Hardwick
Financial Director Kevin Ellis
Marketing Director Gillian Auld
General Manager Nichola Coulthard
Production Manager Mark Lamond
Accountant Bridget Carter

Features in this guide were written and researched by:

Introduction Nigel Kendall. **Tokyo by Season** Tom Carroll. **History** Tom Carroll. **Tokyo Today** Clive Victor France.
Architecture Tom Carroll. **Ikebukuro, Shinjuku, Marunouchi, Ueno Park** François Trahan. **Roppongi** Tom Boatman.
Shibuya, Harajuku Yishane Lee. **Ginza** Jin Fumiko. **Ochanomizu** Nigel Kendall. **Sightseeing** Nigel Kendall, Jordanna
Potter, François Trahan. **Tokyo Walks** François Trahan. **Museums & Galleries** Yishane Lee. **Accommodation** Nigel
Kendall. **Restaurants** Aeve Baldwin (Menu Reader Hosoe Masami). **Bars** Aeve Baldwin, Tom Boatman, Nigel
Kendall, François Trahan. **Coffee Shops** Tom Carroll. **Shops & Services** John Paul Catton. **Business** Neil Buckton.
Children Jordanna Potter. **Dance** Shakti. **Film** Nigel Kendall, Sonobé Yuka, (On Location Matt Wilce). **Gay &
Lesbian** Tom Boatman. **Media** Nigel Kendall. **Music** Steve McClure. **Nightlife** Amano Jun. **Sport** Tom Carroll.
Theatre Jean Wilson. **Yokohama** Neil Buckton. **Kamakura, Mountains, Beaches, Nikko** François Trahan. **Directory**
Bella Katz, Sasha Smith, Amano Jun, Nigel Kendall. **Getting by in Japanese** Hosoe Masami.

The Editor would like to thank the following:

Frank Baldwin, Janice Baldwin, Aeve Baldwin, Sonobé Yuka, Hosoe Masami, Amano Jun, Egashira Fumiyo,
Nakano Miwako, Rhonda Carrier, Nibayashi Maki, François Trahan, Mark Devlin, Mary Devlin, Ito Daisuke, Jeff
Gatov, Steve Walsh, Anji Harkness.

Maps MMGraphics/© Time Out Group Ltd

Photography by Jon Denton except: pages 6, 237 Japan National Tourist Organisation; page 9 Japan Information
and Cultural Centre; page 12 Tokyo Metropolitan Museum of Photography and Japan Local Government Centre,
London; pages 41, 85, 86, 224 Tokyo Metropolitan Government and Japan Local Government Centre, London;
page 83 Clive Victor France; page 197 Youichi Kukuminato; page 199 New World Pictures; page 226 Yokohama
Convention & Visitors Bureau.
The following photographs were supplied by the featured establishments: pages 111, 115, 192.

Contents

About the Guide

This first edition of the *Time Out Tokyo Guide* has been written and researched by a team of Tokyo-based writers. It is one in a fast-expanding series of city guides that includes Paris, London, Berlin, New York, Madrid, Budapest, Sydney and Venice.

USING THE GUIDE

The *Time Out Tokyo Guide* is structured a little differently to other books in the series. As well as listing all the usual sights and places of interest, our Tokyo by Area section (*page 32*), gives something of the flavour of the various mini-cities that make up this metropolis. It also provides additional local suggestions and recommendations.

CHECKED & CORRECT

As far as possible, all the information in this guide was checked and correct at the time of writing. However, Tokyo is a fast-changing city, and establishments, particularly small bars, clubs and restaurants, come and go with a bewildering rapidity. It's always best to phone before visiting.

PRICES

The prices given should be used as guidelines. Inflation in Japan is so low that prices (particularly in shops) tend to go down, rather than up. If prices are significantly greater than those we have quoted, try to ask if there's a good reason. If not, go elsewhere and then let us know. We try to give the best and most up-to-date advice, so we always want to hear if you've been overcharged or badly treated.

CREDIT CARDS

Japan is still a cash-based society. Although the use of credit cards is on the rise, many smaller shops and restaurants still do not accept them. Throughout the guide, the following abbreviations have been used for credit cards: **AmEx** American Express; **DC** Diners' Club; **JCB** Japanese credit card; **MC** Mastercard; **V** Visa/Barclaycard.

PUBLIC TRANSPORT

Every entry in the guidebook contains the name of the nearest train or subway station. On the rare occasions when there is no station, we also give the numbers of connecting buses. For a full explanation of how public transport works in Tokyo, *see page 244*. For the subway map, *see page 270*.

ADDRESSES & MAPS

The complex system of addresses in Tokyo is explained on page 248. If you are set on exploring the city yourself, then a detailed map is an essential purchase (*see* **Further Reading**, *page 258*). Because finding your way around can be difficult, we have included a series of area maps, with relevant entries cross-referenced and clearly marked.

LANGUAGE

Reading, rather than speaking, is the main barrier for foreigners in Japan. To help alleviate the stress, our Restaurants chapter includes a basic menu reader (*page 150*), and our Language chapter (*page 254*) reproduces many of the signs you are likely to encounter, as well as a selection of useful phrases.

RIGHT TO REPLY

In all cases the information we give is impartial. No organisation or enterprise has been included in this guide because its owner or manager has advertised in our publications. We hope you enjoy the *Time Out Tokyo Guide*, but if you disagree with any of our reviews, let us know. Your comments on places you have visited are always welcome and will be taken into account when compiling future editions of the guide. For this purpose, you will find a reader's reply card at the back of the book.

There is an online version of this guide, as well as weekly events listings for several international cities, at
http://www.timeout.com

Introduction

There are two hoary old clichés that appear time and again in books about Tokyo. One is that it's the ultimate city for the twenty-first century; the second is that it's essentially a city of ancient, close-knit village communities. The fact that both are equally true gives you some idea of the split personality of the place; this is a city of contradictions that can fascinate and infuriate, but that give it an energy and drive unlike any city in the west.

It can also make Tokyo a confusing, and even frightening, place for the unprepared first-time visitor. It's not an uncommon reaction for otherwise independent people to arrive here, find that they can't read any of the signs, and be too scared to leave their hotel for fear of getting lost. While it's true that Tokyo can be an assault on the senses, there's nothing to fear. Locals don't expect you to be able to speak or read their language and will always make concessions. Don't be shy about asking directions, or putting your nose around the door of an interesting-looking place.

The guide has been structured to make this vast city easier to understand, but straying off the beaten track can produce unexpected results. The lack of no-go areas, the super-efficient public transport system and the high level of personal safety mean that this is a great city to get lost in. Don't worry about the size of the place, or about not knowing where you are. The areas we have highlighted are just a starting point. Follow our recommendations, but take the time to wander around and breathe in the different atmospheres of the city.

Many western writers have written learned tomes trying to reconcile the contradictions of Tokyo, a city of neon lights, massage parlours and love hotels, where politeness, tradition and formality are still much in evidence. The best way to enjoy the city is to accept its contradictions and revel in them. Even in the centre, where new buildings soar all around, it is not unusual to find tiny shops where people make a living from selling nothing but rice crackers next door to a bank or tower block 100 times its size. It can be confusing, difficult to make sense of. So don't try. More than any western city, Tokyo is what you make it. If you hanker for peace and tranquillity, there are scores of beautiful historic gardens and temples; if you want to hurl yourself into the late-night action, the city provides more places to eat, drink and make merry than one person can visit in five lifetimes.

For all its many attractions, it would be a lie to say that Tokyo is an attractive city. In fact, it is

possibly one of the ugliest cities in the world, without the grand vistas of Paris, London or Budapest. Tokyo is unashamedly chaotic, with buildings thrown up seemingly overnight. Appreciation of an individual building or pocket of beauty often requires a certain mental filtering out of its context. Underlying this chaos is a feeling of impermanence. Here, nothing lasts for ever. The city has been destroyed and rebuilt twice this century and is constantly renewing itself – rare is the building that lasts more than 20 years. Nostalgia or sentiment play no part in this constant reconstruction, and much-loved local monuments are swept away with a vigour unimaginable in the west. Unlike London, which draws heavily on its past for its appeal, Tokyo is constantly looking forward.

Although its global importance as a centre of trade and finance is now well established, Tokyo is often under-appreciated as a major capital for culture and the arts. Yet large museums here are among the best in the world, while the sheer number and variety of smaller museums and galleries put most other cities in the shade. For culture, Tokyo is a centre of excellence. The second biggest market for recorded music in the world, Japan is often a higher priority for touring stars than Europe.

But it is the people who live there who make Tokyo a great place to be. Despite the popular image of crowds and constant rushing, Tokyo-ites have a strong curiosity about visitors, a deep pride in their city and love the gentle art of conversation. Visitors are still a relative novelty, and residents are always keen that people should make the most of their extraordinary home. Sit alone in a restaurant or bar anywhere in this city and you won't have to wait long before someone strikes up a conversation. In a city that's often accused of being dehumanised and impersonal, the people have a warmth and generosity that should be the envy of every other major city. *Nigel Kendall*

In Context

Tokyo by Season

From blossom viewing to bean hurling, Tokyo is a city for all seasons.

Meditate on the fleeting beauty of the cherry blossom in late March and early April.

Public holidays

Japan has 14 public holidays: New Year's Day (Ganjitsu) 1 January; Coming of Age Day (Seijin no Hi) 15 January; National Foundation Day (Kenkoku Kinen no Hi) 11 February; Vernal Equinox Day (Shumbun no Hi) around 21 March; Greenery Day (Midori no Hi) 29 April; Constitution Day (Kempo Kinenbi) 3 May; Children's Day (Kodomo no Hi) 5 May; Marine Day (Umi no Hi) 20 July; Respect for the Aged Day (Keiro no Hi) 15 September; Autumnal Equinox Day (Shubun no Hi) around 23 September; Sports Day (Taiiku no Hi) 10 October; Culture Day (Bunka no Hi) 3 November; Labour Thanksgiving Day (Kinro Kansha no Hi) 23 November; Emperor's Birthday (Tenno Tanjobi) 23 December.

Saturday remains an official workday, but holidays falling on a Sunday shift to Monday. If both 3 May and 5 May fall on weekdays, 4 May also becomes a holiday. From 2000, to encourage domestic tourism, Coming of Age Day and Sports Day will no longer have fixed dates and will be held on the second Mondays of January and October respectively.

Winter

December

Toyota Cup   **early Dec**
National Stadium, Sendagaya station (JR Sobu line). (Ticket Pia 5237 9999).
Soccer's official world club champs are decided at this annual one-off match on neutral Tokyo turf between the holders of Europe and South America's premier club competitions. South American teams dominated for many years, but in recent seasons have been increasingly financially outgunned.

47 Ronin Memorial Service
(Ako Gishi-sai)   **13-14 Dec**
Sengakuji Temple, Sengakuji station. (Info 3441 5560). **Times** various.
The famous vendetta attack took place in the early hours of 31 January 1703, or 15 December by the old calendar. Two days of events, including dances, a parade in period costume and a Buddhist memorial ceremony, take place at the temple where the warriors are buried alongside their former master. There's also a parade in Ginza, with participants in samurai outfits.

Kodo at Theatre Apple   mid-Dec
Theatre Apple, Kabuki-cho, Seibu-Shinjuku station.
(Info 3209 0222).
Sado Island's *taiko* drum troupe has long been wow-
ing audiences worldwide with dynamic stage performances of pounding intensity. The seemingly
endless One Earth Tour hits the metropolis for up
to ten days at this regular pre-Christmas residency.

Battledore Market
(Hagoita Ichi)   17-19 Dec
Sensoji Temple, Asakusa station. (Info 3844 1221).
Hagoita are paddle-shaped bats used to hit the shut-
tlecock in the traditional New Year game of *hanet-
suki.* Ornamental versions come festooned with
colourful pictures and many temples hold markets
selling them in December. The one at Sensoji is
Tokyo's largest.

Emperor's Birthday
(Tenno Tanjobi)   23 Dec
The only day apart from 2 January when the public
is allowed to enter the inner palace grounds.

Beethoven's Ninth   late Dec
Various venues; various times.
An outbreak of Beethoven's ninth in concert halls
across the city. Early post-war radio broadcasts of
the symphony performed by the NHK Orchestra are
supposedly responsible for the custom, and *Ode to
Joy* is still seen as a suitably uplifting note on which
to contemplate the coming year.

Christmas Eve/Day   24-25 Dec
The most romantic day of the year is Christmas Eve:
couples celebrate with extravagant dates, involving
fancy restaurants and love hotels. Not many locals
do anything special to mark the following day,
despite the battery of fairy lights, decorated trees
and piped carols deployed by department stores.

Year End   28-31 Dec
The last official day of work is 28 December; people
then begin a frantic round of last-minute house
cleaning, decoration-hanging and food preparation.
Many stay at home on the last night of the year to
catch NHK's eternally popular *Red and White
Singing Contest*, although huge crowds make it to
shrines and temples for midnight, when bells are
rung 108 times to welcome in the New Year.

January

New Year's Day (Ganjitsu)   1 Jan
*(Tourist info 3201 3331). Many locations, including
Meiji Shrine & Sensoji Temple.*
The most important annual holiday of the year sees
large crowds fill temples and shrines to bursting
point for that all-important first visit of the year.
Otherwise, New Year's Day is a quiet family affair,
except for postmen staggering under enormous
sacks of New Year cards. Only the first day of the
year is an official holiday but most shops and businesses close until 4 January.

Emperor's Cup Final   1 Jan
(Info 5237 9955; Ticket Pia 5237 9999).
The showpiece event of Japan's domestic soccer sea-
son is the climax of the main cup competition. It
takes place at the **National Stadium** (*see chapter*
Sport & Fitness) and kicks off at 1.30pm.

New Year Congratulatory Visit
(Ippan Sanga)   2 Jan
The public is allowed into the inner grounds of the
Imperial Palace (*see chapter* **Sightseeing)** on two

Tradition takes to the modern streets at the Kanda Festival in May of odd-numbered years.

Acrobatic antics at the Tokyo Metropolitan Fire Brigade Parade on 6 January.

days a year; this is one of them (the emperor's birthday in December is the other). Seven times during the day, between 9.30am and 3pm, the symbol of the state appears in person on a balcony of the place with other members of the royal family to wave to the crowds from behind bullet-proof glass.

Tokyo Metropolitan Fire Brigade Parade (Dezome-shiki)   6 Jan
Plaza in front of Tokyo Big Site, 3-21-2 Ariake, Koto-ku. (Tourist info 3201 3331). **Time** morning.
The highlight is a display by members of the Preservation Association of the old Edo Fire Brigade, who dress in traditional *hikeshi* firefighters' garb and perform acrobatic stunts at the top of long ladders. Modern equipment is also featured.

New Year Grand Sumo Tournament (Ozumo Hatsu Basho)   mid-Jan
Kokugikan, Ryogoku station. **Time** 10am-6pm.
First of the year's three full 15-day sumo tournaments in Tokyo. These are held from the second to the fourth Sunday of January, May and September.

Coming of Age Day (Seijin no Hi)   second Mon of Jan
Meiji Shrine & others. (Tourist info 3201 3331).
Those reaching the age of 20 in the 12 months to April make their way to shrines in their best kimono and suits for blessings and commemorative photos. The traditional date generally coincides with New Year's Day under the old lunar calendar.

Chinese New Year   Jan/Feb
Yokohama Chinatown, East Gate, Ishikawacho station (JR Keihin Tohoku line) (Yokohama tourist info 045 641 4759).

Cymbals crash and dragon dancers weave their way along the restaurant-lined streets of Yokohama Chinatown as the local community celebrates its big party of the year.

February

Setsubun   3 Feb
Various locations, including Sensoji Temple & Zojoji Temple. (Tourist info 3201 3331).
Much hurling of soybeans to cries of '*oni wa soto, fuki wa uchi*' ('demons out, good luck in') as the last day of winter by the lunar calendar is celebrated in homes, shrines and temples. The tradition is to eat one bean for every year of one's age. Sumo wrestlers and other celebrities are among those doing the casting out in ceremonies at well-known Tokyo shrines.

National Foundation Day (Kenkoku Kinen no Hi)   11 Feb
A public holiday commemorating the supposed beginnings of Japan's imperial line in 660 BC, the date when mythical first emperor Jimmu, a descendent of sun goddess Amaterasu Omikami, is said to have ascended to the throne. After World War II, the public holiday on 11 February was abolished; this one was inaugurated, amid controversy, in 1966.

Valentine's Day   14 Feb
Introduced into Japan by confectionery company innovators as the day when women give chocolates to men: there's a large heart-shaped treat for that special someone, plus *giri choko* (obligation chocolates) to a wider circle of male associates. In theory, favours get returned in kind one month later, on White Day.

Plum Blossoms　　　**mid-Feb to mid-Mar**
Yushima Tenjin Shrine. (Info 3836 0753).
The delicate white blooms arrive a little earlier than the better-known cherry blossoms, and are generally celebrated in a more restrained fashion. Yushima Tenjin Shrine, a prime viewing spot, also holds a month-long festival featuring traditional arts such as *ikebana* (flower-arranging) and tea ceremony.

March

Dolls Festival (Hina Matsuri)　　**3-4 Mar**
A special festival for girls. Kimono-clad dolls representing traditional court figures are displayed on a multi-tiered red stand, and the arrangement takes pride of place in the home on the big day.

Daruma Fair　　　**3-4 Mar**
Jindaiji Shrine. (Info 0424 86 5511).
Time 9am-5pm.
After meditating in a cave for nine years, Bodhidharma, a Zen monk from ancient India, is reputed to have lost the use of all four limbs. The cuddly red figure of the Daruma doll, which is modelled after him, also lacks eyes; the first gets painted in for good luck when a difficult task is undertaken, the second on its successful completion. Jindaiji was first established in AD 733, making it among the oldest temples in Tokyo, and its Daruma fair is one of the biggest.

Spring

March

**Fire-Walking Ceremony
(Hi-watari)**　　　**mid-Mar**
Kotsu Anzen Kitosho, near Takaosan-guchi station (Keio line).(Info 0426 61 1115).
At the foot of Mount Takao, hardy *yamabushi* mountain monks from Yakuoin Temple walk barefoot across burning coals while chanting incantations. Members of the public are then invited to test their own hardiness of soul and sole by following suit.

White Day　　　**14 Mar**
Male recipients of Valentine's Day confectionery are supposed to show their appreciation with a return gift of white chocolates.

**St Patrick's
Day Parade**　　**17 Mar or nearest Sun**
Omotesando Dori. Harajuku station.
Enthusiastic local devotees of traditional Gaelic culture demonstrate their baton-twirling, drumming, pipe-playing and dancing skills at this popular parade led by Ireland's ambassador. Along the route, friendly representatives of the city's Irish hostelries hand out discount vouchers for liquid refreshment.

Tokyo Game Show　**mid-Mar (& mid-Oct)**
Makuhari Messe Convention Centre, Makuhari-Hongo station (JR Sobu line) or Kaihin Makuhari station (Keiyo line). (Info 3591 1421).
Admission ¥11,200.

The biggest computer and video game show on the planet pulls in crowds of up to 200,000 for two weekends, one in spring and one in autumn.

Tokyo Motorcycle Show　　**mid-Mar**
Pacifico Yokohama, Sakuragicho station. (Info 5357 2106). **Admission** ¥1,500.
Everything to warm any biker's heart, with models from Japan and the rest of the world.

**Vernal Equinox Day
(Shumbun no Hi)**　　**around 21 Mar**
Many people visit family graves on this day, since it falls in the middle of *higan*, a week-long, twice-yearly Buddhist memorial service.

**Cherry-Blossom Viewing
(Hanami)**　　**late Mar-early Apr**
(See box).

April

New Fiscal Year　　　**1 Apr**
April Fool's Day marks the start of Japan's financial and academic calendars. Big companies hold speech-filled ceremonies to welcome the year's graduate intake to the rigours of corporate life.

Start of Baseball Season　　**early Apr**
Tokyo Dome or Jingu Baseball Stadium). (Info 5245 7066; Ticket Pia 5237 9999).
The long and winding road to the October play-offs usually gets underway with a three-game Central League series featuring the Giants, the city's perennial favourite. There's extra spice if the opposition is the Swallows, the capital's other big team, or the Giants' oldest and deadliest rivals, the Hanshin Tigers.

Japan Tennis Open　　　**mid-Apr**
Ariake Coliseum. Ariake station (Yurikamome line). (Info 5474 5944; Ticket Pia 5237 9999).
The international tennis circus hits town for the nation's premier event. Local interest tends to focus on the women's tournament.

Horseback Archery (Yabusame)　**mid-Apr**
Sumida Park. Asakusa station. (Info 5246 1111).
Mounted riders in medieval warrior gear shoot arrows at stationary targets while galloping along at full tilt. There's also a big *yabusame* festival at Tsurugaoka Hachimangu Shrine in Kamakura in mid-September; the practice can also be seen during the autumn festival at Meiji Shrine on 3 November.

**Meiji Jingu Shrine Spring Festival
(Haru no Taisai)**　　**29 Apr, 2-3 May**
Meiji Jingu Shrine, 1-1 Kamizonocho, Yoyogi, Shibuya-ku. Harajuku station. (Info 3379 5511).
Admission free. **Times** various.
Daily free performances of traditional entertainment, including *gagaku* and *bugaku* imperial court music and dance, plus *noh* and *kyogen* drama.

Golden Week　　　**29 Apr-5 May**
Put three public holidays (Greenery Day, Constitution Day and Children's Day) in close

proximity and there's the serious vacation opportunity known as Golden Week. Planes, trains and automobiles hit double gridlock as people flee the big city en masse, then all head home again together. Tokyo remains relatively quiet, with many smaller shops and restaurants closed for the duration.

Greenery Day (Midori no Hi)   29 Apr
A nature appreciation day to begin Golden Week.

May

International Labour Day   1 May
Despite falling in the middle of Golden Week, the day when workers of the world unite in celebration is not an official holiday in Japan. Many vacationing trade unionists meet for a rally in Yoyogi Park.

Constitution Day
(Kempo Kinenbi)   3 May
Commemorates the day in 1947 when the US-imposed pacifist constitution came into operation.

Children's Day (Kodomo no Hi)   5 May
A traditional festival for boys; the corresponding one for girls is the dolls festival on 3-4 March (which isn't a public holiday). Celebrations include the hanging of paper streamers in the shape of carp.

Kanda Festival   mid-May
Organised from Kanda Myojin Shrine.
(Info 3254 0753).
One of the city's traditional 'Big Three' festivals, this is held in odd-numbered years, alternating with the Sanno festival. In Edo days, it was a particular favourite of the local townspeople, due to Kanda Myojin's links with the popular tenth-century rebel Taira no Masakado. Events include *shinkosai* rites with participants parading in Heian costume, plus a gala procession that crisscrosses the Kanda area and features a number of festival floats and *mikoshi* portable shrines.

Sanja Festival   mid-May
Organised from Asakusa Shrine. (Info 3844 1575).
The biggest of the city's annual festivals, Sanja attracts enormous crowds to Asakusa and honours the three seventh-century founders of Sensoji Temple. It climaxes after several days of events with three huge mikoshi portable shrines (*sanja*) that carry the spirits of the three men being paraded around local streets. Each needs dozens of people to carry it.

Summer

June

Sanno Festival   10-16 June
Organised from Hie Shrine. (Info 3581 2471).
Another of the 'Big Three' festivals, Sanno alternates with the Kanda festival and is held in its full splendour on even-numbered years. Hie Shrine, which had close links with the Tokugawa shoguns, is near today's central government district. The main procession goes round the edge of the Imperial Palace, with participants in Heian-period costumes and priests on horses, plus all the usual festival floats and mikoshi.

Iris Viewing   mid-June
Various locations, including Meiji Shrine Inner Garden, Horikiri Iris Garden & Mizumoto Park. (Tourist info 3201 3331).
The annual blooming of the purple and white flowers falls during the grey humid days of the rainy season, but is no less popular for that.

July

Mount Fuji
Climbing Season   1 July-31 Aug
It's claimed that everyone should climb Mount Fuji once in their life, though more than that is said to be excessive. The perfectly formed cone of Japan's favourite dormant volcano is all but lost in the summer haze from most Tokyo vantage points, but many enthusiastic walkers head out for that one-off push to the summit, often at night in order to catch the dawn sunrise.

Ground-Cherry Market
(Hozuchi-ichi)   9-10 July
Sensoji Temple, 2-3-1 Asakusa, Taito-ku. (Info 3842 0181).
On these two days in July, prayers at Sensoji are said to be the spiritual equivalent of 46,000 days' worth at other times. Big crowds are attracted by this spiritual bargain. A ground-cherry market takes place at the temple over the same period.

International Lesbian
& Gay Film Festival   mid-July
Spiral Bldg, 5-6-23 Minami-Aoyama, Minato-ku. (Info 5380 5760).
In 1999 this festival celebrated its eighth year by moving from its traditional May slot to mid-July. Stretching over four or five days, the LGFF offers a rare chance for locals to catch up on the best of gay cinema from around the world.

Marine Day (Umi no Hi)   20 July
Introduced in 1996, this is a public holiday celebrating the benefits and bounty of the sea.

Sumida River Firework   last Sat in July
Asakusa station area. (Info 5246 1111). **Time** 7pm.
First held in 1733, this is the daddy of Tokyo's many summer firework events: the oldest, biggest and most crowded. Up to 20,000 *hanabi* ('flower-fires') light up the night skies, and as many as a million people pack streets, bridges and rooftops, eyes trained upward. Waterfront locations also tend to be favoured for other big displays.

Fuji Rock Festival   late July or early Aug
(Info 3444 6751).
A two-day outdoor music mega-festival that moved to Tokyo in 1998 after a disastrous first event the year before on the slopes of Mount Fuji. In 1999 the

festival moved out to Niigata, but may return closer to Tokyo in future years.

Jump 'n' Splash-Reggae
late July/early Aug

Tokyo Bayside Square, Toyosu station (Yurakucho line). (Info 5467 4833). **Time** from 1pm.
The sweltering Tokyo summer lends itself peculiarly well to the outdoor live reggae experience, as a battery of well attended events proves every year. Jump 'n' Splash, formerly known as Japansplash, is the long-established leader of the pack, with past attractions including everyone from Shaggy to Sugar Minott and Freddy McGregor.

August

Obon
13-15 Aug

The souls of the departed are supposed to return briefly to the world of the living during this Buddhist festival honouring the spirits of ancestors. Observances include welcoming fires, *Bon* dances and night-time floating of lanterns on open water. Although there's no public holiday, many companies give workers time off to visit the folks back home, leaving the capital unusually quiet for a few days.

War-End Anniversary
15 Aug

Yasukuni Shrine, Ichigaya station.
The annual anniversary of Japan's surrender to the allied forces is still a source of diplomatic friction with neighbouring countries, as many leading politicians mark the day by visiting Yasukuni Shrine, where the souls of Japan's war-dead, including those executed as war criminals, are honoured.

Asakusa Samba Carnival
late Aug

Asakusa station area. (Info 3847 0038).
Thousands of gorgeously costumed samba dancers, some Brazilian but most Japanese, shake their stuff in the heart of old downtown Tokyo. It's a startling spectacle, with plenty of competition among teams for the cash prize that goes to the parade's top troupe along with the honour of closing the festival.

Awa Odori
late Aug

Koenji station area. (Info 3312 2111).
Street carnival Japanese-style. This annual shindig features a form of traditional Tokushima folk dance known as the *Fool's Dance*. As the raucous refrain of its light-hearted song puts it, 'You're a fool whether you dance or not, so you may as well dance'.

Autumn

September

Tokyo Earthquake Anniversary
1 Sept

The day when the city authorities test emergency relief preparations and hold practice drills in various locations across the city, on the anniversary of the 1923 disaster.

Toto International Super Track & Field
mid-Sept

National Stadium, Sendagaya station. (Info 5411 9500; Ticket Pia 5237 9999).
The Toto International Super Track& Field event is usually the last big outdoor meeting of the international athletics calendar, so there tends to be a relaxed end-of-term atmosphere among the assembled galaxy of record-setters, medal-winners and other track stars.

Respect for the Aged Day (Keiro no Hi)
15 Sept

Respect for the Aged Day is held on the anniversary of the 1966 enactment of the Law on Welfare for the Aged. Japan has the world's highest life expectancy and a population that is ageing rapidly: in 1997 the number aged 65 or over exceeded those aged 14 or under for the first time.

Autumnal Equinox Day (Shubun no Hi)
around 23 Sept

Like the spring equinox, the autumn equinox coincides with the mid-point of higan, the seven-day Buddhist memorial service.

Moon Viewing (Tsukimi)
late Sept

Outdoor parties to view the harvest moon have been held in the city ever since the Edo era, but the search for clear night-skies means that somewhat less urban venues are favoured nowadays. Some nontraditionalists find solace in the annual 'Tsukimi Burger' promotion, recognising a distinctly lunar quality to the fried egg that comes as an added seasonal ingredient.

Takigi Noh
Sept/Oct

Various venues; various times.
Atmospheric outdoor performances of medieval noh drama are staged at a number of shrines, temples and parks, illuminated by flickering flames from bonfires and torches.

October

Japan Electronics Show
early Oct

Makuhari Messe Convention Centre, Makuhari-Hongo station (JR Sobu line) or Kaihin Makuhari station (Keiyo line). **Admission** ¥1,000.
This is the big exhibition of cutting-edge technology, both industry- and consumer-related, so it's the place to check out all the latest gadgets before they hit the shops.

Sports Day
(Taiku no Hi)
second Mon in Oct

The traditional date commemorates the opening day of the 1964 Tokyo Olympics.

Tokyo Motor Show
late Oct-early Nov

Makuhari Messe Convention Centre, Makuhari-Hongo station (JR Sobu line) or Kaihin Makuhari station (Keiyo line). (Info 3211 8731). **Admission** ¥1,200.
The Tokyo Motor Show is an important showcase for the gleaming new high-tech products of car

Cherry-blossom viewing (Hanami)

One sign that spring is on its way is when the television news shows report the first *sakura* (cherry-blossom) sightings in the south of the country. Daily updates then map the sakura swathe sweeping up the archipelago, until the great day arrives sometime at the end of March, and Tokyo explodes in pink petals.

Hanami is the great outdoor event of the year. New employees often find their first duty is to head out to the nearest park armed with little more than a blue plastic groundsheet and instructions to find a prime spot and guard it with their lives. Popular places such as **Ueno Park** attract literally millions of visitors. Other popular viewing spots include **Sumida Park**, **Yasukuni Shrine**, **Shinjuku-Gyoen** and **Aoyama Cemetery** (for tourist info call 3201 3331).

There are two distinct approaches to enjoying cherry-blossom viewing. Some prefer quiet contemplation of the transient beauty up on the trees; others like to mix appreciation of nature with some serious partying with colleagues, friends or family. This can give the experience a surreal quality, as scenes of excess develop against a backdrop of stunning natural beauty. Ambulance crews remain on alert, as serious injuries and cases of alcohol poisoning are far from unknown.

Then, all too soon, it's over. The first rain or strong wind sends blossoms fluttering earthwards, and after a few days all that's left is the memory. Lanterns come down, pizza delivery men resume regular routes, and life gets back to normal. Until next year.

---

manufacturers both domestic and foreign. Passenger cars are featured in odd-numbered years; commercial vehicles in even ones.

Chrysanthemum Festival
late Oct-late Nov
Meiji Shrine Inner Garden. (Info 3379 5511).
The start of autumn was traditionally marked in Japan by the Chrysanthemum festival on the ninth day of the ninth month of the old lunar calendar. The delicate pale blooms are also represented on the crest of Japan's Imperial family.

November

Culture Day (Bunka no Hi)   3 Nov
A host of leading Japanese artists and writers, plus other luminaries, pick up Order of Culture government awards on a day set aside for cultural activities to celebrate the peace-loving democratic ideals of the postwar constitution, promulgated on this day in 1946.

Meiji Jingu Shrine Grand Autumn Festival (Reisai)   3 Nov
Meiji Jingu Shrine. (Info 3379 5511).
Admission free.
In former times, Culture Day celebrated the birthday of the Meiji Emperor (1852-1912), and the biggest annual festival of the Meiji Shrine still takes place on the same date. There are performances of traditional music and theatre, along with *yabusame* horseback archery.

Tokyo International Film Festival   early Nov
Bunkamura & other venues in Shibuya. (Info 3563 6407).
The largest film festival in Japan attracts a glittering influx of international movie talent for the serious business of the various competitions and special promotional screenings of upcoming Hollywood blockbusters. There are also films from Asia and Japanese cinema classics, in addition to a Fantastic Film Festival, Women's Film Week and a number of other events.

Seven-Five-Three Festival (Shichi-go-san)   15 Nov
Various locations, including Meiji Jingu Shrine. (Tourist info 3201 3331).
Tradition has it that children of certain ages (three, five and seven) are strangely susceptible to misfortune. One way out of this problem is to get any family member with the wrong number of birthday cake candles down to a Shinto shrine on 15 November to pray for divine blessings and protection, so important shrines are besieged by hoards of kids in their best kimono.

Autumn Leaves (Koyo)   second half of Nov
Many locations, including Shinjuku Gyoen, Ueno Park and Meiji Jingu Gaien Park. (Tourist info 3201 3331).
The spectacular autumnal colours of maple and ginko trees transform many of Tokyo's parks and gardens into a blaze of reds and yellows.

Labour Thanksgiving Day (Kinro Kansha no Hi)   23 Nov
This public holiday is when people are supposed to thank one another for all their hard work through the year.

Japan Cup   late Nov
Tokyo Racetrack, Fuchu Keibajo Seimon Mae station (Keio line from Higashi Fuchu). (Info 3591 5251; Ticket Pia 5237 9999).
Top horses and jockeys from round the world race Japan's élite over 2,400m.

Geography

Everybody knows where Tokyo is, but where on earth does it stop?

Tokyo has long since slipped the confines of the city's original boundaries around the present-day Imperial Palace area. Today, it lies at one end of the highly developed Pacific belt that runs west along the coast of Japan's main Honshu island to Osaka and holds around half the national population of 126 million.

In a country where up to two-thirds of the land is mountainous, Tokyo stands at the heart of a vast conurbation that sprawls relentlessly over much of the Kanto plain, Japan's largest and a natural population magnet. The National Capital Region, established for planning purposes in 1954, takes in all seven Kanto prefectures and Yamanashi; together these have a population of over 40 million. The outlying four (Tochigi, Gunma, Ibaraki and Yamanashi) are more rural and mountainous, particularly Yamanashi, which contains Mount Fuji on its southern borders.

Defining just where Tokyo's sprawling metropolis begins and ends sometimes appears to be a matter of arbitrary choice. To travellers on a *shinkansen* bullet train from the capital to Osaka and beyond, the whole of the highly developed Pacific belt running along the coast of Japan's main Honshu island can sometimes seem like one vast, endless conurbation.

The UN Department of Economic and Social Affairs Population Division ranks Tokyo as the world's largest urban agglomoration, defined as 'the population contained within the contours of contiguous territory inhabited at urban levels of residential density without regard to administrative boundaries'.

If the definition is accepted, then the 1996 Tokyo population figure of 27.24 million is far ahead of second-place Mexico City (16.9 million), San Paulo (16.72 million) and New York (16.39 million). This represents over 22 per cent of Japan's entire population, all living on less than two per cent of the nation's land.

Such crowding, of course, puts an enormous strain on housing stock, and in an attempt to escape the fearsome housing prices of more central districts, many long-suffering commuters retreat to distant suburbs and satellite towns. These stretch over the hinterland toward the distant hills of Yamanashi, Gunma, Tochigi and Ibaraki, as well as around Tokyo Bay in both directions. This migration only has the effect of making the city grow still more.

At the heart of this enormous concentration are Tokyo's 23 inner wards, or *ku*. These cover 616 square km and are home to 7.83 million. Tokyo prefecture, the 2,187 square km administered from the skyscraper offices of the Metropolitan Government in Shinjuku, has a population of 11.82 million. As well as the 23 inner wards, this larger area includes what the authorities classify as 27 cities, five towns and eight villages. These are mainly commuter belt and semi-rural districts in the western part of the prefecture. Also under its administration, however, are nine sets of scattered Pacific islands (two towns and seven villages), most of them part of the Izu Islands, but also including the semi-tropical Ogasawara Islands, lying some 1,000 km south of the inner wards.

THE LAND LOCK

In an idle moment back in the halcyon days of the late 1980s, somebody worked out that the tempting chunk of prime Tokyo real estate

Tokyo commuters face long journeys to work.

Earthquake!

Japan is one of the world's most seismically active countries. Small tremors are relatively common in Tokyo, but these usually pass by virtually unnoticed. Experts, however, do warn that the possibility of the capital being hit by a big quake at some point in the future is relatively high. Tokyo residents were shaken out of any complacency they may have had in January 1995, when the port city of Kobe was rocked by tremors that left 6,430 people dead and over 43,000 injured. The Great Kanto Earthquake of 1923, which killed around 100,000 people and destroyed large parts of Tokyo, remains the nation's greatest natural disaster.

The aftermath of the 1923 earthquake.

Earthquake prediction remains a notoriously inexact science, despite the vast amounts of money poured into it, but two separate kinds of threat have been identified as posing a danger to Tokyo. One is a big quake along an active fault directly below the city causing vertical movement, similar to Kobe; it was this kind of tremor that jolted Edo in 1855 and caused as many as 7,000 fatalities in the pre-modern city. The other possibility is a repeat of the phenomenon that caused the great disaster of 1923: a sudden release of tension built up deep beneath the ocean floor as tectonic plates slowly shift against each other.

There have been warnings that either kind of quake could affect Tokyo again. Of most immediate concern to the capital's residents are predictions of a vertical-movement quake beneath the city of a similar magnitude to that experienced by Kobe. Authorities believe this could leave over 7,000 people dead, many more injured, and millions homeless. In a relatively distant location from the capital, but likely to be of greater magnitude at its epicentre, is a Tokai earthquake feared possible beneath the ocean floor off Shizuoka in central Honshu. Other sites considered worrisome, including Sagami Bay (off Kanagawa) and the ocean floor east or southeast of Boso peninsula (Chiba), are believed for the time being to be relatively low risk.

The failure to anticipate the Kobe quake indicates the enormous difficulty of trying to predict where and when a big earthquake might hit, and estimates of likely casualties and damage in the event of any future Tokyo disaster also vary widely. There are a whole range of different scenarios possible, depending on magnitude of tremor, time of day, season, weather conditions, and a whole host of other imponderables. In Kobe, supposedly quake-proof structures, including some transport links, failed to withstand the strain, while emergency planning procedures were revealed to be inadequate in many respects. The majority of victims were crushed by collapsed structures, mainly wooden houses, whereas it had been generally believed since 1923 that the main danger to life came from fire.

occupied by the Imperial Palace was worth as much as all the land in California, Los Angeles and San Francisco included. In fact, such calculations seem to have been a popular occupation; both Florida and Canada are also yardsticks quoted from those happy times. Such statistics might not be true today, with the millennial Japanese economy still stuck in a post-bubble slump. But they do reflect the sky-high land prices that lay behind Tokyo's seemingly insatiable desire to sprawl endlessly out into the surrounding prefectures.

In common with other Japanese cities, Tokyo has felt the effects of the rapid population shift from countryside to city since the end of the war. In 1945, half of all Japanese still lived in rural areas; by 1970 the figure had fallen to under one-fifth. By 1996, less than five per cent of the working population were engaged in agriculture, and more than forty per cent of these were over 65 years old. As the villages emptied, millions flocked to the crowded capital.

But as the rural population came one way, Tokyo itself was heading in the opposite direction. With the height of its buildings traditionally limited by possible earthquakes (*see box above*), the metropolis has tended to grow outward rather than upward, and the paddy fields have been covered over by concrete. Commuters retreating to distant suburbs and satellite cities pay the price of cheaper housing and more spacious living conditions with famously long journeys to work. Tokyo at the turn of the century is a city of very sleepy train passengers.

The capital's head-on meeting with the surrounding countryside hasn't always been a happy one. The city's international airport at Narita in Chiba, for example, was built in a highly inconvenient location 41 miles east of central Tokyo, compared to Heathrow's 15 miles from central London, but still ran into almost immediate problems with local farmers (*see chapters* **History** and **Tokyo Today**). A second runway has also been long delayed by a hold-out group who refuse to sell their land. To avoid running any similar problems, Osaka built Kansai International Airport on an offshore artificial island.

REMODELLED CITY

Tokyo itself has never been averse to improving on its own natural endowments. Furiously remodelled over the centuries, the original physical features of the central parts of the city are often scarcely recognisable in their original form, even allowing for the present-day concrete cladding. Hills and valleys have been evened out; lakes and marshes drained; rivers re-routed. Canals have been created, then filled in again and built over. Land reclamation continues to push the shoreline out, far from its original moorings. The Odaiba waterfront development is only one recent example in a long line going all the way back to the early Edo era and the filling in of Hibiya Inlet.

The traditional Edo division was between the smarter *yamanote* areas on the higher ground to the west and south of the city and the lower-lying *shitamachi* downtown districts. To some extent this split still exists. Many of the more traditional and industrial wards are located in the north and east of the city, clustered around the Sumida, Arakawa and Edogawa rivers that empty into Tokyo Bay. Some areas in the eastern wards lie two or three metres below sea-level. Yet shitamachi is often as much a state of mind as anything else. Ginza, the city's most exclusive district for the best part of a century, was once part of the lower city. Similarly, Nihonbashi used to be the heart of the old downtown, but could hardly be classified as belonging to it today.

The modern transport networks that cut through the city provide modern Tokyo's clearest dividing lines. Notable among these is the Yamanote train line that circles the central area. The name recalls older divisions, but the line itself runs through both old yamanote and old shitamachi districts, as well as through western areas that lay outside the official city limits until as late as 1932. The other major infrastructure feature are the overhead highways, many of them tracing routes that follow the network of waterways for which Edo was once renowned. These have now either been drained or languish sadly in the shadow of the road above. This fate has befallen Nihonbashi River, as well as the bridge over it – in a former incarnation, Edo's most famous landmark.

Such an action would probably have the heritage brigade up in arms in many western countries, and there are those who would claim Tokyo's

Tokyo sprawls so much that no one is really sure where the city ends any more.

Temperatures & rainfall

Month	Mean	Max	Min	Rainfall
Jan	5.2	9.5	1.2	45.1
Feb	5.6	9.7	1.7	60.4
Mar	8.5	12.7	4.4	99.5
Apr	14.1	18.3	10.0	125.0
May	18.6	22.8	14.8	138.0
June	21.7	25.2	18.6	185.0
July	25.2	28.8	22.3	126.1
Aug	27.1	30.9	24.0	147.5
Sept	23.2	26.7	20.2	179.8
Oct	17.2	21.2	14.2	64.1
Nov	12.4	16.6	8.9	89.1
Dec	7.7	12.1	3.9	45.7

Units: Temperatures in degrees centigrade, rainfall in mm
Source: Chronological Scientific Tables

headlong rush for development has succeeded all too well. In a country that takes pride in its closeness to nature, the capital has scarcely a trickling stream without ugly concrete sidings, park area per head remains a mere one-tenth that of New York, and startlingly huge crows grow fat on the pickings of the city's enormous rubbish dumps.

On the other hand, demands for stronger pollution controls were acted upon back in the 1970s, and air cleanliness is much improved. On a clear day, you can see Mount Fuji from city viewing spots. Housing space per person has grown steadily, although still below levels in other developed countries, and there is less talk of people living in 'rabbit hutches'. With the break-neck economic growth of past decades now a memory, perhaps the city will find time to have a good think about how it wants to remake itself next time round.

CLIMATE

The Japanese take great pride in the fact that their country boasts four distinct seasons, something they apparently believe to be unique to Japan. Visitors should be grateful for small mercies: under the old solar calendar in Japan, the year was divided into 24 'mini-seasons', ranging from 'the lesser cold' in January to 'the greater snow' in December.

Implicit in Japanese talk about the seasons is the connection that even hardened city-dwellers feel with nature. In this temperate country, which until recently was composed largely of farmers, the concept of being at one with nature is part of daily life, the life cycles mirroring those of the seasons.

In the city, this celebration of the seasons shows itself most clearly in spring, when first the plum trees, then the cherry trees come into bloom, leading to several weeks of partying and celebration. No less important to the Japanese is autumn: when the leaves change colour in Tokyo's finest parks, it takes a brave person to jostle through the massed ranks of amateur photographers to get to a good viewing spot. Broadly speaking, the four seasons in Tokyo can be summarised as follows.

Winter

Sitting on roughly the same latitude as Los Angeles and Teheran, Tokyo escapes the harsh Siberian winter snows blowing east from the Asian mainland courtesy of the rugged protection given by the mountain ranges that run along the central spine of Japan's main island. Snow may fall for a couple of days in January, but rarely sticks.

Spring

The cherry blossoms of late March to early April are the official harbinger of spring, their arrival giving rise to mass celebrations all over Japan. The mood of people becomes noticeably more optimistic in the face of the annual rebirth of nature.

Summer

This is a good time to be out of the city, and many Tokyoites escape to the mountains from the city's oppressive heat. The hot air blasting out of air-conditioners all over Tokyo makes the capital a couple of degrees hotter than elsewhere. Late June and early July bring the summer rains, rather like walking around in a lukewarm shower. Always carry an umbrella.

Autumn

September to early October can bring typhoons, and when the trees change colour, parks and gardens are crammed with people admiring the spectacular leaves.

History

How a small bay settlement became one of the world's biggest cities.

PRE-HISTORY

Archaeological evidence suggests today's metropolitan area was inhabited as long ago as the late Paleolithic period, and stone tools belonging to hunter-gatherers of pre-ceramic culture have been discovered at sites such as Nogawa in western Tokyo Prefecture.

Pottery featuring rope-cord patterns developed in Japan during the so-called Jomon period (10,000-300BC). Around 6,000 years ago, Tokyo Bay rose as far as the edge of the high ground that makes up the central *yamanote* area of the modern city; its retreat left behind a marshy shoreline that provided a rich food source. The Late Jomon shell mounds at Omori, identified in 1877 by US zoologist ES Morse as he gazed from the window of a Shinbashi-Yokohama train, were the site of Japan's first modern archaeological dig and forerunner to a long line of similar excavations.

The Yayoi period (300BC-AD300) is named after the Yayoi-cho district near Tokyo University in Hongo, where in 1884 the Mukogaoka shell mound yielded the first evidence of a more sophisticated form of pottery. Along with other advances such as wet-rice cultivation and the use of iron, this seems to have been introduced from the Asian mainland. Only after arriving on Kyushu did new techniques spread through Honshu.

BACKWATER

Kanto remained a distant outpost as the early Japanese state started to take shape around the Yamato court, which emerged in the fourth century as a loose confederation of chieftains in what is now Nara Prefecture before gradually extending to other parts of the country. Chinese ideographs and Buddhism both arrived via the Korean peninsula, while members of Japan's ruling elite

*The original **Nihonbashi** ('Japan Bridge') was the point from which distances were measured.*

were buried in large tumuli, similar to tombs found on the nearest part of the continent.

Senso-ji Temple (*see page 72*) is said to date back to AD628, when two fishermen brothers are said to have discovered a gold statue of the bodhisattva Kannon in their nets. Under Taika Reform from 645, the land on which Tokyo now stands became part of Musashi province, governed from Kokufu (modern-day Fuchu City). State administration was centralised in emulation of the Tang imperial model and China's advanced civilisation exerted a strong influence.

After the imperial capital was moved from Nara to Heian (Kyoto) in 794, a Japanese court culture flourished. Emperors became largely figureheads, manipulated by a series of powerful regents from the dominant Fujiwara family. The invention of the *kana* syllabary helped the writing of literary classics such as Sei Shonagon's *Pillow Book* and Lady Murasaki's *Tale of Genji*, but the political power of the Kyoto court nobles went into slow decline as control of the regions fell into the hands of the local military aristocracy.

REBELLION

An early revolt against Kyoto rule was staged by Taira no Masakado, a tenth-century rebel later enshrined at Kanda Myojin (*see page 72*) and cherished locally down the ages as an anti-authority figure. A reputed quarrel over a woman between different members of the 'Eight Bands of Taira from the East' in 931 is reputed to have escalated into a full-scale military conflict, during which Masakado won control of all eight provinces of Kanto. He then declared himself emperor of a new autonomous state.

After defeat by central government forces in 940, grisly evidence of Masakado's demise was dispatched to the capital. Legend has it that his severed head took to the skies one night and flew back to be reunited with his other remains at his grave in the fishing village of Shibasaki. The site is now in the central financial district of Otemachi but has remained untouched by successive generations of city builders, perhaps fearful of Masakado's vengeful spirit.

After Masakado, the power of the Taira family went into decline in Kanto. The Ise branch of the clan flourished, however, and by 1160 Taira no Kiyomori had become the most powerful man at the imperial court in Kyoto.

BIRTH OF EDO

Tokyo's original name, Edo ('Rivergate'), is thought to have derived from a settlement located near where Sumida River enters Tokyo Bay. Its first known use goes back to a minor member of the Taira clan, Edo Shigenaga, who is thought to have adopted it after making his home in the area. In August 1180 Shigenaga attacked the forces of his Minamoto ally, Miura Yoshizumi, but he switched sides three months later, just as *shogun*-to-be Minamoto no Yoritomo entered Musashi province.

KAMAKURA SHOGUNATE

By the late twelfth century, the rise of provincial warrior clans had developed into the struggle between the Taira and Minamoto families later chronicled in *The Tale of Heike*. After Minamoto no Yoritomo wiped out the last Taira remnants in 1185, the emperor designated him Seii Tai Shogun ('Barbarian-Subduing Generalissimo'). Yoritomo shunned the imperial capital of Kyoto, setting up his government in Kamakura (*see page 232*)

This inaugurated a period of military rule that was to last till the nineteenth century. *Bushido*, 'the way of the warrior', emphasised martial virtues, while the *samurai* class emerged as a powerful force in feudal society. Nevertheless, attempted invasions of Japan by the Mongols in 1274 and 1281 were only driven back by stormy seas off Kyushu, something attributed to the *kamikaze*, or 'wind of the gods'. Dissatisfaction grew with the Kamakura government, now controlled by a series of regents, and in 1333 Ashikaga Takauji established a new shogunate in the Muromachi district of Kyoto.

OTA DOKAN

The first castle at Edo was erected in 1457 by Ota Dokan, a *waka* poet known as Ota Sekenaga taking a monk's tonsure in 1478, now celebrated as Tokyo's original founder. Above narrow Hibiya Inlet, he constructed a set of fortifications overlooking the entrance to Kanto plain for northbound travellers along the Pacific sea road. To improve local navigation, he also diverted the Hirakawa east at Kandabashi to form Nihonbashi River.

In 1486, during a military clash between branches of the locally powerful Uesugi family, Ota was falsely accused of betraying his lord, and met his end at the home of Uesugi Sadamasa in Sagami (modern-day Kanagawa).

WARRING STATES

Central government authority largely disappeared following the Onin War (1467-77), as regional lords, or *daimyo*, fought for dominance. Only after a century or so of on-off civil strife did the country begin to regain unity under Oda Nobunaga, although his assassination in 1582 meant that final reunification was left to Toyotomi Hideyoshi. In 1590, Hideyoshi established control of the Kanto region after successfully besieging the Odawara Castle stronghold of the powerful Go-Hojo family.

Hideyoshi ordered his ally Tokugawa Ieyasu to exchange his lands in Shizuoka and Aichi for the former Go-Hojo domains in Kanto. Rather than Odawara, which lies in present-day Kanagawa Prefecture, Ieyasu chose Edo as his headquarters.

Construction started on a new castle on the site of Ota Dokan's crumbling fortifications. After Hideyoshi's death, Ieyasu was victorious in the struggle for national power at the Battle of Sekigahara in 1600, and three years later was named shogun. The emperor remained, as ever, in Kyoto, but Edo became the government capital of Japan.

EDO ERA (1600-1868)

When Ieyasu arrived in 1590, Edo was little more than a few houses at the edge of Hibiya Inlet. This changed quickly with building and land reclamation projects. Divided almost equally between military and townspeople, the population grew dramatically before levelling off in the early eighteenth century at around 1.2 million. In an age when London still had under 1 million people, Edo was probably the world's biggest metropolis.

POWER OF THE SHOGUNS

Fifteen successive Tokugawa shoguns ruled Japan, and their domination lasted for more than 250 years. All roads led to Edo: five major highways radiated out from the city, with communications aided by regular post stations, including Shinagawa, Shinjuku, Itabashi and Senju.

Feudal lords retained local autonomy, but a system of alternate annual residence forced them to divide their time between their own lands and the capital of the shoguns, under the watchful eye of the government. Daimyo finances were drained by the regular journeys with their retinues along the highways, as well as by the need to maintain large Edo residences. There was little chance to foment trouble in the provinces, and as a further inducement to loyalty, family members were kept in Edo as permanent hostages.

Although Tokugawa Ieyasu's advisors had included Englishman Will Adams (whose story is fictionalised in *Shogun*), a policy of national seclusion was introduced in 1639. Contact with western countries was restricted to a small Dutch trade mission on the island of Dejima, far from Edo.

DIVIDED CITY

The layout of Edo reflected the social order, with the yamanote high ground being the preserve of the military classes and the townspeople occupying the *shitamachi*, 'low city', areas outside the castle walls. There was also an attempt to conform to Chinese principles of geomancy; the two temples that would hold the Tokugawa family tombs, Kan'ei-ji and Zojo-ji, lay auspiciously in the north-east and south-west of the city. More problematically, since Mount Fuji lay to the west rather than to the north, Edo Castle's main Ote gate was placed on the east side, instead of the usual south.

Completed in 1638, Edo Castle was the world's largest. Its outer defences extended 16 kilometres (ten miles). The most important of the four sets of fortifications, the *hon-maru* or principle fortress, contained the residence of the shogun, the halls of state and the inner chambers, where the shogun's wife and concubines lived. The castle keep stood on a hill alongside, overlooking the whole city. Between the castle's double set of moats, regional daimyo had their Edo mansions arranged in a strict hierarchy of 'dependent' and 'outside' lords.

Outside the castle walls to the east, the low-lying shitamachi districts were home to the merchants, craftsmen, labourers and others attracted to the wealth and power of Edo. Less than one-fifth of the land of Edo, much of it having been reclaimed, held around half of its population. Nihonbashi's curving wooden bridge was the hub of the nation's highways and the spot from which all distances to Edo were measured.

Nearby were wealthy merchants' residences and grand shops such as Echigoya, forerunner of today's Mitsukoshi; the city's prison; and the fish market. Behind grand thoroughfares, the crowded backstreet tenements of Nihonbashi and Kanda were a breeding ground for disease and were in constant danger of flooding. Fires were common in the largely wooden city.

LONG SLEEVES FIRE

The original castle buildings were just one victim of the disastrous Long Sleeves Fire of 1657. Over 100,000 people died, around a quarter of Edo's total population, in three days of conflagrations that raged across both military and townspeople areas. The flames began at a temple, Hommyo-ji in Hongo, where monks had been burning two long-sleeved kimono belonging to young women who had recently died. By the morning of the fourth day, three-quarters of Edo had been destroyed.

Reconstruction work was soon underway. Roads were widened and new fire breaks introduced. Many people had perished because they couldn't escape across the Sumida River, which, for military reasons, had no bridges: opening up Fukagawa and Honjo for development, a bridge was now erected at Ryogoku. There was also a general dispersal of temples and shrines to outlying areas such as Yanaka and newly reclaimed land in Tsukiji. The Yoshiwara pleasure quarters were moved out, too – from Ningyocho to beyond Asakusa and the newly extended city limits.

New secondary residences for daimyo were established outside the walls of the castle, leading to a more patchwork mix of noble estates and townspeople districts, although the basic pattern of shitamachi areas in the east was retained. Daimyo mansions inside the castle were rebuilt in a more restrained style. The innermost section of the reconstructed castle was more subdued, lacking the high tower of its predecessor.

47 RONIN INCIDENT

One by-product of the stability of the Tokugawa regime was that the large number of military personnel stationed in Edo found themselves with relatively little to do. A complex bureaucracy developed, and there were ceremonial duties, but members of the top strata of the feudal system found themselves outstripped economically by the city's wealthy merchants. In these circumstances, a daring vendetta attack staged by the band of masterless samurai known later as the 47 ronin caused a sensation. In 1701, after being provoked by the shogun's chief of protocol, Lord Ako had drawn his sword inside Edo Castle, an illegal act for which he was forced to commit ritual suicide. Two years later, 46 of his loyal former retainers (one dropped out at the last moment) attacked the Edo mansion of the man they blamed for his death. Emerging with Kira's head, they marched through the city to offer it to Lord Ako's grave at Sengaku-ji Temple (*see page 72*). Despite public acclaim for their actions, the 46 were sentenced to death, but permitted to die in the same way as their master.

The incident forms the basis of one of kabuki's most popular plays, *Kanadehon Chushinjura* (*The Treasury of the Loyal Retainers*), written originally for bunraku puppet theatre and first staged in 1748. The story was diplomatically relocated to fourteenth-century Kamakura.

CULTURE CAPITAL

A vibrant new urban culture grew up in Edo's shitamachi districts. During the long years of peace and relative prosperity, the pursuit of pleasure provided the populace, particularly the city's wealthy merchants, with welcome relief from the feudal system's stifling social confines. Landscape artists such as Hiroshige (1797-1868) depict a city of theatres, temples, scenic bridges, festivals and fairs. There were numerous seasonal celebrations, including big firework displays to celebrate the summer opening of Sumida River, as well as cherry-blossom viewing along its banks in spring.

Kabuki, an Edo favourite, didn't always meet the approval of the high city. In 1842, a government edict banished theatres up the Sumida River to Asakusa, where they stayed until after the fall of the shogunate. As the district already boasted Senso-ji Temple, with its fairs and festivals, and the Yoshiwara pleasure quarters lay only a short distance away, the act merely cemented Asakusa's position as Edo's favoured relaxation centre.

BLACK SHIPS

Notice that Japan could no longer seal itself off from the outside world arrived in Edo Bay in 1853 in the shape of four US 'black ships' under the command of Commodore Matthew Perry. Hastily prepared local defences were helpless, and the treaty signed with Perry the following year proved to be the thin end of the wedge, as western powers forced a series of further concessions. In 1855, Edo suffered a major quake that killed over 7,000 and destroyed large parts of the lower city. In 1859, Townsend Harris, the first US consul-general, arrived to set up a mission at Zenpuku-ji Temple in Azabu.

Voices of discontent had already been raised against the government: there were increasingly frequent famines, and proponents of 'National Learning' called for a return to some purer form of Shinto tradition. The foreign threat now polarised opinion. Feelings ran particularly high in Mito and among youthful samurai from Choshu and Satsuma in the south. In 1860, the senior councillor of the shogunate government, Ii Naosuke, was assassinated outside Edo Castle. Under the slogan 'expel the barbarian, revere the emperor', a series of incidents took place against foreigners. Power drained away from Edo as the government looked to build a unified national policy by securing imperial backing in Kyoto. Daimyo residences and estates in Edo were abandoned after the old alternate residence requirement was abolished in 1862.

The Tokugawa regime was finally overthrown early in 1868, when a coalition of forces from the south declared an imperial 'restoration' in Kyoto in the name of the 15-year-old Meiji emperor, then won a resounding military victory at Toba-Fushimi. Edo's population now fell to around half its former level as remaining residents of the yamanote areas departed. A last stand by shogunate loyalists in Ueno was hopeless, and left in ruins large parts of the Kan'ei-ji Temple complex, which housed several Tokugawa shoguns' tombs.

MEIJI ERA (1868-1912)

Edo was renamed Tokyo ('Eastern Capital') when the emperor's residence was transferred from Kyoto in 1868. It became the political and imperial capital, with the inner section of Edo Castle serving as the new Imperial Palace. The population had reverted to its earlier level by the mid-1880s, but shitamachi lost much of its cultural distinctiveness as wealthier residents moved to smarter locations. Industrialisation continued to bring newcomers from the countryside. By the end of the Meiji era Tokyo housed nearly 2 million people.

RICH COUNTRY, STRONG ARMY

To the south-west of the palace, Nagatacho and Kasumigaseki became the heart of the nation's new government and bureaucratic establishment. 'Rich country, strong army' became the rallying cry, but learning from abroad was recognised to be essential: government missions were dispatched overseas, foreign experts brought in, and radical reforms initiated in everything from education to land ownership.

In Tokyo, tradition and neon go hand in hand.

Laying the foundations of a modern state meant sweeping away much of the old feudal structure. Government was centralised and the daimyo pensioned off. The introduction of conscription in 1873 ended the exclusive role of the warrior class. Disaffected elements, led by Saigo Takamori (*see page 57*, Ueno statue), staged a rebellion in Satsuma in 1877, but were defeated by government forces. The next year, six former samurai from Satsuma staged a revenge attack and murdered Meiji government leader Okubo Toshimichi.

Ending old social restrictions fuelled economic development. The Bank of Japan was established in 1882, bringing greater fiscal and monetary stability. Industrialisation proceeded apace and factories sprang up near the Sumida River and in areas overlooking Tokyo Bay. After 1894, Marunouchi became the site of a business district called 'London Town' after its blocks of Victorian-style office buildings. In 1889, a written constitution declared the emperor 'sacred and inviolable'. Real power remained with existing government leaders but there was a nod to greater popular representation. Elections were held among the top 1.5 per cent of taxpayers, and the first session of the Imperial Diet took place in 1890.

By the early 1890s, the government was making progress on ending the much-hated 'unequal treaties' earlier conceded to the west. Taking a leaf from the imperialists' book, Japan seized Taiwan in 1895 after a war with China. Ten years later its forces defeated Russia. This was the first victory over a western power by an Asian country, but there were riots in Hibiya Park at the perceived leniency of the peace treaty. In 1910, Japan annexed neighbouring Korea.

EAST MEETS WEST

New goods and ideas from overseas started to pour into Tokyo, especially after Japan's first train line started services between Yokohama and Shinbashi station in 1872. Men abandoned traditional topknots; married women followed the lead of the empress and stopped blackening their teeth. There were gas lights, beer halls, the first public parks and department stores, and even ballroom dancing at Hibiya's glittering Rokumeikan, where the elite gathered in their best foreign finery to display their mastery of the advanced new ways.

The former artisan district of Ginza was redeveloped with around 900 brick buildings after a major fire in 1872, and newspaper offices were the first to flock to what would become Tokyo's most fashionable area. Asakusa kept in touch with popular tastes through attractions such as the Ryounkaku, which had the city's first elevator, and was Tokyo's tallest building, with 12 storeys. Asakusa was also home to Japan's first permanent cinema, which opened in 1903, and the cinemas, theatres and music halls of Asakusa's Sixth District remained popular throughout the early decades of the new century.

TAISHO ERA (1912-26)

The funeral of Emperor Meiji was accompanied by the ritual suicide of General Nogi. The new emperor, Taisho, was in constant poor health and his son became regent the same year. There was a brief flowering of 'Taisho Democracy': in 1918 Hara Takashi became the first prime minister from a political party, an appointment that came after a sudden rise in rice prices prompted national disturbances, including five days of rioting in the capital. Hara was assassinated in 1921 by a right-wing extremist, but universal male suffrage was finally introduced in 1925.

The city was starting to spill over its boundaries and part of Shinjuku was brought inside the city limits for the first time in 1920, a first indication of the capital's tendency to westward drift with the growth of suburban train lines. Ginza was enjoying its heyday as a strolling spot for fashionable youth. In nearby Hibiya, a new Imperial Hotel, designed by Frank Lloyd Wright, opened in 1923.

GREAT KANTO EARTHQUAKE

Shortly before noon on 1 September 1923, the Kanto region was hit by a devastating earthquake of 7.9 magnitude on the Japanese scale. High winds fanned the flames of cooking fires and two days of terrible blazes swept through Tokyo and surrounding areas, including Yokohama, leaving over 140,000 dead and devastating large areas. Around 63 per cent of Tokyo homes were destroyed, with the traditional wooden buildings of the old shitamachi areas hardest hit. In the confusion, dark rumours of well-poisoning and other misdeeds led vigilante groups to massacre several thousand Koreans before martial law was imposed.

Temporary structures were quickly in place and there was a short building boom. The destruction in eastern areas accelerated the population movement to the western suburbs, but plans to remodel the city were largely laid aside because of cost.

SHOWA ERA (1926-89)

The longest recorded reign of any Japanese emperor coincided with a period of extraordinary change and turbulence. Tokyo recovered gradually from the effects of the 1923 quake and continued growing, but the country slid into dark days of militarism and war. In March 1945, Allied bombing brought huge devastation to the capital once more. Defeat was followed by occupation, but Tokyo was to rise again as Japan entered a new era of peace and unprecedented economic prosperity.

CITY EXPANSION

Post-quake reconstruction was declared officially over in 1930. In 1932, Tokyo's boundaries underwent major revision to take account of changing population patterns, with growing western districts such as Shibuya and Ikebukuro, and the remaining parts of Shinjuku, coming within the city limits. The total number of wards jumped from 15 to 35 (later simplified to the 23 of today) and the city's land area increased sevenfold. At a stroke, the population doubled to over 5 million, making Tokyo the world's second most populous city after New York.

MILITARISM & WAR

The era of parliamentary government didn't last. Political stability fell victim to the economic depression that followed a domestic banking collapse in 1927 and the Wall Street crash two years later. Extremist nationalist groups saw expansion

overseas as the answer to the nation's problems. In November 1930, after signing a naval disarmament treaty, prime minister Hamaguchi Osachi was killed by a right-wing extremist in Tokyo station (where Hara was killed nine years earlier).

In 1931, dissident army officers staged a Japanese military takeover of Manchuria, bringing conflict with world opinion. Pre-war party government ended after a shortlived rebellion of younger officers on 15 May 1932; prime minister Inukai Tsuyoshi and other members of the cabinet were assassinated and a series of national unity governments took over, dependent on military support. A puppet state, Manchukuo, was declared and Japan left the League of Nations. On 26 February 1936, the army's First Division mutinied and attempted a coup in the name of 'Showa Restoration'. Strategic points were seized in central Tokyo, but the rebellion was put down.

In an atmosphere of increasing nationalist fervour at home, Japan became involved in an ever-widening international conflict. Full-scale hostilities with China broke out in July 1937, but Japanese forces grew bogged down after early rapid advances. Western powers, led by the US, eventually declared a total embargo of Japan in summer 1941. Negotiations between the two sides reached an impasse, and on 7 December 1941, Japan attacked the US Pacific fleet at Pearl Harbor.

After a series of quick successes in the Pacific and south-east Asia, Japanese forces began to be pushed back after the Battle of Midway in June 1942. By late 1944, Tokyo lay within the range of American bombers. Incendiary attacks devastated the capital; the one on 10 March 1945 is estimated to have left 100,000 dead. On 6 August, an atomic bomb was dropped on Hiroshima, followed by another on Nagasaki three days later. Cabinet deadlock was broken by the intervention of the emperor, whose radio broadcast to the nation on 15 August announced Japan's surrender.

POST-WAR

Much of Tokyo lay in ruins; food and shelter posed immediate problems. As many as one in ten slept in temporary shelters during the first post-war

The Constitution of Japan, 1946

Chapter II. Renunciation of War

Article 9. Aspiring sincerely to an international peace based on justice and order, the Japanese people forever renounce war as a sovereign right of the nation and the threat or use of force as a means of settling international disputes.

(2) In order to accomplish the aim of the preceding paragraph, land, sea and air forces, as well as other war potential, will never be maintained. The right of belligerency of the state will not be recognised.

winter. General MacArthur set about demilitarising Japan and promoting democratic reform. The emperor kept his throne, but was forced to renounce his divine status. Article one of the new constitution included strict pacifist provisions (*see box*) and the armed forces were disbanded. In 1948, seven Class A war criminals, including war-time prime minister Tojo Hideki, were executed.

The outbreak of the Korean War in 1950 provided a tremendous boost to the Japanese economy, with large contracts to supply UN forces. Under MacArthur's orders, a limited rearmament took place, leading to the eventual founding of the Self-Defence Forces. Occupation ended in 1952 and there was a new security treaty with the USA.

With national defence left largely in US hands, economic growth was the priority under the long rule of the pro-business Liberal Democratic Party, formed in 1955. Prosperity started to manifest itself in the shape of large new office buildings in central Tokyo. In 1960, prime minister Ikeda Hayato announced a plan to double national income over a decade – a target achieved with ease in the economic miracle years that followed.

The Olympics were held in Tokyo in 1964, the same year *shinkansen* bullet trains started running between the capital and Osaka. Infrastructure improvements were made inside the city. Even after the Olympics, Tokyo's redevelopment continued apace. Frank Lloyd Wright's Imperial Hotel, a survivor of both the 1923 earthquake and the war, was demolished in 1967, the year the city's inner 23 wards achieved their peak population of almost 9 million. To the west of Shinjuku station, Tokyo's first concentration of skyscrapers started to take shape during the early '70s.

Despite the economic progress, there was an undercurrent of social discontent. Hundreds of thousands demonstrated against renewal of the security treaty with the United States in 1960, and the end of the decade saw students in violent revolt. In 1970, novelist Mishima Yukio dramatically ended his life after failing to spark a nationalist uprising at Ichigaya barracks. In Chiba, radical groups from the other end of the political spectrum joined local farmers to battle with riot police, delaying completion of Tokyo's new international airport at Narita from 1971 to 1975 and its opening until 1978.

The post-war fixed exchange rate ended in 1971 and growth came to a temporary halt with the oil crisis of 1974, but the Japanese economy continued to outperform its western competitors. Trade friction developed, particularly with the USA. After the Plaza agreement of 1985, the yen jumped to new highs, inflating the value of Japanese financial assets. Shoppers switched to designer labels as a building frenzy gripped Tokyo, the world's most expensive city. Land values soared and wild speculation fuelled a 'bubble economy'.

HEISEI ERA (1989-)

The death of Hirohito came at the beginning of the sweeping global changes marking the end of the Cold War. As the 1990s wore on, the system that served Japan so well in the post-war era began to stumble. A collapse in land and stock market prices brought the bubble economy to an end in 1990 and left Japanese banks with a mountain of bad debt. An economy that had been the envy of the world a decade earlier became mired in its deepest recession since the end of the war.

Longstanding demands for an end to 'money politics' finally proved irresistible in 1993, after prosecutors discovered 100 kilograms (220 pounds) of gold bars, plus billions of yen in bond certificates and other valuables, in raids on the offices of LDP 'shadow shogun' Kanemaru Shin. The LDP lost power for the first time in 38 years, and a shortlived nine-party coalition under Morihito Hosokawa of the Japan New Party enacted a programme of reform, ending the old multi-seat constituency system. The LDP clawed its way back to government in 1994, in an unlikely partnership with its erstwhile foe, the rapidly declining Socialists, but there was strong evidence of continuing voter dissatisfaction as a kaleidoscope of new parties came and went.

In 1991, Tokyo's metropolitan government had moved to a thrusting new skyscraper in Shinjuku, symbolising the capital's gradual move from its traditional centre. Four years later, in January 1995, the Kobe earthquake provided Tokyo-ites with a reminder of their own vulnerability to natural disaster. Soon after, a sarin gas attack on city subways by members of the Aum Shinrikyo doomsday cult provoked more horror and much agonised debate. In April 1995, in a protest against the established political parties, Tokyo voters elected an independent, former comedian Aoshima Yukio, as their new governor. He promptly scrapped a planned exhibition to inaugurate a waterfront development at Daiba on grounds of cost. Discussions about moving the national government to a less quake-prone location continued.

A consumption tax increase and the knock-on effects of the Asian economic meltdown of 1997 snuffed out the tentative signs of economic recovery. Events such as the sudden collapse of Yamaichi Securities added to a climate of job insecurity, and led to talk of Tokyo losing its position as one of the world's major financial centres. After disappointing results in the July 1998 upper house elections, Hashimoto Ryutaro resigned as PM and LDP leader, leaving Obuchi Keizo to scrabble around for tie-ups with opposition groups while attempting to deal with a worsening economic crisis. In April 1999, attracted by the promise of strong leadership, Tokyo voters elected as new governor Ishihara Shintaro, a hawkish former-LDP independent and co-author of *The Japan that Can Say No*.

Key events

c.10,000-300 BC Jomon period.
660 BC Date given for ascension to throne of Jimmu, Japan's mythical first emperor.
c.300 BC-AD 300 Yayoi period; wet-rice growing, bronze and ironware arrive from continental Asia.
1st century AD Japan ('land of Wa') first mentioned in Chinese chronicles.
4th century Yamato court exists in Nara area.
538 or 552 Buddhism introduced from Korea.
710 Nara becomes imperial capital.
794 Capital moves to Heian (Kyoto).
1002-19 Murasaki Shikibu writes *Tale of Genji*.
1180 First recorded use of name Edo.
1185-1333 Kamakura is site of government.
1274, 1281 Attempted Mongol invasions.
1457 Ota Dokan builds first castle at Edo.
1543 Western firearms introduced by Portuguese.
1549 St Francis Xavier arrives in Japan.
1590 Edo becomes HQ of Tokugawa Ieyasu. Construction of Edo Castle begins.
1592 Hideyoshi invades Korea.
1598 Withdrawal from Korea.
1603 Ieyasu named *shogun*; Edo becomes seat of national government. Bridge built at Nihonbashi.
1616 Death of Tokugawa Ieyasu.
1639 National seclusion policy established.
1657 Long Sleeves Fire destroys much of Edo.
1688-1704 Genroku cultural flowering; Ichikawa Danjuro I creates *aragoto* style of *kabuki* in Edo.
1703 47 *ronin* vendetta carried out.
1707 Mount Fuji erupts; ash falls on Edo.
1720 Ban on import of foreign books lifted.
1742 Floods and storms kill around 4,000 in Edo.
1787-93 Kansei reforms; rice granaries set up in Edo after Tenmei famine and riots in urban areas.
1804-29 Bunka-Bunsei period; peak of Edo merchant culture.
1825 'Order for Repelling of Foreign Ships'.
1841-3 Reforms to strengthen economy following nationwide famine.
1853 Arrival of US 'Black Ships' at Uraga.
1854 Treaty of Kanagawa signed with Perry.
1855 Major quake kills over 7,000 in Edo.
1858 Commercial treaties with western powers.
1860 Ii Naosuke assassinated outside Edo Castle.
1862 End of alternate residence system.
1868 Meiji Restoration. Imperial residence moved from Kyoto; Edo renamed Tokyo.
1869 Yasukuni Shrine built to honour Japan's war dead. Rickshaws appear on Tokyo streets.
1871-3 Meiji leaders tour US and Europe.
1872 Train service from Shinbashi to Yokohama.
1874 Tokyo's first gas lights, on streets of Ginza.
1877 Saigo Takamori leads Satsuma rebellion.
1889 Meiji constitution promulgated.
1890 Ryounkaku brick tower built in Asakusa.
1894-5 Sino-Japanese War.
1902 Anglo-Japanese alliance signed.

1904-5 Russo-Japanese war.
1910 Korea incorporated into Japanese empire.
1912 Death of Emperor Meiji; Taisho era begins.
1922 Lloyd Wright's Imperial Hotel completed.
1923 Great Kanto Earthquake leaves 100,000 dead; fire destroys much of Tokyo.
1925 Universal male suffrage introduced.
1926 Hirohito becomes emperor; Showa era begins.
1927 Asia's first subway line, between Asakusa and Ueno; extended to Ginza and Shibuya by 1939.
1931 Manchurian Incident.
1932 PM Inukai Tsuyoshi assassinated. Major extension of Tokyo boundaries.
1933 Japan leaves League of Nations.
1934 Yomiuri Giants baseball team founded.
1936 Army rebellion in central Tokyo. Completion of Diet building. Arrest of murderess Abe Sada (story told in film *Ai No Corrida*).
1937 Rape of Nanking.
1940 Tripartite Pact with Germany and Italy.
1941 Pearl Harbor attack begins Pacific War.
1945 March: incendiary bombing of Tokyo. August: atom bombs dropped on Hiroshima and Nagasaki. Japan surrenders; occupation begins.
1946 Emperor renounces divinity. New constitution promulgated.
1950-3 Korean War.
1951 Security treaty signed with USA.
1952 Occupation ends.
1954 Release of first *Godzilla* film.
1955 Liberal Democratic Party formed, along with Japan Socialist Party.
1958 Tokyo Tower completed.
1960 Demonstrations against renewal of US-Japan security treaty.
1964 Tokyo Olympic Games. First *shinkansen* bullet train runs between Tokyo and Osaka.
1966 Beatles play at Nippon Budokan.
1968-9 Student unrest.
1970 Writer Mishima Yukio commits suicide.
1971 Yen revalued from 360 to 308/US$. Japan's first McDonald's opens in Ginza.
1973 Oil crisis: panic buying, economic slowdown.
1983 Tokyo Disneyland opens.
1988 Release of *Akira*. Tokyo Dome completed.
1989 Death of Hirohito; Heisei era begins. Recruit scandal forces PM Takeshita Noboru to resign.
1990 End of 'bubble economy'.
1993 LDP loses power after 38 years to political reform coalition under Hosokawa Morihito.
1994 Japan Socialist Party leader Murayama Tomiichi becomes PM in coalition with LDP.
1995 Kobe earthquake. Sarin gas attack on Tokyo subway. Yen briefly reaches 90/US$.
1998 Asian economic crisis spreads from Thailand. Obuchi Keizo replaces Hashimoto Ryutaro as LDP leader and prime minister.
1999 Ishihara Shintaro elected Tokyo governor.

Tokyo Today

It's a brave new world as Tokyo strides into the twenty-first century.

Graffiti: one of the less troubling expressions of youthful alienation in the Tokyo of today.

'More thorough nonsense must be spoken and written about Japan than about any comparably developed nation.'

Introduction to Japan, Alan Booth.

WELCOME TO TOKYO

The big 'Welcome to Tokyo' signs throughout New Tokyo International Airport fail to prepare the visitor for two initial surprises. Firstly, the airport is at Narita, a considerable 66 kilometres (41 miles) from Tokyo. This distance can be covered by the high-speed Skyliner shuttle, which does Narita to Shinjuku in 60 minutes, but the train nixes the second surprise – the controversy that's engulfed the airport since its inception.

Catch the airport limousine bus and the airport's formidable fortifications and riot police presence immediately come into view. They represent one of post-war Japan's longest-running and most documented disputes. During the initiation and expansion of the country's busiest air terminal, farming

Pachinko

Walk down any Tokyo shopping street and you'll soon hear the clatter of steel balls from the local *pachinko* arcade. Pachinko is a national obsession, an industry thought to be worth over ¥30 trillion per year. Players buy buckets of steel ball bearings and then sit at a vertical pinball table watching as they whizz round, in the hope that the balls will fall down the right holes and win them more ball bearings. There's very little skill involved, since all the machines are fully automatic, yet regular players will have their favourite machines and will keep a careful eye on the pachinko parlour to see which ones are paying out. So what's the appeal of this mindless game? In a word, money. Although gambling is mostly illegal in Japan (*see chapter* **Sport**), pachinko parlours get round the law by offering worthless tokens as prizes that can then be exchanged for cash at a little booth around the corner. It's technically illegal, but the authorities continue to turn a blind eye.

Although vast amounts can be lost and won at pachinko, the minimum outlay, at around ¥100, is quite small. If you want to give it a blast, walk into your local parlour, buy ¥500-worth of balls, then watch them disappear, along with your mind and your sense of hearing.

Pachinko: it takes balls of steel.

communities were 'persuaded' to move from land they'd worked for generations. In a country where agricultural land accounts for only 13.4 per cent of its total area, this is no small issue. For two decades local villagers, together with a mixed bag of support from students, Communists and anti-war protesters (who believed the facilities would be used for military flights), fought pitched battles with riot police outside the airport gates and legal battles with the authorities in court. The dispute continues to smoulder, as two families who stubbornly refuse to sell up and leave have frustrated attempts to add a second runway to what is one of the world's most congested airports.

POLITICAL PASSION ON THE WANE

Tokyoites today are less prone to outbursts of political passion than 20 or 30 years ago. The low voter turn-out on election day is a clear indication of the cynicism many have about the goings-on in the corridors of power. National politics is widely viewed as a self-serving world of faceless ministers jostling for wealth and power. Since April 1995, however, when the office of governor in both Tokyo and Osaka fell to two outsiders, the picture of local government has looked rosier.

Running as independents, 'Knock' Yokoyama, a comedian-turned-politician, and Aoshima Yukio, a former scriptwriter, actor and novelist, brought a human face to the seedy world of city politics, and subsequently launched a thousand imitators in local government throughout the country. Knock Yokoyama excelled at his new post as governor of Osaka, and was easily re-elected in April 1999, when only the communists dared field a candidate against him. Aoshima's 'human face' was quickly battered, and by the time he stepped down most Tokyoites had written him off as a pawn of the bureaucrats, Japan's most powerful political class.

In a scramble to fill the vacuum left by Aoshima, 19 candidates ran in the gubernatorial elections held in Tokyo on 11 April 1999. The winner, by a good furlong, was Ishihara Shintaro, a maverick writer-politician known for his nationalistic and anti-American views. A former member of the ruling Liberal Democratic Party until he abruptly quit in 1995, Ishihara's notoriety stems from both his hawkish remarks and his inflammatory book, *The Japan that Can Say No*, co-authored with former Sony chairman Morita Akio. While the book takes aim at the government's spineless acquiescence to anything out of Washington, his angry outbursts have found targets almost everywhere.

'Article 9 should be revised. It is necessary [for Japan] to develop nuclear weapons', he told a news conference in 1997. 'Surrounded by pig pens and chicken coops, the test course is in the least adequate place for exhibiting Japan's technology to the rest of the world', he answered when asked about the test track of the magnetically levitated train in Hyuga, Miyazaki Prefecture. For that one, he later apologised.

TAXING TIMES FOR SHOPPERS

Surprisingly, the Japan Communist Party (which goes to great pains to distance itself from its overseas counterparts) repeatedly garners support in Tokyo. Of late, many of its successful candidates have been middle-aged women – the all-pearls-and-lipstick brigade – who rally their housewife cadres with the cry for retail revolution.

This cash register stumping has found an ideal platform in the consumption tax. In 1989, when the new tax was introduced at three per cent, suburbia rang with loudspeakers calling for a united opposition. When, in 1994, the tax was increased to five per cent, the same candidates were back on the streets calling for a return to the good old days of three per cent. The struggle continues.

On the opposing side, the ballot box holds little attraction for the various parties of the ultra-right. Eschewing democracy, however, does have its rewards, as the nationalists continue to flaunt their *enfant terrible* image with loud pulpit-banging speeches long after the polling booths have closed.

From atop their armoured trucks and buses uniformed lieutenants harangue downtown Tokyo on a near-daily basis with apocalyptic threats against Japan's enemies – Russia, America, China, Communism, the incumbent government, the teachers' union, foreigners staying illegally in the country – while a convoy of nationalist pride converges annually on Yasukuni Shrine (*see chapter* **Museums & Galleries**) to pay homage to the 2.5 million war-dead enshrined there, among whom are convicted war criminals and kamikaze pilots.

Mobile phones: must-haves for teenagers.

ORGANISED CRIME

The far right's affiliations with organised crime are no secret. Many an ardent defender of Japan by day is, by night, a petty gangster and, indeed, the same foot soldiers that rail against Tokyo's burgeoning foreign community gladly reap huge rewards from the lucrative trafficking of Thai prostitutes to Japan.

The notorious *yakuza* have their fingers in most criminal pies (pun not intended). The three main gangs, Yamaguchi-gumi, Sumiyoshi-kai and Inagawa-kai, have between them some 42,000 members nationwide, and their activities, from drug smuggling to gambling, span the underworld's horizon. Their weakness is for extortion, a particularly undemanding task that ensures a regular flow of yen. Many a Tokyo restaurateur, bar owner, street seller, company president, politician and even shareholder can look forward to the eventual knock at the door, and an offer that is near-impossible to refuse. The police, for their part, keep a safe distance, usually intervening only when gang rivalry turns to warfare.

In theatre and film the yakuza still carries hero status. Period dramas depict him as the gentleman thief; a wandering *samurai* driven to crime by his own privation, while in contemporary film he is a moralist, torn between gangland duty and a latent yearning to do good. Back in the real world the average hood is neither.

Gang rights are given young: many members are recent school drop-outs who have passed into the underworld through motorcycle gangs, part-time work or crime. The swaggering confidence of this rank and file does little to conceal its affiliations, and the preening that distinguishes Japanese males is nowhere more obsessive than in the testosterone-fuelled world of gangsterism.

Although it's no surprise to find the yakuza don prefers the godfatherly touch – black Mercedes; coat draped over shoulders; tinted glasses; hair scraped back – it is bizarre that in a profession where facial scars and torso-sized tattoos are de rigueur the chosen look is a tightly knit 'punch' perm, an in-ya-face-coloured trouser suit, sunglasses and heeled sandals – the latter usually a few sizes too small.

CRIME ON THE RISE

Since the mid-'70s crime in Japan has increased dramatically. In 1973 there were fewer than 1,200 offences per 100,000 people; by 1997 the number had reached 1,900. This figure includes offences committed by foreigners, which have skyrocketed from a trifling 1,725 in 1985 to a total of 21,670 in 1997, and serious crimes, such as rape and murder, which have risen steadily since the '80s. But these figures can be misleading. Tokyo is still a remarkably safe place in which to live, work and play – 87.7 per cent of 1997's crimes were thefts, with violent crime accounting for just 2.1 per cent.

Tokyo by numbers

378 deaths from traffic accidents (1997).
614 people aged 100 or over (1999).
13 deaths from AIDS (1997).
75 amusement parks (1996).
76 art museums (1997).
76.73, 83.12 average life expectancy of men and women respectively.
23,536 bars (1996)
857,873,000 beer drunk annually, in litres (1996).
99,620 births (1998).
423 average price in yen, per kilo of bread.
26 prime ministers since end of World War II.
4,222 convenience stores (1997).
688 churches (1996).
552 shrines (1996).
2,722 temples (1996).
25.4 average summer temperature in centigrade (1997).
7.7 average winter temperature in centigrade (1997).
1,583 pachinko parlours (1997).
23,690 divorces (1997).
5,331,773 amount of rubbish, in tonnes (1997).
431,000 average monthly salary of a full-time working male, in yen.
273,700 average monthly salary of a full-time working female, in yen.
6,820 sushi bars (1996).
11,872,031 people (1 Apr, 1999) (*see chapter* **Geography**).
49.9/50.1 male/female ratio, as a percentage.
164/160 average working hours per month of men and women respectively.
695.5 length, km (432 miles) of JR rail track in Tokyo's 23 wards (local track 502.4km/312.2 miles; shinkansen track 193.1km/120 miles).
765,517 number of people who buy a ticket at Shinjuku station in one day (1997).
1,300,000 estimated number of people who pass through Shinjuku station in one day (1997).
275 maximum speed, in kph (172mph), of the Tohoku, Joetsu and Akita shinkansen (1998).
34 average speed, in kph (21mph), of Yamanote line trains.
34.5 length, in km (21.5 miles), of Yamanote line loop.
61 average time, in minutes, it takes to do one loop on the Yamanote Line.
640 number of special express trains arriving and departing from Tokyo station per day.
259 maximum urban commuter train congestion rate, expressed as a percentage, between Oimachi and Shinagawa stations on JR's Keihin Tohoku line, between 7.30 and 8.30am (1995).
26,774 factories (1996).
948,000 landing fee at Narita airport, in yen (1997).
2.9 park area, in sq m, per person in Tokyo (1997).
25.3 park area, in sq m, per person in London (1997).
46 snowfall, in cm, on 8 Feb 1883.
6.693 Imperial Household expenses, in billions of yen (1998).
10,000 cultivated hectares (24,710 acres).
234 height of Opera City tower in m (768 ft).
386,100 average price, in yen, of 1sq m of land (1997).
11,800,000 average price, in yen, of 1sq m of land in Ginza 5-chome (1998).
3.52 average number of rooms per home (1993).
0.72 average number of people per room (1993).
133 deaths in the ANA Boeing 727 crash at Haneda airport on 4 Feb 1966.
142,807 deaths in the Great Kanto Earthquake of 1 Sept 1923.
576,262 buildings destroyed by the above.
91,967 items housed by the Tokyo National Museum (1997).

Yet a more sinister trend has left the country shocked at both the cruelty and cold indifference of its own children. Juvenile crime, which has doubled since 1993, is no longer just about teenage filching or spray-paint graffiti. School rapes, stabbings, suicides, and even the murder of teachers, are no longer horrific tragedies that happen to other people in other countries. For boys the uproar has been about knives: stabbings of fellow students, and even a fatal rage knifing of a young woman teacher by a pupil, revealed a countrywide fascination with carrying, and using, 'butterfly' knives. Fanned by Japan's sensationalist media, the incidents increased in number and viciousness, peaking in 1998 when, it seemed, not a week went by without another stabbing, the news stations falling over themselves to capture the nation's tears on video. The question now is what the next schoolboy prank will entail.

TEENAGE RAMPAGE

For girls, the uproar has been about *enjo kosai*, or 'compensated dating'. Since the start of the '90s a deepening recession has forced drastic changes in consumer habits as workers face an increasingly uncertain future. Having grown up in the boom years of the bubble economy, most Tokyo

A bumpy ride into the future for Tokyo's youth.

teenagers have never known restraint and, egged on by media that dictate what today's youth requires, the shopping list of the average Tokyo teenage girl is a far cry from the spartan days of her parents' youth. Mobile phones, Prada handbags, designer clothes, skiing holidays – all require a budget that flipping hamburgers cannot sustain. This has resulted in an almost Faustian pact: many adult men are willing to pay for casual sex, and many teenage girls happy to deliver. A recent survey of junior high school girls in their final year revealed that 17 per cent found nothing distasteful about compensated dating and 13 per cent felt no reluctance about practising it. In 1998 these figures moved the government to enact a law that left those who encourage minors to sell sex liable to prison terms of up to one year and a fine of ¥500,000. However, encouraged by the materialistic pressures of society and the plenitude of 'love hotels', compensated dating has shown no signs of decline. On the contrary, reports suggest that it has moved up a generation, as young 'office ladies' turn to solicitation to boost their meagre salaries.

On the other hand, the inequality of the sexes has left women in Tokyo with a remarkable amount of independence. Not having the responsibilities and opportunities in the workplace afforded their male counterparts has allowed women a freedom of choice unprecedented in the country's history. Although marriage remains high on a woman's agenda, more and more of Tokyo's young brides are choosing to enjoy the financial privileges of a double income over the restraints of early motherhood. Indeed, marriage itself, when it does happen, is happening later in life. No longer do Tokyo's women fear the 'Christmas cake' moniker, a derogatory term used for a woman still single after 25 (implying that, after the 25th, she would be left on the shelf). The early years of womanhood are now seen as a time for enjoyment and discovery, be that socialising with friends, learning new skills or travelling and studying overseas.

This new-found freedom is in no way restricted to the young. Since the post-war baby boom of 1947, the birth rate has plummeted, with the present figure a perilous all-time low. Older women, free from the shackles that tied an earlier generation of mothers to a legion of offspring, are now reaping the rewards of their husbands' 'employment for life'. Department stores, art galleries, theatres, domestic package holidays and chic 'coffee and cake' shops all cater predominantly to a middle-aged sisterhood that is both affluent and liberated after years of housewife drudgery.

THE TIMES, THEY ARE A CHANGIN'

The Tokyo male, on the other hand, has little to celebrate. With a family tucked away in the suburbs, an undemanding mortgage and a steady job that looked set to last for eternity, the average salaryman's life was, until ten years ago, a carefree one. His days were spent at a desk that, over his working life, he would literally come to know inside out. The evenings, after the mandatory overtime, he could enjoy on Tokyo's neon-lit tiles, secure in the fact that the company would foot the bill, no questions asked. Now he must be wondering what hit him. When the economy nosedived, the first casualty was the much-abused corporate expense account. No longer would the accounts department turn a blind eye to the horrendous sums spent cavorting with young women in hostess clubs and girly bars – if an evening out did not involve entertaining a client integral to company survival, the ¥50,000 and upwards many of the establishments charge for a bottle of whisky would have to come out of his own pocket.

Coinciding with the digital revolution, next up for the chop was the system of promotion based on age and loyal service. In an ironic twist, the same Tokyo companies that preached the success of 'the Japanese way' to their overseas counterparts in the '80s are now, in the '90s, looking to the west for guidance in the unfamiliar climate of meritocracy. This policy shift has left membership of the *madogiwa-zoku* ('tribe by the window': workers waiting for retirement) an enviable alternative to outright expulsion. As companies close one after another, the number of unskilled middle-aged men out of work sadly reflects the naive trust the 'job-for-life' system induced.

Tokyo now looks to the future, perhaps anticipating a period of stability after two decades of boom and bust. But one eye will remain fixed on the past, hoping to find an explanation for the difficulties still to be faced.

Architecture

Earthquakes and fire have shaped this city as much as any architect.

Since it first flung open its doors to the world back in 1868, Tokyo has been a laboratory for the meeting and synthesis of local and western styles that continues to inform the development of Japanese architecture today. Lacking the ancient temples of Kyoto and Nara, Tokyo has also been stripped of much of its own architectural heritage by a history of fires, terrible earthquakes and heavy war-time bombing, compounded by break-neck post-war economic development and an unsentimental lack of attachment to the old.

One of the great attractions of this extraordinary city is its apparent randomness, and this is nowhere more true than in the field of architecture, where multi-billion-yen buildings often stand next to mundane shops or humble convenience stores. Sometimes, to appreciate an individual building, an act of imagination is required to take it out of its context. At other times, its setting makes it stand out all the more.

TRADITIONAL STYLES

Japanese architecture has traditionally been based on the use of wooden materials, but authentic examples of older styles of housing and shops (as well as buildings from the early modern period) are often best looked for at one of the open-air museums that have preserved original structures from destruction (*see chapter* **Sightseeing**).

Very few original structures remain from the city's former incarnation as Edo, capital of the Tokugawa shoguns, although parts of the imposing pre-modern fortifications of Edo Castle can still be seen when walking around the moat and gardens of the Imperial Palace, built on part of the castle site.

The original wooden houses and shops of Edo-era *shitamachi* (downtown) have now almost completely disappeared, although later examples in similar styles can often be found in older residential districts. Outside the very heart of the city, recognisable traditional features, such as eaves and tiled roofs, are still widely used on modern suburban housing, while *tatami* mats and sliding doors are common inside even more western-style apartment blocks.

The city's shrines and temples are overwhelmingly traditional in form. The Meiji Shrine is an impressive example of the austere style and restrained colours typical of Shinto architecture, which is usually quite distinctive from that of Buddhist temples, where the greater influence of

Chinese and Korean styles is usually apparent. Many present-day buildings of older religious institutions are reconstructions of earlier incarnations; the well-known temples of Sensoji and Zojoji are both examples, although in these cases some remnants of earlier structures also survive. The 1605 Sanmon Gate of Zojoji Temple and Gokokuji Temple, which dates from 1681, are rare, unre-constructed survivors.

In contrast, when the wooden building of Honganji temple in Tsukiji burnt down for the ninth time in the temple's long history, after the 1923 earthquake, it was rebuilt in sturdier stone. The design by architect Ito Chita, earlier responsible for the Meiji Shrine, was also quite different: an eye-catching affair recalling Buddhism's roots in ancient India.

WESTERNISATION & REACTION

After the Meiji Restoration of 1868, the twin influences of westernisation and modernisation quickly made themselves felt in Tokyo, the new national capital. Early attempts to combine western and traditional elements by local architects resulted in extraordinary hybrids featuring Japanese-style sloping roofs rising above wooden constructions with ornate front façades of a distinctly western style. Kisuke Shimizu's Hoterukan (1868) at the Foreign Settlement in Tsukiji and his First National Bank (1872) in Nihonbashi were two notable Tokyo examples. Neither survives today.

Tokyo's earliest buildings of a purely western design were chiefly the work of overseas architects brought to Japan by the new Meiji government. Englishman Thomas Waters oversaw the post-1872 redevelopment of Ginza with around 900 red-brick buildings, thought to be sturdier than wooden Japanese houses. Ironically, none of them survived the 1923 earthquake.

Waters' fellow-countryman Josiah Conder, who taught at Tokyo Imperial University, was the most influential western architect of the early Meiji period, with important projects in the capital including ministry buildings, the original Imperial Museum at Ueno (1881) and Hibiya's Rokumeikan reception hall (1883). His Mitsui Club in Mita (1913) and Nikolai Cathedral in Ochanomizu (1891) still exist, although the latter was badly damaged in the 1923 earthquake.

Later Meiji official architecture was often a close reflection of western styles, although it was

The skyscraper city of west Shinjuku grew out of Japan's post-war economic boom.

Japanese architects who increasingly handled the prestige projects. Remaining red-brick structures of the period include the Ministry of Justice (1895), built in Kasumigaseki by the German firm of Ende and Bockman, and the Crafts Gallery of the National Museum of Modern Art (1910), which once housed the administrative headquarters of the Imperial Guard. The imposing Bank of Japan building (1896) was built by one of Conder's former students, Tatsuno Kingo, who was also responsible for the Marunouchi wing of Tokyo Station (1914), modelled on Centraal Station in Amsterdam. A far more grandiose overseas inspiration, that of Versailles, is said to have been used for Akasaka Detached Palace (1909), created by Katayama Tokuma, whose other work includes the Hyokeikan building of the National Museum in Ueno (also completed in 1909).

The era after World War I saw the completion of Frank Lloyd Wright's highly distinctive Imperial Hotel (1922), which famously survived the Tokyo earthquake shortly after its opening, but has since been demolished. The period after the earthquake saw the spread of social housing, and a prominent example that still exists, although now used largely for shops, is the Harajuku tenement apartment blocks (1926) on Omotesando.

The influence of contemporary overseas trends can be discerned in the modernism of Yoshida Tetsuro's Tokyo Central Post Office (1931) and the art deco of Tokyo Metropolitan Teien Art

Museum (1933), built originally as a mansion for Prince Asaka and planned mainly by French designer Henri Rapin. The present-day Diet Building (1936) also shows a strong art deco influence, but its design became a source of heated debate in the increasingly nationalist climate of the period when it was completed.

A reaction against westernisation had already been apparent in the work of Ito Chita (*see above*), who had looked toward Asian models. There were now demands for a distinctive national look. The so-called 'Imperial Crown' style is usually represented by the main building of the National Museum (1938) in Ueno. This was the design of Watanabe Hitoshi, an architect of unusual versatility whose other works include the Hattori Building (1932) of Wako department store at Ginza 4-chome crossing, and the Daiichi Insurance Building (1938). The latter was used by General MacArthur as his Tokyo headquarters after the war, and is now the shorter and older part of the DN Tower 21 complex in Hibiya.

POST-WAR TOKYO

The priority in the early post-war period was often to provide extra office space for companies trying to cope with the demands of an economy hurtling along at double-digit growth rates, or a rapid answer to the pressing housing needs of the city's growing population. Seismic instability meant that tall buildings were not initially an option, and anonymous, box-like structures proliferated.

Even as confidence grew about new construction techniques, designed to provide greater protection against earthquakes, many of the initial results were strangely undistinguished. The city's first and only real cluster of skyscrapers, built in west Shinjuku from the early 1970s, has been described as resembling a set of urban tombstones.

Tokyo ordered itself something of a postmodernist make-over as the bubble economy took hold during the 1980s, and this splurge of 'trophy architecture' has left the city a string of new and enjoyably eye-catching landmarks. One that's particularly difficult to ignore is the Super Dry Hall in Asakusa by Philippe Starck, one of the increasing number of foreign architects to have worked on projects in Tokyo in recent years. These include Rafael Viñoly, responsible for the stunning Tokyo International Forum (1996), and Norman Foster, whose Century Tower (1991) is located near Ochanomizu.

The reclamation of Tokyo Bay has also opened up land for a wide range of projects, such as Tange Kenzo's Fuji TV headquarters (1996) on Odaiba (*see page 62*). The Spiral building in Aoyama is one contribution to the new city look by Maki Fumihiko; another is the strange and low-level Tokyo Metropolitan Gymnasium in Sendagaya. Finally, another municipal project that should be mentioned is Kikutake Kiyonori's Edo-Tokyo Museum (1992) in Ryogoku, its alien spacecraft look comprised of traditional elements recalling the city's past, and its height of 62 metres exactly matching that of Edo Castle.

As for the future, one thing is certain: Tokyo will continue to rebuild itself, as it has for hundreds of years. If the buildings here today aren't to your taste, come back in 20 years and there'll be a whole new set for you to enjoy.

Tange Kenzo

The dominant figure of post-war Japanese architecture is Tange Kenzo. His string of major projects spans the whole era from 1949, when he won the competition to build the Hiroshima Peace Centre (completed in 1956), to 1991, when the Tokyo Metropolitan Government offices opened in the western part of Shinjuku. Tange's landmark twin-tower skyscraper complex became the tallest building in a city with which he had enjoyed a long and close association.

Back in 1957 he had also designed the previous metropolitan offices, a modernist work built on the Yurakucho site now occupied by Rafael Viñoly's Tokyo International Forum. In 1960 Tange presented a plan, never implemented, for a vast reordering of the city, overlaying Tokyo with a grid structure stretching right across Tokyo Bay but reminiscent of older Japanese and Chinese capitals. This reference to more ancient traditions can also be detected in Tange's big work for the 1964 Tokyo Olympics, the Yoyogi National Stadium, but is perhaps less obvious in projects such as the Hanae Mori Building (1978).

Tange's long career connects completely different generations of Japanese architects. One of his collaborators was Maekawa Kunio, a pre-war student of Le Corbusier in Europe who become one of Japan's foremost modern architects with works such as Tokyo Metropolitan Festival Hall (1961) and the Tokyo Metropolitan Art Museum (1975).

Someone who worked with Tange on his 1960 Tokyo Plan is Isozaki Arata, now one of Japan's most distinguished post-modernist architects and known internationally for the Museum of Contemporary Art (1986) in Los Angeles. Examples of his work in Tokyo include the Panasonic Globe (1983) in Okubo and the Ochanomizu Square Building (1987).

Landmark Tower in Yokohama, p224.

Sightseeing

Ikebukuro 池袋

In this fast-growing part of north Tokyo, shopping is king.

Ikebukuro, at the north-west corner of the Yamanote line, ranks alongside Shibuya and Shinjuku as a city within a city. A farming village until the Meiji era, it became a train junction early this century, amd started to grow. As the population expanded, more train and subway lines passed through to make Ikebukuro the shopping and entertainment centre of one of the most densely populated wards in Tokyo.

The credit for this rapid and radical transformation is largely due to rivals Yasujiro Tsutsumi and Kaichiro Nezu, who respectively developed the Seibu and Tobu railway lines. In time, each expanded its stronghold on the area by building a department store. Both ventures have been such successes that today they stand like walls along the station. The east side is dominated by Seibu, one of the largest department stores in the world, and the west side by the equally massive Tobu. Perpetually trying to outdo each other has led Seibu and Tobu to become multi-billion-dollar empires, with interests in transport, tourism, real estate, housing and more.

Many others have joined in the boom in Ikebukuro, most notably the 60-storey **Sunshine City** complex, one of the tallest buildings in Japan. Built on the grounds of the former Sugamo Prison – where executions took place until the late 1940s – it has one of the fastest elevators in the world, whisking you to a top-floor observatory offering views of the city and beyond.

Ikebukuro is a concrete monster, crammed with shops, restaurants and entertainment venues to satisfy the needs of the throngs on its streets, from early-morning commuters to office workers, shoppers and night time pleasure seekers.

The main hurdle is the station, which houses five train lines and two subway lines. There are over 40 exits and no maps indicating where you are or where the exits lead to. The best advice is to go out at the nearest exit and use the department stores to assess your position.

Because of the competition between the two giants and other department stores, as well as the area's less trendy reputation, prices are often lower than in areas closer to the centre. It goes for food, drinks and entertainment too. Don't be surprised to find love hotels offering three-hour rest periods for only ¥3,000. There are thousands of restaurants too, both in the narrow streets around the station and inside Seibu, Tobu and other complexes.

EAST EXIT

The most obvious building is **Seibu** (*see chapter* **Shops & Services**), stretching like a wall along the tracks. Get a floor guide to navigate the maze. The food halls on B1 and B2 have a great selection of Japanese and imported foods and ingredients. The imported foods supermarket has one of the largest selections in Tokyo. The fish and seafood section is amazing, and is one of the few places where you can buy cuts of the whales Japan catches 'for scientific experiments'. Plenty of bento and foods to make up lunch, although places to sit and eat nearby are scarce.

Facing Seibu on your right you'll find **Parco** (*see chapter* **Shops & Services**), the outlet for the young and trendy. There are two stores, one part of the Seibu complex, the other, P'Parco, a minute's walk away. The store outside the complex has a more interesting selection of fashion items. You'll also find **Tower Records** on the fifth and sixth floors, and on the seventh is **Ishibashi** for musical instruments and gear, as well as **S.R.C.** sporting goods on the eighth.

Carrying on the main road will soon take you to the discount store **BIC Camera** (*see chapter* **Shops & Services**); it specialises in cameras but also stocks other electronic and electrical goods. There is also a branch on the main road towards Sunshine 60 Street.

By far the best place for foreign books and magazines in Ikebukuro is across the road from Seibu on the fifth floor of **Junkudo**. The area between Junkudo and Green Odori is full of small shops and restaurants, but the main concentration is across the road towards Sunshine City. The main street, Sunshine 60, leads to **Tokyu Hands** (*see chapter* **Shops & Services**), and the entrance to Sunshine City. Tokyu Hands is the store par excellence for just about anything and worth a visit.

After the department stores, however, the focal point of Ikebukuro is the **Sunshine City** complex, four giant connected buildings which contain everything from an aquarium to a theatre. The information desk has maps to help you around.

The first building is **Sunshine 60**, where you'll find the **observatory** on the sixtieth floor. There is a direct elevator – brace yourself for a psychedelic ride. Mount Fuji is visible on a clear day, but sunset is usually a better time to catch at least a glimpse. At nightfall the neons of Shinjuku are especially striking.

The second building is the **Prince Hotel**, and leads to **World Import Mart**. On the tenth floor there is an **aquarium** and **planetarium**.

The last building is **Bunka Kaikan** (Culture Hall), renowned for the Sunshine Theatre, showing modern Japanese entertainment, and the **Ancient Orient Museum**.

On the way out of the complex, you'll notice **Amlux** (*see page 76*), a giant Toyota showroom. Each of the five floors is devoted to a different style of car. On the first floor, there's a 3-D cinema and computer driving simulator which is so realistic that they check your driving licence before you use it. For an unusual experience check if they have a piano concert going on in the salon on the fourth floor. If you come out at street level, cross under the elevated expressway and you're back at Tokyu Hands.

The streets on the right lead back towards the station. The easiest way to get to the other side, avoiding the station, is via the passage between the two Parco stores. The area away from P'Parco is lined with sex establishments and ramen shops.

WEST EXIT

As with the east exit, you'll find a wall of buildings along the station. This is the **Tobu department store** (*see chapter* **Shops & Services**). As with Seibu on the other side, you could spend a whole day here. Pick up a map at the entrance. There's an English information desk on the first floor of the basement, but finding it takes time. At the southern end of the complex, as you go into the adjacent Metropolitan Plaza, is the entrance to the **Tobu Museum of Art** (*see chapter* **Museums & Galleries**). The plaza is home to more stores, and on the sixth floor is CD emporium **HMV**.

If you haven't yet had enough of Tobu, there's the **Spice2** building, which is full of restaurants.

One block away from the station is the **Tokyo Metropolitan Art Space** (*see chapter* **Music**); the long escalator leads straight to the fifth floor, where an art gallery offers free exhibitions.

At the corner of the two main roads, **OIOI** (the names is a visual pun for Marui) (*see chapter* **Shops & Services**) has eight floors of fashionable clothes and accessories. In the basement is the **Virgin Megastore**. On the street behind is Marui's home furnishings outlet, **In The Room** (*see chapter* **Shops & Services**).

The area north of OIOI, on both sides of the main road is chock full of bars and clubs, restaurants and myriad shops to satisfy the locals' every whim. The scale of it is mind-boggling, and it's amazing to think that all these establishments get enough patrons to keep going.

How to get there

Ikebukuro is on the JR Saikyo and Yamanote lines, the Eidan subway Marunouchi and Yurakucho lines, the Seibu Ikebukuro line and the Tobu Tojo line. See Map 1.

Addresses

Junkudo

2-15-5 Minami-Ikebukuro, Toshima-ku (5956 6111). **Open** 10am-8.30pm daily, closed every second Wed. **Credit** DC, MC, V.

Ancient Orient Museum

Bunka Kaikan 7F, 3-1-4 Higashi-Ikebukuro, Toshima-ku (3989 3491). **Open** 10am-8pm Mon-Fri; 10am-6pm Sat, Sun. **Admission** ¥900.

*The massive **Sunshine City** complex occupies the former site of Sugamo prison.*

Roppongi 六本木

Tokyo's nightlife capital is a 24-hour mini-city of clubs, food and bars.

'High Touch Town' is the phrase chiselled into the concrete on the highway overpass at the epicentre of Roppongi's main crossing (4-*chome*). Mention of this usually brings a smirk to the face of any foreigner who's lived in Tokyo for more than a few months. Most get their first exposure to Japan's venerable nightlife here. It's sometimes called the '*gaijin* ghetto' by snooty locals, even though an astounding number of upscale drinking, dining and entertainment establishments are packed in to Roppongi's six *chome*.

For travellers, Roppongi is a mesmerising glimpse at the energy that makes Tokyo so exciting. A deluge of neon lights, and video message boards reminiscent of *Blade Runner*. A cornucopia of ethnicity, with virtually every nation represented. Narrow streets packed with traffic and bustling with activity until dawn, and just about everything you could imagine to pass the evening in bliss.

TOKYO'S WILD FRONTIER

Located just inside the south-eastern arc of the Yamanote line, Roppongi is actually a bit out of the way. At present, its only subway link is the Hibiya line, although the Chiyoda line stops close-by in Nogizaka. Nevertheless, young and middle-aged alike have flocked to its hilly, zigzagging streets for fun after dark since the early 1960s.

Roppongi's origins are rooted in the military establishment. At one time there was a barracks not far from the main crossing. During the American occupation these were taken over by the US Army and quite a few bars stayed open to cater to the soldiers. The Americans moved out in 1959, a year after Tokyo Tower opened.

It's not easy to come up with a working list of hot spots in Roppongi, because there's no telling how long they'll last. Every season brings a slew of new clubs and bars. The key landmarks given below appear to have gained a foothold on Roppongi's merry-go-round of commerce.

CIRCUIT 1: THE HEART OF THE ACTION

The best way to attack Roppongi is from the main crossing of Gaien-Higashi Dori and Roppongi Dori, also known as 4-chome. You can walk down either main street in either direction and happen upon all kinds of action.

At one point of the intersection you will find the café **Almond** *(see chapter* **Coffee Shops***).* This is *the* Roppongi meeting place. On any evening this corner will be packed with touts and tarts, blind

Roppongi's seedy reputation is well merited.

dates nervously glancing at their watches, business folks and wide-eyed travellers. If you're male, you will almost certainly be approached by a man with a handbill for a strip show or hostess bar. These establishments cater to executives on expense accounts. Prices start at around ¥7,000.

If you exit the subway on the Almond side and head up Roppongi Dori towards Gaien-Higashi Dori, you will pass Almond and then a narrow sloping side street on your right. Don't cross the intersection, but turn right and head down Gaien- Higashi Dori, towards Tokyo Tower. Now drink in the action. You will pass a Starbucks and a Sbarro's pizzeria before you reach McDonald's. Turn right down the side street alongside McDonald's, follow the bend in the road to the left and you'll come to the **Hard Rock Café**, perhaps the most unsettling restaurant in the world. Take in the life-size King Kong climbing the outer wall. If you need souvenirs, the gift shop is a little booth at the front, off the car park.

Across the parking lot in front of the Hard Rock you will see a well-lit building with several establishments vying for your attention. The most prominent is **Charleston & Son Pizzeria**. Besides the fact that it features open-air seating in warm weather, it's an entirely forgettable experience. Forget it but enter the Rein Building and head up the second floor for the **Bauhaus**.

No tour of Roppongi would be complete without a visit here. One of those 'only in Japan' experiences, this is a live music venue that has featured the same band for more than 20 years. Unfortunately, one of the features that made the Bauhaus so charming – the cavern-like firetrap where the band was literally part of the audience – recently changed. The place went upscale. If you're claustrophobic, it's for the better. Yet the spacious 'new' Bauhaus still features the ultimate Japanese garage band, an amazing group of cover artists. Nowhere else in the world can you jam to flawless covers of the Rolling Stones, Pink Floyd, Rainbow and Guns N Roses, by men who can't speak three words of English. Be careful, though: the Bauhaus is on the pricey side, ¥3,500 with one drink. Sets are every hour. Leave the Bauhaus and make a left down the narrow road and you'll come to another Tokyo oddity, the **Cavern Club**, where Beatles covers are the order of the day.

CIRCUIT 2: WEIRD AND WONDERFUL

If you return to Gaien-Higashi Dori and continue towards Tokyo Tower, you will come to one of the weirdest establishments in Roppongi. From the outside it looks like a dilapidated old subway car covered with graffiti. A licence plate over the door reads BB-160. Inside it's no bigger than a subway car. In fact, there's just enough room for the bar and five or six patrons. It's called **Mistral Blue**.

Mistral Blue is actually connected to the **Roi Building**, another important Roppongi landmark and not a bad place to hang out. The Roi Building is loaded from basement to roof with restaurants, bars, meeting facilities and boutiques. Walk past Mistral Blue and you'll come to the front patio-porch. In the basement level, which is actually open-air, but hidden from the street, the place to go is **Paddy Foley's Irish Pub** (*see chapter* **Bars**), a popular gaijin watering hole where you can be served real Irish brews and food by real Irish people. In summer, the patrons spill out on to the basement patio to drink in the balmy summer air, and it gets very crowded. Watch out for broken glasses. Right next to Paddy's is their live music installation, the **Celt**. Unfortunately, it has no outdoor seating.

If you climb the stairs in front of Paddy's to street level and curve around to the right you'll encounter an interesting little bar that's ancient by Tokyo standards. The **Wonder Bar** was established in 1982. It looks like a train coach from an Agatha Christie novel and features a fine selection of spirits behind an oblong bar.

If you go into the Roi Building and take the elevator to the thirteenth floor you'll arrive at one of Roppongi's three excellent Thai restaurants, **Erawan** (*see chapter* **Restaurants**).

Past the Wonder Bar, further down Gaien-Higashi Dori, you'll happen upon a rash of sexually oriented establishments with names like Uprise, Climax and Splash. The pictures on the signs will give you a good idea of what's going on inside. They are not for the thin of wallet and most don't admit foreigners.

The next landmark going toward Tokyo Tower on Gaien-Higashi Dori is the Axis Building. It features a street-front café pretending to be a brasserie called **Les Halles**, and some very expensive home interior shops and boutiques. If you turn right after the Axis Building, on the left side of the street you'll eventually come across a live jazz house called **Bash**.

If you walk back towards Gaien-Higashi, on the same side of the street as Bash, but right on the corner, you will find a delightful little German pub called **Bernd's Bar** (*see chapter* **Bars**). The stairs are on the side street.

After Bernd's there's not much left on Gaien-Higashi Dori. If you continue down to the intersection, Ikura-katamachi, you will come to another elevated highway. If you go right at Ikura-katamachi and walk down a few metres on the right, you'll come to one of the two **Zest** restaurants that mark the gates to Roppongi. Zest features healthy portions of Tex-Mex food, and offers a nice lunch special. It's also not a bad spot for bending elbows and people-watching. Best of all, it's open until 5am.

If you continue through the Ikura-katamachi intersection you will encounter a few more drinking and dining establishments, including a Denny's, the Russian Embassy and after another big intersection, you'll eventually find **Tokyo Tower** (*see chapter* **Sightseeing**). Near the Tower but on the other side of the street is another Tokyo oddity, a Russian restaurant/nightclub called **Volga**. From the outside it looks like a miniature Orthodox church.

CIRCUIT 3: FOREIGNER FRENZY

Back at the Roi Building, closer to the Wonder Bar, if you look across Gaien-Higashi Dori, you'll see the site where the first hamburger made in Japan was served. That is if you believe the proprietors of the **Hamburger Inn**. But you're more likely to get a decent plate of curry there.

If you follow the street sloping down past the Hamburger Inn you'll run into the **Gas Panic Building** (*see chapter* **Bars**), an edifice that looks as if it ought to be on the Las Vegas strip. Gas Panic is a Roppongi institution of depravity. Thankfully, there's a public toilet right across the street, and on the other side of the toilet, there's a

Geronimo: *drink enough and get a plaque.*

spooky little cemetery. If you look out across the cemetery, you might spy the **Charleston Club**, yet another legendary Roppongi dive.

Around the cemetery are some very narrow, twisting paths and streets. Some are so steep that they have stairs. If you're brave, you might encounter an interesting little bar or restaurant hidden away in some alley.

After you've had your curry at the Hamburger Inn, head up Gaien-Higashi Dori towards the main crossing, pass the street that leads to Gas Panic, and at the third street turn right. This will lead you to Roppongi's most famous disco, the **Lexington Queen**. The Stones party there, models party there movie stars party there. Should you? Maybe just once. You might be disappointed, though.

Head back down Gaien-Higashi Dori and at the main crossing, Roppongi Dori, curve around to the right. Just a few metres from the corner you'll find the closest to 1950s America you can get in Japan, **Johnny Rockets**. There you can chow down on real 'authentic American' hamburgers, BLTs, cheese fries and malted milkshakes while listening to the jukebox. Grab a seat by the window.

CIRCUIT 4: MOVIES, SHOPS, CLUBS

If you return to Roppongi crossing and head away from the intersection, towards Tokyo-Mitsubishi Bank, you will come to one of only two cinemas in Roppongi, the **Haiyu-za Talkie Night** (*see chapter* **Film**). This is one of the most charming and unusual spaces in Roppongi. For starters there is a branch of the English-style pub chain, **Hub** (*see chapter* **Bars**), in the middle of the lobby. The cinema itself is a throwback to the days when going to the movies was a cultural experience. Wide sweeping staircases wind up to a most alluring, yet graceful balcony. It's a dreamy place to watch a film, and shows the most offbeat, weird and avant-garde fare that comes to Japan.

Two more establishments in the Tokyo-Mitsubishi Bank block are indicative of the brand of Japan-only entertainment that Roppongi offers. Start at the corner and walk away from the crossing, past the rather large **Hotel Ibis** (*see chapter*

Accommodation) on the other side of the street, towards the Japan Ground Self-Defence facility. Turn right at the third street down. About halfway down the street on the left look up for a gigantic bloodshot eyeball staring at you from above. Welcome to the **Paranoia Café** (*see chapter* **Bars**), where the walls and ceiling are swimming with screaming heads, slasher movies run endlessly and heavy metal blares from the sound system.

From Paranoia Café, go left and head to the next intersection, make a left and then make your next right and you'll find **Ichioku**. It's easy to spot because of the yin-yang symbol on the lighted-sign. 'Ichioku' means 100 million in Japanese, and it's said that the restaurant was established when that was the population of Japan. Ichioku is a delightfully cramped *izakaya* with interesting east-west combinations like cheese harumaki, and tuna sautéed in garlic.

Heading back towards the main intersection on the other side of the road, you'll encounter a pot pourri of bars, restaurants and sex parlours. Continue towards the intersection, but stop at the last street before the intersection and turn right. There will be a large, gaudy strip bar on the corner called Seventh Heaven. Just after Seventh Heaven, on the right side of the street, is **Velfarre** (*see chapter* **Nightlife**), Roppongi's answer to London's Hippodrome. Incredibly, it closes at midnight. Right across the street from Velfarre is a better bet, provided you can samba. **Salsa Sudada** trips the light Latino until 5am. Spanish spoken inside.

Exiting from the subway on the Almond side of the street and facing the crossing, you will find a narrow sloping road just to the right of Almond. If you head down the slope, the street eventually runs parallel to Roppongi Dori. Soon, you'll see an interesting building that looks as if it could be a French restaurant. It's not. **Sweet Basil 139** is a relatively new live house that features French/Italian dining and slightly fading or almost forgotten pop acts from the west. It ain't cheap.

Now take the narrow road that spurs off to the right. You'll be heading back toward Roppongi Dori. First you'll find the notorious **Mogambo** (*see chapter* **Bars**), a place that always seems to be packed with foreign brokers and bankers well into the wee hours. Close by is another establishment run by the same people, **Geronimo** (*see chapter* **Bars**). Almost next door to Mogambo is another watering hole, **Castillo**. It features a sweaty, crowded dance area and '70s and '80s pop music.

Walk all the way up the slope back to Almond, turn left and head down Roppongi Dori towards Nishi-Azabu. You will soon come to another important Roppongi landmark, the **Aoyama Book Centre**, fondly known as 'ABC books'. ABC is open all night and features a healthy selection of foreign, primarily English books, and one of Tokyo's better collections of foreign magazines.

Feel free to do as the locals do, and spend many hours browsing, without buying a thing.

Continue down toward Nishi-Azabu and you'll pass a Nissan dealership and then **Wave** (*see chapter* **Shops & Services**), one of Tokyo's finest music stores and an excellent place to while away a rainy day listening to CD samples. In the basement of the same building you'll find the second of Roppongi's two cinemas, **Ciné Vivant** (*see chapter* **Film**).

CIRCUIT 5: JUST ONE MORE CLUB...

If you've still got the energy for more, then Roppongi still has more to offer. Head back on to the main Roppongi Dori towards Nishi-Azabu, then cross Roppongi Dori at the junction with Terebi Asahi Dori, named after the nearby television station. There will be the entrance to a pedestrian tunnel here. Go right and look on your left for **Acaraje Tropicana**, a lively Latin samba bar. It's a great place to dance away the night without pretence.

Head back down Roppongi Dori until you are almost at the intersection with Gaien-Nishi Dori. At the third street up from the intersection, turn right. You will now attempt to find **Space Lab Yellow** (*see chapter* **Nightlife**), but it won't be easy. It's on the right side of the street. There's not really a sign and it begins at the second basement level. It used to be the closest Tokyo came to a New York-style disco. These days there are others, but Yellow still pulls them in. Inside it's a winding labyrinth of catwalks and halls adjoining random chill-out rooms and bars, spilling into a large dark dance area. Yellow usually features some hot Tokyo DJs and every so often a big star from Europe or America drops by. It doesn't get rolling until 11pm or midnight and goes all night.

Continue down Roppongi Dori to the intersection and cross towards Aoyama a little bit, and you will find the other **Zest**. You walk up the stairs in front and enter at the second floor. Like its cousin at Ikura-katamachi (*see above*), this Zest is open until 5am. It marks the south-western gate of Tokyo's nightlife city.

How to get there

Roppongi is on the Hibiya subway line. See Map 2.

Addresses

Hard Rock Café

5-4-20 Roppongi, Minato-ku (3408 7018). **Open** 11am- 2am Sun-Thur; 11:30am-4am Fri, Sat.

Charleston & Son Pizzeria

Rein Bldg 5-3-4 Roppongi, Minato-ku (3479 0595). **Open** 11:30am-5am Sun-Thur; 11:30am-6am Fri, Sat.

Bauhaus

Rein Bldg, 5-3-4 Roppongi, Minato-ku (3403 0092). **Open** 8pm-1am Mon-Sat.

The Cavern Club

Saito Bldg 1F, 5-3-2 Roppongi, Minato-ku (3405 5207). **Open** 6pm-2.30am Mon-Sat; 6pm-midnight Sun.

Mistral Blue

5-5-1 Roppongi, Minato-ku (3423 0082). **Open** 7:30pm-2am Mon-Thur; 7.30pm-5am Fri and Sat.

The Celt

B1, 5-5-1 Roppongi, Minato-ku (3423 1176). **Open** 6pm-1am Sun-Thur; 6pm-3am Fri, Sat.

Brasserie Les Halles

5-17-1 Roppongi, Minato-ku (3505 8221). **Open** 11am-midnight daily.

Bash

Five Bldg B1, 5-18-20 Roppongi, Minato-ku (3584 8939). **Open** varies.

Zest

Grand-Mer Roppongi 1F, 5-18-19 Roppongi, Minato-ku (5570 6999). **Open** 11:30am-5am daily.

Volga

3-5-11 Shiba Koen, Minato-ku (3433 1766). **Open** 11:30am-2pm, 5:30pm-11:30pm Mon-Sat.

The Hamburger Inn

3-15-22 Roppongi, Minato-ku (3401 9357). **Open** 11:30am-5pm daily. Closed every third Sun.

Charleston Club

3-8-11 Roppongi, Minato-ku (3402 0372). **Open** 6pm-5am daily.

Lexington Queen

Third Goto Bldg B1, 3-13-14 Roppongi, Minato-ku (3401 1661). **Open** 8pm-midnight daily.

Johnny Rockets

Coco Bldg 2F, 3-11-10 Roppongi, Minato-ku (3423 1995). **Open** 11am-11pm Mon-Thur; 24 hrs Fri, Sat, through to 11pm Sun.

Ichioku

4-4-5 Roppongi, Minato-ku (3405 9891). **Open** 5pm-3am Mon-Sat; 5-11pm Sun.

Salsa Sudada

La Palette Bldg 3F, 7-13-8 Roppongi, Minato-ku (5474 8806). **Open** 6pm-5am daily.

Sweet Basil 139

6-7-11 Roppongi, Minato-ku (5474 1395). **Open** varies.

Castillo

6-1-8 Roppongi, Minato-ku (3475 1629). **Open** 8pm-7am Mon-Sat.

Acaraje Tropicana

B1, 1-1-1 Nishi-Azabu, Minato-ku (3479 4690). **Open** 6pm-2am Tue-Thur; 6pm-5am Fri, Sat; 7pm-2am Sun.

Zest

2-13-15 Nishi-Azabu, Minato-ku (3400 2235). **Open** 11:30am-5am daily.

Shinjuku 新宿

Multi-faceted Shinjuku can give you a taste of all of the city's delights, from its seedy alleyways to its high-tech skyscrapers.

The vast **Shinjuku station**, where even Tokyo veterans have been known to lose their way.

If you're looking for one place in Tokyo that captures all the contradictions and contrasts of the city, then look no further. From Tokyo's highest concentration of skyscrapers on one side to thousands of tiny, ancient bars on the other, the mini-city of Shinjuku has the lot.

Shinjuku is three worlds put together: the ultra-modern Nishi-Shinjuku (west Shinjuku), the shopping centres and the seedy neon-lit bustle of Kabuki-cho. In the middle of it all stands Shinjuku station, where nine train and two subway lines spew out passengers from dawn to 1am. Around 2 million people pass through the station every day – approximately twice the population of Brussels.

Shinjuku is a place of contrasts and extremes. Around the station and Kabuki-cho areas, people swarm in such numbers that progress is only possible at a shuffle, yet the wide streets of Nishi-Shinjuku, lined with skyscrapers and hotels, are often totally empty. In the midst of all this conspic-uous consumption and corporate activity, there is the highest concentration of homeless people of any area in Tokyo, sleeping on the pavements or in Shinjuku Central Park. Shinjuku provides a glimpse of what cities might be like in the next century, but it also has a very strong sense of its own past.

FROM BROTHELS TO NEON

Shinjuku (the name means 'new lodging') was born in the early days of Edo, as a travellers' resting place on the Koshu Kaido road to Kyoto. One of five roads out of Edo, it was less well used than the Tokaido route to the old capital, which went closer to the coast. Nevertheless, Naito Shinjuku, as it was known, was busy enough for teahouses, inns, stores and brothels to prosper.

Shinjuku station appeared on the Shinagawa line between Shinagawa and Akabane in 1885. It became a junction four years later when a new line was built to Hachioji, in the west. Both lines were originally used for goods, Shinjuku being a storage depot for firewood and charcoal. But soon other railways – the Komu, Keio and Odakyu lines – followed into Shinjuku and the area became a fast-growing transportation centre and a major junction for travellers and commuters.

From the late nineteenth century until the 1920s, Shinjuku was also a popular residential district. The earthquake of 1923 largely spared the area, and an influx of people followed. By the early Showa era, the late '20s and early '30s, Shinjuku was one of the most crowded places in Tokyo and its reputation as an entertainment area grew with the theatres, which attracted people from all over the city.

Then came World War II. Shinjuku, almost totally destroyed in the firebombing of Tokyo, became home to flourishing black markets operated by rival gangs near the station's exits. One small street on the west side, called Piss Alley, is a remnant of those days, as is Golden Gai (*see page 163*). Everything else has been rebuilt, but the spirit of consumption and the area's reputation for dodgy dealings remain, the latter especially true in the district known as Kabuki-cho.

Despite its name, Kabuki-cho has never had much to do with the Japanese theatrical art. After the destruction of the war, there was a shortlived plan to turn the area into a cultural centre for kabuki. The plan came to nothing, but the name stuck.

Over on the west side of the station, where the skyscrapers now stand, there was a water purification plant and reservoir until the 1960s (*see picture, page 41*). When the reservoir moved west, Tokyo's first skyscrapers appeared on the reclaimed land, the first being the Keio Plaza Hotel in 1971. West Shinjuku is now a dense forest of skyscrapers dominated by the massive twin towers of architect Tange Kenzo's Metropolitan Government Building.

DEALING WITH THE STATION

The best advice on arrival at Shinjuku station is that doled out to hitchhikers all over the galaxy: don't panic. If you rush for the nearest exit, you may end up miles away from where you want to go. Instead, take your time to read the clear, bilingual signs and decide in which of the three main directions – west, east or south – you need to go.

Taking one of the east exits will land you in the main shopping area, with an option to stroll down to Kabuki-cho; west will take you to the skyscrapers, while south and 'new south' will take you in the direction of Takashimaya Times Square, currently the world's biggest department store building. The west side is also where the private train lines Odakyu and Keio terminate.

Should you exit the station in the wrong place, an underground passage, the Metro Promenade, connects the east to west exits, although even Tokyo veterans still get lost en route.

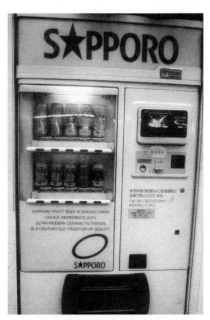

You're never far from a vending machine.

EAST & SOUTH EXITS: SHOPPING CITY

This is the main shopping area and spreads from Shinjuku's main thoroughfare, Yasukuni Dori, in the north to Takashimaya Times Square in the south. There are also plenty of restaurants, amusement centres, sex and gambling establishments to help while away the time.

Right at the 'east south' exit is the **Lumine 2** shopping centre. In the **Flags** building next door is **Tower Records** (*see chapter* **Shops & Services**). Going right at the bottom of the stairs leads past the new south exit and on to **Takashimaya Times Square**, a giant shopping complex containing the upmarket department store **Takashimaya** and **Tokyu Hands** (*see chapter* **Shops & Services**). On the eleventh floor is **Joypolis**, a large Sega amusement theme park, while on the twelfth is a branch of **HMV** and an **IMAX** theatre. The twelfth to fourteenth floors are stuffed with restaurants, some of which have outdoor terraces. Next door to Times Square is **Kinokuniya** (*see chapter* **Shops & Services**), a giant bookshop whose sixth floor has a very large selection of foreign magazines and books. It also stocks a large number of books on Japan, including Japanese novels in English translation.

At the east exit of the station is **MyCity**, another shopping complex full of fashion boutiques. On the ground floor is a branch of **Japan Railways**

*Like its NY namesake, **Shinjuku Central Park** brings a splash of green to skyscraper city.*

(JR) View Travel Service Centre, where staff speak basic English. It's the main counter in the area for tourists and, unusually, credit cards are accepted. This office also validates the JR rail pass (*see chapter* **Directory**). Near this office in the same building is a small **Tokyo Government Tourist Information Centre**.

Outside the JR travel centre, across Shinjuku Dori, is **Studio Alta** (*see chapter* **Shops & Services**), marked by a huge video screen that is the most popular meeting spot in Shinjuku. From here you will see branches of the three electronics retailers that dominate the area: **Yodobashi Camera**, **Bic Camera** and **Sakuraya** (*see chapter* **Shops & Services**).

Head east along Shinjuku Dori and you'll come across a mass of department stores, among them **OIYOUNG** (owned by Marui) and **Isetan** (*for both, see chapter* **Shops & Services**), the latter just about the only building in the area left standing after the war. There is also the original branch of Kinokuniya bookshop (*see chapter* **Shops & Services**), with foreign titles on the sixth floor.

Facing Isetan on Shinjuku Dori is **OICITY** (*see chapter* **Shops & Services**), eight floors of boutiques selling the latest fashions in clothes and accessories. In the basement is a **Virgin Megastore** with a concert ticket counter. On the corner across Meiji Dori is another Marui outlet, **OIZACCA** (*see chapter* **Shops & Services**), this one specialising in accessories, watches and eyewear.

Towards the station is **Mitsukoshi** (*see chapter* **Shops & Services**), which opened just after the 1923 earthquake. For CDs check out **Disk Union**, one branch with three floors of jazz music and the other branch with eight floors divided up into different styles. On the same street is **Raj Mahal**, an Indian restaurant serving good-quality ¥1,000 all-you-can-eat lunches from 11.30am to 3pm. Nearby is the Irish pub the **Dubliners** (*see chapter* **Bars**). There's also a small 'beer garden' called **Sol** stuck between buildings. Back towards MyCity is the **Cinema Qualité** complex, a quirky cinema with three screens showing a mixture of modern and classic films, both domestic and foreign (*see chapter* **Film**).

On Sundays Shinjuku Dori is closed to traffic and the street is taken over by buskers, performers and other street artists. It can make for a lively afternoon out, if you don't mind the crowds.

WEST EXITS: SKYSCRAPER CITY

The most famous of Nishi-Shinjuku's skyscrapers is the **Tokyo Metropolitan Government Offices**, which consist of two main structures divided into five towers. The complex was designed by architect Tange Kenzo (*see chapter* **Architecture**), whose bold neo-Gothic design caused controversy when the building opened in 1991. Still, in its first two years of opening, 6,000 people a day made their way to the forty-fifth-floor observatories. The observatories in the north and south towers are identical, with panoramic views interrupted only by the other tower. Entry is free and the lifts go straight to the observatories from street level. On a clear day Mount Fuji and the mountains to the west are visible on the horizon, while landmark panels inside help to identify the surrounding buildings. On the way out, on the second floor, are two areas showing videos on the history of Tokyo and its government. The south tower shows the 1868-1945 period and the north the period from 1945 to the present. At street level, there's a semi-circular main plaza decorated with sculptures which gives a feeling of spaciousness that's lacking just about everywhere else in Shinjuku.

Adjacent to the towers is **Shinjuku Central Park**, modelled on New York's Central Park. Some of the people evicted from their cardboard dwellings in the station (where an automatic walkway was constructed where they once slept) now live here.

Most of the other skyscrapers have viewing areas, too. In the **Sumitomo Building** across Chuo Dori it's on the fifty-first floor. Most restaurants on that floor or the two below have lunch specials from ¥1,000. The **Shinjuku Centre Building** has an observation area on the fifty-third floor, and the **Nomura Building** on Ome-kaido has one on its fiftieth floor.

Across the road from the **Keio Plaza Hotel** (*see chapter* **Accommodation**), the area's oldest high-rise building, is the **Mitsui Building**, which houses the **Museum of Future Science and Technology**. It's quite small and concentrates on optical illusions and space technology displays, but has a few terminals with free Internet access. It's in the basement, next to the **Pentax** and **Epson** galleries (*see chapter* **Museums & Galleries**) with their free photographic displays.

In the basement plaza in the nearby **I-Land Building** is the Spice Road food hall, offering a choice of Indonesian, Indian, Middle Eastern, African or Italian lunch specials. Inside the building, many Japanese restaurants offer similar lunchtime bargains.

Nearby on Ome Kaido in the **Yasuda Fire Building** is the Togo Seiji Memorial Museum, home to Van Gogh's *Sunflowers* (*see chapter* **Museums & Galleries**). Across Ome-kaido is a branch of **T-Zone** (*see chapter* **Shops & Services**), a huge computer retailer. On the tenth floor, there's an Internet café (*see chapter* **Coffee Shops**).

Near Koshu-kaido, the **NS Building**, with its hollow interior and glass roof, has a lift going to the top floors along the building's exterior, so spectacular views unfurl as you ascend. At the top are several restaurants and a small viewing area looking out over Harajuku and Shibuya. Nearby in the **Shinjuku Park Tower** is the **Ozone Living Design Centre**, where shops and showrooms on the third to seventh floors display new products and home accessories.

Away from Shinjuku on Koshu-kaido is the Opera City complex (*see chapter* **Music**). The building is a 20-minute walk from Shinjuku station's western exits but is right by Hatsudai station on the Keio New line. Also in the main building is the **NTT InterCommunication Centre** (*see chapter* **Museums & Galleries**), with three floors of exhibits connected with communication, art and technology. In the lobby is a small café that offers free Internet access. The third floor houses the **Nambata Art Gallery**, next to a new art gallery that opened in September 1999. On the ground floor is another free Internet access area courtesy of NTT. Next door to the Opera City centre is the

The **Metropolitan Government Building** (*right) stands where water was purified in the '60s.*

Kabuki-cho after dark: a riot of neon, bars, love hotels, massage parlours and more.

New National Theatre (*see chapter* **Theatre**), where opera and ballet are occasionally performed.

Back towards Shinjuku station on Koshu-kaido is **Yamaya**, a good outlet for foreign foods and wines. The area from Koshu-kaido towards Shinjuku post office has many restaurants and a few bars, among them the Irish pub the **Shamrock** (*see chapter* **Bars**). There are also many discount stores selling electronic, video, audio and photographic equipment. Look out for the head branch of **Yodobashi Camera** (*see chapter* **Shops & Services**).

Right by the station are the imposing **Keio** and **Odakyu** department stores (*see chapter* **Shops & Services**), both long-established residents of Shinjuku, offering less trendy but cheaper goods than similar stores on the west side. The Odakyu department store is divided into two buildings, the main one and the Halc building.

On the other side of the Odakyu department store towards Kabuki-cho is a small street called Shomben Yokocho, or **Piss Alley**. It's not as repulsive as it sounds – it's so called because most of its eating places share toilets. It's a narrow 30-metre (98-foot) stretch of *yakitori* bars, ramen shops, *izakayas* and other cheap eateries. Piss Alley, with Golden Gai, are the only two clusters of old buildings left near Shinjuku station. They look daunting, but even the strangest or most drunken characters are harmless. Eating in Piss Alley is a real experience. Most places, despite appearances, serve decent food – choose one that's crowded and you won't go far wrong.

The area across Ome Kaido, parallel to the railway lines, is famous for **record shops**. There are more than 30 shops specialising in bootleg recordings, or in a particular era or style. Serious music fans from all over the world come here to top up their collections of rarities.

KABUKI-CHO: SIN CITY

A stroll in the daytime can give an idea of what goes on after dark, but there's nothing like walking around Kabuki-cho at night. Every building is covered with neon and lights, advertising karaoke, amusement centres, *pachinko* halls, cinemas, restaurants, nightclubs, shot bars, 'pubs', hostess bars, lady's (*sic*) clubs, love hotels and more erotic establishments, including no-pantie coffee shops, lingerie pubs, strip shows, massage parlours and other operations catering to all tastes, fantasies and fetishes.

Yet at the same time Kabuki-cho is a place where people hang out and stroll, especially along the main street from Shinjuku station. It starts to the left of Studio Alta (*see above*) and leads to entertainment complexes, cinemas and a plaza.

Across the plaza is the **Shinjuku Toho Hall** entertainment complex, home to the **Code** nightclub (*see chapter* **Nightlife**), cinemas, bowling alleys and a 24-hour pool hall. Adjacent to this building is the **Shinjuku Koma Stadium** for contemporary Japanese plays and drama. On the right of the plaza is the **Humax Pavilion** containing the **Liquid Room** (*see chapters* **Music** *and* **Nightlife**), a contemporary music party and concert venue, with another pool hall on the fifth floor. Nearby bars include **Café Olé**, **Half Time**, **Mon Chéri** and **Hub** (for all, *see chapter* **Bars**), with **La Scala** coffee shop providing hot drinks in surreal surroundings (*see chapter* **Coffee Shops**).

The area even has a shrine: **Hanazono**. Every Sunday there's a flea market from morning until late afternoon. On the street behind lies the renowned **Golden Gai**, a small corner that has come through the decades unscathed. Walking through can take less than five minutes but there are around 200 bars. Many cater only to members or regular customers, but a few friendly ones will serve anybody as long as there's space. Try **Bon's** or **Shot Bar Shadow** (for both, *see chapter* **Bars**). Golden Gai is bordered by the tree-lined Shiki no michi promenade, leading back up to Yasukuni Dori. In the other direction are hundreds of busy love hotels. Just follow the neon signs.

THE END OF SHINJUKU

From Hanazono Shrine across Meiji Dori is **OIMEN**, with eight floors of fashionable clothes, shoes and accessories for men, from brand names to famous designers. At the back is **Field**, Marui's sports and street wear outlet.

Across Yasukuni Dori along Meiji Dori is one of the most over-the-top department stores in Tokyo, **OIONE**, another Marui outlet. It's worth a look, if only for entertainment value. In the block behind is a trove of bars, clubs and restaurants. One venue that stands out is the **Suehirotei**, an old theatre showing *rakugo* (traditional storytelling) and similar forms of entertainment. Festooned with lanterns, the place is hard to miss.

East across the next main road is **Ni-chome** (2-chome), the most concentrated area of gay and lesbian bars and clubs in Tokyo. As with Golden Gai (*see above*), you might not be welcome in all of the places here (*see chapter* **Gay & Lesbian**).

At the back of Ni-chome is **Taiso-ji** Temple, strangely spacious in the midst of Shinjuku. It was established in 1596, but nothing of those days remains. From here, it's just a short walk to one of Shinjuku's most glorious spots, the landscaped garden **Shinjuku Gyoen** (*see chapter* **Sightseeing**).

How to get there

Shinjuku station is on the JR Chuo, Saikyo, Sobu and Yamanote lines, on the Eidan subway Marunouchi line, the Toei subway Shinjuku and Number 12 lines and the Keio and Odakyu private lines. See Maps 3a and 3b.

Addresses

Shinjuku Joypolis

Takashimaya Times Square 10-11F,
5-24-2 Sendagaya, Shibuya-ku (5361 3040).
Open 10am-midnight daily. **Admission** from ¥300.

Tokyo Imax Theatre

Takashimaya Times Square 12F, 5-24-2 Sendagaya,
Shibuya-ku (5361 3030/reservations 5361 3031).
Open 10am-10pm Mon-Thur, Sun; 10am-11.30pm
Fri, Sat. **Admission** ¥1,300.

JR View Travel Service Centre

Shinjuku station (3354 4826). **Open** 10am-6pm
Mon-Sat; 10am-5pm Sun.

Tokyo Government Tourist Information Centre

Shinjuku station (no phone). **Open** 9am-6pm Mon-Sat.

Disk Union

3-31-2 & 3-31-4 Shinjuku, Shinjuku-ku (3352
2691/jazz 5379 3551). **Open** 11am-8pm Mon-Sat;
11am-7pm Sun.

Raj Mahal

Peace Bldg 5F, 3-34-11 Shinjuku, Shinjuku-ku (5379
2525). **Open** 11.30am-11pm daily.

Beer Terrace Sol

3-36-10 Shinjuku, Shinjuku-ku (5269 7225). **Open**
5pm-midnight Mon-Thur; 5pm-5am Fri, Sat; 4pm-
midnight Sun.

Tokyo Metropolitan Government Building

2-8-1 Nishi-Shinjuku, Shinjuku-ku (5321 1111).

Sumitomo Building

2-6-1 Nishi-Shinjuku, Shinjuku-ku (3344 6941).

The Shinjuku Centre Building

1-25-1 Nishi-Shinjuku, Shinjuku-ku (3345 1218).

Nomura Building

1-26-2 Nishi-Shinjuku, Shinjuku-ku (3345 0616).

Mitsui Building

2-1 Nishi-Shinjuku, Shinjuku-ku (3344 4827).

I-Land Building

6-5-1 Nishi-Shinjuku, Shinjuku-ku (3348 1177).

NS Building

2-4-1 Nishi-Shinjuku, Shinjuku-ku (3342 3755).

Ozone Living Design Centre

Shinjuku Park Tower 3-7F, 3-7 Nishi-Shinjuku,
Shinjuku-ku (5322 6500). **Open** 10.30am-6.30pm
Mon-Thur; 10.30am-7.30pm Fri-Sun.

NTT Intercommunications Centre

Tokyo Opera City Tower 4F, 3-20-2 Nishi-Shinjuku,
Shinjuku-ku (0120 144 199). **Open** 10am-6pm Tue-
Thur, Sat, Sun; 10am-9pm Fri. **Admission** ¥800.

Yamaya

3-2-7 Nishi-Shinjuku, Shinjuku-ku (3342 0601).
Open 10am-9pm daily.

Hanazono Shrine

5-17-3 Shinjuku, Shinjuku-ku (no phone). Shinjuku
San-chome station.

Shinjuku Suehirotei

3-6-12 Shinjuku, Shinjuku-ku (3351 2974). Shinjuku
station. **Open** noon-4.30pm, 5-9.30pm, daily;
additional performance 10-11.30pm Sat only.
Admission ¥2,500.

Taiso-ji Temple

2-9-2 Shinjuku, Shinjuku-ku (no phone). Shinjuku
Gyoenmae station.

Shibuya 渋谷

Looking for a neon-lit, 24-hour fashion parade? Look no further.

There's no sign reading 'All platform shoes lead to Shibuya' hanging in Tokyo station, but there might as well be. To beat the surest path to Shibuya, just follow the clomp of platforms: boots for the unseasonably tanned, bleached-blonde girls wearing bottom-skimming skirts, thick-soled shoes for the apple-cheeked students with inventively bobby-pinned hair. When you find yourself in the middle of hundreds of young people having a smoke, saying *'Ima doko?'* ('Where are you now?') into their cell phones and loitering around a statue of a dog, you've found Shibuya.

Once on the city's western outskirts and now the centre of every trendy young thing's universe, Shibuya is the future of Tokyo, embodying its youthful energy, unbottled creativity and devil-may-care consumerism – the Spice Girls as shopping destination. Stand before **Shibuya Crossing** at the north end of JR Shibuya station, from which four roads radiate, and observe the mass of chattering young people here for the department stores, boutiques, record shops, cafés, karaoke boxes, video-game arcades, bars and restaurants. Recession, what recession? Everyone carries numerous shopping bags, from Barneys and Patagonia and Comme Ça du Mode. Over Shibuya Crossing loom two giant video screens that play music videos and strangely poetic scenes of snowboarders taking leaps off cliffs.

A QUESTION OF STYLE

Is it any surprise that this vibrant area has spawned its own signature music and fashion? *Shibuya-kei* has come to mean a sophisticated soft-rock sound that pays homage to classic Anglo pop, with Pizzicato 5, Cornelius and the roster of hip Trattoria Records a few of the better-known examples. More an attitude than a sound, Shibuya-kei practitioners dress *Shibuya kaji* ('casual'). These days that means plenty of utilitarian high-neck windbreakers and second-hand US college sweatshirts. Shibuya girls, meanwhile, have been emulating Hawaii by way of the tanning salon: frosted make-up, frosted hair and far-from-frosty clothing – all inspired by Okinawan pop super-*idoru* Amuro Namie. Their plucked-eyebrow male counterparts, taking their cue from make-up wearing boy bands such as Glay, exemplify what's called *visual-kei*, with its girlish accent on looks.

In view of the area's present status, it's fitting that a root of the name Shibuya comes from the word *shibui*. Meaning 'coolly elegant', it is grounded in the sublime beauty of the tea ceremony. Together with the *-ya* suffix, it can be read as 'refreshing valley'. Shibuya does indeed lie in a river valley – you'll notice when you walk in any direction from the station that it's all uphill. Today Shibuya River is but a cemented-in trickle to the south-east side of the station, between the Tokyu Toyoko train line and Meiji Dori. It dribbles through Hiroo and Azabu and eventually out to Tokyo Bay.

Another story traces Shibuya's name to Japan's first shogun, Minamoto no Yoritomo. When one of his retainers caught a robber, Yoritomo gave him the robber's name, Shibuya, as thanks. Shibuya's son Konnomaru became a legendary warrior, defending Yoritomo against his brother Yoshitsune in a famous night attack. Yoritomo showed his gratitude by planting a cherry tree, a descendant of which still stands in the grounds of the warrior's namesake shrine in Shibuya. There are original stones from Konnomaru's homestead at **Konno Hachimangu**, built in the seventeenth century. As at many Shinto shrines to warriors, the god of war Hachiman is honoured here.

Konnomaru's loyalty has a modern parallel, though there is no attempted murder involved. The life-size **statue of Hachiko**, an Akita, stands outside the north exit of JR's Shibuya station, among a patch of bricked-in shrubs and trees and benches. It's a popular meeting spot and street musicians set up shop here, the sound of congos and marimbas adding to the festive air. Hachiko – sometimes translated as Octavius, as *hachi* means 'eight' – had the habit of walking his master, a professor at Tokyo University, to the station every morning and home again in the evening. One day in May 1925, the professor died while he was away. Hachiko waited patiently at the station, and when his master failed to materialise he came back the next day, and the following days. Even when the professor's family sent the dog to relatives in Asakusa, he still set off for Shibuya. Finally, he was allowed to live with a family friend in Yoyogi, and his daily travels to the station – spanning a decade – gained him renown for their display of loyalty. His statue was a gift to the city from the professor's granddaughter in 1934. The next year, after a grand funeral, he joined his master in the heavens above. His stuffed body is in the National Science Museum in Ueno.

LOVE FOR SALE

From these two stories you might think Shibuya symbolises loyalty, but there is another side. When you walk out past Hachiko take a left up the hill, keeping to the left after the road forks, and you'll find yourself on **Dogenzaka**, or Dogen Slope, named after a notorious thirteenth-century robber, Owada Dogen. Originally from a clan opposing the shogunate in Kamakura, Dogen liked to spend time on this hill robbing and murdering travellers en route to the western mountains. Some say he repented and became a monk, others that he met the same end as his victims.

You'll notice the coloured numbers 109 on a building where Dogenzaka splits off; the silver, wedge-shaped **109 Building** (*see chapter* **Shops & Services**) – eight storeys of clothing boutiques aimed at the young – is another popular meeting spot. It is one of many enterprises by the Tokyu rail company that mark the Shibuya landscape – Tokyu has three other 109 branches in Shibuya, and Shibuya station was the second station in Tokyo to have a department store inside it. Though people call the building *Ichi-maru-kyuu* ('one zero nine'), an alternative Chinese reading of number ten is 'to' and nine in Japanese is 'kyuu'.

Dogen might have liked how his perch is now also known as **Love Hotel Hill**. The area between Dogenzaka and Bunkamura Dori is dotted with dozens of short-stay hotels with themed rooms, be it western movies or Disney characters. They're a contemporary take on what used to be a geisha area: in the Meiji era Maruyamacho was an elegant district, with 86 geisha houses and 400 geisha in 1921. At the bottom of the hill, near the 109 Building, prostitutes also used to ply their trade, either because of or in spite of the military offices located there. A walk along Dogenzaka means passing dozens of hostess clubs, topless clubs and massage parlours promising 'special amusement time', but there are also several cineplexes and cheap eats (mostly ramen).

Coming from the station up Dogenzaka, if you take a right on the street with a lamp shop on the corner and go up the hill, you'll soon hit **On Air East** and **On Air West** (*see chapter* **Music**), two concert venues that host bands both local and foreign, such as Pulp. With its late-night hours and pan-Asian menu, **Club Asia** (*see chapter* **Nightlife**), just up the street, is a good place for an after-concert drink or snack; it also has its own club downstairs.

CULTURE VULTURES

For a bit of culture among the love hotels, seek out **The Lion** (*see chapter* **Coffee Shops**). In this unique church-like space are two floors of wooden benches and tables facing giant speakers that blast out not rock but the dulcet tones of Mozart or Beethoven, to be listened to as you sip a coffee,

soda or juice. If ever there were a respite from Shibuya's madness, this is it. No talking is allowed. Next door is a more convivial bar, **BYG**, with a pink sign. **Sugar High** (*see chapter* **Nightlife**) on the third floor of a building on the same street, is a small space that hosts bands and DJs. Look for the LifeSavers on the sign.

If you keep walking north you'll hit **Bunkamura** ('culture village') (*see chapters* **Film** and **Music**): cinemas and concert spaces along with a museum, a gallery and shops. Owned by Tokyu, it's next to the main Tokyu store in Shibuya. Bunkamura skirts the edge of the **Shoto** district, where Hachiko's master once lived. If you take Bunkamura Dori back towards the station, on your right you'll pass the **Eyeglass Museum** (*see chapter* **Museums & Galleries**) in the Iris Optical Building. Across the street is the five-floor **Book 1st** bookshop and **Club Sega**, the latter just one of many giant games complexes in Shibuya.

Shoto's name came from a strain of tea. Feudal lords had built their suburban estates along Oyama Kaido, present-day Aoyama Dori. To supplement their income, the *daimyo* planted tea on their plantations on the far western side of the station. Given the evocative name Shoto ('waves of pines'), the tea did well. Eventually, trains – bringing teas from western Japan – proved its downfall.

But what was bad for Shoto tea was good for Shibuya. As with Shinjuku and Ikebukuro to the north, Shibuya's growth came from train travel. The 1907 Tamagawa Densha tramway linked military barracks and a prison in south-western Setagaya ward to offices in Shibuya. It was the first railway line west out of the city. By the 1920s, 30,000 people were using the station daily. In 1920 the station was moved 200 metres north. The **Tokyu Toyoko and Keio Inokashira terminals** plus the Ginza subway line were combined in one building in 1939, with the Toyoko exiting from the fourth floor, the Ginza and the Inokashira from the third and the JR Yamanote from the second. (Ginza subway is a misnomer here; Shibuya is the only one of its stops not underground.) Six lines now converge at Shibuya.

STORE WARS

Shibuya didn't totally come into its own until after the 1923 Great Kanto Earthquake, when the devastation of most of lower Tokyo jumpstarted the move to the higher-elevation western frontier in earnest, with Shibuya, Shinjuku and Ikebukuro absorbing increased populations. Still, Shibuya didn't escape the destruction of World War II; much of it was burned down in air raids. And even before then, the original Hachiko statue had been melted down for its metal.

The only war these days is that among the department stores Tokyu, Seibu and Marui. Every other store, it seems, is owned by one of the three, with the first two dominating. Walking out the Hachiko exit up towards Harajuku, along the road that runs parallel to the Yamanote, you'll pass two **Seibu department stores** (*see chapter* **Shops & Services**) on your left, divided by a road but linked by skywalks. On your right is Marui's glass-faced **Young 0101** (the Japanese love word-play: 'Maru' is one way of saying zero). If you carry on heading north, the road forks off at **01 City**, Marui again (*see chapter* **Shops & Services**). But it was Seibu (which, like Tokyu, first grew as a train line) that was behind the naming of the road that splits off into Koen Dori – **Park Avenue** – in a deliberate attempt to invoke Manhattan chic, with the motto 'Park Avenue in Shibuya, where the people you pass are beautiful'. Seibu's foray into the youth-clothing market thus became its **Parco department stores** (*see chapter* **Shops & Services**), which really function as shopping arcades bringing together a cornucopia of trendy designers and labels under several roofs.

FROM MUSEUMS TO MUSIC
The **Tobacco & Salt Museum** (*see chapter* **Museums & Galleries**) is farther up Koen Dori, on the right, in a building that used to house the government offices in charge of those two former state monopolies.

Across the street from Parco Part 2 is **Cinema Rise** (*see chapter* **Film**), one of the city's best independent film theatres. Surrounding Cinema Rise on either side is a games centre that, along with a panoply of video games, has the latest in 'Print Club' technology, including cool 3-D variations. Spain Dori is the narrow steep alley to the left of Cinema Rise; its name comes from a Barcelona-style façade on one shop that was copied by others.

Take the little road that runs between Parco Part 2 and Part 1 running north, taking an immediate left on the larger road. Just down that block in a building painted green is another Tokyu entry, **Tokyu Hands** (*see chapter* **Shops & Services**), billed as a hands-on, do-it-yourself supply store, which sells everything from incense to camping equipment to dozens of different kinds of glue.

If you follow the shop-filled street running north to south that Tokyu Hands sits on, called Inokashira Dori, you'll eventually hit the **NHK Broadcasting Centre** on your right. It was built on the site of the national broadcaster's 1964 Tokyo Olympics information headquarters, near the game grounds in Yoyogi and Shinjuku. NHK moved here from Shinbashi in 1973, and it's not uncommon to see lines of people waiting to become part of a studio audience.

Following Inokashira Dori back towards the station, you'll pass a number of stores selling bargain (for Tokyo) 'American' goods such as sweat-shirts and coats. Eventually you'll hit a *koban* (policebox), where Inokashira Dori merges with

another street coming from the south. If you turn right on the little road just before the koban, you'll see a big Taiwanese restaurant called **Ryuu no Hige** ('Dragon's Moustache') with a red-brick façade on your immediate right. This is one of many Taiwanese restaurants in the area, a legacy of the immediate post-war years when Shibuya was the home of a Taiwanese-run black market. It's a tad ironic that Ryuu no Hige sits so close to the koban. In July 1946 skirmishes ensued when police tried to force out the Taiwanese; they ended violently, with several deaths.

The road that merges with Inokashira Dori is lined with small shops, bars and restaurants as well. Seibu checks in again with its **Quattro store**, selling more eclectic clothing in a multiple-boutique setting. On the top floor is **Shibuya Club Quattro** (*see chapter* **Music**), a popular club venue for music; bands such as Yo La Tengo and Soul Coughing have played here, along with homegrown indies such as the Velvet Underground-tinged Sugar Plant.

Taking Inokashira Dori down back towards the station, you'll pass the **Loft** store on the left, whose entrance is located on a still-smaller offshoot street. Loft (a Seibu entry) has the **Wave** music store (*see chapter* **Shops & Services**) on its top floor; other floors sell what can best be described as funky junk: small home furnishings and imported goods. It's Seibu's answer to Tokyu Hands (*see above*).

Instead of taking the road forking to the left at Marui, head north parallel to the Yamanote, and you'll come to **Tower Records** (*see chapter* **Shops & Services**) on the right. The seventh floor houses Tower's foreign books department, with an extensive newspaper section featuring the *New York Times*. On the same side of the street is **Doi Camera**. Past yet another Marui, **01 One** (home furnishings), on the left is the free **TEPCO Energy Museum** (*see chapter* **Museums & Galleries**) and its power-mad displays, housed in round mirrored building shaped like R2-D2.

Take a right on the road between Doi and Tower, crossing beneath the Yamanote, where you'll see rare examples of Japanese graffiti, to **Meiji Dori** on the other side. Shops line the street in both directions. If you take a left and then the first right, you'll hit a narrow street that runs parallel with Meiji Dori to Harajuku. **Kyuu-Shibuya-gawa Promenade** lies along what used to be Shibuya River. In both directions are stores with interesting names. Take the promenade south towards Shibuya station and you'll pass a giant golden egg on your left, marking the clothing store **Miracle Woman**. Back out on Meiji Dori on your right lies a sad excuse for a park; **Miyashita Koen** would in other cities be curbside greenery. On the east side of Meiji Dori are bigger boutiques.

If you head left after the corner Armani store and up the hill, you'll find the **Tokyo**

Bright lights and bright colours make Shibuya a magnet for the young, fashionable locals.

Metropolitan Children's Hall (Tokyo-to Jido Kaikan) (*see chapter* **Children**), one of two huge child-focused facilities in the area.

Reach the other, the **National Children's Castle (Kodomo no Shiro)** (*see chapter* **Children**) by following the road the Children's Hall is on until you hit Aoyama Dori; take a left on Aoyama Dori and the castle – which is not really a castle but a big curved building – is on your left after several blocks. A big square marks the area. The difference between this and the hall is that the latter is free; the castle charges ¥400 per child (aged 3-17) and ¥500 for adults to enjoy its play halls. It does have a swimming pool, however. In the same complex down the escalator is **Aoyama Books** (*see chapter* **Shops & Services**).

Taking Aoyama Dori back down the hill into Shibuya you go over Miyamasuzaka again; the streets are lined mostly with coffee shops, banks, cheap ramen and Italian eateries and karaoke boxes. **Fuji Bank** – yet another meeting spot – sits on the north-west corner of the Meiji Dori and Aoyama Dori intersection. A narrow alley on the right just after the bank leads to **Nonbei Yokocho**, recognisable by the sign and Chinese lanterns. In this 'guzzlers' alley' about 40 tiny bars – seating at most ten people each – are lined up in two orderly rows. Foreigners might feel out of place at these bars patronised mainly by middle-aged salarymen, but it's worth a peek to see a slice of Tokyo unchanged for decades.

Also on Shibuya's east side, Tokyu checks in again with its **Tokyu Bunka Kaikan**, connected to the station with an elevated walkway. This 'culture centre' has several cinemas, a rather run-down-looking selection of shops and the equally fading **Gotoh Planetarium** (*see chapter* **Museums & Galleries**) and its sky shows.

How to get there

Shibuya station is on the JR Yamanote line, Eidan Ginza and Hanzomon subway lines, the Keio Inokashira, Tokyu Toyoko and Shin-Tamagawa lines. See Map 4.

Addresses

Book 1st
33-5 Udagawa-cho, Shibuya-ku (3770 1023).
Open 10am-10pm daily.

BYG
2-19-14 Dogenzaka, Shibuya-ku (3461 8574).
Open 3pm-midnight daily.

Club Sega
28-6 Udagawa-cho, Shibuya-ku (3780 2667).
Open 10am-midnight daily.

NHK Broadcasting Centre
2-2-1 Jinnan, Shibuya-ku (3465 1111).

Ryuu no Hige
33-4 Udagawa-cho, Shibuya-ku (3461 5347).
Open 11am-11.30pm Sun-Thur; 11am-midnight Fri, Sat.

Doi Camera
1-11-3 Jinnan, Shibuya-ku (3496 5141).
Open 10am-7pm daily.

Miracle Woman
Pink Dragon Bldg 2-3F, 1-23-23 Shibuya, Shibuya-ku (3498 2592). **Open** 10am-8pm daily.

Harajuku 原宿

What teenagers here wear today, the world wears tomorrow.

If Shibuya is for twentysomethings, then Harajuku is its spirited teenage sibling. Here cries of '*kawaii*' ('Cute!') reach fever pitch, whether to describe an Atom Boy wallet, a Mandarin-speaking wristwatch or a pair of funky striped socks, each an accessory that makes or breaks an outfit, didn't you know?

You can find the right stuff on **Takeshita Dori** (pronounced Ta-ke-shi-ta, by the way), Harajuku's youthful fashion sense distilled. This narrow lane leading from Harajuku station to Meiji Dori overflows with clothing stores and shoe shops, with a generous handful of calorific fast-food joints. It's madhouse-crowded, but it's your best bet for figuring out what's hot, be it duffel coats or nose rings.

Harajuku put the street into Tokyo street fashion; label 20471120, which made its début here, now appears on Paris catwalks. Underground has gone aboveground. You'll see photographers from teenybopper magazines *Cutie* and *Olive* staking out spots on Harajuku streets, as they look to snap locals decked out in their finest. That wide-cuffed, dark-jean look? Invented in Harajuku, years before Gap appropriated it. Have no doubt that Japanese teenagers dictate worldwide trends, even beyond fashion: this is where the Tamagotchi was born.

In front of **Laforet** *(see chapter* **Shops & Services**), in a round tower building around the corner from Takeshita on Meiji Dori, scenesters congregate, with their thick-soled shoes and crinoline skirts topped by fluffy cotton-candy-pink hair. A banner proclaims, 'Nude or Laforet', and inside the motto bursts forward in kaleidoscopic chaos: five storeys of individual boutiques, all brimming with up-to-the-minute fashions. Check out the ground floor's **Nice Claup**, **Antianti** 'life cosmetics' and **OZOC**. If San Francisco has its Haight-Ashbury and London its King's Road, then Tokyo has its Takeshita Dori and Laforet. But in Tokyo the street wear lacks a street edge. It's not so much cutting edge as just plain cute.

Perhaps this is because Harajuku really is an amalgamation of many small neighbourhoods – Jingu-mae ('in front of [Meiji] shrine'), Aoyama, Omotesando – with narrow side streets and alleys that parallel main avenues and allow you to step easily away from crowds. The in-your-face consumerism found in neighbours Shibuya and Shinjuku is diluted. Many of the shops located in side-street buildings find space in converted apartments. Shopping can't be any more low-key than in what feels like someone's living room.

HARAJUKU HISTORY

The entire area benefits from the greenery that surrounds Harajuku on multiple sides: Yoyogi Park (Yoyogi Koen) and Meiji Shrine (Meiji Jingu) to the west, and Meiji Shrine Outer Gardens (Meiji Jingu Gaien) to the east. Each dates back to the Edo period, when feudal lords built their suburban estates on what had been open land. Harajuku's name comes from its history as a lodging stop (*shuku*) along the road from Kamakura heading north; *hara* means field or plain.

The downfall of the shogunate meant that the new Meiji government enjoyed a land windfall from these estates. North of Aoyama Dori, at the present site of the **Meiji Outer Gardens**, it set up a military college, with drilling grounds for troops on parade. Every year on his birthday (3 November), Emperor Meiji watched his troops show their stuff. The parade grounds moved farther west, to what is now **Yoyogi Park**, in 1909. A year later this would be the site of Japan's first foray into the air: a small plane piloted by a lieutenant rose 70 metres (229 feet) in the air for a three-kilometre (1.9-mile) trip.

Following the emperor's death in 1912, **Meiji Shrine** was opened in 1920 in a spot just north of Yoyogi Park. With a treasury museum showcasing items used by Emperor Meiji and Empress Shoken, Meiji Shrine is one of Japan's largest Shinto shrines. Its 72 hectares (178 acres) include flora representatives from around the nation; however, somewhat embarrassingly, its huge cypress *torii* (gates) were made from Taiwanese logs.

The shrine's opening was marred by the collapse of a bridge over the train line; apparently, corrupt officials taking bribes had sanctioned below-par work. Still, the other shrine-related construction remains intact: Omotesando ('outer approach road') thrives today as a mecca of shops, cafés and restaurants. The wide, tree-lined boulevard is often compared to the Champs-Elysées and affords one of the most pleasant walks in Tokyo.

American Occupation forces took over the parade grounds west of the station following World War II, building the residential development Washington Heights there. The billeted soldiers and their families contributed to Omotesando's growth as a lively area, as did visitors to the 1964 Tokyo Olympics. At that time, Washington Heights had been reclaimed by Tokyo and turned into a village housing the game's players. The sev-

Many of the old apartments along Omotesando have now become art galleries or shops.

eral stadiums in the Yoyogi and Shinjuku area too
are an Olympic legacy.

There once was a different kind of play in
Yoyogi Park as well. In a fascinatingly carefree
display of musicianship and dancing, bands of all
sorts, from heavy metal to ska to punk to folk, set
up shop here on fair weekends, performing to the
gathering young before them. Rockabilly Elvis
look-alikes cavorted with poodle-skirted gals, and
even spiky-haired punks lifted a booted heel or
two. City authorities shut down the giant open-
mike session in 1996, but today some bands still
play along the fringes of the park.

HARAJUKU ON FOOT

If you take Harajuku station's **Omotesando exit**
and walk down the north side of the street toward
Meiji Dori, you'll pass stores like **J Crew** and
Benetton and cheap places to eat. You'll soon hit
Meiji Dori. **Anasazi-Santa Fe**, in a small adobe-
style building, sits on prime real estate on the corner; perhaps that's why its south-west American
silver and turquoise jewellery is so expensive.
Across the street is **Condomania** (*see chapter*
Shops & Services), selling both gimmicky and
utilitarian prophylactics. Because they are the
birth-control method of choice, Japanese condoms
enjoy a reputation for variety (though not for generous size). Meiji Dori towards Shibuya affords a
good mix of stores, bars and restaurants, including
Mujirushi Ryohin (known in the UK as Muji) on
the left-hand side. This 'no-brand store' specialises
in casual clothing, basics and home furnishings.

If you opt to go left at the adobe building on Meiji
you'll hit **Laforet** and its milling teenyboppers.
Past Laforet, take another left at the crêperie and
follow the road left up the hill to find the **Ukiyo-e
Ota Museum** (*see chapter* **Museums &
Galleries**). Its collection of woodblock prints is a
slice of old Japan in the midst of its energetic youth.

Furusato Plaza lies on Meiji Dori past the
crêperie; *furusato* means 'hometown', and the shop
sells goods from around Japan, like crab from
Hokkaido, Niigata *sake* and Nagano's dried blue-
berries. Past the intersection between Takeshita
and Meiji is the red-canopied **Aux Bacchanales**
(*see chapter* **Restaurants**), the most popular of
the French-style bakery/cafés that have sprung up
over the past few years.

Across Meiji Dori is another small alleyway that
begins where Takeshita left off; this is **Harajuku
Dori**. Noticeably less packed, it too is lined with
shops worth exploring.

Harajuku Dori intersects **Kyu Shibuyagawa
Promenade**. In the curves of the cemented-in
promenade, you can feel the flow of its namesake
Shibuya River. Stores like **Romantic Standard**,
Vandalize and **Hide & Seek** have set up shop
here. The brand-new **Candy Stripper** clothing
shop stands out with its nail polish-red front, punc-
tuated with bubble-mirror windows. **Café Vasy**
is on the corner of the promenade and Harajuku
Dori and serves latte in giant soup bowls.

The promenade leads back to Omotesando,
where on the north side of this stretch between
Meiji and Aoyama Dori are the **Dojunkai**

Aoyama Apartments, named after the company that built them two years after the 1923 Great Kanto Earthquake. Housing was badly needed and most people could not afford single homes. Today, these first of Tokyo's apartments look like they could be in New York, with their ivy-covered concrete walls and slightly run-down appearance. Tiny boutiques, galleries and beauty salons now use some of the apartments as commercial space, a uniquely intimate setting for shopping.

Across the street, near the pedestrian bridge over Omotesando, you'll find **Perbacco!**, as Italian a coffee bar as Aux Bacchanales (*see above*) is French. Amid cries of 'Ciao!' and air kisses, expatriate Italians line up for an extensive selection of coffees as well as panini, gelato and sorbeto. A table charge makes it more expensive to sit than imbibe at the bar – but the people-watching the former affords is second to none. Perbacco! stands where Omotesando hits the river promenade again; just around that corner you'll find **Todd Oldham** and **Anna Sui** boutiques. To the right of Perbacco! on Omotesando is **Café de Ropé** (*see chapter* **Coffee Shops**), one of the original French cafés along this boulevard (and a little the worse for wear), and toy paradise **KiddyLand** (*see chapter* **Shops & Services**), which correctly predicted that Harajuku is about being a kid at heart.

Further up the street, towards Omotesando station, is **Oriental Bazaar** (*see chapter* **Shops & Services**), a vision in red-, green- and white derivative-Asian architecture and filled with traditional Japanese crafts and antiques. Its English-speaking staff take the pain out of shopping for gifts to take back home. Farther on is the **Tokyo Union Church**, with striking stained-glass art by designer Miura Keiko in its sanctuary.

The enormous glass-covered building down the street, toward Aoyama Dori, is the **Hanae Mori Building** (*see chapter* **Shops & Services**), named for one of Japan's best-known designers. Tange Kenzo (*see chapter* **Architecture**) created the geometrically intricate design; he is also behind numerous other landmarks in the area, among them the striking **United Nations University**.

On both sides of Omotesando you'll usually find a cluster of portraitists and sellers of jewellery and other nick-nacks. At Christmas, the streets here are the most crowded with golden lights decorating the trees. Stripped of any religious connotation in Japan, Christmas is the biggest date holiday of the year (think Valentine's Day plus New Year's Eve times Prom Night), and thousands of romantic-minded couples come to gaze at the lights before exchanging expensive presents. The trees and Omotesando proper end at Aoyama Dori, though the street itself continues through to Roppongi. If you're on the left corner of the street, there's a **koban** (police box) and on the right corner is **Fuji Bank**; both are popular meeting spots. The street

running behind the koban has yet another cluster of shops and restaurants, including the cozy and casual French restaurant **Red Pepper**. If you take a right on to Aoyama Dori you're heading back towards Shibuya. Take a right at the very first alley and look for **News Deli**, which might be the closest thing to a New York deli in this area, albeit with loud music playing. There are bagels, but its honey toast (a cube of toasted bread with honey seeping into it) may end up being your new favourite Sunday brunch option.

ANTIQUES TO HIGH FASHION

Back on Aoyama Dori, the big road almost opposite Kinokuniya is **Kotto Dori**, or Antique Street. Leading to Nishi-Azabu, this street has some 40 antique shops, mostly high-end, though striking a bargain is not unheard of at the smaller establishments. Back out on Aoyama Dori, heading back towards Omotesando, you'll pass the **Spiral Building** (*see chapter* **Museums & Galleries**), noted for its unusual curved achitecture by Maki Fumihiko. Returning to the Omotesando and Meiji Dori intersection, you'll see the popular **Andersen Bakery** (*see chapter* **Restaurants**) on your right, on the south-east corner. Nearby is **Gallery 360** (*see chapter* **Museums & Galleries**), one of many tiny galleries in the area. If you take a right on to the road at the corner, you'll come upon Tokyo's Madison Avenue. Nearly every top Japanese designer (and then some) has a store on this block, among them **Comme des Garçons** and **Issey Miyake** (*see chapter* **Shops & Services**). If you take the second left along this stretch of road and walk two minutes till the alley ends in a three-way intersection, you'll see **Cine City** in front of you. The store comprises two floors of film paraphernalia – videos, T-shirts, books, even mousepads.

Besides giving the name to this swank district, Aoyama is also the name of one of four national cemeteries built during the Meiji era. Like Yanaka Cemetery in Nippori, **Aoyama Cemetery** (Aoyama Bochi) was one of Japan's first public cemeteries. Cherry trees line a central straight road, attracting legions of *hanami* (cherry-blossom viewing) revellers celebrating spring's blooms with the dead. Aoyama in fact had once been covered with a different kind of tree: mulberry. They were planted in an ill-conceived plan to earn revenue by exporting silk. The Meiji government realised its error and by 1876 had uprooted them all.

Walking north along Aoyama Dori towards Gaien Nishi Dori ('outer-garden west avenue'), you'll hit **Plaza 246** and its **Japan Traditional Crafts Centre** on the south-west corner. Like Omotesando's Oriental Bazaar, the second-floor centre sells traditional crafts and caters to foreigners. **Bell Commons** is diagonally across from Plaza 246, a small mall that is a common meeting spot. Making a left down Gaien Nishi Dori puts you on a stretch of road called **Killer Dori**, whose name comes either for the steep hill down and the accidents it precipitates or for the 'killer' fashion boutiques and art galleries. Either way the unusually named street has plenty of distractions, not the least being **Watari-um Museum** (*see chapter* **Museums & Galleries**) and its gift shop. At the bottom of Killer Dori's hill, turn to the left and you'll eventually loop back in the direction of Harajuku station.

How to get there

Harajuku station is on the JR Yamanote line. The station is adjacent to Meiji-Jingumae station on the Eidan subway Chiyoda line. See Maps 5 and 12.

Addresses

J Crew
1-13-9 Jingumae, Shibuya-ku (3475 5088). **Open** noon-8pm daily, closed every third Wed.

Benetton
1-13-11 Jingumae, Shibuya-ku (3470 3158). **Open** 11am-8pm daily.

Anasazi-Santa Fe
1-11-11 Jingumae, Shibuya-ku (3403 6823). **Open** 11.30am-8pm daily.

Mujirushi Ryohin
1-12-7 Jingumae, Shibuya-ku (5414 3531). **Open** 11am-8pm daily.

Furusato Plaza
Laforet Part 2, 1-8-10 Jingumae, Shibuya-ku (5413 2302). **Open** 10am-7pm daily.

Romantic Standard
3-20-10 Jingumae, Shibuya-ku (3405 4562). **Open** 11am-8pm daily.

Vandalize
3-20-5 Jingumae, Shibuya-ku (5413 4864). **Open** noon-8pm daily.

Hide & Seek
3-18-25 Jingumae, Shibuya-ku (5474 4425). **Open** noon-8pm daily.

Candy Stripper
4-26-27 Jingumae, Shibuya-ku (5770 2204). **Open** 11am-8pm daily.

Café Vasy
3-20-9 Jingumae, Shibuya-ku (3401 6757). **Open** 11am-10pm Mon-Thur; 11am-10.30pm Fri, Sat; 11am-8pm Sun.

Perbacco!
Omotesando Vivre 1F, 5-10-1 Jingumae, Shibuya-ku (5466 4666). **Open** 10am-12.30am Mon-Thur; 10am-11pm Fri, Sat.

Todd Oldham
Omotesando Vivre 1F, 5-10-1 Jingumae, Shibuya-ku (3499 1330). **Open** 11am-8pm daily.

Anna Sui
Garden Terrace 1F, 6-1-4 Jingumae, Shibuya-ku (3486 1177). **Open** 11am-8pm daily.

Tokyo Union Church
5-7-7 Jingumae, Shibuya-ku (3400 0047).

United Nations University
5-53-70 Jingumae, Shibuya-ku (3499 2811).

Red Pepper
Shimizu Bldg. 1F, 3-5-25 Kita-Aoyama, Minato-ku (3478 1264). **Open** 5pm-midnight, 5-11.30pm Sat.

News Deli
SJ Bldg 1F, 3-6-26 Kita-Aoyama, Minato-ku (3407 1715). **Open** 11am-11pm daily.

Cine City
3-14-7 Minami-Aoyama, Minato-ku (5411 0838). **Open** noon-8pm daily.

Aoyama Cemetery
2 Minami-Aoyama, Minato-ku.

Japan Traditional Crafts Centre
Plaza 246, 3-1-1 Minami-Aoyama, Minato-ku 3403 2460). **Open** 10am-6pm Mon-Wed, Fri-Sun.

Bell Commons
2-14-6 Kita-Aoyama, Minato-ku (3475 8121). **Open** 11am-10pm daily.

It ain't what you do, it's the way you do it.

Marunouchi 丸の内

The historic centre of Tokyo offers respite from the city's crowds.

The Marunouchi area, which starts in front of Tokyo station, does not buzz with life, like the brasher new towns of Shinjuku and Shibuya, but it is the historic centre of Tokyo, the centre of the city since the establishment of old Edo.

The main feature in the district is the **Imperial Palace**, unfortunately inaccessible to visitors, except on the emperor's birthday, 23 December, and on 2 January (9.30am-3pm only). The grounds where the palace now stands are exactly those where Dokan Ota built the original Edo castle in 1457. When the military government gave way to imperial rule in 1867, the castle grounds became the Imperial Palace. Three sections of the old castle grounds have become public parkland: Higashi Gyoen, still within the walls and open in the daytime only, Kokyo-mae-hiroba along Hibiya Dori and Kitanomaru Park to the north, both open at all times.

The castle grounds were once much larger than they are today, and most of modern Marunouchi and Hibiya lay within the walls. In fact Marunouchi simply means 'within the moat or castle walls'.

MITSUBISHI TAKES OVER

After the Meiji Restoration, the land where Marunouchi now stands belonged to the army and was sold to Mitsubishi in 1890. Many derided the purchase, but the area slowly turned into the financial and business centre of Tokyo and Japan. At first Mitsubishi turned the area into Itcho Rondon, or Londontown, with Mitsubishi No.1 Hall the first London-style building. Many other brick buildings were to follow, the most admired of which was **Tokyo station**, modelled after Amsterdam's Centraal station and completed in 1914. Unlike many of the other brick buildings, it survived the 1923 earthquake and is intact to this day, with the exception of the roof, the original burnt in the air raids of the last war. It is one of only two buildings surviving from that era, the other being the **Banker's Club**, on the road leading to the National Diet.

To the west side of the former castle ground is **Hibiya**, also the residence of feudal lords in Edo. The site adjacent to the castle first became military showgrounds, but was turned into Japan's first western-style park early this century.

Despite the proximity of Tokyo station to the imperial, political and financial centres of power, nothing prepares you for the sight at the Marunouchi exits. It is one of the quietest places

in the whole of Tokyo. Like the City of London, it is a virtual ghost town after office hours.

Inside the station is one of the few points of interest, the **Tokyo Station Gallery**. To the left is **Tokyo Central Post Office**, the principal mail centre in the city.

Heading to the right leads to Otemachi, in reality nothing but an extension of Marunouchi, home to many financial and publishing organisations.

A WALK IN THE PARK

At the end of Eitai Dori, the street that divides Marunouchi from Otemachi is **Ote-mon**, one of three gates to enter **Higashi Gyoen**, the main park area in the old castle grounds. The garden is almost an island, being surrounded by moats, and the gates are probably the most interesting constructions. There is also the Sanno maru-shozukan, or **Museum of Imperial Collections**, displaying Japanese arts and crafts from the imperial family's collection. There are no views of the palace from anywhere in the park. The two main paths in **Higashi Gyoen** lead to Kita-Hanebashi gate. At the exit the foundation stones of the old castle and the moat are at their most dramatic, dropping at a very steep angle.

Across the road is **Kitanomaru Park**. On the right of the main road into the park is the **National Museum of Art**. The park is also home to the **National Science Museum** (*for both, see chapter* **Museums & Galleries**) and the **Nippon Budokan** (*see chapter* **Music**), built for judo competitions in the 1964 Olympics, but now more famous as a music venue.

At the exit to the main road, turning left and left again along **Chidorigafuchi moat** takes you down a 500-metre path lined with cherry trees. It's picturesque and very popular when the trees are in bloom. Boats can be rented between1 March and 15 December (9.30am-4.30pm daily), for ¥300 for 30 minutes.

The path leads to Uchibori Dori, which follows the moats back towards Tokyo station. The road passes along the **National Theatre of Japan** (*see chapter* **Theatre**). Next door is the **Supreme Court**. At the Aoyama Dori crossing, straying away from the moat in almost a straight line leads to the **National Diet Library** on the right and the small **Parliamentary Museum** on the left. Memorabilia on the history of the national government and the National Diet (Japanese parliament) building is on

The gardens of the **Imperial Palace** are the closest you'll get to meeting the emperor.

display. In the Meiji era the Diet was housed in wooden buildings nearby, but after they burnt down twice, the current granite building was constructed in the 1930s. You can visit the **National Diet** but tours are slightly disorganised. To visit, go to the Information Office of the House of Representatives, located at the back of the Diet building, near exit 1 of Kokkai-gijidomae station.

The road continues on to **Hibiya Park**, a very popular hangout, particularly with courting couples. There are a number of good-value restaurants and cafés, some with seats outside. It's a pleasant place for an afternoon stroll.

The pièce de résistance of the area, the **Tokyo International Forum**, is a short distance away. Designed by architect Rafael Viñoly and opened in 1996, it is divided in two buildings, the glass hall being a genuine architectural wonder. Take the lift to the seventh floor from the lobby for a great view of the extraordinary roof. A path descends three floors along the glass wall, not a good idea for vertigo sufferers. The adjacent building has convention and exhibition halls and in the basement you'll find a number of restaurants, as well as the **Tourist Information Centre** (*see chapter Directory*), which provides free maps and infor-

mation in English on destinations and accommodation anywhere in Japan.

How to get there

Tokyo station is on the JR Chuo and Yamanote lines, plus many others, and on the Eidan Marunouchi subway line. See Maps 6 and 18.

Addresses

Tokyo Station Gallery
1-9-1 Marunouchi, Chiyoda-ku (3212 2485). **Open** 10am-8pm Tue-Thur; 10am-6pm Sat, Sun.

Tokyo Central Post Office
2-7-2 Marunouchi, Chiyoda-ku (3284 9500). **Open** 24 hours (postal services only).

Higashi Gyoen
Open *Mar-Oct* 9am-4.30pm Tue-Thur, Sat, Sun; *Nov-Feb* 9am-4pm Tue-Thur, Sat, Sun.

Museum of Imperial Collections
1-1 Chiyoda, Chiyoda-ku (3213 1111). **Open** *Mar-Oct* 9.15-4.15pm; *Nov-Feb* 9.15-3.45pm Tue-Thur, Sat, Sun.

National Diet Building
1-7-1 Nagatacho, Chiyoda-ku. **Open** *museum* 9.30am-4.30pm; *Diet building* by guided tour only. See text for details.

Ginza 銀座

Tokyo's plushest shopping area is surprisingly affordable – if you know where to go.

It's Sunday, just before noon. A police car appears on Ginza Dori and an announcement blares from its loudspeaker: 'This avenue will be turned into *hokosha tengoku* (pedestrian heaven) soon. No vehicles will be allowed between Ginza 1-*chome* and Ginza 8-chome until 7pm. Please remove your parked cars immediately.' As if by magic, the busy traffic vanishes.

At noon, **Ginza Dori** (known officially as Chuo Dori, or Central Avenue) looks wide enough for Godzilla to wander down without touching a building. Nowhere else in centre of the city has the same sense of space and freedom. Tables and chairs are set up on the street, allowing pedestrians to rest, chat, or just watch people pass by. This is the best time to indulge in the favourite Tokyo pastime of *ginbura* (Ginza strolling), first popularised in the early decades of the twentieth century by the fashionably modern youth of a bygone era.

The atmosphere is surprisingly peaceful. Busking is very much frowned upon here, unlike in other areas closed to traffic on Sundays. When Elvis Costello toured Japan for the first time in 1984 he came to Ginza during hokosha tengoku and attempted to drum up interest for his gigs with a live set from the back of a truck. No one took any notice.

Ginza (the name means 'Silver Seat') was originally the Edo-era nickname for the area around the silver mint, built in 1612 near where **Tiffany's** (*see chapter* **Shops & Services**) now stands on Ginza Dori. Although the mint itself was moved to Nihonbashi in 1800, the name Ginza remained. In 1869, the district was officially given the name Ginza by the new Meiji government. Ginza became the symbol of modern, fashionable Tokyo after a major fire cleared the area of many of its wooden buildings in 1872 and the city's first rail hub opened at nearby Shinbashi. Ginza Dori was known as 'Brick Avenue' for its rows of western-style red-brick buildings – shops, offices, restaurants and bars. These were destroyed in the 1923 earthquake, but a monument to 'Ginza Bricktown' stands on a foundation of original red bricks in front of the **Hotel Seiyo Ginza**.

Rising from the ashes after the devastation of the earthquake, and again after the air raids of World War II, Ginza continued to grow, consolidating its reputation as the city's most exclusive district. Today, shopping and dining in Ginza maintain an air of luxury. Compared to places like Shinjuku or Shibuya, the age profile is noticeably higher and the dress code smarter. It can be tough to find a reasonably priced meal after 9pm. Karaoke boxes and convenience shops, very familiar sights in Tokyo's other entertainment quarters, are scarce in Ginza.

Still, this is the only part of Tokyo where older fashions mix easily with the latest trends. There are elegant department stores like **Mitsukoshi** and **Matsuya** (*see chapter* **Shops & Services**), wooden shops selling traditional items, and brand-name boutiques, small old galleries exhibiting avant-garde art, showrooms where you can touch and test the latest high-tech products and a huge number of coffee shops and Japanese-style tea rooms.

The best bargain, however, is the **special lunch offers** of Ginza's up-market restaurants. There are enough lunchtime options in Ginza to provide you with a different meal every day of the year. On weekdays between 11.30am and 2pm, and also at weekends at some establishments, high-quality set meals are offered for around ¥1,000, up to ten times cheaper than the same dishes on evening menus. Explore the back streets and look outside restaurants for signs, together with a list of prices. Chinese, Italian, French, tempura, sushi – you name it. There is certainly no shortage.

GINZA STROLLING

There are many ways to walk around Ginza, but setting off from Yurakucho station is best.

Take the exit for Ginza and walk down the narrow street with the tiny **Cine La Sept** cinema (*see chapter* **Film**) on the corner. Continue straight through the arcade running inside the modern Mullion complex – home to **Seibu** and **Hankyu** department stores (*see chapter* **Shops & Services**), as well as several cinemas – and you come out at the multi-directional zebra crossings of **Sukiyabashi** (Sukiya Bridge). Confusingly, there is no bridge. There used to be one going from the present-day Sukiyabashi Hankyu department store towards Hibiya, across the old outer moat of Edo Castle (now the Imperial Palace), but both bridge and waterway were casualties of 1960s highway construction. Today, only a small monument marks the spot where the bridge stood.

Standing with Sukiyabashi Hankyu department store on your right, you will see a large **Sony** sign on the other side of the crossing. This tall, slim building offers eight floors of entertainment (*see*

At cherry blossom time, Ginza is an especially pleasant place for a weekend stroll.

chapter **Shops & Services**). Technology and games fans can easily spend hours there, but even for non-admirers of machines it is still an enjoyable place to kill time. Sounds, visuals, computers – all the latest Sony models are on display and can be tried out. The sixth floor is dedicated to PlayStation and you can request games to play. This section is packed with kids at weekends, so try to be there during the week. Smokers might find the third floor of Sony a good place to take a break. **Japan Tobacco** has an information section there, with a large table and chairs for smokers to enjoy a care-free drag. You are even offered a free cold drink.

If you carry on walking along **Harumi Dori** (away from Yurakucho) after coming out of the Sony building, you reach Ginza 4-chome crossing in almost no time. Instead, walk down Sotobori Dori (Outer Moat Avenue, once part of Edo Castle's waterway defences), towards Ginza 8-chome and Shinbashi. Ginza streets are laid out in a simple grid and have names rather than numbers, so it's difficult to get lost. On your way down to 8-chome, stop off at some of the many small art galleries, most of which have free admission (*see chapter* **Museums & Galleries**).

When you finally reach the boundary of Ginza at Gomon Dori, turn left towards Ginza Dori, passing the narrower streets of Sony Dori, Namiki Dori, and Nishi Gobangai. Just before Ginza Dori is the start of Konparu Dori, the Edo-era home of the celebrated Konparu school of Noh theatre performers, the most historic of the four troupes who appeared regularly at the shogun's castle. During the nineteenth century, many geisha houses sprang up in the **Konparu-cho** district, along with nearby Shinbashi, as the area became one of the city's main unlicensed pleasure quarters. Although geisha can no longer be seen here, several old wooden Japanese restaurants preserve something of the atmosphere of past times. The area is also home to a public bath-house, **Konparu-yu**, where crewcut chefs from the local restaurants come to bathe during the short break between the end of lunch and evening re-opening.

Whichever route you take, the atmospheric streets between Ginza Dori and Sotobori Dori are probably the best pottering area in Ginza. Take a slow zigzag route toward 4-chome crossing, enjoying the back streets and some window-shopping on Ginza Dori on the way.

*The imposing **Kabuki-za** in Ginza is the home of Japan's venerable theatrical form.*

When you arrive at 4-chome crossing, you will see **Le Café Doutor Espresso**, part of the giant Doutor coffee shop chain (*see chapter* **Coffee shops**), on your left. Next to it is **Kyukyodo**, a traditional stationery shop known not only for its quality Japanese paper products but for marking the spot usually quoted as the nation's most expensive piece of real estate. On the other side of the crossing is **Wako** (*see chapter* **Shops & Services**), a watch and jewellery department store famous for its dazzling window displays, whose mini clock-tower is the popular symbol of Ginza. In a scene in Yasujiro Ozu's film *Tokyo Story* (1953), two women drive past Wako in a chauffeur-driven car, and the store represents the high-class, modern face of Tokyo. The current building dates from 1932, although the original clock tower stood on pre-earthquake premises named for their owner, Seiko watch-company founder Kintaro Hattori. 'Outside Wako at 4-chome crossing' remains the most common phrase for fixing a Ginza meeting spot.

Another popular meeting place is **Nissan Gallery**, also on the corner of the crossing. All the latest Nissan cars are exhibited on the glass-windowed ground floor. Since admission is free, the ground floor gets very busy on rainy days.

Take the last right turning before Miharabashi Crossing, where Harumi Dori meets Showa Dori, and on your right you will see the **Okome Gallery** (Rice Gallery). Here, learn everything about Japanese sticky rice, and eat cheap set meals with a bowl of deliciously cooked rice. *Onigiri* (rice balls) are also available to take away.

Further down Harumi Dori, you will see the **Kabuki-za** theatre, home of kabuki (*see chapter* **Theatre**). Reserved seats cost up to ¥15,000, but a single act of the day-long programme can be enjoyed for around ¥1,000. Although you have to queue for tickets, and good opera glasses are definitely required, this is a good way to get a taste of traditional Japanese performing arts.

Another way of seeing Ginza is to begin the day here, as performances start at 11am, then head off and sample the delights listed above.

How to get there

Ginza station is on the Ginza, Hibiya and Marunouchi subway lines, but the best way to tour the area is to start at Yurakucho station, on the JR Yamanote line, and walk down. See **Map 7**.

Addresses

Hotel Seiyo Ginza
1-11-2 Ginza, Chuo-ku (3535 1111/fax 3535 1110).

Konparu-yu
8-7-5 Ginza, Chuo-ku (3571 5469). **Open** *2pm-midnight Mon-Fri; 2-11pm Sat.* **Admission** *adult* ¥385, *middle schoolchildren* ¥170, *primary schoolchildren* ¥70.

Kyukyodo
5-7-4 Ginza, Chuo-ku (3571 4429). **Open** *10am-7.30pm Mon-Sat; 11am-7pm Sun.*

Nissan Gallery
Nissan Motors Bldg 1F, 6-17-1 Ginza, Chuo-ku (5565 2389). **Open** *8:30am-6:30pm Mon-Fri; 8:30am-5:30pm Sat.*

Okome Gallery
Ginza Crest Bldg 1F, 5-11-4 Ginza, Chuo-ku (3248 4131). **Open** *10am-6pm Mon-Sat.*

Ueno Park 上野公園

Where history, culture and good times go hand in hand.

A rare example of nature run wild in Tokyo, at **Shinobazu pond** *in Ueno Park.*

Ueno Park is one of Tokyo's most popular destinations for a day out. With a collection of world-class museums, a zoo, a boating lake and a pond, as well as several monuments of deep historical significance, it has something for everyone.

The history of Ueno Park is closely linked with that of Edo, the name of Tokyo before the Meiji Restoration. The second Tokugawa *shogun* had Kan'ei-ji temple built in 1625 on what was then Ueno hill, located north-east of the castle, to ward off evil spirits coming from that direction. He also established Toshogu Shrine nearby, dedicated to the first shogun, Ieyasu. Kan'ei-ji became the shrine of the Tokugawa family and the burial place of many a shogun. The temple grounds expanded, and at their apex at the end of the seventeenth century, were home to 36 temples and 36 subsidiary buildings in addition to Kan'ei-ji. Ueno grew as a temple town to support the needs

of the population living in the temple grounds.

Ueno Park is also closely associated with the fall of the shogunate. The last Tokugawa shogun, Yoshinobu, surrendered power to the emperor peacefully in 1867. But when the imperial troops reached Tokyo the following year they were met by a diehard group of 2,000 men, the *shogitai*, at Ueno hill. Outnumbered and using traditional fighting methods against an army with modern weaponry, the shogitai fell by the end of the day. In the fighting almost everything on Ueno hill was destroyed. Yoshinobu used one of the few remaining buildings as a retreat to await the emperor's decision regarding his fate. He was eventually pardoned but exiled.

Ueno hill became Japan's first park in 1873, thanks to the convincing effort of Dutch doctor Antonius Bauduin, who had originally been summoned to Tokyo as a consultant on a scheme to turn the desolate area into a military hospital. As buildings have eaten into all of Tokyo's other parks, only Ueno has been left largely intact. All of Tokyo owes the Dutch doctor a vote of thanks.

Ueno is Tokyo's largest park, and is constantly crowded, but never more so than at cherry-blossom time, when over 2 million people will throng through the park in the week that the blossoms remain on the trees. If you are lucky enough to go at cherry-blossom time (usually at the end of March to early April), prepare yourself for scenes of unimaginable rowdiness and drunkenness as well as the breathtaking beauty of the 1,300 blooming pink cherry trees.

It may be partly due to this notoriety as a good-time place that the Ueno area as a whole has a lowbrow reputation; other contributory factors are its low city origin and the fact that many people coming from the rural north of Japan arrive at Ueno station. Some end up living under tarpaulins in the wooded areas of the park.

This regrettable fact aside, Ueno Park is a great place for a leisurely day. The key to making the most of it is not to try and do too much. It is simply impossible to take in all of the park's attractions in one day. The adjacent areas along the tracks and north of Chuo Dori are covered in the walk from Ueno to Akihabara (*see page 80*).

Our tour of the park starts near Ueno Keisei station, across the road to the right from the JR Shinobazu exit. For information on Ueno Park's museums and galleries, *see page 92*.

MAGICAL HISTORY TOUR

Near the entrance is the statue of **Saigo Takamori**, a leading figure in the negotiations for the transfer of power from the shogun to the emperor. He resigned from the imperial forces a few years later and led the Satsuma rebellion to Tokyo to challenge the government, but failed and then killed himself. For his dual status as hero and rebel the statue depicts him in casual dress. In this way his contribution is marked without compromising the imperial forces' reputation.

Behind to the left is a tomb dedicated to the memory of the shogitai. In the small enclosure there are prints of the battle and a map of the temple grounds before the buildings were destroyed.

Away down a path to the left is **Kiyomizu Temple**, one of the few buildings to escape destruction in the battle. Originally completed in 1631, the main building has been renovated but the small annexe retains a flavour of old.

Going down the steps from the temple leads to **Bentendo Temple** in Shinobazu pond. The island and the original temple were built in the early seventeenth century, the bridge not constructed until many years later. Bentendo is dedicated to Benzaiten, at first goddess of rivers, eventually goddess of wisdom and pursuit of knowledge and the arts, as well as goddess of money. The current building dates from 1958.

Back towards the steps and left up the hill is **Gojoten Shrine**, a concentration of small buildings dedicated to the gods of medicine and learning. The small grey *torii* (gate) leads to a tiny man-made cave with a small shrine. The steps under a row of orange torii on the right lead back to the main avenue in the park.

Turning left after Seiyoken, the small restaurant serving noodles and coffee, there is a bell, the **Bell of Time**, dating from 1666, and a Buddhist stupa almost hidden away in the bushes.

The street leads to the entrance of **Toshogu Shrine**, the undisputed highlight of the historical monuments in the park. The shrine is dedicated to the first shogun, Tokugawa Ieyasu. The style is similar to the one where he is buried, in Nikko. Toshogu was first built in 1627, then remodelled in 1651. It has withstood earthquakes and numerous fires as well as the battle of Ueno hill, and is one of the oldest buildings in Tokyo. The lantern on the left before the first gate is one of Japan's three largest. The path to the entrance is lined with many smaller stone lanterns. There are also some copper lanterns near the temple, used only for purification and sacred fires in religious ceremonies. They were offerings to the memory of the first shogun by feudal lords. On the right along the path are two separate monuments in memory of World War II. **Karamon**, the front gate of the temple, is famous for the carvings of the dragons, which date from 1651 and are said to be so lifelike that they sneak down to the pond to drink at night. The main shrine building is the **Golden Hall** or Konjiki-den, and inside is the armour and sword of the shogun, as well as a few artworks and personal artefacts.

Walking along the path to Toshogu you will see an intriguing-looking five-storey pagoda. Unfortunately, to get a closer look you need to pay to enter the zoo. Following the zoo wall and returning to the main path leads towards the grand fountain, where **Kan'ei-ji Temple** used to stand. To preserve this important memory a small temple was moved in 1879 from Kawagoe (in Tokyo's north) to the park and renamed Kan'ei-ji. This particular structure was chosen because it was the work of the same person who supervised the building of the original Kan'ei-ji. On the grounds are a few stones and mementoes of the past and a monument dedicated to insects. Behind the temple and past the school the road leads along a cemetery to **Chokugakumon gate**, where six of the Tokugawa shogun are buried. It is not open to the public. The road continues back towards the park and at the main road stands **Rinno-ji Temple**. The temple itself is relatively recent, but the small structure and the lanterns on the premises are reminiscent of days before the battle.

protest. The boating section is open from March to November, from 9am to 5pm. Renting a rowing boat or pedal boat costs from ¥300 for 30 minutes. The nature pond, also called Hasu pond, is famed for its lotus, and at flowering time in the summer is a great sight. The rest of the year, it must be said, it's not that attractive, except to the wild black cormorants, ducks, pigeons, crows and seagulls that make their home there. The zoo section, to the north of the pond, houses many breeds of aquatic birds.

Ueno Zoo itself opened over 100 years ago, in the early days of the park. It's home to many animals, including snow leopards, gorillas and tigers, but the most famous are the pandas, who feed daily at 3.30pm, but have a well-deserved day off on Fridays. The zoo is split into two parts connected by a monorail. Those who don't like to see wild beasts in captivity may prefer to hop on the monorail to the children's section, where there is an open-air petting zoo.

Back in the park proper, another attraction for kids is **Kodomo-yuen**, a small area clustered with ferry rides close to the zoo entrance. There is no entrance fee – you pay only for each ride.

More grown-up attractions in the same area include a **peony garden**, which attracts a lot of people during January and February, while the flowers are in bloom. Admission is ¥800.

Finally, if hunger starts to get the better of you, the park has no shortage of places to eat and drink. Close to the Royal Museum is a restaurant and beer terrace, which is open from Monday to Saturday from 11am to 5pm in winter and until 9pm in the summer. The white building to the left of Saigo Takamori's statue has two restaurants, both serving lunch specials for ¥1,000. There are also many stands serving street food at all hours of the day and night.

How to get there

Ueno station is on the Yamanote, Keihin-Tohoku and other JR lines, the Eidan subway Ginza and Hibiya lines and the Keisei line. See Map 8.

Addresses

Toshogu Shrine

Open 9am-5pm daily. **Admission** ¥200.

Tokyo Metropolitan Festival Hall

5-45 Ueno-Koen, Taito-ku (3828 2111). **Open** *library* 10am-8pm Thu-Sat; 10am-5pm Sun. Closed every other Sun; *hall* varies with events.

Ueno Zoo

Open 9.30am-5pm (last admission 4pm) Tue-Sun. **Admission** ¥500;¥200 high schoolchildren.

Tourist Information Booth

Near park entrance from JR Ueno station (5685 1181). **Open** 9am-6pm daily. Free maps in English.

Blossom time in the park: let your hair down.

TAKING IT EASY

Heading down from Rinno-ji Temple, on the other side of the block housing the National Science Museum and National Museum of Western Art, is the massive **Tokyo Metropolitan Festival Hall** (Tokyo Bunka Kaikan). It's a centre for music, with venues for classical music concerts and dance performances. On the fourth floor there is a library with over 10,000 recordings, which is open to the public: you are free to browse and listen for as long as you want.

With your ears still ringing, head back down to **Shinobazu pond**, which is an unchanged remnant of the marshy ground that once covered this area of the city. The pond is divided into three areas: one is part of the zoo, another is for boating and the third is given over to nature. Peaceful though it may appear, the pond is regularly under threat from Tokyo's rapacious developers. Late last century there was a horse-racing track around it, and immediately after World War II, when Tokyo was experiencing acute food shortages, the pond was drained and used to grow food. Most recently, plans to build a huge car park underneath were thwarted by popular

Ochanomizu お茶の水

A place of religion, education, bookshops and electric guitars.

In Ochanomizu, young and old Tokyo co-exist, divided only by the Kanda River, which runs parallel to the train tracks. Once, this river, actually a canal, marked the outer limits of the old castle of Edo, part of a vast outer moat constructed to protect it from invaders. Its origins can still be traced in some of the brickwork that lines its steep banks. To the north of the river stand two of Tokyo's most venerable shrines, while to the south lie the city's tin-pan alley, a motley collection of shops selling guitars, musical instruments and DJ equipment, and the bookshop area of Jinbocho.

Take the east exit from the JR station, towards Hijiribashi, one of two bridges that span the river from the station. If you cross to the far side of the street and look away from the river, you should see the green dome of one of Ochanomizu's odder monuments – the dome of **Nikolai**, a Russian orthodox cathedral dating from 1892 (*see chapter* **Sightseeing**). Its real name is the Resurrection Cathedral of the Orthodox Church of Japan, but it took its nickname from its first archbishop, who administered it until his death in 1912. Although the original designs for the building were drawn up in St Petersburg, the architect responsible for its construction was an Englishman, Josiah Conder, one of the first foreigners to make an impact in Japan. His building was taller than the current one, the original dome having collapsed in the 1923 quake.

The entrance to the cathedral is difficult to find, around the corner from an ornate gateway that looks as if it should be the way in. Above the gate is the Russian inscription *'slava byshnikh bogu'* (praise be to God in the highest). Unfortunately, few Christian virtues seem to have penetrated the reception office, where you will be told in no uncertain terms that the cathedral is not open to visitors. The only way to see it at the time of writing is to attend a service (10am-12.30pm Sun), although rumour has it that its former weekday opening hours are soon to be restored.

On the other side of the Kanda River lie two more buildings of religious significance. The first, on the other side of Hijiribashi, is **Yushima Seido**, a Chinese shrine dedicated to Confucius. Yushima Seido was founded in Ueno Park, and originally stood where the statue of Saigo Takamori is now (*see* **Ueno Park**, *page 57*). Sixty years after its foundation, in 1691, it moved here, its mission to promote the study of Confucian classics. Confucianism appealed to the Japanese of the period because it

seemed to offer a more intellectual approach to the big questions than the largely animistic answers offered by shinto. Whatever the temple's raison d'être, its presence was enough to start a trend. Over the following centuries, the Kanda area (of which Ochanomizu is a part) emerged as Tokyo's academic centre; there are nearly 30 educational institutions making their home here or nearby today.

As with many historic sites, little remains of the original shrine buildings. The shrine has been destroyed four times by fire, and was last rebuilt in 1935. The imposing statue of Confucius that stands in the pleasantly overgrown grounds is said to be the world's largest. At the top of a flight of steps near the statue are two of the rare survivors of the various catastrophes that have overtaken the shrine: a wooden gate dating from 1704, and a water purification trough. On the other side of the gate, a courtyard contains the shrine itself. The hall (open only at weekends) contains an image of Confucius in the company of his disciples.

Because of its academic associations, Yushima Seido (like Yushima Tenjin further north, *see chapter* **Sightseeing**) is a popular place for hopeful students to pray for good exam results towards the end of the academic year. Students will write their wishes on a wooden prayer tablet, or *ema*, which they then attach to a frame. Even among the young in Japan, ancient superstition dies hard.

A short walk from Yushima Seido, on the other side of Hongo Dori, tradition and superstition also live on in Kanda Myojin, a shrine dating back to AD730. The small road that leads to the shrine is dotted with traditional shops selling *amazake*, sake sweetened with ginger. The most famous of these is Amanoya, which looks as if it has slipped into the twentieth century through a time warp.

Unless you visit in March, when the plum blossom is in full bloom, the main shrine building, a post-earthquake reconstruction from 1934, is a disappointment, the most striking feature being a spectacular fountain containing two Chinese lions which date back to the Edo period. Even they haven't come through the years unscathed: their children were destroyed in the 1923 earthquake.

Left of the main hall is a series of smaller buildings used to store the *mikoshi* (portable shrines) that are carried through the streets during the Kanda festival, the shrine's main claim to fame. The festival, one of the largest in Tokyo, takes place in odd-numbered years, around 14 or 15 May,

Nikolai *Russian Orthodox cathedral (1892).*

and local people take to the streets carrying 70 mikoshi (*see also chapter* **Tokyo by Season**).

As well as an occasion for local traders to ask the gods to bless their business, the festival is thought to be an expression of popular affection for Taira-on Masakado, a tenth-century rebel and folk hero who took on the emperor in Kyoto and was beheaded for his pains. His head, displayed as a warning, is said to have flown back to rejoin his body at the shrine's original site, in present-day Otemachi. Such is the awe in which this man is held that when the emperor visited Kanda-Myojin in 1868, advisers insisted that Masakado's spirit be purged from the building. The spirit was returned when the temple was rebuilt, but Masakado's grave in Otemachi remains undeveloped to this day, surrounded by tall buildings owned by multinational corporations too nervous to encroach.

Back on the other side of the Kanda River, over Ochanomizubashi, the area's character changes. In term time, students from the nearby universities swarm through the streets; as a result the area is crammed with bars, coffee shops and places to eat. On the left-hand side of the main road, one of the best budget choices is the long-established kaitenzushi (revolving sushi) restaurant **Himawari**; the sushi is of good quality and just ¥130 per plate. At lunchtime, the queue to get in can stretch round the block. If you want to wait out the lunchtime rush, Miró (*see chapter* **Coffee Shops**), in an alleyway behind Himawari, is a fine place to relax.

As you continue down the main road, the white building on the right houses the Criminal Museum (*see chapter* **Museums & Galleries**). The giant Liberty Tower on the same side of the street opened in 1998 on the site of a splendid old building that was unceremoniously demolished to make way for it. You can get some idea of what the old building was like by looking at the Ochanomizu Square building on the opposite side of the street. This building was painstakingly refurbished in 1987 by Isozaki Arata, with the addition of a new tower protruding from its original fabric. Ochanomizu Square is home to Casals Hall (*see chapter* **Music**), one of Tokyo's premier classical music venues.

On the way down the street, it's impossible not to notice the number of shops selling guitars and other musical equipment. This is where Tokyo's would-be pop stars do their shopping. Towards the intersection with Yasukuni Dori, the character of the area begins to change again. This is the start of the Jinbocho book district, where more than 100 bookshops sell new, used and antique reading matter from all over the world. Many of the shops along Yasukuni Dori and the back streets behind it are cramped and disorganised and, weather permitting, the books spill out on to the street to entice passing browsers. Although most of the books are in Japanese, it's worth stopping to look.

For new English books in the area, check out the huge book store **Sanseido**, which has been in business since 1881, or Charles Tuttle (*for both, see chapter* **Shops & Services**), one of Tokyo's leading English-language publishers whose shop contains a wide selection of English-language books on Japan and the Japanese language. Another shop worth checking out is **Matsumura**, which specialises in books on design from all over the world.

Bunpodo the stationer, near the Yasukuni Dori junction, has one of the most imposing buildings in the area. It dates from 1922 and stands out from the anonymous crowd around it. Unusually it survived the 1923 earthquake, but was gutted by fire and refurbished. The company itself has had a shop on the site since 1887.

For all its points of historical interest, one of the main attractions of the Ochanomizu/Jinbocho area is the way it lends itself to aimless wandering. Parallel to Yasukuni Dori, on both sides of the street, are labyrinthine networks of tiny streets with bookshops, bars and coffee shops by the dozen. Check out beer bar **Brussels** or yakitoriya **Ieyasu Hon-jin** (*for both, see chapter* **Bars**), or if you've bought a book, settle down for a good read in a coffee shop such as **Mironga** or **Saboru** (*for both, see chapter* **Coffee Shops**). You certainly won't be alone.

How to get there

Ochanomizu is on the JR Chuo and Sobu lines and on the Eidan subway Chiyoda and Marunouchi lines. See Map 9.

Addresses

Himawari
2-4 Kanda-Surugadai (3295 9125) **Open** 11am-9pm Mon-Sat.

Matsumura & Co
1-7 Kanda-Jinbocho (3295 5678). **Open** 10.30am-6pm Mon-Sat.

Bunpodo
1-21-1 Kanda-Jinbocho (3291 3441). **Open** 10am-7pm Mon-Sat; 11am-7pm Sun.

Outside the Yamanote Line

There's more to Tokyo than what lies inside the JR Yamanote loop. We start our trek in the city of the future, on a Tokyo Bay island.

Odaiba お台場

It is sometimes easy to forget that Tokyo stands on the sea, and for years the waterfront area was neglected by both locals and town planners. Despite a shaky start, the area known as Odaiba, or Rainbow Town, is changing all that, offering a sense of space that the city lacks. With its futuristic buildings, fairground and beach, it's a strange, fun and spectacular place for a day's sightseeing.

Odaiba is a new district of Tokyo designed at the height of the '80s bubble economy on an island of reclaimed land in Tokyo Bay. The island is connected to one of the nineteenth-century gun emplacements, or *daiba*, that were built to protect old Edo from invasion. By the time the magnificent new **Rainbow Bridge** opened in 1993, connecting Odaiba to the city, the building project was in trouble, and by 1995 Suzuki Shunichi, the Tokyo mayor who had championed Odaiba's development, was booted out of office by disgruntled voters.

By 1999, the picture looked different. Fuji TV's decision to build its astonishing new headquarters on the island encouraged others to follow, and since 1997, shopping malls, luxury hotels and office buildings have been springing up. More are sure to follow: at the time of writing, Sony is constructing a mammoth new building on the waterfront.

The quickest way to Odaiba is via the Yuri-kamome line, from Shinbashi station. This is a fully automatic train line that makes a complete circuit of Odaiba before terminating in Ariake. It's also rather pricey. A single ticket to Daiba station costs ¥380. If you plan to make a day of it, buy a one-day pass for ¥800.

Fuji TV's landmark headquarters is another of architect Tange Kenzo's amazing creations.

The train ride is almost worth the trip in itself. Raised above the street, it loops around before crossing the bay over Rainbow Bridge. Sit at the front of the driverless train if you can, and watch the skyline come looming towards you. If you want to head straight for the action, get off at Daiba Kaihin Koen station. If not, it's worth staying on the train to Ariake, right at the other end of the U-shaped line, which gives you a great perspective of the island. On the way, you will see many shiny new buildings that are becoming landmarks in their own right, among them the **Maritime Museum** (a huge concrete boat), the **Telecom Centre** (all glass, with a reflective satellite dish-like structure at its centre) and **Tokyo Big Site** (also written Big Sight), a giant exhibition and concert venue whose main hall looks like four inverted glass pyramids.

There isn't much of any great interest in Ariake, except for the **Washington Hotel**, which opened in July 1999. One stop back on the train is Kokusai Tenjijoseimon, the stop for Big Site. When the exhibition hall is empty, visitors can take an elevator to the roof. Opposite Big Site, on the other side of the tracks, is a nondescript mall with numerous restaurants and shops. The best bet is to head back for Daiba station, on foot (15 minutes) or by train. The train will drop you off just short of the **Fuji Television** building, Odaiba's major landmark after Rainbow Bridge, which opened in 1997. It's another of architect Tange Kenzo's creations (*see chapter* **Architecture**), and is recognisable by the large metallic ball that seems to be suspended in mid-air in the middle of the building. This is the twenty-fifth-floor viewing platform, and combined view-and-tour tickets are on sale. The tour is unlikely to be of much interest to anyone unfamiliar with Japanese TV. If you want a similar view for free, head for the Sky Lounge on the thirtieth floor of the **Meridien Grand Pacific Hotel** (*see chapter* **Accommodation**) next door.

Back towards Rainbow Bridge, Fuji TV's other neighbour is the **Decks** shopping centre, which houses five floors of shops and restaurants and a giant **Sega Joypolis** amusement centre. Of particular interest on the fifth floor is the **Decks Tokyo Brewery**, which makes its own Daiba brand beer on the premises. You can watch the brewing process take place through giant windows, then retire to the **Sunset Beach Brewing Company** restaurant to sample it with food from a giant western-style buffet. Try to get a seat out on the veranda with a view over the artificial beach, whose three-metre-deep sand was specially shipped in.

The beach itself is a popular venue for courting couples, who'll stroll arm in arm for hours before retiring to one of the European-style bistros that have sprung up a little way back from the seafront.

Heading inland from Decks you'll find another new complex, **Palette Town**, which opened in summer 1999. Just head for the huge ferris wheel.

Palette Town comprises yet another shopping mall with the **MegaWeb funfair** *(see page 68)*, a **Neo-Geo amusement arcade**, and the biggest car showroom in the world, **Toyota City Showcase**. In the basement, there's a small motor museum called **History Garage** with over 30 historic cars from around the world, some of which you are allowed to climb inside. Toyota City Showcase also gives you the chance to 'drive' the company's latest self-driving, electric, radar-guided mini-cars (¥200), plus a range of driving simulators (¥600).

Try to time your visit to Odaiba so as to catch the sunset over Rainbow Bridge, which can be spectacular. Watch as the lights on the giant ferris wheel flicker into life, and then head back from this tranquil future city, with its wide pedestrian walkways, into the sprawling, crowded metropolis on the other side of the water. If you're feeling energetic, you can do it on foot along **Rainbow Bridge's pedestrian walkway**.

How to get there

Odaiba is on the Yurikamome line, which runs from Shinbashi station.

Addresses

Maritime Museum
3-1 Higashi-Yashio, Shinagawa-ku (5500 1111). **Open** 10am-5pm daily. **Admission** ¥1,000.

Telecom Centre
2-38 Aomi, Koto-ku (5565 5734).

Tokyo Big Site
3-21-1 Ariake, Koto-ku (5530 1111).

Tokyo Bay Ariake Washington Hotel
3-1 Ariake, Koto-ku (5564 1015).

Fuji TV Building
2-4-8 Daiba, Minato-ku (info 0180 993 188/5500 8888). **Open** 10am-9pm Tue-Sun. **Admission** *tower/studios* ¥500.

Decks Tokyo Beach
1-6-1 Daiba, Minato-ku (5500 5050). **Open** *shops* 11am-9pm, *restaurants* 11am-11pm, daily.

Sega Joypolis
1-6-1 Daiba, Decks Tokyo Beach 3F-5F, Minato-ku (5500 1801). **Open** 10am-11pm daily. **Admission** ¥500; ¥300 schoolchildren.

Sunset Beach Brewing Company
Decks Tokyo Beach 5F, 1-6-1 Daiba, Minato-ku (5500 5066). **Open** 11am-4pm, 5-11pm, daily.

Neo-Geo World Tokyo Bayside
Palette Town, 1 Aomi, Koto-ku (3599 0800). **Open** 10am-11pm Mon-Thur, Sun; 10am-1am Fri, Sat.

Rainbow Bridge walkway
Open *Apr-Oct* 10am-9pm, *Nov-Mar* 10am-6pm, daily. **Admission** ¥300.

Other Areas

Being out of the centre doesn't mean being out of the action.

Shimo-Kitazawa
下北沢

Shimo-Kitazawa has had a reputation as an arty enclave since at least the 1960s, when a group of small local theatres were experimenting with new, unconventional forms. While few of these venues acquired much of a reputation outside Tokyo, their presence was enough to attract those in search of intellectual stimulation and alternative ideas.

Even today, Shimo-Kitazawa still attracts young people and can claim something of a uniquely bohemian atmosphere. Its busy streets are thronged with teenagers and university students whose easy-going, cool and casual attitude is reflected in the local fashions, shops and venues.

Catering for this young, energetic clientele is a host of restaurants, coffee shops, boutiques and shops with unusual selections of goods, from records to home accessories and gadgets.

Unsurprisingly, Shimo-Kitazawa is also known for its live music houses, of which it has one of the largest concentrations in Tokyo. Every night, several groups of local hopefuls will be found plying their trade. There are plenty of bars, too, varied enough to satisfy the most eclectic tastes.

Best of all, everything is within a ten-minute walk of the station, inside four streets forming an irregular rectangle with the station almost in the middle. The Odakyu line is at street level and effectively divides Shimo-Kitazawa in two. While the layout of the streets is confusing, it's a pedestrian-friendly place. There are two exits from the station, north and south, the south being the busier area at night.

NORTH OF THE ODAKYU LINE

There is no shortage of places for food in Shimo-Kitazawa. In the middle of the area there's **Deli & Baking Co**, a good place to sit down and have a sandwich, bagel or the daily special. It's at street level and upstairs is **Sunday Brunch**, a café/restaurant with European-style food. Across the street a little further down, in the basement, is **Café Plants**, which serves tea in the afternoon and does wining and dining at night. Strangely, it's also a plant shop, which adds a certain vibe to the atmosphere.

On the main road there's an extremely popular crêpe take away shop. It's a very small place with

Shimo-Kitazawa is a mecca for the young.

no name but recognisable by the constant line of people outside, its pink front and pink TV set on the counter. There's a similar place, and just as popular, at the other end by the Odakyu line selling *takoyaki* (chopped octopus in batter). In a lane behind this shop are many restaurants, mainly Japanese, but with one Italian and one Sri Lankan standing out from the pack. All are open in the evenings only. Close to the station is **Tamaiya**, one of the very few old style shops around, selling rice crackers.

If you head into the area after nightfall, there's also a good selection of bars, most of which are along Ichibangai. If you fancy a spot of the local tipple, head for Japanese bar **Kagiya**, which has a good selection of sake. Further up is **Delta Blue**, a third-floor blues, R&B, soul, wine and food bar, as well as **Artist**, a soul, R&B and funk music bar on the second floor.

If you're neither drinking nor eating in Shimo-Kitazawa, chances are that you'll be shopping. This is one of the best places to find young street fashion and alternative music. For new clothes and accessories the coolest place is currently **In Due**, along the Inokashira line tracks. Clothes are from more than 30 young local designers, with plenty of unusual items. Each designer's selection often fits on only one rack. Off the main road nearby there's **Apartment Store**, a group of small shops selling new and second-hand street fashions.

For music, try **Schooler** on Ichibangai for punk and hardcore, while in the same building on the second floor **Time to Galaxy** concentrates on techno, drum'n'bass and ambient. Down the road is **Eq Records** for abstract, drum'n'bass and jazz beats-style LPs and CDs.

SOUTH OF THE ODAKYU LINE

Starting off with food once more, the south side of the station offers just as many options for the discerning diner. Close to the station is **Tarato**, a Thai restaurant with cheap lunches and sets. The small street heading left just before Vietnamese restaurant **Little Saigon** leads to **Shirube**, a very popular *izakaya*. A little further down the street is one of the oddest restaurants in town, **Asa** (*see chapter* **Restaurants**), specialising in dishes prepared with hemp.

For a lighter meal, or just a break, try **Palazzo**, an Italian-style café and bar near the station. Tucked away behind the supermarket is the jazz coffee shop **Masako** (*see chapter* **Coffee Shops**).

The south side really comes alive at night, and a host of bars and clubs line the Odakyu railway tracks. On Azuma Dori there's **Bar Duke**, an American south-west style joint on two floors. Right by the tracks you'll find bar **Idiot Savant**, the rock café **Stories** and night café **Le Grand Ecart**. By Chazawa Dori there's **Shelter**, a live house until 9pm, which then turns into a bar, open until 4am.

On Minamiguchi-shotengai are two well-known places, **Club Que** (*see chapter* **Nightlife**) and **Rock'n'Roll Diner**, with cheap drinks and loud oldies music. One of the most comfortable venues to relax here is off Minamiguchi Dori, in **Heaven's Door**, a recently opened bar run by Englishman Paul Davies and furnished with deep, comfy sofas. If you fancy something a little livelier, down the same street in a basement is **Y-uno**, a jazz and hip-hop bar. The outdoor market by the main intersection turns into a music venue and bar late at night. Further down on the main road is a famous live house, **Club 251** (*see chapter* **Music**).

For shopaholics in search of young, trendy clothes the most interesting goods come from a shop which goes by the unpromising name of **Pile of Trash**. There are second-hand clothes shops on this side too. There's also the outdoor market (*see above*) at the intersection.

Record stores are also a big feature of the area. For Japanese indie punk and rock, try **High Line Records**, a good source of information about upcoming gigs. In the same building on the second floor is **Jazz Cab**, a second-hand jazz specialist. More mainstream tastes are catered for by the branch of **Recofan**, while **Rakstone Records** on Azumi Dori, by the tracks, caters for lovers of ska, roots and R&B. If all this isn't enough, check out the back of the buildings, where dozens of smaller music specialists lurk in the shadows.

No guide to shopping in Shimo-Kitazawa would be complete without **Vilidz Vangard** (Village Vanguard), easily the weirdest shop in the area (and there's a lot of competition). It stocks a wide range of books and magazines, and aims to sell titles not found in conventional bookstores. It also sells motorbikes, toys and gadgets, household goods, and other items too numerous and varied to mention.

Of the theatres left in the area the bigger ones are **Honda Theatre** by the Inokashira line tracks and **The Suzunari** on Chazawa Dori. Two small ones, **Off-Off** and **Ekimae**, are on the third floor, across from the station. There's also the small **Geki Theatre** in the Gallery Geki building.

How to get there

Shimo-Kitazawa is on the Odakyu and Inokashira lines. the former runs from Shinjuku, the latter from Shibuya. See Map 29.

Addresses

Locations mentioned in the text are marked on Map 29.

Nakano 中野

Both Nakano and its near neighbour, Koenji (*see below*), are residential areas, similar to hundreds of others along Tokyo's suburban train lines. The focus is the station, where the local shopping streets, or *shotengai*, originate. They are the centre of activity, typically lined with many small shops selling everything from hand-made tofu to clothes and electrical goods, restaurants of all types and sizes, bars and other entertainment venues.

Nakano is the first main stop on the Chuo line, five minutes west of Shinjuku, and attracts a mixture of locals and crowds on their way home to the suburbs, while Koenji, the next stop, generally caters to its young, studenty residents.

Both exits of Nakano station lead to shotengai, the north side a larger area, with streets too narrow for vehicles and reminiscent of a style from older days. The streets from the north exit are a maze of narrow alleyways, housing hundreds of restaurants, bars and small clubs.

The best way to appreciate the attractions of Nakano is to wander around, the addresses below being only a fraction of the choices available.

One of Nakano's must-see sights is the ancient, ramshackle **Classic** (*see chapter* **Coffee Shops**).

It has survived both the earthquake and the war, and the inside looks as though it hasn't seen daylight or a duster since the turn of the century. Floors are at odd angles, and the staircase is like something from a funhouse. What the coffee lacks in taste, the place makes up for in atmosphere.

From Classic, head for the nearby Nakano Broadway shopping centre, a haven for *manga* and CD collectors (*see chapter* **Shops & Services**). Back out of Broadway is Fureai Road, a great place to eat, with more Chinese, *ramen* and Japanese restaurants than you can count. Disappointingly, Nakano is poorly served when it comes to drinking. The most interesting bar is definitely the **Side Bar**, a place so small that when someone goes to the toilet, the whole bar has to stand up to let them pass. Opening hours depend on the master's mood. Other bars in the area, such as **Bar 300** (*see chapter* **Bars**) and **Brick**, a bit of a salaryman hang-out, lack atmosphere. To make a night out of drinking in the area it's best to move to the adjacent neighbourhood, Koenji.

How to get there

Nakano is on the JR Chuo and Sobu lines and the Eidan subway Tozai line. See Map 26.

Addresses

Locations mentioned in the text are marked on Map 26.

Koenji 高円寺

Koenji may be the next stop on the Chuo line from Nakano, but the atmosphere is totally different, despite the presence of largely similar suburban shops. The feeling is more of a real community, the pace a bit more leisurely. This sense of community finds its best expression every year on 27 and 28 August, from 6.30pm, when hundreds of people dance and sing through the streets for Awa-odori, the local festival. Koenji is also a favourite with students, young musicians and artists, giving it a bohemian feel.

Unlike Nakano, Koenji is a good place for drinking, with many small bars only a few minutes' walk from the station. There are also a number of live houses where bands play every night.

Bars in Koenji tend to be on the small side, accommodating between ten to 20 people, and usually the master is serving drink and food while playing his own CD collection. Most bars, in fact, are little more than an extension of the master's lounge, and most will extend closing time as long as there are customers.

On the north side of the station, one of the most interesting musically is **Asyl**, an Asian music bar. There are Okinawan, Indonesian, Thai, or Indian nights, where customers bring CDs, videos and friends. Along Central Road are **Troubadour** and **Zizitop**, two 1960s-'70s rock bars, and **Bobby's Soul Food Ranch**, a bar and restaurant playing soul music.

The bars carry on, on to Koshin Dori, off Central Road. The first two, **After Hours**, a jazz house, and **White and Black**, play all types of music and cater to a quieter crowd. Across in the plaza is **Cornfields**, an American-style bar which lists a dartboard, table football and a pinball machine among its attractions. Expect to be called upon to play against the locals, some of whom are devastatingly good at darts.

On the south side, only one street off Pal Arcade boasts a similar concentration of bars. Among those are **Club Dolphin**, which has DJs playing J-pop, UK/US indies or big beat and similar stuff on weekends, when it's about ¥1,500 to get in. On weekdays it's free and the master plays 1960s and '70s rock. In the same building is **Funky Flames**, a reggae/black music club.

Like Shimo-Kitazawa, Koenji has a very active live scene, with bands playing somewhere here every night. Most start between 6pm and 7.30pm, and closing time is correspondingly early. Expect to pay around ¥2,000 to get in. Two live houses, **Gear** and **20,000 Volts**, are on top of each other a short distance from the station along Pal Arcade.

Although eating choices in Koenji are slightly restricted, one truly excellent, if pricey, option is **Dachibin**, an Okinawan restaurant on Central Road. The quality of the food and the rowdy atmosphere make it a local favourite, and the place is often packed from 5pm-5am. It's worth waiting for seats downstairs rather than go upstairs. The dress of the staff, the decor and the food are typically Okinawan. Some nights they also have live Okinawan music.

As far as shopping is concerned, Koenji offers nothing special, bar a few second-hand bookshops in the arcade under the station and a few specialised record stores on the south side, the best of which is **Manual of Errors**, which has a vast selection of unusual records and CDs – stuff you'd never find anywhere else.

How to get there

Koenji is on the JR Sobu and Chuo lines. See Map 23.

Addresses

Locations mentioned in the text are marked on Map 23.

Other areas to explore

Other areas outside the Yamanote line worth a look include: Jiyugaoka (Tokyu Toyoko line, good for upmarket fashion); Kichijoji (Chuo line, a great park, restaurants and lively nightlife); Sangenjaya (Tokyu Shin-Tamagawa line, lively and studenty); and Daikanyama (Tokyu Toyoko line, designer shopping).

Sightseeing

From temples to theme parks, Tokyo has an eclectic mix of treasures.

Thanks to the city's frequent destruction and rebuilding, there's relatively little of genuine historic interest in Tokyo. Yet in among the jumble of architectural styles and seemingly unregulated construction, there are some gems, often nestling incongruously against some modern monstrosity. That you have to seek them out somehow makes finding them more rewarding.

As far as other sights go, Tokyo has no shortage of parks and gardens, oases of calm in the middle of the modern city, while funfairs and hi-tech showrooms are sure to appeal to those who like to mix travelling with a little hands-on activity.

Amusement parks

Hanayashiki

*2-28-1 Asakusa, Taito-ku (3842 8780).
Asakusa station.* **Open** 10am-6pm Mon, Wed-Sun.
Admission ¥900; ¥400 children over five. **Map 10**
Japan's oldest amusement park is located right next to Asakusa's Senso-ji Temple (*see* **Asakusa**, *p77*) and has been in business since 1885. It still draws crowds, but while most rides have been upgraded over the years their scope is limited due to the small size of the park. There are about 20 rides, more appealing for nostalgia than for thrills; the rollercoaster is Japan's oldest.

Korakuen

*1-3-61 Koraku, Bunkyo-ku (3817 6098). Suidobashi
station.* **Open** *Jan-June, Sept-Dec* 10am-8pm Mon-Fri;
9.30am-9pm Sat, Sun; *July, Aug* 9.30am-10pm daily.
Admission *all rides* ¥4,100 (¥2,500 after 5pm);
five rides ¥3,100 (¥2,000 after 5pm); *all rides &
attractions* ¥4,900; *admission only* ¥1,500 (¥1000
after 5pm); *each ride costs* ¥200-¥900.
Right next to Tokyo Dome, Korakuen offers close to 30 rides and attractions. Parachute Land and Tower Hacker are fairly big rides in this medium-sized amusement park that's exciting for kids and young teenagers, but tame and limited for adults.

MegaWeb

*1 Aomi, Koto-ku (3599 0808). Odaiba Kaihin Koen
station (Yurikamome line).* **Open** *Futureworld* 11am-
11pm daily; *Toyota City Showcase* 11am-9pm daily;
History Garage 11am-10pm daily. **Admission** free.
Part of a huge development that opened on the island of Odaiba in summer 1999 (*see* **Odaiba**, *p62*), MegaWeb certainly lives up to the promise of its name, with a giant funfair, Futureworld, whose big wheel is visible for miles, and brightly illuminated at night. Part of the MegaWeb complex is the largest

Toyota showroom in Japan, where you can sit in the newest models, take a virtual drive (¥600), or be ferried around in the company's self-driving electric town-car prototypes (¥200). Expect a queue for tickets, especially at weekends. In the basement, there's a small car museum, History Garage.

Toshimaen

*3-25-1 Koyama, Nerima-ku (3990 8800). Toshimaen
station (Seibu Toshima/Toei No.12 subway line).*
Open *17 July-31 Aug* 9am-9pm daily; *other times*
10am-6pm daily. **Admission** *pool/ride ticket* ¥3,500;
¥3,000 children; *entrance only* ¥1,000. **Credit** JCB.
Among the 35 different rides are some of the biggest and most thrilling in Tokyo. Since it's located inside a large leafy park, Toshimaen also provides space to relax, but what really sets it apart is Hydropolis, a swimming pool section that includes a surf pool and a very elaborate set of waterslides. For the more sedate among you, there's also a beautifully restored carousel from the turn of the century.

Theme parks

Nikko Edomura

*470-2 Karakura, Fujiwara-machi, Shioya-gun,
Tochigi-ken (0288 77 1777). Kinugawa Onsen
station (Tobu Kinugawa line).* **Open** 9am-5pm daily.
Admission ¥3,500; ¥2,300 children.
While you won't find samurai and geisha strutting the streets of Tokyo any more, you will find fantastic *ninja* shows, costumed geisha and other exciting attractions to take you back in time at this sprawling theme park that is a fairly accurate reproduction of old Edo. It's a two-hour ride from Asakusa station.

Tokyo Disneyland

*1-1 Maihama, Urayasu-shi, Chiba (English-language
info 047 354 0001). Maihama station.* **Open** varies
with season, and sometimes closed for special events.
Call for details. **Admission** *one-day passport* ¥5,200;
¥4,590 12-17s, ¥3,570 4-11s. Many other ticket
combinations available.
Sitting on 83 ha (204 acres) in Tokyo Bay, Tokyo Disneyland is the most popular theme park in the world, with 16.67 million visitors in 1998. The park, the first Disneyland outside the US, opened in 1983 and is modelled exactly on that in California. Its seven zones – 'Adventureland', 'Westernland', 'Critter Country', 'Fantasyland', 'Toontown', 'Tomorrowland' and 'World Bazaar' – boast 45 attractions, with more to follow in 2000, when 'Pooh's Honey Hunt' and 'Tokyo DisneySea' are scheduled to open. Whatever you may feel about the mighty Disney machine, it's virtually impossible not to have

a great day out here. Go early, and preferably on a weekday, to avoid the queues, although main attractions, such as 'Space Mountain' and 'Pirates of the Caribbean', are likely to require a wait at any time. To get there, take the Keiyo line from Tokyo station. The journey takes around 15 minutes. Tickets may be purchased in advance from the address below.
Ticket office: Tokyo Disneyland Ticket Centre, Hibiya Mitsui Bldg, 1-1-2 Yurakucho, Chiyoda-ku (3595 1777). Open 10am-7pm Mon-Sat.
Website: http://www.tokyodisneyland.co.jp/

Parks & gardens

Aoyama Cemetery
2-33 Minami-Aoyama, Minato-ku. Nogizaka station.
Open 24 hours daily. **Map 12**
This giant necropolis occupies some of the most expensive land in Tokyo. Once part of the local daimyo's estate, it has been a cemetery since 1872. It now contains over 100,000 graves and is a favourite spot for *hanami* (cherry-blossom viewing) in April, when the whole area turns bright pink.

Hama-rikyu Detached Garden
1-1 Hama-rikyu Teien, Chuo-ku (no phone). Shinbashi station, then 15-min walk. **Open** 9am-5pm daily.
Admission ¥300; free to over-65s. **Map 13**
This 25-ha (62-acre) garden was a hunting ground for the Tokugawa shogunate in the seventeenth century. Eventually, it reverted to the emperor, who donated it to the city after World War II. Its main appeal lies in the abundance of water in and around it and the fact that it feels deceptively large, thanks to its beautiful landscaping. The park itself is on an island, surrounded by an ancient walled moat with only one entrance, over the Nanmon Bridge (it's also possible to reach Hama-rikyu by boat from Asakusa; *see* **Messing about on the river**, *p75*). Its focal point is the huge Shiori Pond, which has two islands of its own, connected to the shore by charming wooden bridges. The admission fee makes sure that the park never gets too crowded, making it the perfect place for a contemplative stroll, five minutes from the western edge of Ginza. The surrounding jumble of concrete overpasses and building sites is hideous.

Hibiya Park
1-6 Hibiya Koen, Chiyoda-ku. Hibiya station.
Open 24 hours daily. **Map 7**
Next to the Imperial Palace and five minutes' walk from Ginza, Hibiya Park was once the parade ground for the Japanese army (*see* **Marunouchi**, *p52*), but was turned into the nation's first western-style park in 1903, complete with rose gardens, bandstand and open-air theatre. It's very popular with courting couples and, increasingly, with homeless people.

Imperial Palace East Garden (Kokyo Higashi Gyoen)
Chiyoda, Chiyoda-ku. Otemachi station. **Open** *Mar-Oct* 9am-4.30pm, *Nov-Feb* 9am-4pm Tue-Thur, Sat, Sun. **Admission** free (token collected at gate to be submitted on leaving). **Map 18**

The impressive **Imperial Palace East Garden**.

This is the main park of the Imperial Palace, accessible through three old gates: Ote-mon (near Otemachi station), Hirakawa-mon (Takebashi Bridge) and Kita-Hanebashi (near Kitanomaru Park). The park dates from the early days of Tokyo and is mostly landscaped. Inside is the Museum of Imperial Collections, as well as two old watch-houses and the remains of a dungeon dating from the days of Edo Castle (*see* **Marunouchi**, *p52*).

Inokashira Park
1-18-31 Gotenyama, Musashino-shi (0422 44 3796). Kichijoji station, then a 15-min walk.
Open *park* 24 hours, *zoo & boat rentals* 9.30am-4.30pm, daily. **Admission** *zoo* ¥300; free under-12s.
Map 24
Located just 15 minutes from the centre of Tokyo in the trendy area of Kichijoji, this park has enough to keep you busy for a full afternoon including a zoo (skip it), pond with rental boats, petting zoo and playground facilities. At weekends the park comes alive with street musicians and artists.

Kitanomaru Koen
1-1 Kitanomaru Koen, Chiyoda-ku. Kudanshita station. **Open** 24 hours daily. **Map 18**
Part of the Imperial Palace grounds till 1969, now a beautiful public park. Home to several museums, including the National Museum of Modern Art and the Science and Technology Museum (*see chapter* **Museums & Galleries**).

Koishikawa Botanical Garden (Koishikawa Shokubutsuen)

3-7-1 Hakusan, Bunkyo-ku (3814 0138). Myogadani station, then a 10-min walk. **Open** 9am-4.30pm Tue-Sun. **Admission** ¥330 (tickets from Yoneda Food Shop across the road).

A 7-ha (18-acre) botanical garden with a history stretching back over 300 years, Koishikawa was once a herbal garden attached to a paupers' hospital. It is now beautifully landscaped in a mixture of Japanese and Chinese styles, with bridges, stone monuments and ponds teeming with carp.

Koishikawa Korakuen

1-6-6 Koraku, Bunkyo-ku (3811 3015). Iidabashi station. **Open** 9am-5pm (last admission 4.30pm) daily. **Admission** ¥300.

The oldest garden in Tokyo, first laid out in 1629, Koishikawa once occupied 26 ha (63 acres). Redevelopment, earthquake and war damage have reduced this to just 6 ha (16 acres). On such a relatively small plot, it's difficult to escape the views of the surrounding city (the concrete of the neighbouring Tokyo Dome is particularly off-putting), but this is still an astonishingly beautiful park, with a range of walks, bridges, hills and vistas (often the miniatures of more famous originals) that encourage quiet contemplation. The entrance, tucked away down a side street, can be difficult to find.

Meiji Shrine Park (Meiji Jingu Gyoen)

Yoyogi-kamizono-cho, Shibuya-ku. Harajuku station. **Open** 5am-6pm daily. **Admission** free. **Map 5**

A thickly wooded park with a shrine dedicated to Emperor Meiji and Empress Shoken in the centre (*see below*). The shrine's atmosphere of serenity stretches to encompass the whole park, which has many tranquil paths, as well as dense overhanging foliage that keeps it cool even at the height of summer. The best approach is from the end of Omotesando. In the park there's also a garden (*see below*) and a Treasure Museum.

Meiji Jingu Inner Garden

Yoyogi-kamizono-cho, Shibuya-ku. Harajuku station. **Open** 8am-5pm daily. **Admission** ¥500. **Map 5**

There are two entrances to the garden, just off the main path to Meiji Shrine, yet few people take time to go through it. It's neither large nor especially beautiful but it is quiet – except in June when the iris field attracts many admirers. Vegetation is so dense that access is limited to the few trails, all leading towards the pond and teahouse.

Komazawa Olympic Park

Komazawa Koen, Setagaya-ku (3421 6121). Komazawa Daigaku station (Shin-Tamagawa line). **Open** 24 hours daily. **Admission** free.

Built for the Olympic Games in 1964, this sprawling park has kilometres of bicycle paths that are perfect for beginners and families. Well-equipped playgrounds dot the park, and from July to September several swimming pools open to the public (¥250 for two hours).

Kyu Shiba-Rikyu Garden

1-4-1 Kaigan, Minato-ku (no phone). Hamamatsucho station. **Open** 9am-5pm (last admission 4.30pm) daily. **Admission** ¥150.

Another beautiful landscaped garden, not far from the larger Hama-rikyu (*see above*). This one is laid out around a central pond, with an island connected by a stone walkway (a miniature of an ancient Chinese original) on one side, and a bridge on the other. There's also an archery range, which costs an additional ¥140 per hour.

Rikugien

6-16-3 Hon-Komagome, Bunkyo-ku (3941 2222). Komagome station. **Open** 9am-5pm (last entrance 4.30pm) daily. **Admission** ¥300.

A relatively small but attractive place that combines landscaped gardens and islands in a large pond with trails in the woods around it. Rikugien was established in 1702 and the water, landscapes and flora create 88 scenes described in famous poems. It's hard to see any of the literary connections but it is surprisingly peaceful.

Shiba Park

4-10-17 Shiba Koen, Minato-ku (3431 4359). Hamamatsucho station. **Open** *garden* 8.30am-5pm daily. **Admission** free.

Situated near Tokyo Tower, this park is the spot for great memorial photos of your trip, with the Tower and Zojo-ji Temple (*see below*) framed in a classic Tokyo shot. In the summer several pools open to the public and there are playgrounds, a bowling alley and other attractions all within walking distance, including a very beautiful Japanese garden, Kyu Shiba-Rikyu Garden (*see above*).

Shinjuku Gyoen

Naito-cho, Shinjuku-ku (3350 0151). Shinjuku Gyoenmae station. **Open** *park* 9am-4.30pm Tue-Sun; *greenhouse* 11am-3.30pm Tue-Sun. Open seven days during cherry (early Apr) and chrysanthemum (early Nov) flowering. **Admission** ¥200. **Map 3b**

Shinjuku Gyoen was completed as the imperial garden in 1906, during Japan's great push for westernisation, and was the first place in Japan that many non-indigenous species were planted. The fascination with the west continues into the lay-out of the garden, which contains both English- and French-style sections, as well as a traditional Japanese garden. The greenhouse is home to many interesting tropical plants, while the park itself is spectacular at cherry blossom time, when its 1,500 trees paint the whole place pink.

Showa Memorial Park

Midori-cho, Tachikawa-shi (042 528 1751). Nishi Tachikawa station (Ome line). **Open** 9.30am-5pm Tue-Sun. **Admission** ¥390; ¥80 elementary & middle schoolchildren.

A sprawling oasis of green with bicycle courses, playgrounds and public pools, Showa Memorial Park makes a wonderful day's outing away from the city centre. There is a Japanese traditional garden,

Asakusa's temples *and shrines are Tokyo's most popular and historic tourist attraction.*

a children's forest, a lake with rental rowboats and several athletics areas. Bicycle rental costs ¥310 for three hours (¥210 children).

Yoyogi Park
2-1 Yoyogi-Kamizono-cho, Shibuya-ku (3469 6081). Harajuku station. **Open** 24 hours daily. **Map 5**
Yoyogi Park was until 1996 the Sunday venue for Tokyo's greased-back rock 'n' rollers to come and strut their stuff on Sundays, but since police decided to reopen the road to traffic, some of the action has moved to neighbouring Omotesando, which remains closed to traffic on Sunday afternoons. The park itself is a favourite with couples and families, who spend warm afternoons lounging on the grass. Across Inokashira Dori (where the rockers once played) is architect Tange Kenzo's 1964 Yoyogi National Stadium, still one of Tokyo's most famous modern landmarks (*see chapter* **Architecture**).

Temples & shrines

Asakusa Kannon Temple (Senso-ji)
2-3-1 Asakusa, Taito-ku (3842 0181). Asakusa station. **Open** *temple* 6am-5pm daily; *grounds* 24 hours daily. **Map 10**
The origins of Tokyo's oldest temple are said to date back to the year 628, when three fishermen found a statue of Kannon in their nets. The temple is now the centrepiece of Tokyo's biggest historic tourist attraction (*see* **Asakusa**, *p77*).

Asakusa Shrine (Asakusa Jinja)
2-3-1 Asakusa, Taito-ku (3844 1575). Asakusa station. **Open** 6.30am-5pm daily. **Map 10**
This shrine was established in 1649 to honour the three fishermen who, 1,000 years before, had found the Kannon statue in their nets that led to the founding of the Asakusa Kannon Temple (*see* **Asakusa**, *p77*). Nicknamed 'Sanja-sama' ('the three shrines'), the shrine is host to the annual Sanja *matsuri* (Sanja festival) in May (*see chapter* **Tokyo by Season**), where hundreds of *mikoshi* (portable shrines) are carried boisterously through the neighbouring streets. The building is one of very few in Tokyo to have survived this century's disasters.

Hie Jinja
2-10-15 Nagatacho, Chiyoda-ku (3581 2471). Kokkaidogijido-mae station. **Open** *Apr-Sept* 5am-6pm, *Oct-Mar* 6am-5pm daily. **Map 11**
Nicknamed 'Sanno-sama' ('Mountain god'), the Hie shrine was originally established in the grounds of Edo Castle, to protect it from its enemies. It moved here in 1659, its role as protector of Edo Castle (now the Imperial Palace) unchanged. Every two years, in June, the shrine hosts one of Tokyo's biggest matsuri (*see chapter* **Tokyo by Season**), and participants have the rare privilege of entering the castle gates.

Joren-ji Temple
5-28-3 Akatsuka, Itabashi-ku (3975 3326). Narimasu station (Tobu Tojo line), then a no 2 bus. **Open** *Apr-Sept* 8am-4.30pm, *Oct-Mar* 8am-4pm daily.

A hillside temple way out in northern Tokyo that was once a favourite resting point for travellers. Its main point of interest is a giant Buddha, the third largest in Japan.

Kanda Myojin Shrine
2-16-2 Soto-Kanda, Chiyoda-ku (3254 0753). Ochanomizu station. **Open** *shrine* 9am-4pm, *grounds* 24 hours, daily. **Map 9**
This shrine is said to have been established in Otemachi in 730, but moved here in the early seventeenth century. One legend connected with the shrine is that the head of an executed rebel leader flew back to Kanda Myojin in 935 to rejoin his body. The seventeenth-century building was destroyed in the 1923 earthquake, and the current building, surrounded by a host of smaller shrines, is a concrete replica built in 1924 (*see* **Ochanomizu**, *p60*). The Kanda matsuri, held every two years, is one of Tokyo's biggest. The approach to the shrine has some interesting traditional shops selling *sake* and cakes, but the site itself is a disappointment, save for the dragon fountain in the courtyard.

Kan'ei-ji Temple
1-14-11 Ueno Sakuragi, Taito-ku (3821 1259). Ueno station. **Open** 24 hours daily. **Map 8**
Built in 1625 to protect the Imperial Palace from spirits coming from the north-east, Kan'ei-ji was once the centre of a massive temple town, consisting of 36 temples, most of which were destroyed in the 1868 Ueno battle (*see* **Ueno Park**, *p57*). The current building was moved here in 1875 from Saitama.

Meiji Jingu Shrine
1-1 Kamizonocho, Yoyogi, Shibuya-ku (3379 5511). Harajuku station. **Open** 5.40am-5.20pm (spring, autumn), 4am-5pm (summer), 6am-5pm (winter), daily. **Admission** *shrine* free; *treasure house* ¥200. **Map 5**
Surrounded by the shady trees of Meiji Jingu Park (*see above*), this important shrine is an impressive example of the austere style and restrained colours typical of Shinto architecture. Originally opened in 1920, it is dedicated to Emperor Meiji, whose long reign (1868-1912) coincided with Japan's modernisation after two centuries of seclusion. The current building dates from 1958: a reconstruction after the original was destroyed during the war. At the entrance on the Harajuku side stands an 11m-high (36-ft) *torii* (gate), the largest in the country, built from 1,600-year-old Japanese Cypress trees imported from Taiwan. The Imperial Treasure House near the shrine contains a variety of items associated with Emperor Meiji, including his coronation carriage.

Sengaku-ji Temple
2-11-1 Takanawa, Minato-ku (3441 5560). Sengaku-ji station (Toei Asakusa line). **Open** *temple* 7am-5pm, *museum* 9am-4pm, daily.
The most interesting thing about this otherwise unremarkable temple is its connection with one of Japan's most famous stories – that of 47 samurai attached to a lord called Asano Naganori. After he drew his sword on a rival, Kira Yoshinaka, in Edo Castle

(a serious breach of protocol), Asano was ordered to commit *seppuku* (death by ritual disembowelment). He was buried here. His 47 loyal followers then became *ronin*, or samurai without a master, bent on avenging their master's death. They killed Kira and were then themselves permitted to die in the same manner as their master, and to be buried close to him, here at Sengaku-ji. Their tombs are at the top of a flight of steps. Follow the smoke trails from the incense left by well-wishers and admirers of their courage and honour. A museum on the site contains some of the ronins' personal artefacts.

Toshogu
9-8 Ueno Koen, Taito-ku (3822 3455). Ueno station. **Open** 9am-sunset daily. **Admission** main hall ¥200; otherwise free. **Map 8**
Built in the early seventeenth century, the shrine is a designated National Treasure, and the dragons on its gates, sculpted by Hidari Jingoro ('Lefty' Jingoro), are said to be so life-like that they descend to the nearby *Shinobazu* pond to drink at night (*see* **Ueno Park,** *p57*).

Yasukuni Shrine (Yasukuni Jinja)
3-1-1 Kudankita, Chiyoda-ku (3261 8326). Kudanshita station. **Open** 9am-4.30pm daily. **Admission** ¥500; ¥200 high middle schoolchildren; ¥100 primary schoolchildren. Group discounts. **No credit cards.**
Yasukuni, which means 'peaceful country', annually invites controversy when one high-ranking politician or another visits it on 15 August, the anniversary of Japan's World War II defeat (*see* chapter **Museums & Galleries**).
Website: www.yasukuni.or.jp

Yushima Seido Shrine
1-4-25 Yushima, Bunkyo-ku (no phone). Ochanomizu station. **Open** hall 10am-5pm Sat, Sun; *grounds* 10am-5pm daily. **Map 9**
Founded in Ueno Park in 1631, this shrine, dedicated to Confucius, moved here 60 years later and evolved into an elite academy for the study of the classics. The hall itself was rebuilt in the 1930s. A statue of Confucius stands in the grounds (*see* **Ochanomizu,** *p60*).

Yushima Tenjin Shrine
3-30-1 Yushima, Bunkyo-ku (3836 0753). Yushima station. **Open** 9am-7.30pm daily.
This shrine was founded in the fourteenth century, in honour of ninth-century poet and statesman Michizane Sugawara, who was given the title *tenjin* ('heavenly god') after his death. At exam time, thousands of students from nearby universities come to pray for success, leaving hopeful messages on *ema*, small wooden tablets hung outside the main hall.

Zenpuku-ji Temple
1-6-21 Moto-Azabu, Minato-ku (3451 7402). Hiroo station. **Open** 9am-5pm daily.
This temple, founded in 832, has been repeatedly destroyed by fire, most recently in World War II, after which it was rebuilt again. Its main claim to fame is as the site of the first American legation to Japan under Townsend Harris, from 1859 to 1875.

Zojo-ji Temple
4-7-35 Shiba Koen, Minato-ku (3432 1431). Hamamatsucho station. **Open** *temple* 5.30am-5.30pm, *grounds* 24 hours daily.
Today, Zojo-ji is something of a disappointment: it's hard to imagine that at one point in the seventeenth

What's that for?

On your travels around Tokyo, you're bound to be confronted by hundreds of cartoon-like representations of animals. Probably the most popular is the *maneki-neko* (pictured), a cat with its paw outstretched. In fact, the cat is beckoning, Japanese-style (hand out, fist clenched and wave, moving only the wrist). If the cat is using its left paw, it is beckoning customers into a business or guests into a home, while the right paw is thought to bring riches. A white cat is believed to bring luck, a black one wards off evil spirits.

Other common sights outside restaurants and bars are giant frogs. This is because the Japanese for frog, *kaeru*, sounds the same as the Japanese for 'to return'. The establishment in question is asking you to come back again.

Another cartoonish beast is the Daruma, a red legless doll whose origins lie in the story of a priest who sat in one place for so long he lost the use of

Maneki-neko *bring good luck and cash.*

his legs. The Daruma has blank eyes for you to fill in. Make a wish as you fill in one eye and, when it comes true, fill in the other. Daruma are usually burned for good luck every New Year.

century, there stood 48 temples on this site. The main hall has been destroyed three times by fire in the last century, the current building being a post-war reconstruction. The most interesting thing in the temple grounds is the historic *Sanmon* gate, which in each of its three sections represents three of the stages that are necessary to attain nirvana. The gate, which dates back to 1605, is the oldest wooden structure in Tokyo. At the side of the main temple hall is a huge number of small stone statues wearing red hoods. They look very charming, almost cute, but are in fact rather unsettling: they are in memory of the spirits of dead children, including aborted foetuses.

Historic buildings

Bank of Japan
2-1-1 Nihonbashi Hongoku-cho, Chuo-ku (English tour reservations 3279 1111). Mitsukoshi-mae station. **Open** 10am-3pm Mon-Fri. **Admission** free. **Map 6**
The first western-style building built by Japanese people is modelled on the Bank of England (*see chapter* **Business**).

Akasaka Detached Palace (Geihinkan)
2-1-1 Moto-Asakusa, Minato-ku (3478 1111). Yotsuya station. **Not open to the public. Map 16**
Tokyo is not famous for the uniformity of its architecture, but even in a city as jumbled as this, this building comes as something of a surprise. Its construction, in the early years of the century, was intended to prove that Japan could do anything the west could, including build royal palaces. On the outside, the building is a copy of Buckingham Palace, while inside it's a replica of Versailles. The late emperor Hirohito lived here when he was crown prince, but the only people who are allowed in these days are visiting state dignitaries. A great pity.

Imperial Palace
Chiyoda, Chiyoda-ku. Tokyo station. **Map 18**
Tokyo has been home to the Japanese royal family since 1868 and the Imperial Palace occupies 1.15-sq km of prime real estate slap bang in the centre of the city on part of the former site of Edo Castle, the seat of the Tokugawa shoguns. Unlike Buckingham Palace, there's no chance of seeing inside while the residents are on their summer holidays; indeed, with all the walls and moat you can't really see very much at all. The masses, however, are graciously allowed into part of the grounds twice a year (2 January and the emperor's birthday on 22 December). Otherwise, it's a matter of walking around the outside (a popular jogging course), taking in the Imperial East and Outer Gardens (*see above*), and maybe stopping off for a snap or two of the scenic view at Nijubashi Bridge.

Nikolai Cathedral
4-1 Kanda-Surugadai, Chiyoda-ku (3295 6879). Ochanomizu station. **Open** *visits* 1-4pm Tue-Sat; *service* 10am-12.30pm Sun (in Japanese). **Map 9**

This cruciform Russian Orthodox church, complete with an onion dome, was designed by the British architect Josiah Conder (*see chapter* **Architecture**) and completed in 1891. The original, larger, dome was destroyed in the 1923 earthquake. More recent renovation has meant that visits outside service hours have not been possible for more than a year. At the time of writing, they are supposed to be about to resume.

Nogi Shrine
8-11-27 Akasaka, Minato-ku (3478 3001). Nogizaka station. **Open** *shrine* 10am-5pm, *grounds* 9am-4pm daily; *house* 12-13 Sept 9.30am-4.30pm. **Map 12**
The Nogi Shrine is dedicated to the memory of General Nogi Maresuke, whose house and stables are adjacent to the site where the shrine now stands. When Meiji Emperor died, on 13 September 1912, the loyal general and his wife joined him in death, he by seppuku, she by slitting her throat with a knife. The house in which they did away with themselves is open only two days a year, on the eve of and the anniversary of their deaths, but an elevated walkway around it allows you a voyeuristic peer in through the windows, one of which affords you a glimpse of Nogi's bloodstained shirt. The dedication of a shrine was a posthumous reward for the general's loyalty.

Tokyo Tower
4-2-8 Shiba-Koen, Minato-ku (3433 5111). Hamamatsucho station. **Open** *tower* 16 Mar-31 July, 1 Sept-15 Nov 9am-8pm daily; 1-31 Aug 9am-9pm daily; 16 Nov-15 Mar 9am-7pm daily. *Other attractions* 16 Mar-31 Jul, 1 Sept-15 Nov 10am-8pm daily; 1-31 Aug 10am-9pm daily; 16 Nov-15 Mar 10am-7pm daily. **Admission** *main observatory* ¥820; ¥460 high and primary schoolchildren; ¥310 pre-school children. *Special observatory* (additional charge) ¥600; ¥400 high and primary schoolchildren; ¥350 pre-school children. *Waxwork museum* ¥870; ¥460 children. *Mysterious Walking World* ¥410; ¥300 children. *Trick Art Gallery* ¥400; ¥300 children.
When it was built, in 1958, the Tokyo Tower must have been a monster, its 333m (13m more than the Eiffel Tower) looming over Tokyo's low-rise skyline. Since then, a great deal of the original magic has been lost, as a succession of skyscrapers and high rises have blunted the novelty of high buildings, not to mention taken the edge off the view from the top. The tower itself was designed as a television and radio transmitting tower, a function it still performs today, but it was also intended to echo the more famous tower in Paris – a comparison that Tokyo Tower's current owners are still very fond of making. A more apt one comparison might Britain's Blackpool Tower, since with its waxwork museum (3F), aquarium (1F), Trick Art Gallery (4F) and Mysterious Walking World (3F), a hologram gallery, there's a lot more tack than class about the tower these days. Still, it looks lovely when it's illuminated at night.
Website: http://www.tokyotower.co.jp

Animals & nature

Kasai Seaside Park

6-2-3 Rinkai-cho, Edogawa-ku (5696 1331). Kasai-Rinkai Koen station. **Open** *park* 24 hours daily; *birdwatching centre & viewpoint visitors' centre* 9.30am-4.30pm daily; *beach* 9am-5pm daily. **Admission** free.

Located by the water at the eastern edge of the Tokyo city limits, most of this park was built to recreate a natural seashore environment. While traces of the city are evident on three sides (the Disney castle is especially incongruous) it's a good escape. Inside are the Tokyo Sea Life Park, a couple of small beaches, a Japanese garden and a lotus pond. The birdwatching area includes two bird-shaped ponds as well as tidal flats.

Shinagawa Aquarium

3-2-1 Katsushima, Shinagawa-ku (3762 3431). Omorikaigan station (Keihin Kyuko line). **Open** 10am-5pm Mon, Wed-Sun. **Admission** ¥900; ¥500 high school and primary children/¥300 over-4s.

Divided into sea surface and sea floor levels, Shinagawa Aquarium (which is actually some distance from Shinagawa station) covers most aspects of marine life. The main attractions are the dolphin and sea lion shows (four or five times a day) as well as the tunnel water tank, in which you walk through a tank of fish. Other displays include freshwater fish and river life, corals, fish that make sounds, unusual sealife and the sea at Shinagawa. To get there, take the train from Shinagawa.

Sunshine International Aquarium & Planetarium

Sunshine City, World Import Mart Bldg 10F, 3-1-3 Higashi-Ikebukuro, Toshima-ku (3989 3466). Ikebukuro station. **Open** *aquarium* 10am-5.30pm Mon-Sat; 10-6pm Sun. *Planetarium* 11.45am-6pm Mon-Fri; 10.45am-7pm Sat, Sun. **Admission** *aquarium* ¥1,600; *planetarium* ¥800. **Map 1**

Over 20,000 fish from 400 different species are on show in the aquarium, the first one in the world to be set in a high-rise building. The planetarium, on the same floor, is more hi-tech than Shibuya's rather shabby Gotoh Planetarium (*see chapter* **Museums & Galleries**).

Tokyo Sealife Park

6-2-3 Rinkai-cho, Edogawa-ku (3869 5151). Kasai-Rinkai Koen station. **Open** 9.30am-5pm (no entry after 4pm) Tue-Sun. **Admission** ¥700; ¥250 primary schoolchildren.

An extensive complex in the middle of Kasai Seaside Park (*see above*), the Sealife Park has three floors stacked with displays that include Tokyo Bay, the Izu and Ogasawara islands, the Pacific and other oceans, tuna, penguins, sharks, kelp forests, the shoreline and also a touch pool. The auditorium presents 3-D underwater videos, while in the library there are aquarium videos in English. Outside the main building there's a walk through recreated freshwater environments.

Kan'ei-ji Temple Pagoda: *lost in Ueno Zoo.*

Ueno Zoo

9-83 Ueno Park, Taito-ku (3828 5171). Ueno station. **Open** 9.30am-4.30pm (last entry 4pm) Tue-Sun. **Admission** ¥500. **Map 8**

Over 100 years old, so it has only partly kept up with standards for animals' comfort – some have large enclosures and a semblance of a natural environment (gorillas, tigers, pandas and some birds) but many have basic accommodation. The pandas feed at 3.30pm, but have Friday off . Animals are from all over the world; there's only a few specimens of Japanese fauna. A children's zoo is connected to the main zoo by a monorail. Kan'ei-ji Temple Pagoda is inconveniently stranded in Ueno Zoo.

Messing about on the river

Sea Line Tokyo Company Ltd

Suzue Baydium 2F, 1-15-1 Kaigan, Minato-ku (restaurant reservations 3798 8101/whole boat reservations 3435 8105/sealine@symphony-cruise.co.jp). Hamamatsucho station. **Restaurant average** *¥10,000.*

If you want to take in Tokyo Bay in style, Sea Line offers four departures a day from Hinoda Pier, at 11.50am, 3pm, 4.30pm and 7.10pm. At lunch and dinner there's a choice of Italian or French meals in the ship's plush restaurant (bookings required), though you're free just to take in the scenery, which will include Rainbow Bridge, Disneyland and a glimpse of the open sea. Cruises last 50, 120 or 150 minutes, depending on the time of day. *Website: www.symphony-cruise.co.jp/*

Reach for the clouds at **Sunshine 60**.

Tokyo Cruise Ship Company
(Asakusa:3841 9178/Hinoda Pier:3457 7830).
Five lines of waterbus up and down the Sumida
River, stopping at destinations such as Shinagawa
Aquarium, Odaiba Seaside Park and Kasai Sealife
Park, taking in the old bridges and the new Rainbow
Bridge en route. The lines converge at Hinoda Pier,
a five-minute walk from Hamamatsucho station, but
for many the best point of departure is Asakusa (*see*
Map 10), where the boats leave a pier next to
Azuma Bridge before heading off towards the beau-
tiful Hama-rikyu Detached Garden (*see above*). Boats
depart every 40-45 minutes and tickets cost ¥620
(there's an entry fee for Hama-rikyu).
Website: www.suijobus.co.jp/

Rooms with a view

Sunshine 60 Building
3-1-1 Higashi-Ikebukuro, Toshima-ku (3989 3331).
Ikebukuro station. **Open** 10am-8pm daily.
Admission ¥620; ¥310 children. **Map 1**
One of the fastest lifts in the world will whisk you
to the top of one of the tallest buildings in Asia in
around 35 seconds.

Tokyo Metropolitan Government Building Twin Observatories
2-8-1 Nishi-Shinjuku, Shinjuku-ku (5321 1111).
Shinjuku station. **Open** 9.30am-5.30pm Tue-Fri;
9.30am-7.30pm Sat, Sun. **Map 3a**
One of the best views over Tokyo also has the added
bonus of being free. Each of the TMG twin towers
has an observatory on the 45th floor, an uninter-
rupted view of surroundings obscured only by the
other tower. Admire the view over a coffee from the

cafeteria in the centre of the vast floor. Other buildings in west Shinjuku with free viewing areas
include the Sumitomo Building (51F), the Shinjuku
Centre Building (53F) and the Nomura Building
(49F), all of which are open later than the TMG.

Showrooms

Amlux Toyota Auto Salon
3-3-5 Higashi-Ikebukuro, Toshima-ku (5391 5900).
Ikebukuro station. **Open** 11am-8pm Tue-Sat; 10am-
7.30pm Sun. **Map 1**
Toyota used to claim this was the word's biggest car
showroom, but just to make sure, it opened an even
bigger one in MegaWeb (*see above*). But there's more
to this place than cars. As well as being able to sit
and fiddle with controls in all of Toyota's range, you
can watch free 20-minute films in the Amlux
Theatre, on chairs that vibrate in time with what's
on screen. There's also a virtual driving experience
that's so realistic you're not allowed to use it unless
you can produce a valid driving licence.

Fujita Vente
Fujita Corp Head Office, 4-6-15 Sendagaya, Shibuya-
ku (3796 2486). Yoyogi station. **Open** 10am-6pm
Mon-Wed, Fri-Sun. **Map 17**
This is a very strange showroom indeed. On entry
the first thing you see is a tree growing without soil.
Other attractions include robot guides, interactive
games and a virtual trip through the universe.
Although admission is generally free, a fee can be
charged for special events.

Honda
2-1-1 Minami-Aoyama, Minato-ku (3423 4118).
Aoyama-itchome station. **Open** 10am-6pm daily.
Map 12
All of Honda's cars and motorbikes are on display,
and most can be touched and petted.

Sake Information Centre
Nihon Syuzo Centre Bldg 1F, 4F, 1-1-21 Nishi-
Shinbashi, Minato-ku (3519 2091). Toranomon
station. **Open** 10am-6pm Mon-Fri. **Admission** free.
Map 13
Free booze! There is a theory propounded by cynics
that the sake centre moved its free tasting centre to
out-of-the-way Shinbashi because it was too popular in Ginza. Whatever the truth, the chance to try
ten different types of sake for nothing does have a
small catch. You have to mark them according to
preference on a postcard, which will then be
returned to you to let you know how your palate
measures up against the experts'.

Sony Building
5-3-1 Ginza, Chuo-ku (3573 2371). Ginza station.
Open 11am-7pm daily. **Map 7**
Play around to your heart's content with seven
floors of Sony products. There's a whole floor devoted to PlayStation, where you can request games to
play on the giant screens, while another floor shows
you the insides of many of Sony's best-selling products. *See also* **Ginza**, *p54.*

Tokyo Walks

Whether it's history or high-tech you're after, the four walks below should convince you that Tokyo is a city worth discovering on foot.

Asakusa 浅草

In modern Tokyo, Asakusa is a rare thing – an area with genuine, tangible history, and lots of it. Every year, 30 million tourists flock here, lured by the historic temple and all-pervading sense of tradition. Before the Meiji period, Asakusa was Tokyo's biggest entertainment hotspot, providing *kabuki* and other forms of entertainment, music and even striptease. As a gateway to the red-light district of Yoshiwara, closed down in the late 1950s when prostitution was outlawed, its reputation as the capital of pleasure ensured the area's popularity.

The close proximity of religious grounds and entertainment districts is not unusual in Japan. But today, while the temple continues to pull in the tourists, the entertainment area, Rokku, has lost its former glory. The war brought near total destruction to the area, and even its long history as a pleasure quarter did not bring back the revellers, a fact still lamented by many.

But there is never a quiet day in the temple grounds, with an endless procession making their way to **Senso-ji**, the main temple in Asakusa and the oldest in Tokyo. A sacred statue of Kannon, the goddess of mercy and infinite compassion, is enshrined here. In AD628, the story goes, two brothers caught the statue in their fishing net. Their master recognised its sacred qualities and rebuilt his house, on the spot where the temple now stands, to enshrine the statue. It is said to measure only five or six centimetres (around two inches), but nobody is allowed to see it.

Exit 1 from the Ginza subway line will take you to **Kaminarimon Gate**, the entrance to the temple grounds. The statues of the two gods are to protect Kannon; on the left is Raijin, god of thunder, and on the right, Fujin, god of wind. At the back of the gate are two dragon gods, added in 1978 for the temple's 1,350th anniversary.

Ahead lies **Nakamise Dori**, lined with stalls selling traditional and modern crafts, toys and foods. After the row of shops on the left is a series of paintings depicting the story of the founding of

In Asakusa, local people strive to maintain and celebrate the ancient traditions of the area.

The smoke from the incense burner is believed to heal whatever part of the body it touches.

the temple. Right after and just before the gate, there is a small shrine with a child-sized golden Buddha that people pat as they pray.

Nakamise Dori leads to **Hozomon**, also called Niomon for the pair of guardian Nio figures to frighten evil spirits. The old sutras and some of the temple's treasures are stored in the gate's upper section. The big straw sandals are for the Nio.

The last stage before Senso-ji is the incense burner, or *okoro*, where the smoke is said to cure the body parts it touches. Crowds of people gather round to 'bathe' in the healing smoke.

Senso-ji, affectionately referred to as Kannon-sama, was rebuilt after the war, an exact replica of the structure that stood there for the previous 300 years. This Buddhist temple became the centre of worship to Kannon in the Kamakura period (1188-1333). Kannon allegedly has great power to purify people and help attain true happiness, and the start of the new year is a grand occasion, when throngs of worshippers crowd the area.

On the right of Senso-ji is **Asakusa-jinja**, a Shinto shrine dedicated to the Hinokuma brothers who found the statue, and their master. Also called Sanja-sama, it is the starting point of the Sanja *matsuri*, the greatest annual festival in Tokyo. Held the third weekend of May and lasting three days, around 100 *mikoshi* (portable shrines) are carried through the streets in a frenzied and emotional affair. At the back of the building is another shrine, **Hikan-inari**, one of only three structures that survived the air raids of the war. The other two are **Nitenmon gate**, built in

1618, and the very small **hexagonal temple**, dating from the Muromachi period (1336-1573). Around this small temple you'll find a garden and a number of small shrines.

The **pagoda** dates from AD 942, but this third incarnation was built in 1973. It contains some of Buddha's ashes in a golden globe. Behind the pagoda lies **Denpo-in**, a garden created in the early seventeenth century and home to the abbots serving at Senso-ji. You can go in for a stroll, but must get permission from the office; you'll find it through the door on the left of the pagoda. It is only open 9am-3pm, and is closed on Sundays, on holidays or when in use by the monks. But it is free, and peaceful after Senso-ji.

The entrance is around the corner and if you follow the perimeter you'll get to a small shrine, originally dedicated to *tanuki* (raccoon dogs), called **Chingodo**. Now it is more popular for praying for success in business, the arts and entertainment. Behind the shrine is another, smaller one with many tanuki statues.

The last monuments connected with the temple are back across Nakamise Dori: two **statues of Buddha**, and a little further on **Bentenyama mound** with a temple and a **bell**. The bell used to be rung to tell the time three times a day, but nowadays it is only rung on New Year's Eve, 108 times to cleanse all sins.

Down the small road from Bentenyama mound there are some old shops worth peeking in. The area is still home to many artisans and shops supplying traditional goods. In the block between

Asakusa *has many souvenir shops selling traditional Japanese clothing and accessories.*

Nakamise Dori, Kaminarimon Dori, Kokusai Dori and Denpo-in gardens a bit of aimless walking should take you to some interesting ones. The area's main traditional fare is *senbei* (rice crackers), but you'll find many old food stores and crafts shops, like a comb shop, a *shamisen* (Japanese lute) maker and a restaurant making soba. Remember that many shops close on Monday.

Examples of traditional crafts can be found at the **Gallery Takumi/Edo Shitamachi Traditional Crafts Museum**. It has a different artisan at work on site on weekends, making arrows, prints, lanterns, kites and other traditional goods. Upstairs are examples of their various crafts. Some goods are sold in the annexe a few shops down the road. Both open 10am-8pm daily and are free.

While you're in the area, look out for the **Stars Hall**, which you'll recognise by moulds of hands on the pavement. The hands belong to famous actors and entertainers. From the intersection, the third street on the right is **Tanuki Dori**. On lampposts are replicas of tanuki, and people rub them to invite success.

In between the shopping area and Gallery Takumi, you'll find yourself in **Rokku**, or Sixth District, the entertainment area. It was named Rokku after the division of the temple compound after the Meiji Restoration, and was specifically for entertainment. Literature of the late nineteenth and early twentieth centuries speaks fondly of Asakusa's Rokku. Kabuki was once banished to this area by the shogunate, and other popular arts

such as *rakugo*, *kodan* (forms of storytelling) and *bunraku* (puppet theatre) thrived. It was also famous for its cinemas, dance halls, cabarets, music houses, sex shows and attractions. What's left today, such as the rakugo performances at **Engei Hall**, is a sad echo of this glorious past.

The main form of entertainment in Asakusa today is the festivals. **Sanja matsuri** is the biggest and noisiest, though rivalled by one night of **fireworks** along the river at the end of July. Up to a million people line the banks for an event that has been happening for 250 years. The **Brazilian samba festival** at the end of August is very popular too. Two other traditional festivals worth seeing are the **Kinryu no Mai (Golden Dragon Dance)** on 18 March and 18 October, and the **Shirasagi no Mai (White Heron Dance) on** 3 November. On that day they also have the **Tokyo Jidai matsuri**, which aims to recreate some of the city's history. To make sure you don't miss out on any festival, check the board on the left just before Hozomon Gate.

If your feet are feeling the pace, head for the strange golden thing that's sitting on a roof on the other side of the river. The tall building aims to be like a beer glass, and the small black one with Philippe Starck's golden 'thing' on top is meant to represent the burning heart of Asahi beer. Don't let that put you off – the **Asahi Sky Bar** is a great place for a break, and the view from its 22nd floor location is worth the trip (*see chapter* **Bars**).

For a drink in a slightly more historic location, **Kamiya Bar**, on Kaminarimon Dori right on the corner of Edo Dori, has been in business since 1880 and is said to be the first western-style bar in Tokyo (*see chapter* **Bars**).

Until around 7pm, you can leave the area by boat from Azuma Bridge. They depart every 35 minutes and cost ¥660 to Hanode Pier (a few minutes' walk from JR Hamamatsucho station). Some also go to Hama-rikyu gardens, near Tsukiji, and to Odaiba.

If you need any help in Asakusa, visit the Tourist Information Centre, open 9.30am-8pm, with English help available 10am-5pm, seven days. It is located on the corner, right across the street from Kaminarimon Gate. See also Map 10.

Ueno to Akihabara
上野 – 秋葉原

The Ueno Park area began life as a *monzem-machi*, or temple town, centred on Kan'ei-ji (*see* **Ueno Park**, *page 57*). The temple grounds were home to a great many priests and monks, builders and carpenters, artists and craftpeople, as well as domestic staff, and as the temple grew, so did commerce and the population in the neighbouring town. By the time the battle of Ueno hill and destruction of the temple grounds took place, Ueno had become a fully grown town.

When the grounds were turned into a park with museums and a zoo, many people flooded into the area for sightseeing and entertainment. Ueno also became the terminus for trains coming from the north late last century, bringing a lot of migrants from the countryside.

The 1923 earthquake destroyed most buildings in Ueno, but on the other hand allowed the train tracks to be connected to Tokyo station. In World War II the area was ravaged again, this time by air raids. Black marketeers moved in and the stretch along the train tracks became one of the most famous places to buy goods in Tokyo. Later, when basic foods and goods became available, this makeshift market began to sell small luxuries, and eventually it gained a repututaion for its sweets – hence the current name **Ameya Yokocho or 'Confectioners' Alley'** (though some people say it derives from the American goods available during the subsequent Korean War). Today Ameya Yokocho (or Ameyoko) is famous for its variety – there's seafood, imported foods, clothes and shoes, jewellery and cosmetics, seaweed, tea and rice, to name but a few – low prices and lively, down-to-earth atmosphere. It's more like an Asian market than a typical Japanese shopping street.

Ameyoko follows the JR train tracks, from opposite the Shinobazu exit of Ueno Station to the north exit of Okachimachi Station. The busiest part begins at the junction with Ueno Centre Mall. In the basement of the building that stands at the intersection is a unique food market selling Chinese, Korean, Filipino, Thai and other Asian foods, including live turtles and frogs.

If you turn right at the lane before the traffic lights at Kasuga Dori and Okachimachi Station,

Ueno *is famous for two things – its downtown atmosphere and cherry blossom in the park.*

Just over ten minutes' walk away from Ueno is high-tech **Akihabara**, *'Electric Town'*.

you'll soon see steps leading to Tokudai-ji shrine, which has one of the strangest locations of any religious building: the courtyard with statues and a bell is just metres from the JR train line. However, it is peaceful inside – a rare phenomenon in Ameyoko. The shop across the steps on the second floor sells imported food at low prices.

The first lane on the left, which leads to Kasuga Dori, has a few places to eat, including three sushi restaurants. Two are part of the same chain and have a picture menu to simplify the ordering, the third one (the one with slats in the sliding door) is typically Ueno in atmosphere. It specialises in *negitoro*, a chopped mass of tuna and green onions, dropped on the counter with fresh seaweed, *wasabi* and *nori*, from which you make your own rolls. None of these restaurants is cheap; the last costs up to ¥5,000 per person (including drinks) if you order delicacies such as sea urchin, crab or abalone.

If you carry on down this lane, the next junction you'll come too is **Ueno Centre Mall**, with shoes, clothes and accessories shops, many of them offering bargains. The mall leads back to Ameyoko – look out between the market stalls for the entrances to shops filling the space under the tracks.

The other side of the tracks is quite similar but bigger in scale. There are more restaurants, a lot of amusement centres and hints of a sex district. The **Warrior Celt**, a friendly third-floor spot on the second street parallel to the tracks, has a large selection of imported beers, British food and live bands most nights. Unlike pubs in Britain, it's open from 5pm to 5am daily.

On the corner of Kasuga Dori and Chuo Dori is **Matsuzukaya**, a major department store that's been in the area since the days of the temple town. Also of interest on Chuo Dori is **Suzumoto Engeijo**, the oldest *yose* (a form of variety theatre similar to vaudeville) in Tokyo, dating from 1857. *Rakugo* and *kodan* are also performed here. The drum on top of the ticket counter is banged loudly to announce the next show.

The area behind Suzumoto Engeijo is Ueno's **sex district**, with 'pubs', hostess bars, soaplands and love hotels. It's rather dead in the daytime, although **Yabu Soba** serves fine food (albeit in small portions). You can sit down for a beer at **Hoppel Poppel**, a two-storey 'German castle' with a statue of a pot-bellied man, pint in hand. You'll get charged for nibbles (a disguised cover charge). To get there, take the first left from exit 3 of Ueno-Hirokoji Station on the Ginza line.

Follow Kasuga Dori up the hill to the bend to get to **Yushima Tenjin Shrine**, which looks very recent but has in fact been here for several centuries. In previous times it was one of only three shrines that were allowed to hold lotteries. Yushima is a very important shrine for those praying for good luck and success in learning, and there are often thousands of votive plaques, or *ema*, stacked dozens deep, here. It's also famous for its plum blossoms in winter.

The traditional, ramshackle charm of Ueno provides a strange contrast with Akihabara or 'Electric Town' (*see chapter* **Shops & Services**), a mecca for computers, electronics, games and videos, cameras, audio equipment, household and other electrical goods. The 15-minute walk between the two is quiet and drab but Akihabara itself is an amazing sight, especially at night, with its shop signs and advertising stacked eight floors high. Like Ueno, this area was the site of a black market after World War II, this time involving scrap electrical equipment. The only remnants of those days can be seen under the tracks along the Sobu line, where two floors of cramped stalls sell components, chips and other computer and electrical parts. Akihabara is packed all day with bargain-hunters and anoraks. Competition is fierce and you'll find the latest products all along the footpath, along with stations at which you can play the latest cutting-edge computer games.

For Ueno, see Map 8. Akihabara is on Map 14.

Tsukiji 築地

One of Tokyo's greatest attractions, the **Tsukiji Fish Market** is appropriately located on land reclaimed from the sea. After the great fire of 1657, the shogunate decided to extend Tokyo into the bay to ease cramped living conditions. Tsukiji means simply 'built-up' or 'reclaimed' land.

Despite its location,a short walk down from Ginza, Tsukiji is a rather unattractive area, but it has one fantastic redeeming feature. The Tsukiji Fish Market is the largest in the world, selling just about anything with a fin, at the rate of 2.2 million kg (4.8 million pounds) per day. It's a world unto itself, a fantastic island of frenetic activity and wondrous sights.

Subways and trains start running at around 5am every day and should get you to the market in time to catch all the action. The closest station is Tsukiji on the Hibiya line. Take exit 1 or 2 – if the latter, cross the pedestrian bridge. From the temple gate follow Shin-ohashi Dori to the nearest corner and go straight across the intersection with Harumi Dori. Stay on Shin-ohashi Dori until the shops and restaurants come to an end, then turn left and at the end turn right across the bridge.

The area between the intersection of the two main roads and the market entrance is full of small shops and stalls best visited after you've seen the fish market. In front of you just before you cross the bridge into the market is **Nami-Yoke Inari shrine**. It's small but worth a look for the huge mythical lion's head.

One of the most celebrated sights of Tsukiji Fish Market is row upon row of frozen tuna lying on the ground. This is the **tuna auction**, which starts every day before 6am and is over in under an hour. Achieved without the help of technological wizardry, it is like taking a step back in time. Among the tuna lurk buyers inspecting the catch, while auctioneers bark frantically. Most of the fish are taken away by market stallholders, to be cut, displayed and sold to sushi restaurants and fish shops. The auction is officially closed to visitors but nobody objects to a background presence.

The market itself is adjacent to the site of the auction. Simply housed in an enormous hangar-like structure, it consists of thousands of makeshift tables stacked with styrofoam boxes filled with marine life of every shape and size imaginable – and some that aren't. Buyers and onlookers negotiate narrow paths between the catch. While the activity here starts as early as the tuna auction, there's still plenty happening as late as 9am, but remember that you are competing for space with frenzied fish-buyers, so be prepared to be brushed aside without the customary politeness. Even greater danger awaits you in the wider alleys, which are even busier and patrolled by motorised carts.

The market starts to wind down mid-morning and by early afternoon it's all over for another day. There is no market on Sundays and holidays.

Away from the fish section, you'll find the fruit and vegetable market. More of a distribution centre than a market, it's rather unexciting after the piscine delights of the fish market. There are no auctions, most goods are packed in boxes, and what you can see displayed you've probably seen in any number of greengrocers.

Making the most of their proximity to some of the world's freshest fish are the numerous nearby **sushi restaurants**, some opening as early as the market itself. As you cross the bridge into the market grounds you'll see a row of numbered two-storey buildings away to the right. In the middle of building No.6, two adjacent sushi restaurants with identical *noren* (curtains) are very popular. There's often a queue. Staff are friendly, and if you can't speak Japanese they'll serve you the cheapest set, at ¥2,000, indicating the last pieces by crossing their hands. It's not a big meal by any means, but it's as fresh as it gets. Larger and more expensive sets are also available. Another five or six sushi restaurants are located nearby, with coffee shops and other restaurants, too.

If the idea of sushi this early in the morning fails to attract, you can head back to the row of stalls on the main road. Most are very basic, with metal shelves for eating stands, but two places are especially popular. One is a soba and tempura stall near the corner as you retrace your steps from the market, and it's easily recognisable by the different tempura on the counter. Just point at what you want; you should get away with spending less than ¥800. The other place, further towards Harumi Dori and right next to the Black Sheep coffee shop, serves ramen. You are spared the agony

Get up early for the pick of the catch at **Tsukiji**, *the world's largest fish market.*

of choice by the fact that there's only one thing on the menu, and it costs ¥600.

The numerous stalls and shops behind this side of the street sell mostly food, cutlery and crockery. Check them out early, as most start closing at around lunchtime.

Back near the station entrance is **Hongan-ji Temple**. Founded in 1617 near Asakusa, it burnt down in the 1657 fire and was relocated here. The 1923 earthquake reduced it to rubble and the current structure, greatly influenced by Indian Buddhism, dates from 1935. Services, which take place from 10-11.30am and 1.30-3pm, are open to all.

From the temple, head for **St Luke's observation tower**, the highest building in the area (open 9am-8.30pm). Take the lift to the forty-sixth floor and climb one flight. The observation area doubles as the entrance to a restaurant and the views stretch across Tokyo Bay to Chiba, Odaiba, Haneda airport and as far as Yokohama, to Tokyo Tower and Shinjuku and all the way to the mountains to the west of Tokyo. The reclaimed land areas are clearly delineated, and the sight of so much water quite surprising. The restaurant (open 11am-11pm), which is not too expensive, has a terrace that provides further views to the north.

From St Luke's it's but a hop to **Tsukuda island**. Originally a speck of land, it was expanded into an island by fishermen brought from Kansai by the shogun in the early days of Edo. The attraction is a small area with an atmosphere of days gone by, but the time it takes to walk around it is about the same as it takes to get there from the market in the first place.

Sumiyoshi shrine is the centrepiece of the area and you won't find many old buildings, other than a lighthouse and parts of the temple. Its fishing village atmosphere has all but disappeared, but it is still sufficiently different to make you forget you're in Tokyo for a few minutes. The easiest way to get there is to walk across the bridge after St Luke's; take the steps at the edge of the river and walk under the bridge.

Away from the station and the market following the main road, a ten-minute walk will take you to **Hama-rikyu Detached Garden** (see **Sightseeing**, p69), a pleasant and relatively quiet spot to visit after the fish market. From the gardens you can take a boat to Asakusa. They run every 40 minutes or so and cost ¥620.

Tsukiji is on Map 19.

Yanaka 谷中

Edo (the name of Tokyo before the Meiji Restoration) was divided into three areas: the castle, *yamanote* and *shitamachi*. The latter originally defined the low city, which consisted mainly of the area between the castle and the Sumida River. It was where the common people settled, as opposed to yamanote, the higher grounds west of the castle where the feudal lords and rich merchants lived. Shitamachi stretched from north of Asakusa to Nihonbashi and beyond, but constant destruction and rebuilding resulted in the disappearance of old areas, and today only small pockets of shitamachi remain. The word has now come to mean traditional commercial districts, but all shitamachi areas are still in the low city.

One such area is around the intersection of Shinobazu Dori and Kototoi Dori, near Nezu station on the Chiyoda subway line. Adjacent is **Yanaka**, one of the four first cemeteries in Edo. Many temples were relocated here after the Long Sleeves Fire of 1657. Yanaka became a famous temple town, with Tenno-ji one of the busiest temples in Edo. The area is one of the few to have survived the air raids of World War II. Yanaka is also well known because of the many writers and artists who lived here and were buried in the area. The last shogun, Yoshinobu Tokugawa, was also interred in Yanaka, instead of in nearby Kan'ei-ji (in Ueno Park) where six of his predecessors are buried, because he gave up power to the emperor.

At Nishi-Nippori station on the Yamanote line, take the exit away from Ueno. Once you're outside, turn left. Take the first left, uphill along the tracks, just before the *koban* (policebox). The area at the top near the park, **Dokanyama**, was a popular scenic spot in the Edo period, with its commanding views. Walking away from the park takes you first to **Suwa Jinja**, an unkempt shrine and grounds with old buildings and tombs. It is said to date from 1205. As you exit the *torii*, you're at the gate of Jojoki. A couple of minutes down the road you'll find **Yofuku-ji**. Inside the gate are four old statues: the two in front are Nio figures, sculpted in the Kamakura-era style, and behind are two statues of gods dating from a similar era. The original temple was founded in 1704, but the main building has been rebuilt. There are other stone statues and an old bell in the grounds.

On the left at the intersection at the end of the street is **Kio-ji**, the gate showing bullet holes from the 1868 fighting (see **Ueno Park**, p57). The temple inside is one of the nicest in the area, but it's not possible to get a close look.

If you go to the right at the intersection, you'll find **Enmei-in Temple** just off the street, then some stairs leading to a *shotengai* (shopping street) with some traditional shops and a neighbourly feel. Taking the first right after the steps, you'll come across a number of small temples and eventually arrive at a main road.

Just to the right around the corner is **Daien-ji**, an interesting temple in that the left section is Buddhist and the right Shinto. The building is more than 150 years old and has great carvings. The grounds are famous for containing the grave of

Yanaka cemetery *is an atmospheric part of a long stroll through old Tokyo.*

Kasamori Osen, one of the three beauties of Edo, as well as that of the artist who drew her. Across the road on the corner is **Isetatsu**, a famous paper shop. If you head uphill on the main road, you'll soon come to **Zenshoan**, with its four-metre (13 feet) golden statue of Buddha. Across the road are the grounds of **Tenriu-ji**, divided into two sections. Both have interesting structures and buildings.

If you continue uphill from Zenshoan and turn right at the first intersection, you'll soon reach **Anritsu-ji**, with its attractive small hall. At the end of the street an old gate leads to a compound behind the wall. To the right is a *tsuijibei*, a traditional roof mud wall, about 200 years old.

At the next intersection turn left and very soon you'll arrive at **Kannon-ji**, a temple connected to the 47 *ronin* (samurai without master) allowed to commit ritual suicide for having avenged the murder of their master. In the grounds there's an interesting grave monument and an old well. Further up the street on the right is **Asakura Choso Museum**, the house of sculptor Asakura Fumio, with a superb garden (*see chapter* **Museums & Galleries**).

Turn right at the next road (you're back across Kio-ji, seen earlier) and down the hill. Just before the station, take the steps to the right and follow the long path through the cemetery. It leads to **Tenno-ji**, another casualty of the 1868 battle, but while the temple itself is recent, the Daibutsu (Buddha statue) was cast in 1690. The small old building in the grounds was built recently, too, out of the leftovers from the old five-storey wood-

en pagoda that used to stand on the avenue. A landmark in the area, it was burnt down in the late 1950s in a love suicide. The foundation stones remain next to the koban, at which a right-hand turn up to the next crossing brings you to **Choan-ji**. The main attractions here are three *itabi* (stone board stupa) from the Kamakura period.

As you come out, turn right; opposite is an art gallery and shop in a house dating back to 1847. A few antiques and artworks are sold in three small rooms, but it's worth going in just to see the inside of an old building.

Turn right at the next intersection, then take the first left. You'll soon reach **Shiyamo-ji**. A few metres away across the road is **Saiko-ji**, housing a number of statues and stones. It's only a small temple but worth a look. Walk all the way to the end, turn left and you'll see **Aizen-do** (also known as **Jisho-in**), where your prayers for marriage partners and household harmony might be answered. At the intersection with the main road is **Scai – the Bath-house**, a former public bath turned art gallery (*see chapter* **Museums & Galleries**). Turn right; on the left at the main intersection is the **Shitamachi Museum Annexe**, a traditional late-seventeenth-century shop that's open from 9.30am to 4.30pm Tuesday to Sunday. Admission is free.

As you come out of the annexe turn left and follow Kototoi Dori; in a few minutes you'll arrive at **Jomyoin Temple**, which is famous for its collection of *jizo* (Buddhist saints in search of truth/guardians of children) statues. The grounds

The Yanaka area is one of the few which still boasts rows of traditional-style houses.

are stacked with the small statues, but they still haven't reached their goal of 84,000.

If you turn right coming out of the annexe, at the second street you'll see **Ichio-ji**, a temple resembling a house or inn. Up the side street you'll come across **Daiyo-ji**. At the next corner go left and take the first left again: at the first intersection on the right there's a row of old gates, houses and a small temple. At the end of the street is **Zuirin-ji**, the biggest temple in the area.

Return to the intersection, turn right and you soon come to **Renge-ji**, a small temple with a peaceful atmosphere. If you continue straight ahead and follow the road to the right, you'll arrive at **Ryogen-ji**, a modern concrete temple in the grounds of which tools, pottery and clam shells dating from the Jomon period (3000-1000BC) were found. The area used to be very close to the river and the sea and its current location gives a good idea of how much Tokyo has been subjected to landfill and waterways diversion by successive rulers, town planners and governments.

Across from Renge-ji is **Enjyu-ji**, another small place but definitely worth a look. When you come out, turn right and follow the small street, where a temple a few metres away has a bell tower and statues near its entrance. Continuing along the street you'll pass a small temple, and at the end of a lane to the right you'll see another temple about 20 metres away. Once there, take the path between the walls on your left: at the bottom of some steps you'll see an old hand pump, at which the neighbourhood used to draw its water. You'll soon arrive at the grounds of **Gyokurin-ji**, a leafy and peaceful spot.

Around this area are a number of old-style shops. Taking the main exit from Gyokurin-ji, turn right and then first right. You'll walk past two temples and come to **Rinko-ji**, across the car park. It's untidy but its architecture is quite different from the other temples in the area. As you come out, turn right, then take the first right uphill. At the top there's a modern white temple, on the left a compound with black buildings. Inside this compound is the **Daimyo Clock Museum** (*see chapter* **Museums & Galleries**), which has clocks from the Edo period.

Take the second left after the museum and walk about 200 metres past the main road (Shinobazu Dori) to get to **Nezu Shrine**, which is fairly old, with well-trodden grounds. On the side are rows of orange torii leading to a monument dedicated to Inari, the deity of cereals. It's also popular because of its azaleas, which bloom in early spring. Head back to the main road, cross it again and take the first right, a small street leading to Kototoi Dori. Cross Kototoi Dori at the lights, turn left and take the first right along the main road (Shinobazu Dori). You'll come to two interesting wooden buildings about 50 metres down the street. On the right is **Hantei**, a three-storey restaurant, and right opposite is a two-storey house with flats. The small street just before the wooden block of flats leads to an interesting group of three old buildings.

If you turn left at the corner, you'll be back at Kototoi Dori, and not far away is **Tengen-ji temple**. The nearest subway station is Nezu, back on Shinobazu Dori.

Yanaka is on Map 32.

Museums & Galleries

As well as world-class museums and galleries, Tokyo is home to hundreds of tiny spaces where private obsessions go public.

It is often said that Japan is a nation of *otaku*. The word, with no direct English translation, has been rendered as computer geek or nerd, but the underlying nuance is not limited to technology. It refers to someone (or a group of people) who obsessively indulges in one single interest. You might meet a person who has carpeted his apartment with every *Star Wars* toy, or stumble across a tiny bar dedicated to playing the music of just one band, such as the Rolling Stones or Phish. This otaku mentality – the term isn't, it should be said, derogatory – means there's an incredibly diverse range of museums in Tokyo, including the Button Museum, a museum of luggage and bags, a bonsai museum, the Sword Museum, the Eyeglass Museum and a parasite museum. Each is carefully looked after, informative and, more often than not, representative of one collector's interest.

They come from the same collecting spirit behind more conventional art museums, those that reflect the studious art-collecting efforts of one person. Usually it is a company president who opens a showroom inside his company's HQ – unlike in the west, where large corporations sponsor big-name shows or bequeath their collections to a public museum. Some of Tokyo's world-class museums – the Bridgestone, the Nezu, Yasuda Fire – came into being this way. There are also memorials showcasing one artist's work in the artist's former studio or home, in gorgeous traditional Japanese houses with exquisite gardens.

Of course Tokyo hosts internationally recognised art museums of the traditional sort as well. Those clustered in Ueno Park are a great introduction to Japanese art as well as art from other Asian and western nations. Blockbuster shows from top institutions abroad regularly make stops; Impressionists are a hit here as elsewhere.

Hi-tech Tokyo wouldn't be complete without some of the best in interactive museum-going, from beermaking to the latest in 3-D film-making. In contrast, a trio of museums re-creates aspects of the culture and lifestyles of Edo, present-day Tokyo. A cliché it may be, but for the museum-goer in Tokyo, there's something for everyone.

A few ground rules: museum labels are not always in English but many museums have translated at least a simple introduction to their collections; if you're not handed one, ask for it by saying, '*Eigo no gaido ga arimasu ka?*' You'll also find that you don't always need a full translation to get the gist. As Japan is still a cash-based society, credit cards are generally not accepted, except at some larger gift shops. You generally need ID to get a student or senior citizen's discount on admission; the very young, the disabled and those over 65 usually get in free. Note that, as with most places in Tokyo, disabled access is the exception.

Museums generally shut their doors half an hour before closing, and may take anywhere from a few days to a couple of weeks to change exhibitions. Most are closed on Monday; if a public holiday falls on a Monday, they are open then and closed on Tuesday. (Museums that take their day off on Wednesday follow this rule too.) In addition to closing dates mentioned below, all are closed over the New Year, from about 26 December to 4 January or longer. Some also close during Golden Week in May and Obon in August; others make a point of being open then. When in doubt, call first.

Individual artists

Asakura Sculpture Museum

7-18-10 Yanaka, Taito-ku (3821 4549). Nippori station. **Open** 9.30am-4.30pm Tue-Thur, Sat, Sun. **Admission** ¥300; ¥150 middle & primary schoolchildren. **No credit cards. Map 32**
Regarded as the father of modern Japanese sculpture, Asakura Fumio (1883-1964) designed his combination house and studio with a noble vision: to one day foment 'artistic cultural missions' as a museum. This 1936 building consists of a high-ceilinged concrete portion that was the artist's studio; his living quarters behind it were built in the style of a tea ceremony room. Among the studio's display of life-size (and larger) bronzes are Asakura's award-winning *Grave Keeper* (1909) and a sculpture of Goto Shinpei, former mayor of Tokyo.
Gift shop.

Kume Art Museum

Kume Bldg 8F, 2-25-5 Kami-Osaki, Shinagawa-ku (3491 1510). Meguro station. **Open** 10am-5pm Thur-Tue. **Admission** ¥500; ¥300 university & high school students; ¥200 middle & primary schoolchildren. Group discounts. **No credit cards.** **Map 27**

Kume Kuchiro was one of the first Japanese artists to embrace western-style Impressionism; this museum has changing displays of his paintings, with themes taken from his 1871-72 trek across the globe. *Gift shop.*

Mukai Junkichi Annexe, Setagaya Art Museum

2-5-1 Tsurumaki, Setagaya-ku (5450 9581). Komazawa Daigaku station (Tokyu Shin-Tamagawa line). **Open** 10am-5.30pm Tue-Sun. **Admission** ¥200; ¥100 over-65s; ¥150 university & high school students; ¥100 middle & primary schoolchildren. Group discounts (by appointment). **No credit cards.**

Born in 1901, painter Mukai Junichi made his home and studio in this traditional Japanese house. He donated it along with 500 paintings to the Setagaya Art Museum (*see below*) in July 1993. Mukai's life-long effort to capture in his art Japan's disappearing thatched farmhouses is evident from the oil and watercolour paintings and illustrations, some of which are charred from a 1961 fire. The garden's carefully maintained oaks hark to the Tsurumaki area's past as part of the Musashino forest. *Gift shop.*

Okamoto Taro Memorial Museum

6-1-19 Minami-Aoyama, Minato-ku (3406 0801). Omotesando station. **Open** 10am-6pm Wed-Sun. **Admission** ¥600; ¥300 students. Group discounts. **No credit cards. Map 2**

For a healthy dose of whimsy, check out this two-storey museum, once the studio of artist Okamoto Taro, who died in 1996 at the age of 84. Okamoto's anthropomorphic lithographs, silk screens, oils and sculptures look like something out of *Alice in Wonderland*, with tentacle-like limbs and wacky, blissed-out (or strung-out) visages. Other work includes candy-coloured seats shaped like giant hands and sunburst-inspired abstract paintings. The garden is filled with sculptures as well, hidden among the foliage like madcap gnomes. *Gift shop.* *Website: www.taro-okamoto.or.jp*

Yayoi & Takehisa Yumeji Museum & Tachihara Michizo Memorial Museum

2-4-3 Yayoi, Bunkyo-ku (3812 0012); 2-4-5 Yayoi, Bunkyo-ku (5684 8780). Nezu station. **Open** 10am-5pm Tue-Sun. **Admission** ¥700; ¥600 college & high school students; ¥400 middle & primary schoolchildren. Group discounts. **No credit cards.** **Map 32**

These three small museums face one of Tokyo University's historic entrance gates. The first two are housed under the same roof and are dedicated to Japanese *manga* (cartoons) and illustrations, as

featured on magazine covers and other print media. There are no English translations. The third museum is dedicated to Tachihara Michizo, an artist noted for his works in pastels who died aged 25. *Gift shop. Restaurant.*

Yokoyama Taikan Memorial Hall

1-4-24 Ikenohata, Taito-ku (3821 1017). Ueno station. **Open** 10am-4pm Thur-Sun. **Admission** ¥500; ¥200 primary schoolchildren. Group discounts. **No credit cards. Map 8**

Regarded as one of Japan's great modern painters, Yokoyama Taikan was born in the year of the Meiji Restoration (1868) and saw vast changes in his 89 years. In his traditional Japanese house (rebuilt after damage sustained during World War II firebombings) just outside Ueno Park Yokoyama practised *nihonga* (traditional Japanese painting), taking Mount Fuji and other images from nature as his inspiration. An English pamphlet is available. *Gift shop.*

Science & technology

Communications Museum

2-3-1 Otemachi, Chiyoda-ku (3244 6811). Otemachi station. **Open** 9am-4pm Tue-Sun; 9am-6.30pm Fri. **Admission** ¥110; ¥50 high & primary schoolchildren. Free high school & younger Sun & holidays. Group discounts. **No credit cards.** **Map 6**

This massive museum tells the stories of several of Japan's enormous communications entities: national broadcaster NHK, telecommunications companies NTT and KDD and the Post and Telecommunications Ministry. Histories of each institution, conveyed by artefacts such as early cable wiring and transmitters, combine with state-of-the-art multimedia displays. Each portion of the museum is sponsored by a company or ministry, so the up-with-technology propaganda can be overbearing (there's no talk of harmful monopolies or environmental concerns). Among the most popular items is a bank of TVs with video games and NHK shows. NHK's Hi-Vision theatre is also popular – seats in front of the large, high-definition screen are filled with adults taking a nap. *Gift shop. Lounge.*

Gotoh Planetarium & Astronomical Museum

Tokyu Bunka Kaikan 8F, 2-21-12 Shibuya, Shibuya-ku (3407 7409). Shibuya station. **Open** 11.20am-6pm Tue-Sun. **Admission** ¥900; ¥500 middle & primary schoolchildren. **No credit cards.** **Map 4**

With a rooftop solar telescope, Gotoh Planetarium's 445-person theatre presents an artificial sky depicting the gradual movement of the sun, planets and stars. The one-hour shows, in Japanese, are changed monthly and explain things such as black holes and the Milky Way. The museum on the periphery of the theatre seems like an afterthought but does contain

some interesting artefacts. Among them is a remarkably detailed star map from China dating to 1247. If this taste of space leaves you dissatisfied, there's another planetarium, in Sunshine City, Ikebukuro.
Gift shop.
Website: www.f-space.co.jp/goto-planet

Japan Science Foundation Science Museum

2-1 Kitanomaru Koen, Chiyoda-ku (3212 8544).
Kudanshita station. **Open** 9.30am-4.50pm daily.
Admission ¥600; ¥400 high school & middle schoolchildren; ¥250 primary schoolchildren.
No credit cards. Map 9
This museum takes the maxim 'learning by doing' to the extreme. Located in a corner of Kitanomaru Park, the unique five-spoke structure comprises five floors of interactive exhibits. Don't let its drab, dated entranceway dissuade; it has put real effort into the displays. Kids can learn about science as they stand inside a huge soap bubble, lift a small car using pulleys or generate electricity by jumping or shouting. Naturally, there are plenty of computers, high-definition TVs and other audio-visual aids. There's not a lot of English to be found, though much of the interaction needs no translation.
Gift shop.
Website: www.jsf.or.jp

Nature Study Institute & Park

5-21-5 Shiroganedai, Minato-ku (3441 7176).
Meguro station. **Open** 9am-4pm Tue-Sun; 9am-5pm May-Aug. **Admission** ¥210; ¥60 high & middle schoolchildren. Group discounts. **No credit cards. Map 27**
The institute and park, which fill 20 ha (49 acres), retain the original wildlife characteristics of the historic Musashino (Musashi Plain), which, after six centuries of existence, was turned into a space for the study of nature in 1949. About 750 plants, 100 birds and 1,300 types of insect make their homes here. The one-room museum at the entrance shows how the amount of greenery in Tokyo has decreased since 1677, largely as a result of dwindling temple grounds. Push-buttons allow you to hear the calls of the various stuffed birds in the central display.
Gift shop.

NHK Broadcast Museum

2-1-1 Atago, Minato-ku (5400 6900). Kamiyacho station. **Open** 9.30am-4.30pm Tue-Sun.
Admission free. **No credit cards. Map 2**
Tracing the history of radio and TV, this museum is run by Japan's national broadcaster and is located at the birthplace of Japan's first broadcasting station, which began transmitting radio waves in July 1925. (NHK itself has since moved to bigger digs in Shibuya.) There are two floors of early equipment along with actual examples, such as a refrigerator-sized TV whose images were watched via a mirror. Among the historical microphones, TV cameras and transmitters, vintage TV shows and news broadcasts play (some are available for viewing at the video library). See the vinyl disk containing the

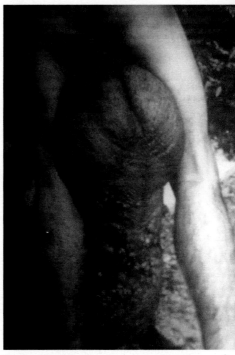

The Parasite Museum: *they start out small.*

recording of Emperor Showa's announcement of Japan's surrender, ending World War II; it was the first time the public had heard the emperor's voice.
Gift shop.
Website: www.nhk.or.jp/bunken/jp/h1-j.html

Parasite Museum

4-1-1 Shimo-Meguro, Meguro-ku (3716 1264).
Meguro station. **Open** 10am-5pm Tue-Sun.
Admission free. **No credit cards. Map 27**
Medical doctor Kamegai Satoru opened this museum in 1953 after he noticed that his post-war practice increasingly dealt with parasites because of widespread unsanitary conditions. The museum now displays some 300 samples of 45,000 parasites he has collected, among them 20 that are his foundation's new discoveries. The second floor has a display of an 8.8m tapeworm taken from the body of a 40-year-old man, with a ribbon next to it showing you how long 8.8m is. Parasites preserved in plastic keychains are available at the gift shop.
Gift shop.

TEPCO Electric Energy Museum

1-12-10 Jinnan, Shibuya-ku (3477 1191). Shibuya station. **Open** 10am-6pm Thur-Tue. **Admission** free. **No credit cards. Map 4**

*Take a fascinating walk through the history of the city at the **Edo-Tokyo Museum**.*

TEPCO (Tokyo Electric Company) has put together seven punchy floors of displays about electricity, including computer games and toys related to energy usage, touch-screen computer quizzes hosted by Enomon (Energy Monster), virtual reality tours of Shibuya by bike and walk-in models of different power generators. Most displays are in Japanese, but there's enough intuitive interactivity to light up any kid's eyes. There's always a queue, so get here early. *Café. Gift shop.*

Transportation Museum
1-25 Kanda-Sudacho, Chiyoda-ku (3251 8481). Akihabara station. **Open** 9.30am-5pm Tue-Sun. **Admission** ¥310; ¥150 middle & primary schoolchildren. Group discounts. **No credit cards. Map 14**
At the crossroads of four subway lines, two train lines and a working river, the huge Transportation Museum couldn't be better located. After starting out as a railway museum in 1921, it has grown to include an exhaustive compendium of transportation over land, sea, air and space, from rockets to rickshaws. Train buffs will have a field day with the oldest train used in Tokyo, an 1872 steam locomotive made in England that travelled between Shinbashi and Yokohama. A must-try among the range of interactive audio-visual displays on offer is steering a Yamanote line train through Tokyo in an actual conductor car, complete with movable knobs and levers.
Café. Gift shop. Lockers.

History

Archaeological Museum of Meiji University
University Hall 4F, 1-1 Kanda Surugadai, Chiyoda-ku (3296 4432). Ochanomizu station. **Open** 10am-4.30pm Mon-Fri; 10am-12.30pm Sat. **Admission** free. **Map 9**
This is an excellent museum replete with objects found on digs around Japan. Detailed English translations describe the results of the excavation and restoration work Meiji University's archaeological institute has undertaken over the past four decades. Represented is every age and region in Japan, including stone tools found in Iwajuku, Gunma Prefecture, which are the earliest proof of human habitation in Japan, dating from the Pleistocene Age.

Banknote & Postage Stamp Museum
9-5 Ichigaya-Honmuracho, Shinjuku-ku (3268 3271). Ichigaya station. **Open** 9.30am-4.30pm Tue-Sun. **Admission** free. **Map 18**
Run by the Finance Ministry, this gives a historical overview of the role of the Printing Bureau, founded in 1871 as the Paper Money Office. First, try to

lift the stack of ¥100 million near the entranceway (it's encased in glass, and stamped *mihon* – 'sample' – in case people get ideas). Japanese currency owes a debt to Edoardo Chiossone, an Italian intaglio plate engraver who did much to improve the look of Japan's money in the late nineteenth century, including making the empress's visage on a banknote look more Japanese. There are also dozens of examples of money and stamps from around the world.

Criminology Museum of Meiji University

University Hall 3F, 1-1 Kanda Surugadai, Chiyoda-ku (3296 4431). Ochanomizu station. **Open** 10am-4.30pm Mon-Fri; 10am-12.30pm Sat. **Admission** free. **No credit cards. Map 9**

Housed in one building on Meiji University's campus in bustling Jinbocho are three interesting (and free) museums. The university was originally the Meiji Judicial School, founded in 1881, so its Criminology Museum is a logical sideshow. It showcases a small selection culled from the school's 250,000 Edo period and Meiji era crime-related objects. A series of enlarged woodblock prints vividly depicts the various punishments – rock throwing, whipping, decapitation – meted out to criminals. *Gift shop.*

Currency Museum

1-3-1 Nihonbashi Hongokucho, Chuo-ku (3277 3037). Mitsukoshimae station. **Open** 9.30am-4.30pm Tue-Sun, second & fourth Sun of month. **Admission** free. Groups by appointment. **Map 6**

The Bank of Japan has put together a sterling museum about Japanese money in its annexe. It traces the long history of money in Japan, from the use of imported Chinese coins in the late Heian period (twelfth century) to the creation of the yen and the central bank in the second half of the nineteenth century. A very good English pamphlet translates most of the exhibition descriptions.

Website: www.imes.boj.go.jp/cum

Daimyo Clock Museum

2-1-27 Yanaka, Taito-ku (3821 6913). Nezu station. **Open** 10am-4pm Tue-Sun except Aug-Sept. **Admission** ¥300; ¥200 students; ¥100 primary schoolchildren. Group discounts. **No credit cards. Map 32**

An unassuming room filled with several dozen clocks, from 200 to 700 years old. *Daimyo* were princely lords during the time of the shogun; since only they could afford these clocks, which required readjusting twice a day, they became known as daimyo clocks. They used a unique way of keeping time, tied to the rising and setting of the sun; the length of an hour changed with the season, becoming longer in the summer and shorter in winter.

Edo-Tokyo Museum

1-4-1 Yokoami, Sumida-ku (3626 9974). Ryogoku station. **Open** 10am-6pm Tue-Sun, till 8pm Thur, Fri. **Admission** ¥600; ¥300 high, middle & primary schoolchildren; additional fee for special exhibitions. Group discounts. **No credit cards. Map 31**

A futuristic eight-storey building that belies the history captured within, the Edo-Tokyo Museum integrates life-size reconstructions of historical buildings, scale models, photographs, audio-visual and high-definition TV presentations, along with an impressive collection of actual artefacts, to trace all aspects of everyday life in Edo, renamed Tokyo ('eastern capital') with the Meiji Restoration in 1868. Everything is covered, from a samurai's everyday life to Tokyo's growing role as Japan's centre of culture and commerce. The museum also shows how disasters both natural (annual floods, the 1657 Meiriki fire, the 1923 Great Kanto earthquake) and manmade (World War II) successively altered the city's landscape. An outdoor outpost (0423 88 3300) in a park in Hanakoganei, western Tokyo, contains over 20 historic buildings saved from the Tokyo bulldozer and open to the public.

Free English and other foreign-language guides. Coffeeshop. Gift shop. Lockers. Restaurant.

Fire Museum

3-10 Yotsuya, Shinjuku-ku (3353 9119). Yotsuya-Sanchome station. **Open** 9.30am-5pm Tue-Sun. **Admission** free. **No credit cards. Map 16**

Between 1603 and 1868, Edo experienced 97 major conflagrations, and large swathes of the city had to be replaced each time. Tokyo Fire Department draws from a great wealth of material for its museum, which includes artefacts such as the thick, heavy-looking coats Edo period firefighters wore, detailed scale models and slick audio-visual displays, one of which uses traditional Japanese puppets to re-enact Edo period blazes. Others use hologram videos to explain how to avoid fire hazards. Kids can guide a firetruck towards a blaze in one of several computer games. An LED display tracks the number of fires that occurred the day before in Tokyo – 13 the day of this visit.

Gift shop.

Fukagawa Edo Museum

1-3-28 Shirakawa, Koto-ku (3630 8625). Monzen-Nakacho station. **Open** 9.30am-5pm daily, closed second & fourth Mon of month. **Admission** ¥300; ¥50 middle & primary schoolchildren. Group discounts. **No credit cards.**

Tokyo has three museums that re-create Edo period *shitamachi* (downtown) existence in life-size reproductions; this one is better than Ueno Park's cramped Shitamachi Museum but pales beside the grandiosity of the Edo-Tokyo Museum (*see above*). Still, it's worth seeking out. Everything about its carefully reproduced corner of a typical 1840 Edo town is accurate: walk along the street and duck into the vegetable store, rice storehouse, boathouse tavern and tenement house. You can even peek into the rubbish bin, next to the outdoor toilets.

Japanese War-Dead Memorial Museum, Yasukuni Shrine

3-1-1 Kudankita, Chiyoda-ku (3261 8326). Kudanshita station. **Open** 9am-4.30pm daily. **Admission** ¥500; ¥200 high & middle

Ueno Park

It's not exactly New York's Central Park, but Ueno Park in north-east Tokyo boasts a similar marriage of nature and edification, with its cluster of world-class museums in a bucolic setting. Ueno Koen (literally 'uphill park') was once the site of an ill-fated last-ditch defence at Kan'ei-ji Temple by samurai loyal to shogun Tokugawa Ieyasu. Their defeat by the Meiji emperor's troops heralded the beginning of the Meiji era in 1868. Kan'ei-ji had been built more than two and a half centuries earlier by the second Tokugawa shogun, Hidetada, to protect Edo at its feng shui-decreed weakest point, 'devil's gate' at the north-east corner. When the samurai sensed defeat they set fire to the hill's protector, the temple buildings.

The Meiji government wanted to build a medical school on the razed grounds; the army preferred a military hospital. A Dutch doctor the government consulted, Antonius Bauduin, managed to persuade both sides that a park would be better use of the hill. (The hospital found a home nearby on the Maeda daimyo estate, now the main campus of Tokyo University. As for the doctor, he got a statue on park grounds.) The nation's first western-style park featured examples of greenery from throughout the empire, all set on manicured grounds that, ever since the park's inception in 1873, have drawn crowds year-round, especially during cherry-blossom season in April.

Museums (and a zoo) were natural extensions of the park's late-nineteenth-century role as host to national exhibitions promoting industry and commerce. The art gallery used at the 1882 show became the main hall of the forerunner of the **Tokyo National Museum**. Now housing a collection of over 89,000 items, the museum is Japan's oldest and largest. If you have just one day to devote to museum-going in Tokyo and are interested in Japanese art and artefacts, the Tokyo National Museum is a good bet.

Its ornate gateway and guardhouses, taken from the Ikeda Mansion in Marunouchi, open up to a wide courtyard and fountain surrounded by three main buildings. The 1937 Chinese-roofed building directly in front is the Honkan, the main gallery, housing Japanese arts and antiquities. With a rotating display of its immense collection – the world's best and biggest – the Honkan's 25 exhibition rooms include paintings, ceramics, metalwork, calligraphy, textiles, lacquerware and sculpture, all organised by genre. Notable are the displays of samurai paraphernalia: curly black bear fur covers one *jinbaori* (a coat worn over armour).

To the entrance's right, in a Japanese log cabin-style building built in 1968, is the Toyokan, featuring three floors of antiquities from Asian countries other than Japan. Among its offerings of Chinese, Korean, Central Asian, Indian and Taiwanese art are Chinese oracle bones and Taiwanese tribal clothing. Ming dynasty-China striped textiles resembles African kente cloth.

Left of the courtyard is the complex's oldest building, the Hyokeikan, which opened in 1909; Tokyo citizens funded the building to celebrate the Taisho emperor's marriage. Inside the domed Renaissance edifice are archaeological finds from Japan. Artefacts range from cord-decorated pottery and bone objects from the pre-Jomon and Jomon periods (Paleolithic and Neolithic, respectively), to Ainu fishing and hunting implements found in Hokkaido and the Sakhalin Islands near Russia, to Kofun period (third to fifth century AD) *haniwa* (tomb figures).

The museum's Horyu-ji Treasure House, behind the Hyokeikan, is home to priceless 1,000-year-old Buddhist objects from Nara's Horyu-ji Temple. The fireproof building had been open to the public only on fair-weather Thursdays in order to preserve the treasures, but a new and more spacious building, completed in 1999, will provide more opportunity to view the antiquities.

Across the street and a short walk to the left of the Tokyo National Museum is the **National Science Museum**, established in 1877. This huge two-building museum requires another full day, but unless you can read Japanese (there is an English guidebook for sale at the entrance) or are keen on spending the afternoon with hundreds of uniformed school kids (cute but noisy), its attractions are limited. Everything is covered here, from astronomy to dinosaurs to mummies, but the general approach of the museum means science buffs are probably better off hitting their museum at home. If you do decide to explore, be sure and look for Hachiko. After the 1935 death of the dog immortalised as a statue outside Shibuya station for its loyalty (*see page 44*), his body was stuffed and is now displayed on the second floor of the museum's Midori Building.

Next door but with an entrance around the corner is the **National Museum of Western Art**. The 1959 Le Corbusier-designed main building houses the Matsukata Collection, named after a president of the Kawasaki Ship Building Company and comprising mostly French Impressionists. A second building by Kunio Maekawa in 1979 augments the collection with other titans of

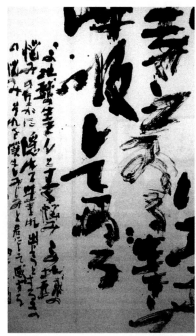

*The writing's on the wall at the **Metropolitan**.*

western art from the museum's permanent collection along with a usually excellent travelling exhibition. Rodin's *The Thinker* contemplates other sculptures in the garden courtyard.

Sculpture-filled gardens aside, if Ueno Park hasn't yet tempted you to stay outside, yet another park museum worth a visit is the **Tokyo Metropolitan Art Museum**. Designed by Maekawa as well, the mainly underground museum (constructed in this way in order to blend in with the park) focuses on modern Japanese art and displays nearly 3,000 items, ranging from *ikebana* (flower arranging) to western-style oils.

Other art museums in Ueno Park are: the **Ueno Royal Museum**, which has no permanent collection of its own, instead showing temporary exhibitions (3833 4191; open 10am-5pm, varying entrance fees and closure days); and the **Tokyo University Art Museum**, featuring a changing display of Japanese and Chinese art

(5841 8452; open April to mid-July, Sept to mid-Dec, 10am-4pm Mon-Fri, 10am-12.30pm Sat).

An antidote to art lies in the southern corner of the park. The **Shitamachi Museum** aims to capture old Edo. On the first floor, the hands-on exhibition recreates *shitamachi* ('downtown'): life-size displays of a merchant's shop, a coppersmith's workshop, a sweetshop and a merchant's home, with outdoor toilet. Open doors and drawers and take your shoes off for a sit on the *tatami*. Upstairs, rotating exhibitions feature aspects of shitamachi life rendered with artefacts and a video.

How to get there

Ueno Park is by Ueno station, on the JR Yamanote line, the Eidan subway Ginza line and the Keisei line. From the JR station, take the park exit. See Map 8.

Addresses

Tokyo National Museum

13-9 Ueno Koen, Taito-ku (3822 1111). **Open** Apr-Sept 9.30am-8pm Tue-Sun; Oct-Mar 9.30am-4.30pm Tue-Sun. **Admission** ¥420; ¥130 university & high school students; ¥70 middle & primary schoolchildren. Free general admission every second Sat. **No credit cards.** *Gift shop. Lockers. Restaurant.*

National Science Museum

7-20 Ueno Koen, Taito-ku (3822 0111). **Open** 9am-4.30pm Tue-Sun. **Admission** ¥420; ¥70 under-18s. Group discounts. Separate admission for observatory (open for the two-hour period following sunset first & third Sat when sky is clear). **No credit cards.** *Café. Gift shop. Lockers. Lounge.*

National Museum of Western Art

7-7 Ueno Koen, Taito-ku (3828 5131). **Open** 9.30am-5pm Tue-Sun; 9.30am-7pm Fri. **Admission** ¥490; ¥450 university & high school students; ¥250 middle & primary schoolchildren; additional charge for special exhibitions. **Credit** shop only MC, V. *Café. Gift shop. Lockers.*

Tokyo Metropolitan Art Museum

8-36 Ueno Koen, Taito-ku (3823 6921). **Open** 9am-5pm daily, closed third Mon of month. **Admission** free. **Credit** shop only, purchases over ¥3,000 JCB, MC, V. *Gift shop.*

Shitamachi Museum

2-1 Ueno Koen, Taito-ku (3823 7451). **Open** 9.30-4.30pm Tue-Sun. **Admission** ¥200; ¥100 all schoolchildren. **No credit cards.**

schoolchildren; ¥100 primary schoolchildren. Group discounts. **No credit cards. Map 9**

Yasukuni ('peaceful country') invites controversy every 15 August, the anniversary of Japan's World War II defeat, when one high-ranking politician or another visits. The Shinto religion honours the spirits of Japan's war dead, from those who died during the Meiji Restoration (1868) on, and the name, date and place of death and address of each of the 2.5 million dead men and women is recorded here. That this list includes convicted war criminals – such as the notorious General Tojo – makes the bald glorification unsettling. Over two floors is a fascinating array of soldiers' personal effects from conflicts such as the Sino-Japanese War (1894-95), the Russo-Japanese War (1904-05) and World War II, with its *kamikaze* suicide pilots. The US army is thanked for letting the museum borrow one of Japan's human torpedoes, found in Hawaii.

Website: www.yasukuni.or.jp

Map Museum

2-1-36 Kudan-Minami, Chiyoda-ku (3261 0075). Kudanshita station. **Open** 10am-4pm Mon-Sat. **Admission** ¥300; ¥200 university & high school students; ¥150 middle & primary schoolchildren. Group discounts. **No credit cards. Map 18**

The illustrious Satakes, a powerful daimyo family living in Hitachi, were punished for remaining neutral in the 1600 Battle of Sekigahara and made to move to Akita, with their fiefdom reduced by half. They thrived, building a castle and ruling for 12 generations, until the Meiji Restoration in 1868 placed the land and people in the emperor's hands. Satake Yoshiharu (34th generation) bequeathed the maps, ancient documents, paintings, personal seals, monograms and stamps used by his family for hundreds of years to form this museum on the site of Lord Satake's Edo residence. Edo period maps detail the shogun's holdings; with their fine detail they appear more like paintings. Included for comparison are maps of present-day Tokyo. You can see how crowded 1960s Tokyo was able to build highways for the 1964 Olympics – by filling in most of its canals. *Gift shop.*

Tobacco & Salt Museum

1-16-8 Jinnan, Shibuya-ku (3476 2041). Shibuya station. **Open** 10am-6pm Tue-Sun. **Admission** ¥100; ¥50 high & primary schoolchildren. Group discounts. **No credit cards. Map 4**

This quirky four-floor museum provides an introduction to two items that, until recently, were held as monopolies by the Japanese government. There's a giant globe tracing the worldwide tobacco business, hundreds of cigarette packets from around the world, touch-screen interactive displays, historical artefacts such as Chinese snuff boxes and a re-creation of Edo period tobacco production and salt harvesting models. At the gift shop purchase some unusual Japanese cigarettes, including Golden Bat, launched in 1906 and recently reintroduced. *Coffee shop. Gift shop.*

*The **Japanese War Dead Memorial Museum***

Tokyo Metropolitan Memorial & Tokyo Reconstruction Memorial Museum

2-3-25 Yokoami, Sumida-ku (3623 1200). Ryogoku station. **Open** 9am-4.30pm Tue-Sun. **Admission** free. **No credit cards. Map 31**

Yokoami Park was the site of an enormous number of deaths following the Great Kanto Earthquake, which took place on 1 September 1923. After the 7.9 Richter scale quake struck, at precisely one minute 16 seconds before noon, firestorms broke out across the whole city, and thousands of panicking citizens gathered at a former military clothing factory here, the only open space in the area. Approximately 40,000 people perished at this spot as sparks set clothing and bedding alight, and the fiery aftermath raged for nearly a day and a half. In the end, three-quarters of the city was destroyed and about 140,000 people died. Seven years after the devastation, a three-storey pagoda-topped building was built in memory of the dead. Designed by architect Ito Chuta, it blends Christian pews and a Buddhist incense-filled altar (Shinto is represented by the exterior stairs). Following World War II, the memorial's name was changed to include the 100,000 people who died in air raids on Tokyo. *Gift shop.*

houses a fascinating collection of artefacts.

Ancient Asian art & artefacts

Hatakeyama Memorial Museum

2-20-12 Shirokanedai, Minato-ku (3447 5787).
Takanawadai station. **Open** 10am-5pm Tue-Sun.
Admission ¥500; ¥350 students. **No credit cards.**
Map 22
The backstreets of tiny Shirokanedai are an apt location for the small but exquisite collection of industrialist Hatakeyama Issei. Changed each season, its exhibitions reflect the Ebara Corporation founder's interest in Noh and the tea ceremony.
Gift shop.

Matsuoka Museum of Art

Matsuoka Tamura Bldg 9F, 5-22-10 Shinbashi,
Minato-ku (3431 8284). Shinbashi station.
Open 10am-5pm Tue-Sun. **Admission** ¥550; ¥200
students. Group discounts. **No credit cards.**
Map 13
Over a lifetime that spanned nearly a century, real-estate developer Matsuoka Seiji became a connoisseur of Japanese paintings, oriental ceramics and ancient sculpture and carvings from China, Rome and Egypt. The quality and condition of the antiquities (with excellent English-language labels) is remarkable. Centuries-old temple carvings, door

jambs and schists from India stand alongside a twelfth-century Khmer sculpture of Uma, Shiva's consort. Various Bodhisattvas and Buddha carvings line the perimeter of displays containing a wealth of Chinese ceramics.
Gift shop.

Nezu Institute of Fine Arts

6-5-1 Minami-Aoyama, Minato-ku (3400 2536).
Omotesando station. **Open** 9.30am-4.30pm Tue-Sun.
Admission ¥1,000; ¥700 students. Group discounts.
No credit cards. Map 2
Set in more than 20 sq km (8 sq miles) of prime real estate in swish Aoyama, the Nezu Institute of Fine Arts represents the wide-ranging collection of Nezu Kaichiro, who died in 1940. The founder of the Tobu Railway founder, he had a penchant for Chinese art, including world-renowned bronzes from the Shang and Zhou dynasties, lacquerware, metalwork and Buddhist figures, all of which are shown in rotated displays. In 1909 a trip to America, of all places, inspired an interest in the tea ceremony, which he began to practise, collecting utensils and related artwork. The grounds are a quiet wooded oasis in the middle of Tokyo, with a pond of carp swimming among stone trails to seven teahouses.
Café gazebo. Gift shop.
Website: www.nezu-muse.or.jp

Okura Museum

2-10-3 Toranomon, Minato-ku (3583 0781).
Kamiyacho station. **Open** 10am-4.30pm Tue-Sun.
Admission ¥700; ¥500 university & high school
students; ¥300 middle & primary schoolchildren.
Group discounts. **No credit cards. Map 2**
Just in front of the famous hilltop Hotel Okura sits a two-storey Chinese-style building whose pagoda décor jars with the hotel's defiantly western retro-modern design. Inside is a dark museum containing a small but interesting mix of Asian antiquities. The collection comprises paintings, calligraphy, Buddhist sculpture, textiles, ceramics, swords, unearthed artefacts, lacquerware and metalwork, and is rotated five or six times a year.
Gift shop.

Takagi Bonsai Museum

Meiko Shokai Bldg 8-9F, 1-1 Gobancho, Chiyoda-ku
(3221 0006). Ichigaya station. **Open** 10am-5pm Tue-
Sun. **Admission** ¥800; ¥500 students. **No credit**
cards. Map 18
Decades ago Takagi Reiki started a business repairing nylon stockings but soon expanded into restoration on a grander scale, with recycling machinery. His company, Meiko Shokai, combines its recycling philosophy with the theme of longevity as exemplified by the art of bonsai. On the ninth floor of the company HQ is a rooftop garden, a serene spot for meditating upon the 500-year-old pine that is the museum's centrepiece. Takagi has some 300 bonsai in his collection, now cared for by a namesake horticultural foundation.
Tearoom. Gift shop.

Little Museums of Sumida-ku

On the eastern side of the Sumida River exists a Tokyo that is worlds away from the crowds of Ginza, Roppongi or Shinjuku. Here life comes more slowly and, though the buildings nowadays are more often concrete than wood, it isn't much changed from hundreds of years ago.

In the midst of this quiet area are a dozen or so very small museums dedicated to traditional Japanese handicrafts, from *tabi* (split-toe socks) to fireworks. Several focus on woodworking. Sumida Ward dubbed these craftspeople 'meisters' in 1987 and made them the focus of a '3M' campaign, along with museums and model shops. Generations-old talent is honoured by having its skills preserved and its wares sold. Calling these places 'museums' stretches the definition of the word; more often than not, they comprise a few display cases taking up a corner of a still-active workshop, where the artisans and families may live as well. A few unique places enshrine a particular obsession, such as cigarette lighters, baseballs or sumo (larger museums located here are listed separately in this chapter).

Spread over a triangular area between the Sumida River to the west and Arakawa River to the east, the museums take some effort to find. Be prepared to feel a bit conspicuous after circling the same block a few times. They're all designated by a rainbow-coloured sign that reads '*Chiisa na Hakubutsukan*'. (Detailed maps in Japanese can be had at the museums, or call Sumida City Office on 5608 6186.) The majority are family-run, and the hours they keep are often not daily; expect unannounced closures.

The Little Museums are listed in order of proximity to one another, moving north to south, from Kanegafuchi (Tobu Isezaki line, from Asakusa station) to Morishita (Toei Shinjuku subway). All addresses are in Sumida-ku.

Rubber Baseball Museum

2-36-10 Sumida (3614 3501). Kanegafuchi station (Tobu Isezaki line). **Open** 10am-4pm Mon-Fri & first, third & fifth Sat of month.
Rubber baseball maker Nagase Kenko shows how they're created, next to displays of those used in historic games such as the 1964 Tokyo Olympics.

Wooden House Museum

1-7-16 Tsutsumi Dori (3612 7724). Higashi-Mukojima station (Tobu Isezaki line). **Open** 10am-4pm Sat & fourth Sun of month.
Surprisingly simple-looking tools of the trade for making traditional wooden houses, with examples of the craftsmanship.

Suzuki Woodwork Museum

6-38-15 Higashi-Mukojima (3616 5008). Higashi-Mukojima station (Tobu Isezaki line). **Open** 10am-4pm, but necessary to call in advance.
Wood carvings such as brightly painted toys displayed; call in advance and you can watch how they're made.

Kobayashi Doll Museum

6-31-2 Yahiro (3612 1644). Yahiro station (Keisei Oshiage line). **Open** 10.30am-5pm Fri-Sun.
This museum spotlights handmade dolls from the Edo period to the present, including a doll given to General MacArthur after World War II.

Ko-Imari Porcelain Museum

A-S Motors 2F, 5-23-9 Yahiro (3619 3867). Yahiro station (Keisei Oshiage line). **Open** 11am-6pm Sat.
The owner of this museum spent more than two decades collecting delicate antique blue-and-white Imari ware from Kyushu.

Battledore Museum

5-43-25 Mukojima (3623 1305). Hikifune station (Tobu Isezaki/Kameido lines). **Open** 10am-5pm Thur-Sat. Closed 15 June-15 July, 1 Nov-20 Jan.
These painted wooden paddles, still made by the father and son Nishiyama team, were used in a badminton-like game favoured by women.

Fortune Seal Museum

2-10-9 Kyojima (3612 1691). Hikifune station (Tobu Isezaki/Kameido lines). **Open** 1-5pm Wed, but necessary to call in advance.
This museum has 5,000 examples of cards left at shrines in the belief they'd bring good luck.

Kawashima Knit Museum

3-9-8 Mukojima (3622 6350). Narihirabashi station (Tobu Isezaki line). **Open** 10am-5pm Mon-Fri.
A brother and sister team shows how traditional clothes were designed and made.

Cigarette Lighter Museum

Ivy Antiques Gallery 3F, 1-27-6 Mukojima (3622 1649). Narihirabashi station (Tobu Isezaki line). **Open** 10am-6.30pm daily.
Several small display cases of cigarette lighters, collected over 20 years (1930s-50s) in Europe, America and Japan occupies the upstairs of a peculiarly British-style antiuque shop.

Portable Folding Screen Museum

1-31-6 Mukojima (3622 4470). Narihirabashi station (Tobu Isezaki line). **Open** 9am-5pm Mon-Sat. Closed second & fourth Sat of month May-Sept.
Screens from the Nara to the Edo periods. Run by a company that makes screens to order. Ask to see the screen with the 'magic' changing pattern.

Noh Mask Museum

5-10-5 Narihira (3623 3055). Narihirabashi station (Tobu Isezaki line). **Open** 9am-5pm Tue, Sat & fourth Sun of month.

This museum takes you through the process of making a Noh mask by hand, from carving the wood to applying the natural stains (horse hair, gold leaf) to form facial characteristics.

Alloy Casting Museum

Lions Mansion Oshige 403, 3-4-13 Harihira (3624 2494). Narihirabashi station (Tobu Isezaki line). **Open** 10am-5pm Fri.

This museum shows, among other things, how the Giant Buddha at Kamakura was made.

Traditional Wood Sculpture Museum

4-7-8 Higashi-Komagata (3623 0273). Narihirabashi station (Tobu Isezaki line). **Open** noon-5pm first, second & third Fri & Sat of month.

A display of intricate wood carvings, made for temples and shrines from the Edo period on.

Takinami Glassware Museum

1-18-19 Taihei (3622 4141). Kinshicho station. **Open** 10am-6.30pm daily. Closed second Mon of month. Factory closes 5pm; classes 10am-4pm.

Glassware dating from the fifteenth century BC. Modern examples are included, with the glassmaking shown in stages. Classes are available.

Woodwork Museum

2-9-11 Kinshi (3625 2401). Kinshicho station. **Open** 10am-5pm, but necessary to call in advance.

Kanso mokuzai refers to furniture made from special 'dry' wood. The proprietor of this museum creates expensive, one-of-a-kind, handmade pieces.

Books on Glassware Museum

4-10-4 Kinshi (3625 3755). Kinshicho station. **Open** 11am-6pm Tue-Fri.

A collection of 700 coffee-table books in English, Japanese, French and German about glassblowing and glassware around the world. A clear winner, if glass is your thing.

Tortoiseshell Work Museum

2-5-5 Yokoami (3625 5875). Ryogoku station. **Open** 10am-5.30pm daily.

A single display case in the entrance of what looks like someone's house. It shows tortoiseshell combs and other hair accessories which date back to the Edo period, over 100 years ago.

Wood Carving Museum

1-13-3 Ishihara (3622 4920). Ryogoku station. **Open** 10am-4pm Sat.

Glass cases in the entrance of this workshop show examples of the carving that goes on upstairs.

Sumo Museum

Ryogoku Kokugikan 1F, 1-3-28 Yokoami (3622 0366). Ryogoku station. **Open** 9.30am-4.30pm Mon-Fri. Open to ticket-holders only during matches in Jan, May & Sept. **Map 31**

Photos, costumes, handprints, dolls, scrolls, woodblock prints, examples of *gunbai* (the ref's wooden paddle) and the art of the topknot.

Sumo Photograph Museum

3-13-2 Ryogoku (3631 2150). Ryogoku station. **Open** 10am-5pm Tue, daily during the Jan, May and Sept tournaments. **Map 31**

One room devoted to a small but changing display of *rikishi* (sumo wrestler) photographs.

Tabi Museum

1-9-3 Midori (3631 0092). Ryogoku station. **Open** 9am-6pm Mon-Sat. **Map 31**

Only three places in Tokyo still make *tabi* (split-toe socks worn with traditional outfits); this is one. Shown are tools used in the 24-step process. Sumo rikishi need custom-made tabi for their big feet, and the museum contains outlines of famous ones, such as those belonging to Akebono.

Paulownia Wood Furniture Museum

4-1-8 Ryogoku (3632 0341). Ryogoku station. **Open** 10am-6pm Thur-Tue.

Musical instruments, furniture and sculpture made from paulownia wood.

Fireworks Museum

Sumitomo Fudosan Ryogoku Bldg 1F, 2-10-8 Ryogoku (5608 1111 ext 3406). Ryogoku station. **Open** noon-4pm Thur-Sat, daily in July & Aug. **Map 31**

The firecrackers in this museum are round, like cannonballs, or like rockets.

Safe & Key Museum

3-4-1 Chitose (3633 9151). Morishita station (Toei Shinjuku line). **Open** 10am-5pm first & third Sat & Sun of month. Closed Aug.

A brief history of security is provided by this collection of safes from the Kamakura and Edo periods and abroad. Included is the safe in which the Japanese army stored its secret codes during World War II.

Construction Tools & Wooden Frame Museum

1-5-3 Kikukawa (3633 0328). Morishita station (Toei Shinjuku line). **Open** 10am-4pm Sat & fourth Sun of month.

No nails were used in the building of traditional Japanese wooden houses; pieces fit together with the use of perfectly measured slats. Tools and wooden frames are on display.

Ukiyo-e Ota Memorial Museum of Art

*1-10-10 Jingumae, Shibuya-ku (3403 0880).
Harajuku station.* **Open** 10.30am-5pm Tue-Sun.
Closed from 26 till end of each month. **Admission**
¥500; ¥400 students; additional fee for special
exhibitions. **No credit cards. Map 5**

Take off your shoes and pad through this tatami-
floored museum, a dimly lit paean to the delicate art
of *ukiyo-e* woodblock prints. The late Ota Seizo,
chairman of Toho Mutual Life Insurance, began collecting the prints after he saw that Japan was losing
examples of its traditional art to museums and collectors in the west. The 12,000-strong Ota collection
includes work by masters Hiroshige and Hokusai.
Gift shop.

Offbeat

Beer Museum Yebisu

*4-20-1 Ebisu Garden Place, Ebisu, Shibuya-ku (5423
7255). Ebisu station.* **Open** 10am-5pm Tue-Sun.
Admission free; beer additional fee. **No credit
cards. Map 20**

Part of the outdoor mall-like Ebisu Garden Place
(built in 1994), this spacious museum was concoct-
ed by Sapporo where one of its breweries once stood.

Lap it up at Ebisu's **Beer Museum**.

Displays recount the history of beer around the
world and the science of brewing. Amid the historical photographs, beer labels and ads are video displays and touch-screen computers, and there's also
a virtual-reality brewery tour. After learning how
beer is made, you can taste the real thing in the bar-
like lounge.
*Gift shop. Tasting lounge.
Website: www.sapporobeer.co.jp*

Drum Museum

*Nishi-Asakusa Bldg 4F, 2-1-1 Nishi-Asakusa, Taito-
ku (3842 5622). Asakusa station.* **Open** 10am-5pm
Wed-Sun. **Admission** ¥300; ¥150 middle & primary
schoolchildren. **No credit cards. Map 10**

Interactive museum-going at its best. Bang away on
hundreds of drums from all over the world in this
well-organised museum above a family-run drum
and Buddhist festival shop. Not all can be played;
look for the blue dot – red means no.
Gift shop.

Eyeglass Museum

*Iris Optical 6-7F, 2-29-18 Dogenzaka, Shibuya-ku
(3496 3315). Shibuya station.* **Open** 11am-5pm Tue-
Sun. **Admission** free. **Map 4**

The first spectacles appeared in Italy in 1280 but
Japan had to endure blurry vision till the sixteenth
century, when Jesuit priest Francis de Xavier
brought a pair over. There's a large statue of him in
the corner, a pair of glasses dangling from his hand.
The 6,000-strong collection is periodically changed.
On the sixth floor the museum has rebuilt an 1800
French eyeglass workshop, shipped over in its
entirety from the French Alps.

Japan Stationery Museum

*1-1-15 Yanagibashi, Taito-ku (3861 4905).
Asakusabashi station.* **Open** 10am-4pm Mon-Fri.
Admission free. **Map 31**

One floor dedicated to the history of writing and cal-
culating implements, ranging from Egyptian
papyrus and abacuses – still widely used all over
Asia – to manual typewriters with interchangeable
kanji keys. In the back is a 14kg (31lb) brush made
from the hair of more than 50 horses; some examples of calligraphy using smaller brushes hang on
the wall. As you walk out, an old gentleman hands
you a free Pilot pen.

Kite Museum

*Taimeiken 5F, 1-12-10 Nihonbashi, Chuo-ku (3271
2465). Nihonbashi station.* **Open** 11am-5pm Mon-
Sat. **Admission** ¥200; ¥100 middle & primary
schoolchildren. **No credit cards. Map 6**

Located in drab Nihonbashi, this museum is a cornucopia of colourful kites. Layered on the walls,
packed in display cases and crowding the ceiling,
the 2,000 kites represent the lifelong collecting
efforts of the former owner of the first-floor restaurant (one of Tokyo's earliest forays into western-
style dining). The global collection ranges from
dried flat leaves from Indonesia to giant woodblock-
drawn samurai kites.
Gift shop.

Toys

Japan Toys Museum

Tsukuda Group Bldg 9F, 1-36-10 Hashiba, Taito-ku (3874 5133). Asakusa station. **Open** 9.30am-5pm Wed-Sun except third Wed of month. **Admission** ¥200; ¥100 high & primary schoolchildren. Group discounts. **No credit cards. Map 10**

Japanese cartoon icon Hello Kitty greets visitors outside this nondescript building. For serious toy collectors, the trek may be worth it, but the 8,000 toys categorised by year sit tantalisingly far from reach, in glass cases. Everything from Meiji era wooden toys and a plastic Astro Boy (c1964) to a remote-controlled Godzilla is here. A small stack of games and toys that can actually be handled sits in one corner.
Gift shop.

Toy Museum

2-12-10 Arai, Nakano-ku (3387 5461). Nakano station. **Open** 10.30am-4.30pm Sat-Thur. **Admission** ¥500 age 3 and over. **No credit cards. Map 26**

More hands-on than the Japan Toys Museum (*see above*), the arts-and-crafts oriented Toy Museum has no shortage of local kids to enjoy its toys. There's not a video game or TV in sight.
Gift shop.

Modern art, Asian & otherwise

Bridgestone Museum of Art

1-10-1 Kyobashi, Chuo-ku (3563 0241). Nihonbashi station. **Open** 10am-6pm Tue-Sun. **Admission** ¥500; ¥400 university & high school students; ¥200 middle & primary schoolchildren. Group discounts. **No credit cards. Map 6**

Industrialist Ishibashi Shojiro had a penchant for Impressionist painters decades before they became all the rage among other wealthy Japanese. The founder of tyre-maker Bridgestone Corp, he opened this museum in his company's building in 1952, by which time his collection had grown to include a number of post-Impressionists, western-style Japanese painters and modern European sculptors. Many western giants are represented, including Manet, Monet, Cézanne, Van Gogh, Picasso, Rodin and Moore.
Gift shop.

Contemporary Sculpture Museum

4-12-18 Naka-Meguro (3792 5858). Meguro/Naka-Meguro stations. **Open** 10am-5pm Tue-Sun. **Admission** free. **Map 27**

Three adjacent tiled-over outdoor areas filled with larger and mostly conceptual works complement the two storeys of figurative studies inside the museum, built in 1982. All are part of the Watanabe Collection, which comprises more than 200 pieces by 56 contemporary Japanese artists. The monolithic marble tombstones in the graveyard next door provide an interesting counterpoint.
Coffeeshop.
Website: www.pp.iij4u.or.jp/~mitu

Gallery Tom

2-11-1 Shoto, Shibuya-ku (3467 8102). Shibuya station. **Open** 10.30am-5.30pm Tue-Sun. **Admission** ¥600; ¥200 middle & primary schoolchildren. **No credit cards. Map 4**

Gallery Tom stands out in this mostly residential area with its sleek concrete-and-glass confines. A flight of wooden stairs leads up into the gallery, which comprises two loft-like floors with plenty of wood and windows. An eclectic roster of exhibitions.

Hara Museum of Contemporary Art

4-7-25 Kita-Shinagawa, Shinagawa-ku (3445 0651). Shinagawa station. **Open** 11am-5pm Tue-Sun; 11am-8pm Wed. **Admission** ¥1000; ¥700 university & high school students; ¥500 middle & primary school children; free high school students second & fourth Sat of month. **Credit** AmEx, DC, MC, V. **Map 22**

Unconventional art in a funky art deco house built by art collector Hara Toshio in 1938. The six rooms and long corridors of this fan-shaped building) are the perfect size for absorbing an eclectic and changing display of contemporary work, among them internationally known bigwigs such as Andy Warhol, Nam June Paik, Tadanori Yokoo, Yanagi Miwa, Robert Mapplethorpe and Christo. Hot architect Isozaki Arata designed the café annex, which overlooks a leafy lawn with more outdoor art.
Café. Gift shop.
Website: www.haramuseum.or.jp

Idemitsu Museum of Arts

Teikoku Gekijo Bldg 9F, 3-1-1 Marunouchi, Chiyoda-ku (3272 8600). Hibiya station. **Open** 10am-5pm Tue-Sun. **Admission** ¥500; ¥300 university & high school students. **No credit cards. Map 6**

Like the nearby Bridgestone Museum (*see above*), the Idemitsu is the collection of a wealthy Japanese industrialist, Idemitsu Sazo, who made his fortune in petroleum. From the collection, which is rotated throughout the year, it's obvious Idemitsu had diverse interests, from Japanese calligraphy and scrollwork to oriental antiquities and ceramics and western art.

Meguro Art Museum

2-4-36 Meguro, Meguro-ku (3714 1201). Meguro station. **Open** 10am-6pm Tue-Sun. **Admission** varies with events. **No credit cards. Map 27**

Part of a complex of buildings, among them a library and citizens' centre, operated by Meguro Ward. As such it has a small-town feel, exemplified by a large annual exhibition featuring local artists. Worth a look if you're in the area.
Café. Lockers.

Museum of Contemporary Art, Tokyo

4-1-1 Miyoshi, Koto-ku (5245 4111). Kiba station. **Open** 10am-6pm Tue-Sun, till 9pm Fri. **Admission** ¥500; ¥250 all schoolchildren; additional fee for special exhibitions. Group discounts. **Credit** shop only JCB, MC, V.

Opened in March 1995, this shrine to modernity is located on reclaimed swampland in one of the older,

Department store museums

Never one to shy away from blending commerce and culture, Japan is home to a particular breed of art museum: that located in a department store. In Tokyo nearly every department store worth its salt has a museum (despite the grand term, it's usually just a floor or two), lending these citadels of consumerism a cultural imprimatur.

Generally speaking, Tokyo's department stores are easy to find because of their sheer girth. They are typically listed as a destination at station exits. The museums share store hours, usually 10am-7pm (*see chapter* **Shops & Services**), and require admission fees that vary according to the individual shows – they're usually a bit higher than regular museums' fees. For more on the stores themselves, *see chapter* **Shops & Services**.

Bunkamura

Bunkamura B1, 2-24-1 Dogenzaka, Shibuya-ku (3477 3244). Shibuya station. **Open** 10am-7pm Tue-Sun, till 9pm Fri-Sat. **Credit** AmEx, DC, JCB, MC, V. **Map 4**
The Bunkamura isn't a department store but a multistorey complex comprising theatres, shops and a concert hall. The museum recently hosted a travelling show featuring highlights from L'Orangerie in Paris.

Daimaru

Daimaru Dept Store 12F, 1-9-1 Marunouchi, Chiyoda-ku (3212 8011). **Credit** AmEx, DC, JCB, MC, V. **Map 6**
Here you can find work by Japanese as well as foreign artists. A good way to kill time before catching a bullet train.

Isetan

Isetan Shinjuku Store 8F, 3-14-1 Shinjuku, Shinjuku-ku (3352 1111). Shinjuku station. **No credit cards. Map 3b**
High-calibre travelling exhibitions; a recent one showcased Egyptian antiquities.

Laforet

Laforet 6F, 1-11-6 Jingumae, Shibuya-ku (3475 0411). Harajuku station. **Credit** varies with events. **Map 5**
Borderline gimmicky mixed-media art is favoured, like watching artist Yokoo Tadanori at work, literally (his office was moved in).

Mitsukoshi

Mitsukoshi Shinjuku South Annexe 7-8F, 3-29-1, Shinjuku, Shinjuku-ku (3354 1111). Shinjuku station. **Open** 11am-8pm daily. **Credit** AmEx, DC, JCB, MC, V. **Map 3b**

You'll find all sorts of things here, from a show of Tiffany's jewellery to an exhibition of celebrity art, featuring work by Donna Summer and Takeshi Kitano.

O Art Museum

Osaki New City 2F, 1-6-2 Osaki, Shinagawa-ku (3495 4040). Osaki station. **Open** 10am-6.30pm Fri-Wed. **No credit cards. Map 21**
Not exactly a department store museum, O Art Museum is located in a new mall adjoining out-of-the-way Osaki station. Shows of uneven quality but worth checking out if you need to kill time in the neighbourhood.

Parco

Shibuya Parco Space Part 1 8F, 15-1 Udagawa-cho, Shibuya-ku (3477 5873) & Shibuya Parco Space Part 3 8F, Shibuya-ku (3477 5905). Shibuya station. **Credit** AmEx, DC, JCB, MC, V. **Map 4**
Reflecting the hip streetwear it sells, Parco has a reputation for showing funky pop-culture-infused art. In two galleries in separate buildings, it also features some headlining international acts, like American photographer Nan Goldin. Another recent show displayed the anime and manga illustrations of Moshino Katsura, whose eye-catching work has been picked up by Nike.

Seibu

Seibu Shibuya B Bldg 8F, 21-1 Udagawa-cho, Shibuya-ku (3462 0111). Shibuya station. **Credit** AmEx, DC, JCB, MC, V. **Map 4**
Seibu closed its respected Sezon Museum in its Ikebukuro branch in early 1999; this one-floor museum can't begin to compare but for now it represents the department store's sole foray into the arts.

Takashimaya

Takashimaya Nihonbashi 6F, 2-4-1 Nihonbashi, Chuo-ku (3211 4111). Nihonbashi station. **Credit** AmEx, DC, JCB, MC, V. **Map 6**
Takashimaya, which is the grandaddy of Japanese department stores, generally shows a range of work by Japanese or Asian artists, such as incense stands by the ceramics artist Takiguchi Kazuo.

Tobu

Tobu Ikebukuro 1-3F, 1-11-1 Nishi-Ikebukuro, Toshima-ku (3981 2211). Ikebukuro station. **No credit cards. Map 1**
A recent show took Mount Fuji as its theme and featured Important Cultural Properties and other artwork; another presented African art and handicrafts.

Take it easy at **Tokyo Metropolitan Teien Art Museum**, *an art deco mansion in fine gardens.*

quainter parts of Tokyo. Supplemented by a searchable database and an extensive video library (both available in English), it has a changing roster of artwork, foreign and Japanese, taken from its 3,500-strong permanent collection. A new MOT Annual, begun in 1999, showcases fresh young artists such as Ozawa Tsuyoshi, who had visitors climb, shoeless, to the top of a mountain of futons and blankets to view his photographs. You won't find a more futuristic setting for the contemplation of art anywhere. *Café. Cloakroom. Gift shop. Lockers. Restaurant.*

National Museum of Modern Art
3 Kitanomaru Koen, Chiyoda-ku (3272 8600). Takebashi station. **Open** 10am-5pm Tue-Sun (till 8pm Fri in summer). **Admission** ¥420; ¥130 university & high school students; ¥70 middle & primary schoolchildren; additional fee for special exhibitions. Group discounts. **No credit cards.** **Map 18**

One of Tokyo's oldest national art museums, this comprises Japanese and foreign paintings, watercolours, sculptures, illustrations, photographs and other genres, from the first decade of the twentieth century on. The first and second floors are devoted to temporary exhibitions, usually headlining acts borrowed from top-flight institutions abroad. *Gift shop. Lockers. Tearoom.*
Website: www.momat.go.jp

NTT InterCommunication Centre
Tokyo Opera City Tower 4F, 3-20-2 Nishi-Shinjuku, Shinjuku-ku (5353 0800). Hatsudai station. **Open** 10am-6pm Tue-Sun; 10am-9pm Fri. Closed second Sun in Feb, first Sun in Aug. **Admission** ¥800; ¥600 university & high school students; ¥400 middle & primary school children. Group discounts. **Credit** AmEx, DC, JCB, MC, V. **Map 3a**

The museum of the future, set in the sparkling-new 54-storey Tokyo Opera City tower complex, opened in 1996. ICC's focus is on multimedia art that combines technology with creativity. Featuring noted Japanese as well as overseas artists, shows explore how machines can be used to create art and can become art themselves. Typically interactive, they're also fun. The permanent collection includes work by Iwai Toshio, whose 1997 *Seven Memories of Media Technology* updates things such as the flip book, kaleidoscope and music box with computer-generated effects.
Gift shop. Internet café. Lockers.
Website: www.ntticc.or.jp

Setagaya Art Museum
1-2 Kinuta Koen, Setagaya-ku (3415 6011). Yoga station (Shin-Tamagawa line). **Open** 10am-6pm; 10am-8pm Sat. Closed Mon. **Admission** ¥200; ¥100 over-65s; ¥150 university & high school students; ¥100 middle & primary school children; additional fee for special exhibitions. Group discounts. **No credit cards.**

On the edge of Tokyo in the middle of a beautifully lawned park. Unlike other ward art museums, this compares favourably to better private museums in Tokyo, with the modern look of its one-storey main

building and its fine selection of temporary exhibitions. Recent shows have featured American artist James Turrell, whose work examines people's relationship to light, and 3,000-year-old excavated artefacts from Sanxingdui, China. The permanent collection focuses on modern Japanese art. *Gift shop. Lockers. Restaurant.*
Website: www.setagayaartmuseum.or.jp

Shoto Museum of Art
2-14-14 Shoto, Shibuya-ku (3465 9421). Shinsen station (Inokashira line). **Open** 9am-5pm Tue-Sun. Closed second Sun. **Admission** ¥300; ¥100 middle & primary schoolchildren; free in Feb and Mar. Group discounts. **No credit cards.** **Map 4**

The Shibuya Ward counterpart to Meguro Ward's art museum, the Shoto Museum of Art shows artwork, largely paintings by local artists, and a changing roster of temporary displays in an unusual building with an atrium. *Tearoom.*

Enjoy shiny high-tech delights at the **Tokyo**

Striped House Museum of Art

5-10-33 Roppongi, Minato-ku (3405 8108).
Roppongi station. **Open** 11am-6.30pm Mon-Sat.
Admission free. **Credit** shop only AmEx, DC,
JCB, V. **Map 2**
This museum's striped exterior, created by alternating rows of brown and white bricks, is modelled on a Byzantine church. Its four airy floors present a display (changed monthly) of contemporary art: paintings, sculpture, even performance art.
Gift shop.

Tokyo Metropolitan Teien Art Museum

5-21-9 Shirokanedai, Minato-ku (3443 0201).
Meguro station. **Open** 10am-6pm. Closed second &
fourth Wed of month. **Admission** varies with
exhibition; ¥100 garden only; ¥50 all schoolchildren.
No credit cards. Map 27
Next to a lovely landscaped garden and teahouse, this 1933 art deco mansion was once the home of Prince Asaka Yasuhiko, the uncle of Emperor

Metropolitan Museum of Photography.

Hirohito, and his wife Princess Nobuko, the eighth daughter of Emperor Meiji. The prince returned from a three-year stint in 1920s Paris enamoured of art deco and decided to build his house in the modern style. Henri Rapin designed most of the interior, while René Lalique added his touch in such things as the crystal chandeliers and the entrance's glass doors. The actual house was completed by architects of the Imperial Household Department, foremost among them Yokichi Gondo. Blueprints and plans hang on the walls, along with photographs of how the rooms looked when it was a home. The second floor plays host to temporary exhibitions.
Gift shop. Lockers. Lounge.

Watari-um

3-7-6 Jingumae, Shibuya-ku (3402 3001). Gaienmae
station. **Open** 11am-7pm Tue-Sun; 11am-9pm Wed.
Admission ¥800; ¥600 students. **Credit** AmEx,
DC, MC, V. **Map 5**
The Watari-um is part of a new breed of museums in Tokyo dedicated to cutting-edge art. Along with sketchbooks, photo albums, T-shirts and other arty goods, its gift shop features a gigantic selection of postcards, arranged by artist.
Café. Gift shop.
Website: www.watarium.co.jp

Yamatane Museum of Art

Sanbancho KS Bldg 1F, 2 Sanbancho, Chiyoda-ku
(3239 5911). Kudanshita station. **Open** 10am-5pm
Tue-Sun. **Admission** ¥500, ¥400 university &
high school students. Group discounts. **Credit** shop
only DC. **Map 18**
Yamatane, which takes its name from Yamatane Securities, opened in 1966. It once resided on the top floors of the company's downtown HQ but will move to Roppongi in 2002. Meanwhile, those interested in modern Japanese art – from nihonga to western-style art – can visit the collection's temporary home.
Gift shop.

Yasuda Fire Museum of Art

Yasuda Fire Bldg 42F, 1-26-1 Nishi-Shinjuku,
Shinjuku-ku (3349 3081). Shinjuku station.
Open 9.30am-5pm Tue-Sun. Closed fourth Sun of
month. **Admission** ¥500; ¥300 university & high
school students; additional fee for special exhibitions.
Group discounts. **No credit cards. Map 3a**
The views from the Yasuda Fire Building's 42nd floor are spectacular. So breathtaking a setting deserves art that holds its own – perhaps that's why Yasuda purchased, at the record-breaking expense of over ¥5 billion (£24 million), Van Gogh's 1889 *Sunflowers* in October 1987. This symbol of Japan's go-go bubble years hangs alongside other gems of western art, including Cézanne's *Pommes et Serviette* (bought in January 1990), although the museum's core work is by Japanese artists, specifically Togo Seiji (1897-1978), who donated 200 of his own pieces and 250 items from his art collection to the museum.
Gift shop.

Photography & film

JCII Camera Museum

JCII Ichibancho Bldg B1, 25 Ichibancho, Chiyoda-ku (3263 7110). Hanzomon station. **Open** 10am-5pm Tue-Sun. **Admission** ¥300; ¥100 middle & primary schoolchildren. Group discounts. **No credit cards. Map 16**

Operated by the organisation that tests and inspects Japanese cameras, the JCII Camera Museum displays around 500 cameras from around the world. The first camera ever made, the 1839 Giroux Daguerrotype, is here; it's a surprisingly compact wooden box. Newer models are represented by pocket-size cameras that use the Advanced Photo System jointly devised (in a rare moment of co-operation) by Fuji Film and Kodak.
Gift shop.

National Film Centre, National Museum of Modern Art

3-7-6 Kyobashi, Chuo-ku (3272 8600). Kyobashi station. **Open** 10.30am-6pm Tue-Fri. **Admission** ¥210; ¥120 university & high school students; ¥90 middle & primary school children. **No credit cards. Map 6**

Japan's only national facility devoted to the preservation and study of films fills its two cinemas for screenings of archival films in themed festivals throughout the year. It has a collection of about 19,000 Japanese and foreign films. Film fanatics can indulge in the film-book library on the fourth floor or take in exhibitions in the seventh-floor gallery, which presents shows of film-related items, photographs and graphic design, often drawn from its own store of posters, screenplays and stills.
Café.

Tokyo Metropolitan Museum of Photography

1-13-3 Mita, Meguro-ku (3280 0031). Ebisu station. **Open** 10am-6pm Tue, Wed, Sat, Sun; 10am-8pm Thur, Fri. **Admission** ¥500; ¥250 high & primary school children; additional fee for special exhibitions. Group discounts. **No credit cards. Map 20**

Tokyo has dozens of interesting little photo galleries, but this museum, filling four shiny floors in a corner of the Ebisu Garden Place complex, outdoes them in terms of sheer scale and technology and benefits from curators who do an excellent job of framing the changing displays of its permanent collection. Photography's natural segue into the moving picture hasn't been neglected: in the basement, the Images & Technology Gallery presents a multimedia history of film as well as temporary exhibitions featuring mixed-media and video artists.
Café. Gift shop. Lockers.
Website: www.tokyo-photo-museum.or.jp

Handicrafts

Commodity Museum of Meiji University

University Hall 3F, 1-1 Kanda-Surugadai, Chiyoda-ku (3296 4431). Ochanomizu station.

Open 10am-4.30pm Mon-Fri; 10am-12.30pm Sat. **Admission** free. **Map 9**

Down the hall from Meiji University's Criminology Museum (*see above*) is this small exhibition room dedicated to Japanese handicrafts. With models and photos, the museum depicts the step-by-step process involved in making lacquerware, from carving the wood to applying the layers of lacquer and polish.

Crafts Gallery, National Museum of Modern Art

1-1 Kitanomaru Koen, Chiyoda-ku (3272 8600). Takebashi station. **Open** 10am-5pm Tue-Sun. **Admission** ¥420; ¥130 university & high school students; ¥70 middle & primary school children. Group discounts. **No credit cards. Map 18**

This 1910 Gothic-style red-brick building was once the base for guards overseeing the Imperial Palace. Now it houses the Crafts Gallery, which exhibits Japanese and foreign handicrafts from the Meiji era to the present. Along with artist demonstration videos and regular talks, it has more than 2,000 pieces on rotating display.
Gift shop. Lockers.
Website: www.momat.go.jp

Japan Folk Crafts Museum

4-3-33 Komaba, Meguro-ku (3467 4527). Komaba-Todaimae station (Inokashira line). **Open** 10am-5pm Tue-Sun. **Admission** ¥1,000; ¥500 university & high school students; ¥200 middle & primary school children. Group discounts. **No credit cards.**

A wonderful antidote to the glitzy, heavy-on-the-high-tech art museums in Tokyo. As befits its contents – pre-industrial Japanese handicrafts – the museum is housed in a 150-year-old traditional residential building awash with dark wood, shoji-screen doors and other subtleties of Japanese architecture. Kyoto University professor Yanagi Soetsu created it in 1936 to spotlight *mingei*, literally 'arts of the people' – the criteria for these were that they were made anonymously, by hand and in large quantities and were inexpensive, functional and representative of the region in which they were made. Yanagi collected ceramics, metalwork, woodwork, textiles, paintings and other everyday items from Japan, China, Korea, Taiwan and Okinawa at a time when their beauty wasn't always recognised. Handwritten labels (all in Japanese) beautifully complement their rustic feel, as do the simple wooden display cases.
Gift shop.

Sword Museum

4-25-10 Yoyogi, Shibuya-ku (3379 1386). Sangubashi station (Odakyu line). **Open** 9am-4pm Tue-Sun. **Admission** ¥525; ¥315 university & high school students. Group discounts. **No credit cards.**

The confiscation of swords during the American occupation as offensive weapons meant that traditional Japanese artform suffered after World War II, so the Society for the Preservation of Japanese Art Swords was set up in 1948. It opened two decades later to display its collection of centuries-old swords

and fittings, which even non-enthusiasts will find mesmerising, as temper patterns used to date the swords appear as mysterious, wave-like shadows on the blade.
Gift shop.

Toguri Museum of Art

1-11-3 Shoto, Shibuya-ku (3465 0070). Shibuya station. **Open** 9.30am-5.30pm Tue-Sun. **Admission** ¥1,030; ¥730 university & high school students; ¥420 middle & primary school children. Group discounts. **Credit** AmEx, DC, JCB, MC, V. **Map 4**
The exquisite art of porcelain is the focus of this quiet museum in the shadow of crowded Shibuya. Its 3,000 pieces of antique Chinese and Japanese porcelain are rotated in four annual shows. Mirrors show the detailed undersides of some pieces; all are accompanied by captions in Japanese and English. *Gift shop. Lounge.*

Fashion

Ace World Bag Museum

Ace Bldg 8F, 1-8-10 Komagata, Taito-ku (3847 5515). Asakusa station. **Open** 10am-4.30pm Mon-Fri. **Admission** free. **Map 10**
Inspired by a leather museum he saw in Germany, Ace Luggage owner Shinkawa Ryusaku opened this museum on the eighth floor of his company's HQ in 1975. The subject may sound dull, but this three-room museum is a fascinating look at materials and fashion through the decades and around the world. Thailand is represented by a 1974 purse made from a patchwork of frog skins and a 1977 handbag graced with the fan-like arcs of anteater leather. If that isn't squirm-inducing, look at the Japanese bag made from the skin of an unborn calf – now illegal.

Bunka Gakuen Costume Museum

Endo Memorial Hall 3F, Bunka Gakuen, 3-22-1 Yoyogi, Shibuya-ku (3299 2387). Shinjuku station. **Open** 10am-4.30pm Mon-Fri; 10am-3pm Sat. **Admission** ¥300; ¥200 university students; ¥100 high & middle school children. Group discounts. **No credit cards. Map 3a**
Women's fashion college Bunka Gakuen founded this museum on its 60th anniversary in 1979. The small collection includes historical Japanese clothing, such as an Edo period firefighting coat and a brightly coloured, 12-layer *karaginumo* outfit, seemingly unchanged from centuries earlier. Kamakura period scrolls include illustrations of dress among different classes of people. It's a shame more of the collection isn't shown.
Gift shop.

Button Museum

Iris Bldg 4F, 1-11-8 Nihonbashi-Hamacho, Chuo-ku (3864 6537) Higashi-Nihonbashi station. **Open** 10am-noon; 1-5pm Mon-Fri. **Admission** ¥300. **No credit cards.**
Iris has been manufacturing buttons for over half a century. Its vast company museum is worthy of the sweeping fourth-floor view of the Sumida River. A 15-minute video introduced the glass-encased objects in the next room. (A sketchy English translation is available.) The first button was discovered in Egypt and dates from 4000 BC; Japan first used buttons, which were imported from Portugal, during the Edo period. Animal horn, embroidered, enamel, porcelain, glass mosaic, gold-plated, ceramic and glass are just some of the types and materials represented. Look for the Halley's Comet, lion's head Chanel and Betty Boop buttons.
Gift shop.
Website: www.iris.co.jp

Sugino Costume Museum

4-6-19 Kami-Osaki, Shinagawa-ku (3491 8151). Meguro station. **Open** 10am-4pm Mon-Sat. Closed mid-Aug to mid-Sept. **Admission** ¥200; ¥160 university & high school students; ¥100 middle & primary school children. Group discounts.
No credit cards. Map 27
Sugino College's four-floor costume museum presents a small collection of old western and Japanese fashions, along with some ethnic costumes from around the world, but it's a bit dingy, with old linoleum floors, fluorescent lighting, chipped mannequins and dusty display cases. (Also, the address on the gate reads 4-6-13 but the museum insists its address ends in 19.) Still, those interested in historical clothing won't be disappointed. A flapper dress from the 1920s greets visitors on the first floor, along with other nineteenth- and twentieth-century western clothing. The fourth floor's Japanese clothing is the most interesting, with Edo period textile swatches, hair accessories, Ainu tribal wear and a reproduction of a Heian period outfit worn by women.
Gift shop.

Tanaka Chiyo College World Folk Costumes Museum

5-30-1 Jingumae, Shibuya-ku (3400 9777). Shibuya station. **Open** 10am-4pm Mon-Sat. Closed Aug. **Admission** ¥300; ¥200 students. Group discounts. **No credit cards. Map 5**
Tanaka Chiyo's interest in folk costumes led her to collect 5,000 examples and found a college of couture. The museum's changing displays are categorised by type rather than origin: a *kufiyah* headcloth and *agal* headrope from Iraq are displayed next to a Taiwanese headdress. English-language labels, photos and diagrams of how the costumes are worn make this the best of the museums showing ethnic wear, but sadly Tanaka seems to have left out folk costumes of her home country.
Gift shop.

Literature

Basho Memorial Museum

1-6-3 Tokiwa, Koto-ku (3631 1448). Morishita station. **Open** 10am-5pm Tue-Sun. **Admission** ¥100; ¥50 middle & primary school children. Group discounts. **No credit cards.**

The seventeenth-century poet Basho Matsuo, most famous for his *haiku*, made this spot on the Sumida River his home, in a corner of timber tycoon (and poetry enthusiast) Sugiyama Sanpu's villa estate. Stone trails near the museum lead to a shrine marking the cottage's location. Plantains (*basho*) grew there; the poet came to like the plain banana's symbolism – its easily-torn leaves rip reminded him of a poet's sensitivity – and he took it as his name. The modest museum holds three floors of Basho's poetry, his personal items such as travel clothes and maps of his routes; you can see haiku in his own handwriting along with paintings and poems by his disciples. The lack of English translations makes this museum for diehard Basho buffs only.

Tokyo Metropolitan Museum of Modern Japanese Literature
4-3-55 Komaba, Meguro-ku (3466 5482).
Komaba-Todaimae station (Inokashira line).
Open 9am-4.30pm. Closed first & third Mon of month. **Admission** free.
Once owned by the royal Maeda family, the large two-storey brick mansion housing this museum was designed as an exemplar of English Tudor architecture in 1929. Wide stairwells, lofty ceilings and dark-wood accents provide the university-library setting for the collection of original manuscripts, first editions, photographs and other memorabilia from modern Japanese writers. None of the descriptions is in English. Next door is the Japan Museum of Modern Literature (3486 4181; 9.30am-4.30pm Tue-Sat), with more manuscripts by famous Japanese authors. Everything here, too, is in Japanese only, and the setting's far less spectacular. *Lockers. Lounge.*

Galleries

Tokyo isn't generally thought of as a walking city, but it can be – within a given neighbourhood – and its vast selection of art galleries are clustered around pedestrian-heavy enclaves. Foremost among them is Ginza, whose grid layout and flagship department stores may remind you of the area around New York's Fifth Avenue. If that's so, then the 400 or so galleries in Ginza and Kyobashi to the north are akin to the brand-name galleries in Manhattan's Midtown area. Concentrated east of the Yamanote line, in Ginza's 8-chome area and moving up towards Tokyo station to Ginza 1-chome, the galleries come in all shapes and sizes and show everything from contemporary photography and traditional Japanese paintings to ceramic ware and Asian antiques.

Chic Ginza hosted British magazine *Dazed & Confused*'s sex-themed photography show, showing it can be edgy too, but the exhibition might have been more at home in the trendy Omotesando, Aoyama or Daikanyama neighbourhoods, near Harajuku and Shibuya stations. A stroll around their backstreets guarantees a gallery discovery or three among the myriad shops and restaurants. Gallery space is often funded through shops selling eclectic art-related merchandise (postcards and coffee-table books) and other adjunct businesses (graphic design studios, restaurants), and smaller galleries may even charge the artists rental fees to show their work.

A selective sample of galleries in these two regions follows, along with a few notables in other areas, such as Shinjuku and its photography galleries. For current listings in English, see Saturday's *Japan Times* or the Thursday editions of *Asahi Evening News* or *Daily Yomiuri*. Gallery hours are generally **11am-6pm** (or noon-7pm); they are closed on Sundays unless noted below.

Ginza

The majority of these galleries are easily reached via the Ginza, Marunouchi and Hibiya subways to Ginza; the Toei Asakusa subway to Higashi-Ginza; Yurakucho subway to Ginza-Itchome, or the JR Yamanote line to Yurakucho (exceptions noted). All are in Chuo Ward (Chuo-ku), and on **Map 7**.

Fuji Photo Salon
Sukibayashi Center 2F, 5-1 Ginza (3571 9411).
Open daily.

Gallery Asuka
Taiyo No. 3 Bldg 3F, 1-5-16 Ginza (5250 0845).
Handicrafts, including exquisite ceramic ware.

Gallery Koyanagi
Koyanagi Bldg 1F, 1-7-5 Ginza (3561 1896).
This gallery can be counted on to show contemporary art that gets talked about; British photo portraitist Gillian Wearing exhibited here in 1999.

Ginza Art Space
7-8-10 Ginza (3571 7741). **Open** daily.
'Outsider art' was the theme of one recent show, borrowed from Lausanne's *Collection de L'Art Brut*. This is also where *Dazed & Confused* sponsored its show of photographs.

Gallery Nikon Salon
Matsushima Gankyo Bldg 3F, 3-5-6 Ginza (3562 5756). **Open** daily (till 2pm Mon).
Nikon also has a 'mini gallery' in Nihonbashi (3281 6810) and two other galleries in Nishi-Shinjuku.

Gallery Q
Tosei Bldg B2, 8-10-7 Ginza (3573 2808).
Two basement galleries showing contemporary Asian art.

INAX Gallery
INAX 2F, 3-6-18 Kyobashi (5250 6530).
Kyobashi station.
This maker of ceramic kitchen fixtures sponsors two galleries in Ginza showing architecture-related and contemporary artworks. INAX also has gallery/showrooms in Roppongi, in the Ark Mori

Gallery Le Déco: *six floors of art in the heart of Shibuya.*

Building's east wing (3505 0311) and in Nishi-Shinjuku (3340 1700). The latter recently featured winners of its INAX design prize.

Kobayashi Gallery
Yamato Bldg B1, 3-8-12 Ginza (3561 0515).
Work in various media by young Japanese artists.

Kyocera Contax Salon
Tokyo Kyukyodo Bldg 5F, 5-7-4 Ginza (3572 1921).
Closed Wed.

Moris Gallery
Taiyo No. 5 Bldg 1F, 7-10-8 Ginza (3573 5328).
Woven work by a Korean artist featured recently.

Pepper's Gallery
Ginza Pine Bldg B1, 7-13-2 Ginza (3544 3240).
One show's theme was 'chic kitsch'.

Satani Gallery
Asahi No. 2 Bldg B1, 4-2-6 Ginza (3564 6733).
Closed Mon, Sun.
Satani represents well known Japanese and foreign artists including Man Ray.

Shirota Gallery
Taiyo No. 5 Bldg B1, 7-10-8 Ginza (3572 7971).
Oils, sculptures and prints, including those by contemporary Japanese printmakers.

Wacoal Ginza Art Space
Miyuki No. 1 Bldg B1, 5-1-15 Ginza (3573 3798).
Art in various media, including metal by four artists and glass by Miyake Michiko.

Aoyama/Shibuya

Bizen Gallery Ko
Asano Bldg B1, 5-18-10 Minami-Aoyama, Minato-ku (3486 8150). Omotesando station. **Map 5**
This gallery/shop specialises in earth-toned Bizen ceramic ware from Okayama Prefecture, western Honshu. In the same building is Maki Textile Studio, featuring an interesting array of fabrics.

Gallery 360°
5-1-27 Minami-Aoyama, Minato-ku (3406 5823). Omotesando station. **Map 5**
Contemporary art, both Japanese and foreign, and a gift shop strong in art postcards.

Gallery Le Déco
Towa Bldg, 3, 5, 6F, 3-16-3 Shibuya, Shibuya-ku (5485 5188). Shibuya station. **Open** daily. **Map 4**
It looks like an office building but each of its six floors showcases a variety of art. One recent group show explored the links between art, design and science. The office and gift shop is on the second floor.

Gallery Ma

TOTO Nogizaka Bldg 3F, 1-24-3 Minami-Aoyama, Minato-ku (3402 1010). Nogizaka station. **Closed** Mon, Sun. **Map 12**
Installations by international architects and those in related professions.

Gallery Rocket

Dojunkai Apt 5-101, 4-12-1 Jingumae, Shibuya-ku (3470 6604). Omotesando station. **Closed** Thur. **Map 5**
Many of the old, slightly rundown Dojunkai Aoyama apartments have been converted into shops, beauty salons and galleries. This one presents contemporary art by young art-school grads.

Hillside Gallery

Hillside Terrace Bldg A, 29-18 Sarugakucho, Shibuya-ku (3476 4795). Daikanyama station (Toyoko line). **Closed** Mon.
Respected for its carefully curated modern art, sculpture and installations and representing such artists as Claes Oldenburg, this gallery is also active on the international art scene. A related space, Hillside Forum in Building F, also shows work; visionary Spanish architect Antonio Gaudi was the focus of a recent show.

Itochu Gallery

2-27-21 Minami-Aoyama, Minato-ku (3497 1261). Gaienmae station. **Map 12**
A larger gallery than most. Acrylic abstract paintings by Shimizu Soichiro were shown recently.

Japan Traditional Crafts Centre

Plaza 246 Bldg 2F, 3-1-1 Minami-Aoyama, Minato-ku (3403 2460). Gaienmae station. **Closed** Thur. **Map 12**
This crafts centre offers a good introduction to traditional handicrafts. Buy examples of what you've seen in museums: lacquerware, ceramics, porcelain, paper, textiles, *kimono*, chopsticks and knives.

Nadiff

4-9-8-B1 Jingumae, Shibuya-ku (3401 8814). Omotesando station. **Open** daily. **Map 5**
A basement one-room gallery in an art bookshop.

Röntgen Kunstraum

Twin Minami-Aoyama 103, 3-14-13 Minami-Aoyama, Minato-ku (3401 1466). Omotesando station. **Map 5**
A tiny gallery showing mixed-media art.

Spiral Garden

Spiral Bldg 1F, 5-6-23 Minami-Aoyama, Minato-ku (3498 1171). Omotesando station. **Open** daily. **Map 5**
This gallery got its name from a spiral ramp around an open central space, designed by Maki Fumihiko.

Toki no Wasuremono

3-3-3 Minami-Aoyama, Minato-ku (3470 2631). Gaienmae station. **Map 12**
'Things that Time Forgot' shows work such as the avant-garde nihonga by the late Mikami Makoto.

Vision Network

5-47-6 Jingumae, Shibuya-ku (3407 6863). Omotesando station. **Map 4**
Vision Network has a bunch of art spaces within its Omotesando complex, either in its narrow gallery area up front or in one of its several bars. Expect pop-culture art: one show's theme was Ultraman, another's centrepiece was a vintage water bed.

Wa Craft Space

2-11-12 Shibuya, Shibuya-ku (3797 3567). Shibuya station. **Map 4**
Contemporary handicrafts, such as ceramics.

Shinjuku

All of these are in Shinjuku Ward (Shinjuku-ku). As with Ginza galleries (*see above*), standard shop opening hours apply unless stated.

Gallery 1

Shinjuku Park Tower Bldg 4F, 3-7-1 Nishi-Shinjuku (5322 6633). Shinjuku station. **Map 3a**
Mostly photography but also other genres, including a touchable sculpture show by Group Sodo and folding-screen nihonga by a western artist.

Konica Plaza

Shinjuku Takano Bldg 4F, 3-26-11 Shinjuku (3225 5001). Shinjuku station. **Open** daily. **Map 3b**
The gallery is attached to a camera museum.

Minolta Photo Space

Kawase Bldg 3F, 3-17-5 Shinjuku (3356 6281). Shinjuku station. **Map 3b**
Linked to a small camera museum and a browsing area for coffee-table books.

Nikon Mini Gallery

Nikon Shinjuku Service Center, Shinjuku NS Bldg 5F, 2-4-1 Nishi-Shinjuku (5321 4466). Shinjuku station. **Open** daily. **Map 3a**
As at Nihonbashi mini gallery, Nikon users can show their works here for free; ask at the gallery for details.

Pentax Forum

Shinjuku Mitsui Bldg 1F, 2-1-1 Nishi-Shinjuku (3348 2941). Shinjuku station. **Open** daily. **Map 3a**
Another photo gallery, called epSITE, is located on the same floor.

Shinjuku Nikon Salon

Keio Plaza Hotel 3F, 2-2-1 Nishi-Shinjuku (3344 0565). Shinjuku station. **Map 3a**
A monthly exam determines what gets shown here.

Elsewhere

Scai – The Bath-house

Kashiwayu-Ato, 6-1-23 Yanaka, Taito-ku (3821 1144). Nippori station. **Closed** Mon, Sun. **Map 32**
Asian and western art in an eighteenth-century bath-house beside Yanaka Cemetery. Art Forum Yanaka is nearby (6-4-7 Yanaka, 3824 0804).

Consumer

Accommodation

For the business traveller, Tokyo offers some of the best hotels in the world. For those on a budget, there are bargains to be had.

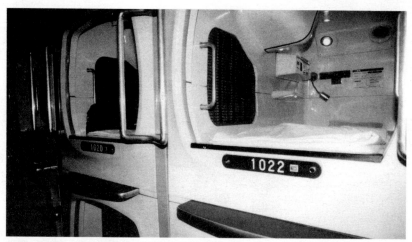

Rooms without a view in one of Shibuya's capsule hotels. Not for the claustrophobic.

Tokyo has a bewildering number of hotels, offering everything from top-class luxury accommodation to a futon on the floor and a tiny capsule (*see below,* **Types of hotel**). During the economic bubble years of the 1980s, new hotels sprang up all over the city, notably in areas such as west Shinjuku. The result is something of an imbalance: if you have the money, there is an embarrassment of expensive luxury accommodation but precious little in the way of reasonably priced rooms.

Given the choice on offer, the most important question facing the first-time traveller is location. If you want to sample the nightlife without spending a fortune on taxis, perhaps a hotel in Shinjuku or Roppongi should be top of your list. If you're after a rather more cultural experience, consider Ueno or Asakusa. Check out our Tokyo area guide section (*see pages 31-85*) and then work out which part of this vast city would suit you best as a base.

Types of hotel

Deluxe

Most deluxe hotels offer western-style rooms; some also have Japanese-style rooms (a bit pricier).

Business hotels

Business hotels are designed with commercial travellers in mind, rather than long-stay tourists. A step down in quality and service, they nevertheless offer solid value for money, though rooms are often on the small side.

Ryokan

Staying at a *ryokan*, or Japanese-style inn, is one of the best ways to enhance your enjoyment of Tokyo (*see* **How to behave in a ryokan***, page 123*). Most offer Japanese-style accommodation – there are *tatami* (woven straw mats) on the floor rather than carpet and you sleep on a futon. One of the bonuses of these rooms for budget travellers is that most ryokan are happy to accommodate several guests in one room, bringing down the price per head. Another plus is that by day the futons are folded away in a cupboard, giving you much more living space. More expensive ryokan usually come with individual bathrooms, but at the cheaper end of the scale you will be expected to bathe Japanese-style in a communal bath. Some *ryokan* expect guests to be back in their room by 11pm. It's advisable to check when you are booking.

Capsule hotels

Traditionally the last resort of the drunk and desperate, a capsule hotel offers a cheap place to put your head down for the night, and not much more. Accommodation is likely to be a small tube barely big enough to sleep in, and extended stays are unheard of. Most capsule hotels are for men only.

Deluxe

Shinjuku

Century Hyatt Tokyo

2-7-2 Nishi-Shinjuku, Shinjuku-ku (3349 0111/fax 3344 5575). Shinjuku station. **Rooms** 800. **Rates** *single* ¥32,000-¥37,000; *double* ¥35,000-¥40,000; *Regency Club single* ¥37,000-¥57,000; *double* ¥40,000-¥60,000; *suite* ¥70,000-¥400,000. **Credit** AmEx, DC, JCB, MC, EE$£TC, V. **Map 3a**
A dull, red 28-storey building in the heart of west Shinjuku, the Century Hyatt is one of Tokyo's finest and most prestigious hotels. The entrance hall, with its huge chandeliers, mirrors and stained glass, is breathtaking, and the standard of accommodation and service is flawless. There are also three floors devoted to the Regency Club, a hotel within a hotel, with bigger rooms, individual service, a private lounge and fax machines and data ports in all rooms.
Hotel services *Air-conditioning. Babysitting on request. Bars (2). Beauty Salon. Business services. Coffeehouse. Conference facilities. Currency exchange. Disabled: access. Fitness centre. Florist. Japanese-style rooms. Karaoke bar. Laundry. Multilingual staff. No-smoking floors. Parking. Restaurants (6). Shopping arcade. Station shuttle bus. Swimming pool. Travel agent.* **Room services** *Cable TV. Fax (on request). Hairdryer. Minibar. Modem line (on request). Radio. Room service (24 hours). Safe. Tea in room (Japanese). Voicemail. Website: www.centuryhyatt.co.jp/en/menu.html*

Keio Plaza Intercontinental

2-2-1 Nishi-Shinjuku, Shinjuku-ku (3344 0111/fax 3345 8269). Shinjuku station. **Rooms** 1,500. **Rates** *single* ¥20,000-¥36,000; *double* ¥24,000-¥39,000; *suite* ¥80,000-¥250,000. **Credit** AmEx, DC, JCB, MC, E$£TC, V. **Map 3a**
One of the first luxury hotels in west Shinjuku, now starting to look a little faded. Service, though, is impeccable, and the bars on the top floors offer commanding views. An executive centre offers a range of services, from translation and interpretation to business card printing and secretarial services.
Hotel services *Air-conditioning. Airport shuttle bus. Babysitting on request. Bars (10). Beauty salon. Business services. Conference facilities. Currency exchange. Disabled: access; rooms (15); toilets. Fax. Laundry. Multilingual staff. No-smoking floors (3). Parking (not free). Pharmacy. Restaurants (19). Safe. Shopping centre. Swimming pool. Wedding chapel.* **Room services** *Cable TV. Hairdryer. Ironing facilities. Minibar. Modem line. Radio. Room service (24 hours). Tea in room (Japanese). Voice mail.*

*A warm reception at the **Century Hyatt**.*

Park Hyatt

3-7-1-2 Nishi-Shinjuku, Shinjuku-ku (5322 1234/fax 5322 1288). Shinjuku station. **Rooms** 178. **Rates** *double* ¥47,000-¥58,000; *suite* ¥82,000-¥500,000. **Credit** AmEx, DC, JCB, MC, E$£TC, V. **Map 3a**
Arguably the finest and most exclusive hotel in Tokyo, and as discreet as a 52-storey building can be. Outside, the smallest of signs tells you you've arrived; inside it's all soft lighting and light wood, with a liberal sprinkling of artworks. It feels like a modern take on a gentlemen's club, and has a dress code to complete the effect. The reception is on the glass-walled 41st floor, with stunning views over the whole of Tokyo. On a clear day you can even see Mount Fuji. Service is attentive but not overly fussy, and the immaculately equipped and furnished rooms are claimed to be the largest in any Tokyo hotel. From the 47th-floor sunlit gymnasium you can watch night descend over Tokyo.
Hotel services *Air-conditioning. Babysitting on request. Bars (2). Beauty salon. Business services. Conference facilities. Currency exchange. Disabled: access. Fitness centre. Laundry. Library. Multilingual staff. No-smoking floors (3). Parking. Restaurants (4). Swimming pool.* **Room services** *CD player. Fax. Hairdryer. Ironing facilities (on request). Laser disc player. Minibar. Modem line. Radio. Room service (24 hours). Safe. Tea in room (Japanese). Voicemail. Satellite TV. Website: www.parkhyatttokyo.com*

Tokyo Hilton

6-2-6 Nishi-Shinjuku, Shinjuku-ku (3344 5111/fax 3342 6094). Shinjuku station. **Rooms** 807.
Rates *single* ¥23,000-¥37,000; *double* ¥27,000-¥41,000; *executive floor single* ¥37,000-¥44,000; *double* ¥43,000-¥50,000; *Japanese-style room single* ¥50,000; *double* ¥90,000; *suite* ¥70,000-¥240,000.
Credit AmEx, DC, JCB, MC, E$£TC, V. **Map 3a**
An unremarkable building that opened in 1984. Guestrooms are of a good size but the views, often blocked by other towers, can be disappointing. The standard of service is high. For business travellers, the hotel offers five executive floors, with separate check-in, a fax in each room and their own guest relations officers. You can even get married here, in either a Christian or Shinto chapel, and have the reception in the 1,100-capacity banqueting suite or one of 17 smaller private function rooms.
Hotel services Air-conditioning. Babysitting on request. Bar (1). Beauty salon. Business services. Conference facilities. Currency exchange. Disabled: access; toilets; rooms (2). Fax. Fitness centre. Laundry. Multilingual staff. No-smoking floors (5). Parking (not free). Pharmacy. Restaurants (6). Safe. Station shuttle bus. Swimming pool. Tennis courts (2). Wedding chapels (2). **Room services** *Fax (executive floors). Hairdryer. Ironing facilities (on request). Minibar. Modem line. Radio. Room service (24 hours). Tea in room (Japanese).Voicemail. Satellite TV.*
Website: www.hilton.com

Roppongi & Akasaka

Akasaka Prince Hotel

1-2 Kioi-cho, Chiyoda-ku (3234 1111/fax 3262 5163). Akasaka Mitsuke/Kojimachi/Nagatacho station. **Rooms** 761. **Rates** *single* ¥27,000-¥36,000; *double* ¥34,000-¥42,000; *business suite* ¥39,000-¥43,000; *Japanese/western suite* ¥100,000-¥120,000.
Credit AmEx, DC, JCB, MC, $£TC, V. **Map 16**
Designed by award-winning architect Tange Kenzo, the 40-storey Akasaka Prince main building is the centrepiece of a complex that also includes a convention centre, European-style guesthouse and banqueting building. Inside the main tower, dating from 1983, it's all glittering light-coloured marble and bright lights, in contrast to the subdued atmosphere of the New Otani (*see below*) over the road. A feature of this hotel is its ingenious stepped design, intended to mirror a Japanese folding screen, which means every guestroom is in a corner. The elegantly simple rooms look like something out of *Star Trek*.
Hotel services *Air-conditioning. Babysitting on request. Bars (3). Beauty salon. Business services. Conference facilities. Currency exchange. Disabled: access; rooms; toilets. Fax. Fitness centre. Laundry. Multilingual staff. No-smoking floor. Parking. Photo studio. Restaurants (8). Safe. Station shuttle bus. Swimming pool (outdoor). Tennis courts (2). Travel desk. Wedding chapel.* **Room services**
Cable/satellite TV. Hairdryer. Minibar. Modem line. Radio. Room service (24 hours). Safe. Tea in room (Japanese). Video player. Voicemail.

ANA Hotel Tokyo

12-33-1 Akasaka, Minato-ku (3505 1111/fax 3505 1155) Tameike Sanno station. **Rooms** 900.
Rates *single* ¥24,000-¥36,000; *double* ¥31,000-¥38,000; *suite* ¥60,000-¥280,000 **Credit** AmEx, DC, JCB, MC, E$£TC, V. **Map 2**
This 13-year-old, 29-storey hotel, owned by All Nippon Airways, is situated in Ark Hills, one of the wealthiest areas of Tokyo, about ten minutes' walk from the nightlife of Roppongi. The brightly lit entrance hall and lobby are vast, while the rooms themselves are spacious, comfortable and well equipped. Room rates rise the higher up in the hotel you wish to stay, and on a clear day, from the side of the open-air pool at the top, you can see Mount Fuji. The lack of 24-hour room service is a curious blemish on a top-class place.
Hotel services Air-conditioning. Babysitting on request. Bars (3). Beauty salon. Business services. Conference facilities. Currency exchange. Disabled: access; rooms (2). Fax. Fitness centre. Japanese/western rooms. Laundry. Multilingual staff. No-smoking floors (5). Parking. Restaurants (8). Safe. Swimming pool (summer only). Wedding chapel. **Room services** *Cable/satellite TV. Fax. Hairdryer. Ironing facilities on request. Minibar. Modem line. Radio. Room service (6am-2am). Tea (Japanese)/coffee in room. Voice Mail.*
Website: www.anaanet.or.jp/anahotels/e/

Capitol Tokyu

2-10-3 Nagatacho, Chiyoda-ku (35811 4511/fax 3581 5822). Kokkaigijido-mae station.
Rooms 459. **Rates** *single* ¥23,000-¥37,500; *double* ¥35,500-¥55,000; *suite* ¥90,000-¥380,000.
Credit AmEx, DC, JCB, MC, $¥TC, V. **Map 11**
For its first 20 years, until 1983, the Capitol Tokyu was the Tokyo Hilton, but when the lease from Tokyu expired the Hilton moved to Shinjuku (*see above*). Ever since it opened, the year before the Tokyo Olympics, the Capitol has attracted the stars. This is where the Beatles stayed in 1966, and more recent guests include Michael Jackson. Its proximity to the Japanese parliament means you also get more than your fair share of politicians. It's close enough to the centre to be interesting but isolated enough, overlooking the Hie Shrine, for peace and quiet.
Hotel services *Air-conditioning. Babysitting on request. Bar. Beauty salon. Business services. Conference facilities. Currency exchange. Disabled: access; rooms (2) toilets. Fax. Fitness centre. Japanese/western rooms. Laundry. Multilingual staff. No-smoking rooms (100). Parking. Restaurants (5). Safe. Swimming pool (summer only). Wedding chapels (2).* **Room services** *Cable TV. Hairdryer. Ironing facilities (on request). Minibar. Modem line (50% of rooms). Radio. Room service (24 hours). Tea in room (Japanese).*
Website: www.capitoltokyu.com

Hotel New Otani

4-1 Kioi-cho, Chiyoda-ku (3265 1111/fax 3221 2619). Akasaka Mitsuke/Nagatacho stations. **Rooms** 1,600. **Rates** *single* ¥28,500; *double* ¥30,000-¥49,000; *suite* ¥70,000-¥180,000. **Credit** AmEx, DC, JCB, MC, $£TC, V. **Map 16**

Ten minutes' walk west of the Imperial Palace, the New Otani bears the unattractive hallmarks of its 1969 construction, but inside the dim lighting and spacious foyers produce the feeling of a luxury cruise ship. To the rear there's a beautiful Japanese garden, the remnants of an ancient garden that was a bequest to one of his generals by Shogun Ieyasu Tokugawa nearly 400 years ago. In it stand several of the hotel's 34 restaurants. Capacity was increased in 1979 by the addition of a 40-storey tower block, but rooms in the older main building are pricier. In an adjoining building, Garden Court offers a designer shopping mall and business/conference facilities.
Hotel services *Air-conditioning. Babysitting. Bars (4). Beauty salon. Business services. Conference facilities. Currency exchange. Disabled: access; rooms (4); toilets. Fax. Fitness centre. Japanese/western rooms. Laundry. Multilingual staff. No-smoking floors (7). Parking. Restaurants (34). Safe. Shopping mall. Swimming pools (2). Wedding chapels (4).*
Room services *Cable TV. Hairdryer. Ironing facilities. Minibar. Modem line. Radio. Room service (24 hours). Tea (Japanese)/coffee in room. Voicemail.*

Hotel Okura

2-10-4 Toranomon, Minato-ku (3582 0111/fax 3582 3707). Toranomon station. **Rooms** *858.* **Rates** *single* ¥28,500-¥41,000; *double* ¥32,000-¥57,000; *suite* ¥75,000-¥500,000; *Japanese room* ¥37,000-¥71,500. **Credit** AmEx, DC, JCB, MC, $£TC, V. **Map 2**
The Okura, next to the US Embassy, oozes opulence in a reassuringly old-fashioned way. This is one of the world's great hotels, and it knows it. Service is formal and efficient and the rooms are of a good size, very well equipped and furnished. The huge wooden lobby evokes the tranquillity of a Japanese garden/ The Okura is also justifiably famous for its food, offering everything from Cantonese and Japanese to French haute cuisine.
Hotel services *Air-conditioning. Babysitting. Bars (4). Beauty salon. Business services. Conference facilities. Currency exchange. Disabled: access; room; toilets. Fax. Fitness centre. Japanese/western rooms. Laundry. Multilingual staff, No-smoking floors (3). Parking. Restaurants (12). Safe. Station shuttle bus. Swimming pools (2). Wedding chapels (2).*
Room services *Cable TV. Fax. Hairdryer. Ironing facilities. Minibar. Modem line. Radio. Room service (24 hours). Tea/coffee in room.*
Website: www.okura.com

Ginza & Imperial Palace

Dai-ichi Hotel Tokyo

2-6-1 Shinbashi, Minato-ku (3501 4411/fax 3595 2634). Shinbashi station. **Rooms** *275.* **Rates** *single* ¥27,000-¥38,000; *double* ¥34,000-¥48,000; *suite* ¥80,000-¥350,000. **Credit** AmEx, DC, JCB, MC, $£¥TC, V. **Map 13**
This 1993 tower rises high above the relatively low skyline of Shinbashi, a ten-minute walk from Ginza. The interior is a mix of styles, the entrance hall a self-conscious echo of the grandness of old European

Live the high life at the **Dai-Ichi**.

luxury hotels. Rooms are immaculate and beautifully decorated, with high ceilings. Elsewhere, the selection of Japanese and foreign restaurants is a tribute to the designers' ability to cram many different styles of interior décor into one building.
Branches: all over Tokyo.
Hotel services *Air-conditioning. Ballroom. Bars (2). Beauty salon. Business services. Conference facilities. Currency exchange. Disabled: access; toilets. Fax. Fitness centre. Laundry. Multilingual staff. No-smoking floors (2). Safe. Shopping arcade. Swimming pool. Wedding chapels (2).* **Room services** *Cable/satellite TV. Hairdryer. Ironing facilities (on request). Minibar. Modem line. Radio. Room service (24 hours). Tea/coffee in room.*
Website: www.daichi-hotel.co.jp

Imperial Hotel

1-1-1 Uchisawaicho, Chiyoda-ku (3504 1111/fax 3581 9146). Hibiya/JR Yurakucho station. **Rooms** *1,059.* **Rates** *single* ¥30,000-¥56,000; *double* ¥35,000-¥61,000; *suite* ¥60,000-¥800,000. **Credit** AmEx, DC, JCB, MC, $£¥TC, UC, V. **Map 7**
There has been an Imperial Hotel on this site overlooking Hibiya Park since 1890. This 1970 tower block-style edifice replaced the glorious 1923 Frank Lloyd Wright building that famously survived the Great Kanto Earthquake shortly after opening. The vast foyer is a popular meeting spot, and though service is impeccable, inside the hotel is starting to show its age; the rooms are blandly furnished and the corridors feel cramped. The newer tower annexe has a slightly less dated feel.
Hotel services *Air-conditioning. Babysitting on request. Bars (3). Beauty salons (2). Business services. Conference facilities. Currency exchange. Disabled: access; rooms (2); toilets. Fax. Fitness centre. Infant care centre. Laundry. Multilingual staff. Music rehearsal room. No-smoking floors (3). Parking. Restaurants (15). Safe. Swimming pool. Wedding chapels (2).* **Room services** *Cable TV. Fax (on request). Hairdryer. Ironing facilities (on request). Minibar. Modem line. Radio. Room service (24 hours). Tea (Japanese)/coffee in room. Voicemail.*
Website: www.imperialhotel.co.jp

Palace Hotel

1-1-1 Marunouchi, Chiyoda-ku (3211 5211/fax 3211 6987). Otemachi/Tokyo stations. **Rooms** 391. **Rates** *single* ¥24,000-¥29,000; *double* ¥29,000-¥41,000; *business suite* ¥56,000; *suite* ¥100,000-¥320,000.* **Credit** AmEx, DC, JCB, MC, V. **Map 6**
Despite its position, on the edge of the moat that skirts the Imperial Palace, something about the Palace doesn't quite strike the right chord. The entrance hall has a dingy, faded feel, and while rooms are comfortable and the views potentially spectacular, the 1970s feel of the décor takes some of the edge off moving in next door to the emperor.
Hotel services *Air-conditioning. Babysitting. Bars (2). Beauty salon. Business services. Conference facilities. Currency exchange. Disabled: access; rooms (2); toilets. Fax. Fitness centre. Laundry. Multilingual staff. No-smoking rooms. Parking. Restaurants (7). Safe. Swimming pool. Wedding chapel. Western rooms.* **Room services** *Cable/satellite TV. Hairdryer. Ironing facilities. Minibar. Modem line. Radio. Room service (24 hours). Tea in room (Japanese). Voicemail.*
Website: www.palacehotel.co.jp

Elsewhere

Four Seasons at Chinzan-so

2-10-8 Sekiguchi, Bunkyo-ku (3943 2222/fax 3943 2300). Mejiro station, then 61 bus. **Rooms** 264. **Rates** *single* ¥33,000-¥43,000; *double* ¥40,000-¥70,000; *suite* ¥62,000-¥450,000.* **Credit** AmEx, DC, JCB, MC, \$£¥TC, V. **Map 25**
Out in the wilds of northern Tokyo but a breathtakingly opulent and beautiful hotel. Stroll around the Japanese garden, with ancient statues from Nara and Kamakura, then enjoy the wide open spaces of the lobby area. Everything here is immaculate, from the service to the size and décor of the rooms, in a mixture of old Japanese and European styles.
Hotel services *Air-conditioning. Babysitting by arrangement. Beauty salon. Business services. Conference facilities. Currency exchange. Disabled: access; rooms (2); toilets. Fax. Fitness centre (paid). Japanese/western rooms. Laundry. Multilingual staff. No-smoking floor. Parking (500). Pets (4). Restaurant. Safe. Swimming pool. Wedding chapel.* **Room services** *Cable/satellite TV. Hairdryer. Ironing facilities (on request). Minibar. Modem line. Radio. Room service (24 hours). Tea in room (Japanese). Voicemail.*
Website: www.fourseasons.com

Hotel Inter-Continental Tokyo Bay

1-16-2 Kaigan, Minato-ku (5404 2222/fax 5404 2111). Takeshiba (Tokyo monorail)/Hamamatsucho station. **Rooms** 339. **Rates** *single* ¥27,000-¥43,000; *double* ¥33,000-¥49,000; *suite* ¥100,000-¥300,000.* **Credit** AmEx, DC, JCB, MC, E\$£¥TC, V.
Not content with providing guests with a view from their bedroom, the Inter-Continental also gives you a view from your bathroom; each one looks out over Tokyo Bay. It strives for European elegance, with soft lighting and acres of marble and wood panelling. Rooms are generously proportioned, though

there is a small premium for a room with a bay view. An extra ¥10,000 per night will get you one of the superior 87 Club Inter-Continental guestrooms, with butler service and full business support.
Hotel services *Air-conditioning. Babysitting. Bar (2). Beauty salon. Business services. Conference facilities (9). Currency exchange. Disabled: access; rooms; toilets. Fax. Laundry. Multilingual staff. No-smoking rooms. Parking. Restaurant (7). Safe. Wedding chapel. Western rooms.* **Room services** *Cable/satellite TV. Hairdryer. Ironing facilities (on request). Minibar. Modem line. Radio (FM only). Room service (24 hours). Tea in room (Japanese). Voicemail.*
Website: www.interconti.com

Royal Park Hotel

2-1-1 Nihonbashi-Kakigara-cho, Chuo-ku (3667 1111/fax 3667 1115/rphfront@pluto.dti.ne.jp). Suitengu-mae station. **Rooms** 450. **Rates** *single* ¥22,000-¥39,000; *double* ¥30,000-¥43,000; *suite* ¥80,000-¥230,000.* **Credit** AmEx, DC, JCB, MC, E\$£¥TC, V.
A glorious hotel ingloriously located next to the Shuto expressway and the TCAT airport check-in terminal. The clientele reflect the location: suits do deals in the impressive lobby. Rooms are spacious and well equipped, and there's a ¥4,000 premium to upgrade your accommodation to executive standard, which includes in-room fax, free translation and interpretation and complimentary cocktails.
Hotel services *Air-conditioning. Babysitting by arrangement. Bars (3). Beauty salon. Business services. Conference facilities. Currency exchange. Disabled: access; rooms; toilets. Fax. Fitness centre. Japanese/western rooms. Laundry. Multilingual staff. No-smoking rooms (139). Parking. Restaurant. Safe. Swimming pool. Wedding chapels (2).* **Room services** *Cable TV. Fax (executive rooms). Hairdryer. Ironing facilities (on request). Minibar. Modem line. Radio. Room service (24 hours). Tea/coffee in room.*

The Westin Tokyo

1-4-1 Mita, Meguro-ku (5423 7000/fax 5423 7600). Ebisu station. **Rooms** 444. **Rates** *single* ¥31,000-¥38,000; *double* ¥36,000-¥43,000; *suite* ¥90,000-¥380,000.* **Credit** AmEx, DC, JCB, MC, \$£¥TC, V. **Map 20**
The Westin, at the far end of Ebisu's giant Garden Place development, opened in 1994. The marbled lobby recreates the feeling of a European palace, while all guestrooms are palatial in size and feature soft lighting and antique-style wooden furniture. A good view is pretty much guaranteed. For a premium of ¥12,000, the Westin Executive Club offers superior accommodation, complimentary breakfast, cocktails and free use of the fitness club.
Hotel services *Air-conditioning. Babysitting by arrangement. Bars (3). Beauty salon. Business services. Conference facilities. Currency exchange. Disabled: access; rooms (2); toilets. Fax. Fitness centre. Laundry. Multilingual staff. No-smoking rooms. Parking (¥1,000/day). Restaurants (6). Safe. Wedding chapels (2).* **Room services** *Cable TV. Fax*

(on request). Hairdryer. Ironing facilities. Minibar. Modem line. Radio. Room service (24 hours). Tea/coffee in room. Voicemail. Website: www.westin.co.jp

Le Meridien Grand Pacific

2-6-1 Daiba, Minato-ku (5500 6711). Daiba station (Yurikamome line). **Rooms** 884. **Rates** *single* ¥23,000; *double* ¥31,000-¥48,000; *suite* ¥70,000-¥400,000. **Credit** AmEx, DC, JCB, MC, E$£¥TC, V.

The Meridien opened in 1998 on the new island area of Odaiba and boasts spectacular views over Rainbow Bridge and the Tokyo skyline (rooms with a view are subject to an extra charge). The only real drawback is its location: Odaiba is a great place for a day out but as a base for touring Tokyo it's inconvenient. Perhaps aware of the lack of much in the way of local character, the hotel supplies some of its own, in the form of an art gallery and, more bizarrely, a museum of music boxes. The Sky Lounge on the 30th floor has one of the best views over Tokyo and the bay. And check out the banquet room on the 29th floor – Victorian railway station meets Versailles palace.

Hotel services *Air conditioning. Bar (2). Beauty salon. Business services. Conference facilities. Currency exchange. Disabled: access; rooms (2); toilets. Fax. Fitness centre. Western rooms. Laundry. Multilingual staff. No-smoking rooms. Parking (438). Restaurant (13). Safe. Tour bus (on demand). Swimming pool. Wedding chapel.* **Room services** *Cable/satellite TV. Hairdryer. Ironing facilities (on request). Minibar. Modem line. Radio. Room service (6am-1am). Tea/coffee in room. Website: www.htl-pacific.co.jp*

Expensive

Asakusa

Asakusa View Hotel

17-1-3 Nishi-Asakusa Taito-ku (3847 1111/fax 3842 2117). Tawaramachi station. **Rooms** 342. **Rates** *single* ¥13,000-¥18,000; *double* ¥21,000-¥31,000; *Japanese-style* ¥40,000-¥63,000; *suite* ¥50,000-¥300,000. **Credit** AmEx, DC, JCB, MC, $¥TC, V.

Map 10

This 15-year-old, 28-storey hotel stands proud on the skyline of low-rise Asakusa. Although smaller and

*The curvaceous **Shinjuku Washington**, where frequent visitors check in with a smart card.*

more compact than many of Tokyo's high-priced hotels, it boasts a high standard of accommodation and its rates reflect its status as the only luxury hotel in this touristy area. Go for a room as high up as you can: the view from the top over Asakusa and the Sumida River is worth catching. The Belvedere lounge on the 28th floor offers the chance to take in the view over a drink. The sixth floor is given over to Japanese-style rooms, complete with their own garden, creating a sort of ryokan within a hotel.
Hotel services *Air-conditioning. Bars (3). Beauty salon. Conference facilities. Disabled: access. Fax. Fitness centre. Karaoke room. Laundry. Multilingual staff. No-smoking rooms. Parking. Pharmacy. Restaurants (6). Safe. Shopping arcade. Swimming pool. Wedding chapels (2).* **Room services** *Hairdryer. Ironing faclities (on request). Minibar. Modem line. Radio. Room service (6am-2am). Satellite TV. Tea in room (Japanese). Voicemail.*

Shinjuku

Shinjuku Washington Hotel

3-2-9 Nishi-Shinjuku, Shinjuku-ku (3343 3111/fax 3342 2575). **Rooms** 1,638. **Rates** *single* ¥11,300-¥14,500; *double* ¥17,000-¥24,000; *suite* ¥30,000.
Credit AmEx, DC, JCB, MC, $TC, V. **Map 3a**
A step down in price and luxury from many hotels in west Shinjuku, the Washington still offers a high standard of accommodation and service. Its main target market is businesspeople, so rooms tend to be small and blandly but efficiently furnished. For frequent visitors, there's an automatic check-in and -out service. The annexe contains 337 of the 1,638 rooms, and is a bit pricier than the main building.
Branch: Akihabara Washington Hotel, 1-8-3 Sakuma-cho, Kanda, Chiyoda-ku (3255 3311/fax 3255 7343).
Hotel services *Air-conditioning. Bar (2). Beauty salon. Conference facilities. Disabled: access; rooms (2). Fax. Laundry. Multilingual staff. No-smoking rooms. Parking (not free). Pharmacy. Restaurants (7). Safe. Travel agent.* **Room services** *Cable TV. Hairdryer. Minibar. Modem line. Radio. Room service (6am-10pm). Tea in room (Japanese). Trouser press. Voicemail.*

Shinjuku Prince Hotel

30-1-1 Kabuki-cho, Shinjuku-ku (3205 1111/fax 3205 1952). Shinjuku station. **Rooms** 571. **Rates** *single* from ¥15,000; *double* from ¥17,000; *twin* from ¥26,000. **Credit** AmEx, JCB, MC, V. **Map 3b**
The Japan-wide Prince chain prides itself on the architecture of its hotels, but this is the ugly duckling, a nondescript red-brick tower rising above the Shinjuku terminus of the Seibu-Shinjuku rail line. The main attraction is its location, in the centre of Shinjuku, two minutes' walk from the Kabuki-cho entertainment area and within striking distance of the rest of Tokyo from the Shinjuku mainline station. Rooms (all western style) are smallish and minimally furnished but spotlessly clean. Enjoy great views over the neon forest of Shinjuku from the 25th-floor Châtelaine French restaurant.
Branches: all over Tokyo.

Hotel services *Air-conditioning. Bar. Beauty salon. Conference rooms (2). Fax. Fitness centre. Laundry. Multilingual staff. No-smoking floor. Parking. Restaurants (9). Safe. Shopping centre. Pool.* **Room services** *Cable TV with evening video on request. Hairdryer. Minibar. Room service (11am-midnight). Website: www.princehotels.co.jp/english/*

Ginza & Imperial Palace

Ginza Renaissance Tobu Hotel

6-14-10 Ginza, Chuo-ku (3546 0111/fax 3546 8990). Higashi Ginza station. **Rooms** 206.
Rates *single* ¥17,000-¥30,000; *double* ¥28,000-¥35,000; *suite* ¥60,000-¥200,000. **Credit** AmEx, DC, JCB, MC, E$£¥TC, V. **Map 7**
A stone's throw from Ginza's Kabuki-za, the Renaissance is an unprepossessing building whose main interior motif is shiny and golden. This may explain its popularity as a venue for young couples to tie the knot. The rooms are comfortable in a functional, bland sort of way, and service is good.
Hotel services *Air-conditioning. Babysitting by arrangement. Bar. Beauty salon. Business services. Conference facilities. Currency exchange. Disabled: access; rooms; toilets. Fax. Laundry. Multilingual staff. Parking (¥1,000/day). Restaurants (3). Safe. Wedding chapels (2).* **Room services** *Cable TV. Hairdryer. Minibar. Modem line. Radio. Room service (6.30am-midnight). Tea in room (Japanese). Voicemail.*

Mitsui Urban Hotel

6-15-8 Ginza, Chuo-ku (3572 4131/fax 3572 4254). Shinbashi station. **Rooms** 265. **Rates** *single* ¥14,000-¥17,000; *double* ¥21,000-¥30,000. **Credit** AmEx, DC, JCB, MC, $£¥TC, V. **Map 7**
An unassuming, practical choice on the edge of Ginza. Rooms are quite small and basically furnished, and the relative lack of facilities is reflected in the price.
Hotel services *Air-conditioning. Bar. Currency exchange. Disabled: access. Fax. Laundry. Multilingual staff. No-smoking floor. Parking (¥1,000/day). Restaurants (2). Safe.* **Room services** *Cable/satellite TV. Hairdryer. Ironing facilities (on request). Minibar. Modem line. Radio. Room service (night only). Tea in room (Japanese). Website: www.mitsuikanko.co.jp*

Ginza Tokyu

5-15-9 Ginza, Chuo-ku (3541 2411/fax 3541 6622). Higashi Ginza station. **Rooms** 437.
Rates *single* ¥16,000-¥41,000; *double* ¥29,800-¥45,000; *Japanese-style* ¥48,000; *suite* ¥100,000-¥150,000. **Credit** AmEx, DC, JCB, MC, V. **Map 7**
Opulence and style, with good-sized rooms with sliding paper screens in the windows. It's particularly proud of its French restaurant, Le Ginza, whose menu was developed in conjunction with Paris restaurant Michel Rostang. For business meetings over lunch or dinner, private dining rooms are available. The communal hot bath is for men only.
Hotel services *Air-conditioning. Airport limousine bus service. Babysitting & child services. Bar. Barber.*

*Beauty shop. Bookstore. Business services. Camera
shop. Car rental. City information desk. Currency
exchange. Disabled: rooms. Doctor (on request).
Dressing and costume rooms. Florist. Kimono shop.
Laundry and valet service. Lounges (2). No-smoking
rooms and facilities. Parking. Pharmacy.
Photography studio. Restaurants (5). Safe. Sauna
and massage service. Shopping arcade. Wedding
chapel.* **Room services** *Cable/satellite TV.
Hairdryer. Ironing facilities. Minibar. Modem line.
Radio. Room service (24 hours). Rooms adapted for
disabled. Tea/coffee in room. Voicemail.
Website: www.tokyuhotel.com/tokyu.html*

Roppongi & Akasaka

Roppongi Prince Hotel

*3-2-7 Roppongi, Minato-ku (3587 1111/fax 3587
0770). Roppongi station.* **Rooms** 216. **Rates** *single*
¥19,500; *double* ¥23,000-¥26,500; *suite* ¥50,000-
¥60,000. **Credit** AmEx, DC, JCB, MC, E$£TC, V.
Map 2
The best way to view this hotel is to stand on the roof
and look down. It was designed by Kurokawa Kisho
around a perspex-sided open-air swimming pool heated to 30°C year round. It's reminiscent of something
from a Spanish package holiday brochure but far more
classily situated, in a backstreet five minutes from the
nightlife of Roppongi. The reception area is so anonymous it's easy to miss it, while the rooms are well furnished, with just enough of the interior designer about
them to remind you you're staying somewhere special.
A favourite with visiting rock stars.
Hotel services *Air-conditioning. Bar. Business
services. Conference facilities. Currency exchange.
Disabled: access; toilets. Fax. Jacuzzi (outdoor).
Multilingual staff. No-smoking floor.
Restaurants (4). Safe. Swimming pool (outdoor).*
Room services *Cable TV. Hairdryer. Modem line.
Radio. Room service (7am-midnight).
Website: www.princehotels.co.jp/english/*

Akasaka Tokyu Hotel

*14-3-2 Nagatacho, Chiyoda-ku (3580 2311/fax 3580
6066). Akasaka-mitsuke station.* **Rooms** 535.
Rates *single* ¥16,000-¥23,000; *double* ¥28,000-
¥37,000; *suite* ¥80,000-¥150,000. **Credit** AmEx, DC,
JCB, MC, E$£TC, V. **Map 11**
A superior business hotel close to the New Otani and
Akasaka Prince (for both, *see above*). Rooms are of
a reasonable size, if unimaginatively furnished. Just
around the corner is the Hie Shrine.
Branches: Capitol Tokyu and Ginza Tokyu are
reviewed above. **Other branches:** Tokyo Bay Hotel
Tokyu, 1-7 Maihama, Urayasu-shi, Chiba-ken (0473
55 2411); Haneda Tokyu, 2-8-6 Haneda Airport, Ota-
ku (3747 0311).
Hotel services *Air-conditioning. Babysitting. Bars
(2). Business services. Conference facilities. Currency
exchange. Fax. Laundry. Multilingual staff. No-
smoking rooms (20). Parking (¥1,000/day).
Restaurants (4). Safe. Wedding chapel.*
Room services *Cable TV. Hairdryer. Minibar.
Modem line. Radio. Room service (7am-midnight).
Tea (Japanese)/coffee in room.*

Elsewhere

New Takanawa Prince Hotel

*10-30-4 Takanawa, Minato-ku (3442 1111/fax 3444
1234). Shinagawa station.* **Rooms** 946 (New
Takanawa Prince) + 309 (Sakura Tower) + 414
(Takanawa Prince). **Rates** *single* ¥22,000; *double*
¥30,000-¥36,000; *suite* ¥70,000-¥85,000.
Credit AmEx, DC, JCB, MC, £¥TC, V. **Map 22**
The Prince chain is owned by the Seibu corporation,
which bought much of the ground its hotels are built
on when Japanese princes were stripped of their lands
during the American occupation. On this piece of land,
there are three Prince hotels, the Takanawa Prince,
the Sakura Tower and the New Takanawa Prince,
which operate as separate hotels, with separate tar-
iffs, but are linked by glorious landscaped grounds.
Guests at one hotel are free to use the facilities of
another. The oldest of the three, the Takanawa Prince,
has a solid, reassuring elegance. The New Takanawa
Prince is gaudy from the outside but impressive within, while the Sakura Tower, a pink monster of a building, offers the most up-to-date facilities and most
expensive accommodation. Service in all three is
impeccable, but the Shinagawa area will disappoint
those seeking nightlife. The European-style house in
which the dispossessed prince originally lived is now
the hotels' Kihinkan guesthouse, where foreign dignitaries and businessmen are often entertained.
Facilities below are for all three hotels combined.
Hotel services *Air-conditioning. Babysitting by
arrangement. Bars (6). Beauty salons (3). Bridal
salon. Business services. Conference facilities.
Convenience store. Currency exchange. Disabled:
access; rooms (2); toilets. Fax. Fitness centre.
Japanese/western rooms. Laundry. Multilingual staff.
No-smoking rooms. Parking. Restaurants (13). Safe.
Station shuttle bus. Swimming pool (summer only).
Wedding chapels (5).* **Room services** *Cable TV.
Hairdryer. Ironing facilities (on request). Minibar.
Modem line. Radio. Room service (24 hours).
Tea/coffee in room. Voicemail.
Website: www.princehotels.co.jp/english/*

Hotel Sofitel Tokyo

*2-1-48 Ikenohata, Taito-ku (5685 7111/fax 5685
6171/info@sofiteltokyo.com). Yushima station.*
Rooms 71. **Rates** *single* ¥17,000-¥27,000; *double*
¥22,000-¥32,000; *suite* ¥36,000-¥70,000.
Credit AmEx, DC, JCB, MC, $¥TC, V. **Map 8**
This looks like a series of white pyramids stacked
one on top of the other. Inside it's no less distinctive,
with soft moody lighting offsetting artworks decorating every surface. The 71 western-style rooms are
good-sized and comfortable, with unusually spacious bathrooms and high-quality furnishings. Each
boasts a view, either over Ueno Park or over the vast
neon cityscapes of Shinjuku and Ikebukuro. Try one
of the tea ceremony rooms on the third floor.
Hotel services *Air-conditioning. Bar. Beauty salon.
Business services. Conference facilities. Currency
exchange. Disabled: access. Fax. Laundry.
Multilingual staff. No-smoking rooms (12). Parking
(¥1,500/day). Restaurants (3). Safe. Wedding chapel.*

Room services *Cable/satellite TV. Hairdryer. Ironing facilities (on request). Minibar. Modem line. Room service (24 hours). Tea (Japanese)/coffee in room. Website: www.sofiteltokyo.com/*

Hilltop Hotel

1-1 Surugadai, Chiyoda-ku (3293 2311/fax 3233 4567). Ochanomizu station. **Rooms** 75.
Rates *single* ¥15,000-¥20,000; *double* ¥22,000-¥32,000; *suite* ¥40,000-¥50,000. **Credit** AmEx, DC, JCB, MC, $¥TC, V. **Map 9**
This has long been a popular haunt of Tokyo's intellectuals and writers, including Yukio Mishima, who stayed here shortly before killing himself in 1971 (the two events are not thought to be connected). The hotel itself spreads over two buildings, the main one atop Surugadai, one of the highest hills in Tokyo. Food in its seven restaurants is of a high standard and the bars are well stocked and unusually comfortable. The Hilltop bills itself as a 'hotel to maintain health', pumping oxygen and negatively charged ions into all rooms.
Hotel services *Air-conditioning. Babysitting by arrangement. Bars (3). Beauty salon. Conference facilities. Currency exchange. Fax. Japanese/western rooms. Laundry. Multilingual staff. Parking (¥1,000/day). Restaurants (7). Safe. Wedding chapel.* **Room services** *Cable/satellite TV. Hairdryer. Ironing facilities (on request). Minibar. Modem line. Radio. Room service (7am-2am). Tea (Japanese)/coffee in room.*

Le Meridien Pacific Tokyo

3-13-3 Takanawa, Minato-ku (3445 6711/fax 3445 5733). Shinagawa station. **Rooms** 954.
Rates *single* ¥21,000-¥25,500; *double* ¥25,000-¥33,000; *suite* ¥50,000-¥300,000. **Credit** AmEx, DC, JCB, MC, $TC, V. **Map 22**
This 1971 monolith benefits from an extensive, pleasant garden that gives it a sense of space. It might look its age from the outside, but within it is immaculate. Rooms are of a good size and facilities are bang up-to-date.
Hotel services *Air-conditioning. Babysitting by arrangement. Bars (3). Beauty salon. Business services. Conference facilities. Currency exchange. Fax. Laundry. Multilingual staff. No-smoking rooms. Parking. Restaurants (6). Safe. Swimming pool (summer only). Wedding chapels (2).* **Room services** *Cable TV. Hairdryer. Ironing facilities (on request). Minibar. Modem line. Radio. Room service (6.30am-1am). Tea/coffee in room.*

Moderate
Shinjuku

New City Hotel

31-1-4 Nishi-Shinjuku, Shinjuku-ku (3375 6511/fax 3375 6535). JR Shinjuku station. **Rooms** 400. **Rates** *single* ¥9,400-¥11,200; *double* ¥16,200-¥19,200; *triple* ¥20,100. **Credit** AmEx, DC, JCB, MC, V. **Map 3a**
The New City has a grand view over Shinjuku central park and the skyscrapers of west Shinjuku but is a poor relation of the many luxury hotels in the area.

The interior has a faded '70s feel, and the rooms, though comfortable, clean and quite spacious, are furnished in the same style. Nevertheless, it's a popular place for Japanese tourists, lured by the area and the prices. Another plus is the natural hot spring bath.
Hotel services *Air-conditioning. Bar. Conference facilities. Fax. Hot spring bath. Laundry. Multilingual staff. No-smoking rooms. Parking (¥1,500/24 hours). Restaurant. Safe. Station shuttle bus.* **Room services** *Hairdryer. Ironing facilities. Modem line. Radio. Room service (5-11pm). Tea in room (Japanese). TV.*

Shinjuku Palace Hotel

2-8-12 Kabuki-cho, Shinjuku-ku (3209 1231). JR Shinjuku station. **Rooms** 34. **Rates** *single* ¥7,000-¥7,200; *double* ¥10,300-¥11,500. **No credit cards.** **Map 3b**
No-frills accommodation aimed primarily at local businessmen or salarymen who've stayed one drink too long and missed the last train home. Still, it's clean and friendly; just don't expect to be able to make much meaningful communication in English.
Hotel services *Air-conditioning. Fax. Japanese-style rooms on request.* **Room services** *Hairdyer. Radio. Tea (Japanese) in room.*

Star Hotel Tokyo

7-10-5 Nishi-Shinjuku, Shinjuku-ku (3361 1111/fax 3369 4216). JR Shinjuku station. **Rooms** 214.
Rates *single* ¥9,000-¥11,500; *double* ¥17,000-¥18,000. **Credit** AmEx, JCB, MC, V. **Map 3a**
The Star offers everything its more expensive west Shinjuku rivals do; in fact it's closer to the station than most of them. In terms of facilities, it has the sort of décor you expect from a business hotel coupled with the standard of service and facilities of a tourist hotel. The rather gaudy bars and restaurants aren't the sort of places you'd want to hang around in long, but five minutes' walk away are the hundreds of restaurants and bars of east Shinjuku.
Hotel services *Air-conditioning. Bars (2). Conference facilities. Fax. Karaoke room. Multilingual staff. No-smoking rooms. Parking (¥1,500/night). Restaurant.* **Room services** *Cable TV. Hairdryer. Minibar. Room service (5-11pm). Trouser press.*

Roppongi & Akasaka

Hotel Ibis

14-4-7 Roppongi, Minato-ku (3403 4411/fax 3479 0609). Roppongi station. **Rooms** 182. **Rates** *single* ¥11,500-¥16,000; *double* ¥14,100-¥23,000; *suite* ¥36,000. **Credit** AmEx, DC, JCB, MC, E$£TC. **Map 2**
The closest hotel to the centre of Roppongi and one of the area's cheapest, the Ibis is functionally furnished and room state is merely adequate. There's one 'designer bedroom' on each floor from the seventh to the 12th, each created by a different interior designer. The Ibis can get particularly busy at weekends, when those too tired or drunk to get home spend the night here before catching the train home.
Hotel services *Air-conditioning. Business services. Conference facilities. Currency exchange. Disabled:*

Hidden extras

When staying in a hotel in Tokyo, you may be liable to a series of hidden charges. All hotels will add the basic rate of tax, five per cent, to the bill. If the hotel charges, including service charge (ten per cent is often added at top hotels) comes to over ¥15,000 per person per night, you will be liable to an extra three per cent local tax.

access. Fax. Multilingual staff. No-smoking floor. Parking (¥2,100/night). Restaurants (3). Safe. Wedding chapel. **Room services** *Cable TV. Hairdryer. Ironing facilities (on request). Minibar. Modem line. Radio. Room service (5am-10.30pm). Tea/coffee free on request.*

Ginza & Imperial Palace

Hotel Ginza Daiei

3-12-1 Ginza, Chuo-ku (3545 1111/fax 3545 1177). Higashi Ginza station. **Rooms** 100. **Rates** *single* ¥11,400-¥13,300; *double* ¥15,600-¥20,800. **Credit** AmEx, DC, JCB, MC, V. **Map 7**
The Hotel Ginza Daiei is a modern, well-furnished and well-situated hotel with a few more comforts than you might expect for the price. Its thoroughly modern-looking rooms are of a good size, with functional pine furniture and inoffensive, light décor. Top price 'Healthy Twin' rooms give you the added bonus of a jet bath.
Hotel services *Air-conditioning. Business services. Conference facilities. Currency exchange ($ only). Fax. Laundry. Multilingual staff. Parking (¥1,000/day). Safe.* **Room services** *Cable TV. Hairdryer. Minibar. Radio.*

Hotel Alcyone

4-14-3 Ginza, Chuo-ku (3541 3621/fax 3541 3263). Higashi Ginza station. **Rooms** 70. **Rates** *single* ¥10,000; *double* ¥17,000-¥23,000. **Credit** AmEx, DC, JCB, MC, $¥TC, V. **Map 7**
One of the cheapest places to stay in Ginza, this superior business hotel offers many of the services found at its larger, more luxurious rivals. The entrance hall and the rooms are clean enough but betray their 1970s origins, though an effort to inject a bit of class has been made in the reproduction furniture. The rooms are adequate in size, but the Japanese-style rooms are the same price as the western-style ones, so you'd be well advised to opt for the former.
Hotel services *Air-conditioning. Conference facilities. Fax. Japanese/western rooms. Laundry. Multilingual staff. Parking (¥1,000/day). Restaurant. Safe. Wedding chapel.* **Room services** *Hairdryer (on request). Ironing facilities (on request). Room service (7am-9.30pm). Tea in room (Japanese). TV.*
Website: www.yin.or.jp/user/syscargo

Nihonbashi

Hotel Kazusaya

4-7-15 Nihonbashi-Honcho, Chuo-ku (3241 1045/fax 3241 1077/Kazusaya@takarabune.or.jp). Shin-Nihonbashi station. **Rooms** 71. **Rates** *single* ¥8,800-¥9,500; *double* ¥12,000-¥14,000; *Japanese-style* (sleeps three) ¥24,000. **Credit** AmEx, DC, JCB, MC, ¥TC, V. **Map 15**
There has been a Hotel Kazusaya in Nihonbashi since 1891, but you'd be hard-pushed to know this from the modern exterior of the current building, in one of the last *shitamachi* areas in the heart of Tokyo's business district. It offers good-sized, functionally furnished rooms decorated in pleasant pastel shades. Service is obliging, though only minimal English is spoken. If you're not in Tokyo on business, you might find the area just a little too restful.
Hotel services *Air-conditioning. Bar. Conference facilities. Disabled: access; toilets. Fax. Japanese/western rooms. Laundry. Parking (¥2,000/day). Restaurant. Safe.* **Room services** *Cable/satellite TV. Hairdryer (on request). Ironing facilities (on request). Tea in room (Japanese). Website: www. takarabune.or.jp/Kazusaya.*

Sumisho Hotel

9-4 Nihonbashi-Kobunacho (3661 4603/fax 3661 4639/Sumisho@po.teleway.ne.jp). Ningyocho station. **Rooms** 63. **Rates** *single* ¥7,000; *double* ¥11,000-¥13,500; *Japanese-style double* ¥13,500 (extra people ¥3,000 each). **Credit** AmEx, DC, JCB, MC, V. **Map 6**
A little tricky to find, off one of Nihonbashi's main thoroughfares, this charming Japanese-style hotel imbues an ugly modern Tokyo building with something quintessentially Japanese – a small pond with slabs for stepping stones ,which you cross to get to the foyer. Good facilities and a high level of service, but non-Japanese speakers may find it difficult to make themselves understood. It's convenient for the TCAT terminal (see chapter **Directory**), but the area has little else to recommend it.
Hotel services *Air-conditioning. Conference facilities. Disabled: access; toilets. Fax. Japanese/western rooms. Laundry. Pets by prior arrangement. Restaurant.* **Room services** *Cable/satellite TV. Hairdryer (on request). Ironing facilities (on request). Modem line (on request). Tea in room (Japanese).*
Website: www.teleway.ne.jp/~sumisho/

Kayabacho Pearl Hotel

1-2-5 Shinkawa, Chuo-ku (3553 8080/fax 3555 1849). Kayabacho station. **Rooms** 268. **Rates** *single* ¥8,500-¥11,200; *double* ¥15,200-¥20,000. **Credit** AmEx, DC, JCB, MC, V.
An upscale canalside business hotel in the heart of the business district, with good-sized, well-furnished rooms and a reasonable level of service. Staff speak some English. Convenient for TCAT air terminal.
Hotel services *Air-conditioning. Bar. Business services. Conference facilities. Currency exchange ($ only). Disabled: access. Fax. Laundry. Multilingual staff. Parking (¥1,500/day). Restaurant. Safe.*

Room services *Hairdryer. Ironing facilities (on request). Modem line. Tea in room (Japanese). TV.*

Asakusa

Sukeroku No Yado Sadachiyo

2-20-1 Asakusa Taito-ku (3842 6431/fax 3842 6433). Asakusa/Tawaramachi stations. **Rooms** 22. **Rates** (basic, *see text*) single ¥10,300; double ¥7,900-¥17,500. **Credit** AmEx, DC, JCB, MC, V. **Map 10**

This smart modern ryokan is wonderfully situated five minutes' walk from Asakusa's temple and pagoda tourist traps. From the outside it looks like a European chalet but within it's pure Japanese. Kimono-clad staff are obliging but speak only minimal English. All rooms are Japanese style and come in a variety of sizes, the smallest being just five mats. The communal Japanese baths, one of which is made of wood, should make for a relaxing stay. Room rates vary according to season, and there's a ¥3,000 supplement for Friday nights or the day before a national holiday. During the high season (30 Dec-5 Jan, 7 May-30 June, 15 Sept-30 Nov) rates rise by an average of ¥1,000. Breakfast costs an extra ¥1,500.
Hotel services *Air-conditioning. Disabled: access. Fax. Japanese rooms. Restaurant. Room service (4-10pm). Safe.* **Room services** *Tea (Japanese)/coffee in room. TV.*

Hotel Sunroute Asakusa

1-8-5 Kaminarimon, Taito-ku (3847 1511/fax 3847 1509/webmaster@sunroute-asakusa.co.jp). Tawaramachi station. **Rooms** 120. **Rates** *single* ¥7,800-¥8,600; *double* ¥13,000-¥17,000.
Credit AmEx, DC, MC, V. **Map 10**

Small rooms and lack of facilities notwithstanding, this business hotel offers reasonable value for money for those determined to sleep in beds rather than on futons. The building's so bland there's a danger of walking past it – look out for the Jonathan's restaurant sign on the street. This second-floor American-style eaterie doubles as the hotel's restaurant and is open 24 hours a day.
Hotel services *Air-conditioning. Disabled: access; rooms; toilets. Fax. Laundry. Multilingual staff. Parking (¥1,500/day). Restaurant. Safe.* **Room services** *Hairdryer. Minibar. Modem line. Radio. Satellite TV. Tea in room (Japanese). Telephone message system.*
Website: www.sunroute-asakusa.co.jp/

Ryokan Shigetsu

1-31-11 Asakusa Taito-ku (3843 2345/fax 3843 2348). Asakusa station. **Rooms** 24. **Rates** *single* ¥7,300-¥8,000; *double* ¥14,000-¥15,000.
Credit AmEx, MC, $¥TC, V. **Map 10**

For the first-time tourist in Tokyo, this hotel could hardly be better located: it's barely 30 seconds' walk from Asakusa's market and temple complex. It offers comfortable rooms in both Japanese and western style, the latter being slightly cheaper, and all rooms have their own bathrooms, although there is a Japanese-style communal bath on the top floor with a view over the surrounding area. Booking

ahead is recommended, particularly around national holidays. Bookings can be made through the Japanese Inn Group (*see* **Booking organisations**).
Hotel services *Air-conditioning. Currency exchange ($ only). Disabled: access; toilets. Fax. Japanese/western rooms. Laundry. Multilingual staff. No-smoking floors (2). Parking. Restaurant. Safe.* **Room services** *Hairdryer (on request). Ironing facilities (on request). Minibar. Radio. Tea in room (Japanese). TV.*

Ueno

Hotel Park Side

2-11-18 Ueno, Taito-ku (3836 5711/fax 3836 3459). Ueno station. **Rooms** 128. **Rates** *single* ¥9,200-¥11,500; *double* ¥14,000-¥18,200. **Credit** AmEx, DC, JCB, MC, ¥TC, V. **Map 8**

The hotel's name is something of a misnomer, as it's one street away from the Shinobazu pond end of Ueno Park, bang in the middle of Ueno's late-night drinking and entertainment district. Still, if you get a park-facing room on one of the upper floors, you might just about be able to convince yourself you're in the countryside. Western-style rooms are a bit small, so go Japanese.
Hotel services *Air-conditioning. Bar. Conference facilities. Disabled: access; rooms. Fax. Japanese/western rooms. Laundry. Multilingual staff. Parking. Restaurants (4). Safe. Wedding chapel.* **Room services** *Hairdryer (on request). Minibar. Modem line. Radio. Room service (3-10.30pm). Tea in room (Japanese). Telephone message system. TV.*
Website: www.parkside.co.jp/

Homeikan Daimachibekkan

5-10-5 Hongo, Bunkyo-ku (3811 1181/fax 3811 1764/homeikan@mcgroup.or.jp). Hongo-sanchome station. **Rooms** 57. **Rates** *single* ¥6,400; *double* ¥11,200 (special long-stay rate available).
Credit AmEx, DC, JCB, MC, ¥TC, UC, V.

A real find, buried in the anonymous residential backstreets around the University of Tokyo medical school. It looks like a Japanese inn ought to – wooden, glass-fronted and with a small ornamental garden. Some of the furnishings look frayed around the edges, but this only adds to the charm. The ryokan is divided into two buildings, which face each other across the street, while the branch (*see below*) is a five-minute walk away. The only drawback is its location, about 20 minutes' walk from the nearest real action around Ueno or Ochanomizu stations.
Branch: Morikawabekkan, 6-23-5 Hongo, Bunkyo ku (3811 1181/fax 3811 8120).
Hotel services *Air-conditioning. Disabled: access. Fax. Japanese rooms. Parking (3 spaces). Safe.* **Room services** *Hairdryer (on request). Ironing facilities (on request). Tea in room (Japanese).*
Website: www.jnto.go.jp/03welcome/ptgroup.html

Ueno First City Hotel

1-14-8 Ueno, Taito-ku (3831 8215/fax 3837 8469). Okachimachi station. **Rooms** 77. **Rates** *single* ¥8,000-¥8,500; *double* ¥13,000-¥16,000.
No credit cards. Map 8

Booking organisations

Hotels and ryokan in Tokyo and the rest of Japan can be booked from abroad, or in Japan, via the following organisations:

Hotel Hotline

This Internet-led service offers substantial discounts – sometimes as much as ¥10,000 per night – on standard rates at many of Tokyo's top hotels, including the Imperial and the Park Hyatt. Reservations can also be made by fax (3433 8388) or phone (5403 7710).
Website: http://jgl.biglobe.ne.jp/english/

Japanese Inn Group

This specialises in providing ryokan accommodation all over Japan, and produces a leaflet of its inns,

available free from Tourist Information Centres (TIC; *see Directory p253*) or by post from the head office: c/o Ryokan Asakusa Shigetsu, 1-31-11 Nishi-Asakusa, Taito-ku, Tokyo 111-0032, Japan.
Website: http://members.aol.com/jinngroup

Welcome Inns

Run by the Japan National Tourist Organisation, this offers both ryokan and western-style accommodation for under ¥8,000 per person per night. A free booklet is available from TIC (*see Directory p253*), and reservations can be made in person at a TIC, by fax (3211 9009) or by e-mail from the website. Note that many of Welcome Inns hotels also feature in the Japanese Inn Group pamphlet.
Website: http://www.jnto.go.jp

A cut above the normal business hotel, this offers comfortable accommodation in an unprepossessing modern red-brick block not far from Ueno Park. Western-style rooms are pleasantly furnished and decorated in pastel shades while Japanese rooms have the usual tatami and olive colour scheme.
Hotel services *Air-conditioning. Banquet hall. Bar. Coffee shop. Conference facilities. Fax. Japanese/western rooms. Restaurant.*
Room services *Hairdryer. Massage (paid). Satellite TV. Tea/coffee in room.*

Elsewhere

Hotel Bellegrande

2-19-1 Ryogoku, Sumida-ku (3631 8111/fax 3631 8112). Ryogoku station. **Rooms** 150. **Rates** *single* ¥8,000-¥16,000; *double* ¥14,000-¥40,000; *suite* ¥80,000. **Credit** AmEx, DC, JCB, V. **Map 31**
A modern business-style hotel barely a wrestler's stride from the sumo stadium in Ryogoku, a quiet area of Tokyo that comes alive during the three annual Tokyo sumo tournaments. Its unglamorous location is reflected in the prices of the rooms, which are small but comfortable. Booking is definitely recommended if your visit coincides with a sumo tournament.
Hotel services *Air-conditioning. Bar. Conference facilities (2). Fax. Japanese/western rooms. Parking (paid). Restaurant (3).* **Room services** *Hairdryer. Radio. Tea in room (Japanese). TV.*

Keihin Hotel

4-10-20 Takanawa, Minato-ku (3449 5711/fax 3441 7230). Shinagawa station. **Rooms** 53. **Rates** *single* ¥8,000-¥8,500; *double* ¥14,000. **Credit** AmEx, DC, JCB, MC, V. **Map 22**
There has been a Keihin Hotel here since 1871, but the current building dates from the 1960s. Long overshadowed by its more illustrious neighbours the Prince hotels and the Meridien Pacific (for both, *see*

above), the Keihin has a certain shabby appeal. It's clean and the rooms are of a reasonable size, but a lick of paint in some quarters wouldn't do any harm. Staff are helpful, but speak only minimal English.
Hotel services *Air-conditioning. Bars (2). Conference facilities. Disabled: access. Fax. Japanese/western rooms. Laundry. Restaurant. Safe.*
Room services *Hairdryer (on request). Minibar. Radio. Room service (24 hours). Tea in room (Japanese). TV. Trouser press.*
Website: gnavi.joy.ne.jp/keihin-h/

River Hotel

2-13-8 Ryogoku, Sumida-ku (3634 1711). Ryogoku station. **Rooms** 97. **Rates** *single* ¥6,600-¥7,200; *double* ¥11,000-¥12,000. **Credit** AmEx, DC, JCB, MC, V. **Map 31**
This offers tiny, slightly shabby western-style, or – much better value – Japanese-style rooms. Booking is recommended if there's a sumo tournament on.
Hotel services *Air-conditioning. Conference room. Fax. Parking. Restaurant (Japanese).* **Room services** *Ironing facilities (on request). Hairdryer. Radio. Tea/coffee in room. TV.*

Ryokan Ryumeikan Honten

3-4 Kanda-Surugadai, Chiyoda-ku (3251 1135/fax 3251 0270/ryumeikan@ma2.justnet.ne.jp). Ochanomizu station. **Rooms** 12. **Rates** *single* ¥10,000; *double* ¥13,000. **Credit** AmEx, DC, JCB, MC, V. **Map 9**
Just south of Ochanomizu's Russian cathedral and 20 minutes' walk north of the Imperial Palace grounds, this ryokan is modern and clean, with helpful staff and good-sized Japanese rooms. Architecturally, it's a nightmare, occupying part of a modern office building that blends so well into the surrounding bank buildings and skyscrapers as to be virtually invisible. The interior is a testament to how ingeniously the Japanese can disguise the shortcomings of a building to produce a pleasant atmosphere,

but you still might wish you'd stayed somewhere a little more traditional. The branch, in Nihonbashi, is slightly cheaper and more imposing.
Branch: Hotel Yaesu Ryumeikan, 1-3-22 Yaesu Chuo-ku (3271 0971/fax 3271 0977).
Hotel services *Air-conditioning. Conference facilities. Fax. Laundry. Multilingual staff. Parking. Restaurant. Safe.* **Room services** *Cable/satellite TV. Hairdryer (rental). Ironing facilities (rental). Room service (7.30am-10pm). Tea in room (Japanese).*

Budget

Ueno

Tsukuba Hotel
2-7-8 Moto Asakusa, Taito-ku (3834 2556/fax 3839 1785). Inaricho station/JR Ueno station. **Rooms** 111. **Rates** *single* ¥3,000-¥5,800; *double* ¥8,000-¥13,500. **No credit cards. Map 8**
A basic business hotel in the downtown area of Ueno, this is clean and good value for money. If you can, opt for a Japanese-style room, partly because it's more fun, partly because tidying the futon away in the morning will make the tiny room seem that much bigger. Western-style rooms come with their own bathing facilities, but if you stay in a Japanese room you'll be expected to bathe in the communal bath on the ground floor. The nearby Ginza subway line can whisk you to all the major tourist sites.
Branch: Iriya Station Hotel, 1-25-1 Iriya, Taito-ku (3872 7111/fax 3872 7111).
Hotel services *Air-conditioning. Japanese/western style rooms. Japanese bath.* **Room services** *Tea in room (Japanese). TV (coin).*

Hotel Edoya
3-20-3 Yushima, Bunkyo-ku (3833 8751/fax 3541 3263). Yushima station. **Rooms** 49. **Rates** *single* ¥7,850-¥8,950 (¥5,890-¥6,930 weekends); *double* ¥12,930 (¥9,930 weekends). **Credit** AmEx, DC, JCB, MC, V. **Map 14**
This mainly Japanese-style ryokan, not far from Ueno Park, offers good accommodation at fair prices. There's a small Japanese tearoom and garden on the first floor, and the roof has an open-air hot bath open to both men and women. The mahjong room package is popular with local gamblers.
Hotel services *Air-conditioning. Fax. Multilingual staff. Parking. Restaurant (Japanese).*
Room services *Hairdryer. Ironing facilities. Modem line. Tea (Japanese)/coffee service.*

Ryokan Katsutaro
4-16-8 Ikenohata, Taito-ku (3821 9808/fax 3821 4789). Nezu station. **Rooms** 7. **Rates** *single* ¥4,500 (no bath); *double* ¥8,400-¥9,000. **Credit** AmEx, MC, V. **Map 8**
In a backstreet on the other side of Ueno Park, Katsutaro is a small, friendly ryokan with good-sized rooms and the atmosphere of a real family home (which it is). Rooms can be occupied by up to four people, at an extra charge of roughly ¥4,000 per person. The owner speaks a little English, but keep a phrasebook handy.

Hotel services *Air-conditioning. Fax. Japanese rooms. Laundry. Safe. Tea/coffee downstairs.*
Room services *Ironing facilities (on request). TV.*

Ryokan Sawanoya
2-3-11 Yanaka, Taito-ku (3822 2251/fax 3822 2252). Nezu station. **Rooms** 12. **Rates** *single* ¥4,700-¥5,000 (no bath); *double* ¥8,800-¥9,400. **Credit** AmEx, MC, ¥TC, V. **Map 32**
One of the few ryokan to encourage foreign visitors, Sawanoya has a small library of English-language guidebooks and novels and the owner is studying to improve her already passable English. Rooms are small but comfortable, and there are signs in English reminding you how to behave and use the bath. It's well situated for the cultural delights of Ueno Park and the old quarters of the Yanaka area. More expensive rooms have their own bath, cheaper ones have access to the communal bath and shower.
Hotel services *Air-conditioning. Coffee shop.*
Room services *Hairdryer (on request). Ironing facilities. Tea in room (Japanese). TV.*

Nihonbashi

Hotel Nihonbashi Saibo
3-16-3 Nihonbashi-Ningyocho, Chuo-ku (3668 2323/fax 3668 1669/saibo@POP12.odn.ne.jp). Ningyocho station. **Rooms** 126. **Rates** *single* ¥7,800-¥8,400; *double* ¥9,000-¥12,000. **No credit cards.**
This squeezes into the budget category on account of its double-room price. The downside is that rooms are quite small, and are western-style. That said, there are business hotels offering a similar standard of accommodation but charging much more. Don't expect to be able to get across anything but the most basic requests in English. Convenient for TCAT, the city-centre airport check-in service.
Hotel services *Air-conditioning. Conference facilities. Fax. Restaurants (2). Safe.* **Room services** *Ironing facilities (on request). Modem line (third floor only). Radio. Tea in room (Japanese). TV.*

Elsewhere

Kimi Ryokan
2-36-8 Ikebukuro, Toshima-ku (3971 3766). Ikebukuro station. **Rooms** 41. **Rates** *single* ¥4,500; *double* ¥6,500-¥7,500. **No credit cards. Map 1**
A foreigner-friendly ryokan with simple Japanese-style rooms. Bathing and toilet facilities are communal but immaculate; there's a Japanese bath for use at set times. Downstairs in the communal lounge, backpackers and travellers exchange gossip, and the noticeboard carries job and long-term accommodation info. Kimi also runs an information and accommodation service for foreigners apartment-hunting in Tokyo (3986 1604), and a telephone answering service for businesspeople (3986 1895). Very popular with budget travellers, so book ahead.
Hotel services *Air-conditioning. Fax. Multilingual staff. Safe. Tea in lounge.*
Room services *Hairdryer (on request). Ironing facilities (on request). TV.*

How to behave in a ryokan

Staying in a ryokan, or Japanese-style inn, is a memorable experience, and although Japanese hosts are always forgiving of westerners' social faux pas, there are some simple rules of conduct. On arrival, you are expected to take off your shoes in the entrance hall and wear the slippers provided. The slippers are for walking through the communal areas. Once you arrive at your room, remove your slippers and walk on the tatami (straw mat floor) barefoot or in stockinged feet. One thing you may notice is the absence of a bed. Later in the evening (usually around 8pm), staff will come to make your futon up for you on the floor.

Inside the room, Japanese green tea and a flask of hot water are provided, perhaps with Japanese biscuits or sweets. The décor will include a *shoji* (paper sliding screen) and a *tokonoma* (alcove), which is for decoration, not luggage storage. Inside the cupboard, you'll find a *yukata* (dressing gown) and *tanzen* (bed jacket), which you can wear around the ryokan and which double as pyjamas. When you don the yukata, put the left side over the right.

Many ryokan have communal bathing facilities, and the usual rules for bathing in Japan apply (*see Directory p247*). After a bath and a good night's sleep, you will usually be awoken at around 8am with a Japanese-style breakfast, and staff will tidy away your futon.

Please note that because most ryokan are small family-run businesses, they tend to lock up early. If you think you may return or arrive late, try to give your hosts fair warning.

Sakura Hotel

2-21-4 Kanda-Jinbocho, Chiyoda-ku (3261 3939/fax 3264 2777/sakusaku@po.iijnet.or.jp). Jinbocho station. **Rooms** 42. **Rates** *single* ¥6,800; *double* ¥8,000. **Credit** AmEx, DC, JCB, MC, V. **Map 9**
A haven for backpackers, Sakura offers the option of shared rooms sleeping six people for ¥3,600 per person per night. Staff speak good English and are on duty 24 hours. Rooms are tiny but clean, and all are non-smoking. Book well in advance.
Hotel services *Air-conditioning. Bar. Coffee shop. Disabled: access. Fax. Laundry. Multilingual staff. No-smoking rooms. Safe.* **Room services** *Hairdryer. Ironing facilities. Modem line (one room). Tea in room (Japanese). TV. Website: www.iijnet.or.jp/yas/sakura/*

Sakura Ryokan

2-6-2 Iriya, Taito-ku (3876 8118/fax 3873 9456). Iriya station. **Rooms** 20. **Rates** *single* ¥5,300-¥6,300; *double* ¥9,600-¥10,600. **Credit** AmEx, JCB, MC, V.
Ten minutes' walk from Asakusa's temple complex, this friendly, traditional family-run ryokan goes back over 70 years. Of the 12 Japanese-style rooms, only two have their own bathrooms, while seven of the eight western-style rooms have baths. There's a communal bath on each floor. By the reception desk there's a rack of tourist leaflets and info in English.
Hotel services *Air-conditioning. Beer vending machine. Disabled: access. Fax. Japanese/western rooms. Laundry.* **Room services** *Cable TV. Hair dryer (on request). Ironing facilities (on request). Tea/coffee in room.*

Asia Center of Japan

8-10-32 Akasaka, Minato-ku (3402 6111/fax 3402 0738). Nogizaka station. **Rooms** 166.
Rates *single* ¥5,100-¥7,500; *double* ¥6,800-¥10,500. **Credit** JCB, MC, V. **Map 12**
Founded by the Ministry of Foreign Affairs in the 1950s as a cheap place for visiting students, this now offers comfortable, no-frills accommodation to all visitors on a budget. The tiny rooms (the cheapest of which don't have baths) still bear the hallmarks of their institutional beginnings, but the backpackers constantly trooping out into the fashionable Aoyama area don't seem to mind. Rooms in the newer wing have been refurbished and have extras that the older rooms lack.
Hotel services *Air-conditioning. Business services. Coffee shop. Conference facilities. Currency exchange. Disabled: access; room; toilets. Fax. Laundry. Multilingual staff. Parking. Restaurant. Safe.* **Room services** *Hairdryer (new wing). Ironing facilities. Modem line (on request). Radio. Tea/coffee in room (new wing). TV.*

YMCA Asia Youth Center

2-5-5 Sarugaku-cho, Chiyoda-ku (3233 0611/fax 3233 0633). Ochanomizu station. **Rooms** 55.
Rates (non-members) *single* ¥7,000; *double* ¥13,000; *triple* ¥16,800; (members) *single* ¥6,500; *double* ¥12,000; *triple* ¥15,300. **Credit** JCB, MC, $¥TC, V. **Map 9**
The YMCA Asia Youth Center offers many of the same facilities and services you'd expect at a regular hotel, a fact that is reflected in its relatively high prices. The smallish rooms are western-style with their own bathrooms.
Hotel services *Air-conditioning. Conference facilities. Disabled: access. Fax. Laundry. Multilingual staff. Restaurant. Safe.* **Room services** *Tea in room (Japanese). TV.*

Minshuku

A *minshuku* is the Japanese equivalent of bed and breakfast accommodation, offering visitors the chance to stay in a real family environment for around ¥5,000 per night. Reserve at least two days in advance.

Love hotels

One of Japan's most famous modern gifts to the world, the love hotel is designed purely for sex. Their success is the direct result of the lack of living space enjoyed by most Tokyo dwellers, and they can equally be used by mum and dad, trying to get away from the kids for a couple of hours, as by the kids, trying to do the reverse. Naturally, they're also popular with co-workers or lovers 'playing away from home'.

For the budget tourist, their appeal rests largely on the price: most charge around ¥8,000 per room per night. For your money, you get a room with a large double bed, a couple of condoms and, probably, a large, immaculately clean bathroom, usually with a tub for two. Other extras may include clean underwear, porn videos, karaoke equipment, vibrating beds, sex toy vending machines, a sauna or even a swimming pool. As with all hotels, the more you pay, the more you can expect in the way of extras. The downside to using a love hotel for accommodation is that you're not usually expected to check in before 10pm, and once you're in, you're not free to come and go as you please. Using one as a base is out of the question. Still, if you're happy to leave your belongings in a station locker all day and retrieve them at night, staying in a different love hotel every night can be fun, if exhausting.

Love hotels tend to flourish close to high concentrations of nightlife, such as Shibuya, Shinjuku and Ikebukuro. They are easily identified from the outside by their garish pink or purple neon signs, blacked-out windows and discreet entrances, often shrouded by shrubbery so customers can avoid the unwanted attention of passers-by. Most offer two rates on a board outside; the cheaper is for a two- or three-hour break (*kyuke*), the more expensive one is the overnight rate. Inside the hotel lobby, you will usually be confronted by illuminated pictures of the rooms on offer. If it's not illuminated, it's busy. Push a button beneath the picture to reserve it, then pay the desk clerk (whose face is usually discreetly hidden by a glass panel) and collect your key (if the doors are not electrically operated). Most love hotels do not accept credit cards. Because they tend to exist in clusters, if you can't get in at the ones below, there'll probably be another option next door.

Ikebukuro

London Hotel
2-3-8 Nishi-Ikebukuro, Toshima-ku (3984 0511). Ikebukuro station. **Rates** *rest* from ¥8,000; *stay* from ¥13,000.
One of the few love hotels that takes bookings, and one of even fewer with its own website.
Website: www.iijnet.or.jp/hotel-london/

En
2-12-2 Ikebukuro, Toshima-ku (3988 3988). Ikebukuro station. **Rates** *rest* from ¥4,500; *stay* from ¥7,500. **Map 1**
Thoroughly respectable from the outside, thoroughly cheeky on the inside. There's few extras and rooms are on the small side, a fact reflected in the price.

Shibuya

Dixy Inn
2-15 Maruyama-cho, Shibuya-ku (3461 7349). Shibuya station. **Rates** *rest* from ¥4,000; *stay* from ¥7,800. **Map 4**
One of a huge number of love hotels in Shibuya's Dogenzaka area, the Dixy has an all-American theme. Games and a Wurlitzer jukebox, for a price.

Villa Giulia
2-27-8 Dogenzaka, Shibuya-ku (3770 7781). Shibuya station. **Rates** *rest* from ¥5,500; *stay* from ¥9,500. **Map 4**
The Giulia's rooms resemble regular hotel rooms more than many of its competitors'.

Shinjuku

G7
2-5-5 Kabuki-cho, Shinjuku-ku (3232 0007). Shinjuku station. **Rates** *rest* from ¥4,500; *stay* from ¥7,500. **Map 3b**
Kabuki-cho probably has more love hotels than any other area. Stepping into this one is like walking out on to the bridge of the Starship Enterprise.

Wako
2-35-9 Kabuki-cho, Shinjuku-ku (3200 2111). Shinjuku station. **Rates** *rest* from ¥4,500; *stay* from ¥7,200. **Map 3b**
Unfortunately named and thoroughly basic.

Japan Minshuku Association
4-10-15 Takadanobaba, Shinjuku-ku (3364 1855). Takadanobaba station. **Open** 10am-5pm Mon-Fri; 10am-1pm Sat. **Map 25**
This is slightly out of the centre, in the studenty Takadanobaba area.

Japan Minshuku Centre
Kotsu Kaikan Bldg B1, 2-10-1 Yurakucho, Chiyoda-ku (3216 6556/fax 3216 6557). Yurakucho station. **Open** 15 June-15 Aug 9am-9pm, closed Sun; rest of year 10am-7pm, closed Sun. **Map 7**
In the basement of the shopping and eating complex

on the Ginza side of Yurakucho station. English-speaking assistants can help you find a minshuku.

Capsule hotels

Business Inn Shinbashi and Annexe
4-12-11 Shinbashi, Minato-ku, 4-12-10 Shinbashi, Minato-ku (3431 1391/annexe 3431 1020). Shinbashi station. **Capsules** 88 (56 annexe). **Rates** *Mon-Fri* ¥4,300; *Sat, Sun* ¥3,950. **Closed** 31 Dec-3 Jan. **No credit cards. Map 13** *Men only. Air-conditioned. Alarm. Daytime shower & siesta service. Radio. Reading lamp. TV. Video.*

Shinjuku Kuyakusyo-Mae Capsule Hotel
1-2-5 Kabuki-cho, Shinjuku-ku (3208 0084). Shinjuku station. **Capsules** 480. **Rates** ¥4,200+. **No credit cards. Map 3b** *Men only. Japanese restaurant. Massage. Sauna.*

Capsule Inn Akasaka
6-14-1 Akasaka, Minato-ku (3588 1811). Akasaka station. **Capsules** 600. **Rate** ¥4,000. **No credit cards. Map 2** *Men only. Bath. Conference room. Massage. Sauna. Shower.*

Capsule Hotel Azuma
3-15-1 Higashi-Ueno, Taito-ku (3831 4047/fax 3831 7103). Ueno station. **Capsules** 144. **Rates** ¥3,500. **No credit cards. Map 8** *Men only. Alarm. Bath. Fax (paid). Intercom. Japanese restaurant. Radio. Satellite TV (paid). Sauna. TV. Toothbrush (free). Towel.*

Central Inn Shibuya
1-19-14 Dogenzaka, Shibuya-ku (3770 5255). Shibuya station. **Capsules** 140. **Rates** ¥3,650. **No credit cards. Map 4** *Men only. Bath (public). Shower.*

Long-term accommodation

For foreigners, finding long-term accommodation in Tokyo can be an absolute nightmare. Many Japanese landlords don't want foreigners living in their houses, and refuse to deal with them. This has led to the appearance of companies specialising in letting to foreigners, some of which let apartment space by the week. When you find an apartment, you will be required to pay a damage deposit (*shikikin*), usually equivalent to 1-3 months' rent, a brokerage fee (*chukairyo*) to the agent, usually another month's rent, and finally and most ridiculously, key money (*reikin*), usually one or two months' rent. The latter often has foreigners (and people from outside Tokyo) chewing the rug in frustration: it's a non-refundable way of saying thank you to the landlord for having you. You then have to find a month's rent in advance.

Many foreigners fall back on so-called *gaijin* houses – apartment buildings full of foreigners who share bathrooms, cooking facilities and, in some cases, rooms. All of the places that are listed below are used

to dealing with foreigners and offer a range of accommodation, from dorm-style to individual apartments. Deposits are refundable.

Crystal Village
1-2-10 Arai, Nakano-ku (3388 7625/fax 3388 7627). Nakano station. **Credit** AmEx, MC, V.
Crystal Village offers private rooms with shared bathroom and kitchen for ¥21,500 per week, or for ¥75,000 per month. Studio apartments cost ¥44,000 per week or ¥130,000 per month (a ¥30,000 deposit is required).

Fontana
Hoyo Daini Bldg, 4-19-7 Kita-Shinjuku, Shinjuku (3382 0151/fax 3382 0018/fontana@hpo.net). Higashi-Nakano station. **No credit cards.**
A bona fide estate agent with a section devoted to English-speaking clients, Fontana can also find medium-term accommodation. Studio apartments are ¥39,000-¥45,000 a week (¥50,000 deposit), family-sized apartments ¥120,000-¥500,000 a month (¥100,000 deposit; for terms of three months or longer, one month's deposit).

Hoyo Tokyo
Hoyo Daini Bldg, 4-19-7 Kita-Shinjuku, Shinjuku (3362 0658/fax 3362 9438). Okubo station. **No credit cards.**
Studio apartments are ¥39,000-¥65,000 per week (¥50,000 deposit) or ¥120,000-¥230,000 per month, family apartments are ¥300,000-¥500,000 a month (¥100,000 deposit; for terms of three months or longer, one month's deposit).

Oak House
4-30-3 Takashimadaira, Itabashi-ku (3979 8810). Shin-Takashimadaira station (Mita line). **No credit cards.**
In the middle of nowhere, closer to Saitama than Shinjuku, this has shared dorm-style rooms for ¥35,000 a week, with private rooms (shared bathroom and kitchen) for ¥47,000- ¥80,000 per month. A ¥30,000 deposit is required.

Sakura House
K-1 Bldg 7F, 7-2-6 Nishi-Shinjuku, Shinjuku-ku (5330 5250/fax 5330 5251/sakurahs@pc4.so-net.ne.jp). Shinjuku station. **No credit cards.**
This is owned by the people who operate the Sakura Hotel (*see above*). A room in a guesthouse with shared bathroom and kitchen costs between ¥60,000 and ¥110,000 a month; apartments run from ¥105,000 to ¥190,000 per month. A ¥30,000 deposit is required.
Website: http://www03.u-page.so-net.ne.jp/pc4/sakurahs/

Town House
508, 2-7-6 Yoyogi, Shibuya-ku (3320 3201/fax 3320 3202). Shinjuku station. **No credit cards.**
A private room with a shared bathroom and kitchen is ¥40,000-¥70,000 a month; apartments are ¥55,000-¥200,000 per month. The deposit depends on individual landlords.

Restaurants

It's possible that Tokyo has more places to eat out than any other city in the world, and the range and quality of food is unbeatable.

Tokyo is a world-class food city and eating out is a big part of the enjoyment of a visit to Japan. Most visitors are familiar with some of the country's better-known specialities, having tried *sushi*, *tempura* or *sukiyaki* on their home turf. But Japanese food at home offers a depth and variety never touched on outside of Japan. With over 100,000 restaurants, it's possible to spend a month eating out in Tokyo, experimenting with food ranging from the ridiculous (octopus balls) to the sublime (¥40,000 multi-course affairs), and never have the same food twice.

The quality of food preparation in Tokyo is very high. Ingredients are usually fresh, while sanitation and hygiene are impeccable. Even street food is quite safe. One common complaint about eating out here is the cost. True, a night out in a fancy *ryotei* is not for the financially faint-hearted, and a walk through the 'gift fruit' departments of Japanese supermarkets can be an exercise in surrealism. ¥10,000 melons, nestled in individual padded boxes, really do exist. But this is the high end and, like anywhere else, there's also a low end and a whole spectrum in between.

The cheapest deals on meals are likely to be found in an **izakaya, nomiya** or **aka-chochin.** These have often been likened to pubs, but the analogy is only partially apt. While lots of drinking does go on, much of the activity also centres around eating – and you'll never find one open at 11am. Izakaya ('*sake* house'), nomiya ('drinking place') and aka-chochin ('red lantern' for the characteristic red chochin lantern that hangs outside) are a unique Japanese institution. They are raucous, crowded, smoky and casual.

Japanese cuisine by type

Japanese restaurants usually concentrate on one type of cuisine, and you're more likely to find the best of that type at a speciality restaurant than at a general eatery. Japanese chefs take justifiable pride in the quality of their food.

FUGU

Fugu, or blowfish, is one of Japan's great delicacies. This obsession is a source of puzzlement to foreigners, because eating fugu, if it has not been prepared by a skilled and licensed chef, is a bit like playing Russian roulette. Fugu contains a deadly neurotoxin that, if not carefully removed, will result in numbness and even death. Deaths are

rare, though, and aficionados will avidly ingest the delicate-tasting fugu between October and March when it is in season.

GRILLS & COUNTER FOODS

Kushiage

Kushiage is skewered pieces of chicken, beef, seafood, shiitake or other vegetables deep fried to a golden brown in a batter and breadcrumbs. Sometimes served with sauce, salt or just plain, kushiage can be ordered as a set but it is more fun to sit at a counter and order one by one or ask for a *moriawase*, or assortment.

Okonomiyaki

Okonomiyaki is often described as a Japanese pancake or pizza, though a more apt description is an omelette. An egg-based batter is cooked on a grill, usually by the customer, and stuffed with seafood, meat and/or vegetables. It's customary to choose your own ingredients.

Teppanyaki

Beef is a luxury item in Japan, but Japanese beef (especially Kobe beef) is exceptionally good. If you're not averse to spending a little money, then teppanyaki (literally 'grilled') is a wonderful way to experience Japanese-style steak. Tender, thin slices of beef, seafood and vegetables will be grilled to sizzling perfection in front of you.

Yakitori

Yakitori are small skewered pieces of chicken cooked over a crackling charcoal grill, served with salt or a slightly sweet soy-based glaze. Usually served in small, smoke-filled izakaya, yakitori is a tasty accompaniment to beer, sake or *shochu*. Though yakitori is literally grilled chicken, most yakitori-ya also do wonderful things with skewered vegetables, grilled until tender with a crust of salt, often served with lemon juice.

HAUTE CUISINE

Kaiseki-ryori

Kaiseki-ryori is Japan's beautiful, formal haute cuisine. It originated over four centuries ago as a light accompaniment to the tea ceremony.

A kaiseki meal is a sequence of small dishes, often simply but stunningly prepared to reflect seasonal bounties. Courses follow one after the other, but slowly; a one-hour parade would be considered

*Try an **izakaya** for cheap eats.*

the one pot: pluck out choice, seasonal titbits with special long chopsticks, drop them into the small bowl provided or dip in sauce before enjoying.

Sukiyaki
Sukiyaki is a dish of tender, thinly sliced beef, vegetables, tofu and other ingredients, such as *shirataki* (devil's tongue noodles) cooked in a soy sauce broth that has been slightly sweetened with mirin (a sweet liquor used in cooking). A raw egg is set before each diner in a small bowl. Break the egg, beat it slightly, then dip sumptuous morsels into the egg.

Shabu-shabu
Another 'national dish', shabu-shabu refers to the sound made as paper-thin beef is swished back and forth in a steaming, bubbling broth cooked at the table in a copper pot.

ODEN
Oden is a simple seasonal dish of fish cakes, tofu, vegetables and *konyaku* (devil's tongue) simmered in a light, kelp-based broth, served with a dash of *karashi* (hot mustard) for flavouring.

RICE & NOODLES

Rice
Japanese rice is short-grained, moist and eaten plain. It is usually served at the end of a meal, with tea and a dish of pickles. Plain rice and alcohol are never consumed together; ordering rice at the end of the meal signifies that you are done drinking.

Noodles
Noodles are very popular, especially at lunchtime, and there are many noodle dishes and restaurants (*soba-ya*). Soba are thin buckwheat noodles served with a light soy-based sauce. When served hot, soba are topped with chopped spring onions, fried tofu, tempura or other ingredients. When cold, they are served on a bamboo 'plate' with a small bowl of sauce. Another noodle found at soba-ya is *udon*, a fatter, wheat noodle that is slightly more filling.

Ramen is perhaps Japan's favourite fast food. Borrowed from the Chinese, these yellow egg noodles are served in a rich, meat-based stock, flavoured with miso, soy sauce or salt, and topped with vegetables or *cha-shu*, barbecued pork.

SUSHI & SASHIMI
Sushi in Japan (except *kaiten zushi*) is only ever prepared by highly trained male chefs (Females are banned because it's thought that the monthly rise in their body temperature affects the flavour of the fish.). The most popular types of raw fish are sashimi and sushi. Sashimi is usually served as an hors d'oeuvre. It is very thinly sliced raw fish, usually one of the milder fishes such as tuna (*maguro*), yellowtail (*hamachi*), sea bream (*tai*) or squid (*ika*).

a 'hurried' kaiseki meal. Most meals will include *sashimi* and cooked fishes, a soup, seasonal and often unusual vegetables such as *sansai* (mountain vegetables) and a small amount of meat, either beef or chicken. Rice comes only at the end of the meal.

Kaiseki is the most expensive of all Japanese foods. It is usually served in ryotei – beautiful rooms or houses set amid stunning carp-filled ponds and gardens meant to conjure up images of historic Kyoto. It's also an evening's entertainment; you will be presented, rather than served, course after course by kimono-clad waitresses bearing neverending flacons of warm or chilled sake. The menu – almost always a set course – will be decided by the ryotei, and usually starts at around ¥8,000.

Shojin-ryori
Shojin-ryori is a form of vegetarian cuisine that was imported from China by a Zen monk and developed in Zen monasteries in Japan. Shojin-ryori eschews not only meat and fish, but onion and garlic as well, resulting in a cuisine that is subtle and delicate, even in a food culture known for its subtlety and delicacy.

NABEMONO & ONE-POT COOKING
Nabemono is a winter cuisine – one-pot stews cooked at the table, in a heavy earthenware pot (*nabe*) over a gas flame. Everyone is served from

Sushi is often incorrectly thought to mean raw fish. It is actually lightly vinegared rice, usually moulded into small mounds and topped with slices of raw fish, roe, shellfish or cooked items including egg, shrimp and seafood.

TEMPURA
Tempura is fish or vegetables delicately deep-fried in *koromo* (batter). The secret to good tempura is thought to lie in the oil. While outside Tokyo, a light vegetable oil is employed, Tokyo chefs prefer the heavier, more aromatic sesame oil. In either style, only high-quality, expensive oil is used, and when properly executed, there is no oily aftertaste.

TONKATSU
The 'katsu' in 'tonkatsu' means cutlet, a widely and wildly popular dish introduced during the Meiji period when eating meat began to catch on. Katsu is now almost always pork, usually very lean cuts of sirloin, dredged in flour, dipped in egg, rolled in breadcrumbs and deep-fried.

UNAGI
Unagi, or eel, is another of Japan's great delicacies. Eels are split open, filleted, basted with an aromatic brown glaze of soy sauce and mirin and very slowly cooked over a charcoal fire. Unagi is thought to be a restorative, and is consumed almost religiously during the hot months of July and August for stamina, to improve eyesight and even virility.

VEGETARIAN
Tokyo has few vegetarian restaurants, but because so much of the diet is based on fish (fish stock in miso soups, for example) even options like soba that contain no meat will not be vegetarian.

One alternative is a shojin-ryori restaurant (*see above*), although these are often quite expensive. Your best bet is the izakaya – although most specialise in various forms of meat on a stick, you can order an incredible variety of foods à la carte. Try grilled vegetables, *onigiri* (rice balls) with *ume* (plum) filling, and tofu dishes.

YAKINIKU
Korean restaurants are very popular, mostly for yakiniku (Korean barbecue). Tender, marinated meats are grilled at the table, then dipped in a slightly sweet sauce and eaten with rice and *kimchee* (pickled veg). When ordering meat, ask for *rosu* (lean beef) or *karubi* (marbled beef from ribs).

Japanese drinks

SAKE
Japan's national brew is made from fermented rice; usually colourless, it has the highest percentage of alcohol (by volume) of any fermented drink, and packs a wallop. Cheap sake, even drunk in small quantity, can result in legendary hangovers.

There are over 1,000 sake breweries in Japan producing thousands of brands and are a number of types and grades of sake. *Junmaishu* contains only white rice and rice *koji* (starter). It is generally full-bodied and pungent. *Honjozo* contains rice, rice koji and brewer's alcohol, and is often smoother. There's also *ginjoshu*, or special brew, which can be either of the two categories. It's distinguished by special techniques or methods used in its brewing, resulting in a distinctive taste.

Sake may be drunk hot or cold. Purists insist that heating it past a certain point destroys its bouquet, but hot sake, or *atsukan*, is very popular; there's nothing like its head-clearing warmth during a bone-chilling Tokyo winter. When hot, it's served from flacons called *tokkuri*. Cold sake, or *reishu*, often arrives in a glass, a small 'box' called *masu*, or a 'snake's eye' *choko* or cup.

SHOCHU
Often likened to vodka or moonshine, shochu is a potent liquor made from grains such as rice, barley or potato. Much cheaper than good sake, it is popular among the young; in summer an ice-cold lemon sour really hits the spot.

BEER
The market has long been ruled by big brewers such as Kirin and Sapporo. The bad news is that most of the beers taste similar. The good news is that they are quite good and relatively inexpensive. Beer can be ordered by the bottle (*bin*) or draught (*nama*). Bottled beer is drunk out of tiny glasses; nama comes in three sizes of mugs (*jokki*): *sho* (small), *chu* (medium) and *dai* (large).

TEA
Japan is famous for its *ocha* (green tea), particularly the intricate tea ceremony. What differentiates ocha from its black-leaf counterpart is that the tea leaves are steamed after picking. Japanese tea is drunk as it is served; no one would ever add milk or sugar. High-quality teas can be tasted at teahouses; most department stores have a tea section.

Restaurants

Unless otherwise noted, prices given are for one person with moderate amounts of alcohol.

Asian
Roppongi

Bangkok
Woo Bldg 3F, 3-8-8 Roppongi, Minato-ku (3408 7353). Roppongi station. **Open** 11.30am-3pm, 5-11pm, Mon-Sat; noon-9pm Sun. Closed every third Sun. **Average** ¥3,500. **No credit cards. Menu in English. Map 2**

The menu is huge, the food is good and service is fast – just the ticket to get you back out into Roppongi play land. Tom kha kai soup arrives in a clay pot, turned a beautiful orange colour from the liberal dose of peppers. Goes well with their minced meat larbs, well flavoured with lemon grass, cooling mint and tangy onion. Plenty of veggie fare, too.

Bengawan Solo

Kaneko Bldg 1F, 7-18-13 Roppongi, Minato-ku (3408 5698). Roppongi station. **Open** 11.30am-2.30pm, 5-11pm daily. **Average** ¥4,000. **Credit** all major cards. **Menu in English. Map 2**
Indonesian fare in Tokyo has long been synonymous with Bengawan Solo. After all, it's been around since 1954, and being one of the first 'ethnic' joints to open, is often credited with single-handedly launching Tokyo's spicy food awakening. While the menu never changes, it remains consistently yummy: great gado gado (a salad smothered in a rich, spicy peanut sauce), shrimp in coconut cream, lots of curries, noodle and fried rice dishes.

Bombay Café

Iida Bldg 1F, 1-8-4 Nishi-Azabu, Minato-ku (3404 9988). Roppongi station. **Open** 11.30-5am Mon-Thur; 11.30-7am (last order 6am) Fri, Sat. **Average** lunch ¥1,000, dinner & late night ¥2,500. **Menu in English. Map 2**
A local favourite. Not only are the prices right and the food good, but if your dining companion fails to entertain, there is non-stop Indian music complete with incredibly cheesy videos that perfectly match the décor and a lively collection of Indian movie posters. The onion pakoras and curries are superb. A ¥350 draft beer happy hour (6-8pm) will send you out smiling without gouging your wallet. If the service seems a little slow, bear in mind everything is made to order.

Erawan

Roi Bldg 13F, 5-5-1 Roppongi, Minato-ku (3404 5741). Roppongi station. **Open** 5-11.30pm daily. **Average** ¥4,000. **Credit** all major cards. **Menu in English. Map 2**
While the quality of food at Erawan has been a little erratic of late, it's still fairly reliable and its place on the 13th floor of Roppongi's Roi Bldg (notorious for the hanky-panky that goes on on some of its other floors) offers one of the best dining views in town. Teak décor, understated Thai decorations, and enviable elbow room if the staff would only get over the (very common in Tokyo) habit of seating all new customers immediately adjacent to the preceding arrival.

Monsoon Café

2-10-1 Nishi-Azabu, Minato-ku (5467 5221). Roppongi station. **Average** ¥4,000. **Credit** all major cards. **Menu in English. Map 2**
The faux-Indonesian jungle décor might be a little contrived, but the bar is good and the food varied, while the mixed foreign/Japanese crowd tends toward the thirtysomething rather than the twenties crowd that haunts much of Shibuya. The menu will please all-comers: curries, salads, soups and satay use free-range chicken, organically grown rice and no MSG, while spice is adjusted to suit your heat tolerance. **Branch** 15-4 Hachiyama-cho, Shibuya-ku (5489 3789).

Phothai Down Under

Five Plaza Bldg 2F, 5-18-21 Roppongi, Minato-ku (3505 1504). Roppongi station. **Open** noon-2.30pm, 5pm-5am, daily. **Average** ¥4,000. **Credit** all major cards. **Menu in English. Map 2**
A Thai-Australian restaurant, a fairly extensive menu of middling-quality Thai food and enormous Aussie steaks. Think of the Thai dishes as starters, choose a cut of meat from the tray brought to your table, and wash it all down with Australian wine or Thai beer. Better yet, try mixing it all together – somehow it works.

Shibuya

Jembatan Merah

Higashi Indo Kan 1, 3F, 1-3 Maruyama-cho, Shibuya-ku (3476 6424). Shibuya station. **Open** 11am-11pm daily (no lunch on Sun). **Average** ¥2,500. **Credit** bills over ¥5,000, all major cards. **Menu in English. Map 4**
The Indonesian fare at JM is not quite as good as at Bengawan Solo (*see above*) and quality does vary from location to location. But with branches dotted conveniently around the Yamanote line, it greatly broadens Tokyo's Indonesian horizon with the added attraction of good vegetarian offerings. There are seven dishes starring tempeh (a fermented soybean patty with a slightly nutty flavour), middling gado gado salad, and an extravagant 12-course 'special menu' for those who can't be troubled to navigate the many pages of the menu.
Branches I-Land Tower B1, 6-5-1 Nishi-Shinjuku, Shinjuku-ku (5323 4214); 3-20-6 Akasaka, Minato-ku (3588 0794); Sunshine City Alpa B1, 3-1 Higashi-Ikebukuro, Toshima-ku (3987 2290).

Shinjuku

Angkor Wat

1-38-13 Yoyogi, Shibuya-ku (3370 3019). Yoyogi station. **Open** 11am-2pm, 5-10pm, Tue-Sun. **Average** ¥2,500. **No credit cards. No English menu. Map 17**
What this place lacks in ambience it makes up for in food. It may look like a cafeteria, and indeed the food comes with amazing dispatch, but that may only be because they're lining up to get in. Cheerful Cambodian waitresses (daughters of the proprietor) will help you navigate the menu; don't leave out an order of chicken salad and chahan (fried rice). **Branch:** 1-16-6 Dogenzaka, Shibuya-ku (3477 1010). Shibuya station.

Ban Thai

Dai-ichi Metro Bldg 3F, 1-23-14 Kabuki-cho, Shinjuku-ku (3207 0068). Shinjuku station. **Open** 5pm-midnight Mon-Fri; 11.30am-midnight Sat, Sun. **Average** ¥3,000. **Credit** all major cards. **Menu in English. Map 3b**

Conveniently situated at the opening end of raunchy Kabuki-cho, this is the longest-standing Thai institution in town, and no wonder: while no longer the best (try Bangkok in Roppongi instead, *see above*), there's nothing on the extensive menu that will disappoint. The curries are especially good.

Hyakunincho Yataimura
2-20-25 Hyakunin-cho, Shinjuku-ku (5386 3320). Okubo station. **Open** 5pm-4am Mon-Sat; 5pm-2am Sun. **Average** ¥2,500. **No credit cards. Menu partially in English.**
If you find yourself out all night or just looking for a break from polite Japanese service, this is the kind of low-rent place where 'waiters' might dish out your rice while puffing on a cigarette. Yataimura is a collection of food stalls, and proprietors will be aggressively for your orders. Sit down and prepare to be swarmed by as many as five people pointing out their specialities. There are pages of choices from places as diverse as Thailand, Indonesia, Taiwan and Fukien. Servings are huge, the 'décor' is atrocious – and this is one of the most fun places in town for a crowd. How many other places in Tokyo reek of duck and have a small herd of cats standing guard outside?

Elsewhere

Namaste Kathmandu
Wakatsuki Bldg B1, 2-34-12 Kichijoji-Honcho, Kichijoji, Musashino-shi (042 221 0057). Kichijoji station. **Open** 11am-3pm, 5-10.30pm, Mon-Wed, Fri-Sun. **Average** ¥3,000. **No credit cards. Menu in English. Map 24**
One of the sincerest places in Tokyo, this cosy little den makes you feel like you've walked into someone's home; the proprietors treat customers like family, passing around snapshots from Nepal and urging you to visit. There's only one chef, six tiny tables and a counter. Stay away from the alu tama – a dish purportedly much loved in Nepal – and you'll do fine.

Ninniku-ya
1-26-12 Ebisu, Shibuya-ku (5488 5540). Ebisu station. **Open** 6.15-10.30pm Mon-Sat. **Average** ¥5,000. **No credit cards. Menu in English. Map 20**
Ninniku is the Japanese word for garlic, and everything on the menu, with the possible exception of the drinks, is laced with copious amounts. The odours of towering garlic bread, vicious Thai curries, mouthwatering pasta and rice dishes with Chinese, Thai, Indian and other ethnic twists waft out on the streets, luring the uncommitted.

Peppermint Café
Grand Maison Kichijoji B1, 1-15-14 Kichijoji Minami-cho, Kichijoji, Musashino-shi (0422 79 3930). Kichijoji station. **Open** 5.30pm-1am daily. **Average** ¥2,500. **No credit cards. Menu in English. Map 24**
An open kitchen, *horikotatsu* table with reclining cushions from Thailand, lights and bamboo lattice-

work from Bali and Hong Kong decorate the interior of this 'Thai, Asian Foods Paradise Restaurant Bar' just a stone's throw from Inokashira Park. Thai mainstays like tom yom koong soup, pad Thai and green curry are Peppa's strengths, but it also serves Korean bibimbap, chicken salad Kampuchea style and Vietnamese vegetable rolls.

Chinese
Aoyama/Harajuku/Omotesando

Fumin
Aoyama Ohara Bldg B1, 5-7-17 Minami-Aoyama, Minato-ku (3498 4466). Omotesando station. **Open** 1-2.30pm, 5.30-9.45pm, Mon-Fri; 5.30-9.45pm Sat. **Average** ¥4,000. **No credit cards. No English menu. Map 12**
Most people in Tokyo haven't actually gone to Fumin; they've tried to go and given up because of a wait made torturous by the heady smells of garlic and Chinese seasonings. But oh how the wait is worth it. An extensive menu of funky home-style Chinese characterised by large servings liberally seasoned. Don't miss the (scallion) wonton or the greasy, garlicky aubergine. Just don't go too hungry.

Kaikatei
Odakyu Minami Aoyama Bldg B1, 7-8-1 Minami-Aoyama, Minato-ku (3499 5872). Omotesando station. **Average** ¥3,500. **No credit cards. No English menu. Map 2**
Like taking a step back in time to 1930s Shanghai: old beer posters, wooden clocks, dated LPs and odd murals of barbarian foreigners lend an air of wartime mystery to this atmospheric Chinese restaurant. Shrimp in crab sauce is delicately flavoured, the flavour of ginger, spring onion and shrimp predominating and a good match with mildly spicy Peking-style chicken with cashew nuts and rich black bean sauce. Avoid the gyoza and flat Heartland beer.

Ginza

Kihachi China
2-3-6 Ginza, Chuo-ku (5524 0761). Ginza station. **Open** for dim sum, à la carte and tea 11.30am-2.30pm, 2.30-4pm, 5-9.30pm, daily; course menu available 11.30am-2.30pm and 6-9pm **Average** lunch ¥2,500, dinner ¥4,000. **Credit** all major cards. **No English menu. Map 7**
If it's Chinese with style you're looking for, this understated, tastefully decorated restaurant near the Ginza shopping strip is the place to go. The dim sum lunch set (¥2,500) is a great choice for a long, filling midday meal. Dim sum, loosely translated, means 'touch your heart' and an afternoon's repast of these little stuffed dumplings nestled in bamboo steamers will no doubt do just that. Don't forget to kowtow when tea is poured: that is, tap your fingers twice on the table, as a gesture of thanks. Reservations rec-

ommended as it's usually packed with women, presumably out shopping.
Branch 2-11-1 Sendagaya, Shibuya-ku (5770 1555). Harajuku station.

Shikawa Hanten

Zenkoku Ryokan Kaikan 5-6F, 2-5-5 Hirakawa-cho, Chiyoda-ku (3263 9371). Nagata-cho station.
Open 11.30-2pm; 5-10pm (last order 9pm) daily. **Average** ¥2,000. **Credit** all major cards. **Menu in English. Map 16**
A popular summer dish is hiyashi chuka, cold Chinese-style noodles and chopped vegetables topped with either a sesame or vinegar sauce. At Shikawa the speciality is sesame, a rich, mildly spicy paste ladled over chilled al dente noodles, topped with sliced chicken and cucumbers. A refreshing summer treat in servings just the right size for lunch. Other Chinese dishes round out the menu.

Shinjuku

China Grill – Xenlon

Odakyu Hotel Century Southern Tower 19F, 2-2-1 Yoyogi, Shibuya-ku (3374 2080). Shinjuku station.
Open 11.30am-4.30pm, 5-11pm, daily.
Average lunch ¥1,500-¥5,000, dinner courses ¥7,000-¥15,000, à la carte about ¥7,000.
Credit all major cards. **Menu in English. Map 17**
Impeccable service and impressive views of the neon skyline make this stylish Chinese restaurant well worth the splurge. Cantonese fare with a nod toward western, rather than Japanese, influences includes dim sum at lunchtime, with over 36 choices, and multi-dish courses and à la carte choices at dinner.

Tokyo Kaisen Market

Tokyo Kaisen Ichiba 1-2F, 2-36-1 Kabuki-cho, Shinjuku-ku (5273 8301). Shinjuku station.
Open 5pm-midnight Mon-Fri; noon-midnight Sat, Sun. **Average** courses ¥4,000-¥6,500, à la carte about ¥2,500. **Credit** all major cards. **Menu in English. Map 3b**
There's something a little dodgy about this place, which is half its charm. It has something to do with the faint whiff of cats that greets diners, or the charcoal haze that limits visibility. Don't let this put you off; wherever there is fresh fish in Tokyo, there are cats. Most of the menu is seafood, prepared Chinese- or Japanese-style, though the kitchen does make forays into other parts of Asia, mainly Thailand. Select your seafood and the method of preparation: raw, broiled, fried, in dumplings and more.

East meets west

Aoyama/Harajuku/Omotesando

Fujimamas

6-3-2 Jingumae, Shibuya-ku (5485 2262). Harajuku station. **Open** 11am-11pm daily. **Average** ¥3,000. **Credit** all major cards. **Menu in English. Map 5**
Confident east-west fusion cuisine in a casual setting. Large servings and good prices, given the swanky address and sunny décor. A jokey menu lets you know they don't take themselves too seriously. Entrées, under the title 'Let's Go For a Wok' or 'Things that Make You Go UMMMMMMMM' won't disappoint. Don't miss Thai-style Caesar salad with crispy calamari croutons and lemon grass dressing.

Kaikatei, *where you can enjoy your Peking duck in an atmosphere of 1930s Shanghai.*

Rojak

*B1, 6-3-14 Minami-Aoyama, Minato-ku (3409
6764). Omotesando station.* **Open** noon-4pm,
6pm-midnight, daily. **Average** lunch ¥1,200,
dinner ¥3,000. **Credit** all major cards.
Menu in English. Map 2

Western-influenced Asian food in a lovely basement with candlelit nooks and crannies, high ceilings and jungle-motif wall coverings. Next to the
dining room is a comfy bar area with soft sofas
and a cigar humidor. Stellar salads with a unique
house dressing are served in large, dark wood
bowls that match the tables. Noodles, curries and
seafood, especially sashimi, get reinvented at
Rojak in sublime ways. Fair selection of wines
(mostly Australian), as well as German and
Belgian beers and the locally brewed Tokyo Ale.

Vision Network/Las Chicas

*5-47-6 Jingumae, Shibuya-ku (3407 6865).
Omotesando station.* **Open** 11am-11pm daily.
Average lunch ¥1,000; dinner ¥4,000.
Credit all major cards. **Menu in English. Map 4**

The most creative, foreigner-friendly space in town,
Vision Network is a gorgeous complex encompass-
ing several restaurants and bars (Las Chicas, Tokyo
Salon, Nude and Crome) that host revolving exhibitions of local talent. The bilingual staff (mostly
Australian) are friendly and helpful, and so on the
cutting edge of fashion as to constitute an exhibition
themselves. Potato wedges with sour cream and
Thai chilli sauce, cheesy polenta chips or homemade
bread with real butter are all meals in themselves,
perfect mates for earthy, sensuous Australian wines.

Shibuya

Sunda

*5-15 Kamiyama-cho, Shibuya-ku (3465 8858).
Shibuya station.* **Open** 6-11.30pm Mon-Sat.
Average ¥3,000. **Credit** all major cards.
Menu in English. Map 4

A mixed bag of east meets west delicacies (softshell
crab in Thai curry sauce) with live music nightly
and great (shaken, not blended) Margaritas.

Elsewhere

Asa

*Kitazawa Bldg 3F, 2-18-5 Kitazawa, Setagaya-ku
(3412 4118). Shimo-Kitazawa station
(Inokashira/Odakyu lines).* **Open** 11.30am-3pm,
6pm-midnight, Mon, Tue, Thur-Sun.
Average lunch ¥1,000, dinner ¥3,000.
No credit cards. No English menu. Map 29

Asa means 'hemp'; the owner has a thing for weed.
Hemp tablecloths, videos of pot growing free in the
wilds of Shizuoka, hemp literature and, in every single dish, crunchy hemp seeds. Try whole baked fish
with hemp seeds, crunchy chips braided like hemp
ropes with seedy salsa, drinks with hemp seeds, curries with hemp seeds... The one-note joke grows a
little tired after a while, but this intriguing place is
an out-of-your-head way to start an evening.

French

Aoyama/Harajuku/Omotesando

Aux Bacchanales

*Palais France 1F, 1-6 Jingumae, Shibuya-ku (5474
0076). Harajuku station.* **Open** 10am-midnight
(brasserie/café), 5.30pm-midnight (restaurant), daily.
Average ¥2,000. **Credit** all major cards (restaurant
only). **Menu in French. Map 5**

One of the rare Tokyo places where the action spills
out on the streets and people go to watch and be
watched – and drink themselves silly on relatively
inexpensive red wine. Features French cooking in a
casual bistro setting, with 'authentic' French café
furniture. All things considered, the food's pretty
good. The less atmospheric branch is in an office
block in the business district; opening hours differ.
Branch Ark Mori Bldg 2F, 1-12-32 Akasaka,
Minato-ku (3582 2225). Tameike-sanno station.

Chez Pierre

*1-23-10 Minami-Aoyama, Minato-ku (3475 1400).
Aoyama-itchome station.* **Open** 11.30am-2.30pm,
6-10pm, Tue-Sun. **Average** ¥7,000. **Credit** all major
cards. **Menu in French. Map 12**

Charming, unpretentious mom and pop place serving French provincial cuisine. The inside is warm
and inviting, while the floor-to-ceiling windows of
the café terrace are perfect for lingering over tea and
pastries. The seafood is popular. Recommended
wines, carefully selected, change regularly.

Elsewhere

La Dinette

*2-6-10 Takadanobaba, Shinjuku-ku (3200 6571).
Takadanobaba station.* **Open** 11.30am-1pm, 6-9pm,
Mon-Sat. **Average** ¥3,000. **No credit cards.**
Menu in French. Map 25

Reservations advised for this authentic bistro in the
low-rent student district of Takadanobaba. La
Dinette has been around for ages because it serves
simple French cuisine at affordable prices in stu-
dent-friendly portions. Almost always crowded, it's
not designed for romantic evenings, but to sate
prodigious appetites and send you out to play.

Health food/natural

Aoyama/Harajuku/Omotesando

Crayonhouse

*3-8-15 Kita-Aoyama, Minato-ku (3406 6409).
Omotesando station.* **Open** 11am-10pm daily.
Average ¥1,500. **No credit cards.**
No English menu. Map 5

This three-storey complex off Omotesando is an
inexpensive, kid-friendly natural food place with a
few meat offerings thrown in to keep carnivores
from grumbling too loudly. Little of the food is stellar, but most is satisfying, and for only ¥1,000 you
can pack up your choice in a box to take away.

Shibuya

Down to Earth

2-5 Sarugaku-cho, Shibuya-ku (3461 5872).
Shibuya station. **Open** 12-3.30pm, 7-10.30pm Mon-
Sat. **Average** ¥1,500. **Credit** all major cards.
Menu in English. Map 4
Down to Earth attracts a mostly young clientele (and
even the occasional celebrity) with its casual atmosphere and wholesome food. While not completely
vegetarian, hefty garden burgers with all the trimmings and a mixed bag of ethnic offerings will satisfy even the vegans.

Elsewhere

Gruppe

5-27-5 Ogikubo, Suginami-ku (3393 1224).
Ogikubo station. **Open** 11.30am-2pm, 5.30-10pm (last
order 9.30pm), Mon-Sat. **Average** ¥1,500.
Credit all major cards. **Menu in English.**
Above a natural food shop, this caters to locals and
regulars. If you speak Japanese, staff will try to
gear your choices toward your ailment or concern.
That's not to say that the food is medicinal – just
healthy Japanese stuff of the brown rice variety. A
white board menu changes frequently. No smoking, but you can imbibe from a selection of organic beers and even brown rice sake.

Nataraj

B1, 5-30-6 Ogikubo, Suginami-ku (3398 5108).
Ogikubo station. **Open** 11.30am-2.30pm, 5-10.30pm
Mon-Fri; 11.30am-10.30pm Sat, Sun. **Average**
¥2,000. **Credit** all major cards. **Menu in English.**
Vegetarian fare is hard to come by in Tokyo, especially food that isn't holier-than-thou. At Nataraj (God of
Dance) the food is sure to satisfy both vegetarians and
carnivores. Servings are moderate, so choose an assortment from the extensive curry menu or select from one
of five special sets with rice, naan , salad, chutney,
popadom, dalwara and a choice of curries.

Roppongi

Moti Darbar

*Roppongi Plaza Bldg 3F, 3-12-6 Roppongi, Minato-
ku (5410 6871). Roppongi station.* **Open** 11am-11pm
Mon-Sat; noon-10pm Sun. **Average** ¥2,000.
Credit all major cards. **Menu in English. Map 2**
One of the better of the Moti chain, with the bonus
of being open late and set smack in disco-central.
Crowded but reliable, with a vast, varied picture
menu of mouthwatering choices, including veggie.

Shibuya

Raj Mahal/Raj Palace

*Jow Bldg 5F, 30-5 Udagawa-cho, Shibuya-ku (3770
7677). Shibuya station.* **Open** 11.30am-10pm daily.
Average ¥3,500. **Credit** all major cards.
Menu in English. Map 4

Moti Darbar: a vast choice of Indian treats.

Despite its chain status, the Raj Mahal/Palace restau-
rants have good service and excellent food. Menus
are extensive.
Branches Urban Bldg 4F, 7-13-2 Roppongi,
Minato-ku (5411 2525). Roppongi station. Peace
Bldg 5F, 3-34-11 Shinjuku, Shinjuku-ku (5379 2525).
Shinjuku station. Hakuba Bldg 4F, 26-11 Udagawa-
cho, Shibuya-ku (3780 6531). Shibuya station. Taiyo
Bldg 4F, 8-8-5 Ginza Chuo Dori, Chuo-ku (5568 8080).
Ginza station.

Aoyama/Harajuku/Omotesando

Giliola

*Aoyama Ohara Kaikan B1, 5-7-17 Minami-Aoyama,
Minato-ku (5485 3516). Omotesando station.*
Open 11.30am-3pm, 5.30-11pm, Mon-Sat.
Average ¥5,000. **Credit** all major cards, evenings
only. **Menu in Italian. Map 2**
This tiny underground trattoria serves up a delightful selection of homestyle Italian cooking. There's a
small list of Italian wines to accompany it, and the
larger selection of grappa to round off the meal. The
grand menu changes three times a year, and seasonal specials are marked up on a chalkboard.
Dishes such as penne with gorgonzola and linguine
al pesto genovese, and main courses of salmon on
mushroom risotto and lamb chops are all fantasti-
cally executed.

La' Grotta Celeste

Aoyama Centre Bldg 1F, 3-8-40 Minami-Aoyama, Minato-ku (3401 1261). Omotesando station.
Open 11.30am-3pm, 5.30-11pm, daily.
Average lunch ¥1,000-¥1,800; dinner ¥5,000.
Credit all major cards. **Menu in Italian. Map 12**
A place for a special-occasion splurge, with excellent service and exquisite Italian food in a lovely pink-hued setting. It's hard to decide which is better: the grotto room with its brick lattice walls and Italianate ceiling fresco or the centre room with a view of the open kitchen and its wood-burning stove.

Tokyo Salon

5-47-6 Jingumae, Shibuya-ku (3407 6865). Omotesando station. **Open** 11am-11pm daily.
Average ¥3,000. **Credit** all major cards.
Menu in English. Map 4
Chef Dante Fazzina would prefer to have his cuisine classified as Mediterranean, but no matter; he'll fulfil any request and happily adapt his cooking to whatever culinary trip you're on. At night a member's club, the yearly fee of ¥10,000 allows you entrée to one of the most creative spaces in Tokyo. Large wooden chairs, a *tatami* room, exquisite flower arrangements, live music and events, dozens of candles and intimately prepared food make this one of the un-stuffiest clubs on earth. Try the sublime baked aubergine, lively vegetable soup or a mixed antipasto platter. Open to non-members until 5pm, and during special events.

Elsewhere

Primi Baci

Inokashira Parkside Bldg 2F, 1-21-1 Kichijoji Minami-cho, Musashino-shi (0422 72 8202). Kichijoji station. **Open** lunch 11.30am-2.30pm, tea 2.30-5pm, dinner 5-10pm, Mon-Fri; 11.30am-10pm Sat, Sun. **Average** ¥4,000. **Credit** all major cards.
Menu in English. Map 24
In a splendid setting overlooking Inokashira Park, Primi Baci (which translates as 'First Kiss') has both exquisite service and well-executed Tuscany cuisine. An open and airy interior boasts well-spaced tables set with fresh flowers and charming, unpretentious waiters who are eager to test their English. For starters don't miss the tartara di tonno, a column of tender tuna tartare garnished with marche salad and slivered fried leeks, or the torretta di melanzane, an aubergine, mozzarella and tomato tower bathed in swirls of basil sauce.

Japanese
Akasaka

Densan

Getsusekai Bldg B1, 3-10-4 Akasaka, Minato-ku (3585 7550). Akasaka-mitsuke station.
Open 4.30pm-5am Mon-Sat; 4.30-11.30pm Sun.
Average ¥2,000. **Credit** all major cards.
No English menu. Map 16

Densan marries two Japanese 'traditions': oden and karaoke. The speciality is Kyoto-style oden. Kyoto cooks wield a much lighter touch than their Tokyo cousins; the broth is delicate and subtle, with only a hint of soy sauce, allowing the flavours of the ingredients to shine. The other specialities are yakitori from free-range chickens and sake, with an emphasis on Niigata Prefecture, where the high quality of rice produces some of Japan's best sake. When your vocal cords are well lubricated, you'll be quite happy that Densan saves you the stumble in search of a karaoke box: the private rooms are equipped with the latest hi-tech system.

Jidaiya

Naritaya Bldg 1F, 3-14-3 Akasaka, Minato-ku (3588 0489/fax 3589 6276). Akasaka-mitsuke station. **Open** 11.30am-2pm, 5pm-4am, Mon-Fri; 5-11pm Sat. **Average** courses ¥3,000-¥6,000, à la carte ¥2,500. **Credit** all major cards.
No English menu. Map 11
Recreates a rustic Japanese farmhouse complete with tatami mats, dried ears of corn, fish-shaped hanging fireplace fixtures and heaps of old-looking wooden furniture. The atmosphere is a bit contrived but fun nevertheless, and large shared tables contribute to the conviviality. The food is all Japanese, with an emphasis on seafood, meat and vegetables cooked at the table. The à la carte menu makes occasional forays into the world of western food; Camembert monja once showed up on the Akasaka menu.
Branches Isomura Bldg B1, 5-1-4 Akasaka, Minato-ku (3224 1505/fax 3586 5089). Akasaka station; Uni Roppongi Bldg B1, 7-15-17 Roppongi (3403 3563/fax 3403 5838). Roppongi station.

Zakuro

TBS Kaikan Bldg B1, 5-3-3 Akasaka, Minato-ku (3582 6841). Akasaka-mitsuke station.
Open 11am-11pm daily. **Average** ¥9,000.
Credit all major cards. **Menu in English. Map 11**
A casual restaurant that captures the best of Japan's traditional haute cuisine: shabu-shabu, sukiyaki, tempura and dishes inspired by fresh seasonal bounties, served in private or common western-style dining rooms, tempura bar or private tatami rooms.
Branches 4-6-1 Ginza, Chuo-ku (3535 4421). Ginza station; Nihon Jitensha Kaikan, 1-9-15 Akasaka, Minato-ku (3582 2661). Akasaka station; Shin Nihonbashi Bldg B1, 3-8-2 Nihonbashi, Chuo-ku (3271 3791). Nihonbashi station; Shin Yaesu Bldg B1, 1-7-1 Kyobashi, Chuo-ku (3563 5031). Kyobashi station; Chiba Bin Bldg B1, Nihonbashi-muromachi 1-5-3, Chuo-ku (3241 4841). Mitsukoshimae station.

Aoyama/Harajuku/Omotesando

Daruma-ya

5-9-5 Minami-Aoyama, Minato-ku (3499 6295). Omotesando station. **Open** 11.30am-9.30pm Mon-Sat. **Average** ¥1,500. **No credit cards.**
Menu in English. Map 2
Daruma-ya takes its name from *daruma*, roly-poly legless caricatures of the fifth-century Indian priest

Takoyaki *(octopus balls): festival favourites but an acquired taste.*

Bodhidarma that are a Japanese good luck charm. Famous for its handmade Chinese noodles (ramen) executed with a Japanese twist, the most popular being takana soba – ramen noodles topped with a leafy domestic vegetable that defies translation.

Denpachi
5-9-9 Minami-Aoyama, Minato-ku (3406 8240).
Omotesando station. **Open** 5pm-midnight daily.
Average ¥2,000. **No credit cards.**
No English menu. Map 2
An izakaya known among regulars as 'the sardine place', Denpachi also serves up a mean array of beef tongue dishes. But mostly it does wicked things to the humble sardine (iwashi). Small strips of very tender fish appear as iwashi sashimi, while iwashi tataki is a tender rendering of sardines into small, carpaccio-like pieces. Don't miss the iwashi wonton soup, a delicately flavoured broth in which swim two wonton stuffed with ground sardine.
Branches 4-8-7 Ginza, Chuo-ku (3562 3957). Ginza station; 1-5 Kabuki-cho, Shinjuku-ku (3200 8003). Shinjuku station.

Gombei
5-9-3 Minami-Aoyama, Minato-ku (3406 5733).
Omotesando station. **Open** 11.30am-10pm daily.
Average ¥1,000. **No credit cards.**
No English menu. Map 2
Known to locals as 'The Grumpy Old Lady Place' because the matriarch treats customers with surly contempt. But she also serves some of the best soba and udon in town. Noodles come in three choices: soba, udon and kishimen, a thin version of the doughy udon noodle. Ikura with kishimen is marvellous; a generous serving of bright red salmon roe nestled in a bed of grated daikon, with a sprinkling of fragrant green trefoil for contrast. Perfect on a cold winter's day is kare-nanban (barbarian's curry), tender pieces of either chicken or pork with onion in

a spicy curry broth. During the hot months try the ikura cold, or go for sansai, a mix of cultivated and wild mountain vegetables. The lunch service menu offers set meals at great prices.

Maisen
4-8-5 Jingumae, Shibuya-ku (3470 0071).
Omotesando station. **Open** 11am-10pm daily.
Average ¥2,000. **Credit** DC, JCB, MC, V.
Menu in English. Map 5
This branch of this chain tonkatsu shop is a converted bath-house. If you're able to get a seat in the huge and airy dining room in the back, you'll notice several tell-tale signs: 30-foot ceilings and a small garden pond. You can't miss with any of the teishoku (set meals); standard *rosu katsu* or lean *hire katsu* are both good choices, each coming with rice, soup and pickled daikon.
Branch Mitsui Bldg B1, 1-1-2 Yurakucho, Chiyoda-ku (3503 1886). Yurakucho station.

Nobu Tokyo
6-10-17 Minami-Aoyama, Minato-ku (5467 0022).
Omotesando station, then a ten-min walk.
Open *restaurant* 11.30am-3.30pm (last order 2.30pm) Mon-Fri; 6-11.30pm (doors close at 10pm) daily.
Bar 5.30pm-4am (last order 3.30am) Mon-Sat; 5.30-11.30pm (last order 11pm) Sun. **Average** lunch ¥5,000, dinner ¥8,000. **Credit** all major cards.
Menu in English. Map 2
Nobu Matsuhisa started as a sushi chef in Tokyo before striking out for Peru, Argentina and the US. His restaurant Nobu electrified jaded New York palates and set the standard for nouvelle Japanese cuisine. In addition to restaurants in New York, London, Beverly Hills and Aspen, Nobu comes home to Japan in an elegant, sophisticated setting serving world-class fusion cuisine. Black cod with miso is purportedly actor Robert De Niro's favourite, though Nobu is most renowned for his sushi rolls.

Candlelight and poetry at romantic Ya-So.

Senba

4-4-7 Jingumae, Shibuya-ku (5474 5977).
Harajuku station. **Open** 11am-10.30pm daily.
Average ¥1,500. **Credit** DC, MC, V.
No English menu. Map 5
Senba specialises in soba, udon and kishimen. The
star of the line-up is kurumi soba, a choice of noodles served with a creamy walnut dipping sauce.
A nice way to sample a number of dips is the
makunouchi: three to five pretty little bowls served
in a (fake) wooden box. You can try oroshi (grated daikon with mushrooms), tororo (grated mountain yam), tempura, walnut and sansai (wild
mountain vegetables).
Branches 4-1-13 Nihonbashi-Honcho, Chuo-ku
(3270 7100). Mitsukoshimae station; 11-1 Kanda
Matsunagacho, Chiyoda-ku (3251 8645). Akihabara
station; 1-4-1 Yurakucho, Chiyoda-ku (3591 7384).
Yurakucho station; Onuki Bldg, 2-9-7 Kanda-Kajicho,
Chiyoda-ku (3251 8007). Kanda station.

Ya-So Poetry Restaurant

Otsuki Bldg 2F, 7-14-7 Minami-Aoyama, Minato-ku
(3499 0233). Omotesando station. **Open** 11.30am-
2.30pm, 5.30pm-3am, Mon-Fri; 11.30am-2.30pm,
5.30pm-1am, Sat. **Average** ¥3,000. **Credit** all major
cards. **No English menu. Map 2**
With walls and room dividers festooned with snip-
pets of poetry, this (at night) upscale izakaya is a
romantic departure from the farmhouse feel most
such places strive for. Lighting is by candle and corner lights wrapped in washi. The food is as distinctive as the interior; classic Japanese with an unusual
approach. Ume no tataki is a creative dish of piquant
ume paste served like sushi, with nori, slivered onion
and ginger. Finish with a delicious twist on a traditional meal-ender: udon chazuke, in which chewy
noodles in tea broth take the place of rice.

Asakusa

Hatsuogawa

2-8-4 Kaminarimon, Taito-ku (3844 2723).
Asakusa station. **Open** noon-2pm (last order
1.30pm), 5-8pm (last order 7.30pm), Mon-Sat;
5-8pm (last order 7.30pm) Sun. **Average** ¥3,000.
No credit cards. No English menu. Map 10
A tradition-steeped unagi restaurant that's located
in tradition-steeped Asakusa. The tiny entrance to
the place is graced with stones, plants, bamboo lat-
ticework and a white *noren* with the word 'unagi'
emblazoned across it. Step into this tiny world of
wooden beams and traditional Japanese décor and
enjoy the taste of succulent unagi, which is prepared by a third-generation family member. The
unaju box set is delicious, or try kabayaki: unagi
on a stick. This place is so popular during festivals and firework displays that the queue winds
down the street.

Ginza

Oshima

Ginza Core Bldg 9F, 5-8-20 Ginza, Chuo-ku (3574
8080). Ginza station. **Open** 11am-10pm (last order
9pm) daily. **Average** lunch courses from ¥1,800,
dinner courses ¥2,800-¥12,000. **Credit** all major
cards. **No English menu. Map 7**
Traditional Japanese food served up in tasteful,
modern, comfortable settings. Not all of the courses
are stellar, but the food is always well prepared and
beautifully presented, and the timing of the waitresses is exquisite.
Branches Odakyu Halc 8F, 1-5-1 Nishi Shinjuku,
Shinjuku-ku (3348 8080). Shinjuku station;
Hotel Pacific Tokyo, 3-13-3 Takanawa, Minato-ku
(3445 6711). Shinagawa station.

Ten-Ichi Deux

Nishi Ginza Depato 1F, Ginza 4-1 (3566 4188).
Ginza station. **Open** 11.30am-10pm daily.
Average lunch ¥1,300-¥2,800, dinner ¥2,800-
¥4,200. **Credit** all major cards. **Menu in English.**
Map 7
A photo of Bill Clinton 'graces' the front counter at
Ten-Ichi Deux, a fairly pricey but famous, and con-
sistently good, tempura chain that specialises in ten-
don (large tempura prawns over rice) as well as
kushiage tempura – deep-fried morsels on sticks.
Branches Ryokoku Hotel Ten-Ichi, 1-1
Uchisaiwaicho, Chiyoda-ku (3503 1001).
Uchisaiwaicho station; Sony Bldg B1, 5-3-1 Ginza,
Chuo-ku (3571 3837). Ginza station.

Yurakucho Under the Tracks

2-1 Yurakucho, Chiyoda-ku (no phones). Yurakucho
station. **Open** early evening to midnight daily.
Average ¥2,000. **No credit cards. Map 7**
For a cheap night's entertainment and a quintessential Japanese experience, don't miss the yakitori
roadshow that takes place nightly beneath the
tracks of the Yamanote line. Little open-air eateries
are wedged into tiny spaces. The master presides
behind the counter, dishing out grilled yakitori and
other tidbits (*see chapter* **Bars**).

Kanda/Ochanomizu

Botan

1-15 Kanda Sudacho, Chiyoda-ku (3251 0577).
Kanda station. **Open** 11.30am-9pm Mon-Sat.
Average ¥7,000. **No credit cards. Map 15**
They serve one thing only here, chicken sukiyaki,
and they do it well, which takes all the guesswork
out of ordering. Botan, meaning both button and
peony, was founded more than 100 years ago by a
button-maker. Four generations on, it still stands in
a fairly well-preserved Tokyo neighbourhood.
Leave your shoes in the hallway, and let yourself
be led to your minuscule table. A kimono-clad
waitress will light the charcoal in the brazier, set a
small iron dish on top, then start cooking: chicken,
onion, tofu and other vegetables simmering in the
house sauce.

Isegen

1-11 Kanda Suda-cho, Chiyoda-ku (3251 1229).
Kanda station. **Open** noon-9pm Mon-Fri.
Average ¥5,000. **No credit cards.**
No English menu. Map 15
In the same bomb-spared neighbourhood as Botan
(*see above*), the sprawling old Isegen has been serving its legendary anko (angler fish) nabe for over 150
years. Anko are only in season from October to
March, which is perfectly fine because that's when
any good Tokyoite worth his sake wants to sit down
to a steaming nabe. Off-season? Still plenty of other
goodies, not the least being Isegen's neighbours –
beautifully preserved old buildings housing some of
the best in traditional Japanese cuisine.

Kandagawa Honten

2-5-11 Soto-Kanda, Chiyoda-ku (3251 5031).
Ochanomizu station. **Open** 11.30am-2pm, 5-7.30pm
Mon-Sat. **Average** ¥4,000. **Credit** DC, MC, V.
No English menu. Map 14
Kimono-clad waitresses serve exquisite unagi (eel)
in one of Tokyo's most famous unagi restaurants.
Charcoal-grilled fillet of eel basted with a sweet
sauce is succulent and tender, and the setting mag-
nificent: an antique Japanese house overlooking a
traditional garden. Reservations are recommended.

Yabu Soba

2-10 Kanda-Awajicho, Chiyoda-ku (3251 0287).
Ochanomizu station. **Open** 11.30am-7pm daily.
Average ¥1,500. **No credit cards. Menu in**
English. Map 14
Indisputably Tokyo's most famous soba shop, locat-
ed in a beautiful old Japanese house decked with
shoji screens, tatami and woodblock prints.

Roppongi

Fukuzushi

5-7-8 Roppongi, Minato-ku (3402 4116). Roppongi
station. **Open** 11.30am-2pm, 5.30-11pm, Mon-Sat.
Average ¥10,000. **Credit** all major cards.
Menu in English. Map 2
Visitors rave about Fukuzushi being the best
sushi in Tokyo. It had better be, as a night at the
counter will put a serious dent in your wallet. But
if you want to get dressed up to eat raw fish – or
see and be seen – this cosmopolitan sushi hang-
out downstairs from Spago (*see below*) is the place
to go. Like the clientele, the sushi is elegant, generous and beautiful and the masters don't shy
away from the occasional western influence
(California roll, anyone?).

Ichiban Sushi

No. 10 Kotobuki Bldg, 2-4-9 Roppongi, Minato-ku
(3585 1256). Roppongi station. **Open** 11am-3am
Mon-Sat; 11am-11pm Sun. **Average** ¥2,000.
No credit cards. No English menu. Map 2
Not the best sushi you'll find in Tokyo; indeed, it's
only a short step up from most kaiten zushi. What
makes Ichiban different is its prices (kaiten-like
¥100 per plate) and the owner's love of Italian cooking. Not only does he serve wine with his sushi but
he explores a few fusion techniques too – you won't
find sashimi carpaccio in any other sushi joint.

Kisso

Axis Bldg B1, 5-17-1 Roppongi, Minato-ku (3582
4191). Roppongi station. **Open** 11.30am-2pm, 5.30-
10pm (last order 9pm), Mon-Sat. **Average** ¥2,500
lunch, ¥10,000 dinner. **Credit** all major cards.
No English menu. Map 2
Kisso is kaiseki in a contemporary setting – the main
dining area is decked out in stylish black, with deep,
comfortable chairs surrounded by artfully arranged
flowers, overhead track lighting and a subtle jazz
soundtrack. Meals are a sequence of small dishes
ordered as a set; most will include sashimi and

cooked fish with grated daikon, miso soup with tofu, wakame (seaweed) and mitsuba (Japanese parsley), seasonal and often unusual vegetables and a small amount of meat, perhaps chicken or pork, with pungent hot mustard.

Yakitori Bincho
Marina Bldg 2F, 3-10-5 Roppongi, Minato-ku (5474 0755). Roppongi station. **Open** 6pm-midnight daily. **Average** ¥5,000. **Credit** all major cards. **Menu in English. Map 2**
Dark, romantic Japanese-style interior complemented by the smoky aroma of charcoal-grilled yakitori and an exhausting array of sake choices. Grilled chicken or vegetables may be ordered by the stick or as part of a course.

Shibuya

Myoko
Shinto Bldg 1F, 1-17-2 Shibuya, Shibuya-ku (3499 3450). Shibuya station. **Open** 11am-11pm daily. **Average** ¥1,200. **Credit** all major cards. **No English menu. Map 4**
Serves hoto, a flat wide udon noodle, in a beautiful traditional setting. Try the hot hoto nabe (oyster, kimchee, mushroom, pork, sansai, etc.), noodles in miso broth and lots of vegetables served bubbling hot in an iron kettle. Or cold 'salad udon', chilled noodles and vegetables available in chicken, tuna, crab, eel or seafood mix. Reasonably priced teishoku as well. A large picture menu makes ordering simple despite the lack of English menu.

Pot & Pot
21-7 Uchidagawa-cho, Shibuya-ku (3461 0788). Shibuya station. **Open** 24 hours daily. **Average** ¥650. **No credit cards. No English menu. Map 4**
Just once every visitor to Tokyo should try the Japanese version of curry; it's a far cry from its Indian ancestor, but yummy in its own way and so ubiquitous it can almost be considered a national dish. Pot & Pot is a small chain that serves decent-quality curry a number of ways. Indicate the hotness you desire; *chu-kara* is hot, *kara-kuchi* is extra hot, while *ama-kuchi* is mild.
Branches Yuwa Bldg 1F, 2-13-6 Yoyogi, Shibuya-ku (5358 7054). Shinjuku station; 5-6-25 Minami-Aoyama, Minato-ku (3400 4920). Omotesando station.

Tamakyu
2-30-4 Dogenzaka, Shibuya-ku (3461 4803). Shibuya station. **Open** 5-10.30pm Mon-Sat. **Average** ¥4,000. **No credit cards. No English menu. Map 4**
This looks from the outside like a shack: an eyesore on the side of Shibuya's landmark 109 Building. Indeed, this little fish restaurant has a story to tell. It opened in 1948, though the land has been owned by the Kamata family for 200 years. World War II destroyed the family's rice business, but out of the rubble a restaurant was born, and survives; despite pressure to sell out to developers, this boisterous izakaya continues at the same incongruous location.

Vingt2
ICI Bldg 1F, 1-6-7 Shibuya, Shibuya-ku (3407 9494). Shibuya station. **Open** 11.30am-2pm, 5-11pm Mon-Sat. **Average** lunch ¥900, dinner ¥3,500. **Credit** AmEx, DC, JCB, V. **No English Menu. Map 4**
An extensive selection of charcoal-grilled fish, meat and vegetable kushi-yaki (skewered foods) near Children's Castle (*see chapter* **Children**) and Aoyama Dori.

Ueno area

Bon
1-2-11 Ryusen, Taito-ku (3872 0234). Iriya station. **Open** noon-2pm, 5-8pm, Mon-Fri; 5-6pm Sat, Sun. **Average** ¥7,000. **Credit** all major cards. **Menu in English.**
Shojin-ryori exquisitely prepared in a style that originated in China. The seasonal menu of Zen vegetarian cuisine at Bon changes regularly. Order by course and enjoy a procession of light delicacies in a simple, quiet tatami setting.

Goemon
1-1-26 Hon-Komagome, Bunkyo-ku (3811 2015). Hon-Komagome station. **Open** 5-10pm Tue-Sat; 3-8pm Sun. **Average** ¥7,000. **No credit cards. No English menu.**
A great introduction to shojin-ryori in a setting that takes you to Kyoto for only half the price. Unimaginable variations on the tofu theme. Try yudofu (tofu nabe) in winter, and hiya yakko (cold tofu with onions and other seasonings) in the warmer months. Especially worth visiting in summer when the shoji screens are pulled away, and you can contemplate the karmic goodness of tofu while overlooking a garden complete with waterfall and carp.

Honke Ponta
3-23-3 Ueno, Taito-ku (3831 2351). Ueno station. **Open** 11am-2pm, 4.30-8pm, Tue-Sun. **Average** ¥4,000. **No credit cards. No English menu. Map 14**
Honke Ponta was the first place in the whole of the city to serve tonkatsu pork cutlet – deep-fried golden nuggets of succulent pork – but it prefers to think of itself as a western-style restaurant and thus serves steak so tender that knives melt in it. But go for the tender katsuretsu (cutlet), ika (squid) or kisu (whiting) fry. Order rice and soup separately and you'll get akadashi soup (red miso, nameko mushrooms and scallions) so dark and viscous it's like eating romantic Brazilian feijoada. There are no prices on the menu, which doesn't seem to bother the housewives with time on their hands who frequent the place.

Ikenohata Yabu Soba
3-44-7 Yushima, Bunkyo-ku (3831 8977). Yushima station. **Open** 11.30am-2pm, 4.30-8pm, Mon, Tue, Thur-Sat; 11.30am-8pm Sun. **Average** ¥1,500. **No credit cards. Menu in English.**
Excellent soba at reasonable prices in a modern Japanese setting. The Yabu Soba flagship in Kanda

is the most famous soba restaurant in Tokyo, and has spawned a host of knock-offs run by former Yabu Soba-ites. While Ikenohata lacks the charm and traditional atmosphere of the original, the soba is still some of the most delectable in Tokyo.

Otafuku

1-6-2 Sento, Taito-ku (3871 2521). Iriya station. **Open** 5-11pm Tue-Sat; 3-10pm Sun. **Average** ¥100-¥500 per piece. **Credit** all major cards. **No English menu.**

This place has been serving oden since the Meiji era. It specialises in Kansai-style oden; the broth is much lighter on soy flavour than the Tokyo version, and the chef takes pride in it. Otafuku also specialises in sake, which goes well with the delicate flavour of vegetables and fish cakes that make up oden.

Sasanoyuki

2-15-10 Negishi, Taito-ku (3873 1145). Nippori station. **Open** 11am-9.30pm Tue-Sun. **Average** ¥4,500. **Credit** all major cards. **Menu in English. Map 32**

Tokyo's most famous tofu restaurant since the Edo period has an imperial legacy: it was founded by a tofu-maker lured from Kyoto by the Kanei-ji Temple's imperial abbot. Most Tokyo tofu restaurants are ridiculously expensive; Sasanoyuki swaps a grand interior for reasonable prices and eye-popping variations on the tofu theme.

Takokyuu

2-11-8 Ueno, Taito-ku (3574 8156). Ueno station. **Open** 6pm-midnight Mon-Sat. **Average** ¥100-¥600 per piece. **No credit cards. No English menu. Map 8**

Four generations have been serving Tokyo-style oden at this Ueno institution for 94 years. Takokyuu is renowned for its heavier, Kanto-type broth, which stews for two days before daikon, onions, oysters and other delicacies are thrown in. The house sake is allegedly available nowhere else in Tokyo.

Elsewhere

Chibo

Ebisu Garden Place Tower 38F, 4-20-3 Ebisu, Shibuya-ku (5424 1011). Ebisu station. **Open** 11am-3pm, 5-11pm (last order 10pm), daily. **Average** ¥2,500. **Credit** all major cards. **Menu in English. Map 20**

This branch of an Osaka okonomiyaki restaurant uses the original Osaka-style recipe (the other major okonomiyaki region is Hiroshima; they stuff theirs with noodles). In addition to the usual meats and seafood, stuffings include asparagus, mochi or cheese and of course mayonnaise. Friendly staff, reasonable prices and a large menu, plus a gorgeous view, make this a popular place for okonomiyaki.

Daigo

2-4-2 Atago, Minato-ku (3431 0811). Kamiyacho station. **Open** noon-3pm, 5-9pm, Mon-Wed, Fri-Sun. **Average** lunch from ¥12,000, dinner from ¥14,000. **Credit** AmEx, DC, JCB. **No English menu.**

Daigo started out as a branch of a ryotei in Hida-Takayama. It now serves a very pricey Buddhist temple kaiseki in private tatami rooms overlooking peaceful gardens. A ten- to 15-course meal revolving around seasonal offerings is lovingly and artfully presented. An elegant slice of Japanese traditional cuisine. Reservations absolutely required.

Edogin

4-5-1 Tsukiji, Chuo-ku (3543 4401). Tsukiji station. **Open** 11am-9.30pm Mon-Sat. **Average** ¥3,500. **Credit** AmEx, DC, MC. **No English menu, but English sushi listing. Map 13**

Famous Tsukiji-area sushi shop renowned for its large, extremely fresh servings and raucous if somewhat sterile atmosphere. The slices are as big as the place itself. Makes up in price and serving size for what it lacks in character

Monja Maruyama

1-4-10 Tsukishima, Chuo-ku (3533 3504). Tsukishima station. **Open** 5-10.30pm Tue-Sun. **Average** ¥2,000. **No credit cards. No English menu. Map 19**

Monja, the crêpe-like concoction of batter, vegetables, seafood and meat cooked on a griddle, is not for everyone. But for those who like it, or want to give it a try, Tsukishima, with its dozens of little monja restaurants, is monja heaven. Mr Maruyama, a Tsukishima native, founded his place ten years ago to experiment with variations on the theme. Thus you'll find rarities such as pitch-black monja with squid's ink, or mochi mochi crêpe, with mochi, the sticky pounded rice that shows up in many Japanese dishes around New Year.

Rera Chise

2-1-19 Nishi-Waseda, Shinjuku-ku (3202 7642). Takadanobaba station. **Open** 11am-2pm, 5-11pm, Mon-Sat. Closed every third Mon. **Average** ¥2,500. **No credit cards. No English menu. Map 25**

This is Tokyo's first Ainu restaurant, and doubles as an unofficial Ainu cultural centre. This casual izakaya is a hangout for local students who come for inexpensive Ainu food and atmosphere. The food is essentially Hokkaido cooking, heavy on salmon, potatoes and spiced with garlic and ginger.

Shirube

Pine Crest Kitazawa Bldg 1F, 2-18-2 Kitazawa, Setagaya-ku (3413 3784). Shimo-Kitazawa station (Inokashira/Odakyu lines). **Open** 5.30-11.30pm daily. **Average** ¥3,000. **No credit cards. No English menu. Map 29**

Anyone who goes to Shirube immediately adopts it as one of their favourite restaurants. A riotous cacophony of mostly young people can be observed having the time of their lives here, ordering dish after dish of izakaya food cooked with flair. Don't let the lack of an English-language menu discourage you from eating here; the offerings change so often that they wouldn't be able to keep up. Just ask for a seat at the counter and point at whatever takes your fancy.

Yukun Sakagura

3-26 Arakicho, Shinjuku-ku (3356 3351). Yotsuya-
sanchome station. **Open** 11.30am-1.45pm Mon-Sat,
5-11pm (last order 10pm), Mon-Fri; 5-9pm Sat.
Average lunch ¥1,000, dinner ¥8,000.
Credit all major cards. **No English menu.**

A friendly Kyushu nomiya with cheerful Kyushu
waitresses and delightful Kyushu cuisine. Many
of the names on the washi menu sound foreign
even to Japanese ears and indeed there's something undeniably exotic – and southern – about the
food that's on offer at Yukun Sakagura. The lunch
sets are absolutely fantastic: onigiri teishoku has
two enormous onigiri (rice balls), while the inaka
udon teishoku will net you a very generous bowl-
ful of udon with rice and mysterious little side
dishes; all dishes come with a little snake's-eye
sampler of sake. In the evening take your pick
from the extensive selection of sashimi, grilled and
simmered goodies. The smooth house sake, which
is also called Yukun Sakagura, is available
nowhere else.
Branches Seio Bldg B1, 2-2-18 Ginza Chuo-ku (3561
6672). Ginza station; Tokyo Tatemono Dai 5 Yaesu
Bldg B1, 1-4-14 Yaesu, Chuo-ku (3271 8231). Tokyo
station; Jitsugyo Kaikan Bldg 2F, 1-1-21 Toranomon,
Minato-ku (3508 9298). Toranomon station; Akasaka
Tokyu Plaza 3F, 2-14-3 Nagatacho, Chiyoda-ku (3592
0393). Nagatacho station.

Korean

Akasaka

Shinmasan-ya

Namiki Bldg 1F, 3-12-5 Akasaka, Minato-ku (3583
6120). Akasaka-mitsuke station. **Open** 11.30-3am
Mon-Sat; 4.30-11.30pm Sun. **Average** ¥3,500.
Credit AmEx, JCB, MC, V. **No English menu.**
Map 11

There may be better Korean restaurants in the
Akasaka-mitsuke area than this one; Tamachi Dori
in particular is crowded with Korean restaurants,
and for good reason – a lot of Koreans work in the
area. But Shinmasan-ya is a Korean-run place that
serves honest home-style cooking which places an
emphasis on dishes other than on the ubiquitous
yakiniku, and there are always Korean customers. It
serves Tokyo's best bibimbap. Ask to be seated on
the floor; your legs can dangle under the table, while
the heated floor warms the parts of you that the food
can't reach.

Roppongi

Kusa no Ya

Mita Bldg 3F, 2-14-33 Akasaka, Minato-ku (3589
0779). Akasaka station. **Open** 11.30am-2.30pm,
5-10.30pm, Mon-Sat; 11.30am-2.30pm, 5-10pm, Sun.
Average ¥4,000. **Credit** all major cards.
No English menu. Map 11

This popular and famous Korean restaurant started out in the Azabu Juban area. People come for the
yakiniku, thinly sliced marinated beef cooked at the
table and devoured family-style with side dishes of
pickled kimchee and copious amounts of beer.
Branches A&K Bldg 8F, 4-6-8 Azabu Juban,
Minato-ku (3455 8356). Roppongi station; 2-10-1
Shinbashi, Minato-ku (3591 4569). Shinbashi station.

Shinjuku

Jojoen Opera City 53

Tokyo Opera City Tower 53F, 3-20-2 Nishi-
Shinjuku, Shinjuku-ku (5353 0089). Hatsudai
station. **Open** 11.30am-11.30pm (last order 10.45pm)
daily. **Average** ¥5,000. **Credit** all major cards.
Menu in English. Map 3a

This is not honest, down-home Korean cooking; it's
yakiniku with a view. And what a view! Perched on
the fifty-third floor, the view of the Shinjuku skyline at night is breathtaking. If there are only two
of you, make a reservation (Mon-Sat only) for the
'pair seats' – ten sets of two comfortable chairs facing the window (weekends and holidays you might
have to wait an hour).

Tokaien

1-6-3 Kabuki-cho, Shinjuku-ku (3200 2924).
Shinjuku station. **Open** 11am-4am daily.
Average All-you-can-eat ¥2,250/90 mins, à la carte
varies. **Credit** all major cards. **No English menu.**
Map 3b

If yakiniku is a religion, then Tokaien is its temple:
nine floors of this building in Kabuki-cho are turned
over to yakiniku and home-style Korean cooking.
The sixth floor features all-you-can-eat ('Viking' in
Japanese) yakiniku.

Mexican & South American

El Quixico

3-15-14 Nishiogi-minami, Suginami-ku (3332 7590).
Nishi-Ogikubo station. **Open** 6pm-2am Tue-Sun.
Closed every third Tue. **Average** ¥3,000.
No credit cards. Menu in English.

'Offbeat' and 'creative' best describe chef Yoshioka
of El Quixico. He comes to Mexican cooking via
Kyoto, where he was once a tortilla-maker, and it
may be this Kyoto influence that explains both the
Japanese twist to his food and the light touch. Here
you'll find no heavy cheese-laden bean fests. Start
with one of the selection of frozen Margaritas that
give new meaning to 'brain freeze'. Don't forget to
try the 'original salad', served with two warm tortillas and a secret salad dressing. Authentic
Mexican? No, but cosy and friendly, with large
servings, an amusing menu, and mixed crowds of
twenty- and thirtysomethings.

La Casita

Selsa Daikanyama 2F, 13-4 Daikanyama-cho,
Shibuya-ku (3496 1850). Daikanyama station
(Tokyu Toyoko line). **Open** 11am-10pm daily (last
order 9.30pm). **Average** courses from ¥2,500, à la
carte ¥3,500. **No credit cards. Menu in English.**
Map 20

Street food

Japan is not an eat-on-the-street country. Food bought hot from carts and eaten on the go are hard to come by. In fact, it is generally considered rude to eat or drink in public, but there are exceptions. During festivals an entire street might be lined with vendors serving some of the foods below out of *yatai*, small portable carts equipped with stoves and, sometimes, a little counter space.

Taiyaki are extremely popular with school kids, though they're making a comeback with adults. A pancake-like batter is stuffed with sweet red bean jam and cooked in fish-shaped molds (tai means sea bream).

An acquired taste, **takoyaki** are diced octopus cooked in an egg batter and moulded into balls, often with small bits of pickled ginger or other condiments, and a sweet glaze sauce. Takoyaki is found either at festival stalls or special takoyaki stands, denoted by a cheerful red octopus icon.

The **yakisoba** available from street stalls is a far cry from the yakisoba, or lo mein, available in Chinese eateries. These noodles, grill-fried with small amounts of cabbage, bean sprouts, or carrot, are doused in a sweet, dark sauce and sprinkled with red pickled ginger and nori (seaweed).

Yaki-imo are charcoal-cooked sweet potatoes, roasted until the skin is flaky and the inside soft and remarkably hot. Some take them home and eat them with a little butter, though most Japanese eat them just as they are. The plaintive song sung by the vendor, exhorting you to 'get your charcoal roasted yaki-imo while it's hot' can bring a nostalgic tear to the eye of even the most cynical old-timer.

Like most of Tokyo's south-of-the-border restaurants, La Casita isn't authentically Mexican. But the heady aroma of corn tortillas grabs you upon entering this airy 'little house' and won't let go until you've sampled the near-perfect camarones al mojo de ajo (grilled shrimp with garlic Acapulco style) or the enchiladas rojos bathed in spicy tomato sauce.

Middle Eastern

Ankara
Social Dogenzaka B1, 1-14-9 Dogenzaka, Shibuya-ku (3780 1366). Shibuya station. **Open** 11.30am-3pm, 5.30-11.30pm, daily. **Average** ¥2,500. **Credit** MC, V. **Menu in English. Map 4**

Tucked away in the backstreets of Shibuya, this snug little Turkish restaurant serves up an array of delicious and healthy meze and a range of other Turkish delights.

North American
Aoyama/Harajuku/Omotesando

Bagels & More Espresso Bar
Coxy 188 Bldg 2F, 1-8-8 Jingumae, Shibuya-ku (3479 0978). Harajuku station. **Open** 11am-10pm daily. **Average** ¥600. **No credit cards.** **Menu in English. Map 5**

Bagels are imported from the famous H & H in New York; while they suffer as much as we do in the trip over, they're still a welcome break from Japanese 'sandwiches'. The coffee is excellent, much better – and warmer – than the stuff they serve with all that fanfare at the neighbouring Starbucks.

Roppongi

Brendan's Pizzakaya
Daiichi Koyama Bldg 203, 3-1-19 Nishi-Azabu, Minato-ku (3479 8383). Roppongi station. **Open** 6-11pm Tue-Thur; 6pm-2am Fri; 6pm-midnight Sat, Sun. **Average** ¥3,500 for two. **Credit** JCB, MC, V. **Menu in English. Map 2**

You didn't come all the way to Tokyo for pizza. But let's say you've been here a while, and absolutely have to have a pizza with two kinds of olives or vegetarian or Santa Fe, with chicken, onions and guacamole, washed down with beer and a Caesar salad on the side. Well, that's what Brendan's is here for.

Rellenos
Trinity Bldg B1, 4-22-7 Nishi-Azabu, Minato-ku (3400 7251). Roppongi station. **Open** 11.30am-2pm, 6-11pm, Mon-Sat. **Average** ¥6,000. **Credit** all major cards. **Menu in English. Map 2**

Chef Kenji Sugawara draws inspiration from California, the Southwest, New Orleans Cajun and views it all through an Asian filter, resulting in a fusion cuisine with flavours that will dance on your tongue. What sets Rellenos apart is its electrifying reinvention of classic dishes, such as salmon with spinach fettuccini in a Thai green curry and coconut sauce. Lemony Caesar salad is a great twist on a California classic, combining tangy lemon with the crunch of corn tortilla strips. Starters such as tempura-style soft-shell crab on basmati rice with Thai chilli sauce not only taste sublime but carry a visual wallop as well. The wines, mostly Californian, are well worth lingering over, and start at ¥3,800 a bottle.

Roy's
Riviera Minami-Aoyama Bldg 1F, 3-3-3 Minami-Aoyama, Minato-ku (5474 8181). Omotesando station. **Open** 11.30am-3.30pm, 5.45-11pm, Mon-Fri; 11am-3.30pm Sat, Sun. **Average** ¥5,000. **Credit** all major cards. **Menu in English. Map 12**

Kaiten zushi

Even in Japan, sushi is expensive. Expect a night out at a decent place, with sake or beer, to run to at least ¥6,000 per person. One alternative is kaiten zushi. Located everywhere, especially in arcades near train stations, kaiten zushi ('revolving sushi') is sushi served on moving conveyor belts. Sushi chefs stand in the middle of the island replenishing the quickly disappearing plates, ready to take special orders. While the quality isn't as good as at a sushi restaurant, it's usually fairly consistent, and the price is right. Most plates run about ¥120-¥240. They are colour-coded for price, and there should be a sign indicating the price per plate.

When you walk in, grab a seat at the counter. Cups for tea are often located overhead. Plop a bag of green tea in the cup, and fill it from the push-button spigot on the counter. Some places provide small dipping saucers for soy sauce, but if not, use one of the sushi plates. Ginger is also self-serve and will be on the counter in a box with small tongs for serving. When you've finished a plate, stack it in a pile. If you don't see what you want, ask for it.

When you're ready to leave, your bill will be tallied up, and you pay at the register. The average kaiten bill, excluding beer, is approximately ¥1,000.

Fresh fish going round in circles at a 'revolving sushi'.

A fabulous selection of simple but exciting Euro-Asian-Pacific cuisine that's combined with intimate service. At Roy's you'll find traditional Japanese flavours – shoyu, ginger and miso – featuring in exquisitely arranged masterpieces such as seared shrimp with a spicy miso butter sauce or Mediterranean-style seafood fritata accompanied by pickled ginger and spicy sprouts. The weekend brunch that's served here is one of the very best ways to start a weekend – or to end it. There's all-you-can-drink wine to wash down home-made muffins, dim sum-style appetisers, devastating entrées and some scrumptious desserts.
Branch Roy's Hiroo, 1-1-40 Hiroo, Shibuya-ku (3406 2277). Hiroo station.

Spago
5-7-8 Roppongi, Minato-ku (3423 4025).
Roppongi station. **Open** 6-10pm Mon-Fri; 6-9.30pm Sat. **Average** ¥8,000. **Credit** all major cards.
Menu in English. Map 2
Launched in California by Wolfgang Puck, the man hailed as the creator of California cuisine, Spago's fusion of US cooking with European, Asian and Latin influences has found a home in Tokyo. Spago has one small fridge, so its ingredients must be bought and used daily. The menu is therefore almost Japanese in its seasonality. Grilled meats and creative fish dishes rely on locally available produce, like Yamagata chicken with double blanched garlic and Italian parsley.

Shibuya

Little Tribeca

1-5 Shibuya, Shibuya-ku (3400 0555). Shibuya station. **Open** 8.30am-10pm daily. **Average** ¥500. **No credit cards. Menu in English. Map** 4
Good for breakfast or a mid-afternoon shopping pick-me-up. Bagels, sandwiches and good coffee.

Lunchan

1-2-5 Shibuya, Shibuya-ku (5466 1398). Shibuya station. **Open** lunch 11.30am-2.30pm, tea 2.30-5.30pm, dinner 5.30-11pm, Mon-Sat; 11am-10pm Sun. **Average** ¥2,500.
Credit all major cards. **Menu in English. Map** 4
No one can figure out the name. Is it a misspelling? Or is it diminutive of someone named Lun? Why is

Chain izakaya

While lacking the mom and pop atmosphere of the local, chain izakaya are a great introduction to the world of Japanese pub foods. The scope of their offerings, from standard Japanese fare such as yakitori and sushi, to western (or westernised) dishes such as pizza and chips, and their large picture menus make them easy choices for the reading-impaired visitor. There's guaranteed to be something on the menu for everyone.

What's more, the price is right; you'd be hard put to spend more than ¥3,000-¥4,000 for a night of eating and drinking at any one of these popular chains:
Jinpachi 1-16-4 Higashi-Gotanda, Shinagawa-ku (3473 2883). Gotanda station.
Kaasan Mochizuki Bldg B1, 1-3 Yotsuya, Shinjuku-ku (3226 0551). Yotsuya station.
Kazoku Nisshin Bldg 1F, 2-37-5 Kabuki-cho, Shinjuku-ku (3232 3353). Shinjuku station.
Kurofune Hara Bldg 1-2F, 3-5-17 Kita-Aoyama,

Minato-ku (3572 9628). Omotesando station.
Kushinobo Isetan Kaikan 6F, 3-15-17 Shinjuku, Shinjuku-ku (3356-3865). Shinjuku station.
Watami Seibu Shinjuku Ekimae Bldg 4F, 1-25-3 Kabuki-cho, Shinjuku-ku (5292 7921). Shinjuku station.
Sakanaya Itcho 1-2-3 Ginza, Chuo-ku (3564 2555). Ginza station.
Shirokiya San Tropez Ikebukuro Bldg 6F, 1-29-1 Ikebukuro, Toshima-ku (5951 4388). Ikebukuro station.
Tengu Nisshin Bldg 1-2F, 7-10-20 Nishi-Shinjuku, Shinjuku-ku (3227 1761). Shinjuku station.
Torigin 4-12-6 Roppongi, Minato-ku (3403 5829). Roppongi station.
Tsubohachi Pick Peck Bldg 6-7F, 1-17-13 Kabuki-cho, Shinjuku-ku (3208 9535). Shinjuku station.
Uotami Aoyama Center Bldg 2F, 3-8-40 Minami-Aoyama, Minato-ku (3408 4288). Omotesando station.

Pub grub gives you the option of Japanese and western staples at a nice price.

the interior so ugly? Ah well, no matter. Aside from the reasonably priced Sunday brunch of ample proportions with complimentary champagne or Mimosa, Lunchan does a credible array of California-meets-Asia curries, pizza and pasta complemented by a friendly little wine list.

Tim's N.Y.
1-10-11, Ebisu Minami, Shibuya-ku (3793 5656). Ebisu station. **Open** 11.30am-2pm, 6-11.30pm, Mon-Sat; 12-3pm Sat brunch. **Average** lunch ¥1,200, dinner ¥4,000. **Credit** all major cards. **Menu in English. Map 20**
Asian and European-influenced American cuisine served up in a casual setting close to Ebisu station. Lunch specials revolve around pasta, salads and sandwiches. At night the lights dim and the frequently changing chalkboard menu offers sublime selections such as basil, blue cheese and walnut bruschetta. There's a nice (and reasonably priced) selection of California wines available by the glass or by the bottle.

Shinjuku

New York Grill
Park Hyatt Tokyo 52F, 3-7-1-2 Nishi-Shinjuku, Shinjuku-ku (5323-3458). Shinjuku station. **Open** 11.30am-2.30pm, 5.30-10.30pm, Mon-Sat; 11.30am-2.30pm, 5.30-10pm, Sun. **Average** dinner ¥10,000, lunch ¥5,000, brunch ¥6,000. **Credit** all major cards. **Menu in English. Map 3a**
The New York Grill offers a sky-high view and has prices to match, but there's no denying that the food here is excellent and the skyline hard to beat. There's an extensive menu of seafood and meat dishes, highlights of which include baked black mussels, lobster ceviche with ginger, tomato and coriander, and home-grown Maezawa tenderloins and sirloins. If your finances won't stretch quite this far, a less expensive alternative in the Park Hyatt is the highly acclaimed Sunday brunch, or you could imbibe a cocktail or two in the adjoining New York Bar (open 5pm-midnight Monday-Saturday, 4-11pm Sunday; cover charge ¥1,700).

Breakfast

Getting going first thing in the morning can be tough. Getting breakfast can be tougher. If you're staying in a place that provides a Japanese breakfast, by all means try it. Even if rice, miso soup, pickles and room temperature fish are not your idea of morning bliss, bear in mind that there's little more nutritious than a Japanese breakfast.

For those whose accommodations don't provide a morning repast (or those who can't get past the raw egg squeamies) there are a small number of places around Tokyo that serve a western morning meal. For a Japan-ised version, try almost any Japanese coffee shop, where a 'morningu setto' (morning set) will net you bitter coffee, slabs of white toast inches thick with jam, a salad and sometimes an egg (cooked!) for less than ¥500.

There are plenty of places that open from 11am; we've limited our selection to those that are open in time to get you up and going before 10am.

Andersen
Ark Mori Bldg 2F, 1-12-32 Akasaka, Minato-ku (3585 0879). Tameike-sanno station. **Open** bakery 8am-10pm Mon-Fri; 8am-7pm Sat, Sun; restaurant 1am-10pm daily. **Average** ¥1,000. **No credit cards. Map 11**
There are two branches of the popular Andersen chain that serve breakfast. A choice of continental or a morning set with eggs, bacon, toast and coffee will set you back about ¥1,000. Great bread and pastries and good sandwiches may be purchased from the on-premises bakery all day long.

Branch: 5-1-26 Minami-Aoyama, Minato-ku (3407-4833). Open bakery 7am-9pm daily; restaurant 8am-9pm Mon-Fri; 9am-9pm Sat, Sun.

Apetito
4-3-24 Jingumae, Shibuya-ku (3497 0170). Harajuku station. **Open** 8am-10pm, Mon-Sat; 8am-9pm Sun. **Average** ¥500. **No credit cards. Map 5**
This Fukuoka chain has recently ventured into Tokyo with the opening of one shop, and we hope they venture further. Bagels, muffins, pastries, salads, soups, some deli items, eggs and toast, mineral waters and herbal teas. Most available to take away.

Chef's Table
3-20-6 Toranomon, Minato-ku (5405 4473). Toranomon station. **Open** 7am-9pm Mon-Fri. **Average** ¥500. **No credit cards.**
Freshly baked croissants and pain au chocolat, plus teas and coffees, soups, salads and other deli items. Better to take away any of their items; while there are a couple tables and a bench, the bench is too low to sit on while using the table, and there are no high stools when using the table.

Harbor Deli
Intercity Bldg D-105, 2-15-2 Konan, Minato-ku (3472 0585). Shinagawa station. **Open** 8am-9pm Mon-Fri; 9am-8pm Sat; 11am-5pm Sun. **Average** ¥800. **Credit** all major cards.
Deli with California-style food: organic juice bar, wrap sandwiches, bagels, salads, coffee and more. Eat in or take-away. Microbrews from Tokyo's own T.Y. Harbor Brewery, plus a happy hour from 4pm to 7pm.

Eating etiquette

When you enter a restaurant you'll be greeted with a shouted chorus of *'irasshaimase!'* ('welcome!'). The waiter will ask you how many people there are – *'nanmei sama?'* Answer by holding up the appropriate number of fingers.

After you have been seated you will be given an *oshibori* (hot towel) to wipe your hands. You'll also be given a menu and asked if you would like anything to drink (*'o-nomimono wa?'*).

Hands cleaned and drinks on the way, it's now time to decide what to order. If you're in a speciality restaurant, a good deal of the guesswork has already been done for you. You know you'll be eating tempura, for instance; the only decision is what kind. After you've ordered a small round, say *'toriaezu'* ('for now' or 'for starters'). If all else fails and you're feeling trusting, say *'omakaseshimasu'* ('I leave it up to you').

Just like anywhere else, Japan has its own dining etiquette. As a foreigner, you will usually be forgiven minor gaffs. However, paying heed to the following guidelines will ensure that you don't make any unintended insult to your hosts.

Slurping, talking with your mouth full and consuming your food at grand prix speed are all quite acceptable, but it is considered the height of rudeness to blow one's nose at the table.

It is perfectly acceptable to lift a bowl towards your mouth. Soups, like miso, are drunk straight from the bowl. Drinking miso with a spoon is like enjoying a fine wine with a straw.

Much of Japanese food, especially food eaten in izakaya, is intended to be shared with your fellow diners. Even in western restaurants, particularly Italian ones, groups of Japanese people will order dishes to be shared, and kitchens will provide small dishes so that each person can help themselves.

There is almost nothing a foreigner can do wrong with chopsticks. Even the most ham-fisted user will be rewarded with a hearty (and quite sincere) *'o-hashi jozu desu ne!'* ('My, you're so good at using chopsticks!').

There are two things one should never do with chopsticks, as they are related to funeral rituals and will genuinely shock fellow diners. First, never plant your chopsticks upright in a bowl of rice. Second, never pass food from one pair of chopsticks to another, as this mimics the act of conveying the bones of a recently departed from cremation tray to urn.

In most places you pay as you leave, at the cash register by the door. The bill will often be at the table, either a slip of paper or an itemised list attached to a small clipboard; if there is no bill, it is being held at the cash register. In some upscale joints (mostly western) the bill is paid at the table. You can signal for it by making an 'X' sign with two index fingers crossed one over the other, or say *'o-kanjo kudasai'* ('the bill, please'). On the way out, it's polite to nod your head and say *'Gochisosama deshita'* ('I enjoyed the meal').

There is no tipping in Japanese eateries. Many restaurants and hotel bills include a 10 per cent service charge.

Elsewhere

T.Y. Harbor Brewery
2-1-3 Higashi-Shinagawa, Bond Street, Shinagawa-ku (5479 4555). Tennozu Isle station (Tokyo monorail). **Open** 5.30-10.30pm Mon-Fri; 11.30am-5pm Sat, Sun. **Average** ¥2,500. **Credit** AmEx, DC, JCB, V. **Menu in English.**

The food that's served up at T.Y. Harbor Brewery, a bayside brewery and restaurant, is hardly what you'd call inspiring, consisting as it does mainly of casual California-style pasta dishes and a range of sandwiches. But the brews that are on offer here (a selection of porter, pale and amber ales and wheat beer, with the occasional foray into the realm of the bizarre – you could sample a coffee stout, for instance) are all quite drinkable, and the outdoor terrace, which overlooks a canal, provides something that's sorely lacking in Tokyo – a place to hang out by the water.

Ramen
Aoyama/Harajuku/Omotesando

Hokuto
Haruki Bldg B1, 3-5-17 Kita-Aoyama, Minato-ku (3403 0078). Omotesando station. **Open** 11am-midnight Mon-Fri; 11am-10pm Sat, Sun. **Average** ¥1,500. **No credit cards. No English menu.** **Map 5**

Hokuto is really a Chinese restaurant, but its ramen are so good it deserves to be in a class all by itself. The atmosphere, too, is a step above what you find in the average ramen joint; large wooden tables allow more space than the usual pack-'em-in approach. The goma ramen (sesame noodles) have been known to send people into raptures. Other Chinese dishes round out the menu.

Branches Ponte Bldg 1F, 1-17-1 Jingumae, Shibuya-ku (3405 9015). Harajuku station; Fuso Bldg B1, 7-8-8 Ginza, Chuo-ku (3289 8683). Shinbashi station.

Kuramoto

3-11 Kita-Aoyama, Minato-ku (5469 1289).
Omotesando station. **Open** 11.30am-3pm,
5-11.30pm Mon-Thur; 11.30am-3pm, 5pm-4am Fri;
11.30am-3pm, 5-9pm Sat. **Average** ¥700.
No credit cards. No English menu. Map 5
Kuramoto is a tiny ramen shack that resembles a
railroad car with a table set outside it. It specialises
in tonkotsu, which is a thick, creamy, fatty pork
stock, and in loud and raucous music. Tickets for
food have to be purchased at the vending machine;
you then leave your ticket on the counter to order.
Red tickets (for aka ramen) will get you shoyu-
based broth, while blue tickets (for ao ramen) will
get you salt-based broth. Yellow (abura ramen) has
no broth.

Kyushu Jangara Ramen

Shanzeru Harajuku Ni-go-kan 1-2F, 1-13-21
Jingumae, Shibuya-ku (3404 5572). Harajuku
station. **Open** 11am-midnight Mon-Thur; 11-3am
Fri, Sat; 11am-11.30pm Sun. **Average** ¥1,000.
No credit cards. No English menu. Map 5
Extremely popular with the late-teen and early
twenties set that congregates around the Meiji Jingu
end of Omotesando, this whimsically decorated
ramen restaurant always has queues that snake
down the stairs. Don't worry: with 73 seats, an opening will quickly appear. Kyushu ramen from
Fukuoka City is the speciality here, but it comes with
a little twist: the customer selects whether they want
the broth light or heavier, the noodles thin, thick or
somewhere in between, and finally the volume – big
or little, take your pick.

Elsewhere

Jigoku Ramen Hyottoko

Okumiya Bldg B1, 1-8-4 Ebisu Minami, Shibuya-ku
(3791 7376). Ebisu station. **Open** 2-10pm Mon-Fri;
2-7pm Sat. **Average** ¥1,000. **No credit cards.**
No English menu. Map 20
Jigoku means 'hell', and the house speciality at
Jigoku Ramen Hyottoko is ramen in a bright red
soup in varying degrees of heat, with equally colourful names: *aka-oni* (red ogre, shoyu broth), *ao-oni*
(green ogre, salt broth), *enma* (King of Hell, spicy
miso), *jigoku* (hell, spicy miso) and jigoku ramen special (spicy miso). A sign on the wall warns that if
you order the special and can't finish it, you have to
wash dishes.

Theme restaurants

Average prices at the following theme restaurants
have been omitted; the total bill will depend on
how much you imbibe.

Ginza

Ganesa

Pacific Ginza Bldg 6F, 7-2-20 Ginza, Chuo-ku
(5568 4312). Ginza station. **Open** 6pm-5am

(last order 4am) Mon-Fri; 6-11.30pm (last order
10.30pm) Sat. **Cover charge** ¥1,000.
Credit all major cards. **Map 7**
World cuisine cooked up in an exotic interior is the
theme at Ganesa. Descend into a world of lush
Balinese draperies and cushions, with low tables
tucked away in veiled tents and intimate little nooks
where you can hide away. The food leans toward the
exotic as well: Balinese fried rice, samosas, Thai
soups and grilled meat tacos are all cooked up at
very reasonable prices. The quality of the food is
erratic but the prices are reasonable and the ambience unbeatable.
Branches Hotel P&A Plaza B1, 1-17-9 Dogenzaka,
Shibuya-ku (5458 0475). Shibuya station; The
Catalina Bldg 3F, 1-3-15 Kabuki-cho, Shinjuku-ku
(5291 8533). Shinjuku station.

Roppongi

Alcatraz B.C

Elsa Bldg 2F, 3-13-12 Roppongi, Minato-ku
(5410 0012). Roppongi station. **Open** 6pm-5am
(last order 4am) Mon-Sat; 6pm-midnight (last order
11.30pm) Sun. Course menu only 6-8pm.
Cover charge ¥1,000, groups of females after
midnight get in free. **Credit** all major cards. **Map 2**
San Francisco's infamous Alcatraz is the inspiration
behind this Roppongi nightspot. A bevy of beautiful jailers will serve you behind bars in a cell from
which you can order thematic drinks. Prices here are
friendly, so you can leave the bail bondsmen's number at home.

Shibuya

Bobby's Café

The Prime Bldg 4F, 2-29-5 Dogenzaka, Shibuya-ku
(3463 8866). Shibuya station. **Open** 5pm-5am
(last order 4.30am) Mon-Sat; 5-11pm (last order
10.30pm) Sun. **Credit** all major cards. **Map 4**
Bobby's Café is a monstrously large late-night
dining spot (it is capable of seating literally hundreds of customers) that is hoping to make the same
kind of impact here in Tokyo as it did in its native
Osaka, by serving around-the-world cuisine alongside a very extensive drinks menu. The menu boasts
a total of 55 dishes representing 30 countries from
nine separate food areas. The wine starts at ¥2,800
per bottle.

World Sports Café Tokyo

World Sports Plaza B1, 1-16-9 Shibuya-ku
(3407 7337). Shibuya station. **Open** 11.30am-
11.30pm Mon-Thur; 11.30am-4.30am Fri, Sat;
11.30am-10pm Sun. **No cover charge.**
Credit all major cards. **Map 4**
Sports, sports and more sports: MLB, NBA, NFL,
lineup. The flagship monitor is a 1,000-inch projec-
tor, and numerous smaller monitors dot the room
and are visible from all of the tables. Perversely grin-
ning life-size mannequins greet you as you enter.
The menu is a hodgepodge of Japanese and
Japanised western grub.

Menu reader

MAIN TYPES OF RESTAURANT

寿司屋 *sushi-ya*
sushi restaurants

イクラ *ikura* salmon roe

タコ *tako* octopus

マグロ *maguro* tuna

こはだ *kohada* punctatus

トロ *toro* belly of tuna

ホタテ *hotate* scallop

ウニ *uni* sea urchin roe

エビ *ebi* prawn

ヒラメ *hirame* flounder

アナゴ *anago* ark shell

イカ *ika* squid

玉子焼き *tamago-yaki* sweet egg omelette

かっぱ巻き *kappa maki* rolled cucumber

鉄火巻き *tekka maki* rolled tuna

お新香巻き *oshinko maki* rolled pickles

蕎麦屋（そば屋） *soba-ya*
Japanese noodle restaurants

天ぷらそば うどん *tempura soba, udon*
noodles topped with shrimp tempura

ざるそば うどん *zaru soba, udon*
noodles served on a bamboo rack in a lacquer box

きつねそば うどん *kitsune soba, udon*
noodles in hot broth topped with spring onion and fried tofu

たぬきそば うどん *tanuki soba, udon*
noodles in hot broth with fried tempura batter

月見そば うどん *tsukimi soba, udon*
raw egg broken over noodles in their hot broth

あんかけうどん *ankake udon*
wheat noodles in a thick fish bouillon/soy sauce soup with fishcake slices and vegetables

鍋焼きうどん *nabeyaki udon*
noodles boiled in an earthenware pot with other ingredients and stock. Mainly eaten in winter.

居酒屋 *izakaya*
Japanese-style bars

日本酒 *nihon-shu* Japanese sake

冷酒 *rei-shu* cold sake

焼酎 *shoochuu* grain wine

チュウハイ *chuuhai*
grain wine with soda pop

生ビール *nama-biiru* draft beer

黒ビール *kuro-biiru* dark beer

梅酒 *ume-shu* plum wine

ひれ酒 *hirezake*
sake with toasted blowfish fins

焼き魚 *yaki zakana* grilled fish

煮魚 *ni zakana*
fish cooked in various sauces

刺し身 *sashimi*
raw fish in bite-sized pieces, served with soy sauce and horseradish

揚げ出し豆腐 *agedasi doofu*
lightly fried plain tofu

枝豆 *edamame*
boiled young soybeans in the pod

おにぎり *onigiri*
rice parcel with savoury filling

焼きおにぎり *yaki onigiri*
grilled rice balls

フグ刺し *fugusashi*
thinly sliced sashimi, usually spectacularly arranged and served with ponzu sauce

フグちり　*fuguchiri*
chunks of fugu in a vegetable stew

雑炊　*zosui*
cooked rice and egg added to the above

焼き鳥屋　*yakitori-ya*
yakitori restaurants

焼き鳥　*yakitori*
barbecued chicken pieces marinated in sweet soy
sauce

つくね　*tsukune*　minced chicken balls

タン　*tan*　tongue

ハツ　*hatsu*　heart

シロ　*shiro*　tripe

レバー　*reba*　liver

ガツ　*gatsu*　intestines

鳥皮　*tori-kawa*　skin

ネギ間　*negima*　chicken with spring onions

おでん屋　*oden-ya*
oden restaurants or street stalls

さつま揚げ　*satsuma-age*　fish cake

昆布　*konbu*　kelp rolls

大根　*daikon*　radish

厚揚げ　*atsu-age*　fried tofu

OTHER TYPES OF RESTAURANT

料亭　*ryotei*
high-class, traditional restaurants

ラーメン屋　*ramen-ya*
Japanese-style ramen or Chinese noodle restaurants

天ぷら屋　*tempura-ya*　tempura restaurants

すき焼き屋　*sukiyaki-ya*
sukiyaki restaurants

トンカツ屋　*tonkatsu-ya*
tonkatsu restaurants

お好み焼き屋　*okonomi yaki-ya*
okonomiyaki restaurants

ESSENTIAL VOCABULARY

A table for..., please　***...onegai shimasu***

one/two/three/four
hitori/futari/san-nin/yo-nin

Is this seat free?　***kono seki aite masu ka***

Could we sit...?　***...ni suware masu ka***

over there　***soko***

outside　***soto***

in a non-smoking area　***kin-en-seki***

by the window　***madogiwa***

Excuse me
sumimasen/onegai shimasu

May I see the menu, please
menyuu o onegai shimasu

Do you have a set menu?
setto menyuu/teishoku wa arimasu ka

I'd like...　***...o kudasai***

I'll have...　***...ni shimasu***

a bottle/glass...
...o ippon/ippai kudasai

I can't eat food containing...
...ga haitte iru mono wa taberare masen

Do you have vegetarian meals?
bejitarian no shokuji wa arimasu ka

Do you have a children's menu?
kodomo-yoo no menyuu wa arimasu ka

The bill, please
o-kanjyoo onegai shimasu

That was delicious, thank you
gochisou sama deshita

We'd like to pay separately
betsubetsu ni onegai shimasu

It's all together, please
issho ni onegai shimasu

Is service included?
saabisu-ryoo komi desu ka

Can I pay with a credit card?
kurejitto caado o tsukae masu ka

Could I have a receipt, please?
reshiito onegai shimasu

For pronunciation guidelines, *see p254*.

Bars

Alcohol keeps Tokyo going, and there's no shortage of places to get it.

Drinking is a major activity in Japan and a great social lubricant. It binds business deals, loosens the reserve of the buttoned-up salarymen, and has evolved its own culture and rules of etiquette (*see* **Drinking Etiquette**, *below*), though as the night wears on, committing a social faux pas becomes much less a concern than finding your way home.

Drinking is almost always accompanied by food. The western notion of sitting in a bar and having a drink, while slowly catching on (*see* **The real pub boom**, *p164*), was for a long time non-existent in Japan. It would be unusual to venture into an *izakaya*, for example, and order just a beverage. It would also be a bit of a waste, as Japanese beer and sake go uncommonly well with food.

This means that the dividing line between bars and restaurants is less clear than in the west. Nearly all of the places recommended here offer some sort of food, although the main purpose of each is drinking. Many bars in Tokyo make a table charge (usually around ¥500 per person) for customers, and provide a plate of nuts or rice crackers to justify it. This makes having one quick drink less economical, encouraging you to stay longer. Most of the bars below make no cover charge. Generally speaking, if a bar does not make a cover charge, it advertises the fact on the sign outside (often in English). Always check prices before going into any bar in Tokyo. One wrong turn and you could end up paying the price of a plane ticket home for a round of beers. As a rule, if you can't see a price list, don't go in.

In addition to the bars below, most of Tokyo's top hotels (*see chapter* **Accommodation**) have bars that are open to non-residents, some of which boast spectacular views over the city. Another interesting, and potentially hazardous, feature of drinking in Tokyo is the lack of licensing hours. Bars can, and frequently do, stay open until empty, particularly at weekends. As the evening wears on, it can be easy to lose track of time. Whatever you do, don't miss that last train home, unless you don't mind spending the rest of the night in a 24-hour karaoke box or capsule hotel.

One thing you don't have to worry about is being drunk in public; the Japanese are very kind to over-indulgers, willing to forgive transgressions ranging from maudlin displays of affection, to recycling one's dinner on railway platforms. Sharing a drink is one of the surest ways to get to know your hosts. For more suggestions for places to eat and drink, *see chapter* **Restaurants**.

Bars

Bernd's Bar
Pure 2F, 5-18-1 Roppongi, Minato-ku (5563 9232). Roppongi station. **Open** 5-11pm Mon-Sat (bar open till empty). **Credit** AmEx, MC. **Map 2**
If you're German, you'll feel right at home in this friendly second-floor bar. Fresh pretzels are stacked on the tables; Bitburger and Erdinger, among other beers, are ready at the tap for washing down your Wiener schnitzel. Even if you're not German you'll like it. Try and get a table by the window, for the view over the nightlife area of Roppongi is worth catching. If you happen to meet the owner, Bernd Haag, you'll find he can chat with you in English, German, Spanish, as well as Japanese.

Bon's
1-1-10 Kabuki-cho, Shinjuku-ku (3209 6334). Shinjuku station. **Open** 7pm-5am daily. **No credit cards**. **Map 3b**
Two minutes' walk away from the neon of Shinjuku is Golden Gai (*see* **Golden Gai**, *above right*), an area of barely one square kilometre that houses around 200 *nomiya*, or Japanese bars. Most bars here do not welcome foreigners, but this is one of the few that does, even though you'll have to pay a ¥600 cover charge for the privilege. It's bigger than most, too.

Golden Gai

Nestling in the shadows of the ultra-modern, neon-lit skyscrapers of east Shinjuku, Golden Gai is a place that shouldn't really exist in Tokyo, yet exist it does, and it's still thriving. This tiny area, consisting of three streets of ramshackle buildings, was constructed 50 years ago, at the end of the war. It hasn't changed since. Walking around, you are instantly transported back to post-war Tokyo, where the black market thrived and temporary accommodation was hastily knocked up to provide shelter for the homeless. Somehow, here, they forgot to knock the buildings down again.

It's hard to believe, but crammed into this warren of streets are around 200 *nomiya*, or Japanese-style bars, many with room for only four customers at a time. Most cater to a regular clientele, and are unlikely to welcome strangers (for exceptions, *see listings*). Just walking into a bar at random here is likely to produce an awkward silence at best, and a hideously expensive bill at worst, so tread carefully. Instead, take the time to wander around and ponder how it is that this piece of prime Tokyo real estate has so far managed to escape the clutches of property developers. Rumours of Golden Gai's demise have been circulating for over 20 years, but still the bars refuse to buckle

under. Towards the end of 1998 a fire in three buildings destroyed 16 bars and raised the possibility once again that Golden Gai's days were numbered. Go there while you can.

Brussels

3-16-1 Kanda-Ogawa-cho, Chiyoda-ku (3233 4247).
Jinbocho station. **Open** 5.30pm-2am Mon-Fri; 5.30-11pm Sat. **No credit cards**. **Map 9**

One of a small chain of Belgian-style bars with a dazzling array of over 30 beers imported from the old country and served in their proper glasses. The Jinbocho branch, which spreads over three wood-panelled floors of a very narrow building, is a favourite with local university students and journalists from the many magazines based in the area. Should the urge take you, there's great Belgian-style food on offer (around ¥1,000), but there's no obligation to eat, and no cover charge.

Branches: 1-10-23 Jingumae, Shibuya-ku (3403 3972). Harajuku station; 1-3-4 Nihonbashi-Kayabacho, Chuo-ku (5641 1929). Kayabacho station; 75 Yarai-cho, Shinjuku-ku (3235 1890). Kagurazaka station.

Café Olé

Metro Building 1F, 22-38-2 Kabuki-cho, Shinjuku-ku (3200 2249). Shinjuku station. **Open** 8pm until empty, daily. **No credit cards**. **Map 3b**

Barcelona-born bar owner Miguel is one of Tokyo's more eccentric barmen. On a night out in this tiny bar (seating for 12), anything can happen, and often does. Recent visits have produced an impromptu demonstration of flamenco dancing with a passing troupe of Spanish guitarists, and an early-morning darts tournament, with free drinks on offer to the winner (Miguel always wins). Prices, for Tokyo, are rock bottom, and he mixes a mean cocktail, too.

Double-Decker Bus

1-7-1 Nishi-Shinbashi, Minato-ku (3597 0242). Shinbashi station. **Open** 11-4am Mon-Fri; 6-11pm Sat. **No credit cards**. **Map 13**

Turn a corner in between Shinbashi and Toranomon and you won't believe your eyes. A number 10 London double-decker bus has been roughly converted and serves as a coffee shop by day and bar by night. Seating and interior is all original, complete with no-smoking signs (to be ignored) and that musty London bus pong. The bar is at the front of the bottom deck. Toilets are out back, in a trailer.

The Dubliners

Shinjuku Lion Hall 2F, 3-28-9 Shinjuku, Shinjuku-ku (3352 6606). Shinjuku station. **Open** 11.30am-11.30pm Mon-Sat; 11.30am-10pm Sun.
Credit AmEx, MC, V. **Map 3b**

Owned and operated by Japanese brewing giant Sapporo, this popular Irish pub serves reasonable pub-style food. The only inauthentic touch is very welcome – waiter service. Downstairs is a branch of Sapporo's Lion Hall, a near-ubiquitous chain of izakaya serving passable Japanese food and lots of Sapporo beer. Another Dubliners branch is scheduled to open in late 1999 in Ebisu.

Branch: Sun Grow Bldg B1, 1-10-8 Nishi-Ikebukuro, Toshima-ku (5951 3614). Ikebukuro station.

The Fiddler

2-1-2 Takadanobaba B1, Shinjuku-ku (3204 2698). Takadanobaba station. **Open** 6pm-3am Mon-Thur, Sun; 6pm-5am Fri, Sat. **No credit cards. Map 25**
This place run by two UK expats smells like pubs back home, only it's open every night until the wee hours. Live music or comedy acts almost every night at no extra charge. Most of the acts are local *gaijin* groups, but the occasional up-and-coming Japanese band plays the Fiddler as well. The food is fairly acceptable, the kitchen staying open till midnight.

Flamme d'Or

Asahi Super Dry Building 1F, 2F, 1-25 Azumabashi, Taito-ku (5608 5381). Asakusa station. **Open** 11.30am-11pm daily. **Credit** AmEx, MC, V. **Map 10**
One of Tokyo's quirkier landmarks, the enormous gold-coloured object lying atop French architect Philippe Starck's ultra-modern building across the river from the temples of Asakusa is most often compared with some as-yet-undiscovered form of giant root vegetable. The dark tetrahedral Super Dry Building itself is said to be modelled on the shape of a cut-off beer glass, and it was named after a brand

of beer. The beer hall inside is also quite distinctive: oddly shaped pillars, tiny porthole windows high overhead and sweeping curved walls covered in soft grey cushioning. English menus are available with a choice of German-style bar snacks and Asahi draught beers. On the twenty-second floor is another bar, the Asahi Sky Room, serving beer and coffee from 10am to 9pm.

Footnik

Marujo Building B1, 3-12-8 Takadanobaba, Shinjuku-ku (5330 5301). Takadanobaba station. **Open** 5pm-1am daily. **No credit cards. Map 25**
In the days before that nice Mr Murdoch brought Sky to Japan, the opening of Footnik in summer 1996 came as manna from heaven for sad souls deprived of their regular Premiership football fix. Since then, others have followed, but only Footnik retains the dingy appeal of a genuine British pub. It boasts a 56-inch TV screen, walls plastered with banners, and it screens live matches on Saturday and Sunday nights, with highlights and taped *Match of the Day* later in the week.

Gas Panic

3-15-24 Roppongi, Minato-ku (3405 0633). Roppongi station. **Open** 6pm-5am daily. **No credit cards. Map 2**
Gas Panic is a Roppongi institution of depravity. More like an American fraternity party than a bar, it's primarily for the young and immature, or those who wish to reclaim their salad days. If you can talk the talk, it's an excellent place for men to 'meet' young Japanese women looking for foreigners (who can pay, if they choose, in American dollars). The

*Take in the view of Asakusa from the **Asahi Sky Room,** in Philippe Starck's Flamme d'Or.*

It's cheap, it's cheerful, it's incredibly popular. It must be **Gas Panic**.

drinks are among the cheapest in town, particularly on Thursdays, when everything is ¥300 all day. There are several Gas Panic installations, three in the Gas Panic Building and one closer to Roppongi Dori, Gas Panic Club (3402 7054).

George's Bar
Misuzu Bldg 2F, 2-19-7 Kichijoji-Honcho, Musashino-shi (0422 22 8002). Kichijoji station. **Open** 7pm-midnight daily. **Credit** AmEx, MC, V. **Map 24**
Pricey (around ¥1,000) but lovingly prepared cocktails served by George Saeki, who used to work on a US military base and thus speaks quite good English. Each cocktail served at this tiny counter bar comes in a unique, carefully selected glass, and is served with a plate of beer nuts and nibbles.

Geronimo
Yamamuro Bldg 2F, 7-14-10 Roppongi, Minato-ku (3478 7449). Roppongi station. **Open** 7pm-6am daily. **No credit cards. Map 2**
This place and its sister bar, Mogambo, are two of the liveliest bars for foreigners in Tokyo, skirting the ridiculous excess of nearby Gas Panic (*see above*), but only just. Like most places in Roppongi, Geronimo doesn't really get going until 1am. If you can drink 20 different shots here, you'll make your way into the hall of fame, get your name on a plaque, a free T-shirt and a terrible hangover.
Branch: Mogambo, Osawa Bldg 1F, 6-1-7 Roppongi, Minato-ku (3403 4833), Roppongi station.

Half Time
1-19-4 Kabuki-cho, Shinjuku-ku (3209 7114). Shinjuku station. **Open** 4pm-5am daily. **No credit cards. Map 3b**

This small hole-in-the-wall, a short hop from Tokyo Kaisen Market and Koma Stadium, as well as clubs such as Code, Liquid Room and the new Loft, offers no-frills drinks at reasonable prices in a no-frills setting: the bar stools are decidedly ratty, and the long counter scratched and pockmarked. There's often a drink promotion, mostly recently vodka and tequila, where a quick drink can be had on the cheap. Not the kind of place where people linger, but a good spot for meeting up or a quiet quick one before moving on. There's almost always sport on the TVs.

Hanezawa Beer Garden
3-12-15 Hiroo, Shibuya-ku (3400 6500). Hiroo station. **Open** 5-9pm daily in summer. **Credit** AmEx, MC, V.
Hanezawa is a real garden (most beer 'gardens' are concrete monstrosities) that was established in the Meiji era. The property was once owned by a feudal lord but was converted into a public beer garden without losing its special touches: a carp pond, hanging lanterns and attentive, if slightly surly, service. It's now a Tokyo institution in the hot, sticky summer months. The food is unremarkable but the beer is cold and comes in enormous mugs (*dai jokki*). Feel free to traipse around among the lanterns, dodging cats underfoot and mosquitoes overhead. One complaint – it closes way too early.

Hub
Poan Shibuya Bldg B1, 3-10 Udagawa-cho, Shibuya-ku (3496 0765). Shibuya station. **Open** noon-midnight Mon-Thur, Sun; noon-2am Fri, Sat. **No credit cards. Map 4**

One of a medium-sized chain of British-style pubs which boasts one of the finest happy hours in Tokyo, with cocktails just ¥180 from 5-7pm every day. This branch also has the added attraction of a real table football table.
Branches: Nobara Bldg B1, 25-9 Udagawa-cho, Shibuya-ku (3770 4524). Shibuya station; Matsui Bldg B1, 1-6-8 Yurakucho, Chiyoda-ku (3592 0310). Hibiya station; Haiyuza Bldg. 1F, 4-9-2 Roppongi, Minato-ku (3478 0393). Roppongi station; 1F, 4-7-22 Kudan-Minami, Chiyoda-ku (5276 3288). Ichigaya station; Kojima Bldg B1, 1-22-8 Kabuki-cho, Shinjuku-ku (3208 1451). Shinjuku station;

Shinjuku Uchino Bldg B1, 3-36-16 Shinjuku, Shinjuku-ku (5379 4067). Shinjuku station; Sushi-Hatsu Bldg 1F, 1-12-2 Asakusa, Taito-ku (3847 8896). Tawaramachi station; Fuji Bldg B1, 1-23-1 Minami-Ikebukuro, Toshima-ku (5952 0621). Ikebukuro station.

Hungry Humphrey
1-1-10 Kabuki-cho, Shinjuku-ku (3200 6156). Shinjuku station. **Open** 6.30pm-1.30am Mon-Sat. **No credit cards. Map 3b**
Another foreigner-friendly small bar in the Golden Gai area of Shinjuku (*see* **Golden Gai**, *p153*).

Karaoke

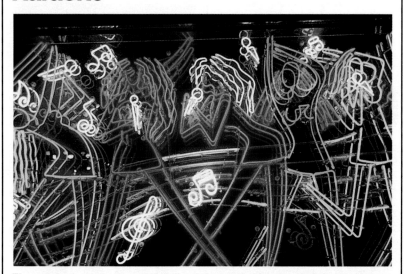

The craze that has swept the world is believed to have been started in the 1970s by a hard-up Japanese bar owner who hit upon the idea of getting his customers to sing along to instrumental backing tracks. Today, almost every street in Tokyo offers passers-by the chance to stretch their tonsils and massacre their favourite songs.

While singing in public bars is still a favourite pastime of middle-aged Japanese businessmen, for young people the venue of preference is usually a karaoke box, a small room rented by the hour where you can sing along with friends while the staff continue to ply you with drink. As night falls near large stations such as Shinjuku or Shibuya, you will be continually approached by young people with leaflets, saying '*Karaoke ikaga desu ka?*' ('How about some

karaoke?'). Often these leaflets will give some discount off the standard price. Most big karaoke box complexes are open 24 hours, all are licensed and some even include all-you-can-drink deals as part of the package. Average price is around ¥500 per person per hour.

The laser disc technology that powers karaoke (literal translation: 'empty orchestra') is provided by a number of companies. All of them offer a selection of English songs (usually at the back of the song book), although the DAM and Songoku systems have a wider variety than most. As a way of breaking the ice, karaoke is hard to beat, and the experience of yelling into a mike is strangely addictive once you overcome your initial shyness. Don't leave Tokyo without giving it a try.

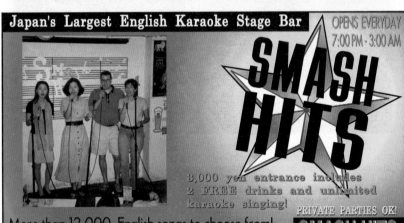

Enjoy British beer, pub atmosphere and the cheapest happy hour in town at the **Hub**.

Ieyasu Hon-jin

1-30 Jinbocho, Kanda, Chiyoda-ku (3291 6228).
Jinbocho station. **Open** 5-10pm Mon-Fri.
No credit cards. Map 9

Genial host Taisho bangs the drum behind the bar to greet each new customer to this cosy, top-class *yakitori* bar named after the first of the Tokugawa shoguns. There are only a dozen seats, so everyone crowds around the counter, where a wide choice of foodstuffs (including mushrooms and beef as well as the usual chicken) lies in glass cases, already on sticks, ready to be popped on the coals and grilled. All the food is excellent, as is the beer (Kirin Brau Meister) and sake, which Taisho dispenses with natural flair, pouring into small cups from a great height. Not cheap (expect around ¥4,000-¥7,000 for a couple of hours' eating and drinking), but still good value. Try to avoid the 6-8pm after-work rush and don't go in a group of more than two or three.

The Irish House

Daishi Yoshikawa Bldg 2F, 2-8-9 Shinbashi, Minato-ku (3503 4494). Shinbashi station. **Open** 11.30am-11pm Mon-Fri; 5pm-11pm Sat. **Credit** AmEx, MC, V.
Map 13

Of the recent rash of new Irish bars, this is possibly the best. Professional, friendly service by bar staff specially flown over from Ireland is matched by a menu featuring Tokyo's best fish and chips.

Kaga-ya

B1, 2-15-12 Shinbashi, Minato-ku (3591 2347).
Shinbashi station. **Open** 5.30-11.30pm Mon-Sat.
No credit cards. Map 13

When the awards for the strangest place in Tokyo are handed out, the master of this bar, who goes by the very un-Japanese name of Michael, will be somewhere near the front of the queue. On arrival, you will be handed a cocktail list which is nothing more than a list of countries. Once you've placed your order, the master will disappear into a cupboard and reappear dressed in a costume which reflects the country you've chosen. The drink itself may be in a vibrating glass, a glass that moos when picked up, or a soup bowl. Once the drinks round is over, you will be encouraged to play games and dress up. Small portions of delicious food are provided as part of the ¥500 cover charge, cooked by the master's tolerant mother. Go with a party of at least six people (call to book, it's a small place) and you'll have the time of your life. The billing system is mysterious; no matter how much you eat and drink here, it always seems to come to ¥2,500 a head.

Kamiya Bar

1-1-1 Asakusa, Taito-ku (3841 5400). Asakusa station. **Open** 11.30am-10pm daily.
No credit cards. Map 10

Established in the late 1800s, Kamiya is the oldest Western-style bar in Tokyo and quintessential Asakusa. The crowds aren't there for decor or even drink: the interior is Formica-table coffee shop and too-bright lighting. But the atmosphere – loud, smoky, sometimes raucous – is, in a word, *shita-machi*. Try the house Denki Bran (Electric Brandy) – not so much for its taste, but for the experience of having tried the domestic stuff. Makes a dubious gift to take home as well.

Monday
Tuesday
Time Out
Thursday
Friday
Saturday
Sunday

Kind House Ruins

B1, 1-8-5 Kichijoji-Honcho, Musashino-shi (0422 21 6269). Kichijoji station. **Open** 5pm-2am daily (last orders 1am). **Credit** V. **Map 24**

Tokyo is not short of theme bars, but even connoisseurs of the tacky will be impressed by this place, a short ride out of the centre. From the outside, Ruins looks like nothing special. It's not until you descend the staircase to the cavernous basement that the first shock really hits you. You're climbing down a dinosaur's gullet. Once inside, you may need a drink (from around ¥700) while you take in the surroundings. In one corner a dead dinosaur (possibly a brontosaurus) lies on its back while locals happily tuck into izakaya-style food sitting at tables in its ribcage. At centre of the room there's a fountain with an ichthyosaur in it, while the far wall boasts a stegosaurus, a triceratops and a variety of trilobites. After all this, you probably won't notice the food, which is good, but unremarkable. You will, however, almost certainly need another drink to steady your nerves before getting up that staircase.

Lion Beer Hall

7-9-20 Ginza, Chuo-ku (3571 2590). Ginza station. **Open** 11.30am-11pm Mon-Sat; 11.30am-10.30pm Sun. **Credit** AmEx, MC, V. **Map 7**

This 1930s beer hall, part of the Sapporo Lion chain, is a tourist attraction in itself. The tiled, wood-panelled interior looks for all the world as if it's been transplanted from Bavaria. The menu, with its plethora of sausage choices, adds to the effect. For those who want to eat more than drink, there is a restaurant upstairs.

Lunchan

1-2-5 Shibuya, Shibuya-ku (5466 1398). Shibuya station. **Open** 11.30am-11pm Mon-Sat; 11am-10pm Sun. **Credit** AmEx, MC, V. **Map 4**

Primarily a restaurant serving fine California-style cuisine, Lunchan has a lovely, modern bar facing floor-to-ceiling glass windows that peek out towards Aoyama Dori. A good assortment of Californian wines and cocktails start at about ¥800. A short walk from Shibuya station, this is a good stopping-off point for those heading to Harajuku and Omotesando, or a quiet place to catch your breath before clubbing it into the wee hours at Loop across Aoyama Dori.

Millgram Underline

JR Yamanotesen-shita, 3-29-70 Shibuya, Shibuya-ku (5458 2366). Shibuya station. **Open** 6pm-2am Mon-Thur; 6pm-5am Fri, Sat. **No credit cards**. **Map 4**

This very small lounge, half bar, half tiny club (*see chapter* **Nightlife**) is located under the JR Yamanote line. You can 'feel' the trains go above your head, the noise subdued only by the sound system. Music ranges from jazz to pop, and drinks start at ¥500. A favourite hangout for people on their way out in a spectacularly sleazy-looking part of Shibuya.

Mon

B1, 28-13 Udagawa-cho, Shibuya-ku (3476 7236). Shibuya station. **Open** 4.30pm-1am Mon-Thur, Sun; 4.30pm-2am Fri, Sat. **No credit cards**. **Map 4**

A long-established bar on one of Shibuya's main drags with a good reputation for cocktails and super-efficient service. Every order is greeted with a shouted chorus of 'Hai!' and then repeated across the bar

*Of the many recently opened Irish bars, the **Irish House** is arguably the best.*

Japanese-style eating meets German-style drinking at Ginza's **Lion Beer Hall**.

until it finally reaches the ears of the uniformed barmen. Prices are firmly mid-range, with beer at ¥600, gin and tonic ¥700 and frozen Margaritas ¥800. There is, however, a ¥500 table charge.

Mon Chéri

B1, 2-37-2 Kabuki-cho, Shinjuku-ku (3209 9718). Shinjuku station. **Open** *6pm-5am daily.* **No credit cards. Map 3b**
A small basement cocktail bar with friendly, uniformed staff and no cover charge. Cocktails cost around ¥700, and on a good night the bearded master will run through his repertoire of magic tricks behind the bar. Head here later in the evening and you're almost guaranteed to become embroiled in conversation with one of the regulars as they teeter precariously on their bar stools. Come alone, and the bar staff will keep you talking.

O'Carolan's

3F, 2-15-22 Jiyugaoka, Meguro-ku (3723 5533). Jiyugaoka station (Tokyu Toyoko line). **Open** *11am-midnight daily.* **No credit cards. Map 28**
An unusually spacious Irish bar in the former premises of an Italian restaurant, which explains the bizarre mural of angels and cherubs on the far wall. Guinness and Kilkenny are on tap, and during happy hour (Mon-Thur 5-7pm) all drinks are ¥500. Away from the cherubs at the other end of the room there's a pleasant greenhouse area where you can sip your drinks on wicker sofas as the sunshine comes through the ceiling.

Oh God!

B1, 6-7-18 Jingumae, Shibuya-ku (3406 3206). Harajuku station. **Open** *6pm-6am daily.* **No credit cards. Map 5**
The nearest Tokyo has to the bars on Bangkok's Khao-san Road. Films are shown nightly on a giant screen to an audience more interested in knocking back the ¥700 beer. Also has pool and pinball tables. A schedule for the week's films is posted outside.

Paddy Foley's Irish Pub

B1, 5-5-1 Roppongi, Minato-ku (3423 2250). Roppongi station. **Open** *5pm-2.30am Mon-Sat; 4.30pm-12.30am Sun.* **Credit** *AmEx, MC, V.* **Map 2**
Just about every bar owner worth his salt is opening an Irish pub in Tokyo these days, but it's this place that takes the credit for getting the ball rolling. Step in and you find yourself transported halfway round the world. Guinness, naturally, is the house speciality and the food is good. Can get as crowded as a London pub at weekends, something the locals (who always sit down to drink) regard with mild bemusement.

Paranoia Café

Victory Bldg 3F, 4-12-5 Roppongi, Minato-ku (5411 8018). Roppongi station. **Open** *7pm-midnight Mon-Thur; 7pm-5am Fri, Sat.* **No credit cards. Map 2**
One of the partners of Paranoia is Crazy George, who was a make-up artist for the cult zombie thriller *Dawn of the Dead*. Being here is like being an extra in that film. The walls and ceiling are liberally 'decorated' with screaming heads, and slasher movies run endlessly on monitors as Goth-rock and heavy

metal blares from the sound system. If that isn't enough, you can look through a catalogue of cuts, contusions and full-scale weirdnesses to decide how you want to get made up. For free. One of the assistants will create a strikingly realistic gash on your forehead. A lot of laughs on the train ride home.

Radio Bar

2-31-7 Jingumae, Shibuya-ku (3405 5490).
Harajuku station. **Open** 7pm-2am Mon-Sat.
No credit cards. Map 5
Dazzlingly designed, in a nineteenth-meets-twenty-first-century style, and dazzlingly expensive, Radio Bar is a wonderful place to enjoy superior cocktails or sample a wide range of Scotch whiskies. For the money (around ¥1,500 per cocktail plus ¥1,500 cover charge), you get attentive service by tuxedo-clad barmen. There are nine tall bar stools at the long wood counter, and in a corner, under a dim light, sits the star of the show – an antique shortwave radio. The cover charge includes a beautifully precious arrangement of fruits, vegetables and cheese.

Rock 'n' Roll Diner

Big Ben Bldg B1, 2-5-2 Kitazawa, Setagaya-ku
(3411 6565). Shimo-Kitazawa station (Odakyu/
Inokashira lines). **Open** 5pm-midnight Mon-Fri; 4pm-2am Sat; 4pm-midnight Sun. **Credit** AmEx, MC, V.
Map 29
Loud, large, popular bar and restaurant in the heart of trendy young Shimo-Kitazawa with 1950s/'60s music and motif, non-stop videos and loud rock 'n' roll. American-style food, heavy on pseudo Tex-Mex fare, like fajitas. Huge drinks selection includes Margaritas by the pitcher. Good place to meet people before you head off to explore the neighbourhood.

The Rising Sun

Shinsei Building 2F, 1-9-3 Yotsuya, Shinjuku-ku
(3352 8842). Yotsuya station. **Open** 6pm-midnight daily. **No credit cards. Map 16**

When is a pub not a pub?

On your travels around Tokyo, you will certainly encounter places calling themselves either 'Pub' or 'Snack'. Such places are likely to be very small, with bright signs and either no windows or heavy curtains. Do not be misled by the signs. These establishments are either hostess bars or small members' clubs whose clients pay for the privilege of being entertained by hostesses or a *mama-san*. If you do decide to go into one of these places, be prepared to pay dearly for the experience, and to speak Japanese.

The longest-established British pub in Tokyo is up a flight of stairs in an anonymous office block. Inside, it's all dark and wooden, the walls covered with framed prints of horses, like a tiny Yorkshire pub. The Rising Sun also operates an unofficial lending library from its bookshelves. Promise to bring it back and you'll be allowed to take it away. Live football screened on request.

The Shamrock

B1, 1-13-3 Nishi-Shinjuku, Shinjuku-ku (3348
4609). Shinjuku station. **Open** noon-11pm Mon-Thur; noon-12.30am Fri, Sat; noon-10.30pm Sun.
No credit cards. Map 3a
A strangely shaped basement bar with genuine Irish fittings that opened for business in 1998. All the usual beers, good food and great Irish coffee, although the happy hour (5-7pm daily) only applies to cocktails.

Shot Bar Shadow

1-1-8 Kabuki-cho, Shinjuku-ku (3209 9530).
Shinjuku station. **Open** 5pm-midnight Mon-Fri; 6pm-midnight Sat (members only after midnight).
No credit cards. Map 3b
The eccentric master of this tiny, foreigner-friendly bar in Golden Gai (*see* **Golden Gai**, *p153*) will speak to you in fluent Japanese, French, Spanish, Russian or Arabic. But not English: 'That's too obvious.' Seating room for eight people, at a pinch.

Smash Hits

M2 Building B1, 5-2-26 Hiroo, Shibuya-ku (3444
0432). Hiroo station. **Open** 8pm-3am Mon-Sat, 7pm-midnight Sun. **Credit** AmEx, MC, V.
There are literally thousands of karaoke bars and boxes in Tokyo, all of them with a smattering of English songs, but this place is one of the few that cater specifically for the foreign market, with over 10,000 English-language songs to choose from. There's a stage where you can strut your stuff while murdering your favourite music, and even a small selection of props, like guitars, for that extra touch of authenticity. The only thing they can't help you with, sadly, is your voice. Admission price of ¥3,000 includes one drink and as much singing as your audience's eardrums can handle.

Sunny Side Jigger Bar

3-28-7 Shinjuku, Shinjuku-ku (3350 6860). Shinjuku
station. **Open** 11.30am-3pm, 5.30pm-12.30am daily.
No credit cards. Map 3b
One of a venerable chain of bars operated by drinks company Suntory, this Shinjuku branch is more spacious than most. Food is of a good standard, and from 5 to 7.30pm they offer a special set menu, incuding beer or a cocktail, for around ¥3,000. A relatively inexpensive place to try out new cocktails.
Branches too numerous to list.

300 Bar

B1, 5-48-9 Nakano, Nakano-ku (3387 0671).
Nakano station. **Open** 11.30am-3am daily.
No credit cards. Map 26
In the warren of streets that surrounds the north side of Nakano station, there are over 200 places to

eat and drink, but none of them is as cheap as this recent addition to the scene. Everything in the place is ¥300, all day, every day, from beer to cocktails to food. Bizarrely, you pay with tickets (¥300 each), purchased from a machine to the left of the bar. It's self-service, and the place has as much atmosphere as the moon, but at this price what do you expect?

Tokyo Sports Café

7-15-31 Roppongi, Minato-ku (3404 3675).
Roppongi station. **Open** 6pm-late daily.
Credit AmEx, MC, V. **Map 2**
This large, friendly bar, run by genial Yorkshireman Paul Wagstaff, has widescreen TVs showing live sporting events from all over the world, including Premiership soccer and NFL American football. The happy hour, 6-9pm, is notable for being one of the few in Tokyo to include Guinness. There's also a pool table, electronic darts and a craps table.

Uluru/125

3-22-6 Jingumae, Shibuya-ku (3403 0125). Harajuku station. **Open** 6pm-3am Mon-Fri; 6pm-midnight Sat.
No credit cards. Map 5
Just as you'd expect from a place named after an Aboriginal word, Uluru's focus is on things antipodean – in this case, wine. At what has to be the cosiest bar in Tokyo (three stools) in a tiny house tucked into an alley near Harajuku, you can choose from a 38-page wine list and a one-page cigar menu. If you're ordering by the glass, you might be limited to what's already open, so it's better to buy by the bottle or go later; this is a consideration for smokers as well, as it's non-smoking before 11pm.

Vision Network

5-47-6 Jingumae, Shibuya-ku (3407 6865).
Omotesando station. **Open** 11am-11pm daily (bar hours vary). **Credit** AmEx, MC, V. **Map 4**
More a concept than a bar, the Vision Network complex off Aoyama Dori houses restaurant/bars Tokyo Salon, Nude and Las Chicas. There is a good selection of wine (emphasis on Australian), beer and cocktails. Most of the food, especially appetisers, is excellent. Menus and service are all bilingual and frequent art exhibits constantly change the look. Las Chicas boasts a Tokyo anomaly: a crackling wood fire in the cold months. Adjacent to Las Chicas is Crome, a dimly lit bar with a DJ occasionally in residence. One caveat: don't take your drinks and food from one spot to the next; though it may seem communal, each of these places is individually run.

What the Dickens

Roob 6 Bldg 4F, 1-13-3 Ebisu-nishi, Shibuya-ku (3780 2099). Ebisu station. **Open** 5pm-1am Tue-Wed; 5pm-2am Thur-Sat; 3pm-midnight Sun.
No credit cards. Map 20
At the top of the building that houses nightclub Milk (*see chapter* **Nightlife**) is this giant and wildly popular British-style pub, on two floors. The walls are decorated with illustrated Dickens manuscripts, which have been liberally re-captioned in the gents' toilets. Food is, unfortunately, of genuine British pub standard – cottage pie and boiled veg kept warm on a hot-plate under glass. Local bands of varying quality play live nightly on a small stage in the corner.

Yurakucho Under the Tracks

2-1 Yurakucho, Chiyoda-ku (no phone). Yurakucho station. **Open** early evening-midnight daily.
No credit cards. Map 7
The sun goes down and the beer and yakitori stands come out under the arches beneath the railway tracks near Yurakucho station. In the years immediately after the war, this area (literal translation: 'Have Fun Town') was alive with a black market of goods from the nearby Allied military headquarters and nighttime activity spilling over from Ginza. The crowds have gone elsewhere, but the trains overhead, the rickety tables, yelling stall-holders and swirling clouds of smoke make this an outdoor drinking spot with an atmosphere all of its own.

The real pub boom

Until relatively recently, it was all but unheard of for Japanese people to drink without eating something at the same time. Judging by the number of British- and Irish-style pubs that have opened in the capital in the last two years, all that is changing.

Long-time Tokyo residents claim that the ball really got rolling when Guinness was first imported on draught, back in the early 1990s. It wasn't long before brewery giant Sapporo got in on the act with its Dubliners pubs in Shinjuku and Ikebukuro, while elsewhere a host of independent operators started setting up their own places, offering 'genuine' Irish atmosphere and 'the craic'. The best of the recent additions are the Shamrock in west Shinjuku, the Irish House in Shinbashi and O'Carolan's in Jiyugaoka, all of which serve superior food as well as the usual range of imported beers.

Longer-established favourites include the Fiddler in Takadanobaba, Paddy Foley's in Roppongi, What the Dickens in Ebisu and the Rising Sun in Yotsuya. One rather pleasant refinement at many (but not all) of these places is table service. Some of them, with their imported fixtures, fittings and even staff, pull off the pub trick so convincingly that only the price of a pint (around ¥1,000) reminds you that you're in Tokyo.

Coffee Shops

From espresso to bizarro, Tokyo's coffee shops have the right blend.

Already buzzing on its own brand of caffeine delirium, Tokyo caters to devotees of the mighty bean with coffee shops (*kissaten*) in profusion. Kissaten are everywhere, with wood-panelled traditionalists, cosy family-run operations and grand cafés jostling for attention against booming franchise outlets and an eclectic mix of strange specialists.

Café society has reflected Tokyo's changing fads and fashions since the city's first coffee shop opened in Ueno back in 1888. Meiji modernisation gave way to the elegant Ginza cafés of the jazz age, post-war havens for music fans and courting couples, and smoky Shinjuku student dives of the 1960s. During the halcyon days of the bubble era, it is claimed that ultra-swanky establishments even put flecks of gold leaf into the coffee. More recently, the economic downturn has helped the rise of a new breed of cheaper chains espousing an unfamiliar gulp-and-run ethos.

Expense is always a consideration in Tokyo. At an average of ¥500-¥600, the price of a cup of coffee is frequently quoted as conclusive proof of the city's outrageous cost of living. But this is to ignore the essential function of the traditional coffee shop, and the reason for its enduring popularity. Here, once you've ordered a single cup, you're free to sit all day on some of the world's most expensive real estate. With the city rushing by outside, the pleasant surroundings, constantly topped-up iced water and unlimited sitting time make the price of that single cup a bargain.

Coffee shops

Angelus
1-17-6 Asakusa, Taito-ku (3841 2208). Asakusa station. **Open** 10am-9.30pm Tue-Sun. **No credit cards. Map 10**
Perhaps, at some point in the distant past, this was the way local upmarket operations got to grips with handling new-fangled foreign delicacies. Out front is a smart counter selling a fancy selection of Western-style cakes; further inside, the coffee shop section is a more Spartan affair of plain walls and dark-wood trimmings.

Ben's Café
1-29-21 Takadanobaba, Shinjuku-ku (3202 2445). Takadanobaba station. **Open** 11am-10pm daily. **No credit cards. Map 25**
A New York-style café, famed locally for its cakes and bagels and easy going ambience. Also hosts

occasional art shows. Friendly staff speak English and serve great coffee.
Website: www.benscafe.com

Bon
B1, 3-23-1 Shinjuku, Shinjuku-ku (3341 0179). Shinjuku station. **Open** noon-11pm Mon-Thur, Sun; 12.30-11.30pm Fri, Sat. **No credit cards. Map 3b**
The search for true coffee excellence is pursued with surprising vigour at this pricey but popular Shinjuku basement. Cheapest choice from the menu sets you back a cool ¥1,000, but cups are selected from an enormous bone china collection. Special tasting events are held periodically for connoisseurs.

Café de Flore
5-1-2 Jingumae, Shibuya-ku (3406 8605). Omotesando station. **Open** 10am-11pm daily. **No credit cards. Map 5**
The Parisian original was a favourite of Sartre and the existentialist crowd, but the busy Tokyo branch remains free of too many intellectual pretensions. The street-level terrace is the fashionable people-watching option. At least the coffee is good, and the separate jugs of espresso and milk provide more than one cup of café au lait for ¥850.

Café Fontana
Abe Building B1, 5-5-9 Ginza, Chuo-ku (3572 7320). Ginza station. **Open** 11am-midnight Mon-Fri; 2-11pm Sat, Sun. **No credit cards. Map 7**
A typically genteel Ginza basement establishment, but one where the individually served apple pies come in distinctly non-dainty proportions. Each steaming specimen contains a whole fruit, thinly covered in pastry, then doused thoroughly in cream.

Café Paulista
Nagasaki Centre, 8-9-16 Ginza, Chuo-ku (3572 6160). Ginza station. **Open** 8.30am-10.30pm Mon-Sat; noon-8pm Sun. **No credit cards. Map 7**
Brazil's national flag hangs proudly both outside and within this veteran Ginza establishment, founded all the way back in 1914. All-natural beans are directly imported, keeping blend coffee prices down to ¥450, a bargain for the area. Low leather seats, plants and wall engravings feature in a brown and green décor motif, while softly playing samba keeps things nice and relaxed.

Café de Ropé
6-1-8 Jingumae, Shibuya-ku (3406 6845). Omotesando station. **Open** 11.30am-11pm daily. **No credit cards. Map 5**
Another Tokyo institution, a short walk down Omotesando from Café de Flore (*see above*). Pleas-

Cybercafés

The Internet has been slower in taking over Tokyo than many cities, possibly owing to the relative shortage of sites in Japanese. There is now, however, a growing number of cybercafés where you can sip a hot drink while surfing the Net.

Click On Café
Koike Bldg 5F, 2-23-1 Dogenzaka, Shibuya-ku (5489 2282). Shibuya station. **Open** 11am-11pm daily. **No credit cards. Map 4**
A thriving café. Net service is ¥500 for 30 mins, with obligatory drinks from ¥250.

Cyberia Tokyo
Scala Bldg 1F, 1-14-17 Nishi-Azabu, Minato-ku (3423 0318). Nogizaka station. **Open** 11am-11pm daily. **No credit cards. Map 2**
Net service is ¥500 for 30 mins, while a ¥600 coffee buys you 30 mins of free time.

Cyber Net Café
Face Bldg 6F, 2-32-5 Jingumae, Shibuya-ku (3423 7406). Harajuku station. **Open** noon-10pm Tue-Thur, Sat, Sun; noon-11pm Fri. **No credit cards. Map 5**
Coffee, at ¥350 per cup, comes in plastic cups. Net service is ¥500 per 30 mins.

T-Zone Shinjuku
T-Zone Shinjuku 10F, 7-11-1 Nishi-Shinjuku, Shinjuku-ku (5330 7219). Shinjuku station. **Open** 11am-8.30pm Mon-Sat; 11am-7.30pm Sun. **No credit cards. Map 3a**
Espresso for ¥250. Internet access is ¥500 for 30 mins and drinks are obligatory.
Branch: T-Zone Minami-kan Bldg 7F, 4-3-3 Soto-kanda, Chiyoda-ku (3526 7711). Akihabara station.

antly light and airy, and a great place for watching the fashion parade up Omotesando. Café au lait so thick you can rest your sugar lump on it.

Classic
5-66-9 Nakano, Nakano-ku (3387 0571). Nakano station. **Open** noon-9.30pm Tue-Sun. **No credit cards. Map 26**
This ramshackle relic of eccentricity is a creaky one-off that's survived the winds of change since 1930. Classical music drifts eerily over the sound system as the ill-lit gothic gloom gradually reveals strangely sloping floors, ancient leather chairs, long-deceased and undusted clocks. The paintings that adorn the walls are all by the shop's original, now dead, owner. Tickets for coffee, tea or juice are ¥350 and purchased at the entrance; cream has been known to arrive in bottle caps.

Coffee 3.4 Sunsea
Takano Bldg 1F, 10-2 Udagawacho, Shibuya-ku (3496 2295). Shibuya station. **Open** noon-11pm daily. **No credit cards. Map 4**
Kathmandu hippy chic and postmodern Shibuya cool meet in this laid-back retreat, with classical Indian sitar and tabla on soundtrack. Cushion-strewn sofas, ethnic wooden carvings and a large tank of hypnotic tropical fish all add to the dreamy effect. Self-indulgent sensory overload guaranteed from the sensational coffee float. It's somehow in keeping with the mood of the place that the owners don't have fixed days off; they close whenever they feel like it, so call ahead to confirm.

Daibo
2F, 3-13-20 Minami-Aoyama, Minato-ku (3403 7155). Omotesando station. **Open** 9am-10pm Mon-Sat; noon-8pm Sun. **No credit cards. Map 5**
The biggest treat at this cosy wood-bedecked outpost is the excellent milk coffee, which comes lovingly hand-dripped into large pottery bowls. Even the regular blend coffee reveals a true craftsman's pride, and comes in four separate varieties. Just one long wooden counter plus a couple of tables, but the restrained decoration and low-volume jazz on the stereo combine to soothing and restful effect.

Danwashitsu Takizawa
B1, 3-35 Shinjuku, Shinjuku-ku (3356 5661). Shinjuku station. **Open** 9am-9.50pm Mon-Sat; 9am-9.30pm Sun. **No credit cards. Map 3b**
Just in case you ever want to experience the perverse pleasure of blowing ¥1,000 on a single cup of coffee, this is where to do it. Artfully simple yet completely comfortable, it's the kind of place you could stay all day: water trickles over rocks for a vaguely Zen-like sense of tranquillity, staff bow with quite extraordinary politeness, and colours combine to mysteriously soothing effect.

él
2-19-18 Kaminarimon, Taito-ku (3841 0114/gallery 3841 0442). Asakusa station. **Open** 11am-midnight (gallery to 7pm) Mon, Wed, Thur; 11am-2am Fri; 11am-10pm Sun. **No credit cards. Map 10**
This retrofitted hang-out is a welcome attempt to inject a little Harajuku-style cool into musty Asakusa, but among its more surprising attractions is a small art gallery converted from a 130-year-old warehouse. Duck through the low entrance way at the back and suddenly you're out of the 1950s Americana and into *tatami* territory, admittance to the main exhibits being up a steep set of traditional wooden steps. A place to try when you're tired of the local temples.

Jazz Coffee Masako
2-20-2 Kitazawa, Setagaya-ku (3410 7994). Shimo-Kitazawa station (Odakyu/Inokashira lines). **Open** 11am-11pm daily. **No credit cards. Map 29**
A real homely feel, as well as all the jazz coffee shop essentials present and correct: excellent sound system, enormous stack of records and CDs behind the

counter, walls and low ceiling painted black and all plastered in posters and pictures. The noticeboard at the flower-filled entrance proudly announces newly obtained recordings; inside, there are bookcases and sofas among the well lived-in furnishings.

Ki No Hana

4-13-1 Ginza, Chuo-ku (3543 5280). Higashi-Ginza station. **Open** 10.30am-9pm Mon-Fri. **No credit cards. Map 7**

The pair of signed John Lennon cartoons on the walls is the legacy of a chance visit by the former Beatle one afternoon in 1978. With its peaceful atmosphere, tasteful floral decorations, herbal teas and lunchtime vegetarian curries, it isn't too difficult to understand Lennon's appreciation of the place. Apparently, the overawed son of the former owner also preserved the great man's full ashtray, including butts. Alas, he kept this as a personal memento, so it isn't on display.

Lion

2-19-13 Dogenzaka, Shibuya-ku (3461 6858). Shibuya station. **Open** 10am-10.30pm daily. **No credit cards. Map 4**

There's a church-like air of reverence at this sleepy shrine to classical music. A pamphlet listing stereophonic offerings is laid out helpfully before the customer, seating is arranged in pew-style rows facing an enormous pair of speakers, and conversations are discouraged. If you must talk, do so in whispers. The imposing grey building is an unexpected period piece set amid the gaudy love hotels of Dogenzaka.

Miró

2-4-6 Kanda-Surugadai, Chiyoda-ku (3291 3088/3089). Ochanomizu station. **Open** 8am-11pm Mon-Sat. **No credit cards. Map 9**

Named after Catalan surrealist Joan Miró (1893-1983), several of whose works adorn the walls. Ambience and décor appear untouched by the passing decades. The location is pretty well hidden, down a tiny alley opposite Ochanomizu station.

Mironga

1-3 Kanda-Jinbocho, Chiyoda-ku (3295 1716). Jinbocho station. **Open** 10.30am-11pm Mon-Fri; 11.30am-7pm Sat, Sun. **No credit cards. Map 9**

Probably the only place in the metropolis where nonstop tango provides seductive old-style dance music accompaniment to the liquid refreshments. Argentina's finest exponents feature in the impressive array of fading monochromes up on the walls, and there's also a useful selection of printed works on related subjects lining the bookshelves. Of the two rooms, the larger and darker gets the nod for atmosphere. A good selection of imported beers and reasonable food, as well as a wide range of coffees.

New Dug

B1, 3-15-12 Shinjuku, Shinjuku-ku (3341 9339). Shinjuku station. **Open** noon-2am Mon-Sat; noon-11.30pm Sun. **No credit cards. Map 3b**

Way back in the 1960s and early '70s, Shinjuku was sprinkled with jazz coffee shops. Celebrated names of that bygone era include Dug, an establishment

whose present-day incarnation is a cramped brick-lined basement on Yasukuni Dori. Everything about the place speaks serious jazz credentials, but amid the carefully crafted authenticity and assorted memorabilia something vital seems lacking in the way of atmosphere. An annexe is used for performances.

Pow Wow

2-7 Kagurazaka, Shinjuku-ku (3267 8324). Iidabashi station. **Open** 10.30am-10.30pm Mon-Sat; 12.30-6.30pm Sun. **No credit cards.**

Heavy on the old-fashioned virtues of dark wood and tastefully chosen pottery, this spacious traditionalist features an extraordinary coffee-brewing performance in its narrow counter section, where large glass flasks bubble merrily away over tiny glass candles in the manner of some mysterious chemistry experiment. Blend coffee is ¥650.

Chain gang

Probably the single best-known coffee shop in Tokyo is the Roppongi crossing branch of **Almond**, a pink-hued landmark that's provided an instantly recognisable meeting spot for many years. **Renoir** is another venerable member of the multi-outlet brigade, a long-running salaryman hit, its patented combination of soothing music and gently tilted soft chairs perfect for power-napping.

The city's caffeine scene was shaken up in the post-bubble 1990s by **Doutor**. The cheap and cheerful fast-food approach of this swift-rising innovator, along with its ever-mushrooming number of branches, continues to pose a stern threat to the high-margin virtues of more traditional operators, particularly small independents. Another form of competition arrived in the shape of dual-role pioneers **Pronto**, where the budget coffee shutters come down at six, and outlets become night-time purveyors of alcoholic drinks and bar snacks.

International developments have also left their mark. Spotting an entirely untapped demand for more exotic Seattle-style flavours, **Starbucks** opened its first Japanese branch in Ginza in 1996, and this has swiftly been followed by dozens more in the metropolitan area. More recently, the brand-name Italian-style cappuccino of **Segafredo Zanetti** has established a beachhead in fashionable Shibuya. Faced with these overseas heavyweights, in late 1998 the local champion opened its first up-market outlet under the name Le Café Doutor Espresso on a prime spot at Ginza 4-chome crossing.

*In the heart of Kabuki-cho, walk through the doors of **La Scala** and step back in time.*

Rihaku

2-24 Kanda-Jinbocho, Chiyoda-ku (3264 6292).
Jinbocho station. **Open** 11am-8pm Mon-Sat.
No credit cards. Map 9
Named after Sung dynasty Chinese poet Li Po (AD
701-62), whose works include the celebrated lament
'Drinking Alone', this is a place more attuned to
Eastern tradition than most. The high ceiling and
wooden layout of the interior are reminiscent of
some old Japanese farmhouse, but resist the temp-
tation to slip off the shoes as you enter.

Saboru

1-2 Kanda-Jinbocho, Chiyoda-ku (3391 8404).
Jinbocho station. **Open** 9am-11pm daily.
No credit cards. Map 9
Wooden masks on the walls, tree pillars rising to the
ceiling, and a menu that features banana juice all
lend a strangely South Sea island air to this cosy
triple-level establishment squeezed into a brick
building reverting to jungle on a Jinbocho back
street. It's cheap, too, with blend coffee a snip at
¥400. Next door is the less extravagantly furnished
sequel, Saboru 2.

La Scala

1-14-1 Kabuki-cho, Shinjuku-ku (3200 3320).
Shinjuku station. **Open** 10am-11pm Mon-Thur;
10am-11:30pm Fri, Sat; 10am-10pm Sun.
No credit cards. Map 3b
Step inside the ivy-covered building of this impec-
cably maintained establishment and it's another century altogether. Graced by a glittering chandelier,
antique furniture, enormous mirrors and plush seating, this proud purveyor of 'coffee and classical

mood music' keeps up an old-world grandeur at
odds with its neon-clad neighbours on the back
streets of Kabuki-cho. Window tables are best for
appreciating the contrast, and this is a great place
to linger over a cuppa. Café au lait is ¥700.

Tajimaya

1-2-6 Nishi-Shinjuku, Shinjuku-ku (3342 0881).
Shinjuku station. **Open** 10am-11pm daily.
No credit cards. Map 3a
Caught between the early post-war grunge of its
immediate neighbours and the skyscraper bustle of
the rest of west Shinjuku, Tajimaya responds with
abundant bone china, coffees from all over the
world, non-fetishist use of classical music, and milk
in the best copperware. Scones on the menu and the
unusual selection of ornaments provide further evidence of advanced sensibilities, but the deeply yel-
lowed walls and battered wood suggest a struggle
to keep up appearances.

Yomu-yomu

Kawase Bldg B2, 3-17-5 Shinjuku, Shinjuku-ku
(3352 6065). Shinjuku station. **Open** 9am-9.50pm
daily. **No credit cards. Map 3b**
Usually credited as being the first of the capital's
many *manga* coffee shops, Yomu-yomu ('Read-
read') opened only in 1994 but has sparked an amazing boom in copycat places offering the same
winning combination of coffee and Japanese comic
books. Non-*otaku* interlopers might find the serried
rows of heads poring over vintage volumes a bit
intimidating, but there are plenty of magazines to
flick through as well. ¥600 for the first 90 mins, then
¥30 for every extra ten mins.

Shops & Services

Tokyo is bursting at the seams with shops catering to everything from your most everyday needs to your wildest fantasies.

Westerners who have interacted with Japanese society are familiar with the archetype of the young 'office lady', who lists her hobbies as 'sleeping, eating and shopping'. It may be facetious, but it's no joke that in recent years the Japanese have defined themselves by what they consume.

Consumer service and the all-important catchword 'convenience' have been pursued with an almost religious fervour. Corner stores such as am-pm and Lawson have proliferated to the point where convenience stores, in 1998, were the only growing sector in the Japanese economy. A survey in the mid-1990s found that the average walking distance from any point in Tokyo to the nearest convenience store was four-and-a-half minutes.

All this means that in Tokyo you can find anything you want, and many things you never knew existed. The stores in this section are only the tip of the iceberg, a selection of shops that are of special interest to the visitor.

Department stores

The giant department stores of Tokyo, a city tradition, have seen good times and bad, and are doing their best to weather the current economic blues. The oldest and most venerable, Mitsukoshi in Ginza and Takashimaya in Nihonbashi, started about 300 years ago as humble dry goods stores. Their innovations, such as displaying merchandise and creating set prices instead of haggling with customers, are now the rule.

Isetan

3-14-1 Shinjuku, Shinjuku-ku (3352 1111). Shinjuku station. **Open** 10am-7.30pm daily. Closed occasional Wed. Call to check. **Credit** AmEx, DC, JCB, V.
Map 3b
Isetan ontains the I-Club, a special service for foreign customers (*see* **Department stores**, *p171*). Membership enquiries can be made at the Customer Services desk on the seventh floor. The monthly

*Shinjuku's **Takashimaya Times Square** is Japan's biggest single department store.*

Going store crazy at Sogo.

newsletter contains comprehensive news of forth-
coming sales, discounts and special promotions. It
also contains details of the clothing ranges available
in sizes larger than the usual Japanese ones – these
are named Clover Town for ladies and Super Men's
for men. Isetan is split into seven buildings very close
to each other: the Main Building, the Annexe building, Isetan Kaikan (for restaurants), the parking lot
on the West side, and Park City 3, 4 and 5. Both the
Isetan Museum of Art and the Fine Art salon are
located on the eighth floor of the Annexe building.
The foreign exchange counter is on the Main
Building first floor, the overseas shipping service is
in the basement, and the tax exemption counter is on
the seventh floor.
Branch: 1-11-5 Kichijoji Honcho, Musashino-shi,
Kichijoji (0422 211 111). Kichijoji station.

Keio
1-1-4 Nishi-Shinjuku, Shinjuku-ku (3342 2111).
Shinjuku station. **Open** 10am-7.30pm daily.
Credit all major cards. **Map 3a**
Situated between Odakyu, My Lord and Lumine (for
all, *see below*), with exits leading directly from
Shinjuku station, Keio offers ladies' accessories on
the first four floors, menswear on the fifth, home furnishings on the sixth, children's clothes and toys on
the seventh and books and stationery on the eighth.
What may well be worth a visit is a recycle shop
called 'With You' on the third floor – in Japan, 'recycle' means second-hand. The tax exemption and currency exchange counters are on the sixth floor.
Branch: Keio Seiseki-Sakuragaoka, 1-10-1 Sekido,
Tama-shi (042 337 2111). Seiseki-Sakuragaoka
station (Keio line).

Lumine 1 & 2
1-1-5 Nishi-Shinjuku, Shinjuku-ku (3348 5211).
Shinjuku station. **Open** 11am-9pm daily.
Credit all major cards. **Map 3a**
This confusingly laid-out store takes up two sides
of Shinjuku station's south exit. Lumine 1 contains
clothes and jewellery for ladies. Lumine 2 sells
menswear and has a branch of the Aoyama Book
Centre on the fourth floor (for books in English, you
have to go to the branches in Aoyama or Roppongi).
Unfortunately, no English store guide is available.

Matsuya
3-6-1 Ginza, Chuo-ku (3567 1211). Ginza station.
Open 10.30am-8pm Tue; 10.30am-7.30pm Wed-Mon.
Credit all major cards. **Map 7**
There is a special section for men's and ladies' clothing designed by Issey Miyake on the fourth floor.
Traditional Japanese souvenirs are on the fifth floor,
while the Matsuya Art Gallery is on the seventh. The
tax exemption, currency exchange and overseas
shipping services are on the first floor. Watch out
for the confusing English-language store guide.

Matsuzakaya Ginza

6-1-10 Ginza (3572 1111). Ginza station.
Open 10.30am-7.30pm Mon-Sat; 10.30am-7pm Sun.
Credit all major cards. **Map 7**

The main branch of the Matsuzakaya Ginza department store is actually situated in Ueno, but foreign visitors are usually more familiar with this branch in Ginza. Tax exemption and currency exchange counters are located on the basement second floor, while Japanese handicrafts can be found on the sixth floor. The store's annexe building contains a beauty and massage salon, an art gallery, an exhibition hall and even a deportment school for ladies.
Branch: 3-29-5 Ueno, Taito-ku (3832 1111). Ueno station.

Mitsukoshi

1-4-1 Nihonbashi-Muromachi Chuo-ku (3241 3311).
Mitsukoshi mae station. **Open** 10am-7pm daily.
Credit all major cards. **Map 6**

The oldest surviving department store in Japan, Mitsukoshi remodelled itself on Harrods in the early twentieth century, intending to add European elegance to excellent customer service. Visitors to the main store are greeted by a huge statue of Tennyo Magokoro, the Buddhist goddess of sincerity. Mitsukoshi own the Tokyo franchise to the Tiffany's – the stores are on the first floor of all three branches. The Ginza branch has a tax exemption counter in the basement third floor, a currency exchange counter and Japanese souvenirs (the

Department stores

Most westerners are familiar with the reputation of the Japanese department store, or *depato*: the opulent prices, the exquisite service. Some of the stories that travellers bring back are true – for example, all the staff really do line up by the doors and bow to the morning's first customers.

But like everywhere else in Japan, department stores are feeling the effects of the recession. In early 1999, **Mitsukoshi** declared losses of ¥26 billion due to a disastrous golf course project, while another giant, **Tokyu**, actually closed down one unprofitable Tokyo branch. The advent of sober reality is sometimes good news for the consumer, however. Prices are down, sales are plentiful, and the stores are constantly trying new ideas to bring in customers.

What makes these places so special? In a land where the word 'convenience' is a mantra, the big-name depato have become the ultimate in one-stop shopping. You can find any category of product you want to buy – food, clothes from the stylish designers of Japan and Europe, furniture, toys, traditional souvenirs. They also provide services to take care of every aspect of your life – they'll open your bank account, give you a haircut, arrange your wedding. Not only will they take care of you in this life, but also prepare you for the next; some of them also arrange funerals.

Japanese depato share certain basic similarities. Food is always in the basement, sometimes accompanied by restaurants and cafés. The first couple of floors are women's clothes and accessories, with menswear beginning on either the third or the fourth. The higher levels will include restaurants of a slightly up-market nature, while the rooftops are often used as beer gardens in the summer (just don't expect much of a garden). It's worth bearing in mind that while the stores close for business at around 7pm or 8pm, the restaurants inside usually stay open until 11pm.

Perhaps the most salutary features, however, are the art galleries and museums that have been founded by the largest companies (*see chapter* **Museums & Galleries**). These places, usually attached to the main store, hold exhibitions from all around the world, giving the average customer access to a stunning variety of cultural influences, both obscure and famous. It's one example of how corporate sponsorship of the arts can, sometimes, benefit all concerned.

The department stores in **Ginza**, being the most famous, attract their fair share of foreign visitors, and so there are certain services for the non-Japanese customer, although perhaps not as many as you might expect. Most stores offer tax-exemption and currency exchange services at special counters, and can deliver purchases to any part of the world. All Ginza department stores have a section, of varying sizes, where traditional Japanese crafts can be bought as souvenirs. Most of them have store guides available in English, although sometimes you have to ask for them.

Perhaps the best value for money, however, is provided not in Ginza, but in Shinjuku, by the store named **Isetan**. The Foreign Customer Service (or I Club) gives its members five per cent discount on certain goods within the store (mainly clothing), as well as two hours of free parking, complimentary tickets to every exhibition at the Isetan Museum of Art, a monthly newsletter in English and, last but not least, free membership. The I Club can be joined by visiting the Foreign Customer Service counter on the seventh floor of Isetan's main building, or by calling 3225 2514.

Tokyu department store's 109 Building.

store is called 'Japanesque') on the seventh. A theatre and gardening shop can be found on the roof garden, while a small annexe building contains a pharmacy, a florist and furniture. The Shinjuku branch contains the Mitsukoshi Museum of Art, and hosts collections of a quality that rival the national museums in Ueno Park.
Branches: 4-6-16 Ginza, Chuo-ku (3562 1111). Ginza station; 3-29-1 Shinjuku, Shinjuku-ku (3354 1111). Shinjuku station; 1-5-7 Higashi-Ikebukuro, Toshima-ku (3987 1111). Ikebukuro station.

Odakyu
1-1-3 Nishi-Shinjuku, Shinjuku-ku (3342 1111). Shinjuku station. **Open** 10am-7.30pm daily. **Credit** all major cards. **Map 3a**
The store is split into two buildings, the main building and the annexr (Halc) building, which are connected by an elevated walkway and underground passageways. The main building sells ladieswear with kimono on the seventh floor and haberdashery on the eighth, while the Halc building has menswear, sportswear and Japanese furniture on the sixth, a

Ladies' Club on the seventh, a beauty salon on the eighth and a golf school on the roof. The tenth to fourteenth floors of the main buildings are given the name of Manhattan Hills, and contain a dental clinic, a barber for men, three floors of restaurants and the Odakyu Museum. The currency exchange counter is on the first floor of the main building, and the tax exemption counter is on the sixth.

Seibu
21-1 Udagawa-cho, Shibuya-ku (3462 0111). Shibuya station. **Open** 10am-8pm daily. **Credit** all major cards. **Map 4**
The Shibuya main store is split into two buildings, A and B, which face each other across the street. A Building sells mainly ladieswear, with B building selling menswear, children's clothes and accessories. The tax exemption counter is on the M2 (Mezzanine) floor of A building. Seibu also runs Loft and Seed, both of which are within easy walking distance of the Shibuya store. Loft is designed for the 18-35 age range, selling goods for household and beauty care, with novelty goods on the fifth and Wave record store on the sixth. Seed is a collection of boutiques aimed at Japanese in their teens and twenties.
Branches: Ikebukuro: 1-28-1 Minami-Ikebukuro, Toshima-ku (3981 0111). Ikebukuro station; 2-5-1 Yurakucho, Chiyoda-ku (3286 0111). Yurakucho station.

Sogo
1-11-1 Yurakucho, Chiyoda-ku (3284 6711). Yurakucho station. **Open** 10.30am-7.30pm Mon-Fri; 10.30am-7pm Sat, Sun. **Credit** all major cards. **Map 7**
This store is between the high-class boutiques of Ginza and the no-frills bars of Yurakucho. Among the goods on offer on its seven storeys are formal wear for men and ladies, jewellery, pearls, traditional Japanese toys and dolls. The tax exemption and currency exchange counters are on the first floor.

Takashimaya
2-4-1 Nihonbashi, Chuo-ku (3211 4111). Nihonbashi station. **Open** 10am-7pm daily. **Credit** all major cards. **Map 6**
This store has much of the opulence and grandeur of its near neighbour Mitsukoshi (*see above*), having based a lot of its interior style on Harrods. Menswear is on the first and second floor, ladieswear on the third and fourth, children's on the fifth, furniture on the sixth and kimono on the seventh. The tax-free counter is on the first floor and the overseas shipping service is on the basement first floor. The Shinjuku branch, Takashimaya Times Square (*see below*), is now the largest single department store building in Japan, and contains a large number of boutiques, a branch of hardware store Tokyu Hands, Kinokuniya International Bookshop in the annexe building, a Sega game centre, Joypolis, on the tenth floor and an IMAX digitally enhanced 3-D cinema on the 13th.
Branch: Takashimaya Times Square, 5-24-2 Sendagaya, Shibuya-ku (5361 1122). Shinjuku station.

Tokyu Plaza International Food Store

1-2-2 Dogenzaka, Shibuya-ku (3463 3851). Shibuya station. **Open** 10am-8pm daily. **No credit cards.** **Map 4**

Of special interest is the Shibuya Food Market in the basement. Not only is it huge, but it also has refrigerated lockers. You can stash your grub for ¥100, nip off to see a movie and come back later.

Tobu

1-1-25 Nishi-Ikebukuro, Toshima-ku (3981 2211). Ikebukuro station. **Open** 10am-8pm daily. **Credit** all major cards. **Map 1**

This sprawling complex, comprising three connected buildings and the Tobu Museum of Art, was until recently the largest department store in the world. The main building houses clothing for all occasions and restaurants from the 11th to the 17th floors. The Central Building sells clothing in larger sizes, interior goods and office supplies. The Plaza Building contains the designer collection; lines by Prada, Versace and Calvin Klein, and also the Tobu Museum of Art, accessible from the first, second and third floors. The currency exchange and tax exemption counters are on the basement first floor of the central building.

Tokyu Honten

2-24-1 Dogenzaka, Shibuya-ku (3477 3111). Shibuya station. **Open** 10am-8pm Mon, Wed-Sun. **Credit** all major cards. **Map 4**

The main store sells designer fashions for men and women and interior goods for the home. The Tokyu Toyoko store is situated directly above JR Shibuya station, consisting of a south wing, a west wing and an east wing. Some shops in this branch close on Thursdays. Goods on sale include clothes, electrical appliances and porcelain. It can be hazardous trying to find your way around the station to get to the place you want, so try to go at an off-peak time (if you can find one). The Tokyu Plaza store, opposite Shibuya station, sells ladies' fashion, cosmetics and accessories, and has a CD shop on the fifth floor. For the food market in Tokyu Honten, *see* international food store section *above*.

Branches: Tokyu Toyoko-ten, 2-24-1 Shibuya, Shibuya-ku (3477 3111). Shibuya station; 7-69-1 Nishi-Kamata, Ota-ku (3733 3281). Kamata station.

Fashion

Looking good is an obsession with Tokyoites, and even if they can't walk down the city streets laden with designer bags any more, they try their best. Over the last ten years, the predilection has been for the famous European designers, with an unhealthy fixation on Louis Vuitton and Prada. On the other side of the coin, Japanese designers have gained recognition internationally and at home, the most notable being Issey Miyake and his bold work with pleated fabrics, and Hanae Mori with her versions of classic styles.

Opening times

Stores in Tokyo open a little later than you are probably used to, but stay open a lot later too. The department stores and most shops open at 10am, with a few opening at 11am or noon. As most shopping is done after office hours, the closing times for most stores are between 7pm and 9pm, with some stores staying open later depending on the season (for example, just before the New Year and O-Bon summer holidays).

Sunday is a normal shopping day in Japan, as it has no religious significance. This means, however, that the large stores are usually very crowded, becoming almost unbearable on Sundays during the sales seasons and just before New Year. Although Japan has fallen prey to the custom of overloading the shelves with seasonal tack during the Christmas season, 25 December is a normal working day, with ordinary shopping hours. What's more, the festive decorations come down on the stroke of midnight, to make space for the more traditional New Year merchandise – a practice that can be bewildering to foreign visitors.

As far as the national holidays (*see chapter* **Tokyo by Season**) are concerned, most large stores will be open – but if you have a specific place in mind, it's worth calling before you go just to make sure. Just about every shop has been trying to beat the recession, so most will be welcoming customers in during the fixed national holidays. Most places are closed, though, on both 1 and 2 January, with the department store sales beginning on 3 January.

If, on the other hand, you like wearing something weird and anachronistic that's going for a song, head to Harajuku, where there are dozens of import and second-hand shops aimed at teenagers and rock 'n' roll types: it's eye-opening to check out what the customers are wearing. Aim for Takeshita Dori, the street leading from Harajuku station to Meiji Dori, and for the Meiji-Dori intersection with Omotesando (*see* **Map 5**).

Barneys New York

3-18-5 Shinjuku, Shinjuku-ku (3352 1200). Shinjuku station. **Open** 11am-8pm daily. **Credit** all major cards. **Map 3b**

A little bit of American style, plus a lot of European designers. Sells an impressive range of neckties and fragrances for men.

Comme des Garçons

5-2-1 Minami-Aoyama, Minato-ku (3406 3951).
Omotesando station. **Open** 11am-8pm daily.
Credit all major cards. **Map 2**
Despite the French name, this extraordinary rat's
maze of a shop contains the designs of Rei Kawa-
kubo. She gained fame (or perhaps notoriety) in the
fashion world with her 1981 Paris show, which featured shapeless fashions in ironically titled 'funeral black', seams laid bare and necklines frayed.
Needless to say, her range of clothing has since then
concentrated on the elegant and stylish, displaying
a European elegance that befits the name.
Branch: Comme des Garçons 2, 5-12-3 Minami-
Aoyama, Minato-ku (3498 1400). Omotesando station.

GAP

FLAGS Bldg, 3-37-1 Shinjuku, Shinjuku-ku (5360
7800). **Shinjuku station. Open** 11am-9pm daily.
Credit all major cards. **Map 3b**
The US clothing giant brings preppy style to the
streets of Tokyo. One of the few places westerners
can regularly find clothes to fit them. Stores are usually crowded and noisy.
Branches: all over Tokyo. Call 3499 8600 for details.

Hanae Mori

3-6-1 Kita-Aoyama, Minato-ku (3423 1448).
Omotesando station. **Open** 11am-7pm daily.
Credit all major cards. **Map 5**
Mori is globally renowned for combining classical
European flair with traditional oriental touches,
such as evening gowns decorated with the brush-
strokes of Japanese calligraphy, and dresses combining features of the kimono. She has designed
outfits for the Japanese Imperial family, and costumes for the late film director Akira Kurosawa.
Mori was the first non-French designer to be admitted into the Chambre Syndicale de la Haute Couture,
and is still the only Japanese member.
Branch: 3-27-1 Shinjuku, Shinjuku-ku (3352 7611).
Shinjuku station.

Hysteric Glamour

6-23-2 Jingumae, Shibuya-ku (3409 7227). Harajuku
station. **Open** 11am-8pm daily. **Credit** all major
cards. **Map 5**
Modern Japanese youth fashion is increasingly dic-
tated by the street, with designers picking up on
what Japanese teens are doing and modifying it.
One of the most successful youth designers of
recent years is Hysteric Glamour (followed closely by Super Lovers). Its boldly decorated T-shirts,
shirts and jeans have proved a winner not just
here, but also with visitors – many pop stars here
on tour go home wearing Hysteric Glamour.
Branches: all over Tokyo. Look for the name in
fashion buildings and department stores.

Issey Miyake

3-18-11 Minami-Aoyama, Minato-ku (3423
1407/1408). **Omotesando station. Open** 10am-8pm
daily. **Credit** all major cards. **Map 2**
If Hanae Mori represents Japan's traditional past,
Miyake represents its mixed-up present and its

chaotic future. His innovative designs are made
from unusual materials such as oilcloth, paper and
molded plastic but feel natural and comfortable.
His range of pleated hemp material and polyester
jersey fabric, 'Pleats Please', developed in the early
'90s, is perhaps the best known internationally.

Jeans Mate

30-1 Udagawa-cho, Shibuya-ku (3477 0921).
Shibuya station. **Open** 24 hours daily.
Credit all major cards. **Map 4**
This branch of the jeans boutique is open 24 hours
every day. If you split your strides on the dancefloor
at 2am, you know where to come.
Branches: all over Tokyo.

Laforet

1-11-6 Jingumae, Shibuya-ku (3475 0411). Harajuku
station. **Open** Laforet 1 11am-8pm daily; Laforet 2
10am-7pm daily. **Credit** MC, V. **Map 5**
This store is situated in the teen capital of
Harajuku, close to the schoolgirl mecca of
Takeshita Dori, so you've already got a pretty good
idea of who its main customers are. Laforet contains over 100 small boutiques spread over two
stores and aimed at young wearers of garish, eccentric fashion.

Marui

3-18-1 Shinjuku, Shinjuku-ku (3354 0101). Shinjuku
station. **Open** 10am-8pm daily. **Credit** all major
cards. **Map 3b**
This is a great haunt for young Japanese. The rather
confusing logo looks like 'oh-one oh-one'; the idea
being that 'maru' means 'circle' or 'zero' in Japanese.
There are five large stores in Shinjuku alone, very
close to each other. They sell a mixture of contemporary men's and ladieswear, accessories, imported
designer and sportswear.
Branches: 3-28-13 Nishi-Ikebukuro, Toshima-ku
(3989 0101/fax 3989 1785). Ikebukuro station; 21-1
Udagawa-cho, Shibuya-ku (3464 0101). Shibuya
station; 6-15-1 Ueno, Taito-ku (3833 0101). Ueno
station; many others all over Tokyo.

NEXT

Kuriyama Bldg, 2-10-16 Jiyugaoka, Meguro-ku
(5731 2227). Jiyugaoka station (Toyoko line). **Open**
10am-7.30pm daily. **Credit** all major cards. **Map 28**
The British clothing retailer is slowly expanding its
presence in Japan, but at present only ladieswear is
sold in Next Tokyo.
Branch: Ebisu Mitsukoshi B1, Ebisu Garden Place,
4-27-7 Ebisu, Shibuya-ku (3280 1851). Ebisu station.

Parco

15-1 Udagawa-cho. Shibuya-ku (3464 5111). Shibuya
station. **Open** 10am-8.30pm daily. **Credit** all major
cards. **Map 4**
The main branch of this mid-range clothing store
in Shibuya is split into three buildings. Part 1 houses a theatre on the top floor and a bookshop (mainly art books in English and other languages), while
Part 3 contains an exhibition hall hosting weird
and wonderful touring exhibitions. Another branch

Bargain-hunting

Now that the 1980s bubble economy has well and truly deflated, it's refreshing to note an atmosphere of back-to-basics aesthetics in Japan. Tokyo dwellers have proved that they can come up with useful, ingenious ways to save money; and if you know where to look, the traveller can come up with some terrific, and often unexpected, bargains.

There are certain seasons when Japan's retail monoliths, the department stores, have their sales. The **New Year Sales** start 3 January and, thanks to the recession, now go on until the beginning of February. One gimmick that the different stores all share is the *fukubukuro*, or Lucky Bag. They sell at various prices, and contain a lucky dip of designer accessories. The **summer sales** start in either July or August, and there are sometimes special **one-off sales**, for example if a baseball team sponsored by the store wins the Japan series.

There are discount shops and stores in every Tokyo neighbourhood. There are the ubiquitous **100 Yen Shops**, selling cutlery, toys and assorted nick-nacks for the stated price (usually plus five per cent tax). Recently, there has been an increase in the number of **recycle shops** (the Japanese term for second-hand), which sell mainly clothes and electronic goods. Your nearest one can be found by calling the **Citizens Recycle Association** (3226 6800).

For foreign residents who find the department stores and international supermarkets too expensive, the **Foreign Buyers Club** (www.fbcusa.com), operating from an island off Kobe, imports food and many other goods in bulk at discount prices. For cheap reads, you can spend a day browsing among the **second-hand bookshops** of the Yasukuni Dori near Jinbocho station.

Last but not least, in the expatriate community people are always moving in and out. **Sayonara sales** are a regular feature of classified advertisements, the best of which are in *Tokyo Classified* and its rival, *Tokyo Notice Board* (*see chapter* **Media**), both of which are distributed free around foreigner-friendly bars and hotels.

As the recession bites, the 'pile it high, sell it cheap' ethic has arrived in Tokyo.

Hawaiian duds are always a hot choice for swingers in Tokyo's fashion jungle.

in Shibuya is the home of the concert hall Club Quattro (*see chapter* **Music**). The designers are a mix of Japanese, British and European fashions. **Branches**: 1-28-2 Minami-Ikebukuro, Toshima-ku (5391 8000). Ikebukuro station; 1-5-1 Honcho, Kichijoji, Musashino-shi (0422 21 8111). Kichijoji station.

Ricky Sarani

3-3-12 Azabudai, Minato-ku (3587 1648). Roppongi station. **Open** 10am-6pm Tue-Sun. **Credit** all major cards. **Map 2**

If you need to rent a tuxedo or formal dress, this is the place to go – call to make an appointment first.

Tokyo Frederick

7-5-7 Roppongi, Minato-ku (3479 4511). Roppongi station. **Open** 3pm-3am Mon-Sat. **Credit** all major cards. **Map 2**

The Japanese branch of the Hollywood boutique, with opening hours to suit those times when you just have to have a new outfit at two in the morning.

Touch Your All

1-14-27 Jingumae, Shibuya-ku (Snoopy Town 5770 4501/Mono Comme Ça 3423 8051). Harajuku station. **Open** 11am-8pm daily. **Credit** all major cards. **Map 5**

A recently opened fashion emporium whose many stalls cater for the young trendies of Harajuku. Contains some designer and more reasonably priced fashions, but mainly noted for the unbearably kitsch 'Snoopy Town' devoted to 'Peanuts' merchandise. Guaranteed to have you gagging within seconds.

Gifts & souvenirs

Bingo-ya

10-6 Wakamatsu-cho, Shinjuku-ku (3202 8778). 76 bus from Shinjuku station west exit. Get off at Yochomachi. **Open** 10am-7pm Tue-Sun. **Credit** all major cards.

Although this is a little off the beaten track, it's worth a visit. Bingo-ya stocks folk crafts from all over Japan and has a wide variety of traditional toys.

Fuji Torii

6-1-10 Jingumae, Shibuya-ku (3400 2777). Meiji-Jingumae station. **Open** 11am-6pm Mon-Wed, Fri-Sun. **Credit** all major cards. **Map 5**

This store is just a few doors up from Oriental Bazaar (*see below*), heading in the direction of Harajuku station. They are particularly good on paper goods, greetings cards and *kakejiku* (hanging scrolls).

Gift Centre Japan

Daiko Asahi Bldg, 3-8-2 Ginza, Chuo-ku (3564 0302). Ginza station. **Open** 10am-6pm Mon-Sat. **Credit** all major cards. **Map 7**

Gift Centre Japan runs a mail order service as well, with next-day delivery for catalogue orders. The catalogues are free and fully detailed.

International Arcade

2-1-1 Yurakucho, Chiyoda-ku (various phones). Yurakucho station. **Open** 9.30am-6.30pm daily. **Credit** AmEx, MC, V. **Map 7**

This arcade is located opposite the Imperial Hotel, actually under the Yamanote line train tracks. Notable shops inside are SI Brothers, which sell a wide range of small Japanese souvenirs of high quality, and Hayashi Kimono, which claims to be the largest kimono boutique for non-Japanese. They offer tax-free shopping for non-residents, and run a mail order service.

Kathryn Milan

3-1-14 Nishi-Azabu, Minato-ku (3408 1532). Roppongi station. **Open** 10.30am-6pm Sat, Sun; by appointment on weekdays. **Credit** all major cards. **Map 2**

A strange name for a Japanese gift shop, but this classy place offers a range of screen paintings, furniture, fans and other decorative accessories.

Ohya-Shobo

1-1 Kanda-Jinbocho,Chiyoda-ku (3291 0062). Jinbocho station. **Open** 10am-6pm Mon-Sat. **Credit** all major cards. **Map 9**

Boasts the world's largest stock of old illustrated books (some dating back 300 years), also *ukiyo-e* and other prints, old maps, early manga, and any kind of Japanese graphic art.

Oji Paper

3-7-12 Ginza, Chuo-ku (3562 6200). Ginza station. **Open** 9.30am-7pm daily. **Credit** all major cards. **Map 7**

Japanese origami paper has a mysterious, organic feel. If you crumple it, it doesn't make a sound. While you are pondering the philosophical implications of this, browse through the Oji Gallery, just around the corner from Matsuya department store (*see above*), and purchase something from the shop, which is on the third floor of the same building.

Oriental Bazaar

5-9-13 Jingumae, Shibuya-ku (3400 3933). Meiji-Jingumae station. **Open** 9.30am-6.30pm Mon-Wed, Fri-Sun. **Credit** all major cards. **Map 5**

This is Tokyo's largest store selling gifts and crafts, ranging from the cheap and cheerful to ivory antiques and traditional Japanese furniture. The higher up you go (it has four floors), the more expensive it gets. There is an impressive room of Buddhist art and statuary on the top floor.

Branch: Narita Airport, No.1 Terminal Bldg 4F, 1-1 Goryo-Bokujo, Sanrizuka, Narita-shi, Chiba-ken (0476 32 9333).

Tolman Collection

2-2-18 Shiba-Daimon, Minato-ku (3434 1300). Hamamatsu cho station. **Open** 11am-7pm Mon, Wed-Sun. **Credit** all major cards.

Specialises in high-quality prints, including ukiyo-e.

Vines

1-8-5 Higashi, Shibuya-ku (3406 5357). Shibuya station. **Open** 10am-7pm Mon-Sat. **Credit** all major cards. **Map 4**

Contains a selection of larger items of furniture, such as lacquerware (also known as Japanware). The most famous varieties are Wajima, Ishikawa prefecture, and Kiso, from Nagano.

Jewellery

Lloyd

2F Ryu Bldg, 1-16-5 Jingumae, Shibuya-ku (3470 2013). Shibuya station. **Open** 10am-8pm daily. **Credit** AmEx, V. **Map 5**

Although Gothic seems a fairer description than ethnic, the quality of this shop lifts it well above average. Staff here are llso very knowledgeable about body piercing.

Branches: all over Tokyo.

Lumine Market

1-1-5 Nishi-Shinjuku, Shinjuku-ku (3348 5211). Shinjuku station. **Open** 10am-7pm daily. **Credit** all major cards. **Map 3a**

Twenty-five famous-name stores are gathered on the second floor of this department store, actually part of Shinjuku station.

Mikimoto

5-5-4 Ginza, Chuo-ku (3535 4611). Ginza station. **Open** 9.30am-6.30pm daily. **Credit** all major cards. **Map 7**

This company calls itself the 'Pearl King', and with good reason. It has branches in the US, Paris and London. The story of the company's origins in the early Meiji period reads like a bestseller; ask one of the staff, who speak fluent English, and take a look at the exhibits in the pearl museum upstairs.

Branches: Akasaka: Akasaka Tokyu Plaza 1F, 2-14-3, Nagata cho, Chiyoda-ku (3581 9585). Akasaka-mitsuke station; Imperial Hotel Arcade, 1-1-1 Uchisaiwaicho, Chiyoda-ku (3591 5001). Hibiya station; Hotel Okura Arcade, 2-10-4 Toranomon, Minato-ku (3584 4664). Kamiyacho station.

Tasaki Shinju

5-7-5 Ginza, Chuo-ku (3289 1111). Ginza station. **Open** 10.30am-7.30pm daily. **Credit** all major cards. **Map 7**

This sumptuous shop, opposite the Ginza Nissan showroom, offers tax-free shopping.

Branch: 8-9-15 Ginza, Chuo-ku (3575 4180). Shinbashi station.

Tiffany's

3-29-1 Shinjuku, Shinjuku-ku (3225 7820). Shinjuku station. **Open** 10am-7pm daily. **Credit** all major cards. **Map 3b**

An obsession with Japanese couples, along with the Audrey Hepburn movie that eulogises it. Favourite purchase is the open-heart necklace.

Branch: Ginza: 2-7-17 Ginza, Chuo-ku (5250 2924). Ginza station.

Wako

4-5-11 Ginza, Chuo-ku (3562 2111). Ginza station.
Open 10am-6pm Mon-Sat. **Credit** all major cards.
Map 7
The hushed ambience of the interior is matched by
the grandeur of the exterior. The shop also sells
designer wear and ornaments.

Music

Japan is the world's second biggest market for
recorded music after the US, and fans can be obsessive about tracking down latest releases and rare
pressings from the past. Needless to say, there are
thousands of record stores in Tokyo, and most are
based in the youth-oriented districts of Shibuya
(best for dance and techno), west Shinjuku (live
bootlegs) and Shimo-Kitazawa (second-hand).

These stores consist of internationally famous
names and much smaller, independently run
stores. All of them are worth a visit by collectors
and casual buyers, but try to do too many in one
go and your head will be spinning faster than the
shop assistant's turntables.

In addition to the major outlets listed below,
Tokyo has several independent record chains, the
biggest of which are **Disk Union**, **Recofan** and
Cisco. Disk Union has its main shop opposite the
Beam Building in Shinjuku, and has seven floors
of new releases and second-hand bargains,
including rarities that will have record collectors
in a cold sweat. Recofan also has a large used CD
section, mostly junk but worth a look because of

the unbelievably low prices. Cisco sells only new
releases but is geared towards the serious consumer; this is where most of Tokyo DJs pick up
their stock. Cisco has five outlets in Shibuya –
techno, house, hip hop, reggae and a mail-order
specialist shop – and two more outlets in
Shinjuku and Ueno.

HMV

24-1 Udagawa-cho, Shibuya-ku (5458 3411).
Shibuya station. **Open** 10am-10pm daily.
Credit all major cards. **Map 4**
This store, which opened late 1998, is obviously
designed to give nearby Tower (*see below*) a run for
its money. Of special interest is the viewing area on
the fifth floor, where shoppers can chill out and
watch the latest video previews.
Branches: all over Tokyo. Call above number for
details.

Tower Records

1-22-14 Jinnan, Shibuya-ku (3496 3661). Shibuya
station. **Open** 10am-10pm daily. **Credit** all major
cards. **Map 4**
This is the favourite shop of many a Tokyo music-
lover. It's not just the six floors devoted to music and
video; it also has one of the best bookshops in Tokyo
on the seventh floor, with an eclectic range of books,
magazines and newspapers in English. Prices are
much lower than in Kinokuniya (*see below*).
Branches: Flags 7-10F, 3-37 Shinjuku, Shinjuku-ku
(5360 7811). Shinjuku station; Ikebukuro Parco 5-6F,
1-50-35 Higashi-Ikebukuro, Toshima-ku (3983 2010).
Ikebukuro station; also branches in Hachioji, Kichijoji
and Machida. Call above numbers for details.

Tower Records: *seven storeys of music, videos, books and more.*

Virgin Megastore

Marui Fashion B1F, 3-30-16 Shinjuku, Shinjuku-ku (5952 5600). Shinjuku San-chome station. **Open** 11am-8pm daily. **Credit** all major cards. **Map 3b**

This arm of the Branson global empire can be found in the basement of Marui City Building, Shinjuku. Although confining its goods to one floor, what it misses in quantity it makes up for in quality and variety. It also has in-store DJs broadcasting on FM radio during opening hours, a service that is better than most of the other commercial FM stations.

Branches: Marui City Ikebukuro B1, 3-28-13 Nishi-Ikebukuro, Toshima-ku (5952 5600). Ikebukuro station; also has a branch in Hachioji. Call above number for details.

Wave Records

6-2-27 Roppongi, Minato-ku (3408 0111). Roppongi station. **Open** 11am-8pm Mon-Thur, Sun; 11am-9pm Fri, Sat. **Credit** all major cards. **Map 2**

Wave has tended to lag behind the others in terms of modernisation, but its stores in Roppongi and Shibuya still have pulling power.

Branches: Ikebukuro 12F, 1-28-1 Minami-Ikebukuro, Toshima-ku (5992 0600). Ikebukuro station; Loft 6F, 21-1 Udagawa-cho, Shibuya-ku (3462 3118). Shibuya station; Seibu 7F, 4-27-14 Koto-bashi, Sumida-ku (3632 7133). Kinshi cho station; also branches in Kichijoji and Hikarigaoka. Call above numbers for details.

Shopping malls & streets

In recent years, a trend has developed to convert run-down, characterless parts of Tokyo into massive modern developments. The first area to undergo such a massive change was Ebisu, formerly a quiet suburb that has now become a shoppers' playground. Most recently, in 1999, a quiet station on the Yamanote line, Osaki, has acquired a massive shopping city complex, containing everything from department stores to restaurants and an Irish pub. In contrast, there is a small shopping street, or *shotengai*, in virtually every neighbourhood and suburb of Tokyo, again usually opposite the station. Most sell takeaway food and cut-price suits, but some have a character all of their own.

Atre Shopping Mall

Ebisu station, Shibuya-ku (5475 8500). Ebisu station. **Open** 10am-9pm Mon-Sat; 10am-8pm Sun. **Credit** varies. **Map 20**

Atre was the first of the recent large-scale urban redevelopments, in the formerly quiet backwater of Ebisu. The JR station exit is on the second floor, and food and pharmaceuticals are in the basement. Restaurants are on the sixth, clothes on the fourth and fifth, while of special interest to the expatriate is Seijo Ishii on the second, a small but well-stocked and reasonably priced food import shop.

Gate City Plaza Shopping Mall

1-11-1 Osaki, Shinagawa-ku (5496 3131). Osaki station. **Open** 11am-10pm daily. **Credit** varies.

This massive new redevelopment, in a quiet area famous for being the terminus of the last Yamanote line train, and therefore always full of lost, drunken salarymen, contains an event hall, office buildings, numerous restaurants, residential apartments, an Irish pub and a garden in a 5.9-ha (14-acre) area.

Kappa-bashi

Taito-ku. A five-minute walk from Tawaramachi station, along Asakusa Dori. **Open** varies. **Credit** varies, but cash usually preferred. **Map 10**

This area boasts not only a host of shops selling old Japanese curios, but also the largest selection of traditional kitchen equipment in one area. This can be surmised from the building with the giant chef's head on top of it, which spectacularly fails to blend in with the surrounding buildings. Look out for Maizuru, a shop that sells the plastic displays of food you see outside the high street restaurants, which make great souvenirs. The sushi is uncannily real. Don't go on an empty stomach.

Nakano Broadway

Nakano-ku. Opposite the north exit of Nakano station. **Open** varies. **Credit** varies. **Map 26**

Broadway is the second of two connected shopping malls that reach out from Nakano station. While the ground floor offers the usual mix of cut-price clothing and foods, the third floor, reached by escalator, is a haven for the collector of manga (comics) and manga-related materials. Three shops sell second-hand and collectors' manga, while on the fourth floor manga-related models and merchandise can be purchased. There are also several toyshops and arguably the best second-hand CD shop in Tokyo, Fujiya, on the third floor.

Sunshine City Shopping Mall

3-1-3 Nishi-Ikebukuro, Toshima-ku (3989 3331). Ikebukuro station. **Open** 10am-8pm daily. **Credit** varies. **Map 1**

A department store with delusions of grandeur, built on the site of Sugamo Prison, where Japan's war criminals awaited trial. This towering edifice holds an import supermarket, a branch of the Mitsukoshi department store, a museum, an aquarium, a planetarium, and an express elevator that will whisk you up to the observation room on the 60th floor. Can you see Mount Fuji yet?

Street markets

Ameyoko Plaza Food & Clothes Market

6-10-7 Ueno, Taito-ku. Ueno station. **Open** 9am-7pm daily. **No credit cards. Map 8**

This hive of activity is two markets, Ueno Centre Mall and Ameyoko itself. The Centre Mall sells souvenirs and clothes, the other market specialises in fresh food, especially fish. Go at the end of the day, when the vendors are knocking down their prices. Indian food freaks may like to know that this is one of the few places in Tokyo where you can buy basmati rice.

Nakamise Dori Shopping Street & Market

1 Asakusa, Taito-ku. Asakusa station. **Open** 8am-8pm daily. **No credit cards. Map 10**
This maze of stalls and tiny shops in and around Kaminarimon in Asakusa sells Japanese souvenirs, both elaborate and tacky. It also sells the kind of snack foods usually sold at festivals, and on some stalls brand-name watches, jeans and so on.

Antique & flea markets

Iidabashi Antique Market

Central Plaza, Ramia Square (info 3260 8211). Iidabashi station. **Open** dawn to dusk, first Sat of the month. **No credit cards.**
A lot of furniture, accessories, and some kimonos.

Nishi-Ogikubo Antique Shopping Street

Suginami-ku. Nishi-Ogikubo station. **Open** varies. **Credit** varies.
Nishi-Ogikubo station is on the Chuo line around 20 minutes west of Shinjuku. It lies at the intersection of four main roads; Kita-Ginza Dori, Shinmei Dori, Heiwa Dori and Fushimi Dori. Around the area are some 75 antique and second-hand shops, selling everything from Japanese objets d'art to Americana. A map of the area is available from most shops.

Roppongi Flea Market

5-5-1 Roppongi, Minato-ku (info 3583 2081). Roppongi station. **Open** dawn to dusk, the last Thur and Fri of the month. **No credit cards. Map 2**
From Roppongi station on the Hibiya line, outside the Roi building.

Salvation Army Bazaar

2-21-2 Wada, Suginami-ku (3384 3769). Shinjuku station, then a 19 bus from the west exit to Boshibyo-mae. **Open** 9am-1pm Sat. **No credit cards.**
This place's full name is the Kyuseiugun Danshi Shakai Hoshi Centre. This is an Aladdin's cave of household wares, furnishings, records, computers and household appliances, all sold at bargain prices. It is immensely popular with local residents and there can be unseemly scrambles for bargains. Be sure to get there good and early.

Togo Shrine Flea Market

1-5-3 Jingumae, Shibuya-ku (info 3403 3591). Harajuku station. **Open** dawn to dusk, first, fourth and fifth Sun of the month. **No credit cards. Map 5**
From Harajuku station, take the Takeshita Dori exit. Togo Shrine is on a road parallel to Takeshita Dori, to the left as you exit the station. A lot of furniture and kimono, not to mention an excellent chance to admire the shrine gardens.

Electronics & cameras

For the visitor, the place of interest is Akihabara (*see* **Akihabara**, *p181*). Of course, there are other stores almost matching the prices there, located in the main urban thoroughfares. The most notable of these are Sakuraya, Yodobashi Camera and Bic Camera. They are also big sellers of cameras, and if photography is your bag, just try a wander around the main shopping streets of Shinjuku. This area has dozens of small

Sakuraya *is just one of many cut-price electrical retailers in Shinjuku.*

Akihabara

Together in electric dreams: Akihabara is the best place in town to get really wired.

Movie directors such as Ridley Scott and SF writers such as William Gibson have often claimed Tokyo as one of their inspirations. Coming out of Akihabara station, dazzled by advertising screens the size of buildings, beguiled by sing-song ad slogans not quite drowned out by the rolling thunder of the trains on the overhead gantry, it's easy to see why. Akihabara is two square kilometres (0.8 square miles) of retail stores devoted to electrical goods. The locals call it 'Electric Town'.

The Japanese were renowned in the '60s for their tiny radios and charming, clunky robots, and now that the Transistor Age has been superseded by the Digital Age the process of miniaturisation has increased with mind-boggling speed. Japan is producing ever-smaller **Mini-Disc** players, **PlayStation** has become **Pocket Station**, laptop PCs have been followed by **palm-size e-mail readers**. **Pagers**, known here as Pocket Bells, can transmit messages written by a special light-pen, most often used by schoolgirls to send cutesy messages to their pals. All this pales, of course, in comparison with that Frankenstein's monster of miniaturisation, which has grabbed the Japanese by the hearts and the wallets – the **mobile phone**. In mid-1999, it was estimated that 40 million Japanese, or one third of the population, carried a mobile phone, or *keitai denwa*, and the number is still increasing at the rate of 10 million per year. If you're tempted to sign up, beware – Japanese mobile phones will not work outside Japan.

For Europeans, buying Japanese-standard electrical goods poses some problems. The mains voltage here runs, like America, at 100-110 volts, rather than the 220-240v standard in Europe. Also, Japanese **TVs** and **videos** use the **NTSC** colour system, and can play videos brought from the USA, but are incompatible with the European PAL/SECAM colour systems. If you're shopping for something like a video or camcorder, then make sure it is compatible with your home country's system. If your wallet stretches to it, it may be worth investing in a multi-system machine. For smaller appliances, like **Walkmans**, mains adapters are readily available. This means that you can buy something in Tokyo, take it home, and use it there with no inconvenience.

Also, you can buy them duty-free! Not all of the shops in Akihabara offer tax-free sales, but the ones that do advertise themselves loud and clear. The requirements are that you must be resident in Japan for less than six months, bring a copy of your passport with you and make a minimum purchase of ¥10,000.

In this city where techno-fads bloom and fade faster than cherry blossom, the latest craze is for new health-related products, such as devices that can measure your body-fat ratio, and give you diet advice. The marketing is aimed squarely at schoolgirls and young working women, buying such gadgets as the 'Slim de Major', 'CalorieMac' and 'BodyMon' to take them, shapely figures digitally enhanced, into the twenty-first century.

second-hand camera shops dotted around corners and small alleys.

Bic Camera

3-35-18 Shinjuku, Shinjuku-ku (5360 0002). Shinjuku station. **Open** 10am-8pm daily. **Credit** all major cards. **Map 3b**

There's not much to distinguish between this store and Yodobashi Camera (*see below*). Both are equally good value.

Branches: 3-26-14 Ikebukuro, Toshima-ku (5396 1111). Ikebukuro station; 1-24-12 Shibuya, Shibuya-ku (5466 1111). Shibuya station.

Kigawa

2-28 Kanda-Jinbocho, Chiyoda-ku (3261 3685). Jinbocho station. **Open** 10am-8pm Mon-Fri; 10am-7pm Sat(closed every other Sat). **Credit** all major cards. **Map 9**

A bargain-hunter's bargain shop, Kigawa sells end-of-the-line and second-hand electrical equipment, PCs, cameras, watches and videos. If it's not crucial that you have the latest model, then this is the place to come. Portable CD players start at ¥4,000, hi-fi stereo videos (NTSC system) at ¥10,000 and portable Mini-Disc players at ¥10,000. It's also the cheapest place in Tokyo for batteries (¥77 for two).

Laox

1-2-9 Soto-Kanda, Chiyoda-ku (3255 9041). Akihabara station. **Open** 10am-7.30pm daily. **Credit** all major cards. **Map 14**

In the main store, the duty-free section is located on the fourth to the seventh floors. A global delivery service is available, and most of the staff speak fair to middling English.

Branches: 1-7-6 Soto-Kanda, Chiyoda-ku (3255 5301). Akihabara station; 1-24 Kanda-Sakuma-cho, Chiyoda-ku (3253 5371). Akihabara station.

Minami Musen Denki

4-3-3 Soto-Kanda, Chiyoda-ku (3255 8030). Akihabara station. **Open** 10am-7.30pm daily. **Credit** all major cards. **Map 14**

Look for the sign that says T-Zone, a few doors up from Yamagiwa (*see below*) on Chuo Dori. Minami Musen Denki is on the first few floors of the T-Zone building, the duty-free counter is on the second.

Sakuraya

3-17-2 Shinjuku, Shinjuku-ku (3354 3636). Shinjuku station. **Open** 10am-8pm daily. **Credit** all major cards. **Map 3b**

Sakuraya is steadily gaining ground on its competitors, thanks to the variety of services it offers. These include relatively inexpensive delivery, repair and support services, and trade-in systems for cameras and mobile phones. Bear in mind, however, that some knowledge of Japanese is required. Among the cheapest places in town for electronic goods.

Branches: all over Tokyo.

Sony Building

5-3-1 Ginza, Chuo-ku (3573 2371). Ginza station. **Open** 11am-8pm daily. **Credit** all major cards. **Map 7**

This eye-catching building contains a number of fascinating showrooms displaying Sony products and a high-vision theatre, which screens films for free

Break out of the malls with a cooling drink in a shotengai, or small shopping street.

every Saturday and Sunday afternoon (to apply for tickets, call 3573 5234/fax 3573 7439). In the basement are the Sony shop (usually more expensive than Akihabara) and Soundmarket Hunter, a record shop. There are cafés and bars scattered throughout the building (*see chapter* **Ginza**).

Takarada

1-14-7 Soto-Kanda, Chiyoda-ku (3253 0101).
Akihabara station. **Open** 10am-7pm daily.
Credit all major cards. **Map 14**
Bilingual Japanese are on hand to help you find your way around.
Branches: duty-free shop 1: 1-14-7 Soto-Kanda, Chiyoda-ku (3251 5408). Akihabara station; duty-free shop 2: 1-15-6 Soto-Kanda, Chiyoda-ku (3253 6253). Akihabara station.

Yamagiwa

4-1-1 Soto-Kanda, Chiyoda-ku (3253 2111).
Akihabara station. **Open** 10.30am-7.30pm daily.
Credit all major cards. **Map 14**
The duty-free store is on the corner of the Chuo Dori, a few minutes' walk from Akihabara station.

Yodobashi Camera

1-11-1 Nishi-Shinjuku, Shinjuku-ku (3346 1010).
Shinjuku station. **Open** 9.30am-9pm daily.
Credit all major cards. **Map 3a**
Contains a bewildering array of electronic products. Particularly hot on video games.
Branches: 1-3-2 Nishi-Shinjuku, Shinjuku-ku (3346 8585). Shinjuku station; 3-26-3 Shinjuku, Shinjuku-ku (3356 1010). Shinjuku station; 4-9-8 Ueno, Taito-ku (3837 1010). Ueno station.

Imported food & supermarkets

If your stay in Japan is longer than a few weeks, you'll undoubtedly develop a hankering for a few home comforts. When was the last time you had a Marmite sandwich, for instance? If you're here for the Christmas period, will it be an overly stuffed turkey or chicken on a stick? Listed below are the stores that cater to expatriates and to Japanese people who are in the mood for something a little bit different.

Kinokuniya Supermarket

3-11-7 Kita-Aoyama, Minato-ku (3409 1231).
Omotesando station. **Open** 9.30am-8pm daily.
Credit all major cards. **Map 12**
The most popular international supermarket in Tokyo among foreign residents. If you can't find what you're looking for in among the racks of baked beans and breakfast cereals, staff here will be happy to order it for you. Kinokuniya also sells cards and foreign magazines and newspapers on the second floor, but the latter are overpriced so do your magazine shopping at Tower Records (*see above*) in Shibuya instead.
Branches: in Kichijoji and Kunitachi. Call above number for details.

Meidiya Hiroo Store

Hiroo Plaza 1F, 5-6-6 Hiroo, Minato-ku (3444 6221). Hiroo station. **Open** 10am-9pm daily.
Credit all major cards.
Smaller than National Azabu (*see below*), but still a good range of goodies.

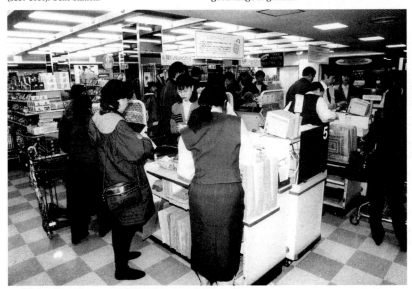

Missing your Marmite? – **Kinokuniya Supermarket** *will soothe away those expat blues.*

Vending machines

The Tokyo dweller's dual obsession with technology and convenience finds its most universal expression in the concept of vending machines, and if you look hard enough, you'll find that almost anything can be purchased from a vending machine in Tokyo.

The city's most common vending machines sell **cigarettes**, **soft drinks** and **hot and cold coffee or tea**, although in a token effort to combat underage smoking and drinking, machines that sell cigarettes and alcohol are closed down every night between the hours of 11pm and 5am. Meanwhile, alcohol vending machines are slowly being phased out, and are set to disappear completely within the next two years. Legions of grateful, drunken salarymen will mourn their passing.

Tokyo's most famous vending machine is probably the one that purports to sell **used schoolgirls' underwear**, but other 'weird' machines abound. A short walk around the Shibuya area will uncover machines selling everything from **disposable cameras** to **magazines**, **fresh flowers** to **rice**, **whisky** to **porn videos**, **sex aids** to the **batteries** needed to power them.

This being Japan, vending machines always work, and all of them give the right change, although most will not accept denominations higher than ¥1,000.

National Azabu

4-5-2 Minami-Azabu, Minato-ku (3442 3181). Hiroo station. **Open** 9.30am-7pm daily. **Credit** all major cards.

This one is a favourite for diplomats, as it's in the heart of the embassy district, and prices tend to reflect this. Rare bargains are available.
Branches: 2-6-21 Tamagawa-Denenchofu, Setagaya-ku (3721 4161). Denenchofu station (Toyoko line); Takashimaya Times Square, 5-24-2 Sendagaya, Shibuya-ku (fruit and vegetables only) (5361 1357). Shinjuku station.

Sun Market

4-10 Udagawa-cho, Shibuya-ku (3464 7770). Shibuya station. **Open** 11am-8pm daily. **No credit cards. Map 4**

Not easy to find, but a little gem. Lots of surprising munchies from all over the world at reasonable prices. It's on a hill near Tokyu Hands (*see below*), in an alley decorated with graffiti.

Confectionery

When the Japanese talk of American or European candies they have tried, the complaint is invariably that they are 'too sweet'. There is certainly something distinctive about the flavour of traditional Japanese *wagashi*, and the sweet paste made from *azuki* beans called *anko*. Many shops will allow you to try before you buy.

Akebono

Akebono Bldg, 2-39-2 Nihonbashi Hama cho, Chuo-ku (3571 0483). Hamacho station (Toei Shinjuku line). **Open** 10am-7pm daily. **Credit** AmEx, JCB, V.

This shop's variety of mouthwatering Japanese sweets is also available in the major Tokyo department stores, on sale in the basement food halls.
Branches: all over Tokyo.

Demel

1-13-12 Jingumae, Shibuya-ku (3478 1251). Harajuku station. **Open** 10am-7pm daily.
Credit AmEx, DC, JCB, V. **Map 5**

Set back from Omotesando, Demel confectionery shop specialises in German and Austrian chocolate and cakes.

Kimuraya

4-5-7 Ginza, Chuo-ku (3561 0368). Ginza station. **Open** 10am-7pm daily. **Credit** AmEx, JCB, V. **Map 7**

This splendid store, next door to Wako jewellers (*see above*), has the distinction of being the first Tokyo store to sell *anpan* – bread rolls filled with anko.

Qu'il Fait Bon

3-18-5 Minami-Aoyama, Minato-ku (5414 7741). Omotesando station. **Open** 11am-8pm daily. **Credit** all major cards. **Map 2**

This shop also has a café where you can sit back and sample the wares, waited on by staff in Victorian maids' costumes. It's all a stone's throw from Omotesando.
Branch: 2-18-2 Ebisu-Nishi, Shibuya-ku (5457 2191). Daikanyama station (Toyoko line).

Toraya

7-8-6 Ginza, Chuo-ku (3571 3679). Ginza station. **Open** 10am-6pm Mon-Sat. **Credit** all major cards. **Map 7**

This store also sells its wagashi in Paris and New York. If you're thinking of buying some as presents, watch out – they are intended to be eaten on the day they are made.
Branches: 4-9-22 Akasaka, Minato-ku (3408 4121). Akasaka-mitsuke station; 1-2-6 Nihonbashi, Chuo-ku (3271 8856). Nihonbashi station; 1-5-1 Marunouchi, Chiyoda-ku (3271 0786). Tokyo station; 1-1-1 Minami-Aoyama, Minato-ku (3475 1754). Aoyama-itchome station.

Tokyu Hands: *DIY paradise with a fabulous gimmicks, gifts and fancy dress department.*

Miscellaneous

American Pharmacy

Hibiya Park Bldg 1F, 1-8-1 Yurakucho, Chiyoda-ku (3211 4111). Hibiya station. **Open** 10am-7pm daily. **Credit** AmEx, DC, MC, V. **Map 7**

Although this shop sells Japanese medicines, the staff speak English, and are very helpful in times of emergency. Also has a small selection of paperback books and imported foods.

Condomania

6-30-1 Jingumae, Shibuya-ku (3797 6131). Harajuku station. **Open** 10.30am-10pm Sun-Thur; 10.30am-11pm Fri, Sat. **No credit cards. Map 5**

Something for the weekend? This store imports condoms for ladies and gentlemen wary of the local products. Also sells novelty goods on a condom theme. **Branch**: 2-23-9 Udagawa-cho, Shibuya-ku (3770 6345). Shibuya station.

In The Room

3-29-1 Nishi-Ikebukuro, Toshima-ku (3989 0270). Ikebukuro station. **Open** 10am-7pm daily. **Credit** all major cards. **Map 1**

This is the home and office furniture branch of the Marui corporation. Looking for something stylish to add to your apartment or your office? Look no further.

KiddyLand

6-1-9 Jingumae, Shibuya-ku (3409 3431). Harajuku station. **Open** 10am-6pm daily. Closed third Tue of the month. **Credit** AmEx, JCB, V. **Map 5**

Welcome to the kingdom of the cute. Contains everything from soft toys for babies to ultra-violent *anime* figures for teenagers. Although ostensibly a children's shop, its main clientele seems to be Japanese couples in their twenties. A great place to shop for offbeat souvenirs, or that Godzilla alarm clock you've always been promising yourself.
Branches: all over Tokyo.

My Lord

1-1-3 Shinjuku, Shinjuku-ku (3349 5611). Shinjuku station. **Open** varies from store to store. **Credit** MC, V. **Map 3a**

Although My Lord could be classified as a fashion building, the sloping terraced street between Keio and Odakyu department stores (for both, *see above*) contains many shops devoted to kitsch, retro, and cute cartoon characters from around the world. Specialist products available are the French Pingu, the American Sesame Street and Muppets, die-cast models of American and Japanese cartoon characters, and an entire shop devoted to the Sony Post Pet e-mail phenomenon.

Okadaya

3-23-17 Shinjuku, Shinjuku-ku (3352 5411). Shinjuku station. **Open** 10am-8.30pm daily. **Credit** AmEx, JCB, V. **Map 3b**
The main store, near Seibu Shinjuku station, is seven floors and an annexe building full of everything you may need to repair or make your own clothes. **Branches**: all over Tokyo.

Pokemon Museum

Kawasaki Teitoku Bldg 1F, 3-2-5 Nihonbashi, Chuo-ku (5200 0707). Nihonbashi station. **Open** 11am-8pm Mon, Tue, Thur-Sun. **Credit** MC, V. **Map 6**
Pokemon (a contraction of Pocket Monster) began life as a Nintendo game and went on to become an incredibly successful children's cartoon series. There is a huge range of items featuring characters from the show, the main mascot being the yellow rabbit-eared creature called Pikachu.

Sekaido Stationery

3-1-1 Shinjuku, Shinjuku-ku (3356 1515). Shinjuku station. **Open** 10am-7.30pm. **Credit** all major cards. **Map 3b**
The main store has a vast range of draughtsman's tools, and a rather interesting selection of wares for manga (comic) artists. Useful if you want to learn more about manga.
Branches: 1-11-11 Nishi-Shinjuku, Shinjuku-ku (3346 1515). Shinjuku station; Parco 5F, 1-28-2 Minami-Ikebukuro, Toshima-ku (3989 1515). Ikebukuro station.

Snoopy Town

1-14-27 Jingumae, Shibuya-ku (5770 4501). Harajuku station. **Open** 11am-8pm daily. **Credit** all major cards. **Map 5**
Everything you could possibly want, and many things you couldn't possibly want, connected with the wonderful world of Snoopy. In the same building as Touch Your All (*see above*).

Tokyu Hands

12-18 Udagawa-cho, Shibuya-ku (5489 5111). Shibuya station. **Open** 10am-8pm daily. **Closed** second and third Mon of the month. **Credit** all major cards. **Map 4**
This is the largest hardware store in Tokyo. If you need something for your apartment, whatever it is, you'll find it here. The basement contains novelty goods, fancy dress outfits and games and is a perfect introduction to the Japanese sense of humour. Be warned, however; the main Shibuya store contains about a dozen mezzanine floors and is very confusing. Unless you want to get lost, head for the easier-to-handle Takashimaya branch in Shinjuku (*see above*, **Department Stores**). Store guides in English are available by the entrance.

Branches: Takashimaya Times Square, 5-24-2 Sendagaya, Shibuya-ku (5361 3111). Shinjuku station; 1-28-10 Higashi Ikebukuro, Toshima-ku (3980 6111). Ikebukuro station.

Victoria Sportswear

3-4 Kanda-Ogawa-machi, Chiyoda-ku (3295 2955). Jinbocho station. **Open** 11am-8pm Mon-Sat; 10.30am-7.30pm Sun. **Credit** all major cards. **Map 9**
This is not the only discount sports shop in Tokyo but it is the cheapest. If you go to the main address (*above*), you'll be able to compare prices, as the area is awash with similar stores, whose specialities change with the season. A change of season usually brings a sale.
Branches: Shinjuku A: 4-1-11 Shinjuku, Shinjuku-ku (3354 8811). Shinjuku station; Shinjuku B: 4-1-10 Shinjuku, Shinjuku-ku (3354 8311). Shinjuku station; 3-10 Udagawa-cho, Shibuya-ku (3463 4211). Shibuya station.

YS Park

5-10-31 Roppongi, Minato-ku (3423 2244). Roppongi station. **Open** 10am-8pm daily. **No credit cards. Map 2**
A hair salon with English-speaking staff. It makes and sells its own range of environmentally friendly hair products.
Branches: 4-29-3 Meiji-Jingumae, Shibuya-ku (3746 2244). Omotesando station; 10-8 Sarugaku-cho, Shibuya-ku (3461 2244). Daikanyama station (Toyoko line).

Books

Below are the some of the stores that sell new books, in English and other languages, on any subject. If you're looking for curiosities and bargains, and have an afternoon to spare, head for the Kanda/Jinbocho area and browse among the second-hand bookstores that line the Yasukuni Dori.

Aoyama Book Centre

Cosmos Bldg, 5-53-67 Jingumae, Shibuya-ku (3479 0479). Omotesando station. **Open** 10am-5.30pm Mon-Sat; 10am-10pm Sun. **Credit** all major cards. **Map 4**
The head store is in Aoyama behind the United Nations University building, but of special interest to book-loving clubbers is the Roppongi branch, open at weekends until 5am. Have a bleary-eyed browse while you're waiting for the first train home.
Branches: 6-1-20 Roppongi, Minato-ku (5485 5511). Roppongi station; Hiroo Garden 2F, 4-1-29 Minami-Azabu, Minato-ku (3442 1651). Hiroo station; Lumine 1 5F, 1-1-5 Nishi-Shinjuku, Shinjuku-ku (3344 0881). Shinjuku station; Lumine 2 4F, 3-38-2 Shinjuku, Shinjuku-ku (3340 2420). Shinjuku station; B1, 1-8-21 Jiyugaoka, Meguro-ku (5701 6651). Jiyugaoka station (Toyoko line).

Charles E Tuttle

1-3 Kanda-Jinbocho, Chiyoda-ku (3291 7071). Jinbocho station. **Open** 10:30am-6:30pm Mon-Sat. **Credit** all major cards. **Map 9**

Long-established bookshop run by Japan's leading English-language publisher. As well as its own guidebooks and language aids, there's a good selection of paperbacks, including some real bargains.

Good Day Books

3F, 1-11-2 Ebisu, Shibuya-ku (5421 0957). Ebisu station. **Open** 11am-8pm Mon-Sat; 11am-6pm Sun. **No credit cards. Map 20**

Stocks 30,000 used books and 7,000 new, mostly in English. An extensive selection of second-hand

books on Japan and Japanese language texts. It's a must for anyone looking for a bargain.

Kinokuniya Bookstore

3-17-7 Shinjuku, Shinjuku-ku (3354 0131). Shinjuku station. **Open** 10am-8pm daily. **Credit** all major cards. **Map 3b**

Kinokuniya Bookstore has what is perhaps the largest selection of imported books in the whole of Tokyo – but this vast choice comes at a price. You should expect to pay around ¥1,500 for a recent

Japanese crafts

Until around 150 years ago, there was no clear distinction between fine art and crafts in Japan. Being an artist wasn't defined by attitude or lifestyle, but by what people did, and how they did it.

Although some aspects of craftsmanship were regarded as the preserve of the political and intellectual elite, others were in the public domain, and familiar to the entire population. This led to the famous occurrence of Japanese exporters using prints of *ukiyo-e* **woodblocks** as packing materials to ship ceramics to the west. Upon delivery, the prints caused as much of a sensation as the ceramics, introducing the west to the now world-famous works by artists Hiroshige and Hokusai.

What exactly do we mean by Japanese crafts? The traditional materials used in larger objects would be wood lacquered with the sap from the urushi tree, bamboo and occasionally worked metal. **Ceramics** consist of glazed or unglazed stoneware, and the recent addition of porcelain. **Kimono** display a variety of textiles and designs, with the most sought-after fabric being reeled silk. Also there is the incredibly resilient **Japanese paper**, of which toys, lanterns, Edo-style umbrellas and even doors are made.

Crafts also fall into two broad categories. *Dento kogei* are the fine traditional crafts, where what matters is the quality of technique and refinement of finish. *Mingei* are the folk crafts intended for everyday use, although frequently they end up as objects of decoration and veneration. One case in point is the highly valuable *netsuke*. In the Edo period, it was forbidden for lower-ranking samurai to overdo the decorations on their kimono, so the more artistically inclined turned to decorating the tiny accessories they carried with them – the bamboo or ivory holders of tobacco or medicine.

In addition, every prefecture in Japan has its own version of the making of dento kogei and

mingei, sometimes with only slight variations, sometimes with bizarre flights of fancy such as the pottery raccoon-dogs of Shigaraki. **The Japan Traditional Craft Centre**, which can be found opposite the Bell Commons building in Aoyama (*see* **Map 12**), performs a valuable service in that it holds both touring and permanent exhibitions of such regional arts, or *meibutsu*, which serve as a handy introduction to newcomers to the subject.

Japanese crafts operate on a system of master and apprentice, with the novice carefully watching and copying the movements of their senior. The fruits of the work are inseparable from the nation's culture, especially the Shinto belief in regarding even inanimate objects as part of a holistic consciousness. The beauty of Japanese art is meant to draw the observer in, forming a unified whole, short-cutting the intellect and appealing directly to the senses. The Japanese say that when they're successful, such objects have *yugen* – they hold the essence of beauty itself.

In the twentieth century, the Japanese government has recognised the effort made by these solitary experts by awarding the title of 'Living Cultural Treasures' to selected individuals. For aspiring artisans, the highest accolade would be to become an apprentice to one of them.

What of the future? It's true that the number of skilled craftsmen producing traditional objects in traditional ways is in decline. However, the market for such products remains undiminished, both at home and abroad. In an age where mass consumerism appears to be driving us down a social and environmental dead end, perhaps the time may be right for a massive decentralisation of industry – with people again realising the value of a few, simple, carefully made products, which represent something far beyond the paper tokens that purchased them.

Browse in Jinbocho's second-hand bookshops: you'll be surprised what you might find.

paperback. The owners claim to have approximately 1 million books in stock, in English and in a range of other languages, and can order other titles from the UK and the USA. The original Shinjuku branch, situated close to the station's east exit, is rather cramped, and the waiting time between lifts can be frustratingly long. A newer, more user-friendly branch is located in the giant Takashimaya Times Square complex.
Branch: Takashimaya Times Square, 5-24-2 Sendagaya, Shibuya-ku (5361 3301). Shinjuku station.

Kitazawa

2-5 Kanda-Jinbocho, Chiyoda-ku (3263 0011).
Jinbocho station. **Open** 10am-6pm Mon-Sat.
Credit all major cards. **Map 9**
Kitazawa, which is without doubt the most handsome bookshop in the Jinbocho area, stands out because of its massive granite exterior and its brass spiral staircase, which is just inside the entrance. A small plaza outside the bookshop contains a number of boxes of paperbacks on offer at knock-down prices. Inside, there's a very scholarly atmosphere, with new works of literature, history and philosophy to be found on the first floor,

and a section of rare and antique books on the second floor.

Maruzen

2F, 2-3-10 Nihonbashi, Chuo-ku (3272 7211).
Nihonbashi station. **Open** 10am-7pm Mon-Sat;
10am-6pm Sun. **Credit** all major cards. **Map 6**
After Kinokuniya Bookstore (*see above*), Maruzen offers what is probably the second largest selection of new books in Tokyo. It also sells books in European languages (French, German, Spanish and Italian). Orders for books can be placed from the UK and the USA. The children's book department is on the fourth floor.
Branches: all over Tokyo.

Sanseido Books

1-1 Kanda-Jinbocho, Chiyoda-ku (3233 3312).
Jinbocho station. **Open** *Jan, Feb, May-Dec* 10am-6.30pm Mon, Wed-Sun; *Mar, Apr* 10am-6.30pm daily.
Credit all major cards. **Map 9**
Sanseido Books is of the longest-established bookshops in this area. It offers a good choice of foreign books on the fifth floor. Prices are slightly lower than those at Kinokuniya Bookstore (*see above*).

Business

Top tips for successful wheeling and dealing.

In the post-war years, following demilitarisation, Japan no longer had the option to focus on developing a strong military, so Japanese leaders were forced to throw themselves into the economic arena, a task they executed with gusto.

With a high degree of government support through low-cost loans and protection of the domestic market and industries from foreign competition, the stable development of the economy was guaranteed. As a result, by the 1970s Japan had emerged as one of the world's economic superpowers. Today its economic muscle is second only to that of the United States and, according to recent statistics, it produces nearly 18 per cent of the world's goods. What happens in Japan has economic ramifications worldwide; as recently witnessed in the Far East, fluctuations in the Japanese economy can influence and even topple the economies of countries around the world.

TOKYO STOCK EXCHANGE

The financial system nurtured in Japan has been one lynchpin in the vast economic success of the country. The origins of this system are credited as being the trading exchanges in Osaka and Tokyo (then called Edo), established in the early eighteenth century and owned by rice merchants. From these came the Stock Exchanges of both cities.

Over 80 per cent of Japan's stock market trading volume takes place on the Tokyo Stock Exchange (TSE) and it is now one of the world's largest equity markets.

There are two indices that measure the performance of the TSE. These are the 'Nikkei Stock Average' (Nikkei 225) and the Tokyo Stock Price Index (TOPIX). The Nikkei is simply the arithmetic mean of the stock prices of 225 (hence Nikkei 225) selected stocks. This is not fully representative of the average price of the stock market price and is similar to the Dow Jones Index Average.

The power of Japanese corporations is phenomenal. In 1996 Mitsubishi was the largest corporation in the world. Not only that, but it ranked as the twenty-second largest economy, larger than major nations like India, Argentina or Switzerland.

Doing Business in Japan

There are crucial differences in business practices and customs between Japan and other countries. Many foreigners who come to Japan to do business are unaware of these deep-rooted traditions and practices. An understanding of the fundamental concepts underlying Japanese business practices can increase your chances of success appreciably.

WA (GROUP HARMONY)

Often touted by the Japanese as the 'secret of their success', the idea of harmony, unity and peace in a social group (or *wa*) is an important concept and something all Japanese strive for. The resulting need for consensus within a group is manifested in the business sphere by the *ringi* system. This is a multi-step procedure for building consensus during business negotiations. It is time-consuming as proposals are circulated to interested parties at the sectional, divisional and corporate levels. It does have the advantage of preventing disagreement once a consensus has been reached.

NAGAI TSUKIAI
(LONG-TERM RELATIONSHIPS)

It's crucial for the foreign businessperson to understand the Japanese desire for lasting relationships

Special challenges for women

Japan's economy may have changed out of all recognition in the last 30 years, but its attitude to women hasn't. The traditional Japanese view of the woman in the workplace is as decoration. Being accepted as an equal and being taken seriously may be the biggest problems for foreign businesswomen coming to Japan. Useful strategies to overcome these problems are:

● An early introduction by as senior a male colleague as possible.
● Having the male members of the team seek a woman's advice signifies her authority.
● The senior executive should always support her if any questions arise.
● During informal socialising it is wise to make an early exit.

and it is critical for business success in Japan. The Japanese will want to gauge your level of commitment so will want to spend a long time getting to know prospective associates. This is the purpose of the 'Getting to know you' stage of negotiations (*see below* **Meeting Structure**) and the time spent socialising (*see below* **Socialising**).

SHINYO (TRUST)

Before entering into a long-term relationship with someone, business or otherwise, the Japanese seek to find a deep feeling of trust between themselves and the other party. Following on from *nagai tsukiai*, in order to achieve *shinyo* a great amount of time is spent getting to know individuals on both a professional and personal level.

'NO' MEANS 'YES' MEANS 'NO'

To avoid confrontation that would disrupt the group's *wa* the Japanese prefer ambiguity to being too direct (which is considered rude). This ambiguity is highlighted by the Japanese use of 'yes' and 'no', which can drive a westerner mad. The English 'yes' is seen as a decision to commit, whereas the Japanese 'yes' (*hai*) means 'yes, I understand you'. 'No' is used little by the Japanese as it could cause disharmony.

MIND YOUR MANNERS!

The traditional Japanese greeting is the bow, but many people greet westerners with a handshake. If shaking hands, the host usually offers his hand first. Westerners are not expected to bow, but if someone bows to you, give a bow of the same depth. There is no eye contact when bowing. Lower your eyes and keep your palms flat at your sides.

The exchange of business cards or *meishi* is an important part of Japanese business protocol and takes place at the same time as the introductory bow. *Meishi* are exchanged when meeting someone for the first time. When receiving a card, it is considered common courtesy to offer one in return. Not returning a card gives the impression that you are not committed to a long-term relationship.

Present the *meishi* Japanese side up and make sure that your name is not upside down from the recipient's point of view. Handle cards you are given with care and place all cards on the table in front of you for the duration of the meeting. Never fold, tear or write on a card.

In introductions, last names are used, followed by *san*, which is the equivalent of 'Mr' or 'Ms'. So, 'Mr Suzuki' becomes 'Suzuki-san'. Do not suggest that the Japanese call you by your first name.

The seating arrangement in a meeting follows strict protocol in Japan and is done according to *sekiji*, the system of ordering rank within an organisation. To avoid making the Japanese uncomfortable by sitting in the wrong place, allow a Japanese colleague to show you to your seat.

MEETING STRUCTURE

The structure of formal business meetings differs significantly between Japan and the west. To reach an agreement satisfactory to all sides, one must undergo a four-stage process, each with a specific task. This may require several meetings.

One: 'Getting acquainted' (Aisatsu)

This is where Japanese attempt to forge the personal foundation with the other party. The temptation for westerners is to dispense with 'small talk' and get straight down to business. This will make the Japanese very uncomfortable, so do not rush this phase of the meeting.

After introductions and the exchange of business cards, the Japanese will ask general questions about your trip, your country, hobbies, travels abroad. Ask similar questions in return and don't worry if the conversation strays on to a personal level; this is appreciated.

The 'getting to know you' stage is at an end when the highest ranking person (the one you were introduced to first) excuses himself. The cue for the second 'discussion' stage to begin is when tea or coffee is served.

If your Japanese hosts invite you to dinner (which they invariably will), accept if possible. Business socialising (*see below* **Socialising**) is a crucial part of trust-building and establishing a long-term business relationship.

At the end of this first visit it is traditional for the guest to offer a gift to the hosts.

Two: Exchange of information

The primary function of this stage is fact-gathering to allow the Japanese to build a total picture of you and your company. It is vital that they get the information they want from you to commit. Prepare details of your proposal thoroughly and expect to provide a lot of technical data. This is also a test of your credibility.

Three: Negotiation

Typically if you reach this stage the Japanese are close to a decision, so avoid the hard-sell approach, which will be received coolly. Proceed slowly, focus on long-term business relations, observe the Japanese use of silence, pauses and body language, expect and accept ambiguity and delay.

Four: Reaching an agreement

The first offer the Japanese make is likely to be the one that they feel best suits both parties. If you disagree and concessions are sought, it is best to present yours before asking theirs. Prepare well and present a united front, because any disagreement within your team will be interpreted as a sign of insufficient preparation.

Once an agreement has been reached and formalised on paper you should plan on attending the contract-signing ceremony as it is considered rude to do this by post after returning home.

SOCIALISING

A vital yet underestimated part of the Japanese business process, socialising is essential for developing the strong and long-lasting relationships that the Japanese prize.

Dining out is a chance for the Japanese to let their hair down and to relax but there are a few formalities that must be observed. Again, seating is determined by rank, so wait for another to indicate your seat to you. Allow your host to order for you, be enthusiastic while eating, and show great thanks afterwards. Never point your chopsticks at another person and never offer to split the bill. If you were invited out, let the host pay.

Business services

Accommodation addresses

Kimi Information Centre

Oscar Bldg 8F, 2-42-3 Ikebukuro, Toshima-ku (3986 1604/kimi529@iac.co.jp).
Website: www.gsquare.or.jp/kimi

Business cards

Many top-class hotels can arrange the printing of business cards, but there are also printers specialising in foreigners' *meishi*. Do not go to a meeting in Japan without a business card.

Kazui Press

11-1 Nishi-goken-cho, Shinjuku-ku (3268 1961/fax 3268 1962).
Offers business cards in any language from English to Hebrew, but orders taken only in Japanese.

Mode International

#303 Etanser Ikebukuro Bldg, 4-13-8 Higashi Ikebukuro, Toshima-ku (3983 3605/fax 3983 3678).
Offers translation and name card printing service, with orders taken in English, Japanese and Urdu.
Website: http://www.asahi-net.or.jp/~YN2A-MSD

Interpretation

Using an interpreter has two important benefits: ensuring that language differences do not become an obstacle to communication and translating the complicated unspoken messages used throughout. When using an interpreter, try to meet beforehand to explain your objectives and perhaps provide a list of words specific to your industry/company.

Communication Facilitator

Opus 1-401, 8-1 Yochomachi, Shinjuku-ku (3354 0516/fax 3354 0516).
Website: www.bekkoame.or.jp/~ryosaito

DHC Corp, Translation & Interpretation Division

Landic Roppongi Bldg 3F, 4-11-13 Roppongi, Minato-ku (3478 2061/fax 3478 3808).
Website: www.dhc.co.jp

Japan Convention Services Inc

Nippon Press Centre Bldg, 2-2-1 Uchisaiwaicho, Chiyoda-ku (3508 1211/fax 3508 0820).
Website: www.convention.co.jp/

Simul International

Shinjuku Green Tower Bldg 9F, 6-14-1 Nishi-Shinjuku (5324 6640/fax 5323 7023).

Limousine hire

Hinomaru Limousine

Ark Hills Mori Bldg, 1-12-32 Akasaka, Minato-ku (3505 1717/fax 3589 2445/ uehara@tpost1.netspace.or.jp).
If arriving in style is crucial, Hinomaru offers stretch

Japanese communication

The Japanese style of communication is significantly different from that in the west. Relying more heavily on a non-verbal style, the Japanese have a rich system of cues that may be lost or, worse, misunderstood by a foreign person. It stems from the belief that *kokoro*, the core of the inner self, cannot be expressed sufficiently with words alone.

These are a few rules of thumb:

Them

● A smile is multipurpose, concealing embarrassment and pain as well as expressing happiness.
● Leaning forward with elbows on the table is a sign of confidence and interest.
● Sitting back in your chair is a sign of uninterest or disagreement.
● Closing one's eyes is a sign of concentration.
● When a senior person falls asleep, this (believe it or not) means that everything is going well.
● A hand on the back of the neck may mean that there is a problem with the negotiations.
● An outstretched hand waving downwards means 'Please come this way'.

You

● Constant eye contact is considered rude and aggressive.
● Keep a greater physical distance when talking with a Japanese person.
● Speaking loudly is threatening.
● Pointing is considered rude.
● Physical contact makes the Japanese uncomfortable, though in informal situations this may be allowed.

limos and the like, driven by English-speaking chauffeurs.
Website: www.netspace.or.jp/~hinomaru

Mailbox rental

Mail Station Ebisu
Lions Plaza Ebisu 807, 3-25-3 Higashi, Shibuya-ku (5469 1408/prepynet@tky.threewebnet.or.jp).
Website: www.tky.threewebnet.or.jp/~prepynet

Nishi Shinjuku Rental Mailbox
Togawa Bldg, 7-12-1 Nishi Shinjuku, Shinjuku-ku (3371 6066).

Mobile phone rental

Japan Direct Dialling Company
(0120 33 4630). **Lines open** 10am-8pm Mon-Fri. International and domestic mobile phones for hire. Prices start at ¥2,000 per day (plus call charges).

Sony Finance International
(0120 116323/3475 5721). **Lines open** 24 hours. Rental by phone or at a desk in the Shinagawa Prince Hotel, open to non-residents. Domestic and international models are available. Prices around ¥2,000 per day (plus call charges).

Newspapers

The Financial Times
Britain's pink business bible prints daily in Tokyo and is available from subway newsstands in the business areas of Tokyo at ¥600. Longer-term subscriptions of three months, six months and one year are available. Call 3295 1711 for details.

Nikkei Weekly
The English version of Japan's premier financial newspaper is published weekly at ¥500. For subscriptions, call 0120 009907.

Office space rental
Despite the fall in office rental costs following the burst of the bubble economy, it's expensive to start up here. Several companies specialise in providing compact space, equipment and other essentials.

Century 21 SKY Realty Inc
Yatsuka Bldg 1F, 1-3-8 Higashi Azabu, Minato-ku (3585 0021/fax 3585 0399).
E-mail: c21@beehive.twics.com

KDD Business Quarters
KDD Otemachi Bldg 21F, 1-8-1 Otemachi, Chiyoda-ku (3243 9180/fax 3243 9190).
Website: www1.kcom.ne.jp/kbq/index/

Servcorp
Shinjuku Nomura Bldg 32F, 1-26-2 Nishi-Shinjuku, Shinjuku-ku (5322 2900).
Website: www.servcorp.com.au

The western-style **Bank of Japan.**

Telephone answering

Telephone Secretary Centre
9-1-7-1020 Akasaka, Minato-ku (5413 7320/gh6m-situ@asahi-net.or.jp).
Answering service for ¥10,000 a month. Service includes bilingual secretaries, word processing and typing. Free Japanese lessons for new customers.
Website: www.mmjp.or.jp/Telease/

Business sights

Bank of Japan
2-1-1 Nihonbashi Hongoku-cho, Chuo-ku (English tour reservations 3279 1111). Mitsukoshi-mae station. **Open** 10am-3pm Mon-Fri. **Admission** free.
Map 6
It's no accident that the Bank of Japan looks like the Bank of England. Built in 1896, this was the first western-style building in Tokyo constructed entirely by Japanese people. If the idea was to bring western-style prosperity, it worked. The Bank of Japan dominates the Japanese financial system and has tremendous sway over the world's economies. This tour in English includes a video about the Bank, a look at the operations and international departments, and a chance to view banking exhibits of historical interest. If you still find yourself hungering for cash, take a look in the Bank's nearby Currency Museum (*see chapter* **Museums & Galleries**).

Tokyo Stock Exchange
2-1 Nihonbashi Kabuto-cho, Chuo-ku (3666 0141). Kayabacho station. **Open** 9am-4pm Mon-Fri; English tours 1.30pm. **Admission** free. **Map 6**
There are two ways to see the throbbing engine room of the Japanese economy: you can go on your own, or ring ahead to join the English-language guided tour. From the mezzanine you can see the frantic activity on the trading floor below, while elsewhere a selection of videos, telephone information booths and even robots explain the mysterious workings of the world markets. The Stock Exchange Museum on the main floor explains the history of stocks and trading in Japan. Trading hours are between 9.00am and 11.00am and 1.00pm to 3.00pm. Exhibits in English describing the history and present activities of TSE keep visitors occupied during the breaks. Full information on the trading rules and layout of the floor, as well as guided tours, are also available in English.

Arts & Entertainment

Children

The big city offers big fun and games for little people, too.

Tokyo is an adult's paradise, and at times it's hard to see where children fit in. Yet in spite of its formidable appearance, the city does offer a variety of distractions, including parks, shops, entertainment centres, cinemas, games centres, children's theatre, museums, planetariums and zoos.

Furry friends

Pony Land

3-12-17 Shinozaki-cho, Edogawa-ku (3678 7520). Koiwa station, then a 72 bus bound for Mizue or Ichinoe. **Open** 9.30-11.30am, 1.30-3.30pm Tue-Sun.
Here kids can ride ponies and enjoy covered carriage rides all for free. A great place to teach your child about horses and spark an interest in riding.

Tama Zoo

7-1-1 Hodokubo, Hino-shi (0425 91 1611). Tama Dobutsu Koen station (Keio Dobutsu line). **Open** 9.30am-5pm Tue-Sun. **Admission** ¥500; ¥200 junior & high school students; free for young children & over-65s.
Tokyo's best zoo is situated on 53 ha (130 acres) of rolling countryside a 45-minute train ride out of Tokyo. Baby changing facilities and plenty of rest areas make this a popular place with parents with small children.

Making a splash

If you're here in the sweltering summer months, you may decide to take a day or two off from sightseeing and take a break at one of Tokyo's many outdoor pools that open only in summer. Tokyo pools are strict. Keep the following rules in mind: no T-shirts in the pool, sunglasses must have straps, no jewellery in the pool, some pools frown on tattoos, no oils and lotions, no radios and in some pools no toys or floats.

Seibu-en

2964 Yamaguchi, Tokorozawa-shi, Saitama-ken (042 922 1371). Seibu-en station (Seibu-en line). **Open** 10am-5pm Mon-Fri, Sun; 10am-8pm Sat. **Admission** ¥1,800; ¥900 elementary schoolchildren; ¥700 4-6s.
This sprawling amusement park in west Tokyo is home not only to several huge pools including a wave pool, a flowing river pool and some thrilling water slides, it also has a giant dinosaur ride, amusement park rides, places to eat, a raceway and fireworks shows on summer weekends.

Tokyo Summerland

600 Kamiyotsugi, Akiruno-shi (0425 58 6511). Hachioji station, then a special shuttle bus. **Open** 10am-5pm Mon-Wed, Sat, Sun. **Admission** ¥2,000; ¥1,000 children.
With the addition of several new water attractions in 1998, Summerland has become the place to get your spills and thrills in the water. Unlike Toshimaen (*see chapter* **Sightseeing**), the park isn't big on jet coasters and the like but there are flowing pools, water slides, waterfalls and all kinds of crazy wet fun.

Amusement parks

Kodomo no Kuni

700 Nara-machi, Aoba-ku, Yokohama-shi, Kanagawa-ken (045 961 2111). Nagatsuda station (Shin-Tamagawa line), then a special train from platform seven. **Open** 9.30am-4.30pm Tue-Sun. **Admission** ¥600; ¥200 middle & elementary schoolchildren; ¥100 pre-school age over 3.
Pool, cycle & boat rental charged separately.
No rides, no superhero shows, what is the point? As the name says, 'This is Kid's Country!' and the point at Kodomo no Kuni is a whole day of exploring nature, bicycling through acres of greenery, boating on the lake, taking pony rides, visiting lots of farm animals and a real working dairy.

Sanrio Puroland

1-31 Ochiai, Tama-shi (042 339 1111). Tama Centre station (Keio/Odakyu lines). **Open** 10am-8pm daily. **Admission** ¥3,000; ¥2,700 12-17s; ¥2,000 4-11s.
In Puroland (the Japanese reading of English 'pure'), you will find the Kingdom of Kitty – Hello Kitty, that is. This is not so much a ride-oriented park as a place where visitors can watch Kitty shows, eat Kitty food, ride Kitty rides and participate in Kitty events.

Sesame Place

600 Kamiyotsugi, Akiruno-shi (042 558 6511). Akikawa station (Itsukaichi line), then two shuttle buses, first to Summerland, then on to Sesame Place bus. **Open** 10am-5pm Mon-Wed, Sat, Sun. **Admission** ¥2,000; ¥1,000 3-12s.
If you like *Sesame Street*, you'll love this theme park, where children of all ages get to play with their TV heroes. The attractions and shows are designed for parent/child interaction with the aim of stimulating a child's learning process. In the summertime a series of water attractions and pools opens up.

Toys, games and books

Crayon House
3-8-15 Kita-Aoyama, Minato-ku (3406 6492).
Omotesando station. **Open** 11am-8pm daily.
Credit all major cards. **Map 5**
Located in the centre of trendy Omotesando, this is
more than just a bookshop; there is also an organic
restaurant with an all-you-can-eat buffet, a bakery
and toys on the upper floors. Skip the toys as most
are imports but browse for beautiful Japanese children's books and games by famous artists.

Hakuhinkan Toy Park
8-8-11 Ginza, Chuo-ku (3571 8008). Ginza station.
Open 11am-8pm daily. **Credit** all major cards. **Map 7**
To children this place in the heart of Ginza is heav-
en. You will find Japanese toys like Ultraman and
Pikachu here, in addition to many imported ones.
There is also a very child-friendly restaurant.

Rainy day remedies

National Children's Castle
5-53-1 Jingumae, Shibuya-ku (3797 5665).
Omotesando station. **Open** 12.30-5.30pm Tue-Fri;
10am-5.30pm weekends & holidays. **Admission**
¥500; ¥400 children. **Map 4**
This large complex contains floor after floor of recre-
ational and educational facilities including a huge
indoor play area, a roof garden play area complete
with ball pool, a video library, an art room and a
music room where kids can try their hand at all
kinds of instruments. There are puppet shows, story
hours, origami classes and many art classes – all
included in the price of admission. There are computers and pool tables for bigger kids too.

Tokyo Metropolitan Children's Museum
1-18-24 Shibuya, Shibuya-ku (3409 6361). Shibuya
station. **Open** 9am-5pm daily. **Map 4**
Another fabulous play hall for children, built by the
government in an effort to make Tokyo easier for
parents with small children. Here you will find several floors of fantastic ways to spend a day, no matter what the weather is doing outside. After the hall
closes at night the area outside becomes one of
Tokyo's biggest open-air dance classes with hip hop
and house dancers practising their moves. Closed
the second Monday of the month.

Babysitting

The following babysitter services are reputable
and each one comes highly recommended by
Tokyo parents. Your hotel may be able to arrange
such a service for you, but just in case the following agencies all have qualified, well-trained and
caring staff.

Rates vary but expect to pay between ¥1,500
and ¥2,200 per hour. Some agencies request you
to order a minimum of three hours at a set rate

Tokyo tots enjoy a bit of parklife.

before they agree to send out a sitter, then you pay
for each additional hour, with different rates for
late-night and early-morning services.

As a rule do not expect the agencies to speak a
wide variety of languages, even though from time
to time some do have babysitters on staff who
speak a little English or French.

Japan Baby-Sitter Service
(3423 1251). **Open** 9am-6pm Mon-Fri.
One of the oldest services in Tokyo, specialising in
grandmotherly types. Reserve 24 hours in advance.

Little Mate
Keio Plaza Hotel (3345 1439). **Open** 24 hours daily.
Okura Hotel (3582 0111 ext 3838). **Open** 10am-
8pm daily.
Little Mate is a day nursery where you can drop
your children off for an hour or longer. Reservations
are required by 7pm of the previous day. For hotel
addresses, *see chapter* **Accommodation**.

Poppins Service
(3447 2100). **Open** 9.30 am-5.30pm Mon-Sat.
Expect either a young lady trained in early child-
hood education or a retired veteran teacher when
you request a sitter from Poppins. One of the best,
one of the most expensive.

Tom Sawyer Agency
(3770 9530). **Open** 9am-10.30pm Mon-Fri; 12.30-
9.30pm Sat, Sun. 24-hour reservation system.
This very reputable Shibuya agency has branches
all over Japan. Reserve by 8pm the night before you
plan to go out.

Dance

Everything from ballet and traditional styles to flamenco and hula.

Ballet and modern dance are the cornerstones of mainstream dance in Tokyo, but the numbers of young dancers, combined with an explosion of interest in foreign or ethnic styles, mean that the wider scene is a much more varied and exciting than ever before.

Thus, while the young dancers of the Tokyo Ballet dance to Maurice Béjart's choreography (Tokyo Ballet is the only company here with the rights to his pieces), on the other side of town anything from hi-tech theatrical pieces to wild Spanish flamenco parties might be taking place.

The new wave of Japanese dancers have taken the basics of the Japanese traditional styles and adapted them for their own ends, cutting themselves off from the iemoto ('original house') of the traditional styles and performing only contemporary dance, but with a Japanese twist. Leading exponents of this style include Senrei Nishikawa and Egiku Hanayagi.

Using traditional movements, Senrei takes a minimalist approach. Watching her is like viewing a painting. Each pose is calculated and each moment suspended in space and time. Egiku, on the other hand, is in constant motion, using jumps, turns, and even some floor movements you won't see in the traditional style. Born into a traditional Japanese dance family, she has faced opposition, but has also received the Japanese government's National Arts Award for her choreography of *The Weaving Crane*, which she also performed at the Edinburgh Festival and in London.

Another area currently enjoying a boom is ethnic dance. The Japanese have discovered an affinity with flamenco that has people flocking to schools to learn it. Artists are regularly invited from Spain, while flamenco dancers, students and lovers flock to the theatres to shout 'Olé!'. Every summer Yoko Komatsubara and her flamenco group puts on a midsummer's night flamenco concert on Hibiya Park's open-air stage.

Other ethnic dances are popping up all over. Tokyo has a large number of Japanese Indian dancers who have studied in India and have come back to open dance schools. There are probably more Indian dance performers and schools in Japan than in the UK. Not exactly ethnic, but in a category of her own (because nobody knew where to dump her) is Shakti. Her movements are based on Indian dance and yoga, but with a certain eroticism added into the mix.

Other ethnic dance forms such as Balinese, belly dancing and Hawaiian hula feature less prominently but are slowly finding a small, loyal following. You probably won't find them in the mainstream theatres in Tokyo (certainly no belly or hula dancing) but dancers are quietly doing their thing and generating interest.

On the modern dance side, acts such as H Art Chaos, Agua Gala, Kim Itoh (better known in London than in Tokyo), Dumb Type Idevian Crew, OM2, DAM and Ku Na'uka Theatre Company are the best known on the Tokyo scene. H Art Chaos has toured extensively in America, where audiences warmed to its pure modern dance with Japanese elegance and flow. Kim Itoh is known for his collaborations with other artists from different countries. Agua Gala combines vocals, music and dance, often inviting audience participation. Dumb Type Idevian Crew, OM2, DAM and Ku Na'uka Theatre Company belong as much in the physical theatre category as in dance, combining highly visual sets with advanced projection and lighting techniques.

Another indicator of the health of the Tokyo scene is the number of small dance festivals cropping up all over the city. Each dancer pays to participate and is given ten or 20 minutes (depending on the programme) to do their thing. 'Lucy no Shokutaku' ('Lucy's Table') is a popular one run by the Roku Hasegawa. A dance critic and writer for years in Tokyo, she is now attempting to nurture new young artists by encouraging them to be creative and 'do their thing'.

Venues

Aoyama Round Theatre

5-53-1 Jingumae, Shibuya-ku (3797 5678).
Omotesando station. **Box office** 10am-6pm daily (3797 1400). **Tickets** prices vary. **No credit cards.** **Map 4**

As its name suggests, this is a theatre that can be used in the round, one of very few in Tokyo. It attracts Dumb Type, H Art Chaos, Agua Gala, Kim Itoh and Shakti, among others.

Art Sphere

2-3-16 Higashi-Shinagawa, Shinagawa-ku (5460 9999). Tennozu Isle station (Tokyo Monorail).
Box office 10am-6pm daily. **Tickets** prices vary. **No credit cards.**

This theatre caters to the whims of well-off young fans of contemporary modern dance and is sure to book things that are considered 'in', but not too avant-garde or risqué. It's located at Tennozu Isle on the Tokyo Waterfront, a fashionable area with many restaurants and cafés overlooking Tokyo Bay. The larger of Art Sphere's two theatres seats 746, while Sphere Mex seats from 100 to 300. Dance critic turned talent spotter Roku Hasegawa puts her 'Lucy no Shokutaku' (*see above*) on here.

Bunkamura Theatre Cocoon

2-24-1 Dogenzaka, Shibuya-ku (3477 3244).
Shibuya station. **Box office** 10am-7pm daily; *phone bookings* 10am-5.30pm. **Tickets** prices vary. **Credit** AmEx, DC, JCB, MC, V. **Map 4**
The giant arts centre's mid-sized venue, with 750 seats, is used mainly for musicals, but stages the occasional dance performance.

Hibiya Outdoor Theatre (Hibiya Yagai Ongaku-do)

1-5 Hibiya Koen, Chuo-ku (3591 6388).
Hibiya station. **Map 7**
This large open-air arena, used mainly for music concerts and open only during the summer months, plays host to Yoko Komatsubara and her flamenco group for one night every summer.

Jean-Jean

B1F, 19-5 Udagawa-cho, Shibuya-ku (3462 0641).
Shibuya station. **Box office** from 10am daily (closing time varies). **Tickets** ¥2,500-¥3,000. **No credit cards. Map 4**
This tiny underground theatre has become a near legend in the Tokyo dance world. It's owned and run by Susumu Takashima, a man with a vision, who believes that theatre (or dance) should be performed by an artist capable of putting on a show without recourse to elaborate sets or lighting. Sadly, financial pressures mean that the space is to close at the end of April 2000.

National Theatre

4-1 Hayabusa-cho, Chiyoda-ku (3265 7411/ticketing 3230 3000). Hanzomon station. **Box office** 10am-6pm daily. **Tickets** ¥1,500-¥9,500. **No credit cards. Map 16**
It's old, it's established, but it's still the best place to see traditional and contemporary Japanese dance. The National has three theatres, of which one is devoted to puppet theatre, while the other two have capacities of 1,616 and 594 (*see chapter* **Theatre**). Since getting into the theatre is very difficult and the selection process quite severe, what you will see here will generally be of a high standard.

New National Theatre

1-1-1 Honmachi, Shibuya-ku (5351 3011). Hatsudai station (Keio Shinsen line). **Box office** 10am-7pm daily. **Tickets** prices vary. **Credit** AmEx, MC, V. **Map 3a**
While the National Theatre was and is for traditional dance and theatre, the New National Theatre caters to the modern generation. It has called its spaces the Opera House, the Playhouse and the Pit rather than follow the normal tradition of calling

Local dancer **Shakti** *fuses east and west.*

them Dai Gekijo (big theatre), Chu Gekijo (medium theatre) and Sho Gekijo (small theatre). The latter two spaces cater to dance, mostly modern, although the Opera House does at times stage classical ballet. The Pit, holding over 500 people, is a leading venue on the contemporary dance circuit.

Session House

158 Yaraicho, Shinjuku-ku (3266 0461).
Kagurazaka station. **Box office** 10am-11pm daily. **Tickets** ¥2,000-¥2,500. **No credit cards.**
This is a pure contemporary dance venue, a small, intimate and well-run studio-style theatre owned and run by Naoko Itoh, herself a modern dancer with her own company. She started Session House in order to give solo dancers the opportunity to experiment and express themselves freely. She presents not only local contemporary dancers, but also those from Europe and America. The aim is to showcase pure dance without extensive use of theatrical props and high-tech lighting.

Setagaya Public Theatre

4-1-1 Taishido, Setagaya-ku (5432 1526).
Sangenjaya station (Shin-Tamagawa line).
Box office 10am-7pm daily. **Tickets** prices vary. **No credit cards. Map 30**
Like the New National Theatre (*see above*), this venue is a great favourite with fans and performers. Although modelled on a Greek open-air theatre, the space can be changed to proscenium-style. The theatre contains two auditoria, the smaller of which, Theatre Tram, is a popular venue for dance and physical theatre.

Space Zero

2-12-10 Yoyogi, Shibuya-ku (3375 8741). Shinjuku station. **Box office** 10am-6pm Mon-Fri. **Tickets** prices vary. **No credit cards. Map 3a**
A mid-sized venue (capacity around 550) that specialises in modern jazz dance; performers include the Alok Dance Company.

Film

Indie cinemas offer the best chance of a good film-going experience.

There are many things that the Japanese do better than westerners, but cinema-going is not one of them. Going to a film can be chaotic. Tickets are often sold at convenience stores for the film, not the cinema (although tickets can also be purchased at the box office). Thus, any number of people can turn up with a valid ticket. If you want to book a seat, you will have to pay a premium of around ¥500 on the already inflated price of ¥1,800-¥2,000. Queues often start two hours early, and once the previous show is over, the next wave of viewers rushes in to grab the best seats.

The highlight of the cinematic year is the Tokyo Film Festival, which takes place in the cinemas of Shibuya every August. This was where *Titanic* received its world première, in 1997.

Shibuya, Ginza and Shinjuku have the largest concentration of cinema screens (more than 70 between them) in the city, most of them showing Hollywood blockbusters. A few cinemas show more alternative fare. These are the ones we've picked out below.

Cinemas

ACT
Waseda-Dori Bldg 2F, 3-14-2 Nishi-Waseda, Shinjuku-ku (3208 4733). Takadanobaba station. Tickets ¥1,700/¥1,500 (depending on show). **Map 25**
A tiny cinema (capacity 50) with no seats that shows whatever takes the manager's fancy.

Box Higashi Nakano
Polepoleza Bldg B1F, 4-4-1 Higashi Nakano, Nakano-ku (5389 6780). Higashi-Nakano station. Tickets ¥1,700.
Small and subterranean, and shows everything from Japanese classics to *The Rocky Horror Picture Show*.

Ciné Amuse
4F, 2-23-12 Dogenzaka, Shibuya-ku (3496 2888). Shibuya station. Tickets ¥1,800. **Map 4**
Divided into two screens, East and West, this cinema shows classics and new films from around the world.

Ciné La Sept
2-8-6 Yurakucho, Chiyoda-ku (3212 3761). Yurakucho station. Tickets ¥1,800. **Map 7**

On location

Tokyo has seen its fair share of movie mayhem through the years, from giant lizards (*see* **Movie monsters**) to Bond baddies and *yakuza*.

Tokyo Tower has made several appearances, including the popular romance *Tokyo Love Story* (Jap 1994). Fans of the romantic hit *Shall We Dance?* (Jap 1996) should head to the area around **Ekoda** station, the film's main location. On their way back into town they may pass by **Rikkyo University**, scene of the comedy *Sumo Do, Sumo Don't!* (Jap 1992).

In Michael Anderson's epic *Around the World in 80 Days* (US 1957) Passepartout strolled round **Asakusa Kannon Temple** but after a few steps ended up at the Heian Shrine in Kyoto – a feat no visitor will be able to reproduce.

For somewhere that's had a number of cameo appearances, head to **Shinjuku**, scene of the classic *Diary of a Shinjuku Thief* (Jap 1969). In Wim Wenders' *Until the End of the World* (Ger 1991) Sam Neill hunts for his wife in **Nishi-Shinjuku**. Wenders had already ventured to Tokyo for *Tokyo-Ga* (US/W Ger 1985), inspired by Yusujiro Ozu's *Tokyo Story* (Jap 1953), and *Notebook on Cities and Clothes* (W Ger 1989) which profiles Yohji Yamamoto. For two unconventional views of the area check out *Shinjuku Boys* (UK 1995), which shows the gay area **Ni-chome** after-hours, and the documentary *Baraka* (UK 1996), which puts a eco-friendly spin on Shinjuku life. Hal Hartley's *Flirt* (US, W Ger, Jap 1985) is also set in Shinjuku.

In **Ginza**, Robert Mitchum met a long-lost love at a bar in *Yakuza* (US 1975) and took a walk past the Kabuki-za before landing in trouble at a public bath. His compatriot Jerry Lewis also experienced bathing problems in *Geisha Boy* (US 1958).

Some visitors may even be lucky enough to sleep in a famous movie location: guests at the **Hotel New Otani** in Akasaka may not realise they're actually in the offices of the Osato Chemical Corporation, which 007 breaks into in *You Only Live Twice* (UK 1967). Bond also pops over to a hotel in Hakone and rides the subway.

A mixture of home-grown films and small charmers from abroad in this authentic-looking arthouse.

Ciné Pathos
4-8-7 Ginza, Chuo-ku (3561 4660). Ginza station.
Tickets ¥1,800. **Map 7**
Three screens showing recent independent films.

Cinema Qualité
Shinjuku Musashinokan 3F, 3-27-10 Shinjuku, Shinjuku-ku (3354 5670). Shinjuku station.
Tickets ¥1,800. **Map 3b**
Three-screen cinema that mixes new films with classic revivals. Great for black-and-white classics.

Cinema Rise
13-17 Udagawa-cho, Shibuya-ku (3464 0052). Shibuya station. **Tickets** ¥1,800. **Map 4**
A champion of independent cinema, this is the place where *Trainspotting* first hit Tokyo. Two screens.

Ciné Saison Shibuya
109 Prime Bldg 6F, 2-29-5 Dogenzaka, Shibuya-ku (3770 1721). Shibuya station. **Tickets** ¥1,800. **Map 4**
Revivals, mini-festivals and independent productions are the lifeblood of this comfortable cinema.

Ciné Vivant
Wave Bldg B1F, 6-2-27 Roppongi, Minato-ku (3403 6061). Roppongi station. **Tickets** ¥1,800. **Map 2**
Screens mainly French films.

Ebisu Garden Cinema
4-20-2 Ebisu Garden Place, Ebisu, Shibuya-ku (5420 6161). Ebisu station. **Tickets** ¥1,800. **Map 20**
Two comfortable screens in Garden Place show a mix of blockbusters and limited-release foreign films.

Euro Space
Tobu-Fuji Bldg. 2F, 24-4 Sakuragaoka-cho, Shibuya-ku (3461 0211). Shibuya station.
Tickets ¥1,700. **Map 4**
Two-screen venue that specialises in European film.

Haiyu-za Talkie Night
4-9-2 Roppongi, Minato-ku (3401 4073). Roppongi station. **Tickets** ¥1,700. **Map 2**
Weird and avant-garde film from all over the world.

Le Cinéma
Bunkamura 6F, 2-24-1 Dogenzaka, Shibuya-ku (3477 9264). Shibuya station. **Tickets** ¥1,800. **Map 4**
Two screens in the giant Bunkamura arts complex.

Shibuya Hermitage
Shibuya Toei Plaza 9F, 1-24-12 Shibuya, Shibuya-ku (5467 5774). Shibuya station. **Tickets** ¥1,800. **Map 4**
Independent American and European films.

Shimo-Takaido Cinema
3-27-26 Matsubara, Setagaya-ku (3328 1008). Shimo-Takaido station (Keio line). **Tickets** ¥1,600.
Repertory cinema with an interesting programme.

Waseda Shochiku
1-5-16 Takadanobaba, Shinjuku-ku (3200 8968). Takadanobaba station. **Tickets** ¥1,300. **Map 25**
Arty fleapit in the studenty area of Takadanobaba.

Movie monsters

Godzilla flopped in New York, but in Japan he and his monster chums Mothra, Gamera and King Ghidora are every bit as big (and bad) as ever. One of the more interesting stamps of approval for modern Tokyo architecture often comes from the foot of a marauding monster. Should Godzilla or his cohorts attack during your stay, head for the Imperial Palace – it's the only Tokyo landmark they haven't flattened.

Shibuya
In *Gamera 3* (1999), the turbo-powered turtle smashes through the roof of the Yamanote line station before slicing the 109 Building in half.

Tokyo Tower
Well mangled in *Godzilla v King Ghidora* (1991).

West Shinjuku
Watch those high-rises tumble in *Godzilla 1985*.

Odaiba
Comes a cropper in *Godzilla v Destroyah* (1995).

National Diet Building
Giant insect larvae pupate in the seat of government in *Godzilla v Mothra* (1992).

Tokyo City Hall
Shinjuku's twin towers were the shiny new symbol of Tokyo government until Godzilla nobbled them in *Godzilla v King Ghidora* (1991).

Yurakucho
Railway bridge torn up in *Godzilla, King of the Monsters* (1954), then again in *Godzilla 1985*.

Gay & Lesbian

The capital's gay scene is small, but incredibly lively.

Ask a typical Japanese person about the gay scene in Tokyo and you're likely to draw a blank. Some might go so far as to say that they know of no gays in Japan. Such is the nature of the society: minorities remain unseen and unheard, and social 'problems' are kept behind closed doors. Nevertheless, there is a vibrant and active gay scene. This is a culture based on Buddhist rather than Christian values, so there are no religious prohibitions against homosexuality. Still, you aren't very likely to see many men walking down the street arm in arm, and, even among heterosexuals, kissing in public is still not common.

Tap into the scene via the various gay Internet sites (*see chapter* **Media**). Alternatively, pick up *Tokyo Classified*, which features announcements for gay and lesbian parties and bicultural mixers.

Shinjuku Ni-chome   Map 3b

Arty Farty
Lily Mansion 1F, 2-4-17 Shinjuku, Shinjuku-ku (3356 5388). Shinjuku San-chome station. **Open** 4pm-5am Mon-Fri; 1pm-5am Sat, Sun.
Young, laid-back and mixed crowd.

Club Dragon
Accord Bldg B1F, 2-12-4 Shinjuku, Shinjuku-ku (3341 0606). Shinjuku San-chome station. **Open** 8pm-5am Tue-Thur, Sun; 9pm-5am Fri, Sat.

Ni-chome

The second *chome* of Shinjuku, always referred to as Ni-chome, is the throbbing heart of Tokyo's gay scene, with over 300 establishments catering to gay men and women. Unfortunately, like a microcosm of Japanese society, the gay community in Tokyo is somewhat xenophobic. At many places, if you don't speak Japanese you will not be allowed in. Yet don't let that discourage you; there are many places that welcome foreigners and many gay Japanese are interested in meeting foreigners, some especially so. The best way to reach Ni-chome is from Shinjuku San-chome station. Ni-chome's central street is Naka Dori and most of the addresses given in this section are close to it.

A hard leather meet-market, definitely for the young at heart. Women less welcome at weekends.

Gamos
2-chome Centre Bldg B1, 2-11-10 Shinjuku, Shinjuku-ku (3354 5519). Shinjuku-Gyoenmae station. **Open** 9pm-5am daily. **Admission** varies. Mixed crowd, with a DJ (*see chapter* **Nightlife**).

GB
Business Hotel T Bldg B1F, 2-12-3 (3352 8972). Shinjuku San-chome station. **Open** 8pm-1am Mon; 8pm-2am Tue-Thur; 8pm-3am Fri; 8pm-4am Sat, Sun.
The most famous foreigner-friendly meet-market. Men only; handily connected to a 'business' hotel.

Gen's Bar
Dai Nana Tenka Bldg 1F, 2-18-1 Shinjuku, Shinjuku-ku (3359 3633). Shinjuku San-chome station. **Open** 7pm-2am Mon, Tue, Thur-Sun.
Welcomes gays, transvestites, *onabe* (women who dress and act like men). Good for people-watching.

Hug
2-15-8 Shinjuku, Shinjuku-ku (5379 5085). Shinjuku San-chome station. **Open** 9pm-6am daily.
Women-only karaoke bar.

Kinsmen
2F, 2-18-5 Shinjuku, Shinjuku-ku (3354 4949). Shinjuku San-chome station. **Open** 9pm-5am Mon, Wed-Sun.
Long-established, very mixed, very relaxed bar with a peaceful lounge atmosphere.

Kins Womyn
Daiichi Tenka Bldg 3F, 2-15-10 Shinjuku, Shinjuku-ku (3354 8720). Shinjuku San-chome station. **Open** 7pm-3am Mon-Sat.
Named after the men's bar (*see above*), this place is for women only. kd lang has been known to stop by.

Lamp Post
Yamahara Heights #201, 2-21-15 Shinjuku, Shinjuku-ku (3354 0436). Shinjuku San-chome station. **Open** 7pm-3am daily.
A mixed piano bar with a relaxed atmosphere.

New Sazae
Ishikawa Bldg 2F, 2-18-5 Shinjuku, Shinjuku-ku (3354 1754). Shinjuku San-chome station. **Open** 10pm-5am Mon-Thur, Sun; 10pm-6am Fri, Sat.
One of the oldest clubs in the area, New Sazae has been going more than 30 years. Soul music backdrop.

Rainbow Café
2-13-10 Shinjuku, Shinjuku-ku (3356 6687). Shinjuku San-chome station. **Open** 2pm-5am daily.

*In the centre of Ni-chome, **Shinjuku Park** is a popular late-night cruising ground.*

A small café with a mixed clientele, Rainbow serves great cakes, coffee, teas and even liqueurs.

Tamago Bar
Nakae Bldg 1F, 2-15-13 Shinjuku, Shinjuku-ku (3351 4838). Shinjuku San-chome station. **Open** 9pm-5am daily.
Women-only bar, where *onabe* host(esse)s tend to the clientele. Prices similar to those in hostess bars.

Zinc
Daini-Hayakawa Bldg B1F, 2-14-6, Shinjuku, Shinjuku-ku (3352 6297). Shinjuku San-chome station. **Open** 8pm-5am Tue-Sat; 8pm-3am Sun.
A friendly, popular and reasonably priced bar that welcomes people of both sexes and all persuasions.

Sex clubs

King of College
2-14-5 Shinjuku, Shinjuku-ku (3352 3930). Shinjuku San-chome station. **Open** 6pm-10am daily. **Map 3b**
Here hosts can be rented by the hour in the bar's private room or for take-out to your home or hotel room.

Treffpunkt
Maeda Bldg 4F, 5-4-17, Akasaka, Minato-ku (5563 0523). Akasaka station. **Open** noon-midnight Mon-Thur, Sat, Sun; noon-5am Fri. **Admission** ¥1,700 (¥1,000, noon-3pm Mon-Thur). **Map 11**
Every Sunday is 'all-naked day' at Treffpunkt: 'No age limit. All nationalities welcome,' says their ad.

Bathhouses & saunas

The scene is very active – hardly surprising in a country that worships getting wet and soaping up.

24 Kaikan Asakusa
2-29-16 Asakusa, Taito-ku (3844 7715). Asakusa station. **Open** 24 hours daily. **Admission** ¥2,400. **Map 10**
You'll need the help of a Japanese to get along here. Active, especially at weekends. Most of the cruising involving non-Japanese takes place in the bath/sauna/steam/shower area. Condoms available at front desk.

24 Kaikan Ueno
1-8-7 Kita-Ueno, Taito-ku (3847 2424). Ueno station. **Open** 24 hours daily. **Admission** ¥2,400. **Map 8**
Six floors of fun, including gift store, sun roof, gym, showers, bath, sauna/steam room, private rooms, 'mix rooms' with bunks and futons, and a restaurant and karaoke bar. Special room for S&M lovers.

Jinya
2-30-19 Ikebukuro, Toshima-ku (5951 0995). Ikebukuro station. **Open** 2pm-11am Mon-Fri; 24 hours Sat, Sun. **Admission** ¥2,200. **Map 1**
Caters to an older crowd and looks like a well-kept business hotel. Large refreshment/TV room, private rooms and a porno viewing area.

Paragon
1F, 2-17-4 Shinjuku, Shinjuku-ku (3353 3306). Shinjuku San-chome station. **Open** 3pm-noon Mon-Sat; 24 hours Sun. **Admission** ¥1,800; ¥1,500 short-haired, moustaches and whiskers; ¥1,300 students. **Map 3b**
Conveniently located sauna, with a bizarre pricing policy. Small but well equipped, featuring private rooms, an exhibitionist room with a raised platform and some curtained-off areas in complete darkness. When you arrive, a voice behind the counter will ask if you speak Japanese. Just say '*hai*'.

Play it safe

The Japanese are still lax about protecting themselves against sexually transmitted diseases, including HIV. Foreign visitors and residents (gay and straight) are often shocked at the activities people engage in here without protection. The number of HIV-carrying citizens continues to rise every year, but Japan still ranks among the world's lowest in AIDS patients and deaths per capita. So far, the government has done little to increase public awareness. Take your own precautions.

Media

For information or recreation, here's how.

Newspapers

The Japanese are among the world's keenest newspaper readers, with daily sales of over 70 million copies, and *Yomiuri Shinbun* is the world's largest-circulation newspaper, selling 14.5 million copies a day. For those who don't read Japanese, the choice of papers is small. The most venerable English-language daily is *Japan Times*, started in 1897. The others are *Daily Yomiuri, Mainichi* and *Asahi Evening News*. All are largely compiled from press agency reports and seem unsure as to whether to focus on events in Japan, since around half the readership is English-speaking Japanese, or in Europe/the USA. On Thursday both *Asahi Evening News* and *Daily Yomiuri* publish what's on guides with arts reviews and film listings, and on Sunday *Yomiuri* carries an eight-page supplement from Britain's *Independent*. On Friday it takes a similar supplement from the *Washington Post*.

Free reads

Tokyo Classified, published on Friday and distributed via some subway kiosks and foreigner-friendly bars and restaurants, started in 1994 as a freesheet and has grown into a 56-page mag with club, concert, film and TV listings. Classified ads are its backbone, forming a valuable resource for people wishing to settle in Tokyo. *TC* has its imitators, *Tokyo Notice Board* being the most visible.

Other free publications can be more difficult to track down. Monthlies *Nippon View, Tokyo Day & Night* and *City Life News* focus on cultural events and carry general-interest features about Japan. *Day & Night*'s listings and community pages are useful; its distribution is largely via big hotels. The others can be found at World Magazine Gallery (*see below*). A more oblique look at life in Japan comes courtesy of *The Alien*, a satirical monthly about life in Japan as experienced by foreigners.

Popular distribution points are HMV in Shibuya (*see chapter* **Shops & Services**) and the Dubliners bar in Shinjuku (*see chapter* **Bars**).

World Magazine Gallery
3-13-10 Ginza, Chuo-ku (3545 7227). Ginza station. **Open** 11am-7pm Mon-Fri. **Map 7**
A reference-only magazine library, with over 800 titles from all over the world; read them at a table or take them to the coffeeshop on the second floor. Also a distribution point for Tokyo's free publications.

Making news on the streets of Tokyo.

Magazines

If you read Japanese, there's a wealth of publications to help you find your way around the city; the best known are *Pia* and *Tokyo Walker* (¥320, weekly). If you don't, *Tokyo Journal* (¥600) is a monthly English-language listings mag.

Radio

InterFM (76.1MHz) is the first station designed for non-Japanese, but there's been an increase in the amount of Japanese spoken. Plays rock and pop.

Television

State broadcaster NHK runs two commercial-free terrestrial channels – NHK General (channel 1) and NHK Educational (channel 3) – and two satellite channels, BS1 and BS2. The five remaining terrestrial channels in Tokyo – Nihon TV (channel 4), Tokyo Broadcasting (channel 6), Fuji Television (channel 8), Television Asahi (channel 10) and TV Tokyo (channel 12) – have commercials and show pap, illuminated occasionally by a good drama or documentary. NHK 1 news at 7pm and 9pm daily is broadcast in English and Japanese: to access the English sound channel, push a button on the remote to a bilingual TV set (most rooms in big hotels have them). Many non-Japanese films and TV series are also broadcast bilingually.

Japan has been slow to catch on to satellite TV. Two organisations, DirecTV and SkyPerfect TV, offer a range of channels, including CNN, BBC World, Sky News and Sky Sports. Most top hotels provide satellite channels.

Tokyo's best websites

Gay

Cruising
www.best.com/~dkg2/elsewherelistings.html
Information on sex clubs and cruising spots from all over the world. Lengthy section on Tokyo.
Gay Net Japan
http://webx.gnj.or.jp
Home page of a support group founded in 1988. Classified ads, links to other sites, and live events.
Shinjuku Ni-chome
www.geocities.com/WestHollywood/4248/&e=26
On-line guide to Shinjuku's Ni-chome area.

Getting around

Cinema Maps
www.asahi-net.or.jp/~cg2k-isi/index-e.html
How to get to Tokyo's cinemas.
Japan Atlas
www.jinjapan.org/atlas/index.html
Maps of the regions with a point and click facility.
Japan Travel Updates
www.jnto.go.jp
Japan National Tourist Organisation's site, with travel info, tips and on-line hotel booking service.
NTT Townpage
english.townpage.isp.ntt.co.jp/
NTT's English-language phone book on-line.
Schauwecker's Japan Guide
www.japan-guide.com/
Schauwecker's guide to Japan on-line. Practical information covering the whole of the country.
Tokyo Subway Maps
www.tokyometro.go.jp/metnet/3600e.html
Plan your trip around town.

Media

Asahi Shinbun
www.asahi.com/english/english.html
Basic daily news from Japan.
Daily Yomiuri
www.yomiuri.co.jp/index-e.htm
A small but well-maintained site from the *Japan Times*' main rival.
Inter FM
www.interfm.co.jp/
Tokyo's first radio station for foreigners on-line.
Japan Times
www.japantimes.co.jp
Japan's venerable English-language daily. Events section only sporadically updated.
Sumo World Magazine
iac.co.jp/~sumowrld/
The complete resource for the sumo fiend. Has a full list of stables and major wrestlers.
Tokyo Classified
www.tokyoclassified.com/Welcome.html
The home page of Tokyo's premier free weekly magazine. Classifieds, features and entertainment information. Advertisements accepted by e-mail.
Weekly Post
www.weeklypost.com/
News and gossip from Japan on the home page of one of the country's biggest-selling magazines.

Music & clubs

CyberJapan
www.so-net.ne.jp/CYBERJAPAN/front.html
The best site for up-to-date information on the Tokyo club scene.
Come on you blues
www.netlaputa.ne.jp/~bginza/
Check out the Tokyo blues scene with Masahiro Sumori's page. Or join the blues ring.
Shaun and Hiromi's Rock Page
www.atrium.com/concert/
Up-to-date information on gigs in Tokyo plus information on booking agencies and venues.
Saison
www.saison.co.jp/ticket/index.html
Large ticket agency offers up-to-date information on music and more.
Smash
smash-jpn.com/
Home page in English and Japanese of one of Tokyo's biggest concert promoters.

What's on

Insite
www.insite-tokyo.com/
A recent addition whose aim is to be 'the most comprehensive guide to Tokyo on the net'. Still has a way to go to match Tokyo Meltdown or Tokyo Q (*see below*).
Neo Tokyo
www.neo-tokyo.com/core.html
Cultural look at life in the city. Heavy on pop music, language and travel.
Toilets on line
www.asahi-net.or.jp/~AD8Y-HYS/index_e.htm
Every toilet at every station on the Yamanote line photographed for your pleasure.
Tokyo Meltdown
www.bento.com/tleisure.html
A towering work of genius. Record shops, a phone book, restaurants and more. Maintained by long-time resident and food expert Robb Satterwhite.
Tokyo Now
www.tokyonow.com/
Information about shopping, music and more, rendered in charmingly eccentric English.
Tokyo Q
www.so-net.ne.jp/tokyoq/
Like Meltdown, Tokyo Q aims to provide a complete guide to going out, from gigs to bathhouses. Can also be reached at *www.tokyoq.com*

Music

Tokyo's live music scene is as varied and exciting as any in the world.

Classical music

Tokyo, as befits one of the world's great cities, boasts several superb venues specialising in classical music, which has enjoyed a firm foothold in Japan since the country opened to the outside world in the mid-nineteenth century. Besides producing world-renowned conductors (Seiji Ozawa), composers (Toru Takemitsu) and soloists (pianist Mitsuko Uchida), Japan is a regular – and highly lucrative – stop on the international concert circuit, and many of the world's top orchestras stop off here as they trip around the globe.

Traditional Japanese classical music can be harder to track down, although occasionally concerts of traditional instruments such as the *shamisen* (a kind of guitar) and *shakuhachi* (Japanese flute) are held at Bunkamura.

Major venues

Casals Hall

1-6 Kanda-Surugadai, Chiyoda-ku (3294 1229). Ochanomizu station. **Capacity** 511. **Map 9**

What's on?

The best way to find out about upcoming concerts or gigs in the Tokyo area is to look through the listings of weekly entertainment guide *Pia* – but if you don't read Japanese, you're out of luck. Actually, trying to decipher *Pia*'s concert listings is a great incentive to gain a working knowledge of written Japanese, and since much of the information is in the phonetic katakana script, it's not really that difficult. You can also phone *Pia*'s ticket information service, Ticket Pia, on 5237 9999, or another major ticket agency, Ticket Saison, on 3250 9999, to get more information. Both offer an English-language service. Saison (http://www.saison.co.jp/ticket/index.html) also has a website with tons of concert info (*see chapter* **Media**). Otherwise, consult *Daily Yomiuri* on a Thursday, or free mag *Tokyo Classified* (*see chapter* **Media**).

A very beautiful hall with marvellous acoustics in the heart of Tokyo's university/bookshop district. For an appropriately *fin-de-siècle* experience, treat yourself to an exquisitely formal meal at Sarafan, a nearby Russian restaurant where the staff don't seem to have heard of the tsar's abdication, and then head over to Casals Hall for a relaxing dose of baroque sounds.

Katsushika Symphony Hills

6-33-1 Tateishi, Katsushika-ku (5670 2222). Aoto station (Toei Asakusa line). **Capacity** big hall, 1,318; small hall 298.

One of many local government-operated classical music halls that have sprung up in less-than-fashionable areas of Tokyo over the past few years. One of the big advantages of these halls is their reasonably priced tickets – you don't have to take out a mortgage to enjoy an evening of classical music.

Orchard Hall

2-24-1 Dogenzaka, Shibuya-ku (3477 9150). Shibuya station. **Capacity** 1,300. **Map 4**

Beautiful concert hall in the Bunkamura complex that's sometimes used for pop/rock concerts, mainly by domestic acts. Bunkamura also contains the smaller (737-seat) Theatre Cocoon, where veteran Japanese singer/songwriter Miyuki Nakajima puts on her always interesting – and sometimes bizarre – Yakai ('evening meeting') revues every winter.

Sogetsu Hall

7-2-21 Akasaka, Minato-ku (3408 9113). Aoyama-Itchome station. **Capacity** 530. **Map 12**

Pleasant, intimate hall that belongs to the Sogetsu *ikebana* (flower-arranging) school. A great place for an evening of refined classical, jazz or traditional Japanese music, apart from the annoying intrusion of noise from the subway that passes below the hall.

Sumida Triphony

1-2-3 Kinshi, Sumida-ku (5608 1212). Kinshicho station. **Capacity** 1,801.

Very new hall with a warm, welcoming atmosphere. Features regular concerts by the New Japan Philharmonic and visiting international artists such as flautist James Galway.

Suntory Hall

1-13-1 Akasaka, Minato-ku (3584 3100). Tameike-sanno station. **Capacity** big hall 2,006; small hall 432. **Map 2**

Very prestigious, ultra-luxurious classical concert hall, available in two sizes for your listening pleasure. A bit too corporate in style for some, but the small hall isn't a bad space at all.

Tokyo Bunka Kaikan

5-45 Ueno Koen, Taito-ku (3828 2111). Ueno station.
Capacity big hall 2,303; small hall 653. **Map 8**
Pleasantly located amid Ueno Park's greenery, this non-descript concert facility has been eclipsed as Tokyo's premier classical venue in recent years by upstarts such as Casals Hall (*see above*) and Tokyo Opera City (*see below*).

Tokyo Metropolitan Art Space (Tokyo Geijutsu Gekijo)

1-8-1 Nishi-Ikebukuro, Toshima-ku (5391 2111). Ikebukuro station. **Capacity** big hall 1,999; middle hall 841; small hall 300. **Map 1**
Very new, acoustically quite good concert hall complex somewhat incongruously located in the midst of Tokyo's depressing Ikebukuro district. Its single-most remarkable feature is the extremely long escalator set in the middle of the vast lobby, inducing vertigo in many concert-goers.

Tokyo Opera City

3-2-2 Nishi-Shinjuku, Shinjuku-ku (5353 0770). Hatsudai station (Keio line). **Capacity** 1,632. **Map 3a**
Brand spanking-new concert hall in the sprawling and rapidly changing west Shinjuku area. Good acoustics, according to those with well-trained ears, but what really makes this an exciting venue is the innovative and varied concert programme.

Rock, roots & jazz

Tokyo is one of the great rock music cities of the world. It's a fantastic place to buy music, as anyone who's ever explored the city's myriad record/CD stores knows. It's a great source of musical talent, as a growing number of pop music fans around the world are beginning to appreciate thanks to the efforts of Tokyo-based acts such as Pizzicato Five, Cornelius, Hi-Standard and the Boom Boom Satellites.

It's also one of the best places on the planet for live music, with venues ranging from the cavernous 60,000-capacity Tokyo Dome to concrete bunker style 'live houses' that lend new meaning to the word 'cramped'.

While Japan's recession has taken some of the shine off the concert business, Tokyo's live music scene remains incredibly active. Japan, it should be pointed out, is the world's second-biggest market for pre-recorded music after the US, and the concert business is correspondingly huge. And since foreign music accounts for roughly a quarter of the Japanese music market, non-Japanese acts – both big names and cult faves – regularly perform in Japan.

Going to a concert in Tokyo is a serious business. First, it's going to cost you: a ticket to a top-ranking domestic or foreign act can easily set you back ¥8,000 or so, and even then it might be an all-standing event. At some venues, such as Nakano Sun Plaza, patrons are treated to a long announce-

ment describing in detail things one shouldn't do during the show: no standing, no dancing, no smoking, no photography, no recording, no lighting matches or cigarette lighters, no eating, no drinking – and oh yes, *do* enjoy the show (which will start precisely at 7pm and end at 9pm)!

Concerts in Tokyo begin and end early because of the long commutes endured by most residents. Miss the last train home and you're looking at a taxi fare of ¥10,000 or even more.

Major venues

Akasaka Blitz

TBS Square, 5-3-6 Akasaka, Minato-ku (3224 0567). Akasaka station. **Capacity** 1,944 all standing; 910 all seated. **Map 11**
Mid-sized venue that Japanese record labels often use for showcase gigs by big-name domestic acts that usually play bigger venues. The biggest problem with Blitz is the precipitous outdoor staircase on the way from the station to the entrance – bloody dangerous in the rain.

Budokan

2-3 Kitanomaru-Koen, Chiyoda-ku (3216 5100). Kudanshita station. **Capacity** 14,310. **Map 18**
Famous for being the place where the Beatles played when they came to Japan in 1966 as well as for Cheap Trick's *Live at Budokan* album, this is a somewhat tatty– but venerable – venue. The Budokan was designed as a venue for traditional martial-arts competitions, which might explain its somewhat funky ambience. The big problem is that no alcohol is sold on the premises.

Ebisu Garden Hall

Ebisu Garden Place, 1-13-2 Mita, Meguro-ku (5424 0111). Ebisu station. **Capacity** 763. **Map 20**
Newish venue in the vaguely upscale Ebisu Garden Place complex. Another box in which punters can be stuffed, but less oppressive and dark than places such as On Air East or the Liquid Room (for both, *see below*). Has a good 'vibe', that mysterious quality that can bring out the best in a performer.

Hibiya Kokaido

1-3 Hibiya Koen, Chiyoda-ku (3591 6388). Hibiya station. **Capacity** 2,074. **Map 7**
Often used for political rallies and other serious gatherings, this pre-war venue is occasionally used for rock concerts. A bit down-at-heel, but refreshingly unpretentious. Mind your head – the Kokaido was built with shorter pre-war Japanese in mind, and the doorways and ceilings are dangerously low.

Hibiya Outdoor Theatre (Hibiya Yagai Ongaku-do)

1-5 Hibiya Koen, Chiyoda-ku (3591 6388). Hibiya station. **Capacity** 2,644. **Map 7**
One of Tokyo's few decent outdoor music venues, the venerable 'Ya-on', despite its posterior-unfriendly concrete benches, is one of the more pleasant

places in Tokyo to soak up some sounds – and rain, especially if a show is booked in the June-July rainy season. Site of the annual Japan Blues Carnival, which offers a chance to see leading US blues artists in a relaxed, quasi-bucolic setting.

Kan'i Hoken Hall
8-4-13 Nishi-Gotanda, Shinagawa-ku (3490 5111). Gotanda station. **Capacity** 1,826. **Map 21**
Bland, somewhat acoustically challenged, run-of-the-mill concert hall. Books a fair number of jazz acts, who seem out of place in its sterile confines.

Koseinenkin Kaikan
5-3-1 Shinjuku, Shinjuku-ku (3356 1111). Shinjuku station. **Capacity** 2,062. **Map 3b**
Shinjuku's version of the Shibuya Kokaido (*see below*) – a mid-size, standard-issue concert hall that's comfy but not classy. The biggest problem with the Koseinenkin is that it's so far from the station.

Liquid Room
Humax Pavilion 7F, 1-20-1 Kabuki-cho, Shinjuku-ku (3200 6831). Shinjuku station. **Capacity** 800. **Map 3b**
Shinjuku's version of On Air East (*see below*) – in the heart of the sleazy Kabuki-cho district. Basically just a box up seven very long flights of stairs. The Liquid Room tends to feature local techno acts and other cutting-edge stuff (*see also chapter* **Nightlife**).

Nakano Sun Plaza Hall
4-1-1 Nakano, Nakano-ku (3388 1151). Nakano station. **Capacity** 2,222. **Map 26**
Suburban venue known for its announcements instructing concert-goers not to stand up, dance, take pictures, make recordings, or do anything else that could disturb the performance.

National Yoyogi Stadium
2-1-1 Jinnan, Shibuya-ku (3468 1171). Harajuku station. **Capacity** 8,000. **Map 5**
Additional proof, if any were needed, that stadiums are not good places to have concerts. The acoustics, if such a term can be used, in Yoyogi Stadium are horrendous. Liberal consumption of intoxicants before taking one's seat is recommended.

NHK Hall
2-2-1 Jinnan, Shibuya-ku (3465 1751). Shibuya station. **Capacity** 3,744. **Map 4**
The public TV/radio network's main concert hall often features great bands, Japanese and foreign, just before they move on to larger venues.

On Air East
2-14-9 Dogenzaka, Shibuya-ku (3476 8787). Shibuya station. **Capacity** 800-1,000. **Map 4**
Another well-known mid-sized Shibuya concert venue, smack in the middle of the love hotel district, making On Air convenient for post-gig assignations. Like Quattro (*see below*), On Air East can sometimes be uncomfortably crowded, and getting to the exit can be quite an ordeal. Gigs here are all-standing events, which is OK if the act plays music you dance to, but a drag if the music is more subdued.

On Air West
2-3 Maruyama-cho, Shibuya-ku (5458 4646). Shibuya station. **Capacity** 500. **Map 4**
Smaller cousin of On Air East (*see above*) immediately across the street that features Japanese and foreign acts from the more cultish end of the pop-music spectrum. Small, but not usually crowded.

Shibuya Kokaido
1-1 Udagawa-cho, Shibuya-ku (3463 1211). Shibuya station. **Capacity** 2,318. **Map 4**
Pleasantly down-at-heel ward government-run hall, just down the road from NHK Hall (*see above*), that many Japanese bands use to kick off their nationwide tours. Comfy seats. Acts performing here tend to put on above-average shows, probably because so many industry/media people tend to come along.

Tokyo Bay NK Hall
1-8 Maihama, Urayasu-shi, Chiba (0473 55 7000). Maihama station (Keiyo line). **Capacity** 6,000.
Inconveniently located out near Disneyland on Tokyo Bay. The kind of place you'd go to only if you're a diehard fan of the act playing there.

Tokyo Dome (aka 'Big Egg')
1-3 Koraku, Bunkyo-ku (5800 9999). Suidobashi station. **Capacity** 60,000. **Map 9**
Cavernous, acoustically challenged venue designed for baseball games, not concerts. So vast that if you're sitting in the cheap seats at the back, there's a discernible delay between the movement of the singer's lips on the huge screens that often flank the stage and the sound of his or her voice. Favoured by mega-acts such as the Rolling Stones.

Tokyo International Forum
3-5-1 Marunouchi, Chiyoda-ku (5221 9000). Yurakucho station. **Capacity** Hall A 5,012; Hall B 1200; Hall C 1,502; Hall D 305. **Map 7**
New concert/event facility right in the heart of Tokyo. Acoustics are less than wonderful, but this hasn't prevented various big-name acts (Bob Dylan, for one) from doing shows here.

Live houses

Blue Note Tokyo
Raika Bldg, 6-3-16 Minami-Aoyama, Minato-ku (5485 0088). Omotesando station. **Capacity** 300. **Map 12**
Classy – and pricey – place to check out top jazz acts visiting Japan, which recently moved down the road to this larger venue. The tables are arranged in rows at 90 degrees to the stage, which may result in sore necks for some patrons.

Club 251
B1, 5-29-15 Daizawa, Setagaya-ku (5481-4141). Shimo-Kitazawa station (Inokashira/Odakyu lines). **Capacity** 400. **Map 29**
Comfortable, reasonably spacious (you might actually find room to dance!) club/mini-theatre in funky Shimo-Kitazawa, a very cool district much favoured by students and other non-conformist types.

Club Q

B2, 2-5-2 Kitazawa, Setagaya-ku (3412 9979).
Shimo-Kitazawa station (Inokashira/Odakyu lines).
Capacity 250. **Map 29**
Another concrete bunker-type live house, where the
emphasis is on fringy or up-and-coming indie bands.

Club CAY

*Spiral Bldg B1, 5-6-23 Minami-Aoyama, Minato-ku
(3498 5790). Omotesando station.* **Capacity** 450.
Map 12
Great space that specialises in rootsy ethnic music
from Japan and abroad. The vibe is sunny and tropical, despite the fact that CAY is hidden away in the
basement of the Spiral Building. Good bar, too.

Club Quattro Shibuya

*5F, Quattro by Parco, 32-13 Udagawa-cho, Shibuya-ku
(3477 8750). Shibuya station.* **Capacity** 1,000. **Map 4**
Quattro is one of the best places in Tokyo's vibrant
Shibuya district to hear live music. Crowded, smoky
and noisy, but a great place to get a close-up look at
top-notch Japanese and foreign acts.

Crocodile Shibuya

*Sekiguchi Bldg B1, 6-18-8 Jingu-mae, Shibuya-ku
(3499 5205). Harajuku station.* **Capacity** 200. **Map 5**
Good, hard-rockin' live house with a friendly vibe.
The setup is more like a club than a live house, with
tables and a bar, and a rather cramped stage that
ensures very close audience-performer contact.

Eggman Shibuya

*1-6-8 Jinnan, Shibuya-ku (3496 1561). Shibuya
station.* **Capacity** 350. **Map 4**
Good place to see Japanese bands just before they
hit it big, or as a venue for bigger acts doing 'showcase' gigs for the media. Usually incredibly crowded – moving across the room to get to the beer
machine can require a Herculean effort.

Heaven's Door

*Keio Hallo Bldg B1, 1-33-19 Sangenjaya, Setagaya-
ku (3410 9581). Sangenjaya station (Shin-
Tamagawa line).* **Capacity** 300. **Map 30**
One of Tokyo's more prestigious live houses, where
cutting-edge Japanese indies and alternative bands
hone their chops. If you're concerned about the possibility of long-term hearing loss, be sure to stuff
your ears with something, because the folks at
Heaven's Door like VERY LOUD music.

Key Note

*Harajuku Ash B1, 1-19-11 Jingu-mae, Shibuya-ku
(3470 6101). Harajuku station.* **Capacity** 130. **Map 5**
Jazz-going in Tokyo can be an expensive pastime,
but the Key Note, with its standard ¥2,500 music
charge (more for famous foreign acts), is a breath of
fresh air. The club opened in 1998 on the abandoned
yet atmospheric premises of a former jazz club
(check the famous-name graffiti on the walls), and
its main mission is to promote local talent. Every
night bar Monday there's a different band or artist,
with styles ranging from flamenco to Dixie to
Japanese folk. Great food and mean cocktails, too.

DJ/remixer **Cornelius** *is hitting the big time.*

Milk

*Roob6 Bldg, 1-13-3 Ebisu-nishi, Shibuya-ku (5458
2826). Ebisu station.* **Capacity** live floor 100. **Map 20**
One of Tokyo's best live houses, whose décor recalls
the Korova milk bar from *A Clockwork Orange*. The
music is cutting-edge indie/alternative, mainly by
local artists. Great layout, featuring all sorts of
rooms in which to ensconce oneself. The 'intestine
room', featuring wallpaper with a digestive-tract
motif, is not recommended for those with ulcers or
similar maladies (*see also chapter* **Nightlife**).

Shinjuku Loft

*B2, 1-12-9 Kabuki-cho, Shinjuku-ku (3365 2664).
Shinjuku station.* **Capacity** 500. **Map 3b**
Despite being called 'Loft', this well-known live
house (which relocated from west Shinjuku in April
1999) is in a basement. While many Tokyo live houses have all the ambience of an air-raid shelter, Loft
uses this space well, dividing it into two stage areas.
A great place to check out Japanese musical talent.

Velfarre

*7-14-22 Roppongi, Minato-ku (3402 8000).
Roppongi station.* **Capacity** 1,500. **Map 2**
Primarily a disco, Velfarre also hosts live acts, mainly of the dance/techno ilk. The emphasis is on glitz,
with an elaborate lighting system, a huge video-mon-
itor display behind the stage and décor that recalls
the excesses of the late '80s. If you're tired of the dance
floor, there are various bars and 'mini-clubs' scattered
throughout the building (*see also chapter* **Nightlife**).

Zepp Tokyo

*Palette Town 1F, Odaiba, Koto-ku (3529 1015).
Daiba Kaihin Koen station (Yurikamome line).*
Capacity 2,709.
A new venue, opened in summer 1999, Zepp is on
the out-of-the-way island of Odaiba and hosts visit-
ing international acts, such as Kula Shaker.

Nightlife

Tokyo's nightclubs change as fast as the rest of the city, and there's a huge number of places where you can dance until dawn, or beyond.

Tokyo's nightclub scene is as wild and varied as the city itself. As Tokyo has become more international in recent years, the scene has adopted a wide variety of global influences. It is also notoriously changeable – as one club springs up, another one closes, and the high and spiralling rents charged for premises make it all but impossible for a club to survive forever.

The club scene is at its hottest in summer. During winter, many clubs struggle to attract the crowds, deterred presumably by the cold trip home at 5am, when most clubs close.

Broadly speaking, Tokyo venues fall into two distinct categories: disco and club. Discos usually charge an entrance fee of around ¥4,000, including one or two drinks. They have relatively large dancefloors, cloakrooms, bars and stages for those who want to show off their moves. There is also often a dress code, and other restrictions, such as no lone men, may apply. A club, by contrast, usually charges around ¥2,500, including one or two drinks, has smaller dancefloors, cloakrooms and bars than a disco, and no dress code. Over the last ten years, many of Tokyo's large clubs have gone out of business due to the recession or downsized their management style to that of a club. The two notable exceptions are the discos Velfarre and Club Tatou (for both, *see below*).

But even these established names are making changes, thanks to the growth of the party concept, which means that the same club night can be had at a variety of different venues. A consequence of this is that the venues themselves change character almost nightly. The Liquid Room (*see below*), for instance, hosts some of the hottest club nights in town, but doubles as a concert venue.

Alcohol is sold till 5am in most clubs. Although it's technically illegal for most clubs to open after midnight (this is connected with a ridiculous law about dancing after the witching hour), most clubs ignore the rules, and some even reopen at 5am for after-hours parties, which last until noon. Maniac Love (*see below*), which starts at 5am on Sunday morning, is one of the most famous in Tokyo, and it's not unusual to see the place full at 6am.

As in most cities, the best source of club information in Tokyo is flyers, many of which are in English as well as Japanese. A good source is HMV in Shibuya (*see chapter* **Shops & Services**). They often double as discount vouchers, so keep them.

Bigger clubs usually post their schedules near the entrance. Weekly free magazine *Tokyo Classified* (*see chapter* **Media**) also keeps you up to date in its 'After Dark' section. For club information on the Internet, see page 202.

Venues

328

B1, 3-24-20 Nishi-Azabu, Minato-ku (3401 4968). Roppongi station. **Open** 8pm-5am daily. **Admission** ¥2,000 Mon-Thur (incl two drinks); ¥2,500 Fri-Sun (incl two drinks). **Dress code** none. **Map 2**
This first opened back in 1979, and in 1998 underwent total refurbishment. From the street, you'll spot its large neon sign from Nishi-Azabu crossing. Music is a mixture of genres, ranging from soul to dance classics, and there are live performances of drums and blues harp at weekends.

Afromania

Black Aoyama Bldg 5F, 3-2-7 Minami-Aoyama, Minato-ku (3408 1546). Gaienmae station. **Open** 9pm-5am Mon-Sat. **Admission** ¥2,000 Mon-Thur (incl two drinks); ¥2,500 Fri, Sat (incl two drinks). **Dress code** none. **Map 12**
As the name implies, Afromania's main dish is reggae. Inside, tropical rainforest décor carries on the theme. It's small, holding only around 80, but it has such a loyal hardcore audience that it's not unusual to have to queue to get in. Drinks start at ¥700.

Ball

Kuretake Bldg 4F, 4-9 Udagawa-cho, Shibuya-ku (3476 6533). Shibuya station. **Open** 9pm-5am Mon-Sat. **Admission** ¥1,000 (before 11pm, incl two drinks); ¥2,000 (after 11pm, incl two drinks). **Dress code** none. **Map 4**
There's a great night view of Shibuya to be had from this small venue, but sadly that is its best feature, despite the reasonably priced bar (drinks from ¥600). The PA isn't up to scratch – given that the choice of music is house, this is a very serious shortcoming indeed. What's more, the dancefloor is tiny.

Bar Drop

Ichibe Bldg 2F, 1-29-6 Kichijoji-Honcho, Musashino-shi (0422 20 0737). Kichijoji station. **Open** 9pm-5am daily. **Admission** varies. **Dress code** none. **Map 24**
On its two dancefloors (2F and B1), Bar Drop features a variety of '90s US and UK pop music, with the downstairs floor offering a slightly more eclec-

Happy clappy clubbers keep Tokyo burning.

tic choice of sounds. Unusually for Tokyo, there's a large lounge space, with tables and chairs to cool off at when you've danced till you dropped.

Bed

Fukuri Bldg B1, 3-29-9 Nishi-Ikebukuro, Toshima-ku (3981 5300). Ikebukuro station. **Open** 10pm-5am daily. **Admission** ¥2,000 Mon-Fri (incl two drinks); ¥2,500 Sat, Sun (incl two drinks).
Dress code none. **Map 1**
As you descend to Bed, you will be greeted by photo montages of previous, presumably satisfied, customers. Clientele here is young, and the music is mainly hip hop, plus occasional techno and warp house.

Cafe & Club Fura

3-26-25 Shibuya, Shibuya-ku (5485 4011). Shibuya station. **Open** 5pm-5am daily. **Admission** free Mon, Wed for women, Tue-Thur before 10pm, Fri-Sun before 9pm; ¥2,500 after 10pm Tue-Thur (incl two drinks); *men* ¥3,000 after 9pm Fri-Sun (incl two drinks); *women* ¥2,500 after 9pm Fri-Sun (incl two drinks). **Dress code** not too casual. **Map 4**

Fura is a four-storey complex with an Italian restaurant on the first floor, a relatively roomy dancefloor on the second and a bar-cum-lounge space on the floor above. The entry charge system is complex, but must be working: the place is heaving, even on weekdays, with Thursday nights the busiest.

The Cave

M&I Bldg B1/B2, 34-6 Udagawa-cho, Shibuya-ku (3780 0715). Shibuya station. **Open** 9pm-5am daily. **Admission** ¥2,000 Mon-Thur (incl two drinks); ¥3,000 Fri-Sun (incl three drinks). **Dress code** none. **Map 4**
Cave has two dancefloors and two bars on two floors, although neither is particularly large. The place is often packed with Japanese bikers, rastas and ko-gals (high-school girls with fake tans). Although The Cave was last redecorated in January 1998, some of the décor is showing signs of age, perhaps as a result of being harshly treated by the young clientele. Even so, the mixture of R&B, hip hop and soul continues to draw the crowds, even during the week.

Club Acid Tokyo

Kowa Bldg B1, 2-3-12 Shinjuku, Shinjuku-ku (3352 3338). Shinjuku-Gyoenmae station. **Open** 8pm-midnight daily. **Admission** varies. **Dress code** none. **Map 3b**
Finding the entrance to Club Acid is a challenge in itself. Only a small sign on Shinjuku Dori gives any hint of its existence. What's more, the surrounding area, just out of Kabuki-cho, is rather quiet by Shinjuku standards. The best way of finding it is to follow your ears: on different nights you can hear anything booming out of here, from ska to rock, hip hop to Latin, R&B to techno to drum 'n' bass. Check the schedule to see what's on when.

Club Asia

1-8 Maruyama-cho, Shibuya-ku (5458 1996). Shibuya station. **Open** 11pm-5am daily. **Admission** around ¥2,500, but varies with events. **Dress code** none. **Map 4**
Club Asia is a current favourite space with party organisers, so for individual events you should be sure to check out the schedule by the entrance. There is a bar and cloakroom on the first floor, a small dancefloor and bar on the second, and by the stairway that leads from the second floor there's a moderately roomy dancefloor and bar. The stairway to the main hall is an unusual feature, but it can get crowded, particularly on Friday nights. The main hall's high ceiling looks great but can make the sound a bit uneven.

Club Bar Family

Shimizu Bldg B1, 1-10-2 Shibuya, Shibuya-ku (3400 9182). Shibuya station. **Open** 10pm-5am daily. **Admission** varies with events. **Dress code** none. **Map 4**
A small, appealing venue with a bar, lounge and dancefloor where you can dance the night away to soul and dance classics, R&B and hip hop. Drinks are around ¥600.

Club Chu

*Oba B-Bldg B1, 28-5 Maruyama-cho, Shibuya-ku
(3770 3780). Shibuya station.* **Open** 9pm-5am Sun
only. **Admission** ¥2,000 (incl two drinks).
Dress code none. **Map 4**

The small lounge opens irregularly, and only on
Sundays. In Japanese, the word *chu* means sky or
space, and the décor at this club is designed to give
you the feeling that you're floating in space. The cool
ambience is designed to attract a more adult clientele than many other clubs – people who are seeking a lounge space with good music and drink,
rather than serious dance nuts or people hunting for
a partner.

Club Complex Code

*Shinjuku Toho Kaikan 4F, 1-19-2 Kabuki-cho,
Shinjuku-ku (3209 0702). Shinjuku station.*
Open varies with event. **Admission** ¥2,500 Mon-
Thur (incl two drinks); *men* ¥3,000 Fri-Sun (incl two
drinks); *women* ¥2,500 Fri-Sun (incl two drinks).
Dress code no sandals. **Map 3b**

With three dancefloors (two small, one gigantic),
Club Complex Code is a monster nightclub that can
host a variety of different events and special nights
(sometimes at the same time). Its location on the
fourth floor of a Kabuki-cho building means that
from the outside you get no impression of its size:
with a capacity of 2,000 people, Code is one of the
biggest clubs in Japan. The biggest of the three
dancefloors is called 'En-Code', and is sometimes
used as a live stage. En-Code itself has a capacity of
1,000 people and four gigantic screens where you
can watch the VJs doing their stuff. Sub-floor 'De-
Code' holds 120 people and has terminals for those
who'd rather surf the Net than strut their stuff.
There is also a main bar room and lounge, 'Ba-Code',
and a snack bar beside the main floor, where a ¥500
token buys you anything from a bottle of mineral
water to a small buffet. On Friday Tokyo's No.1
house DJ, Ko Kimura, fills up the space with
'Passion', and on Thursday nights DJ Yo-C, Nao
Nakamura, Take and Monobe take the helm of a
warp house and hard house party, 'Nu-Disko'. Nao
Nakamura also spins on a regular gay night,
'Friends', on the last Sunday of the month. Although
Code hosts many popular events, it is slightly let
down by the sound system, which suffers from the
size of the dancefloor.
Website: http://www.so-net.ne.jp/CYBERJAPAN/

Club Hachi

*Daikyo Bldg, 4-5-9 Shibuya, Shibuya-ku (5469 1676).
Omotesando station.* **Open** *café* from 7pm, *club* 9pm-
5am Mon-Sat. **Admission** ¥1,000 Mon-Thur (before
11pm, incl one drink); ¥2,000 Mon-Thur (incl two
drinks); ¥1,000 Fri, Sat (before 10pm, incl one drink);
¥2,500 Fri, Sat (incl two drinks).
Dress code none. **Map 4**

Club Hachi occupies the whole of a three-storey
building on Roppongi Dori. The first floor is the bar
and snack bar, where drinks start at ¥500. The club
space is upstairs. Unusually, you are allowed to leave
and re-enter if things start to get too hot and sticky.

Tripping the late-night light fantastic.

Club J Trip Bar

*The Wall Bldg B1/B2, 4-2-4 Nishi-Azabu,
Minato-ku (3409 7607). Hiroo station.*
Open 8pm-5am Wed-Sat. **Admission** ¥2,500 Wed,
Thur (incl two drinks); *men* ¥3,000 Fri, Sat (incl two
drinks); *women* ¥2,500 Fri, Sat (incl two drinks).
Dress code not too casual. **Map 2**

Back in the bubble years of the '80s, J Trip Bar was
a Tokyo legend. Then, like all legends, it began to
fade. In January last year, it reopened as Club J Trip
Bar, and it hasn't looked back since. Gone are the
young high-school kids who made real clubbers'
lives a misery, and the average age of the punters
has shot up to the mid-20s. The club has five massive dancefloors where you can get down to music
from the '80s and early '90s, and a café, Hi-Ball, that
serves Italian food.

Club Jamaica

*Nishi-Azabu Ishibashi Bldg B1, 4-16-14 Nishi-Azabu,
Minato-ku (3407 8844). Roppongi station.* **Open**
10pm-5am Mon-Sat. **Admission** ¥1,000
Mon-Wed (incl one drink); ¥2,500 Thur-Sat (incl two
drinks). **Dress code** none. **Map 2**

Opened by a reggae fanatic in 1989, Club Jamaica is
still blasting out the booming sounds of Jamaica's
finest. It's a small venue with an entrance that can
be difficult to find, but the atmosphere is friendly
and the sound system excellent.

Club Kuaile

*Square Bldg 10F, 3-10-3 Roppongi, Minato-ku
(3470 7421). Roppongi station.* **Open** 9pm-5am
daily. **Admission** ¥3,000. **Dress code** no sandals
or shorts. **Map 2**

Club Kuaile's main bill of fare is speed garage,
pumped out at high volume through a superior
sound system. A roomy venue with great views over
Roppongi from its tenth-floor vantage point.

relax. Other than 'Bump', it features NY house, techno and dance classics. Drinks are all ¥500.

Core

MT Bldg B2, 3-8-18 Roppongi, Minato-ku (3470 5944). Roppongi station. **Open** 9pm-5am daily. **Admission** varies with events. **Dress code** none. **Map 2**

Discretion is taken to new heights at Core, whose owner claims he didn't put a sign outside because he didn't want everyone to know it was there. The dancefloor is surprisingly roomy given its sub-basement location. For a club, the bar snacks are impressive; there's even steak. Drinks are all ¥800. Core features mostly house and techno, and it has proved popular with TV and sports personalities on their nights off. On Saturdays, Subhead and Tokyo's No.1 female minimal techno DJ, Mayuri, appear at Core.

Fai

B2F, 5-10-1 Minami-Aoyama, Minato-ku (3486 4910). Omotesando station. **Open** 7pm-5am daily. **Admission** ¥2,000 Mon-Thur (incl two drinks); ¥2,500 Fri-Sun (incl three drinks). **Dress code** none. **Map 2**

Only punk and techno are left off the musical menu at Fai, whose speciality is music from the '70s and '80s. Fine drinks start at ¥700.

Gamos

2-chome Centre Bldg B1, 2-11-10 Shinjuku, Shinjuku-ku (3354 5519). Shinjuku-Gyoenmae station. **Open** 9pm-5am daily. **Admission** varies with events. **Dress code** no sandals. **Map 3b**

This area of Shinjuku is famous for its gay and lesbian bars and clubs (*see chapter* **Gay & Lesbian**), although Gamos welcomes people of all sexual persuasions, depending on the night. The club features mainly house and techno, but every Saturday and Sunday a gay night, 'Otoko-Matsuri' (male festival), takes up the space. On every second Friday, the space is taken by a lesbian party. Both parties are same-sex only, so check the schedule. 'Gamos is open to everybody,' says owner Ozeki-san, 'but be sure to check the flyer before stopping by.'

Harlem

Dr Jeekan's 2F/3F, 2-4 Maruyama-cho, Shibuya-ku (3461 8806). Shibuya station. **Open** 9pm-5am daily. **Admission** varies with event. **Dress code** none. **Map 4**

Harlem is dedicated to hip hop, rap, soul and R&B. It has two dancefloors, both relatively big. Upstairs the atmosphere is mellow, with a backdrop of soul and R&B, while downstairs in hip hop land, the pace is frenetic. Drinks start at ¥500. The area around Harlem is one of Tokyo's main clubbing centres, and Harlem has Club Asia (*see above*) and Vuenos Bar Tokyo (*see below*) for neighbours.

Liquid Room

Humax Pavilion 7F, 1-20-1 Kabuki-cho, Shinjuku-ku (3200 6831/fax 3200 7350). Shinjuku station. **Open** varies with events. **Admission** varies with events. **Dress code** none. **Map 3b**

Club Que Shimo-Kitazawa

Big Ben Bldg B2F, 2-5-2 Kitazawa, Setagaya-ku (3412 9979). Shimo-Kitazawa station (Inokashira/Odakyu lines). **Open** 10pm-5am Mon, Wed, Thur; 9pm-5am Tue, Fri, Sat. **Admission** ¥2,000 Mon, Wed, Thur (incl two drinks); ¥2,500 Tue, Fri, Sat (incl two drinks). **Dress code** none. **Map 29**

Club Que's main raison d'être is as a live house for rock bands, but once the weekend gigs are over it transforms itself into a club. Music tends to be rock-oriented, with healthy doses of alternative rock, guitar pop and vintage rock thrown in. Worth a trip.

Club Tatou

7-6-2 Roppongi, Minato-ku (5411 4433). Roppongi station. **Open** 9pm-5am Thur-Sat. **Admission** Thur *men* ¥3,000 (incl two drinks), *women* free; Fri, Sat ¥3,000 (incl two drinks), free before 10pm. **Dress code** smart. **Map 2**

Once an exclusive French diner, Tatou Tokyo recently transformed itself into a disco. It hasn't lost any of its exclusivity, though, and you have to dress smart, otherwise they won't let you in. Music is mainly soul, with occasional live performances on Friday nights.

Club Vivian

Azabu Palace Bldg B1, 2-25-18 Nishi-Azabu, Minato-ku (3406 8477). Roppongi station. **Open** 10pm-5am Mon-Sat. **Admission** ¥2,000 Mon-Thur (incl one drink); ¥2,500 Fri, Sat (incl two drinks). **Dress code** none. **Map 2**

Club Vivian, which opened in September 1998, has already become home to one of Tokyo's most famous house events, NY House Night 'Bump', which fills the room two Saturdays a month. Vivian is a small but very attractive venue, with enough lounge space for those who want to sit back, talk and

Liquid Room is a big club and live house located in the middle of frantic Kabuki-cho. Although it does host its own events two or three times a month, most of the time the space is rented out, so you never know what might be happening: it could be a live house one night and a hip hop club the next. Recently, bands such as Massive Attack and Super Furry Animals have played here, while on the party front Liquid Room has hosted Hardfloor, Loopa and Viva. It has two bars and, thankfully, plenty of toilets. Liquid Room's monthly schedule is available free from big record stores such as Tower or HMV (*see chapter* **Shops & Services**).

Loop

Nihon Fudo Bldg B1, 2-1-13 Shibuya, Shibuya-ku (3797 9933). Shibuya station. **Open** 10pm-5am daily. **Admission** varies. **Dress code** none. **Map 4**
Although Loop is not far from Shibuya station, first-time goers who don't want to spend hours wandering the streets might be well advised to take a taxi, which will cost somewhere in the region of ¥700. Many small clubs can feel unwelcoming to the first-time visitor, but that's definitely not the case here. Loop has a friendly vibe, moody lighting and an excellent sound system. It features all kinds of dance music, including minimal techno, hard house and happy house. DJ Patrick's night is one of the best parties in Tokyo.

Lust

MS-EBIS4 2F, 4-4-6 Ebisu, Shibuya-ku (5424 1483). Ebisu station. **Open** 10pm-5am daily. **Admission** varies with events. **Dress code** none. **Map 20**
Not a very big venue, and most of what space there is is given over to a lounge area and the dancefloor. The contrast between the ultra-violet lit, tunnel-like hallway to the dancefloor and the spacious dancefloor itself comes as something of a surprise. Music is house, techno and trance, and the admission fee (usually around ¥2,500) includes two drinks, with extras reasonably priced at ¥500 each.

Maniac Love

Tera-Oasis Omotesando Bldg B1, 5-10-6 Minami-Aoyama, Minato-ku (3406 1166). Omotesando station. **Open** 10pm-5am Mon-Sat; 5am-noon Sun. **Admission** ¥2,000 Mon-Thur (incl one drink); ¥2,500 Fri, Sat (incl one drink); ¥1,000 Sun from 5am (incl free coffee). **Dress code** none. **Map 4**
With its immense sound system and cool lighting effects, Maniac Love was designed to be the mecca for dance music in Tokyo. Its main clientele is serious dance music lovers, so don't come here if you're looking for a date. On every fourth Friday, Q'Hey, Eno, Mayuri and Takami fill the space with their minimal-techno event, 'Re-Boot'. Drinks, at ¥800 each, are expensive, even for Tokyo, and the heat that builds up on busy nights is sure to mean several trips to the bar. The after-hours party on Sunday mornings has built up a loyal following, and it's not unusual to see the place full to bursting at 7am. Yet another attraction is the Saturday party, 'Cycle', which features a number of well-known local

DJs, including Phil Free, Kazu, Mase, Rie, Yasuzawa, Yo-C, Shinkawa, Toby, Take and Owada.

Milk

Roob 6 Bldg B1/B2, 1-13-3 Ebisu-Nishi, Shibuya-ku (5458 2826). Ebisu station. **Open** 8pm-5am daily. **Admission** ¥3,000 Mon-Thur (incl two drinks); ¥3,500 Fri-Sun (incl two drinks). **Dress code** none. **Map 20**
Milk's mission when it opened in 1995 was to bring the best of rock, punk and hardcore to Tokyo. These days, however, even Milk has succumbed to the techno and house sound that has swept Tokyo clubland, although on Saturday nights it goes back to its roots and occasionally hosts live rock acts. The venue itself is maze-like, occupying three floors below ground of the same building as pub What The Dickens (*see chapter* **Bars**). At the bottom of the club is a lounge area where you can have a quiet conversation while up above the dancing continues on the cramped, small dancefloor. A ¥1,500 ticket will buy you two drinks. If you're feeling adventurous, try a Sachiko cocktail. It's not on the menu, and we're not sure what's in it, but we can vouch for its effects.

Millgram Underline

JR Yamanotesen-Shita, 3-29-70 Shibuya, Shibuya-ku (5458 2366). Shibuya station. **Open** 6pm-2am Mon-Thur; 6pm-5am Fri, Sat. **Admission** free. **Dress code** none. **Map 4**
This very small lounge is located under the Yamanote line. You can actually 'feel' the trains go above your head, though the fine sound system stops you from actually hearing them. Music is an eclectic mix, ranging from jazz to pop, and drinks start at ¥500.

Organ Bar

Kuretake Bldg 3F, 4-9 Udagawa-cho, Shibuya-ku (5489 5460). Shibuya station. **Open** 9pm-5am daily. **Admission** ¥1,000 Mon-Thur; ¥2,000 Fri-Sun (incl two drinks). **Dress code** none. **Map 4**
Another small joint in the same building as Ball (*see above*). It features soul and jazz, and its party on the first Thursday of the month, 'A Ready Made Night', organised by DJ Como Esta Yaegashi, is everybody's favourite. Extra drinks are all ¥600.

Oto

Wadakyu Bldg 2F, 1-17-5 Kabuki-cho, Shinjuku-ku (5273 8264). Shinjuku station. **Open** 10pm-midnight daily. **Admission** ¥2,000 Mon-Thur; ¥2,500 Fri-Sun. **Dress code** none. **Map 3b**
Oto (meaning 'sound' in Japanese) lives up to its name, with a sound system that would do a much larger place credit. Music runs from hip hop to hardcore techno, and drinks are all ¥600.

Pylon

Dr Jeekan's 4F/5F/6F, 2-4 Maruyama-cho, Shibuya-ku (3497 1818). Shibuya station. **Open** 10pm-5am Fri-Sun. **Admission** men ¥3,500 (incl two drinks); women ¥2,500 (incl two drinks). **Dress code** none. **Map 4**
Pylon is a recently renovated club in the same building as Harlem (*see above*). The entry charge system

is bizarre. The first time you go, you'll be given a membership card, which costs ¥3,500 (men) or ¥2,500 (women). From your second visit, the card entitles men to ¥1,000 off the price of admission, while women get a discount of ¥500. Pylon attracts an extremely young crowd, mainly 16- to 22-year-olds out for a wild night on the town.

Ring

Kohama Bldg 1F/2F, 1-8-8 Nishi-Azabu, Minato-ku (5411 4300). Roppongi station. **Open** 8pm-5am daily. **Admission** ¥2,500 Mon-Thur (incl two drinks); *men* ¥3,000 Fri-Sun (incl two drinks); *women* ¥2,500 Fri, Sat (incl two drinks); *women* free Sun. **Dress code** not too casual. **Map 2**

Look out for a small sign on Roppongi Dori that says 'Ring' and you've found this place, which plays soul and R&B classics to an appreciative crowd. After its low-key exterior, the size of the dancefloor and bar areas is a pleasant surprise. Expect crowds on Friday and Saturday.

Rockwest

Tosen Udagawa-cho Bldg 7F, 4-7 Udagawa-cho, Shibuya-ku (5459 7988). Shibuya station. **Open** 10pm-5am daily. **Admission** ¥2,500 (incl two drinks); ¥2,000 (with flyer or advance ticket, incl one drink). **Dress code** none. **Map 4**

By day, Rockwest is a café/restaurant (11am-3pm daily), by night it's one of the best places in town for a happy hardcore night out, with Hardcore Kitchen every fourth Friday the highlight. There's a good sound system, air-conditioning and a relatively roomy dancefloor, and re-entry is allowed.

The Room

Jinwa Bldg B1, 15-19 Sakura-oka, Shibuya-ku (3461 7167). Shibuya station. **Open** 9pm-5am Mon-Sat. **Admission** ¥1,000 Mon; ¥1,000 Tue-Sat before 9pm (incl one drink); ¥2,000 Tue-Thur (incl two drinks); ¥2,500 Fri, Sat (incl two drinks). **Dress code** none. **Map 4**

A small, wood-panelled venue, famous for its cocktails. Sometimes plays host to top DJs who come here to practise new routines on their nights off.

Space Lab Yellow

1-10-11 Nishi-Azabu, Minato-ku (3479 0690). Roppongi station. **Open** varies with events. **Admission** varies with events. **Dress code** none. **Map 2**

This relatively big space is a popular venue for events and parties, and the dancefloor is big enough to accommodate the occasional live act. There's also a snack bar and roomy lounge. On Saturday, guest appearances by visiting foreign DJs fill the place. *Website: http://www.space-lab-yellow.com/*

Sugar High DJ Bar & Club

Yubun Bldg 3F, 2-16-3 Dogenzaka, Shibuya-ku (3780 3022). Shibuya station. **Open** 7pm-2am Tue-Thur, Sun; 7pm-5am Fri, Sat. **Admission** varies with events. **Dress code** none. **Map 4**

From Shibuya station, head left at the intersection of 109, climb up the Dogenzaka slope for about 200m, and you'll see the Sugar High sign on your left. The admission charge varies with events, from zero to ¥2,500. Cocktails are all ¥500.

Sugar Hill

Azabudai Mansion 101, 3-4-14 Azabudai, Minato-ku (3583 6223). Roppongi station. **Open** 8pm-5am daily. **Admission** ¥700. **Dress code** none. **Map 2**

A lounge style hideout in Roppongi. One apartment room is stuffed with thousands of classic records from the late '70s and early '80s. As well as finding your favourite dance track at Sugar Hill, you can also indulge in your favourite Japanese food: tempura and udon are brought in from neighbouring restaurants and sold at reasonable prices.

Velfarre

Velfarre Bldg, 7-14-22 Roppongi, Minato-ku (3402 8000). Roppongi station. **Open** 6pm-1am Fri, Sat; 6pm-midnight Thur, Sun. **Admission** Thur *men* ¥3,000 (incl two drinks), *women* ¥2,000 (incl two drinks); Fri-Sun *men* ¥4,000 (incl three drinks), *women* ¥3,000 (incl three drinks). **Dress code** not too casual. **Map 2**

The largest disco in Asia, Velfarre reopened for business in March 1998. This gigantic disco and live house space, with a capacity of over 2,000, is a real throwback to the mirrorball days of the '80s, with marble staircases and other extravagances thrown in. It has a vast dancefloor with an automated movable stage and giant mirror ball at the bottom, and more bars, restrooms and snack bars than you can count. If you're feeling brave, try and blag your way into one of the VIP lounges, from where you can watch the action without actually having to dance. *Website: http://velfarre.avex.co.jp/*

Vuenos Bar Tokyo

1F/B1, 2-21-7 Dogenzaka, Shibuya-ku (5458 5963). Shibuya station. **Open** 10pm-5am daily; *bar* 7pm-5am daily. **Admission** varies. **Dress code** none. **Map 4**

A Latin music club across from Club Asia (*see above*), owned and operated by the same company as its neighbour. Vuenos opened in October 1998 with a mission to spread the word about Latin, soul and dance music, in contrast with Club Asia's mainly techno and house events. Clubbers who come here tend be older than average for Tokyo, mostly around 25 or above, and a ¥1,000 ticket buys two drinks. The admission charge varies with events but is usually around ¥2,500. *Website: http://www.clubasia.co.jp/*

Web

Sano Bldg B1, 3-30-10 Ikejiri, Setagaya-ku (3422 1405). Ikejiri-Ohashi station (Shin-Tamagawa line). **Open** 10pm-5am Mon, Wed, Thur; 9pm-5am Tue, Fri, Sat. **Admission** ¥2,000 Mon, Wed, Thur (incl two drinks); ¥2,500 Tue, Fri, Sat (incl two drinks). **Dress code** none. **Map 30**

A small joint that squeezes in nearly 200 people on weekday nights. Web proudly serves a variety of cocktails, and the menu changes monthly. The DJs spin music of all genres.

Sport

With international events and native specialities such as sumo stable visits and indoor skiing, Tokyo will tickle every sports fan's fancy.

Spectator sports

Japan's mass spectator sports have traditionally been baseball and sumo; these have been joined by soccer, since the founding of the J-League in 1993. Golf and tennis also retain devoted followings.

There are strong links between companies and the top teams of many popular sports. Only baseball and soccer lie outside the semi-professional company-based sports world, though the strength of baseball's corporate connections can be judged by the names of the teams. When soccer turned fully professional, it tried to move away from this and sink the roots of its teams into their local areas.

Athletics

Tokyo's biggest athletics meeting takes place at the National Stadium (*see below* **Football**) in September (*see chapter* **Tokyo by Season**). Tokyo's two marathons have strict entrance requirements and attract some of the world's best runners.

Tokyo International Marathon

Usually held in mid-Feb, starting and finishing at the National Stadium. The 1999 event attracted top international runners, including Abebe Mekonnen.

Tokyo International Women's Marathon

This marathon follows the same route in November. It was the world's first women's marathon.

Baseball

Introduced to Japan by Horace Wilson in 1873, baseball has long held a grip on Japanese hearts and minds, and on corporate wallets: each professional team is owned and sponsored by a large corporation. The first professional team, the Yomiuri Giants, was founded in 1934, and by 1950 a professional competition had been set up, comprising 12 teams in two leagues. Each team plays the other five in its league 26 times a season (Apr-Oct). The two teams with the highest winning percentages in each league then face each other to decide the title. Tokyo has three teams: the Yomiuri Giants, the Nippon Ham Fighters and the Yakult Swallows. Interest is high at amateur level, too. The national high-school baseball tournament is televised live and brings the country to a virtual standstill.

Kokugikan *hosts three sumo bouts a year.*

Tokyo Dome

1-3 Koraku, Bunkyo-ku (3811 2111). Suidobashi station. **Capacity** 55,000. **Tickets** ¥1,200-¥5,900.
Map 9
The Dome, or Big Egg, is home to the Yomiuri Giants and the Nippon Ham Fighters.

Jingu Stadium

Kasumigaoka, Shinjuku-ku (3402 2111). Sendagaya station. **Capacity** 46,000. **Tickets** ¥1,500-¥3,900.
Map 12
This stadium, part of the complex that includes the National Stadium, was built for the 1964 Olympics, and is now home to the Yakult Swallows.

Football

Standards have risen since the start of the J-League in 1993, and the national team secured its first World Cup finals qualification at France 98. In spring 1999 the national under-20 team made the final of the World Youth Cup. This promising crop of youngsters is likely to form the basis for the national co-squad when Japan co-hosts the World Cup with South Korea in 2002. None of the planned venues for 2002 is in Tokyo: the final will be played at Yokohama National Stadium or a new 70,000-seater facility in Omiya, Saitama prefecture. The capital is also left on the sidelines when it comes to J-League action: Tokyo still doesn't have its own team in the J-League top division, but the National Stadium regularly hosts 'home' matches of sides from the Kanto region, such as Kashima Antlers and Jubilo Iwata.

National Stadium

Kasumigaoka-machi, Shinjuku-ku (3403 1151). Sendagaya station. **Map 17**
Tickets for J-League matches cost ¥3,000-¥5,000.

Horse racing

Horse racing in Japan is run under the auspices of the Japan Racing Association (JRA), which manages the ten national tracks, and the National Association of Racing (NAR), which oversees local courses. Race tracks are one of the few places where gambling is legal.

Tokyo Racecourse

1-1 Hiyoshi-cho, Fuchu City (0423 63 3141). Fuchu-honmachi station (JR Nambu line).
One of the ten national tracks run by the JRA. There are 40 days' racing a year, all at weekends. Many of the country's most famous races are held here, including the Japan Derby in June and the Japan Cup in November. The latter is an international invitational race that attracts top riders and horses from around the world. Major JRA races are graded (GI, GII, GIII), with the top one being 'GI'.

Oi Racecourse

2-1-2 Katsushima, Shinagawa-ku (3763 2151). Oikeibajomae station (Tokyo monorail).
Run under the auspices of the NAR, with 116 days' racing a year. 'Twinkle Races' are evening events that Oi pioneered in the 1990s, which have proved popular among office workers. Other NAR courses in the Tokyo region include Funabashi in Chiba.

Hydroplane racing (Kyotei)

Next to horse racing, this is the most popular focus of betting in Japan. The race itself is between six motor-driven boats in what is essentially a very large swimming pool; boats go round the 600m course three times, regularly reaching speeds of over 80kph (50mph). Edogawa Kyotei is the big favourite among Tokyo fans; the race schedule is published in Japanese sports newspapers and on the website *http://www.edogawa-kyotei.co.jp/schedule/schedule.html.* Betting starts at just ¥100.

Edogawa Kyotei

3-1-1 Higashi-Komatsugawa, Edogawa-ku (3250 3500/live telecast 0180 99 3703). Shin-koiwa station, then a 21 bus. **Admission** ¥50.

Ice hockey

There are 131 ice hockey teams in the Tokyo area, but only five – Seibu Tetsudo, Oji Seishi, Kokudo, Yukijirushi, Nihon Seishi and Furukawa Denko – have semi-professional status. Only Kokudo and Seibu Tetsudo play anywhere near Tokyo. The season runs from October to March.

Higashi-Fushimi Ice Arena

3-1-25 Higashi-Fushimi, Hoya-shi (0427 67 7171). Higashi-Fushimi station (Seibu Shinjuku line).
Home of Seibu Tetsudo.

Shin-Yokohama Prince Hotel Skate Centre

2-11 Shin-Yokohama, Kohoku-ku, Yokohama-shi, Kanagawa (045 474 1112). Shin-Yokohama station.
Home of Kokudo.

Martial arts

With the exception of sumo (*see below*), martial arts are not major spectator sports in Japan; judo is the only one competed at Olympic level. Nevertheless, if you wish to watch rather than take part, opportunities exist. The Nippon Budokan stages demonstrations and championships in all the martial arts except sumo. Advance tickets are not required, and in most cases admission is free. Major events include the following (the date is approximate if it's not a national holiday; *see chapter* **Tokyo by Season** for public holiday dates):

18 Mar: Japan Kobudo Demonstration Event
18 Apr: All-Japan Jukendo Championships
29 Apr: All-Japan Judo Championships
23 May: All-Japan Akido Demonstration Event
29-30 May: Kanto Student Kyudo Championships
3 Nov: All-Japan Kendo Championships
5 Dec: All-Japan Naginata Championships (Emperor's Cup)
12 Dec: All-Japan Karate Championships

Martial arts classes may be viewed at Budokan Gakuen school, in the same complex as the Nippon Budokan (*see below*); phone for details (3216 5143). The national associations of the different disciplines (*see below* **Participation sports: Martial Arts**) may have training facilities where spectators can view practice sessions, or can point you in the direction of individual *dojo* that may welcome interested visitors.

Nippon Budokan

2-3 Kitanomaru Koen, Chiyoda-ku (3216 5100/fax 3216 5118). Kudanshita station. **Map 18**

Motor sports

Motor sports have a devoted following in Japan. The Suzuka circuit (in Mie prefecture towards Nagoya; 0593 78 1111) is the venue of the annual Formula 1 Japan Grand Prix. Many fans from Tokyo make the return-trip in a day.

Closer to the capital, Twin Ring Motegi boasts two types of circuit, including an oval course suitable for US-style motor sports. Major events include a late autumn NASCAR invitation race, which attracts many leading drivers from the other side of the Pacific, and a CART championship series race in April. The permanent circuit hosts the motorbike Japan Grand Prix in April of odd-numbered years, alternating with Suzuka.

Twin Ring Motegi

120-1 Hiyama, Oaza, Motegi-cho, Hoga-gun, Tochigi-ken (0285 64 0080). Motegi station (Maoka line).

Rugby

Japanese rugby is divided between corporate- and university-level teams. The Japan championship is held in Jan/Feb, with the top four sides from the corporate and university worlds playing a knock-out competition at the National Stadium in Sendagaya. (This stages the annual Waseda-Meiji match, the big university fixture that has traditionally been the season's most popular game.) Japan championship games of recent years show that the standard of university rugby is now far below that of the corporate game. Corporate sides often feature imported talent, some of whom now appear in the Japanese national side. Major games are held at the National Stadium (*see below* **Football**).

Sumo

With a history dating back 2,000 years, Japan's national sport uniquely blends tradition, athleticism and religion. Its rules are simple: each combatant must try to force the other out of the ring (*dohyo*) or make him touch the floor with a part of his anatomy other than his feet. Tournaments take place over 15 days, with wrestlers fighting once a day. Those who achieve regular majorities (winning more than they lose) progress up through the rankings, the top of which is *yokozuna*. Wrestlers failing to achieve a majority are demoted. Yokozuna must achieve a majority in every tournament or are expected to retire.

Bouts take place in Tokyo three times a year, in January, May and September, at the Kokugikan (*see below*), which opened in 1985. It also hosts one-day tournaments and retirement ceremonies.

If you want to know more about sumo, and witness the rigorous training wrestlers undergo, you can visit a sumo stable, or *beya*. Most Tokyo beya

allow visitors, on condition that you remain quiet. It's a good idea to bring along a small gift, such as a bottle of *sake*, for the stablemaster, to show your appreciation. Be warned: the day starts early. Junior wrestlers are up and about at 4am, and gruelling practice sessions start at around 5am. The higher ranked wrestlers start to appear at around 8am.

Kokugikan

1-3-28 Yokoami, Sumida-ku (3623 5111). Ryogoku station. **Tickets** ¥2,100-¥11,300. **Map 31**
Advance tickets go on sale at the box office and regular ticket outlets about a month before the start of each tournament. Balcony seats usually sell out quickly, and box seats, the most expensive, can be difficult to obtain without corporate connections. A number of unreserved seats are held back for sale on the day of the tournament, going on sale from 8am at ¥2,100 (one per person). Arriving early to join the queue may not always be a necessity, but unreserved tickets do go quickly. Many people watch bouts between younger fighters from downstairs box seats until the ticket-holders arrive mid-afternoon. Many stables are situated close to the Kokugikan. Before visiting a stable, call ahead to ask permission, in Japanese if possible. There are over 40 stables in Tokyo: see the website of *Sumo World* magazine (*http://iac.co.jp/~sumowrld/*).

Azumazeki Beya

4-6-4 Higashi-Komagata, Sumida-ku (3625 0033). Honjo-azumabashi station.

Dewanoumi Beya

2-3-15 Ryogoku, Sumida-ku (3632 4920). Ryogoku station.

Izutsu Beya

2-2-7 Ryogoku, Sumida-ku (3634 9827). Ryogoku station. **Map 31**

Oshima Beya

3-5-3 Ryogoku, Sumida-ku (3632 6578). Ryogoku station. **Map 31**

Tennis

Attention on professional tennis in Japan is focused on the women's game. The biggest professional event is the annual Japan Open, held at Ariake Coliseum and the adjacent Metropolitan Ariake Tennis Woods Park every April (*see chapter* **Tokyo by Season**).

Metropolitan Ariake Tennis Woods Park/Ariake Coliseum

2-2-22 Ariake, Koto-ku (3529 3301). Ariake station (Yurikamome line).

Volleyball

Doffing its cap to soccer's J-League, in name at least, volleyball's V-League has been rather less successful, with stories circulating about teams' financial problems in 1999. The V-League is divided into two leagues of ten teams, one for women, one for men. Many games are televised live.

Tokyo Gymnasium
1-17-1 Sendagaya, Shibuya-ku (5474 2111). Sendagaya station. **Map 17**
The only place within Tokyo that regularly hosts V-League volleyball matches.

Participation sports

Baseball cages

Oslo Batting Centre
2-34-5 Kabuki-cho, Shinjuku-ku (3208 8130). Shinjuku station. **Open** 10am-6am daily. **Admission** ¥300 for 20 balls. **Map 3b**
The not-so-gentle thwack of wood on rubber can be heard through the night at this practice cage surrounded by Kabuki-cho's love hotels. Ten lanes, and ball speed can be varied from 70 to 120kph.

Meiji Jingu Gaien Batting Cage
12 Kasumigaoka-machi, Shinjuku-ku (3478 6800). Shinanomachi station. **Open** 9am-8.30pm daily. **Admission** ¥400 for 20 balls. **Map 17**
Eleven cages. Ball speed variable from 70 to 140kph.

Bowling, pool & snooker

Est
1-14-14 Shibuya, Shibuya-ku (3409 4721). Shibuya station. **Open** *bowling* 10am-4.30am Sun-Thur; 10am-5.30am Fri, Sat; *karaoke* 10am-5am daily; *table tennis* 10am-4am Sun-Thur; 10am-5am Fri, Sat; *pool* 10am-5.30am Sun-Thur; 10am-6am Fri, Sat; *Internet café* 11am-11pm daily. **Admission** ¥500-¥800 per hour. **Map 4**
Est houses 42 bowling lanes, 34 karaoke boxes, 15 table tennis tables, 50 pool tables, arcade games and an Internet café. On weekdays (not Friday) many activities cost less before 5pm.

Fitness

Membership of most private gyms is prohibitively expensive. Large hotels may have swimming pools or gyms, but if you are in need of some muscle-pumping action, head for one of these:

Private gyms

Tipness
Enquiries 3464 3531.
Eleven branches in the Tokyo area, at Shibuya, Akasaka, Kichijoji, Gotanda, Machida, Nakano, Roppongi, Shinjuku, Ikebukuro, Kasai and Shimo-Kitazawa. Most have a swimming pool, aerobics classes and weight gyms and are open 7am-10pm.

Membership starts from ¥11,000 per month; guests can use the facilities for ¥3,000 (¥2,000 Sat, Sun and holidays) if accompanied by a member.

People Xax
Enquiries 3475 4471.
This has 22 branches, most with swimming pool, sauna and weight gyms. Membership and monthly fees vary. Guests are allowed in only with members for ¥3,000. Most branches are open 7am-11pm Mon-Fri; 10am-9pm Sat, Sun.

Nautilus Club
Enquiries 3293 0181/fax 3293 0188.
Seven branches. Facilities typically include shower, aerobics, sauna, weight machines, tanning machine. Akasaka, Shibuya and Suidobashi branches have swimming pools. Except for the Shibuya branch, visitors are allowed in unaccompanied for ¥5,000.

Public facilities

Each of the 23 wards of Tokyo has sports facilities, with bargain prices for residents and commuters. Except for those in Shibuya-ku, they're also open to others, for higher fees, as listed below.

Chiyoda Kuritsu Sogo Taiikukan Pool
2-1-8 Uchi-Kanda, Chiyoda-ku (3256 8444). Kanda station. **Open** noon-8.30pm Mon, Tue, Thur, Sat; 5.30-8.30pm Wed, Fri; 9am-5pm Sun. Closed every third Mon & Sun. **Admission** ¥500 (2 hours). **Map 15**
Swimming pool and gym within a weight's throw of Tokyo's business district.

Chuo-ku Sogo Sports Centre
Hama-cho Koen Nai, 2-59-1 Nihonbashi-Hama-cho, Chuo-ku (3666 1501). Hama-cho station. **Open** 9am-9.30pm daily. Closed every third Thur. **Admission** ¥500 (2 hours).
With a swimming pool, studio and weight gym.

Minato-ku Sports Centre
3-1-19 Shibaura, Minato-ku (3578 2111). Tamachi station. **Open** 9am-9pm Tue-Sun. **Admission** ¥600.
Has a swimming pool, sauna, studio, weight gym, aerobics studio and in-line skating yard.

Shinagawa Sogo Taiikukan Pool
5-6-11 Kita-Shinagawa, Shinagawa-ku (3449 4400). Osaki station. **Open** 9.30am-9pm daily. Closed every third Mon. **Admission** ¥350 (2 hours). **Map 21**
No-frills swimming pool.

Shinjuku-ku Sports Centre
3-5-1 Okubo, Shinjuku-ku (3232 0171). Takadanobaba station. **Open** 9am-9pm daily. Closed every fourth Mon. **Admission** ¥300 (2 hours). **Map 25**
Swimming pool and gym.

Tokyo Metropolitan Gymnasium Pool
1-17-1 Sendagaya, Shibuya-ku (5474 2111). Sendagaya station. **Open** 9.30am-9pm daily. Closed every third Mon. **Admission** ¥450. **Map 17**
Run by Tokyo Metropolitan Government, this has a weight gym (¥380 extra), arena and athletics field.

Ten-pin bowling *is right up Tokyo's alley.*

Golf

Shiba Golf

4-8-2 Shiba-Koen, Minato-ku (5470 1111). Shiba-Koen station. **Open** 6am-11pm daily. **Admission** ¥500-¥900; varies according to box and ball charge.
The Japanese obsession with golf seems to have waned slightly, but Tokyo is still dotted with ranges.

Horse riding

Tokyo Horse Riding Club

4-8 Kamizono-cho, Yoyogi, Shibuya-ku (3370 0984/ fax 3370 2714). Sangubashi station (Odakyu line). **Open** 9am-5.45pm Tue-Sun (*Dec-Feb* 9am-4.45pm). **Admission** ¥7,550 Tue-Fri; ¥8,550 Sat, Sun. **Map 17**
The oldest riding club in Japan boasts 45 horses and six instructors. Luckily, visitors don't have to pay the annual membership fee of ¥96,000 (after a joining fee of ¥2 million; you also need to be recommended by two members). Book a day in advance.

Indoor skiing

In Chiba there's an indoor ski slope with people walking around in puffa jackets and gloves when the temperature's 30°C outside. Time on the slope is divided between snowboarding and skiing. The timetable is complex; study it well before you go.

Ski Dome SSAWS

2-3-1 Hama-cho, Funabashi-shi, Chiba (047 432 7000). Minami-Funabashi station (JR Keiyo line). **Open** 8am-9.30pm Mon-Wed (8am-12.30pm snowboarding; 12.30-9.30pm skiing); 10am-4pm Thur, Fri (10am-4pm skiing; 4-10pm snowboarding); 8am-10pm Sat (8am-4pm skiing; 4-10pm snowboarding); 8am-10pm Sun (8am-12.30pm snowboarding; 12.30-10pm skiing). **Admission** ¥5,400; ¥4,800 under-18s; ¥4,100 under 12s.
At half a kilometre long, this giant steel structure is impossible to miss. Never fear if you come without gear: everything, except socks, can be rented for about ¥1,500 per item. SSAWS, if you're wondering, stands for Spring, Summer, Autumn, Winter Snow.

Jogging

The most celebrated course is the 5km route marked out at 100m intervals around the Imperial Palace. The big one for hobby runners is in spring, out in Ome in the north-western part of Tokyo prefecture.

Martial arts

There are nine recognised modern martial arts – aikido, judo, jukendo, karate, kendo, kyudo, naginata, shorinji kempo and sumo – and a series of older and more traditional forms, known collectively as *kobudo*. The number of people practising them in Japan is put at almost 5 million.

Aikido

Aikikai Federation, 17-18 Wakamatsu-cho, Shinjuku-ku (3203 9236).

Jukendo

All-Japan Jukendo Federation, 2-3 Kitanomaru Koen, Chiyoda-ku (3201 1020).

Judo

All-Japan Judo Federation, 1-16-30 Kasuga, Bunkyo-ku (3818 4199).

Karate

Japan Karate Federation, No. 2 Senpaku Shinko Bldg, 1-11-2 Toranomon, Minato-ku (3503 6637).

Kendo

All-Japan Kendo Federation, Yasukuni Kyudan Minami Bldg 2F, 2-3-14 Kudan Minami, Chiyoda-ku (3234 6271).

Kobuto

Nippon Kobuto Association, 2-3 Kitanomaru Koen, Chiyoda-ku (3216 5114).

Kyudo

All-Japan Kyudo Association, Kishi Kinen Taiikukaikan, 1-1-1 Jinnan, Shibuya-ku (3481 2387).

Naginata

All-Japan Naginata Federation (Tokyo office), Kishi Kinen Taiikukaikan, 1-1-1 Jinnan, Shibuya-ku (3481 2411).

Shorinji Kempo

Shorinji Kempo Federation (Tokyo Office), 1-3-5 Uehara, Shibuya-ku (3481 5191).

Sumo (Amateur)

Japan Sumo Federation, Kishi Kinen Taiikukaikan, 1-1-1 Jinnan, Shibuya-ku (3481 2377).

The Nippon Budokan (*see above* **Spectator sports: Martial arts**) can also provide information.

Team sports

Amateur teams are always on the lookout for new members. Try *Tokyo Classified* (*see chapter* **Media**).

Tennis

Municipal courts exist, but waiting lists are long.

Metropolitan Ariake Tennis Woods Park

2-2-22 Ariake, Koto-ku (3529 3301). Ariake station (Yurikamome line). **Open** 9am-9pm daily. **Admission** ¥1,500 per hour.
Big, new – home to the Japan Open tournament.

Theatre

Indulge your senses in the exquisite traditions of Japanese drama.

Japanese theatre is a visual feast of colour and texture: the exquisite costumes, the white or vivid make-up, the colourful backdrops, even the embroidered fire curtains lowered in the intervals. To the colour and texture add sound and smell – the exotic tones of various instruments that accompany the actors' intriguing speech patterns and impassioned exchanges, and in some plays the perfume or incense, which wafts over the audience. And Japanese theatre is to be felt too – in the tingling of your scalp, the stirred emotions, the held breath and the collective tension of the audience.

In common with the performing arts throughout Asia, Japanese traditional theatre genres integrate dance, music and lyrical narrative. The emphasis is on aesthetic beauty, symbolism and imagery as opposed to western theatre's concentration on realism and logic. Another important element distinguishing Japanese theatre from that of the west is *ma*, perhaps best translated as a 'pregnant pause'. It is not considered silence; rather it is the space between musical notes or words and is used to heighten the intensity of the dramatic moment. It occurs, for example, when actors or puppets perform stop-motion poses (*mie*) between the beats of wooden clappers or between the notes of *shamisen* (three-stringed banjo) strumming.

The various genres of Japanese drama tend to share certain popular themes, the most common of which are clan squabbles; family, group or servant-master loyalty; commitment to or longing for one's home town or homeland; conflicts between duty and feelings; revenge; corruption and justice; and the supernatural.

Types of theatre

Noh & Kyogen

Sombre, slow and deliberate, *noh* is ritualistic and formulaic, with themes invariably centred on religion. The secondary character (*waki*), who enters the stage first, is usually attired as a priest, and plays explore the transience of this world, the sin of killing and the spiritual comfort to be found in Buddhism. Plays are grouped roughly into five categories whose subject matter is gods, warrior-ghosts, women, insanity and demons.

There are no group rehearsals: there is a pre-performance meeting, but the actors and musicians do not play together until the performance. This spontaneity is one of the appeals of this kind of theatre.

Kyogen are short, humorous interludes that make fun of human frailties. They are interspersed with noh pieces to provide comic relief, but can be staged independently. Many of them involve the character of a servant and his lord, who is held up to ridicule but usually proved right in the end.

Bunraku

The puppets used in *bunraku* are a half to two-thirds human size and require great skill and strength to operate. Each puppet is operated by two assistants and one chief puppeteer. Becoming a master puppeteer is a lengthy process, beginning with ten years operating the legs, followed by another ten on the left arm before being permitted to manipulate the right arm, head and eyebrows.

Four main elements comprise a bunraku performance: the puppets themselves; the movements they make; the vocal delivery of the *tayu*, who chants the narrative and speaks the lines for every character, changing his voice to suit the role, and the solo *shamisen* accompaniment.

The weird and wonderful world of kabuki.

History of theatre

The drama performed in Japan is the result of a long history of assimilation and borrowings. This is true of both the classical drama, consisting primarily of noh, kyogen, bunraku and kabuki, and modern drama, which has been heavily influenced by Western notions of acting.

Noh was the first of the classical dramas to be created. In 1374, Kan'ami and his son Zeami performed for the shogun Ashikaga Yoshimitsu, who immediately liked it and thereafter sponsored the troupe. Over time noh became the entertainment of choice of the military and the aristocracy, and in 1647, the shogun Tokugawa Ieyasu placed the art under his control and issued strict regulations governing its form and staging. The art has continued virtually unchanged since.

While the samurai class patronised and sustained noh, the commoners were developing new performing arts, of which one was bunraku, the puppet theatre, then called *joruri*, from a kind of recitation accompanied by the *shamisen*, a three-stringed guitar-like instrument. Around the middle of the seventeenth century, a new, more forceful and exciting narrative style was developed by Gidayu Takemoto, who opened the first puppet theatre, the Takemotoza in Osaka. He collaborated closely with Japan's greatest playwright, Chikamatsu Monzaemon (1653-1724) who became the chief writer for the puppet theatre and for its rival, kabuki. Particularly popular were his love-suicide plays, usually based on the insoluble emotional conflict of a pair of lovers due to a clash between duty or social codes and their personal desires.

The puppet theatre held its ascendancy until the eighteenth century, when kabuki borrowed many of the bunraku stories, especially those of Chikamatsu, and kabuki actors started to mimic some of the actions of the puppets. This novelty drew audiences away and bunraku fell into decline. By the 1960s it had almost disappeared. Its present survival is due largely to governmental support.

Kabuki was started in 1603 by Okuni, an attendant at the Izumo Shrine, and her troupe of entertainers, who also sold their favours off stage. However, in 1629 the Tokugawa government prohibited women from appearing on stage because their sexually provocative dances had begun to cause public disturbances. The women were succeeded by groups of attractive young boys, but in 1653 they were banned for similar reasons, and it was decreed that actors of all roles should be adult men. This became the historical precursor of the unique art we see today, which employs the highly skilled female-role impersonators called *onnagata*.

Historically, two different styles of kabuki evolved. In Kanto (present-day Tokyo), the leading actor was Ichikawa Danjuro (1660-1704) and

Kabuki

Of all the traditional performing arts in Japan, probably the most exciting is *kabuki*. The most important element in kabuki is the actor: everything that happens on stage is a vehicle for displaying his prowess.

Because the actor is central, the props are used only as long as they show him to his greatest advantage. *Koken*, stage hands dressed in black, symbolising their supposed invisibility, hand the actor props, make adjustments to his costume and wig, and bring him a stool to perch on during long speeches or periods of inactivity.

The *onnagata* female role specialists portray a stylised feminine beauty. There is no pretence at realism, so the actor's real age is irrelevant, and there is no incongruity in a 75-year-old actor portraying an 18-year-old maiden.

The three main types of kabuki are *shosagoto* dance pieces, *jidaimono* and *sewamono*. Jidaimono are historical dramas set in pre-Edo Japan, which usually feature gorgeous costumes and colourful make-up called *kumadori*, which is painted along the muscle and blood vessel lines of the actor's face. Jidaimono originated in the puppet theatre and feature accompaniment from a chanter who relates the storyline and emotions of the character while the actor expresses them in movement, facial expressions or poses (mie). Sewamono are stories of everyday life during the Edo period (1603-1867). They are closer to western drama in that the storyline and portrayal are more realistic.

In every kabuki theatre there is a *hanamichi*, an elevated pathway for the performers that runs through the audience from the back of the theatre to the main stage. This is used for dramatic entrances and exits and contains a traplift through which supernatural characters can emerge. The proximity of the audience seating creates an intimacy between the actor and spectators, and this mood is heightened by *kakegoe*, the shouting out of an actor's name by audience members to show appreciation of his adroitness.

Most kabuki programmes feature one jidaimono, one dance and one sewamono, or, less often, a full-length play.

he developed a brash, bravura, bombastic style of acting called *aragoto*, literally 'rough business'. By contrast, in Kansai (present-day Kyoto/Osaka/Kobe region) Sakata Tojuro (1647-1709) practised *wagoto*, a softer, more feminine style used to portray gentle, romantic heroes. Both of these styles are still practised today.

Kabuki's repertoire includes plays taken from the puppet theatre, dances and acts copied from the noh theatre, as well as plays written especially for kabuki. In the 1900s, under the influence of Western drama, *Shin-Kabuki* (New Kabuki) emerged. These were kabuki plays without the *ka* (song, that is narrative recitation and the use of *shamisen*, hand drums and wooden clappers) or the *bu* (dance and stylised fight scenes), leaving only the *ki* ([acting) skill). These are still frequently performed.

Nevertheless, despite kabuki's rich history and refined artistic techniques, the fact is that the majority of Japanese people have never seen it. Kabuki has somehow gained a reputation with the general populace for being boring and difficult to understand. Because of this, some kabuki actors are experimenting with new ways of energising their art. In particular, since 1986, Ichikawa Ennosuke (1939-) has been producing 'Super-Kabuki' spectaculars. Branded by some as a heretic, Ichikawa has sought to recapture the excitement of Edo-period kabuki by reviving various theatrical stunts from that period, such as flying on wires over the heads of the audience to the top floor of the theatre and using cascades of real water on stage. His productions use modern Japanese with speeded-up delivery, hi-tech special effects, dynamic lighting, stunning costumes and minimalist sets. His shows have proved hugely popular with people who would never normally set foot in a kabuki theatre.

The beginning of the popularity of samurai dramas came in the Taisho period (1912-26), when popular novels were adapted for the stage and the New National Theatre was founded by the actor Sawada Shojiro (1892-1929). His troupe produced historical dramas about popular outlaw heroes and emphasised *chambara* (swordplay). After World War II the Occupation forces discouraged chambara and any other historical dramas with feudalistic themes, but since the 1950s they have returned, albeit with a more limited audience.

Western cultural influences have been felt in Japan since the Meiji period (1868-1911), but the flood of Western music, films, plays and musicals that has filled Japan since the end of World War II has affected the choice of material presented in the theatre. A relatively small number of modern domestic dramas are written and produced, but Japanese versions of existing Western plays and musicals account for the majority of productions in commercial theatres.

Samurai & historical dramas

The most frequently portrayed type of historical drama on stage are *jidai geki*, which literally means period dramas, but in practice refers to samurai dramas set in the Edo period. Unlike in kabuki, female roles are played by women.

No matter how tragic, jidai geki must end with a satisfactory resolution, a kind of release, whether it is the successful revenge of a murder or the ascent into heaven of the dead heroine aloft a podium with smoke billowing around her spotlit body.

Modern dramas & musicals

Famous western plays and musicals translated into Japanese are the major source for domestic modern theatre productions. In particular, the New National Theatre in the Opera City complex provides a forum for the most respected Japanese directors, who take a contemporary approach to western classics and other productions.

Musicals are particularly popular and are often staged annually. Long-time favourites include *Fiddler on the Roof* and *The Wizard of Oz*.

There is also a thriving underground avant-garde theatre subculture in the suburb of Shimo-Kitazawa (*see page 65*), with dozens of small venues.

For a city as cosmopolitan as Tokyo, it may come as a surprise to learn that only a handful of productions in English are available each year, and some of those are possible only because of touring troupes from Britain or America.

Theatres to visit

Kabuki-za

4-12-15 Ginza, Chuo-ku (info 3541 3131/box office 5565 6000). Higashi-Ginza station. **Box office** 10am-6pm daily. **Tickets** ¥2,520-¥16,800. **Credit** AmEx, DC, JCB, MC, V. **Map 7**
The best place to see kabuki. An English-language programme (¥1,000) and earphone guide (¥650 plus a refundable deposit of ¥1,000) are invaluable. Performances last up to five hours, including intervals. Tickets to watch one act from the fourth floor can be bought from one hour beforehand. The earphone guide cannot be used on the fourth floor.

Tips for theatregoing

Most theatre tickets go on sale one month or more before the day of the performance. Most theatres reserve a small number of tickets to be sold on the day of the performance, but be sure to get to the box office early.

Theatre doors usually open 20 to 30 minutes before curtain up. There is no bar in Japanese theatres, although some do sell Japanese sake and cans of beer. Almost every theatre has stalls selling a variety of goods, souvenirs and food. Biscuits or sweet bean-filled cakes featuring the star's face are common, as well as sweatshirts, ties, towels, handkerchiefs, lighters, keyrings and other items bearing the star's autograph, name or face.

Theatres have their own restaurants and also sell boxed meals, but eating this way can be costly. Take your own food and drink to save expense. Soft drinks and beverages are available from service counters or vending machines at all theatres. If you do want to eat in the restaurant, make a reservation as soon as you arrive at the theatre.

Be forewarned that many theatres still have only one or two Western-style toilets, and the remainder are the Japanese squat type (see chapter **Directory**).

Lastly, do not expect to sit and watch a performance in silence. Theatregoing is a social outing, and Japanese people go armed with packed meals, flasks and rustling vinyl bags full of goodies. In many theatres, eating in the theatre seat during or between acts, and making comments on the players and their performances during the show, is all part of the enjoyment. Tokyo audiences are much quieter now than they were 20 years ago, but they can still be noisy by Western standards. Be warned – shushing will have little effect, so instead of getting irritated, sit back and enjoy the experience.

Koma Gekijo

1-19-1 Kabuki-cho, Shinjuku-ku (3200 2213).
Shinjuku station. **Box office** 10am-6pm daily.
Tickets ¥2,600-¥11,000. **Credit** JCB, V. **Map 3b**
A famous theatre with a revolving stage. Most performers are famous singers who appear in a period drama, then give a concert. No English.

Meiji-za

2-31-1 Nihonbashi-hamacho, Chuo-ku (3660 3939).
Hamacho station. **Box office** 10am-5pm daily.
Tickets ¥5,000-¥12,000. **Credit** DC, JCB, V.
Usually stages samurai dramas, often starring actors who play similar roles on TV. No English.

National Theatre Large Hall

4-1 Hayabusa-cho, Chiyoda-ku (3230 3000).
Hanzomon station. **Box office** 10am-6pm daily.
Tickets ¥1,500-¥9,500. No credit cards. **Map 16**
Kabuki is staged approximately eight months a year in the Large Hall. The programme (¥800) includes the story in English; an earphone guide is available.

National Theatre Small Hall

4-1 Hayabusa-cho, Chiyoda-ku (3230 3000).
Hanzomon station. **Box office** 10am-6pm daily.
Tickets ¥4,800-¥5,800. No credit cards. **Map 16**
Bunraku for about four months a year. Programme with story in English and earphone guide.

National Noh Theatre

4-18-1 Sendagaya, Shibuya-ku (3423 1331).
Sendagaya station. **Box office** 10am-6pm daily.
Tickets ¥2,300-¥4,300. No credit cards. **Map 17**
Noh performances four or five times a month. A one-page explanation of the story in English is available.

Shinbashi Embujo

6-18-2 Ginza, Chuo-ku (3541 2600). Higashi-Ginza station. **Box office** 10am-6pm daily. **Tickets** ¥2,100-¥15,750. **Credit** AmEx, DC, JCB, MC, V. **Map 13**
Programme features English explanation of story when Ichikawa Ennosuke stages his 'Super-Kabuki' (usually April–May). Samurai dramas other months.

Takarazuka

3-8-3 Marunouchi, Chiyoda-ku (5251 2001).
Yurakucho station. **Box office** 10am-6pm Mon, Tue, Thur-Sun. **Tickets** ¥2,000-¥8,000. No credit cards. **Map 7**
Musicals by glam all-female review troupes. Programme includes the story in English.

Western theatres

Panasonic Globe-za

3-1-2 Hyakunincho, Shinjuku-ku (info in English 3360 3540/box office in Japanese 3360 3240).
Shin-Okubo station. **Box office** 10am-6pm Mon-Fri.
Tickets ¥4,000-¥8,000. No credit cards. **Map 25**
Performances in English for ten days each in June and October by visiting UK Shakespearean actors.

Tokyo International Players

c/o The Asia Foundation, 32 Kowa Building 2F, 5-2 Minami Azabu, Minato-ku (3447 1981/fax 3447 3842). Hiroo station. No credit cards.
Keen amateurs. Season (late September to late May) includes UK and US plays, musicals and readings. Productions are in English and usually take place at the Tokyo American Club (see Map 2).
Website: www2.gol.com/users/tip

Trips Out of Town

Yokohama 横浜

A bright future is taking shape in Japan's second biggest city.

The port of Yokohama, about 30 minutes' train ride out of Tokyo, is the second largest city in the country. It was here that Japan was forced to end its international isolation and open itself up to foreign trade in the nineteenth century, and the centre of Yokohama is dotted with architectural remnants of that period, from waterside warehouses to banks in the business quarter.

Despite its population of over 3.25 million, Yokohama exudes a sense of spaciousness that Tokyo often lacks, largely thanks to its glorious waterfront position. Like Liverpool or San Francisco, Yokohama is also home to a large immigrant community, and it boasts the largest Chinatown in Japan. The newly developed waterfront area also has some of the most striking modern architecture in the country.

HOW TO GET THERE

Yokohama is on a peninsula facing the western coast of Tokyo Bay, just 30 kilometres (18.6 miles) south-west of Tokyo. It's very easy to get to from Tokyo: Shin-Yokohama station is only one stop and 17 minutes on the main Tokyo-Osaka *shinkansen* (bullet train) line, or it takes 25 minutes from Tokyo station to Yokohama station on the JR Tokaido line (cheaper than the shinkansen). The JR Keihin Tohoku and JR Yokosuka lines also go to Yokohama station. Another option is the Toyoko line, which goes from Shibuya to Yokohama (25 minutes) and Sakuragi-cho (30 minutes). It's also easily reached from Narita International Airport by both bus and train (Sogo line). For Kannai and Ishikawa-cho stations change to JR Negishi line at Yokohama station.

Tourist information

Yokohama Kanko Convention Bureau

1-1 Sakuragi-cho, Naka-ku (045 211 0111).
Sakuragi-cho station. **Open** 10am-6pm Mon-Fri;
9am-9pm Sat, Sun.
Next to Sakuragi-cho station, YKCB has free maps of the Yokohama area and several English-speaking staff members. Maps are also available in Tokyo from the Tourist Centre in Yurakucho (*see chapter* **Directory**). The Sanbo Centre branch is open Monday-Friday and has one English-speaker.
Branch: 1F, Sanbo Centre, 2 Yamashita-cho, Naka-ku (045 641 5824).

Yokohama's neon-lit **Chinatown** *is Japan's largest.*

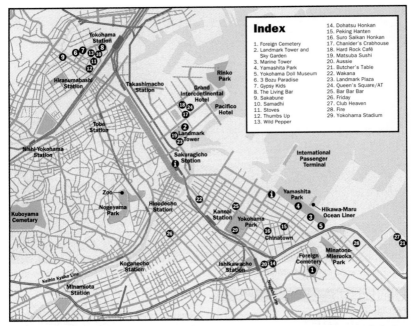

In context

History

Yokohama was little more than a small fishing village when special US envoy Commodore Perry arrived in his black ships in 1853 and demanded that Japan open itself up to international trade, ending 300 years of self-imposed national isolation. Under threat of force, the Japanese government signed the US-Japan Treaty of Amity in 1858, opening the port of Yokohama the following year. A tax office was set up to deal with trade and to serve as a boundary dividing the village up into two areas: a southern, foreign quarter for traders and their families (now the Motomachi and Yamate areas) and a northern, Japanese area. A period of mutual distrust followed, glamourised in the popular James Clavell book *Gaijin*. In 1868 the Edo shogunate was overthrown and replaced by the Meiji government, who believed that to compete with foreigners they had to learn and employ their secrets instead of trying to ignore them.

Yokohama subsequently underwent a wave of modernisation, quickly developing into a major trading port. The first railway in Japan was built between Shinbashi in Tokyo to Yokohama, as Yokohama rapidly became Japan's window onto the outside world. Development seemed, then as now, to be the buzzword in Yokohama. It became a city in 1889, when its population exceeded 120,000, and despite two major calamities that occurred during the twentieth century, it has developed into a port that more foreign vessels enter and that more domestic exports leave than any other in Japan.

Yokohama today

Modern Yokohama has a dream, the 'Yumehama 2010 Plan' (literally, 'Dream Yokohama 2010 Programme'). This vision of a bright tomorrow, which aims at 'fulfilling…residents' dreams' and creating a 'lovely resonance', has culminated in a programme of aggressive urban development. Centred in and around the bay area, it is starting to take shape with the completion of the Minato Mirai 21 (21 as in the new century) area and its stunning skyline. At present one is never more than a stone's throw away from the construction and the port with its tankers, gantries and warehouses, so a certain suspension of disbelief is required if you want to enjoy the bayfront area. The relative sanctuaries of the Chinatown and Motomachi communities do offer some respite, so if you crave escape from the relentless Japanese industrial machine, these are the places you should head for.

*Millennial magic at **Minato Mirai 21**, Yokohama's dream made reality for the next century.*

Sightseeing

Foreign Cemetery

126 Yamate-cho, Naka-ku (045 622 1311). Ishikawa-cho station, then a 15-min walk. **Open** 10am-5pm Tue-Sun. Closed Monday and the day after national holidays. **Admission** free.

Originally established in 1854 for the burial of US sailors from the fleet that accompanied Commodore Perry, the foreign cemetery is now the last resting place of some 4,500 souls from more than 40 countries, dating from the founding of the trading settlement. A rather austere and sombre place, but still interesting in a creepy kind of way. The display in the exhibition hall catalogues the achievements of the foreign settlement in Yamate, one of the first areas in modern Japan to be settled by foreigners.

Hakkeijima Sea Paradise

Hakkeijima, Kanazawa-ku (045 788 8888). Hakkeijima station (Kanazawa Seaside line), then a two-min walk. **Open** 8.30am-10.30pm daily (winter times subject to change; call for details). **Admission** *Aqua Museum only* ¥2,450; ¥1,400 6-15s; ¥700 under-5s. *Rides* ¥300-¥1,000. *Pass to Aqua Museum & riding passport* ¥4,300; ¥3,800 school age; ¥3,000 children.

An artificial island with an array of attractions, including a 'white-knuckle' Jet Coaster and the 107-m (350-ft) 'Blue Fall' freefall ride. The impressive Aqua Museum is in the pyramid at the corner of the island; as well as having a jaw-dropping escalator ride up through one of the biggest indoor aquariums in the world, it also puts on free shows featuring killer whales, dolphins and an annoying group of singing and dancing aqua-girls.

Landmark Tower & Sky Garden

2-2-1-1 Minato-Mirai, Nishi-ku (045 222 5030). Sakuragi-cho station, then a five-min walk. **Open** *(Sky Garden)* Oct-June 10am-9pm, July-Sept 10am-10pm daily. **Admission** ¥1,000; ¥500-¥800 concs.

At 296m (970ft) and 70 storeys in height, Japan's tallest building is visible for miles around. In the years since its completion in 1993 it's become the symbol of the new Yokohama. The earpopping lift ride to the 69th floor is the fastest in the world: at 750m a minute, it takes just 35 seconds to reach the top. Vertigo sufferers should check out the highest observatory in Japan, the confusingly named Sky Garden (there is no garden).

Marine Tower

15 Yamashita-cho, Naka-ku (045 641 7838). Ishikawa-cho station, then a 15-min walk. **Open** 10am-9.30pm Sun-Thur; 10am-10pm Fri, Sat. **Admission** ¥700; ¥350 children; ¥250 small children.

Opposite Yamashita Park, this decagonal inland lighthouse was built to commemorate the centenary of the Port of Yokohama and offers an unexciting and uninspiring view of the area, largely because taller buildings have been built around it. Its amusement arcade has seen better days.

Sankeien Garden

58-1 Honmoku-Sannotani, Naka-ku (045 621 0635). Bus 8 or 125 from Sakuragi-cho station, alight at Honmoku Sankeien-mae; bus 8 or 25 from Yokohama station (platform 2 station East Exit). **Open** 9am-5pm (outer garden), 9am-4.30pm (inner garden) daily except 29-31 Dec. **Admission** *outer garden* ¥300;¥60 children; *inner garden* ¥300;¥120 children).

A beautiful, traditional Japanese garden that was constructed by a wealthy silk merchant in 1906. The extensive grounds contain the famous Rinshun-kaku, which was built by shogun Tokugawa Yoshinobu, a three-storey pagoda and a number of other historical buildings from Kyoto and Nara designated as national cultural properties. In autumn this is one of the best gardens in Japan to see leaves changing colour from green to red and yellow, while in winter the garden comes alive with plum blossoms, and crowds jostling to see them.

Yamashita Park

Yamashita Koen, Yamashita-cho, Naka-ku. **Open** *park* 24 hours daily; *Hikawa-Maru* 9.30am-8pm daily; *winter* 9.30am-7pm daily. **Admission** ¥800; ¥400 children. Bay cruises from the park ¥1,400;¥700 children (60-min cruise); ¥2,000/¥1,250 children (90-min cruise).

A mediocre bayside park that, in the evening, becomes a mecca for amorous couples too young to have their own apartment and too poor to afford a love hotel. Winter winds are arctic but a toothless man sells hot sake from a stall inside the park. The cruise ship *Hikawa-Maru,* anchored in front of the park, once ruled the waves between Japan and America: its luxurious interior, much still in its original condition, is open to the public, including the guestroom once used by Charlie Chaplin. This may be the closest you'll come to seeing how life was aboard the *Titanic,* whose most famous pose tourists are constantly imitating on the prow. Take a stroll on deck, and peek in through the windows of the old captain's cabin. Next to this is a pier from which a number of boats set out on bay cruises. A riverbus service can ferry you to Yokohama station in around 20 minutes.

Yokohama Bay Bridge & Sky Walk

1 Daikoku-Futo, Tsurumi-ku (045 506 0500). Bus 109 from No.6 bus terminal at east exit of Sakuragicho station. **Open** *Sky Walk* 9.30am-8pm Wed-Mon (10am-6pm Wed-Mon Oct-Mar). Closed Tue, and Wed if Tue is a national holiday. **Admission** ¥500; ¥300 children.

This 860-metre high (2,823-ft) monster is the gateway to the Port of Yokohama. The 360-metre (1,080-ft) Sky Walk promenade leading to the observatory slung under the bridge is, like the Landmark Tower (*see above*), an absolute must for height junkies.

Yokohama Doll Museum

18 Yamashita-cho, Naka-ku (045 671 9361). Ishikawa-cho station, then a 13-min walk. **Open** 10am-5pm Tue-Sun; *mid-July-Aug* 10am-6.30pm Tue-Sun. Closed Tue when Mon is a national holiday. **Admission** ¥300; ¥150 children (Red Shoes Theatre puppet show requires extra fee).

The Yokohama Doll Museum is the biggest dolls' house in the world, populated by more than 9,000 dolls from 135 countries. Check out the Iranian doll looking like a bald action man with a bizarre Freddie Mercury 'tache. The dynamic puppet show is definitely worth a look.

Yokohama by neighbourhood

Yokohama

Whichever exit you take from the station, you're likely to find yourself lost in the bowels of a department store before being belched out into the sunlight, such is the nature of this area, with branches of most large shops and department stores crowded around, behind, under and on top of the station. Try not to wander aimlessly or you may get lost. Besides being the main shopping area in Yokohama it's also the entertainment centre, with hundreds of bars and restaurants. This is undiscovered country for many Tokyo-ites, so take the time out to visit and sample the nightlife.

Sakuragi-cho/Minato Mirai 21

The town planners' vision of a twenty-first-century Utopia (hence the name Minato Mirai 21), this is certainly awe-inspiring. As you exit the station you see the neck-aching Landmark Tower directly ahead and fanning out to its right the triple towers of the Queen's Square complex, the Pan Pacific Hotel, the sail-like Pacifico Yokohama and the world's largest ferris wheel. Packed with shops and restaurants, and a great place to spend a day.

Kannai/Chinatown

The most that can be said for Kannai is that it's close to Yokohama Stadium and a only a ten-minute walk to Chinatown (follow the signs). On the far side of Chinatown you arrive at the Yamashita Park area and the attractions there. Between the station and bayfront are plenty of bars, coffee shops and restaurants.

Motomachi

Touted as a trendy shopping area, Motomachi shopping street is lined with boutiques, pâtisseries, delis and coffee shops. It's a good place to relax and people-watch, to explore the sidestreets with their Eurasian feel. It also offers walking access to the city's best clubs and restaurants, hidden in the ugly industrial area of Shin-Yamashita, some 20 minutes' walk from Ishikawa-cho station. Catch a taxi from the station's main entrance; it takes five minutes and costs around ¥800 (more on Friday and Saturday nights).

Consumer

Yokohama has been an important gateway to the world since the port opened in 1859. Japan's first western-style hotel and restaurant were opened here, and the city also saw Japan's first bakery. Together with the influx of Chinese, this means that Yokohama has a selection of food and entertainment to rival that of Tokyo. You may have to look a little harder, but the scene in Yokohama is well worth sampling.

Bars & restaurants

In Japan people like to eat when they drink, so bars are also usually to some degree restaurants and vice versa. Almost every restaurant and bar gets busy from 7pm onwards, so be prepared to wait for up to 30 minutes. Expect to pay a *sekiriyou* (seating charge) or *otoshidai* (cover charge), usually around ¥300 per head, in bars. Some places charge for both and there may also be a maximum stay of two hours.

In & around Yokohama station

3 Bozu Paradise

Taiyou Bldg 1F, 2-20-12 Minami-saiwai, Nishi-ku (045 320 3066). **Open** 5pm-midnight daily. **Credit** AmEx, DC, JCB, MC, V. **Average** ¥3,500.
An Italian restaurant disguised as a horror museum. Original cocktails include Dracula's Fangs (wait for the shot of Dracula's blood from a meaty looking syringe), Freddie and Frankenstein's Love. You might feel like you're being buried alive when there are more than ten people eating, the food is overpriced and under par and the service is truly shocking. The bathroom is worth a visit, though, so maybe have a quick tour of the place then leave.

Gypsy Kids

Taiyou Bldg 1F, 2-20-12 Minami-saiwai, Nishi-ku (045 314 4994). **Open** 5pm-midnight daily.
Credit AmEx, DC, JCB, MC, V. **Average** ¥3,500.
The Mexican brother of 3 Bozu Paradise (*see above*), this fares better on the service stakes and has a homely Latin tinge. There are vegetarian options, while carnivores can feast on Oh! Chinchin (which roughly translates as Oh! Dick). The servings are a little on the stingy side. There's no English menu but the manager speaks a little English. Between 7pm and 9pm expect to wait for up to 30 minutes. There's a ¥300 seating charge. Original cocktails worth trying are Mineruba and Pandra.

Laffits

YT16 Bldg 5F, 2-16-2 Tsuruya-cho, Kanagawa-ku (045 322 3232). **Open** 7pm-4am daily; *happy hour* 5-7pm Sun-Tue. **Credit** DC, JCB, MC, V.
Average ¥2,500.
If feasting beside dead poker-playing pirates is your idea of fun, you'll fit right in at Laffits. From the full-size, wooden-legged Blackbeard at the door to the skull and crossbones flag on the wall and Death cigarettes on sale at the bar, this is pirate world. The service is a tad slow but the food is good. Sample the fantastic seafood salad. During happy hour everything is half price. There's no English menu but staff speak enough English to help you make a choice.

The Living Bar

Miyamoto Bldg 2F, 1-10-3 Minami-saiwai, Nishi-ku (045 311 5125). **Open** 5.30-11.30pm Mon-Thur; 5.30pm-2am Fri, Sat; 5-11.30pm Sun & holidays.
Credit AmEx, DC, JCB, MC, V. **Average** ¥2,500.
Classy joint with such a whiff of European elegance it's hard to believe it's part of a chain. Excellent service from the alert staff. Killer fondue for two at only ¥1,800 and some of the nicest cocktails in the city. There's a two-hour stay limit on weekends. Cover charge is ¥300, including a bread stick appetiser.

Sakabune

1-5-6 Sengen-cho, Nishi-ku (045 411 0810). **Open** 5pm-1am Thur-Tue. **No credit cards**. **Average** ¥3,500.
A cosy Japanese restaurant with a reputation for fresh fish. The owner buys from fishermen in Yamaguchi Prefecture on Kyushu, a two-hour flight away. The menu ranges from tempura to seasonal vegetables and Korean-style yakitori (try the original *tsukune*, a kind of chicken kebab). Dishes range from a reasonable ¥500 to the ¥2,000 'flat fish' sashimi, a speciality. Reserve in advance.

Samadhi

1-10-8 Minami-saiwai, Nishi-ku (045 311 4422). **Open** 5.30pm-midnight daily. **Credit** AmEx, JCB, MC, V. **Average** ¥3,000.
It defies belief seeing how many people can comfortably fit into a space the size of the average European front room. Samadhi does it and does it well, with a tree-house theme seating upwards of 40 people as deep reggae, house and hip hop plus subtle lighting take you to somewhere altogether more relaxing. In its 20-year history, Samadhi has become an institution in Yokohama, so between 7pm and 10pm you might have to wait up to an hour for a table. It's worth the wait, and the seating charge and snack charge totalling ¥600. Last orders for food are at 10.30pm, 11pm for alcohol.

Stoves

2-1-13 Minami-saiwai, Nishi-ku (045 312 2203). **Open** 4pm-2am Mon-Fri; noon-2am Sat, Sun, holidays. **No credit cards**. **Average** ¥3,000.
A laid-back hippie groove with a staff of Japanese deadheads and a background of '60s and '70s music make this an appetising place to eat. The usual American bar and grill menu but some exceptional, original cocktails: try wrestling with an Indian Death Lock. The 70 seats are packed with hungry customers nightly between 7pm and 10pm. A wait of 20-30 minutes is not uncommon, and there's a ¥300 seat charge.

Thumbs Up

Sohtetsu Movil 3F, 2-1-22 Minami-saiwai, Nishi-ku (045 314 8705). **Open** noon-2am daily.
Credit MC, V. **Average** ¥3,000.
Another branch of the Stoves empire (*see above*), this serves up the same fare but throws in a generous helping of live music and a drunken atmosphere. Watch Japanese rockabillies snarling out *Blue Suede Shoes* one night and jazz hipsters a *Blues Brothers* tribute the next. The crowd of students, salarymen and *gaijin* love it, and it's been known for the whole place to get up and get down. There's no music on Sunday. Be prepared to wait between 7pm and 10pm and pay a ¥300 seat charge.

Chinatown

Dancing in the Chinese New Year.

Step through any of four dazzling entrance gates and you'll be transported into what feels like the set of a Jackie Chan movie, with pagoda-style buildings coated in vibrant gold and red, fresh produce cascading from tiny stalls into narrow streets, and cooks and stall-holders haggling over the price of today's catch. There's also a range of fascinating shops selling clothing, knick-knacks and retro-style goods imported from the People's Republic.

But the main reason to visit Chinatown is the food: the aroma permeating the streets from the countless tiny restaurants serving up Cantonese, Peking, Shanghai, Hunan and Szechwan dishes is overpowering. Try a plump *niku-man* meat roll from a street-vendor: look for the huge bamboo steamers at the roadside, and expect to pay around ¥300. In the centre of the town sits Kantei-Byo temple, the symbol of Chinatown. Dedicated to the Chinese God of Business, the glittering structure is best visited at night when illuminated.

In mid-February Chinatown plays host to the Chinese New Year Celebrations, which last about a week. If you're lucky enough to be here at the right time, you'll see famed 'dragon dancers' as parading the streets collecting green packages containing money.

Chinatown is seven minutes' walk from Ishikawa-cho station on the JR Negishi line.

Wild Pepper

Ginzaya Bldg 5F, 2-7-8 Minami-saiwai, Nishi-ku (045 314 4444). **Open** 5pm-3am daily; *happy hour* 5-7pm. **No credit cards**. **Average** ¥2,500.
An indoor jungle. As the name suggests, every dish is hot, with garlic, chilli or spicy sauce. Basic Chinese and Korean dishes are the speciality, and there's a handwritten English menu. At weekends there's a two-hour limit. During happy hour, only food is half price, but it's also worth trying some of the cocktails, including the Dennis Hopper. Arrive just before 7pm to order half-price food until 9pm.

Chinatown

Dohatsu Honkan

1-48 Ishikawa-cho, Naka-ku (045 681 7273). **Open** 11.30am-9.30pm daily. **Credit** DC, V. **Average** ¥5,000.
Delicious Cantonese fare in a cosy atmosphere. Popular for its Hong Kong-style seafood dishes: at lunchtime customers jostle for seats as the strict *mama-san* at the door tries to keep everyone in check.

Peking Hanten

79 Yamashita-cho, Naka-ku (045 681 3535/fax 045 681 8489). **Open** 11.30am-2am daily. **Credit** AmEx, DC, JCB, V. **Average** ¥3,000.
This charming restaurant claims to be the first in Japan to serve Peking duck, the house speciality. A whole duck costs about ¥13,000; smaller portions are ¥2,000. There's an English-language menu with pictures – you'll need it, as the staff here take the art of nonchalance to new levels. The lunchtime special courses, served from 11.30am to 2pm, are ¥1,000 and ¥1,500 respectively, but this menu is in Japanese only. Busy times are noon-2pm and 6-8pm.

Suro Saikan Honkan

190 Yamashita-cho, Naka-ku (045 681 3456). **Open** 11.30am-midnight daily. **Credit** AmEx, DC, JCB, MC, V. **Average** ¥4,000.
A little hard to find but worth the effort for its quality Shanghai cuisine at reasonable prices. The huge fried carp for ¥3,300 is probably the best deal. The Chinese chef, Son Kanri, was a long-running winner on the Japanese TV show *Ryoori no Tetsujin* (*Cooking Championship*). Expect to wait at lunch.

Minato Mirai 21

Chandler's Crabhouse

202 Queen's Square, 2-3-8 Minato Mirai, Nishi-ku (045 682 2805). **Open** 11am-10pm daily. **Credit** AmEx, DC, JCB, MC, V. **Average** lunch ¥1,200; dinner ¥3,500.
Yokohama incarnation of the famous Seattle-based seafood restaurant, serving up some of the freshest seafood on the planet. It can become crowded between noon and 1.30pm and from 7pm; a 20-minute wait is usual. There's an English-language menu. The smoked seafood sampler (¥3,680, serves four), the most popular dish in the house, contains five kinds of sea fare. The lunch special of old-fashioned clam chowder, grilled halibut and Dungeness crab cake costs only ¥2,500, and is delicious. Fish fans can buy a Chandler's Crabhouse fish tie.

Hard Rock Café

Yokohama Queen's Tower A-1F, 2-3 Minato Mirai, Nishi-ku (045 682 5626). **Open** 11am-11.30pm Sun-Thur; 11am-4am Fri, Sat. **Credit** AmEx, BC, DC, JCB, MC, V. **Average** lunch ¥1,000; dinner ¥2,500.

The largest plates of nachos you've ever seen and half-price cocktails between 4pm and 6pm from Monday to Friday. Has a superior collection of rock memorabilia, including Jimi Hendrix's Woodstock bandana and some Beatles stuff.

Matsuba Sushi
Landmark Tower 1F, 2-2 Minato Mirai, Nishi-ku (045 222 526). **Open** 11.30am-10pm daily. **Credit** DC, JCB, MC, V. **Average** lunch ¥1,000; dinner ¥3,000.
A favourite of girls who lunch, Matsuba serves up its top-quality sushi in unusually decorative ways. Even at dinner time, the prices shouldn't put too much of a dent in your wallet.

Motomachi/Ishikawa-cho station

Aussie
1-12 Ishikawa-cho, Naka-ku (045 681 3671). **Open** 5pm-midnight daily; *happy hour* 5-7pm. **Credit** AmEx, JCB, MC, V. **Average** ¥3,500.
This little restaurant has gained a big reputation, receiving several visits from the Australian ambassador. It serves anything Australian, the most popular dish being barbecued kangaroo and crocodile. It's often packed by 7.30pm: get here early for half-price wine, then sit back and soak up the hearty atmosphere. Take the smaller exit from Ishikawa-cho station, turning left and walking past the post office. Aussie is on the left side of the street.

Butcher's Table
3-7 Shin-Yamashita, Naka-ku (045 622 6084). **Open** 6pm-3am Mon-Fri; 5pm-4am Sat & day before national holiday; 4pm-3am Sun & holidays. **Credit** AmEx, DC, JCB, MC, V. **Average** ¥2,500.
Once you've negotiated the surrounding industrial wasteland you'll find yourself in a cavernous restaurant that's packed with a funky crowd but never seems to have much of an atmosphere, despite the blaring hip hop and house. The food is a cheap but uninspiring selection of trad Tex-Mex and American dishes. You may have to wait to be seated on Saturday nights as the place gets packed out with people intending to move on, to dance the night and early morning away in Club Heaven (*see below*) next door later in the evening.

*Funky fare at **Butcher's Table**.*

Wakana
5-20 Minato-cho, Naka-ku (045 681 1404). Kannai station. **Open** 11am-9pm Thur-Tue. **No credit cards**. **Average** ¥2,700.
If you visit Japan during the hot, sticky summer months, you might like to try the Japanese remedy: eel, or *unagi*, the speciality of this small restaurant. Japanese people believe the vitamins contained in eel help combat the sapping effects of the heat and humidity. Here you can sample its restorative effects in over 120 different sauces.

Elsewhere

Shin-Yokohama Ramen Museum
2-14-21 Shin-Yokohama, Kohoku-ku, Yokohama (045 471 0503). **Open** 11am-11pm Wed-Mon (& national holiday Tue). **Average** ¥800. **No credit cards**. No English menu.
Not technically a restaurant, but fans of ramen, the film *Tampopo* or 1950s Japanalia should make a pilgrimage to the world's only museum dedicated to the humble noodle. Between exhibits, collections and a painstaking replica of a *shitamachi* neighbourhood of 1958 are eight ramen shops from the four major ramen centres, Sapporo, Hakata, Kumamoto and Kyoto, plus four Tokyo/Yokohama shops. Each serves several different types of ramen representative of its region: Sumire, a branch of a famous Sapporo shop, specialises in miso ramen; Komurasaki, the Kumamoto shop, specialises in *tonkotsu*, a broth simmered till the pork has melted to a creamy, white soup. Can't decide? Get a three- or six-month free pass and try them all.

Shopping

Landmark Plaza
2-2-1 Minato-Mirai, Nishi-ku (045 222 5015). Sakuragi-cho station. **Open** 11am-8pm daily; *restaurants/cafés* hours vary. **Credit** varies.
Babbling brooks and soothing grand piano recitals provide entertainment and distraction from the hard slog of trawling five floors of shops ranging from Michel Klein to Octopus Army. Relief comes at every turn, with restaurants, cafés and coffee shops. The Dockyard Garden, a restoration of former Yokohama Dock no. 2, offers the best Japanese and western lunch options (follow the signs and don't be fazed when you have to walk through the underground car park – you're going the right way). Try the New Tokyo Beer Dock (B1F; 045 222 5626) for draught beer direct from the brewery.

Queen's Square/AT
2-3 Minato Mirai, Nishi-ku (045 682 1000). Sakuragi-cho station. **Open** *shops* 11am-8pm daily; *restaurants/cafés* times vary. **Credit** varies.
Chimes gently greet you from deftly positioned speakers as you enter from the Landmark Plaza side, and on the hour expect an unearthly sound only describable as bell ringers on acid. At the heart of the complex is a cavernous atrium stretching from

basement level three to the fifth floor, lined with all kinds of cuisine. Try the 'all you can eat' 11am-2pm lunch special at Khazana Indian Restaurant (B1; 045 682 2873) for only ¥980. An abundance of upmarket shopping, a concert hall and an abundance of decorative indoor greenery make this an extremely relaxing place to shop.

Yokohama Bayside Marina

5-2 Shiraho, Kanazawa-ku (045 775 4446/fax 045 775 4446). Torihama station. **Open** 10am-8pm daily. **Credit** varies.

A Legoland-style bayside village. Great bargains year round on major labels, including Guess, Timberland and Nike. Sample lunch specials in one of eight quayside restaurants. The Bayside Deli (045 770 5230) has a filling burger set for ¥1,000. Expect to wait up to 20 minutes for lunch in some restaurants; if you can't, try the street stalls between the Wine Warehouse and Supermarket at the far end of the shopping building. Crammed at weekends so head out on a weekday. Take the Keihin-Tohoku line from Yokohama station, get off at Shinsugita station and transfer to the Seaside line (monorail). Get off at Torihama station (two stops) and follow the stream of shoppers.

Arts & Entertainment

Live music

Bar Bar Bar

Wakaba Unyu Bldg 1 2F, 1-25 Aioi-cho, Naka-ku (045 662 6868). Kannai station. **Open** 6pm-3am Mon-Sat; 5pm-midnight Sun & holidays.

Jazz, blues and pop, by mainly local artists, four times a day from 7.30pm. There's a table charge (¥500) and music charge (from ¥600).

Friday

Sagamiya Bldg 3F, 8-123 Chojamachi, Naka-ku (045 252 8033). Isezaki-chojamachi station.
Open 6pm-1am daily.

This '60s American-style live house provides retro live music on a daily basis. Drinks are relatively cheap, from ¥600.

Yokohama Arena

3-10 Shin-Yokohama, Kohoku-ku (045 474 4000). Shin-Yokohama station.

One of Japan's largest multipurpose arenas, seating 17,000 people. Recent acts who have graced the stage here include the Beastie Boys and Whitney Houston. Tickets for live concerts by international bands are expensive, around ¥7,000 (¥4,000 for domestic acts), and are available through the usual agencies (*see p204*). This is also a popular venue for pro-wrestling events. To get there, take the east exit from the station, keeping the cylindrical Prince Hotel on your right. The arena is on the left side.

Nightlife

Club Heaven

3-7 Shin-Yamashita, Naka-ku (045 622 6042/fax 045 622 6084). Ishikawa-cho station. **Open** 9pm-5am Fri-Sat. **Admission** ¥2,000 (includes one drink).

A pick-up joint for the US military. Drinks are cheap (a ¥1,000 drink ticket buys two), presumably to get you so drunk you don't notice the shoddy décor. The staple musical diet is hip hop, reggae, R&B and hardcore, with occasional foreign DJs. Bikers, rastas and dolled-up high-school girls party in the car park from about midnight. Come here to find a date, not if you already have one. There's no dress code.

Fire

1-14-24 Shin-Yamashita, Naka-ku (045 621 0818/fax 045 621 1828). Ishikawa-cho station. **Open** 10pm-5am Wed-Sat. **Admission** ¥3,000 (includes two drinks).

'We expect only formal wear; if you are not Japanese you have to be with a lady' reads a sign at the entrance of Yokohama's newest and hippest club. Saturdays regularly see a 1,000-strong crowd of beautiful people going crazy. Drinks are quite cheap. The best way to get here is by car Shuto Expressway Kanagawa line no.3 to Shin-Yamashita) or taxi (around ¥800 from Ishikawa-cho station).

Sport

Yokohama Stadium

Yokohama Koen, Naka-ku (045 661 1251). Kannai station. **Admission** varies.

The first amphitheatre-style stadium with movable seats in Japan. Seats 30,000 and is home to the BayStars, the Central League Baseball Champions in 1998. The season is March-October but you can catch pre-season games from mid/late February.

International Stadium Yokohama

3302 Kozukue-cho, Kohoku-ku (045 477 5000). Kozukue station, then a 10-min walk. **Open** *pool* 9am-9pm Mon-Sat; 9am-5pm Sun. **Admission** *pool* ¥500/hour, then ¥200/30 mins.

Where every soccer fan will want to be on the eve of the World Cup Soccer Final in 2002. This, the venue, is Japan's largest stadium, with swimming and paddling pools open to the public.

Hama Bowl

2-2-14 Kita-saiwai, Nishi-ku (045 311 4321). Yokohama station. **Open** 10am-3am Sun-Thur; 10am-5am Fri, Sat. **Admission** ¥530 per game; *shoe hire* ¥300.

Bowling alleys, an archery field, golf driving range, skating rink and karaoke boxes, all in one building.

Kanagawa Skating Rink

1-1 Ota-cho, Kodai, Kanagawa-ku (045 321 0847). Higashi-Kanagawa station. **Open** 10am-7pm daily. **Admission** ¥1,600 (includes skate hire).

Biggest indoor skating rink in Yokohama.

Kamakura 鎌倉

The much-contested former capital of Japan is now a peaceful suburb with a rural feel and religious significance.

For almost 150 years Kamakura was the military and administrative centre of Japan, generating great religious and artistic fervour. What made it a strategic location for the first military government – the fact that it has hills on three sides and Sagami Bay on the other – has also kept the city from creeping in. The feeling in Kamakura is very much that of the country, despite its being only 55 minutes from Tokyo station (¥890; Yokosuka line, underground platform on Marunouchi side).

ZEN CALM TO BLOODY BETRAYAL

The enduring appeal of Kamakura is religious; it has more than 70 temples and shrines, from the large and flamboyant to the small and secluded. They represent different Buddhist sects, among them Rinnai, Pure Land and Nichiren, and many are within walking distance of Kamakura or Kita Kamakura stations. The grounds of most temples have been lost through fires and earthquakes, or, in the case of Engaku-ji in Kita Kamakura, to make way for the railway line. But many buildings have survived since the Kamakura period (1185-1333), giving you the opportunity to view historical and artistic features of old Japan.

Kamakura came to prominence as two warrior clans of eastern Japan, the Taira and Minamoto, fought for supremacy. The Taira originally gained the upper hand, receiving the title of *shogun* from the emperor and establishing the first military government in Japan. But they failed to exterminate the Minamoto, and Yorimoto, the third son, raised armies and gained power within two decades. He installed the government in Kamakura in 1192 and set about making it the most important city in Japan.

The Minamoto and succeeding rulers supported Buddhism generously, inviting Chinese priests and monks to introduce Zen Buddhism to Japan and to establish temples, mainly in the Kamakura area. This period of religious ferment had a strong impact on the arts because many temples were grandiose affairs. The main figure to emerge from this period is the priest Nichiren. Questioning the esoteric nature and rigidity of Buddhism, he preached on the streets of Kamakura for 20 years, defying the authorities with his brazen style and winning many converts. His popularity among the common people did not stop him being exiled twice, but his appeal endured and today there are still many Nichiren sect temples in Kamakura.

The Minamoto did not fare so well. Treachery, intrigues and murder put an end to the family line after two generations and three shogun. The power was transferred to the Hojo, the family of Yorimoto's wife Masakom, and while they retained power for generations the quality of leadership declined. Its prestige diminished after the Mongol attacks in the fourteenth century, and Emperor Go-Daigo sent imperial troops to take Kamakura in 1333, bringing the family's and area's reign to an end.

FESTIVALS & FIREWORKS

Kamakura is now a major tourist destination, and the temples and grounds are well looked after. Most temples require a small fee (¥100-¥300), which you should see as a contribution towards upkeep rather than an admission charge. The directions and distances to temples in each vicinity are marked in English at regular intervals all around town. For a detailed map ask the Tourist Information Centre (0467 22 3350; *Apr-Sept* 9am-6pm daily; *Oct-Mar* 9am-5pm daily) right of the station gates at the east exit. Most temples are open daily, but museums and some shops close on Mondays, and the town and the main attractions should be avoided at weekends.

Festival days are also very busy. The main ones are the Grand Festival (14-16 Sept) and the Kamakura festival (from the second to the third Sunday in April). Both take place at Tsurugaoka Hachiman (*see below*). On the last day of the Grand Festival is *yabusame* (mounted archery) in Kamakura-era hunting attire, but viewpoints are scarce. The fireworks on the beach on 10 August attract big crowds, too. As well as these, each temple and shrine holds its own festival.

The area is also well known for its flowers and blossoms, and many people come to see plums, cherries, irises, azaleas and many others throughout the year.

KAMAKURA BY AREA

Kamakura's main attractions are scattered around and take a day to see in themselves; you may do better to pick an area and check out the temples and sights there. The sightseeing spots each have big and small temples, interesting things to see and their own atmosphere.

Walking to temples in any area will take you through small streets in quiet residential areas, with well-tended gardens, old wooden houses, and traditional and second-hand shops. There's often a smell of incense floating on the air. Many temples have been built on the sides of mountains, so be prepared to climb a few stairs. There are also some hiking courses on ridges leading to temples. Most are fairly easy. The starting points are indicated on the road, as are destinations and estimated durations. You could also rent bicycles to increase the number of sights you can get around. The rental office is behind the *koban* (policebox) on the right at the east exit of the station. It's open daily from 8.30am to 5pm (¥550 one hour, ¥1,500 five hours or more).

Walking around temples may inspire you to eat at a Zen restaurant. In Kita Kamakura, Hachinoki has two restaurants, one near Kencho-ji (22 8719), one close to Engaku-ji (23 3722). In the same area is Monzen (25 1121). On Komachi Dori in Kamakura there's Saami (25 0048). All open for lunch only.

The following list of temples, shrines and other sights is only a selection; check with the Tourist Information Centre (*see above*) for more details.

Tsurugaoka Hachiman

The main and most popular shrine in Kamakura, Tsurugaoka Hachiman is 15 minutes' walk from the station. The guardian shrine of the Minamoto family, it's always busy and contains many attractions. Hachiman is seen today as the god of war, but in the past was recognised as the guardian of the Japanese nation.

If you come out of the station at the east exit, there are two ways of reaching the shrine. The first is Komachi Dori, through the *torii* (gate) on the left. It's a pedestrian mall, full of souvenirs and craft shops, boutiques, food stalls and shops, as well as restaurants. At the end turn right and you'll soon get to the shrine. The second way is the main thoroughfare to the shrine, Wakamiya Dori, which starts at the first torii near the sea and proceeds in a straight line. If you go straight ahead from the station gates (east exit), you'll reach it in one minute. On the left is the second torii, fronted by two guardian lions; from this point either walk through the torii and along the path flanked by cherry trees all the way to the shrine, or follow the footpaths, where there are more shops and restaurants. Some shops specialise in *Kamakura-bori*, a wood carving style particular to the area, derived from religious carvings (as the construction of temples slowed down, sculptors turned their skills into a commercial venture). The third torii is the start of the temple grounds.

The shrine and grounds were built to very strict specifications, the most striking example of which is found near the entrance. On the right (the east, the rising sun) is a large pond with three islands

The **ginkgo tree** *that concealed a murderer.*

(a propitious number) symbolising the Morimoto family. On the left (the west, the setting sun) is a smaller pond with four islands (an unlucky number) symbolising the defeated Taira clan.

Going straight you'll come to a dancing stage, then to the steps to the main hall. The two guardian figures in the gate are Yadaijin and Sadaijin, but the ginkgo tree on the left of the steps dwarfs them in majesty. It's reported to be at least as old as the shrine, which was here even before the arrival of the Minamoto. The tree is also famous for having concealed the murderer of the third Minamoto shogun, taken by surprise and beheaded on the spot. Past the gate on the left in the temple you'll see some very old *mikoshi* (portable shrines) and the entrance to a tiny museum (¥100) displaying a small number of artefacts from the days of the Minamoto reign.

There's a bigger museum on the right after the pond as you walk towards the shrine, **Houmotsuden**, housing old items from neighbouring temples. It's open daily from 8.30am to 4.30pm (¥100). It has an annexe behind the shrine towards Kita Kamakura. There is also the **Kamakura Museum of Modern Art**, open 9.30am-5pm Tuesday to Sunday, next to the pond on the left after you cross the bridge.

Kita Kamakura

This area is home to many Rinzai sect temples, the HQ of which is the famous Engaku-ji, the largest Zen establishment in Kamakura, a few metres from Kita Kamakura station. It's known in the west for the many books written by Daisetsu Suzuki. The temple was founded in 1282, but the main gate, housing statues of Kannon and Rakan, was reconstructed in 1780. Engaku-ji is also famous for having the largest bell in Kamakura. It's a fine establishment with a serene atmosphere.

On the road along the tracks is the **Kamakura Old Pottery Museum** (10am-5pm Tue-Sun) and across the tracks is **Tokei-ji**, for a long time a nunnery offering asylum to women wanting a divorce. Men could easily divorce their wives but the opposite was impossible unless the women stayed in Tokei-ji for three years. Early this century it reverted to a temple. It's worth a visit for its beautiful garden and grounds as well as the Treasure House, which keeps old sutras and scrolls.

Nearby is **Jochi-ji**, interesting for its old bridge and steps at the entrance, its bell tower, the burial caves at the back and a tunnel between cemeteries. On the other side of the road is **Meigetsuin**, approached by a pleasant street. The temple has the biggest *yagura* (burial cave) in the area, a small stone garden and statues carved out of the rock in the caves.

On the road towards Kamakura you'll find **Kencho-ji**, the first great Zen temple of Kamakura. It's an imposing place with large buildings and grounds, though only ten of the original 49 sub-temples survive. The oldest Zen temple in Japan, its arrangement has not changed for over 700 years. In the second floor of the main gate are the statues of 500 *rakan* (Buddha's disciples). Behind the last building there's a garden, and, further along, the path leads to steps climbing to **Hanso-bo**, the shrine protecting the temple. Up the stairs near the tunnel on the road is **Eno-ji**, a very small temple housing statues representing the judges of hell. It's not especially worth the admission charge.

West of Tsurugaoka Hachiman

Eisho-ji, the only active Buddhist nunnery in the area, is closed to the public. At nearby **Jufuku-ji**, the temple grounds are closed, too, but you can wander in the old cemetery behind by following the path on the left of the gate. It's a quiet place with many burial caves, some reputed to date from Kamakura's early days as the capital of Japan.

About 30 minutes away by foot is **Zeniarai Benten ('Money-washing Shrine')**, a must-see. Go through a tunnel under a mountain and enter another world, with small shrines carved in the cliffs, ponds and eerie music. In the cave straight ahead of the entrance you'll find containers to put your money in, notes and all. The more you wash the more you'll get. Use the incense burner if you need to dry the notes.

Back towards the town at a nearby crossing is a lane leading to **Sasuke Inari Shrine**, up steps through more than 100 torii. There's not much up here, but it's very peaceful at the end of the valley.

Another 30 minutes' walk will take you to **Kotokuin Temple**, home of the **Daibutsu** or **Great Buddha**. The temple dates from AD 741 and the statue of Buddha from 1252. Nobody really-ly knows how the statue was cast and put together. It was once in a hall that suffered fires and earthquakes and was finally demolished by a tsunami in 1495. The statue was unscathed and has been in the open ever since. You can go inside it for ¥20. You can get here from Kamakura station via the Enoden railway line, getting off at Hase (¥190). One of the oldest train lines in Japan, the single tracks barely fit between houses along the way.

A few minutes away is **Hase Kannon or Hase Dera** (3-11-2 Hase, Kamakura-shi, Kanagawa-ken; 0467 22 6300), with many interesting sights. Entry costs ¥300. The main feature is a 9m, 11-faced statue of Kannon (goddess of mercy and compassion), reputedly the tallest in Japan. It was carved in AD 721 out of a single camphor tree. The temple is especially well known for its thousands of small *jizo* figures offered in memory of deceased children and babies. There's also a revolving sutra library containing Buddhist scriptures – worshippers rotating the library receive merit equivalent to reading the entire Buddhist canon – and a small network of caves with statues carved out of the rock. The **Treasure House** (9am-4pm; closed irregular days) contains possessions and artefacts excavated from the temple during rebuilding. Entry is included in the fee for the temple. From Hase Kannon there's a panoramic view of the town, the beach and Sagami Bay.

East of Tsurugaoka Hachiman

This least grandiose of the sightseeing areas is quieter with many smaller temples. The first shrine as you come from Tsurugaoka Hachiman

Kamakura, *an hour from Tokyo, feels rural.*

The much visited guardian shrine of the Minamoto family – **Tsurugaoka Hachiman**.

is **Egara Tenjin**, founded in 1104. Tenjin is the patron deity of scholarship and literature, so every 25 January there is a burning of writing brushes here. Nearby is **Kamakura Shrine**, founded by the Meiji Emperor in 1869, so very new compared with the other religious buildings in the area.

Turn left up the small road leading to **Kakuon-ji**. This looks a small temple but the tour by the priest (on the hour from 10am to 3pm; about 40 minutes long) gives you the chance to see the extent of the grounds and other buildings. The tour is in Japanese only but the thatched roof buildings and old wooden statues speak for themselves and are worth the detour.

A 15-minute walk from Kamakura Shrine is **Zuisen-ji**, famous for its flowers, especially the plum blossoms in February. It's a small temple, with an old Zen garden created in the fourteenth century by famous priest and garden designer Muso-Kokushi.

From the intersection near Kamakura shrine you can reach **Sugimotodera**, the oldest temple in Kamakura. The gate and temple have thatched roofs and were built in AD 734. Further up across the road is **Hokoku-ji**, known as the Bamboo Temple because of its large bamboo grove. From here it's a short walk to the famous **Shakado Tunnel**. It is closed to traffic, but pedestrians still use it to cross the ridge.

Back towards the city on the road parallel to Wakamiya Dori, you'll see signs for the **Harakiri cave**, where the last Hojo regent and over 800 of his retainers killed themselves after Kamakura fell

to the imperial forces. There's only a small burial cave, but it's a far cry from the tragedy the name and story evoke.

Down the road (15 minutes from the station) is **Hongaku-ji**, a small temple with a very old gate. Shortly after is **Myohon-ji**, founded in 1260. Between this temple and the beach are many Nichiren sect temples; this is the oldest and largest. There are only a few buildings in the grounds and despite being so close to the station it's surprisingly quiet.

Another 15 minutes or so away is **Myoho-ji**, also known as Moss Temple. You can visit the small grounds but the gate leading to the back and top of the hill is generally closed. The priest Nichiren is said to have resided here and the top of the hill was reputedly one of his favourite spots.

Towards the beach along the main road you'll come to **Choso-ji**, a recently renovated structure (though there's been a temple here since 1345). There's a large statue of Nichiren between the statues of four celestial kings to protect the place against evil. Very close to the beach is **Komyo-ji**, a big temple established in 1243. There is a path on the right between the temple and the playground leading to the back and up to the road above. You can see the beach, ocean, Enoshima Island and Mount Fuji, although there's nowhere to sit to enjoy the sight.

Down by the beach to the east are the remains of **Wakaejima**, the first artificial port in Japan, built in 1232. It was once busy but declined as soon as the seat of power moved back to Kyoto.

The Mountains

Just an hour or two from Tokyo, two sacred mountains offer scenic respite from the city.

Mount Fuji

Once a religious pilgrimage, the climb to the summit of Mount Fuji is now an experience that anyone can enjoy. Japan's highest mountain, Fuji is renowned for its beauty and spiritual significance. Pilgrimages used to start at **Hongu Fuji Sengen Shrine**. Established in AD 788, the shrine is dedicated to Konohanasakuyahime, the patron of Fuji and goddess of the volcano. Mount Fuji is dormant and these days only a wisp of smoke emanates from the crater. The last eruption in 1707 covered Edo (now Tokyo), 100 kilometres (62 miles) away, with a layer of ash.

The pilgrimage was restricted to men only until a few years after the Meiji Restoration. The shrines on the way up doubled as inns; pilgrims would pray and rest at each stage before reaching the summit in time for *goraiko*, the sunrise. People still go up the mountain to see the sunrise, but may use transport to the fifth stage, where the road stops.

Since Fuji is covered in snow most of the year, the climbing season is officially restricted to July and August (outside the season the trails are open but facilities are closed; in theory, people should enjoy the views from the fifth stage). The best time is the middle four weeks of that period. There is a saying that there are two kinds of fools: those who never climb Fuji and those who climb it twice.

The climb typically starts from the fifth stage in the afternoon, and includes a sleep in the huts along the way before an early rise to reach the summit in time for goraiko. There are a number of different ways of getting to Mount Fuji but the main gateway is Kawaguchiko, 30 kilometres (19 miles) to the north in the Fuji Five Lakes district. Buses and trains leaving Shinjuku go directly to the bus terminal leading to the fifth stage. It's best to book transport early in the climbing season. At the bus terminal in Kawaguchiko the Tourist Information Centre (0555 72 6700; 9am-5.30pm daily) is a good source of information, including a vital weather forecast: you don't want to get to the top and find the view obscured by cloud.

The temperature at the summit can be 20°C lower than at the base. The average in July is 4.9°C and in August 2.7°C. It's often below zero before sunrise, so dress accordingly. Essential items include a raincoat, torch, water and food (available at huts but not cheap). Don't forget to bring along some toilet paper and some bags to take your rubbish back in.

The fastest and cheapest way to Kawaguchiko is by bus from Nishi Shinjuku's Keio Shinjuku Expressway Bus Terminal. The fare is ¥1,700 each way and buses leave regularly from the Yasuda Seimei Building No.2, just in front of the Yodobashi Camera store. The ticket office is open 6am-11pm and bookings can be made on the spot. During the climbing season there are also three buses daily directly to the fifth stage: reserve with Fuji Kyuko (3374 2221). It costs ¥2,600 from Shinjuku. One or two buses a day also leave from JR Hamamatsucho station (¥1,900): for info, schedules and bookings call Keio Teito reservation centre (5376 2222). The journey takes 1 hour 45 minutes and the first stop of the highway is Highland Resort by Fuji-Q Highland; from there it's ten minutes to Kawaguchiko station. Kawaguchiko is also accessible by train, but it's more expensive and takes longer. Kaisoku Rapid (¥2,390) leaves Shinjuku in the early evening and takes two hours. There's an extra service in the morning on weekends and holidays. Trains are busy in summer, so book early.

Many trains go from Shinjuku to Otsuki, where a transfer to the Fuji Kyuko line for Kawaguchiko is necessary. The fastest trains to Otsuki are the Asuza or Kaiji Limited Express. They depart from Shinjuku about once an hour and cost ¥4,050 each way, including the journey on the Fuji Kyuko train, which leaves Otsuki every 15-30 minutes and takes 50 minutes to reach Kawaguchiko.

Once you're at Kawaguchiko station it's almost another hour to the fifth stage by bus, which departs from the station. Tickets are available at the office, ¥1,700 one way/¥3,060 return. In season there are up to five buses a day (none at all between December and March). Timetables can be checked with Fuji Kyuko Line Office in Shibuya (3374 2221) or Kawaguchiko (0555 72 2911).

You can also get to the top of Fuji from the south side, starting from one of two new fifth stages. One is near Gotemba, the other further west. There are four daily direct trains on the Odakyu line (express Asagiri) to Gotemba from Shinjuku, taking two hours and costing ¥2,650. From Gotemba there are four buses a day to the new fifth stage (only in season); they take 45 minutes and cost ¥1,080.

Some *shinkansen* heading towards Kyoto stop at Mishima or Shin-Fuji, where buses leave to the new western fifth stage. Buses cost ¥2,400 each way and take over two hours. From 22 July-20 August there are four to six buses a day.

From any fifth stage the only way up is to walk. On the Kawaguchiko side the 7.5-kilometre (4.7-mile) climb takes five hours, the descent about three. From Gotemba it's six and a half hours up and three down. From the western new fifth stage it's a five-hour ascent and three and a half hours to come down. The huts along the trails are only open in season.

Some people start the climb quite late from the fifth stages to avoid staying at huts. The latter often cost over ¥7,000 for the few hours, and are basic and noisy. Don't expect a good night's sleep. Camping on the mountain is prohibited.

It's still possible to do the climb from the base through the nine stages. You start at Hongu Fuji Sengen Shrine and follow the old pilgrim route, the Yoshidaguchi trail. The shrine is in Fujiyoshida (20 minutes' walk from the station, two stops from Kawaguchiko) and takes up to five hours to the fifth stage. The trail is quiet, passing numerous historical buildings and monuments.

There's not much to do on the summit but enjoy the views and walk around the 220-metre-deep (722 feet) crater.

Kawaguchiko is a resort in its own right, with the lake a major attraction. Most popular are boat tours, fishing, riding the cable car to the top of **Mount Tenjoyama** and visiting the many museums. From the station there are buses to **Lake Yamanaka** (popular with campers), **Lake Shoji**, **Lake Motosu**, **Ice Cave (Fuketsu)**, **Lava Cave (Hyuketsu)** and **Midorino Kyukamura onsen (hot springs)** and **Lake Saiko**.

Mount Takao

Most of Tokyo lies in the Kanto Plain and is surrounded by mountains, which, with the exception of the main valleys, have remained in their natural state. Mount Takao, less than an hour west of Shinjuku, is a favourite getaway. A sacred mountain, it has retained some tranquillity despite attracting many visitors. The main route to the 600m summit is often busy and has been turned into a tourist attraction, but other paths leading to the top and circling the mountain are more peaceful. Even so, Takao is not too crowded, and it's the sort of place where passers-by will smile and say *'konnichiwa'*. On a clear day you can see the sprawl of the city on one side and on the other a mountain range with Fuji towering in the background.

Getting to Takao is simple. The easiest way is to catch the Keio line from Shinjuku station to the end of the line at Takaosanguchi. It takes less than an hour and costs only ¥370. Another option is to take the JR Chuo line from to the terminal at Mount

Mount Fuji: *a once-in-a-lifetime climb.*

Takao: a special rapid from Tokyo will take a little over an hour and cost ¥890. You then transfer to the Keio line for Takaosanguchi (a further ¥120).

From the station a brick-lined path leads to the base of the mountain. Restaurants and shops sell food and souvenirs. This is also the boarding area for the cable car and chairlifts to the observatory. The main path (hiking course No.1) to the observatory is very steep, so it's worth spending the ¥470 on the cable car or chairlift.

The principal attraction along the main path, **Yakuoin Temple** was founded in 744 and has large grounds. It's one of few temples around Tokyo dedicated to Tengu, the long-nosed goblin. Also along the path is **Takaosan Wild Grass and Monkey Park** (0426 61 2381), a nature garden open 9.30am-4.30pm Monday-Saturday, 9.30am-5pm Sunday and holidays. Admission is ¥500 for adults, ¥250 for primary schoolchildren. It has two observation platforms.

The other path leading to the top (hiking course No.6) starts to the left of the cable car and is a slow steady climb, except for the last stretch. It's a popular but quiet path that runs alongside a stream, and there are religious artefacts in the woods along the way, plus a temple by a waterfall. Information boards describe the local flora and fauna. The course can be done in about an hour.

Just past the main shopping area is the **Takao Museum of Natural History** (free entry; open *Apr-Nov* 9am-5pm daily; *Dec-Mar* 9am-4pm daily; closed the first and third Monday of each month).

For a special Japanese dining experience, **Ukai Toriyama** (0426 61 0739) is the place. Nestled in a valley a few minutes from town, it consists of many buildings, seating two to 25 people, in a large manicured garden with ponds. It's very quiet, with the tinkle of the stream and old music drifting down from the mountainside. Free buses run from the station. It serves seasonal food from the area for around ¥7,000 a head. Menus are in English and reservations are recommended.

Beaches

The nearest beaches may be an hour away, but they draw the crowds.

The official beach season falls in July and August, and in typically strange Japanese fashion, beaches are quiet and almost deserted outside this period, though surfers and other sporty types congregate even in winter. The infrastructure and facilities are well organised and dependable, every popular beach having plenty of shops where you can buy and hire equipment for sports and activities, and loads of restaurants and cafés. Tokyo's nearest beaches are just over an hour away; as a rule, the further away the beach the more attractive it is, though it won't necessarily be any less crowded.

Kamakura

Closest to Tokyo, Kamakura's beaches are also some of the busiest. In summer it's hard to find a spot to lie in, and, in part due to their popularity, the beaches are a bit dirty.

Trains go directly to Kamakura from Tokyo station (¥890; Yokosuka line) in 55 minutes. The east exit leads to Wakamiya-dori, Kamakura's main street, from which a right turn and a 15-minute walk leads to the shore. On the right is **Yuigahama beach** and on the other side of the Nameri River on the left is **Zaimokuza beach**.

From Inamuragasaki Point, at the western end of Yuigahama beach, there is a long sandy stretch to Koyurugi Point, just before Enoshima.

Katase Enoshima

The road west along the coast from Kamakura goes to Enoshima, another popular summer resort. The beach on the other side of Enoshima Island is

Surfers take time out to shoot the breeze.

nicknamed the **Oriental Miami Beach**, but, despite its tourist attractions and facilities, this is a misnomer. It's as busy as Kamakura, with similar sands, and you should arrive early to get a good spot. Popular activities are yachting, surfing and fishing. The town itself has little to offer.

The Odakyu line goes directly from Shinjuku to Katase Enoshima. The local train takes around 85 minutes and costs ¥610. Express trains run regularly, cost ¥1100 and take about 15 minutes less. The other option is to go via Kamakura, then take the Enoden line (23 minutes; five times an hour; ¥250), or take a bus from the east exit. The latter runs once or twice an hour, takes 35 minutes and costs ¥280.

The 5km beach has been popular since the Meiji era. Near Katase Enoshima station is **Enoshima Marineland** (2-17-25 Katase-Kaigan, Fujisawa-shi, Kanagawa-ken; 0466 22 8111), with a pool for dolphins and whales and two marine zoos. It's open 9.30am-5.30pm daily except 31 Dec. Admission costs ¥1,890 for adults, ¥840 for primary schoolchildren and ¥525 for infants.

Further west by the beach lies a 8.4km cycling course and the **Kagenuma Pool Garden** (4-4-1 Kugenuma-Kaigan, Fuisawa-shi, Kanagawa-ken; 0466 36 7639. Kugenuma-Kaigan station) with pools and water slides. It's open 9am-5pm daily from 29 June to 7 Sept and admission costs ¥1,800 for adults, ¥900 for primary schoolchildren. Among the dunes is **Tsujido Marine Park** (3-2 Tsujido-Nishi Kaigan, Fujisawa-shi, Kanagawa-ken; 0466 34 0011. Tsujido station) with running-water swimming pools. The park is open 9am-6pm daily from 10 July to 15 Sept. Admission is ¥ 810 for adults, ¥200 for primary schoolchildren.

In the town the main attraction is **Ryuko-ji (Dragon's Mouth) Temple** (3-13-37 Katase, Fujisawa-shi, Kanagawa-ken; 0466 25 7357), where the priest Nichiren escaped execution as lightning broke the sword that was about to behead him. The temple was founded in 1337 in his memory and has many old wooden buildings, including a five-storey pagoda. The temple is open daily from 10am to 4pm.

Another very popular attraction is **Enoshima Island**, a religious site with a history going back 1,000 years. The main approach across the bridge turns into a shopping street that goes across the island to reach the western side. The island has three shrines: **Hetsunomiya**, rebuilt just over 20 years ago, **Nakatsunomiya**, founded in AD 853 and rebuilt in 1689, and **Okutsunomiya**. The main path up and across the island leads through the three shrines. There are escalators, each costing ¥100 to ¥200, but they only go a short distance. At the top are botanical gardens with 300 types of plants. Entry costs ¥200, and access to a viewing tower to look at Mount Fuji is an additional ¥280. Restaurants on the left of the path soon after Okutsunomiya offer similar views of Mount Fuji, as do the rocks by the sea at the end of the path. From the rocks, another path leads to caves hollowed out by waves; they can be visited in about 20 minutes for ¥500.

The JR 'Kamakura-Enoshima Free Kippu' ticket, valid for two days, gives unlimited free access to JR trains, Enoden railway and Shonan monorail between Ofuna, Fujisawa, Enoshima and Kamakura. It costs ¥1,970 and allows only one trip from and back to Tokyo.

Izu Peninsula

This popular resort area is one of the most seismically active regions in Japan, though most of the quakes that occur are too small to be felt. As a result of this activity there are many *onsen* (natural hot spring baths), the most accessible in towns along the east coast, which the train line follows. The terminus is at Shimoda, where special US envoy Commodore Perry arrived with the Black Ships in 1854. A ship's replica sails the waters in the bay. Other attractions in Shimoda include a small castle, a floating aquarium and a cable car up **Mount Nesugata**, from which the peninsula and the Izu Islands (*see below*) are visible.

The main beach around Shimoda is **Shirahama**, 3km north-east of the town and accessible by bus from the railway station. It stretches over 700m and is divided in the middle by a rocky outcrop topped by a *torii* (Chinese-style gate). The side nearest town has restaurants and shops along the road and is the closest thing to a 'beach town' near Tokyo. It's packed with swimmers and surfers, even outside the beach season. Closer to Shimoda in a small bay is **Sotoura Beach**, with quiet waters that are especially good for swimming.

There are beaches on the south side of Shimoda, too. **Yumigahama** is 40 minutes from town by bus and a popular spot with bathers in summer. Another small beach, **Kisami-Ohama**, is closer to town and free of large concrete buildings. It's a ten-minute taxi ride from the town. Between the town and Kisami-Ohama are **Nabetahama**, **Tatadohama** and **Iritahama** beaches.

To get to Shimoda directly take the Odoriko train from Tokyo or Shinagawa stations. It takes about two and a half hours and costs ¥6,160 each way. The other option is to take the *shinkansen* to Atami and then the local train; this takes about the same time but is a bit more expensive.

Izu Islands

These are officially called the Seven Izu Islands, but in reality they are more numerous. Geologically part of the Izu Peninsula, they're administered by the Tokyo Metropolitan Government. The main island is **Oshima**, famous for its volcano (an eruption forced the island's evacuation in 1986), beaches, camping and onsen. The main surfing beaches are **Kobohama**, **Sanohama** and **Fudeshima**. Nearby lie the smaller **Niijima** and **Shikinejima** **islands**, the former with many beautiful clean beaches with good waves for surfing and the latter with small beaches for swimming. These three islands are easier to access than ones further south.

A ferry leaves Takeshiba Pier near Hamamatsucho station at 10pm every night, arriving in Oshima at 6am (from ¥3,810 to ¥11,430), Niijima at 8am (an extra ¥1,030) and Shikinejima at 8.40am (an extra ¥1,130). The return boat leaves in the late morning or early afternoon and arrives in Tokyo at around 8pm. Oshima is also accessible by boat from Atami (four times a day; from ¥2,750) and Ito (twice a day; from ¥2,390) on the Izu Peninsula. There are three daily flights to Oshima and back from Haneda airport in Tokyo (¥8,500 each way).

Boso Peninsula

East of Tokyo on the other side of the bay lies the Boso Peninsula, a favourite destination of daytrippers because of its mountains and beaches. The beaches are concentrated near the towns of Tateyama, Chikura, Katsura and Onjuku, but the most famous beach is **Kujukurihama**, a 60km stretch of sand facing the Pacific on the east coast.

It's possible to do a circular trip of the peninsula on the JR Uchibo and Sotobo lines, which meet at Awa-Kamogawa (¥4,090 either way) on the east coast. Both lines leave from Tokyo station; the Uchibo goes along Tokyo Bay while the Sotobo cuts across the peninsula to follow the Pacific shore south of Kujukurihama.

Kujukurihama stretches between Cape Taito and Cape Gyobu and can get rough (good news for surfers). Take the Sotobo line to Oami, change to the Togane line at Togane (¥2,770), then get a bus (35 minutes) to Kujukuri town. To the south on the Sotobo line are Katsura (¥3,990) and Onjuku (¥3,990), both of which have a number of beaches. Every morning except Wednesday, **Katsura** has a fair dating back 400 years. **Onjuku** is well known for its *ama* (women divers) and its sandy hills for skiing. Further south on the Uchibo line, there are good surfing beaches around **Chikura** (¥4,090). **Setohama** and **Maebara**. On the other side of the peninsula, **Tateyama** (¥4,090) has bathing beaches, **Kagamigaura** being the busiest. Between Tateyama and Chikura at the tip of the peninsula are more beaches accessible only by road.

Nikko 日光

Of all the amazing sights in Japan, the frozen Kegon Falls and 'mysterious statues of Jizo' are among the most memorable.

Nikko has been famous for its natural beauty since it became a centre of mountain worship more than 1,200 years ago. Centuries later, the first shogun, Tokugawa Ieyasu, was so impressed by the place that he chose to be enshrined and buried here. Today Toshogu Shrine and Shinkyo, the sacred bridge across the river, are one of the biggest attractions in Japan. And the beauty of Nikko has not dimmed: large crowds throughout the year attest to the local proverb 'Never say *kekko* [splendid] until you've seen Nikko'.

Nikko, which means 'sunlight', derives from Futarasan, now called Mount Nantai, where the goddess Kannon lived. A priest, Shodo Shonin, established a centre for Buddhist asceticism on the mountain, and temples flourished over the years, drawing many religious, military and government figures to the area.

The main sights in Nikko are **Shinkyo Bridge**, **Toshogu** and **Taiyuin** shrines, **Lake Chuzenji** and **Kegon Falls**. Around town are also **Rinno-ji** and **Futarasan** temples, **Cryptomeria Avenue**, **Ganmangafuchi Abyss**, several museums and the **Botanical Gardens**. Further out is a vast national park, a popular place for sightseeing, *onsen* (natural hot springs), hiking, camping, boating, skiing and skating.

Nikko is two hours from Tokyo, right at the edge of the Kanto Plain, where the mountains start to rise. Tall cryptomeria (Japanese cedar) dominate the landscape. The town is fairly small, with a population of only 20,000, but gets 7 million visitors a year.

Two rail lines, Tobu and Japan Railways (JR) go to Nikko; the stations are close to each other in the centre of town. Tobu trains are generally faster and cheaper, and their bus service to the sights more regular. The Tobu terminal in Tokyo is at Asakusa. Limited Express trains go directly to Tobu Nikko station, leaving about every hour from 7am. They cost ¥2,740 each way and take around 1 hour 45 minutes. The Express trains to Shimo-Imaichi, followed by a local train to Tobu Nikko (a few minutes away), cost only ¥200 less. Local trains from Asakusa are the cheapest, at ¥1,320, but they take longer, stopping at most stations and requiring a change at Shimo-Imaichi. Tickets for local trains are always available before departure, but Limited Express trains can be full, so you should book, especially on weekends and holidays.

JR trains leave from Tokyo or Ueno stations, but require a transfer at Utsonomiya. From there it's almost 45 minutes on a local train. To get to Utsonomiya there's a *shinkansen* (Tohoku line) from Tokyo station; the whole journey takes around two hours and costs ¥4,920. The Tohoku (Utsonomiya) line trains leave from Ueno station, cost ¥2,520 and take 15-20 minutes more, not including waiting time for the connecting train. Express trains from Ueno to Utsonomiya cost an extra ¥910.

Each station has a bus terminal with regular services to Lake Chuzenji and beyond via Shinkyo and Nikko National Park. The Tobu ticket counter is in the train station, where there's also a Tourist Information Centre, open from 9-5pm daily. There's another one on the main road towards Shinkyo and Toshogu, used mainly for accommodation bookings, though maps and other printed information are readily available. It's closed on Wednesdays.

From the stations it's a 25-minute walk or five-minute bus ride (¥190; from either platform at Tobu station) to Shinkyo. Antique shops and restaurants line the main road, many with signs in English. The local delicacy, *yuba* (soy milk skin), features prominently on menus and in souvenir shops. The road to the left at Shinkyo leads to Lake Chuzenji via the newer part of Nikko, which is filled with souvenir shops. Toshogu is in the national park across the road, ten minutes away.

Shinkyo Bridge

According to legend, the first bridge across the Daiyagawa River was made by two snakes to allow priest Shodo Shonin through on his pilgrimage to Futarasan. In reality, the bridge was built at the same time as Toshogu and is its main approach. Destroyed by floods in 1902 and rebuilt five years later, it has proved so popular with tourists that it's being reconstructed again and is due to reopen in March 2003. The structure is currently completely hidden, but there's a large picture of Shinkyo on a panel.

Rinno-ji, Toshogu, Futarasan & Taiyuin

The cluster of religious buildings includes Rinno-ji, Toshogu, Futarasan and Taiyuin. The entrance fees are ¥380, ¥1,250, ¥200 and ¥500, but discount

Nikko – *a region of natural beauty – offers magnificent views and peaceful resting places.*

tickets for ¥900 are available in the car park in front of Rinno-ji. The ticket also allows entry to Yakushido (inside Toshogu Shrine), though not to the Sleeping Cat, Tokugawa Ieyasu's mausoleum, or Shin'en in the grounds of Futarasan.

Rinno-ji's main hall is called **Sanbutsudo** (Three Buddhas). Founded in AD 766, it's the largest temple in the area. Inside there are a few artefacts and statues, including the large golden-wood statues of the Three Buddhas. They stand over 5 metres (16 feet) high, and depict the Thousand-armed Kannon, Amida Buddha and the Horse-headed Kannon. The exit leads to Sorinto, a tall pillar to repel evil, built in 1643, as well as another hall.

In front of Sanbutsudo is **Rinno-ji Treasure House**, where more artefacts from the temple are displayed. It's open from 8am to 4.40pm (¥300). Next door is the Edo-style **Shoyo-en Garden** (also ¥300), where a revered 200-year-old cherry tree has been declared a national monument. On the left of Sanbutsudo stands a black gate, Kuremon, and the path leading to Toshogu.

Toshogu is the main attraction, but its flamboyance gets mixed reviews. It was built during the reign of the third shogun, Iemitsu, according to instructions left by Tokugawa Ieyasu himself, who died in 1616. It's not clear when work began, but Toshogu was completed in 1636. The finest craftspeople were brought in and it's said that as many as 15,000 people took part in the construction. The buildings include both Shinto and Buddhist elements, and some are more Chinese than Japanese in design. Nearly all are brightly painted with extremely ornate and intricate carv-

ings. The grounds are often packed, but do quieten down a bit towards the end of the afternoon. It's open from 8am to 5pm (last entrance 4.30pm).

After the first *torii* (gate) is a five-storey pagoda built in 1818. Up the stairs is **Otemon**, also called the Deva gate after its statues, which are said to scare away evil spirits. The building on the left after the gate is **Shinkyusha** (Sacred Stable), where the sacred horse lives. It's the only unpainted building in the grounds, famous for its set of eight carvings of the **Sanzaru** (Three Monkeys) representing the ideal way of life ('hear no evil, see no evil, speak no evil'). The three buildings from the right of Otemon are repositories for costumes and other items used in festivals.

To the left at the top of the stairs is **Yakushido**, famous for its dragon painting on the ceiling and for its echo, which is regularly demonstrated by the priest. For this reason it's called the Roaring Dragon. There are also a dozen old statues inside.

The next gate is **Yomeimon**, meaning 'twilight gate'. Its 400 carvings reputedly make it the most elaborate in Japan. Then there's **Karamon**, leading to the oratory and the main hall. These two gates are decorated in the Chinese style with a dragon, phoenix and other imaginary creatures. The oratory's entrance has dragon carvings, while inside are paintings of another 100 dragons.

To the right of Karamon is the entrance to the **shogun's mausoleum** (an extra ¥500). At the top of the first door is the carving of the **Nemurineko** (Sleeping Cat), famed for its depiction of the Buddhist question and answer 'What about a sleeping kitten under peonies in bloom? I would have nothing to do with it.' The stairs lead up the mountain to a quiet and secluded area with two small buildings simply painted in blue and gold, and behind is the mausoleum.

Toshogu's festivals take place from 17 to 18 May and on 17 October. On 17 May there's horseback archery in hunting attire of the Middle Ages, held in front of the shrine, while on 18 May the Sennin Gyoretsu procession recreates the bringing of the remains of Ieyasu. The 1,000 people taking part are dressed as *samurai*, priests and others in the style of the days of the shogun. The 17 October festival is similar but on a smaller scale.

The path leading to the left before the entrance torii goes to the **Toshogu Treasure Museum**, only a small part of whose treasures are exhibited at any one time. It's open *Apr-Nov* 8.30am-5pm, *Dec-Mar* 8.30am-4pm daily (last entrance 30 minutes before closing). Entrance costs ¥500.

The path to the left between the pagoda and Otemon leads to **Futarasan Temple**, which includes another three shrines, on the summit of Mount Nantai, the shore of Lake Chuzenji and the bank of the Daiyagawa River. Exhibits and access inside this temple are quite limited. To the left is Shin'en, a small compound with a few little shrines and a teahouse/coffee shop. It costs an extra ¥300.

Next is **Taiyuin Shrine**, where the third shogun, Iemitsu, is buried. It was built in 1652, in the Buddhist style only, and while it's similar in tone to Toshogu, it's not as extravagant and extensive. The first gate has Nio guardian figures; soon after comes **Nitenmon Gate**, with statues of Komokuten and Jikokuten, two Buddhist deities. The next gate is **Yashamon**, with four statues of Yashan, and the last is **Karamon**, before the hall of worship. A few artefacts and old treasures are displayed inside. A walk around the main hall leads to **Kokamon Gate** and towards the mausoleum, which isn't accessible. Taiyuin is open *Apr-Nov* 8am-4.30pm, *Dec-Mar* 8am-3.30pm daily.

Lake Chuzenji & Kegon Falls

The Lake Chuzenji area is the prime example of Nikko's famed natural beauty. The lake is popular for swimming, fishing and boating, while nearby are campsites and hiking trails.

The most popular sight is **Kegon Falls**, where the lake's waters plunge 100 metres (328 feet) to the Daiyagawa River. An elevator descends to the base of the gorge. The falls, which include 12 minor cascades, are said to be one of Japan's finest. They freeze in winter and look quite magical. Nearby is the **Chanokidaira ropeway**, and from the top are good views of the lake, Kegon Falls, Mount Nantai and surrounding areas. There's also a botanical garden with alpine plants and a rock garden.

North of the lake, **Mount Nantai** rises almost 2,400 metres (7,877 feet). There's a crater on top, but most climbers making the five-hour ascent

(between May and October) do so for religious reasons, to visit **Okumiya Shrine**. The side of the mountain is crowded with worshippers during its festival (31 July-8 August).

There are buses from both train stations to Chuzenji Spa. The Tobu buses cost ¥1,100 each way and depart from either platform. **Irohazaka Drive**, a series of hairpin bends in the road, is a well-known feature of the area.

Others

Close to the train stations a 37-kilometre (23-mile) road lined with more than 13,000 cryptomeria trees, planted more than 350 years ago by a warlord as an offering to Toshogu, ends. **Cryptomeria Avenue**, as it's known, is pedestrian unfriendly so it's difficult to appreciate its beauty.

On the other side of town, to the left of Shinkyo Bridge, is **Ganmangafuchi Abyss**, a narrow stretch of river made of lava from an eruption of Mount Nantai. Along the path leading to the abyss and beyond are many mossy and crumbling *Jizo* statues, called 'the mysterious statues of Jizo' because their number changes every time they're counted. To get there, follow the road nearest to the river, pass by a small bridge: shortly afterwards the road leads to a path. The abyss is a ten-minute walk.

Nearby is **Joko-ji Temple**, which boasts many tombstones and statues, including the head of a big Jizo statue, discovered after the major flood of 1902, and a Jizo with a straw hat, in the building right in front of the entrance gate. Towards the back of the graveyard there's a small structure with three other statues of Jizo. The middle one is Michibiki or 'divine guidance', the oldest statue of Buddha in Nikko, dating from 1550. Both smaller statues are called Mimidare Jizo. To reach Joko-ji take the first left after the bridge coming back from the abyss, then the first left on top of the hill.

Along the main road to Lake Chuzenji is the former **Imperial Villa**, where Emperor Taisho (1912-26) used to spend every summer. It was built early this century and part of it has been turned into a museum. It's open *Apr-Oct* 8.30am-5pm, *Nov-Mar* 9am-4.30pm daily, and entrance costs ¥400.

Further on down the main road you will find the **Botanical Gardens**, with 2,300 varieties of plants, including 150 types of alpine flora. It's open 9am-4.30pm and costs ¥330.

On the other side of the road is **Shaka Temple**, with a number of 3-metre-high tombstones, the **Graves of Self-immolation**. This is where many of Iemitsu's retainers where buried after they committed *hara-kiri* to show their loyalty upon his death.

On the right of Shinkyo Bridge are **Honju Shrine**, established in AD 766 and housing a statue of the Thousand-armed Kannon, a three-storey pagoda and the **Kosugi Hoan Museum of Art**, open 9.30am-5pm Tue-Sun (¥700).

Directory

Directory

Getting Around

Narita International Airport

Almost certainly the airport you'll arrive at (English-language enquiries: 0476 34 5000), Narita International is nearly 70km (43 miles) from Tokyo and is well served by rail and bus links to the city.

JR's **Narita Express** (info 3423 0111) is the fastest way to get to Tokyo but also the most expensive. Seats must be reserved and there's no standing room, so at busy times you may have to wait. All trains go to Tokyo station (¥2,940), with some also serving Shinjuku (¥3,110), Ikebukuro (¥3,110), Omiya (¥3,740) and Yokohama (¥4,180). Trains depart every 30-40 minutes.

The **Keisei Skyliner** (info 0476 32 8505/3831 0131), operated by a private rail company, is cheaper. Trains take you into Ueno station (¥1,920) in around one hour. Cheaper still is a Keisei Limited Express (Tokkyu), a regular train that makes a few stops on its 75-minute route to Ueno station (¥1,000).

Limousine buses (info 3665 7220) run regularly from the airport to the city, costing around ¥3,000. Airport shuttle buses (info 0476 32 7981) cost about the same and drop off at many of Tokyo's top hotels.

Taxis from the airport are recommended only for those with bottomless wallets: the journey will cost from ¥30,000 and may take longer than the train.

Haneda Airport

It's highly unlikely you'll arrive at Haneda, which handles mainly internal flights. There is talk of expanding international services, but local residents currently seem determined to block the move.

The **monorail** leaves every five to ten minutes (5.20am-11.15pm) and links up to Hamamatsucho station on the JR Yamanote line in 20 minutes. At ¥470, this is the cheapest, quickest way into Tokyo.

Limousine buses from Haneda cost about ¥1,000, depending on which part of the city you want to go to.

A **taxi** will cost a minimum of ¥5,000.

Going home

Tokyo City Air Terminal (T-CAT)

42-1 Nihonbashi-Hakozaki-cho, Chuo-ku (3665 7111). Suitengu-mae station.

If you can't face lugging your luggage to Narita or Haneda, T-CAT, in Tokyo's business district, offers a check-in and passport control service, with buses to the airport leaving every ten minutes (one-way is ¥2,900). Call to check that your airline is served there.

Trains & subway

Tokyo has one of the world's most efficient train systems: in the rare event of delays in the morning rush, staff give out apology slips to office workers to show their bosses. Trains and subways are fast, clean, safe and reliable. Most stations have signs in English as well as Japanese, and signs telling you which exit to take. Subways and train lines are colour-coded.

Subways and trains operate from 5am to around midnight (JR lines slightly later). Rush hours are 7.30-9.30am and 5-7pm. The last train can be a nightmare.

Tokyo's rail network is run by a variety of companies, and changing trains between competing systems can mean paying for two tickets. When travelling in Tokyo, try to stay on one network.

Tickets & passes

Japan Rail Pass

This provides for virtually unlimited travel on the national JR network, including *shinkansen* (bullet trains), except the new 'Nozomi' super-express and all JR lines in Tokyo. It's available only to visitors from abroad travelling under the entry status of 'temporary visitor', and must be purchased before coming to Japan. You have to show your passport when changing the Exchange Order to a ticket. It costs from ¥28,300 for a week, about the same price as a middle-distance shinkansen return ticket. JR East, which runs trains in and around Tokyo, has its own version of the pass, which costs from ¥20,000 for five days. The same conditions apply.

Exchange Orders for the pass can be purchased at overseas offices of the Japan Travel Bureau International, Nippon Travel Agency, Kinki Nippon Tourist, Tokyu Tourist Corporation and other

Women travellers

The crime rate in Japan is very low compared to that in many countries. Women should exercise standard precautions, but the risk of rape or assault is not high, and women can ride the subways at night or wander the streets with little concern. A woman alone might be harassed by drunken, staggering salarymen, but they are rarely serious, and ignoring them will generally do the trick.

This said, Tokyo is not immune from urban dangers, and boys will be boys even in Japan. The low incidence of rape is often attributed by some to under-reporting rather than respect for women. Don't let fear spoil your vacation, but do exercise a little caution at night, particularly in areas such as Roppongi and Shinjuku's Kabuki-cho.

A less serious type of assault occurs every day on packed rush-hour trains, where women are sometimes groped (or worse). Many Japanese women ignore the offence, hesitant to draw attention to themselves. It's pointless to vocalise anyway, as rarely will anyone step in to assist. This doesn't mean you have to stand there and take it: the best recourse is quiet retaliation; dig your nails into the offending hand or, if you're certain of the perpetrator, a swift kick to the shins or a jab in the gut with your handbag or umbrella should do the trick. But before taking any action, be sure there really is something happening. What might feel like a hand between your legs often turns out to be just a briefcase – or a woman's handbag. Avoiding rush hour is the best strategy.

Some public toilets are not sex-segregated. This doesn't pose any particular danger, but some women (and men) find it disconcerting to do their business in mixed company. If this is a concern, look for restrooms clearly marked with 'male' and 'female' symbols.

associated local travel agents, or at an overseas Japan Airlines office if you're travelling by Japan Airlines.

Regular tickets

Regular tickets for travelling in Tokyo can be purchased from station vending machines, many of which have symbols saying which notes they accept; otherwise, the ticket collector can change your notes. At JR stations, the touch-screen vending machines can display info in English, but if you're unsure of your destination (or unable to read it from the Japanese map), buy a ticket for the minimum fare (¥130) and settle up in a fare adjustment machine at the other end. All stations have them. Tokyo does not have punitive fines for travellers with incorrect tickets. Children under six travel free, under-12s pay half price.

Transferring from one line to another, provided it is run by the same operator (*see below*), will be covered in the price of your ticket. If your journey involves transferring from one network to another, you will have to buy a transfer ticket, if available. Or buy another ticket when you arrive at your transfer point.

Subways

Most subways are run by the Teito Rapid Transit Authority, which is often referred to as Eidan. Its eight lines are: Chiyoda (dark green), Ginza (orange), Hanzomon (purple), Hibiya (grey), Marunouchi (red), Namboku (light green), Tozai (turquoise) and Yurakucho (yellow).

Four subway lines are run by the metropolitan government. These 'Toei' lines are slightly more expensive. They are: Toei Asakusa line (pale pink), Toei Mita line (blue), Toei No 12 (bright pink) and Toei Shinjuku line (green). For subway map, *see page 270*.

JR trains

Overland trains in Tokyo are operated by Japan Railways East (JR). It's impossible to stay in Tokyo for more than a few hours without using JR's Yamanote line, the loop that defines the city centre. All Tokyo's subway and rail lines connect at some point with the Yamanote.

JR's major lines in Tokyo are: Yamanote (green), Chuo (orange), Sobu (yellow) and Keihin Tohoku (blue).

JR also operates the long-distance trains and shinkansen, which run from Tokyo or Ueno stations.

Private lines

Tokyo's private lines mainly ferry commuters to the outlying districts of the city. Because most were founded by companies that also run department stores, they usually terminate inside, or next to, one of their branches.

The major private lines are run by Keio, Odakyu, Seibu,

Smoking

Japan is a smoker's paradise. An estimated 60 per cent of the population indulge in the evil weed, and cigarettes are both cheap, at around ¥250 per packet, and readily available from vending machines, specialist shops and convenience stores.

The major supplier of cigarettes in Japan is Japan Tobacco (JT), formerly a state monopoly that was partially privatised in 1985. Ranked by declared income for 1997, JT was the nineteenth biggest company in Japan, one place ahead of Sony. JT's Mild Seven brand is the second most popular brand of cigarettes in the world, after Marlboro.

The practical upshot of all this is that you can smoke almost everywhere in Japan. Non-smoking areas include entertainment auditoria and the subway network, though JR train platforms have designated smoking areas. Some larger restaurants offer non-smoking sections, and the US coffee chain Starbucks is puritanically non-smoking.

Tobu and Tokyu. You can pick up a full map showing all lines and subways from the Airport Information counter on arrival.

Discount tickets

There's a huge number of discount tickets available, from pre-paid cards to 11-for-the-price-of-ten trip tickets. There are also combination tickets and one-day passes for one, two or three networks, though these are unlikely to be worth buying. For more details, call the JR East Infoline (3423 0111; *see* **Tourist services**, *p253, for hours*).

Taxis

The flagfall starts at ¥660 for the first 2km and keeps on climbing. Prices rise at weekends and between 11pm and 5am. Ranks are near stations, department stores, most hotels and main junctions. Doors open automatically.

Buses

Travelling by bus can be confusing if you're new to Japan, as signs are rarely in English. Fares cost around ¥200, no matter what the distance (half

price for kids). Get on the bus at the front, and off at the back, dropping the exact fare into the slot in front of the driver. If you don't have it, use the change machine, normally located to the right, which will deduct your fare from the change. Fare machines accept ¥50, ¥100 and ¥500 coins, and ¥1,000 notes. Stops are usually announced by a pre-recorded voice.

Bicycle hire

Eight Rent

Koshin Bldg 1F, 31-16 Sakuragaoka-cho, Shibuya-ku (3462 2383). Shibuya station. **Open** 10am-7pm Mon-Sat **Credit** MC, V
¥1,000 a day, with a ¥5,000 deposit. Bring your passport.

Driving

Tokyo drivers are notorious lane-weavers, making driving here stressful. Add to this the problem of reading street signs and the super-efficiency of the public transport system, and renting a car becomes a waste of time and money. Outside the city, toll charges on highways often compare unfavourably to the price of a rail ticket. If you rent a car, you'll be obliged to

pay astronomical parking fees (usually around ¥100 for 30 minutes, more in the centre).

If you persist in renting a car, you'll need an international driving licence and at least six months' driving experience. **Japan Automobile Federation** publishes a 'Rules of the Road' guide in English. Phone JAF (3436 2811) and ask for the International Affairs Department for further info. A Metropolitan Expressway map in English is available from the **Metropolitan Expressway Public Corporation** (3502 7311). English-speaking rental assistance is available at many large hotels and at the airport.

Hertz/Toyota Rent-a-car

Narita International Airport Terminal 1 & 2 (0476 32 1020/ fax 0476 32 1088). **Open** 7am-10pm daily.
If you want to drive outside Tokyo (much safer), JR offers rail and car rental packages. Call the **JR East Infoline** (3423 0111) for details.

Walking

Despite its size, Tokyo is a great city for walking. All areas are safe, and you're never far from a station. Straying from the main routes is a great way of discovering the thousands of hidden delights. The **TIC** (*see* **Tourist services**, *p253*) offers info on free walking tours of parts of Tokyo.

Always cross the road at marked crossings and always wait for the green man. If you cross on red, you may be responsible for the death of those behind you, some of whom will blindly follow you into the traffic.

Leaving town

Shinkansen

One of the fastest but most expensive ways to travel Japan's elongated countryside is by bullet train. Tickets can be purchased at JR reservation

'Green Window' areas or travel agents. Trains depart from different stations depending on destination; most leave from Tokyo, Shin-Yokohama, or Ueno. Slower, cheaper trains go to many destinations. Train platforms show where the numbered carriages will stop.

Long-distance buses

One of the cheapest ways to travel, though anyone over 5'6" tall may find the seats small. Most long-distance buses leave at midnight and arrive early the next morning. All are air-conditioned and have ample space for luggage. Seats can be reserved through a travel agent or a bus company such as JR Bus Kanto (7-1-1 Ueno, Taito-ku; 5806 1051; open 10am-6pm Mon-Fri, closed holidays) or Seibu Bus (1-28-1 Minami-Ikebukuro, Toshima-ku; 3981 2525; open 9.30am-6pm Mon-Fri, closed holidays.

Directory A-Z

Banks & money

The yen is not divided into smaller units, and comes in denominations of ¥1, ¥5, ¥10, ¥50, ¥100 and ¥500 (coins) and ¥1,000, ¥5,000 and ¥10,000 (notes). Prices on display do not usually include the five per cent purchase tax.

Banks

Opening a bank account is relatively easy if you have an Alien Registration number. With savings accounts you will be issued a book and card. Getting a card usually takes up to two weeks. It's generally delivered to your address, so you have to be home to sign for it; alternatively, get the bank to inform you when it arrives and pick it up.

You can open an account at the Tokyo Central Post Office and withdraw money from any other post office branch.

Banks are open 9am-3pm Monday-Friday, closed public holidays. Queues are long, especially on Fridays, and procedures involve taking a number and waiting around.

Changing money

You can cash travellers' cheques or change foreign currency at any Authorised Foreign Exchange Bank (look for the signs). Every main street in Tokyo is littered with banks. If you want to exchange money outside regular banking hours, most large hotels exchange travellers' cheques and currency, as do large department stores, which are open until about 8pm. Narita Airport has several bureaux de change staffed by English-speakers, open daily from 7am to 10pm.

Credit cards & cash machines

Japan is a cash-based society, and restaurants and bars may refuse cards. Larger shops, restaurants and hotels accept major cards, but you should always keep some cash on you.

ATMs are rarely open after 8pm and often close at 5pm on Saturdays. Many banks also charge for withdrawals made after 6pm. Still, there is a growing number of 24-hour ATMs in Tokyo, mostly around major train stations. All ATMs have stickers or logos showing which cards are accepted. Some will not accept foreign-issued cards; Citibank is your best bet, with 24-hour ATMs all over Tokyo (info 0120 504 189). Sumitomo Bank (head office 3282 5111) has a good reputation for dealing with foreigners.

To report lost or stolen credit cards, dial one of the following 24-hour numbers:
American Express 3220 6100/0120 020 120 (toll free)
Diners' Club 3797 7311
MasterCard 5350 8051
Visa 0120 133 173.

Etiquette

Japanese people are generally forgiving of visitors' clumsy attempts at correct behaviour, but there are certain rules that must be followed to avoid offending your hosts.

Shoes: when entering a house, temple or Japanese-style hotel, remove your shoes. Wear shoes that are easy to pull off and on, and make sure your socks are in good condition.

Bathing: bathing is one of the great delights of Japanese life, and every area has a public bath or *sento*, identified by a sign that looks like flames coming out of a handleless frying pan. When bathing, wash and rinse before getting in: the bath is for soaking in, not washing in. Never put your head underwater or immerse your washcloth.

Blowing your nose: while it's common to hear old men hawking up great gobs of phlegm, for some reason it's considered impolite to blow one's nose in public. If you must do it, go to the toilet.

For etiquette connected with business, eating or drinking, see the relevant chapters.

Directory

What's that address again?

The Japanese system of writing addresses is based on numbers rather than street names. Central Tokyo is divided into 23 wards, called *ku*. Within each ku, there are many smaller districts, or *cho*, which also have their own names. Most cho are further subdivided into numbered areas, or *chome*, then into blocks, and finally into individual buildings, which sometimes have names of their own. Japan uses the continental system of floor numbering. The abbreviation 1F is the ground floor, English style; 2F means second floor, or first floor English style.

Thus, the address of the Ban Thai restaurant (*see chapter* **Restaurants**) – Dai-ichi Metro Bldg 3F, 1-23-14 Kabuki-cho, Shinjuku-ku – means it's on the third floor (or second floor, English style) of the Metro building, which is the 14th building of the 23rd block of the first area of Kabuki-cho, in Shinjuku ward.

To help keep track of where you are, look out for the (usually bilingual) metal plaques affixed to lamp-posts. Individual buildings usually have small metal numbers that designate their address.

Confused? Don't worry. Few Tokyo-ites know the city well enough to navigate by address alone, and providing directions is one of the main functions of the local policeman in his *koban* (policebox). Few policemen speak English, but all koban are equipped with detailed maps of their area. Maps of areas with individual district and block numbers can also be found at or near the entrances to stations.

If you're serious about finding your way around by address, it's a good idea to buy a bilingual atlas, such as Shobunsha's Tokyo Metropolitan Atlas (*see* **Further Reading**), that shows all the cho, chome and numbered blocks within each ku.

If you have access to a fax machine, it's common practice in Tokyo to call up your destination and ask them to fax you a map of how to get there. If you're staying at a hotel, they'll be happy to let you receive a fax on their machine.

Money transfers

When you're having money sent to a Japanese bank account, you will need to give your bank account number, bank, branch and location. Mail transfers are cheaper than telex/telegraphic but they may take longer.

Customs

The following limits are imposed on travellers coming into Japan: 200 cigarettes or 250g of tobacco; three 750ml bottles of spirits; 57g of perfume; gifts or souvenirs up to ¥200,000.

Penalties for drug importation are severe: deportation is the lenient penalty. Porn laws are very strict, too; anything showing pubic hair may be confiscated.

There's no limit on bringing Japanese or foreign currency into the country.

Disabled travellers

Tokyo is not easy for those with disabilities, particularly when it comes to public transport, though some train stations have wheelchair moving facilities (when lifts aren't available) and raised dots on the ground guide those with vision problems.

Train workers will assist those in need. There are often special 'Silver Seats' near train exits for those requiring them.

For a copy of *Accessible Tokyo* contact: Red Cross Language Service Volunteers, c/o Volunteers Division, Japanese Red Cross Society, 1-1-3 Shiba Daimon, Minato-ku, Tokyo 105 (3438 1311/ fax 3432 5507).

Drinking

There's a lot of it in Tokyo, and the legal age for it to start at is 20, as it is for smoking.

Electricity & gas

Electric current in Japan runs, like the USA, at 100v AC, rather than the 220-240v European standard. If bringing electrical appliances from Europe, you need to purchase an adapter. Electricity in Tokyo is provided by Tokyo Electric Power Company (TEPCO; info 3501 8111); gas by Tokyo Gas (info 3433 2111).

Embassies

Embassies usually open from 9am to 5pm Monday-Friday; visa sections may vary.
Australian Embassy, 2-1-14 Mita, Minato-ku (5232 4111). Mita/ Tamachi stations.
British Embassy, 1 Ichibancho, Chiyoda-ku (3265 5511). Hanzomon station.
Canadian Embassy, 7-3-38 Akasaka, Minato-ku (3408 2101). Aoyama-itchome station.
Irish Embassy, 2-10-7 Kojimachi, Chiyoda-ku (3263 0695). Hanzomon station.

New Zealand Embassy,
20-40 Kamiyamacho, Shibuya-ku
(3467 2271). Yoyogikoen station.
US Embassy, 1-10-5 Akasaka,
Minato-ku (3224 5000).
Toranomon station.

Emergencies

110 police
119 ambulance and fire

The following organisations have an
English-speaking service:
Japan Helpline
0120 461 997 (24-hour emergency-
only number)
**TELL (Tokyo English Life
Line)** *5721 4347*
Tokyo Fire Department
3212 2323 (24 hours)
Helps callers find medical
centres and provides consultations
on emergencies.
Emergency Translation Service
5285 8185 (5am-10pm Mon-Fri;
9am-10pm Sat, Sun).
Telephone interpretation for
communication problems that stop
institutions from providing
emergency care for foreign nationals.
Service available in English, Chinese,
Korean, Thai and Spanish.

Health

Contraception

Condoms reign supreme,
largely because until 1999 the
pill was available only to
women with menstrual
problems. Condom machines
are on many street corners,
often near pharmacies.

Hospitals & insurance

Japanese are covered by
medical insurance, provided by
their employers or the state,
covering 70-90 per cent of the
cost of treatment. People over
70 pay a token amount towards
healthcare. Travellers are
expected to pay the full
amount, and should take out
medical insurance before
leaving their own countries.
    All calls to the numbers
below (except Tokyo Medical
Clinic) are answered in
Japanese. Say *'Eigo de hanashte
yoroshi dess ka?'* ('May I speak
English?') to be transferred to
an English-speaker.

General

Metropolitan Health & Medical Information Centre 'Himawari' service

5285 8181 (9am-8pm Mon-Fri).
Medical and health info in English,
Spanish, Chinese, Korean and Thai.
Also provides an emergency
interpretation service (*see above*).

English-speaking hospitals

Tokyo Sanitarium Hospital

*3-17-3 Amanuma, Suginami-ku
(3392 6151). Ogikubo station.*
Open 8.30am-11pm Mon-Fri.
No emergencies.

International Catholic Hospital

*2-5-1 Naka-Ochiai, Shinjuku-ku
(3951 1111). Shimo-Ochiai station
(Seibu Shinjuku line).* **Open** 8am-
11pm Mon-Sat for consultations.
Closed third Sat of month.
Emergency service 24 hours daily.

Japan Red Cross Medical Centre

*4-1-22 Hiroo, Shibuya-ku
(3400 1311). Hiroo station.*
Open 8.30am-11pm Mon-Fri for
consultations. Emergency service 24
hours daily.

St Luke's International Hospital

*9-1 Akashicho, Chuo-ku (3541
5151). Tsukiji station.* **Open** 8.30-
11pm Mon-Fri for consultations.
Emergency service 24 hours daily.

Tokyo Medical Clinic

*32 Mori Bldg, 3-4-30 Shiba Koen,
Minato-ku (3436 3028). Kamiyacho
station.* **Open** 9am-5pm Mon-Fri;
9am-1pm Sat. Emergency service
24 hours daily.
Doctors here are all from the UK,
America or Japan; all of them speak
English. There's also a pharmacy on
the first floor.

English-speaking pharmacies

American Pharmacy

*Hibiya Park Bldg, 1-8-1 Yurakucho,
Chiyoda-ku (3271 4034). Hibiya
station.* **Open** 9.30am-7.30pm Mon-
Sat; 10am-6.30pm Sun.

Kaken International Pharmacy

*Kaken Tsukiji Bldg, 11-6 Akashicho,
Chuo-ku (3248 6631). Tsukiji
station.* **Open** 8.30am-5.45pm Mon-
Fri; 8.30am-4.15pm Sat.

Late-night pharmacies

Many pharmacies in major
centres or near busy stations
are open till midnight. Some
branches of the 24-hour
convenience store chain AM-
PM have in-store pharmacies.
Basic items, such as sanitary
towels, condoms or sticking
plasters, can be purchased at
any convenience store, but the
law forbids them from selling
pharmaceuticals. Most
convenience stores are open
24 hours daily.

English-speaking opticians

Fuji Optical Service International

*Otemachi Bldg 1F, 1-6-1 Otemachi,
Chiyoda-ku (3214 4751). Otemachi
station.* **Open** 10am-7pm Mon-Fri;
10am-6pm Sat.
Call to make an appointment, as only
one optician speaks English.

Hitch-hiking

Illegal in Japan, but anecdotal
evidence suggests the law is
rarely enforced and drivers are
happy to pick people up.

Language

For information on Japanese
language and pronunciation,
and a list of useful words and
phrases, *see page 254*.
    Hundreds of schools in
Tokyo run courses in Japanese.
Most offer intensive studies for
those who want to learn
Japanese as quickly as possible
or need Japanese for work or
school. They may offer longer
courses, too. Private schools
tend to be expensive so check
out lessons run by your ward
office. Ward lessons cost from
¥100 a month to ¥500 every
two months – a bargain
compared to ¥3,000 an hour for
group lessons.

Arc Academy

3409 0157
Offers a wide variety of courses.
Website: http://www.arc.ac.jp

GABA

3725 7220
Established; offers lessons at home.

Temple University

0120 861 026
Fairly cheap evening classes, plus a
continuing education programme
with business Japanese. A few
undergraduate Japanese classes.

Legal advice

Legal Counselling Centre

Bar Association Bldg, 1-1-3
Kasumigaseki, Chiyoda-ku (3581
2302). Kasumigaseki station. **Open**
1-4pm Mon-Fri (appointment only).
English-language consultations for
¥5,150/half-hour, free for the
impoverished on Thursday
afternoon. A range of issues,
including crime, immigration matters
and labour problems, are covered.
Appointments are on a first-come,
first-served basis, from 1pm to 3pm.

Libraries

Each ward has a central
lending library with a limited
number of English-language
books. You need an Alien
Registration Card to borrow
books. The following reference
libraries have a healthy number
of books in English. All
libraries close for Japanese
national holidays.

British Council Library & Information Centre

Kenkyusha Eigo Center Bldg 1F, 1-2
Kagurazaka, Shinjuku-ku (3235
8031). Iidabashi station.
Open 11am-8pm Mon-Fri.
Info is limited to the UK, but there's
Internet access and BBC World is
always on TV. For ¥500 a day you
can use all the facilities. Loans for
members only. Closes for UK bank
holidays as well as Japanese
holidays. Call ahead to confirm it's
open. People under 18 not admitted.

Japan Foundation Library

Ark Mori Bldg, West Wing 20F,
1-12-32 Akasaka, Minato-ku (5562
3527). Tameike-sanno station.
Open 10am-5pm Mon-Fri; closed last
Mon of month.
Books, mags, reference material and
doctoral works on all aspects of
Japan. Specialises in humanities and
social sciences, and has translations
of Japanese novels. Houses about
25,000 books and 300 magazine titles.
Lending as well as reference. People
under 18 not admitted.

JETRO Library

Kyodo Tsushin Bldg 6F, 2-2-5
Toranomon, Minato-ku (3582 1775).
Toranomon station. **Open**
9am-4.30pm Mon-Fri; closed third
Tue & Wed.
Japan External Trade Organisation
library houses info about trade, the
economy and investment for just
about any country. Lots of statistics
as well as basic business directories.
There are 150,000 titles in all
languages. No entry to under-18s.

National Diet Library

1-10-1 Nagatacho, Chiyoda-ku
¦(3581 2331). Nagatacho station.
Open 9.30am-5pm Mon-Fri; closed
third & fourth Mon of month.
Japan's main library, with the largest
number of foreign-language books
and materials. To get a book you fill
in a form to gain admittance, go
through the catalogues and submit
forms to have the book brought to
you. Over 2 million books, 50,000
mags and 1,500 newspapers and
periodicals. No under-20s.
Website: http://www.ndl.go.jp

Tokyo Metropolitan Central Library

5-7-13 Minami-Azabu, Minato-ku
(3442 8451). Hiroo station.
Open 1-8pm Mon; 9.30am-8pm
Tue-Fri; 9.30am-5pm Sat, Sun;
closed first Thur & third Sun.
Main library for the Tokyo
government, with the largest
collection about Tokyo. Over 150,000
titles in foreign languages. People
under 16 not admitted.

Lost property

If you leave a bag or package
somewhere, go back: it will
probably still be there.
If you left it in a train station or
other public area, go to the
stationmaster's office or nearest
policebox and ask for English-
language assistance. Items
left in the station are logged
in a book. You will have to
sign in order to receive your
item. If it was left in a taxi on
the way to or from the hotel,
try the hotel reception – taxi
drivers often bring the lost item
straight back to your hotel.

Lost property offices

The following numbers will all
be answered in Japanese, so be
sure to ask a Japanese person to
call for you.

Eidan subway: 3834 5577
JR Shinjuku station: 3354 4019
JR Tokyo station: 3231 1880
JR Ueno station: 3841 8069
Metropolitan Police: 3814 4151
Narita Airport: 0476 322802
Taxi: 3648 0300
Toei subway and buses: 3815 7229

Opening hours

Larger stores are open daily
from 9.30/10am to around 8pm.
Smaller shops are open the
same hours six days a week,
Monday and Wednesday being
the most common closing days.
Most restaurants open around
11am and close around
midnight, though some *izakaya*
are open all night and many
bars open till 5am, or till they're
empty. Office hours
are 9am-5pm. The ubiquitous
convenience stores offer
24-hour shopping at
slightly higher prices than
supermarkets. The major
chains are 7-Eleven, AM-PM,
Family Mart and Lawson's. On
national holidays, most places
keep Sunday hours, but on 1
and 2 January most are closed.

Police & security

Japan is one of the safest places
to visit, though crime does
occur and normal precautions
should be taken. Policeboxes
(*koban*) are everywhere, though
officers don't usually speak
English (and may not be overly
friendly to non-Japanese).
City centres such as Shibuya
and Shinjuku have people
wandering about at all hours.
In notorious areas such as
Roppongi, or Shinjuku's
Kabuki-cho, be cautious.
Theft is still miraculously
uncommon in Japan, so it's not
unusual to walk around with
the equivalent of hundreds of
pounds in your wallet without
giving the matter a second
thought. Places in which
you should be careful are
airports and packed trains –
pickpockets may well be at
work there.

Japanese + English = ?

You wake up in your Tokyo *manshon* and consider the possibility of heading out for *mo-ningu saabisu* at your local coffee shop. Are you living in aristocratic splendour in one of the world's most cramped cities? Not exactly. In fact, your residence is a small *apaato* in an anonymous block. You decide against *koohi* and *toosto*, and go back to sleep.

An hour later, you awake again with a start. The *terebi* comes on, but you don't watch the *nyuusu*. Reminding yourself to take it easy on the *biiru* in future, you throw on your *suutsu* and *T-shatsu* (although only one of each). A *neku-tai* is crammed into a pocket, and you head for the *doa*. A schoolgirl wearing baggy white *ruuzu sokkusu* shares the *erebe-taa*, but your only thought is whether you'll be able to grab a *hamu-sando* at the *con-bini* on the corner.

It's Monday morning. You are a *sarari-man*.

Postal services

A red-and-white T sign marks a post office. Most large streets have one. Postcards overseas cost ¥70; aerograms cost ¥90; letters under 25g cost ¥90 (Asian countries), ¥110 (North America, Europe, Oceania) or ¥120 (Africa, South America).

Sending parcels by surface mail is cheaper than by air. Larger department stores can arrange postage if you purchase major items.

Local post offices are open 9am-5pm weekdays (closed public holidays). District post offices (the main ones) are open 9am-7pm Monday to Friday, 9am-3pm Saturday (closed public holidays).

For poste restante, contact the Central Tokyo Post Office on 3284 9539. You can receive mail at the main international post office (3241 4891), in Otemachi by the subway, A4 exit. Mail is held for up to 30 days; the PO is open 9am-7pm weekdays, 9am-5pm Saturday, 9am-noon Sundays and public holidays.

When you're writing addresses, English script is acceptable, as long as it's clearly written.

Express delivery services

Federal Express 0120 003 200
Nippon Express 3572 4305
Overseas Courier Service 5476 8106
Takyubin 3789 5131 (a convenient and cheap same-day, door-to-door service available through convenience stores; costs around ¥1,500 for small packages)

Public holidays

See page 5 for details.

Religion

According to the *Religion Yearbook* issued by the Agency for Cultural Affairs, 208 million Japanese are members of religious organisations – almost twice the population. It's not unusual for a family to celebrate birth with Shinto rites, have a Christian marriage, and pay last respects at a Buddhist ceremony. Freedom of worship is a constitutional right.

Rubbish

After the subway sarin gas attack in March 1995, most bins were removed from subway stations. All JR stations have rubbish bins near the exits. These are divided into three sections: cans; newspapers and magazines; and other rubbish. If you can't find a bin, carry your rubbish home with you.

All domestic rubbish should be divided into burnable, unburnable and large items. To arrange to have large items removed, call 5296 7000 (info 5320 5761).

Telephones

The area code for Tokyo is 03. If you're calling from outside Japan, dial 00 81 3, followed by the number. For domestic calls from outside Tokyo, dial 03 followed by the number. Throughout this book, we've omitted the 03 from Tokyo telephone numbers.

The Japanese public telephone system is expensive: calls within the city cost ¥10 for the first three minutes then ¥10 for every minute. NTT (Nippon Telegraph & Telephone Corporation) is the major national telephone company; ITJ and KDD are the larger international call operators.

International calls can be made only from phoneboxes with 'International' or 'ISDN' marked on the side in English. These phones also have sockets for PCs. The grey monitor displays instructions in English as well as Japanese. To make an international call, dial 001 (KDD), 0041 (ITJ) or 0061 (IDC), followed by your country's access code and the telephone number. NTT phonecards cannot be used to make international calls, so buy a prepaid card or have a lot of change handy. Rates between the three companies differ, but only slightly. The cheapest time to call is 11pm-8am, when a 40% off-peak discount applies. The 'home country direct' service allows you to charge the call to your home telephone bill, provided

Guided tours

If getting around under your own steam is too much like hard work, the following companies offer guided tours of Tokyo in English. Detailed leaflets are on display at TIC (*see below* **Tourist services**) and most big hotels.

By bus

Hato Bus Tokyo Sightseeing Tour Company

World Trade Centre Bldg, 2-4-1 Hamamatsucho, Minato-ku (3435 6081/fax 3433 1972). Hamamatsucho station. **Bookings** 9am-7pm daily. **Credit** all major cards.

One of Tokyo's main sightseeing tour operators, in business since 1948. Offers a variety of tours, including half-day, full-day and night tours with English-speaking guides. One snag is that all bookings must be made by fax 14 days before the tour date, to avoid incurring a booking fee. Prices for tours start at around ¥3,500; the Amazing Night Tour is the most expensive, at ¥13,000.

Website: www.hatobus.co.jp/english/index.html

Japan Gray Line Company

3-3-3 Nishi-Shinbashi, Minato-ku (3433 5745/fax 3433 8388/ easy5@tky3.3web.ne.jp). Shinbashi station. **Bookings** 24 hours. **Credit** all major cards.

Morning, afternoon and full-day tours of Tokyo's sights, in English. From ¥3,300 to ¥10,500. Buses pick up at many of Tokyo's top hotels.

Sunrise Tours

5-5-2 Kiba, Koto-ku (5620 9500). Kiba station. **Bookings** 9am-8pm daily. **Credit** all major cards.

Run by Japan Travel Bureau. Offers the widest range of English-language tours, including trips out of town to Mount Fuji, Disneyland and the hot springs of Hakone, plus the usual full-day, half-day or night tours of Tokyo.

By taxi

Tokyo Jumbo Hire

7-16-23 Iriya, Adachi-ku (3896 0818/fax 3896 8181). **Bookings** 9am-6pm Mon-Fri; 9am-3pm Sat. **No credit cards**.

If you feel like seeing the city in style, splash out on a taxi tour. Three-hour courses start at ¥12,000; an eight-hour ride will set you back ¥31,300. English-speaking drivers can be provided.

By helicopter

Helicopter Night Cruising

(3761 1100). **Bookings** 8am-6.30pm daily. **Credit** all major cards.

A Japanese-only service, operated by Hato Bus (*see above*), this four-hour tour involves a flight over the city and an Indian meal. The flight time is ten minutes. Tours take place on Friday, Saturday and Sunday holidays, starting at 6pm. The ¥18,900 fee includes transfers to and from your hotel. Foreigners not accompanied by Japanese are not allowed on the tour.

Directory

---

you set up the service in your home country first.

Operator assisted international calls **0051**
Home country direct **0039**
Directory assistance **104** (local, in Japanese)
Directory assistance **0120 364 463** (English, 9am-5pm Mon-Fri)
International directory **0057**
Phone installation NTT **0120 364 463**

Toll-free numbers

Numbers starting with 0120 are receiver-paid calls under NTT's 'Free Dial 0120' service.

Telephone cards

Many cards have pictures on the front and are collector's items. You should note that some special edition cards will cost more than the number of telephone calls you can use them for.

Two kinds of telephone card are available. KDD produces a 'Super World' prepaid card for international phone calls, which is sold at most major convenience stores. Valued at ¥1,000, ¥3,000 and ¥5,000, they can be used with any push button phone. Dial 0055 to make the call.

NTT produces a card primarily for the domestic market: a ¥1,000 card contains 105 ¥10 units. They're available from most convenience stores and vending machines inside some phoneboxes. Insert in the direction of the arrow.

If someone offers to sell you a card on the street, do not buy it. Forgeries are common, and the penalties for selling or using them can be severe.

Telephone directories

Unless you're fluent, using a Japanese phonebook is out of the question. NTT publishes an English-language phonebook, *Townpage*, but it's far from comprehensive. You can get it free from NTT (3356 8511) or Tourist Information Centre (TIC) in Yurakucho, or on the web at *http://english. townpage.isp.ntt.co.jp*

Telephone helplines

The following offer info, advice or counselling in English.

AIDS Hotline
0120 461 995 (24 hours daily)

Alcoholics Anonymous
3971 1471 (10am-6pm Mon-Fri)

Immigration Information Centre
3213 8523 (9.30am-4pm Mon-Fri)

Tokyo English Lifeline
3968 4099 (9am-4pm, 7-11pm, daily)

Tokyo Foreign Residents Advisory Centre
5320 7744 (9.30am-noon, 1-4pm, Mon-Fri)

HELP Asian Women's Shelter
3368 8855 (24 hours daily)

Time & seasons

Time zones

All of Japan is in the same time zone, nine hours ahead of GMT. Daylight Saving Time is not practised, but is a constant topic of debate.

Seasons

In Tokyo, winter is marked by clear skies, cold days and the occasional snowstorm. Spring begins with winds and cherry-blossom viewing. The rainy season for Honshu (the main island) begins in June. This is followed by summer with its hot and humid days. Finally, autumn is marked by the changing of the leaves. Temperatures in Tokyo range from around 3°C in January to 32°C in July/August. The summer months can be unbearable for those not used to humidity. It's advisable to travel during summer with a small hand-held fan, a bottle of water and a wet cotton cloth or small washcloth. Fans are often handed out in the street as part of ad campaigns.

Tipping

People will generally be embarrassed if you try to tip them. If you leave money on a restaurant table, for example, you will probably be pursued down the street by a member of staff trying to return it.

Toilets

Public toilets can be found in and around most train stations.

If there's not one in the station, there probably is one near the entrance or just outside the exit.

Station toilets usually offer Japanese-style commodes. The way to use them is to squat over them, facing the back wall. Many public toilets do not have toilet tissue. You can buy tissue from machines outside the doors, or keep an eye out for part-time workers handing out free tissues on the street. The packets are ads for companies and services around Tokyo.

If you don't fancy squatting Japanese-style, you should head for a large shop or department store, where western-style toilets are the norm. In some women's toilets there might be a small box with a button on the wall: pushing it produces the sound of flushing. Many Japanese women flush the toilet two or three times to cover the sounds they make, and the fake flush was designed to save water.

If you happen to be staying in a Japanese home or good hotel, you may find that your toilet looks like the command seat on the Starship Enterprise. The controls to the right of the seat usually operate its heating and in-built bidet controls.

Tourist services

TIC Tokyo Office

Tokyo International Forum B1, 3-5-1 Marunouchi, Chiyoda-ku (3201 3331). Yurakucho station. **Open** 9am-5pm Mon-Fri; 9am-noon Sat. Tourist Information Centres (TIC) are affiliated with Japan National Tourist Organisation (JNTO). The TIC in Tokyo is a must-see on any traveller's list as it's located in Rafael Viñoly's brilliant Tokyo International Forum building, which opened in 1996. The Tokyo office also has a Welcome Inn Reservation Centre (*see chapter* **Accommodation**), open 9.15am-noon and 1-5.15pm (last booking half an hour before closing). TIC has friendly multilingual staff and a wealth of info: maps, event booklets, books on Japanese customs, even NTT English phonebooks.

TIC Narita Offices

Arrival floor, Terminal 2, New Tokyo International Airport (0476 34 6251). **Open** 9am-8pm daily.
Arrival floor, Terminal 1, New Tokyo International Airport (0476 30 3383). **Open** 9am-8pm daily.

Japan Railways East Infoline

3423 0111 (10am-6pm Mon-Fri)

Japan Travel Phone

0088 22 4800 (outside Tokyo & Kyoto); *3201 3331* (in Tokyo); *371 5649* (in Kyoto). **Available** 9am-5pm daily.
A nationwide service for those in need of English-language assistance and travel info. Outside Tokyo and Kyoto, it's free; within the two cities, normal phone rates apply.

Teletourist Service

3201 2911 (24 hours)
Taped info on current events.

Visas

By August 1998, Japan had concluded general visa exemption arrangements with 56 countries, including the USA, Canada, the UK and the Republic of Ireland. Citizens of these countries can stay in Japan for up to 90 days. Japan also has working holiday visa arrangements with Australia, New Zealand and Canada for people aged 18-30.

The following types of visa are available (for more info, contact Tokyo Immigration Office, Daisan Godo Chosha Bldg 2F, 1-3 Otemachi, Chiyoda-ku; 3213 8111).

• Tourist Visa. A 'short-term stay' visa, good for anyone not intending to work in Japan.

• Working Visa. It's illegal to work here without a visa. If you arrive on a tourist visa and find work, your company has to sponsor you for a work visa. You must then go abroad to make the application (South Korea is the cheapest option).

If you plan to stay in Japan for more than 90 days, you need an Alien Registration Card. For this, you need three passport-sized photos, a passport and an address.

Getting by in Japanese

JAPANESE LANGUAGE

Pronunciation

Japanese pronunciation presents few problems for native English speakers, the most difficult trick to master being the doubling of vowels or consonants (see below).

Vowels

a as in bad
e as in bed
i as in feet
o as in long
u as in look

Long vowels

aa as in father
ee as in fair
ii as in feet, but longer
oo as in fought
uu as in chute

Consonants

Consonants in Japanese are pronounced the same as in English, but are always hard ('g' as in 'girl', rather than 'gyrate', for example). The only exceptions are the 'l/r' sound, which is one sound in Japanese, and falls halfway between the English pronunciation of the two letters, and 'v', which is pronounced as a 'b'. When consonants are doubled, they are pronounced as such: a 'tt' as in 'matte' (wait) is pronounced more like the 't' sound in 'get to' than in 'getting'.

Reading the phrases

When reading the phrases given below, remember to separate the syllables. Despite the amusing way it looks in English, the common name Takeshita is pronounced Ta-ke-shi-ta. Similarly, made (until) is 'ma-de', not the English word 'made', and shite (doing) is 'shi-te', rather than anything else. When a 'u' falls at the end of the word, it is barely pronounced: 'desu' is closer to 'dess' than to 'de-su'.

Reading & writing

The Japanese writing system is fiendishly complicated and is the main deterrent to learning the language. Japanese uses two syllabaries (not alphabets, because the letters represent complete sounds), hiragana and katakana, in conjunction with kanji, characters imported from China many centuries ago. The average Japanese person will be able to read over 6,000 kanji. For all but the most determined visitor, learning to read before you go is out of the question. However, learning katakana is relatively simple and will yield quick results, since it is used mainly to spell out foreign words (many imported from English). For books on learning Japanese, *see* **Further Reading**, page 258.

Numbers

1	*ichi*	2	*ni*	3	*san*
4	*yon*	5	*go*	6	*roku*
7	*nana*	8	*hachi*	9	*kyuu*
10	*juu*	11	*juu-ichi*	12	*juu-ni*
100	*hyaku*	1,000	*sen*	10,000	*man*

Days

Monday *getsu-yoobi*   Tuesday *ka-yoobi*
Wednesday *sui-yoobi*   Thursday *moku-yoobi*
Friday *kin-yoobi*   Saturday *do-yoobi*
Sunday *nichi-yoobi*

Time

It's at ...o'clock.   *...ji desu*
Excuse me, do you have the time?
sumimasen, ima nan-ji desu ka

Months

January *ichi-gatsu*   July *shichi-gatsu*
February *ni-gatsu*   August *hachi-gatsu*
March *san-gatsu*   September *ku-gatsu*
April *shi-gatsu*   October *juu-gatsu*
May *go-gatsu*   November *juu-ichi-gatsu*
June *roku-gatsu*   December *juu-ni-gatsu*

Dates

yesterday/today/tomorrow
kinoo/kyoo/ashita

last week/this week/next week
sen-shuu/kon-shuu/rai-shuu

the weekend   *shuumatsu*

Basic expressions

Yes/no **hai/iie**

Okay **ookee**

Please (asking for a favour) **onegai shimasu**

Please (offering a favour) **doozo**

Thank you (very much) **(doomo) arigatoo**

Hello/hi **kon nichiwa**

Good morning **ohayoo gozaimasu**

Good afternoon **kon nichi wa**

Good evening **kon ban wa**

Goodnight **oyasumi nasai**

Goodbye **sayonara**

Excuse me (getting attention) **sumimasen**

Excuse me (may I get past?) **shitsurei shimasu**

Excuse me/sorry **gomen nasai**

Don't mention it/never mind
ki ni shinai de kudasai

It's okay **daijyoobu desu**

Communication

Do you speak English?
Eigo o hanashi masu ka

I don't speak (much) Japanese
Nihongo o (amari) hanashi masen

Could you speak more slowly?
yukkuri itte kudasai

Could you repeat that? **moo ichido itte kudasai**

I understand **wakari mashita**

I don't understand **wakari masen**

Do you understand? **wakari masu ka?**

Where is it? **doko desu ka**

When is it? **itsu desu ka**

What is it? **nan desu ka**

SIGNS

General

左 *hidari* left

右 *migi* right

入口 *iriguchi* entrance

出口 *deguchi* exit

トイレ/お手洗い *toire/o-tearai* toilets

男/男性 *otoko/dansei* men

女/女性 *onna/jyosei* women

禁煙 *kin-en* no smoking

危険 *kiken* danger

立ち入り禁止 *tachiiri kinshi* no entry

引く/押す *hiku/osu* pull/push

遺失物取扱所 *ishitsu butsu toriatsukai jo*
lost property

水泳禁止 *suiei kinshi* no swimming

飲料水 *inryoosui* drinking water

関係者以外立ち入り禁止
kankeisha igai tachiiri kinshi private

地下道 *chikadoo* underpass (subway)

足元注意 *ashimoto chuui* mind the step

ペンキ塗り立て *penki nuritate* wet paint

頭上注意 *zujoo chuui* mind your head

Road signs

止まれ *tomare* stop

徐行 *jokoo* slow

一方通行 *ippoo tsuukoo* one way

駐車禁止 *chuusha kinshi* no parking

高速道路 *koosoku dooro* motorway

料金 *ryookin* toll

信号 *shingoo* traffic lights

交差点 *koosaten* junction

Airport/station

案内 *an-nai* information

免税 *menzee* duty free

入国管理 *nyuukoku kanri* immigration

到着 *touchaku* arrivals

出発 *shuppatsu* departures

コインロッカー *koin rokkaa* luggage lockers

荷物引き渡し所 *nimotsu hikiwatashi jo*
luggage reclaim

手荷物カート *tenimotsu kaato* trolleys

バス/鉄道 *basu/tetsudoo* bus/train

レンタカー *rentakaa* car rental

地下鉄 *chikatetsu* underground

Hotels/restaurants

フロント *furonto* reception

予約 *yoyaku* reservation

非常口 *hijyooguchi* emergency/fire exit

湯 *yu* hot (water)

冷 *ree* cold (water)
バー *baa* bar

Shops

営業中 *eegyoo chuu* open
閉店 *heeten* closed
階 *kai* floor
地下 *chika* basement
エレベーター *erebeetaa* lift
エスカレーター *esukareetaa* escalator
会計 *kaikee* cashier

Sightseeing

入場無料 *nyuujoo muryoo* free admission
大人/子供 小人 *otona/kodomo* adults/children
割引（学生/高齢者）*waribiki (gakusei/koureisha)* reduction (students/senior citizens)
お土産 *o-miyage* souvenirs
手を触れないでください *te o furenai de kudasai* do not touch
撮影禁止 *satsuei kinshi* no photography

Public buildings

病院 *byooin* hospital
交番 *kouban* police box
銀行 *ginkoo* bank
郵便局 *yuubin kyoku* post office
プール *puuru* swimming pool
博物館 *hakubutsu-kan* museum

ESSENTIAL WORDS & PHRASES

Hotels

Do you have a room?
heya wa arimasu ka

I'd like a single/double room
shinguru/daburu no heya o onegai shimasu

I'd like a room with...
...tsuki no heya o onegai shimasu

a bath/shower **furo/shawa**

Reception

I have a reservation
yoyaku shite arimasu

My name is...
(watashi no namae wa)...desu

Is there...in the room?
heya ni...wa arimasu ka

air-conditioning **eakon**
TV/telephone **terebi/denwa**

We'll be staying... **...tomari masu**
one night only **ippaku dake**
a week **isshuu-kan**

I don't know yet **mada wakari masen**

I'd like to stay an extra night
moo ippaku sasete kudasai

How much is it...? **...ikura desu ka**

including/excluding breakfast
chooshoku komi/nuki de

Does the price include...?
kono nedan wa...komi desu ka

sales tax (VAT) **shoohi zee**
breakfast/meal **chooshoku/shokuji**

Is there a reduction for children?
kodomo no waribiki wa arimasu ka

What time is breakfast served?
chooshoku wa nan-ji desu ka

Is there room service?
ruumu saabisu wa arimasu ka

The key to room..., please.
...goo-shitsu no kagi o kudasai

I've lost my key **kagi o nakushi mashita**

Could you wake me up at...?
...ji ni okoshite kudasai

bath towel/blanket/pillow
basu taoru/moofu/makura

Are there any messages for me?
messeeji wa arimasu ka

What time do we have to checkout by?
chekkuauto wa nan-ji made desu ka

Could I have my bill, please?
kaikei o onegai shimasu

Could I have a receipt please?
reshiito o onegai shimasu

Could you order me a taxi, please?
takushii o yonde kudasai

Shops & services

pharmacy **yakkyoku/doraggu sutoaa**
off-licence/liquor store **saka-ya**
newsstand **kiosuku**
department store **depaato**

bookshop **hon-ya**

supermarket **supaa**

camera store **kamera-ya**

I'd like... **...o kudasai**

Do you have...? **...wa arimasu ka**

How much is that? **ikura desu ka**

Could you help me? **onegai shimasu**

I'm looking for... **...o sagashite imasu**

larger/smaller **motto ookii/motto chiisai**

I'll take it **sore ni shimasu**

That's all, thank you **sore de zenbu desu**

Bank/currency exchange

dollars **doru**

pounds **pondo**

yen **en**

currency exchange **ryoogae-jo**

I'd like to change some pounds into yen
pondo o en ni kaetain desu ga

Could I have some small change, please?
kozeni o kudasai

Health

Where can I find a hospital/dental surgery?
byooin/hai-sha wa doko desu ka

Is there a doctor/dentist who speaks English?
eego ga dekiru isha/ha-isha wa imasu ka

What are the surgery hours?
shinryoo jikan wa nan-zi desu ka

Could the doctor come to see me here?
ooshin shite kuremasu ka

Could I make an appointment for...?
...yoyaku shitain desu ga

as soon as possible **dekirudake hayaku**

It's urgent **shikyuu onegai shimasu**

Symptoms

I feel faint **memai ga shimasu**

I have a fever **netsu ga arimasu**

I've been vomiting **modoshi mashita**

I've got diarrhoea **geri shitemasu**

It hurts here **koko ga itai desu**

I have a headache **zutsu ga shimasu**

I have a sore throat **nodo ga itai desu**

I have a stomach ache **onaka ga itai**

I have toothache **ha ga itai desu**

I've lost a filling/tooth
tsumemono/ha ga toremashita

I don't want it extracted **nukanaide kudasai**

Sightseeing

Where's the tourist office?
kankoo annai-jo wa doko desu ka

Do you have any information on...?
...no annai wa arimasu ka

sightseeing tour **kankoo tsuaa**

Are there any trips to...?
...e no tsuaa wa arimasu ka

On tour

We'd like to have a look at the...
...o mitain desu ga

to take photographs **shasin o toritain desu ga**

to buy souvenirs **omiyage o kaitain desu ga**

to use the toilets **toire ni ikitain desu ga**

Can we stop here? **koko de tomare masu ka**

Could you take a photo of us, please?
shasin o totte kudasai

Travel

To..., please. **...made onegai shimasu**

Single/return tickets **katamichi/oofuku kippu**

How much...? **...wa ikura desu ka?**

I'm here on holiday/business
kankoo/shigoto de kimashita

I'm going to... **...ni ikimasu**

on my own **hitori**

with my family **kazoku to issho**

I'm with a group **guruupu de kimashita**

ticket office **kippu-uriba**

ticket gate **kaisatsu-guchi**

ticket vending machines **kenbai-ki**

shinkansen **bullet train**

Where's the nearest underground station?
chikatetsu no eki wa doko desu ka

Where can I buy a ticket?
kippu wa doko de kaemasu ka

Could I have a map of the underground?
chikatetsu no rosenzu o kudasai

Further Reading

Architecture

Tajima, Noriyuki *Tokyo: Guide to Recent Architecture*
Pocket-sized guide with great pictures.
Tajima, Noriyuki & Powell, Catherine *Tokyo: Labyrinth City*
LP-sized guide to more recent projects.

Fiction

Abe, Kobe *The Woman in the Dunes*
Weird classic about a lost village of sand.
Birnbaum, Alfred (ed) *Monkey Brain Sushi*
Decent selection of 'younger' Japanese writers.
Erickson, Steve *The Sea Came in at Midnight*
American novel set partly in a Tokyo 'memory hotel'.
Kawabata, Yasuwari *Snow Country*
Japan's first Nobel prize winner for literature.
Mishima, Yukio *Confessions of a Mask* & others
Japan's most famous novelist, 20 years after his suicide.
Murakami, Haruki *Norwegian Wood* & others
Most of Murakami's books are set in Tokyo.
Murakami, Ryu *Coin Locker Babies* & others
Hip modern novelist, unrelated to Haruki.
Oe, Kenzoburo *A Personal Matter* & others
Japan's second winner of the Nobel prize.
Yoshimoto, Banana *Kitchen* & others
Modern writer who's made a splash in the west.

Food & drink

Harper, Philip *The Insider's Guide to Sake*
Readable introduction to Japan's national libation.
Okakura, Kazuko *The Book of Tea*
Tea as the answer to life, the universe and everything.
Satterwhite, Robb *What's What in Japanese Restaurants*
An invaluable guide to navigating the menu maze.

History & politics

Kaplan, David & Marshall, Andrew *The Cult At The End Of The World*
Terrifying story of Aum and the subway gas attacks.
Schlesinger, Jacob M *Shadow Shoguns: The Rise and Fall of Japan's Postwar Political Machine*
Pretty good non-academic read.
Seidensticker, Edward *Tokyo Rising* & *Low City, High City*
Eminently readable histories of the city.

Language

Three A Network/Minna no Nihongo Shokyuu
Book 1 for beginners, 2 for pre-intermediate.
Integrated Approach to Intermediate Japanese
Well balanced in grammar, reading and conversation.

A Dictionary of Basic Japanese Grammar
Standard reference book from the *Japan Times*.

Maps & guides

Shobunsha Tokyo Metropolitan Atlas
Negotiate those tricky addresses with confidence.
Kennedy, Rick *Little Adventures in Tokyo*
Entertaining trips through the off-beat side of the city.
Martin, John H & Phyllis G *Tokyo: A Cultural Guide to Japan's Capital City*
Enjoyable ramble through Tokyo.
Pompian, Susan *Tokyo For Free*
Immaculately researched guide for skinflints.
Walters, Gary DA *Day Walks Near Tokyo* & *More Day Walks Near Tokyo*
Detailed routes for escaping the crowds.

Miscellaneous

Japan As It Is
Eccentric explanations of all things Japanese.
Asahi Shinbun's Japan Almanac
The ultimate book of lists, published annually.
Bird, Isabella *Unbeaten Tracks in Japan*
Amazing memoirs of intrepid Victorian explorer.
Bornoff, Nicholas *Pink Samurai: Love, Marriage and Sex in Contemporary Japan*
All you ever wanted to know about the subjects.
Whitting, Robert *Tokyo Underworld: The Fast Life and Times of an American Gangster in Japan*
Enthralling story of underworld life.

Sport

Sharnoff, Lora *Grand Sumo*
Exhaustive account, if a little on the dry side.
Whitting, Robert *You Gotta Have Wa*
US baseball stars + Japan = culture clash.

Style & culture

Galbraith, Stuart *Giants Monsters Are Attacking Tokyo: Incredible World of Japanese Fantasy Films*
The ultimate guide to the weird and wacky world of the city-stomping giants of Japanese cinema.
Kawakami, Kenji & Don Papia *101 Unuseless Japanese Inventions: The Art of Chindogu*
Everything you never knew you needed.
Richie, Donald *Public People, Private People* and *Tokyo: A View of the City*
Acclaimed writer on the Japanese and their capital.
Schilling, Mark *Enyclopedia of Japanese Pop Culture*
From karaoke to Hello Kitty, ramen to Doraemon.
Schodt, Fredrick L *Dreamland Japan: Writings on Modern Manga*
Leading western authority on publishing phenomenon.

Index

Advertisers' Index

Please refer to the relevant sections for
addresses/telephone numbers

Maps

The 23 wards of Tokyo

Tokyo Transportation

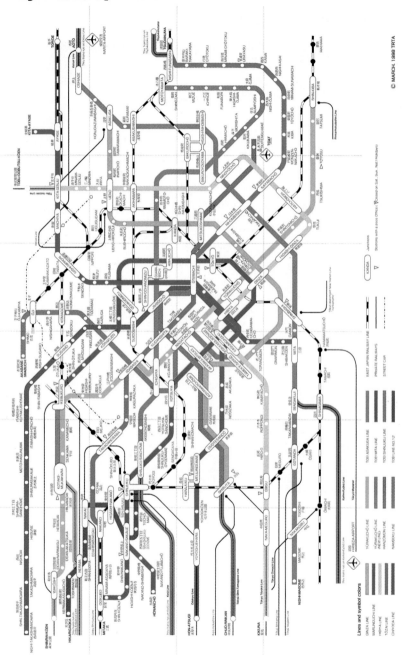

Out of the loop?

Where to catch the trains that connect with the
JR Yamanote line loop

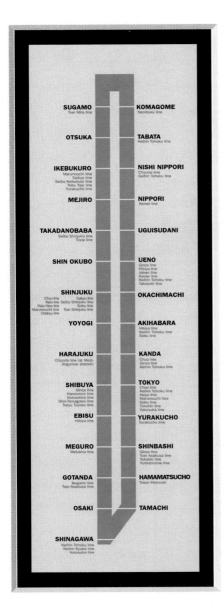

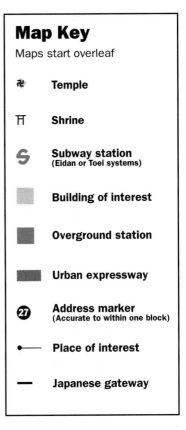

Map Key

Maps start overleaf

卍 **Temple**

丌 **Shrine**

Ｓ **Subway station**
(Eidan or Toei systems)

Building of interest

Overground station

Urban expressway

㉗ **Address marker**
(Accurate to within one block)

●— **Place of interest**

— **Japanese gateway**

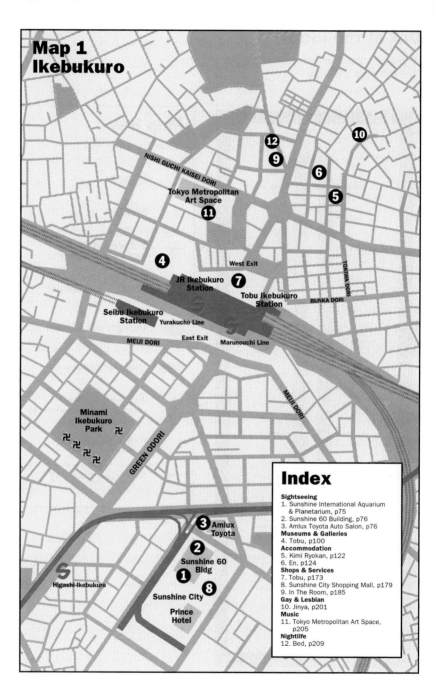

Map 1
Ikebukuro

NISHI GUCHI KAISEI DORI

Tokyo Metropolitan
Art Space

⑪

⑫

⑨

⑥

⑤

⑩

④

West Exit

JR Ikebukuro
Station

⑦

Tobu Ikebukuro
Station

BUNKA DORI

TOKIWA DORI

Seibu Ikebukuro
Station   Yurakucho Line

MEIJI DORI

East Exit

Marunouchi Line

Minami
Ikebukuro
Park   卍

卍 卍 卍 卍

GREEN ODORI

MEIJI DORI

③ Amlux
Toyota

②

Sunshine 60
Bldg

①

⑧

Sunshine City

Higashi-Ikebukuro

Prince
Hotel

Index

Sightseeing
1. Sunshine International Aquarium
   & Planetarium, p75
2. Sunshine 60 Building, p76
3. Amlux Toyota Auto Salon, p76
Museums & Galleries
4. Tobu, p100
Accommodation
5. Kimi Ryokan, p122
6. En, p124
Shops & Services
7. Tobu, p173
8. Sunshine City Shopping Mall, p179
9. In The Room, p185
Gay & Lesbian
10. Jinya, p201
Music
11. Tokyo Metropolitan Art Space,
    p205
Nightlife
12. Bed, p209

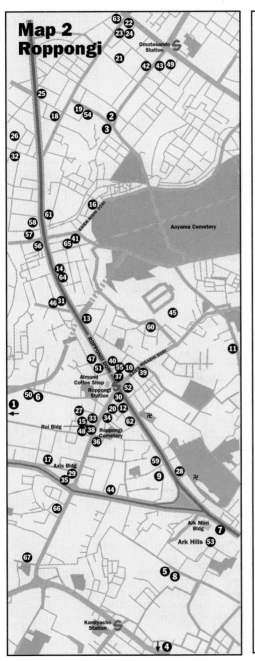

Map 2
Roppongi

Omotesando Station

GAIEN-NISHI DORI

Aoyama Cemetery

ROPPONGI DORI

Almond Coffee Shop
Roppongi Station

GAIEN-HIGASHI DORI

Roi Bldg

Roppongi Cemetery

Axis Bldg

Ark Mori Bldg
Ark Hills

Kamiyacho Station

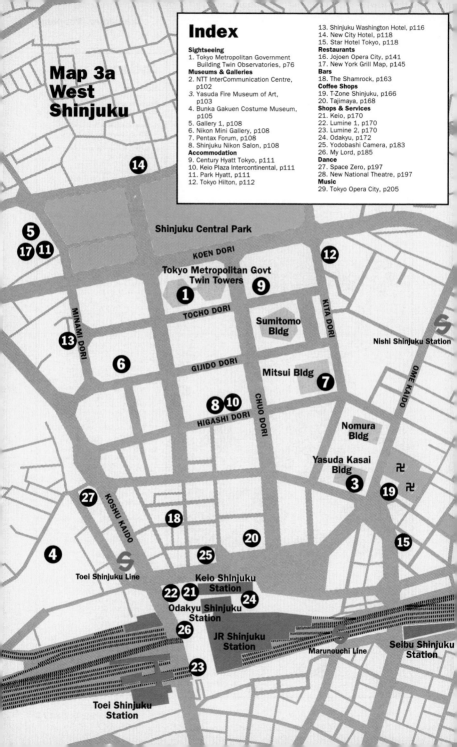

Map 3a West Shinjuku

Index

Sightseeing
1. Tokyo Metropolitan Government Building Twin Observatories, p76

Museums & Galleries
2. NTT InterCommunication Centre, p102
3. Yasuda Fire Museum of Art, p103
4. Bunka Gakuen Costume Museum, p105
5. Gallery 1, p108
6. Nikon Mini Gallery, p108
7. Pentax Forum, p108
8. Shinjuku Nikon Salon, p108

Accommodation
9. Century Hyatt Tokyo, p111
10. Keio Plaza Intercontinental, p111
11. Park Hyatt, p111
12. Tokyo Hilton, p112
13. Shinjuku Washington Hotel, p116
14. New City Hotel, p118
15. Star Hotel Tokyo, p118

Restaurants
16. Jojoen Opera City, p141
17. New York Grill Map, p145

Bars
18. The Shamrock, p163

Coffee Shops
19. T-Zone Shinjuku, p166
20. Tajimaya, p168

Shops & Services
21. Keio, p170
22. Lumine 1, p170
23. Lumine 2, p170
24. Odakyu, p172
25. Yodobashi Camera, p183
26. My Lord, p185

Dance
27. Space Zero, p197
28. New National Theatre, p197

Music
29. Tokyo Opera City, p205

Shinjuku Central Park

KOEN DORI

Tokyo Metropolitan Govt Twin Towers

TOCHO DORI

Sumitomo Bldg

KITA DORI

MINAMI DORI

Nishi Shinjuku Station

GIJIDO DORI

Mitsui Bldg

CHUO DORI

HIGASHI DORI

OME KAIDO

Nomura Bldg

Yasuda Kasai Bldg

KOSHU KAIDO

Toei Shinjuku Line

Keio Shinjuku Station

Odakyu Shinjuku Station

JR Shinjuku Station

Marunouchi Line

Seibu Shinjuku Station

Toei Shinjuku Station

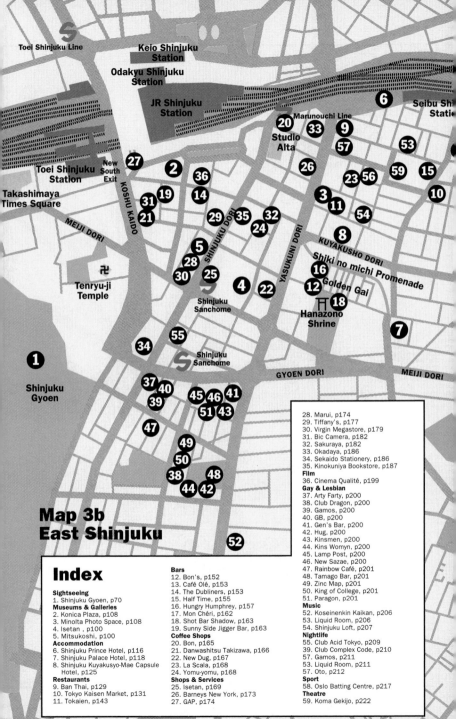

Toei Shinjuku Line

Keio Shinjuku Station

Odakyu Shinjuku Station

JR Shinjuku Station

Marunouchi Line

Seibu Shi Stati

Studio Alta

Toei Shinjuku Station

New South Exit

KOSHU KAIDO

Takashimaya Times Square

MEIJI DORI

Tenryu-ji Temple

SHINJUKU DORI

YASUKUNI DORI

KUYAKUSHO DORI

Shiki no michi Promenade

Golden Gai

Hanazono Shrine

Shinjuku Sanchome

Shinjuku Sanchome

GYOEN DORI

MEIJI DORI

Shinjuku Gyoen

Map 3b
East Shinjuku

Index

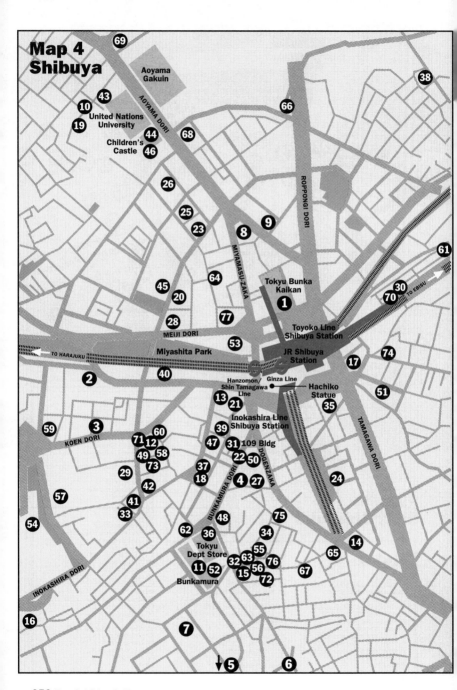

Map 4
Shibuya

Aoyama
Gakuin

69

38

43

10

19

United Nations
University

44

Children's
Castle

46

66

68

26

25

23

8

9

64

45

20

28

77

53

AOYAMA DORI

ROPPONGI DORI

MIYAMASU-ZAKA

Tokyu Bunka
Kaikan

1

61

30

70

TO EBISU

Toyoko Line
Shibuya Station

MEIJI DORI

TO HARAJUKU

Miyashita Park

2

40

13

21

Hanzomon /
Shin Tamagawa
Line

Ginza Line

JR Shibuya
Station

17

74

51

Hachiko
Statue

35

Inokashira Line
Shibuya Station

59

3

KOEN DORI

71

60

12

49

58

73

39

47

31

22

109 Bldg

50

DOGENZAKA

29

37

18

42

4

27

24

41

33

BUNKAMURA DORI

48

75

57

54

62

36

34

14

65

Tokyu
Dept Store

32

63

55

76

11

52

15

56

72

67

Bunkamura

INOKASHIRA DORI

TAMAGAWA DORI

16

7

5

6

Index

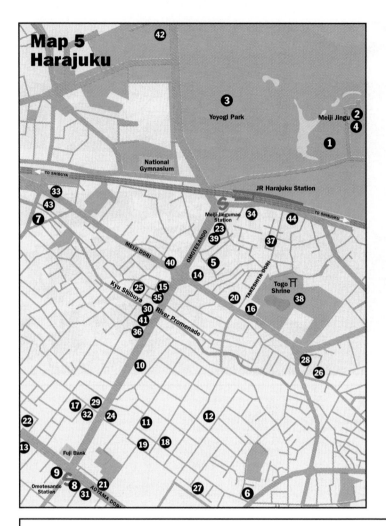

Map 5
Harajuku

Yoyogi Park

Meiji Jingu

National
Gymnasium

TO SHIBUYA

JR Harajuku Station

Meiji-Jingumae
Station

TO SHINJUKU

MEIJI DORI

OMOTESANDO

TAKESHITA DORI

Togo 卍
Shrine

Kyu Shibuya

River Promenade

Fuji Bank

Omotesando
Station

AOYAMA DORI

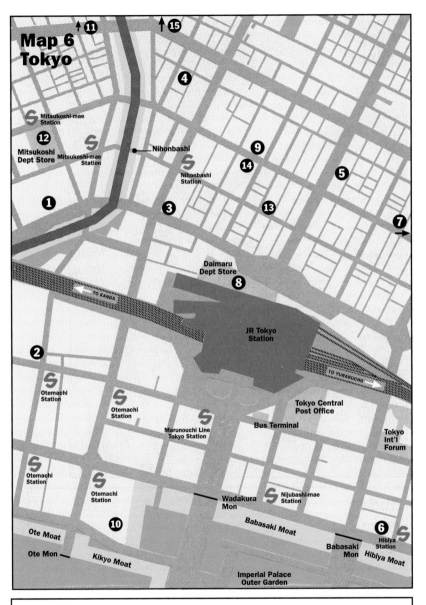

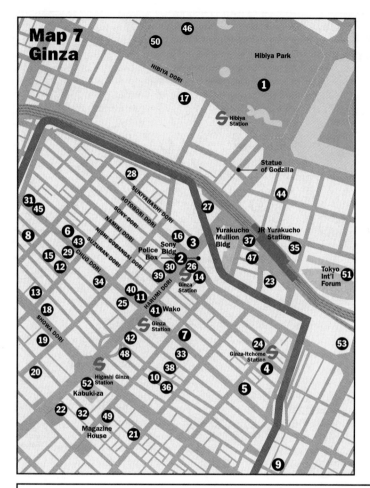

**Map 7
Ginza**

Hibiya Park

HIBIYA DORI

Hibiya Station

Statue of Godzilla

SUKIYABASHI DORI
SOTOBORI DORI
SONY DORI
NAMIKI DORI
NISHI GOBANGAI DORI
SUZURAN DORI
CHUO DORI

Yurakucho Mullion Bldg
JR Yurakucho Station

Police Box
Sony Bldg
Ginza Station

Tokyo Int'l Forum

Wako
Ginza Station

Ginza-Itchome Station

SHOWA DORI
HARUMI DORI

Higashi Ginza Station
Kabuki-za

Magazine House

Index

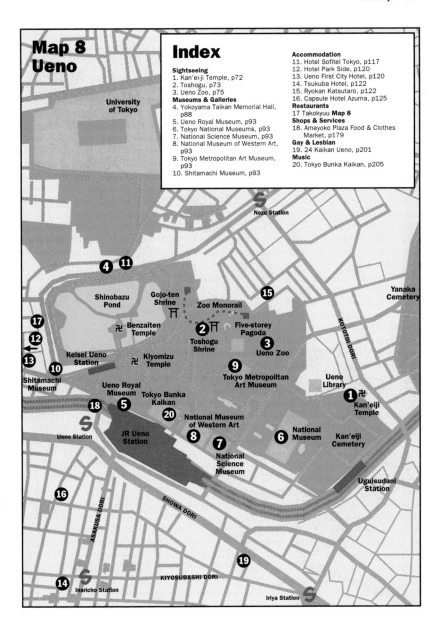

Map 8
Ueno

University of Tokyo

Index

Sightseeing
1. Kan'ei-ji Temple, p72
2. Toshogu, p73
3. Ueno Zoo, p75

Museums & Galleries
4. Yokoyama Taikan Memorial Hall, p88
5. Ueno Royal Museum, p93
6. Tokyo National Museums, p93
7. National Science Museum, p93
8. National Museum of Western Art, p93
9. Tokyo Metropolitan Art Museum, p93
10. Shitamachi Museum, p93

Accommodation
11. Hotel Sofitel Tokyo, p117
12. Hotel Park Side, p120
13. Ueno First City Hotel, p120
14. Tsukuba Hotel, p122
15. Ryokan Katsutaro, p122
16. Capsule Hotel Azuma, p125

Restaurants
17 Takokyuu **Map 8**

Shops & Services
18. Ameyoko Plaza Food & Clothes Market, p179

Gay & Lesbian
19. 24 Kaikan Ueno, p201

Music
20. Tokyo Bunka Kaikan, p205

Nezu Station

Yanaka Cemetery

Shinobazu Pond

Gojo-ten Shrine

Zoo Monorail

Benzaiten Temple

Five-storey Pagoda

Toshogu Shrine

Ueno Zoo

Keisei Ueno Station

Kiyomizu Temple

Ueno Library

Shitamachi Museum

Ueno Royal Museum

Tokyo Metropolitan Art Museum

Kan'eiji Temple

Tokyo Bunka Kaikan

National Museum of Western Art

National Museum

Kan'eiji Cemetery

Ueno Station

JR Ueno Station

National Science Museum

Uguisudani Station

ASAKUSA DORI

SHOWA DORI

KOTOTOI DORI

KIYOSUBASHI DORI

Inaricho Station

Iriya Station

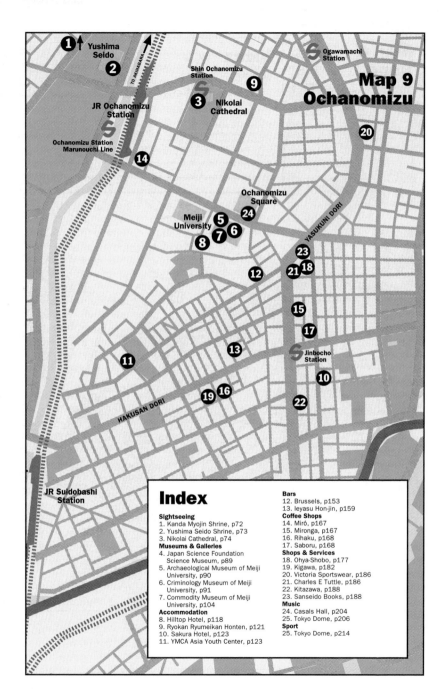

Map 9
Ochanomizu

Yushima
Seido

Ogawamachi
Station

Shin Ochanomizu
Station

JR Ochanomizu
Station

Nikolai
Cathedral

Ochanomizu Station
Marunouchi Line

TO AKIHABARA

YASUKUNI DORI

Ochanomizu
Square

Meiji
University

Jinbocho
Station

HAKUSAN DORI

JR Suidobashi
Station

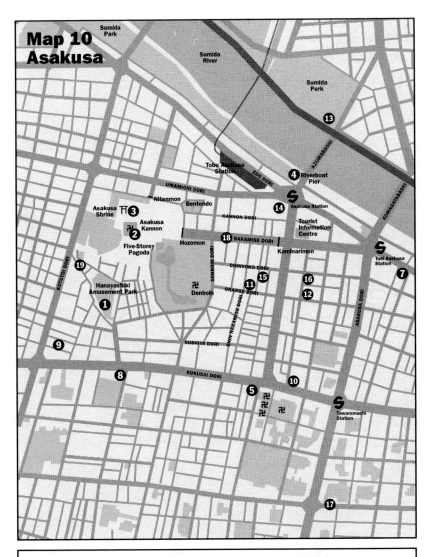

Map 10
Asakusa

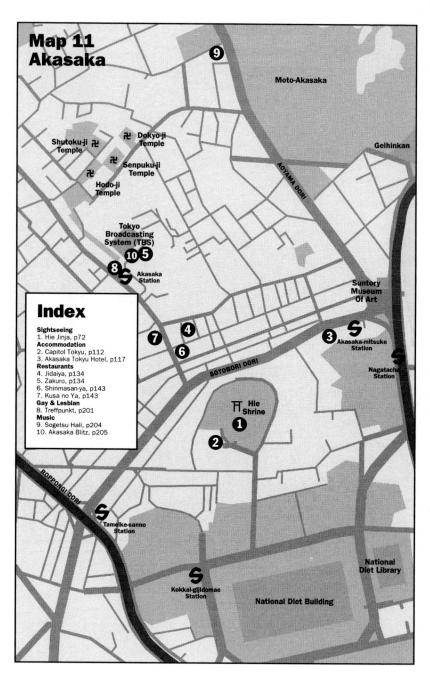

Map 11
Akasaka

Moto-Akasaka

Geihinkan

AOYAMA DORI

Shutoku-ji 卍 卍 Dokyo-ji
Temple   Temple

卍 Senpuku-ji
     Temple

卍 Hodo-ji
     Temple

Tokyo
Broadcasting
System (TBS)

10 **5**

8 S
     Akasaka
     Station

Suntory
Museum
Of Art

Index

Sightseeing
1. Hie Jinja, p72
Accommodation
2. Capitol Tokyu, p112
3. Akasaka Tokyu Hotel, p117
Restaurants
4. Jidaiya, p134
5. Zakuro, p134
6. Shinmasan-ya, p143
7. Kusa no Ya, p143
Gay & Lesbian
8. Treffpunkt, p201
Music
9. Sogetsu Hall, p204
10. Akasaka Blitz, p205

7 **4**
     6

3 S
     Akasaka-mitsuke
     Station

SOTOBORI DORI

S
Nagatacho
Station

卅 Hie
   Shrine

1

2

ROPPONGI DORI

S
Tamelke-sanno
Station

National
Diet Library

S
Kokkai-gijidomae
Station

National Diet Building

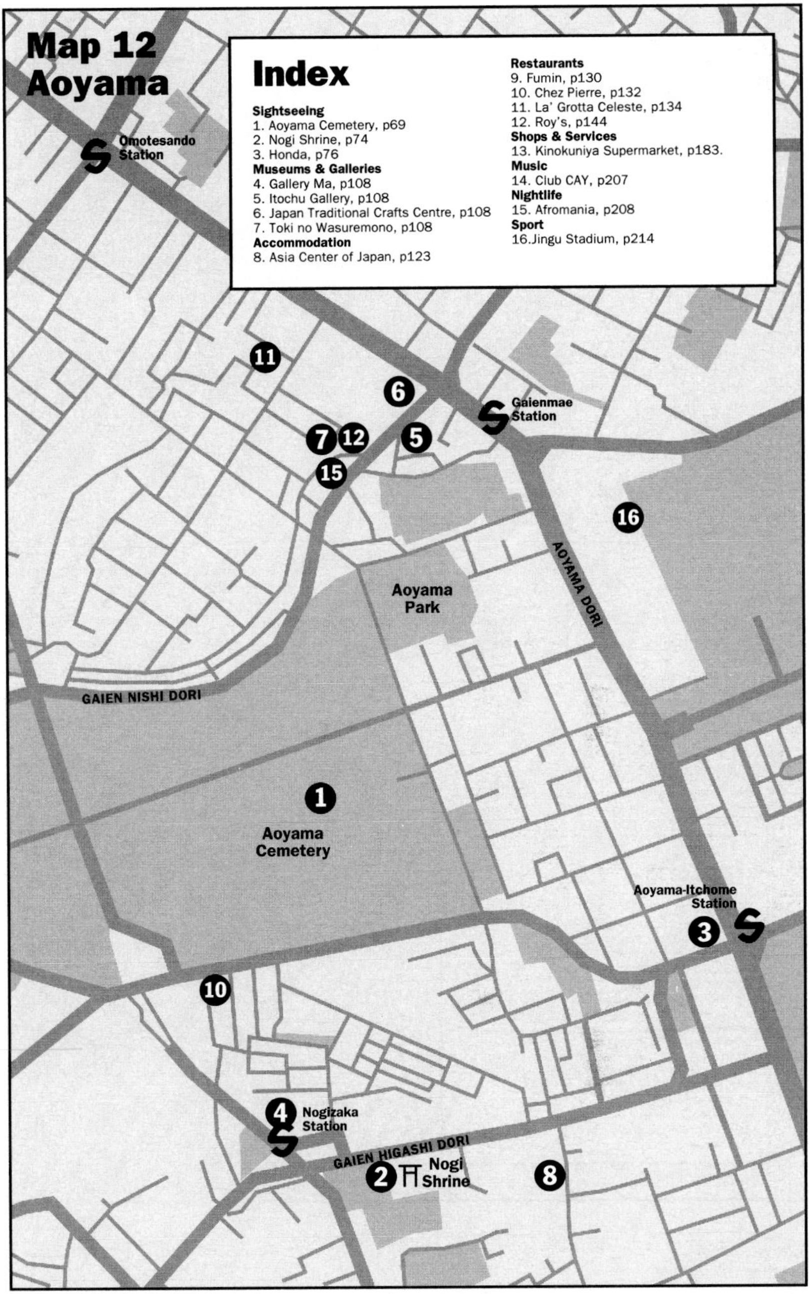

Map 12
Aoyama

Index

Sightseeing
1. Aoyama Cemetery, p69
2. Nogi Shrine, p74
3. Honda, p76
Museums & Galleries
4. Gallery Ma, p108
5. Itochu Gallery, p108
6. Japan Traditional Crafts Centre, p108
7. Toki no Wasuremono, p108
Accommodation
8. Asia Center of Japan, p123

Restaurants
9. Fumin, p130
10. Chez Pierre, p132
11. La' Grotta Celeste, p134
12. Roy's, p144
Shops & Services
13. Kinokuniya Supermarket, p183.
Music
14. Club CAY, p207
Nightlife
15. Afromania, p208
Sport
16.Jingu Stadium, p214

Omotesando
Station

11

6

Gaienmae
Station

7 12   5

15

16

Aoyama
Park

AOYAMA DORI

GAIEN NISHI DORI

1

Aoyama
Cemetery

Aoyama-Itchome
Station

3

10

4 Nogizaka
Station

GAIEN HIGASHI DORI

2 ⛩ Nogi
Shrine

8

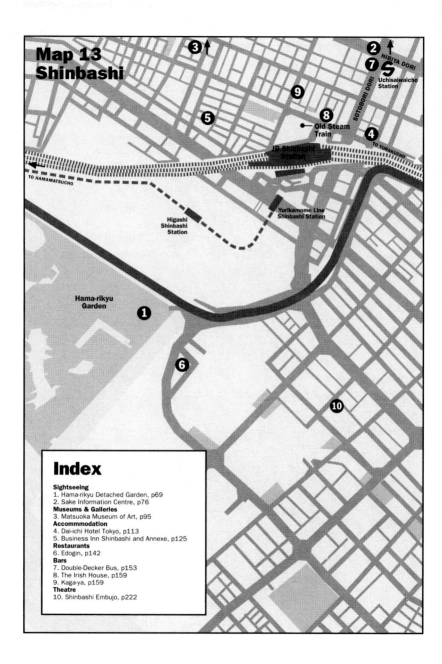

Map 13
Shinbashi

TO HAMAMATSUCHO

Higashi
Shinbashi
Station

Hama-rikyu
Garden

Old Steam
Train

JR Shinbashi
Station

Yurikamome Line
Shinbashi Station

HIBIYA DORI

SOTOBORI DORI

Uchisaiwaicho
Station

TO YURAKUCHO

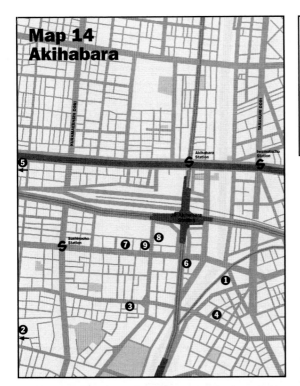

Map 14
Akihabara

Index

Museums & Galleries
1. Transportation Museum, p90
Accommodation
2. Hotel Edoya, p122
Restaurants
3. Kandagawa Honten, p139
4. Yabu Soba, p139
5. Honke Ponta, p141
Shops & Services
6. Laox, p182
7. Minami Musen Denki, p182
8. Takarada, p183
9. Yamagiwa, p183

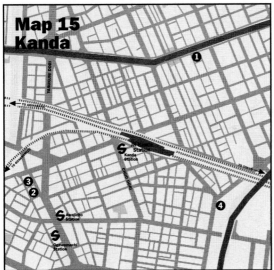

Map 15
Kanda

Index

Accommodation
1. Hotel Kazusaya, p119
Restaurants
2. Botan, p139
3. Isegen, p139
Sport
4. Chiyoda Kuritsu Sogo
   Taiikukan Pool, p217

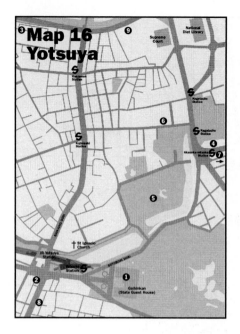

Map 16
Yotsuya

Index

Sightseeing
1. Akasaka Detached Palace, p74
Museums & Galleries
2. Fire Museum, p91
3. JCII Camera Museum, p104
4. Akasaka Prince Hotel, p112
5. Hotel New Otani, p112
Restaurants
6. Shikawa Hanten, p131
7. Densan, p134
Bars
8. The Rising Sun, p163
Dance
9. National Theatre, p197
Theatre
9. National Theatre Large Hall, p222
9. National Theatre Small Hall, p222

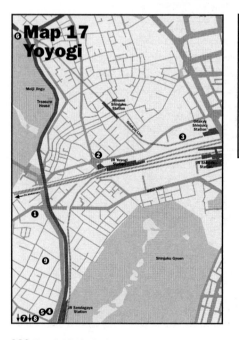

Map 17
Yoyogi

Index

Sightseeing
1. Fujita Vente, p76
Restaurants
2. Angkor Wat, p129
3. China Grill – Xenlon, p131
Sport
4. Tokyo Gymnasium, p217
5. Tokyo Metropolitan Gymnasium Pool, p217
6. Tokyo Horse Riding Club, p218
7. Meiji Jingu Gaien Batting Cage, p217
8. National Stadium, p215
Theatre
9. National Noh Theatre, p222

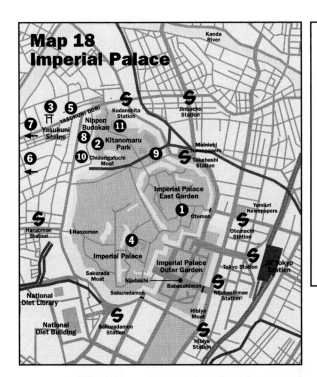

Map 18
Imperial Palace

Kanda River

VASUKUNI DORI

③ ⑤

⑦ 〒
Yasukuni
Shrine

Nippon
Budokan

Kudanshita
Station

⑪

⑧ ② Kitanomaru
Park

⑥

⑩ Chidorigafuchi
Moat

Jinbocho
Station

Mainichi
Newspapers

⑨

Takebashi
Station

Imperial Palace
East Garden

①

Otemon

Yomiuri
Newspapers

Otemachi
Station

Hanzomon
Station

Hanzomon

④

JR Tokyo
Station

Imperial Palace

Sakurada
Moat

Nijubashi

Imperial Palace
Outer Garden

Tokyo Station

Babasakimon

National
Diet Library

Sakuradamon

Nijubashimae
Station

National
Diet Building

Sakuradamon
Station

Hibiya
Moat

Hibiya
Station

Index

Sightseeing
1. Imperial Palace East Garden, p69
2. Kitanomaru Koen, p69
3. Yasukuni Shrine (Yasukuni Jinja), p73
4. Imperial Palace, p74

Museums & Galleries
5. Japanese War-Dead Memorial Museum, p91
6. Takagi Bonsai Museum, p95
7. Banknote & Postage Stamp Museum, p90
8. Map Museum, p94
9. National Museum of Modern Art, p102
10. Yamatane Museum of Art, p103
8. Crafts Gallery, National Museum of Modern Art, p104

Music
11. Budokan, p205

Sport
11. Budokan, p215

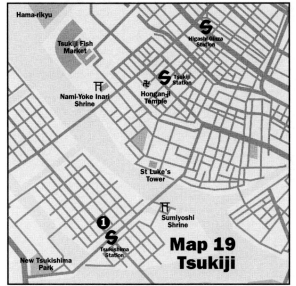

Hama-rikyu

Tsukiji Fish
Market

Higashi-Ginza
Station

Nami-Yoke Inari
Shrine

〒

卍 Tsukiji
Station

Hongan-ji
Temple

St Luke's
Tower

Sumiyoshi
Shrine

〒

①

Map 19
Tsukiji

Tsukishima
Station

New Tsukishima
Park

Index

Restaurants
1. Monja Maruyama, p142

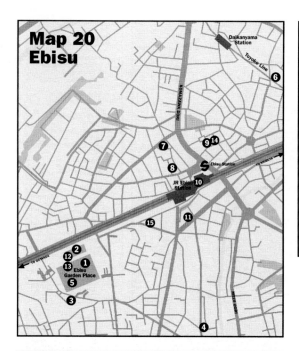

Map 20
Ebisu

Daikanyama Station

Toyoko Line

KOMAZAWA DORI

Ebisu Station

JR Ebisu Station

TO SHIBUYA

TO GOTANDA

Ebisu Garden Place

TO GOTANDA

MEJI DORI

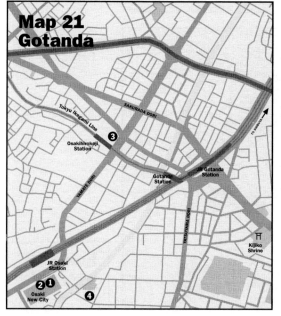

Map 21
Gotanda

Tokyu Ikegami Line

SAKURADA DORI

Osakihirokoji Station

YAMATE DORI

TO SHIBUYA

Gotanda Station

JR Gotanda Station

Kijiko Shrine

JR Osaki Station

Osaki New City

TATSUYAMA DORI

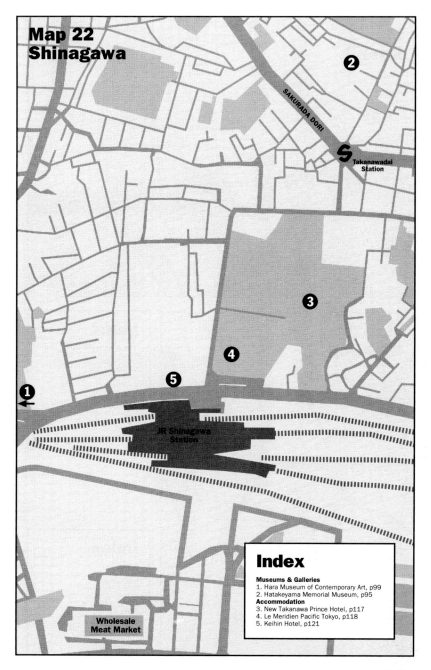

**Map 22
Shinagawa**

SAKURADA DORI

Takanawadai
Station

❷

❸

❹

❺

JR Shinagawa
Station

❶

Wholesale
Meat Market

Index

Museums & Galleries
1. Hara Museum of Contemporary Art, p99
2. Hatakeyama Memorial Museum, p95
Accommodation
3. New Takanawa Prince Hotel, p117
4. Le Meridien Pacific Tokyo, p118
5. Keihin Hotel, p121

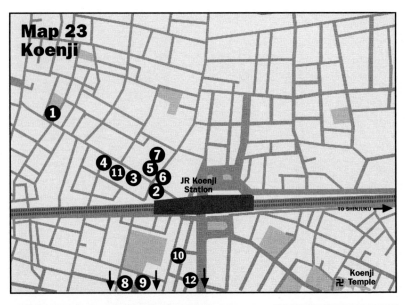

Map 23
Koenji

①

④ **⑦**
⑪ **⑤**
③ **⑥**
②

JR Koenji
Station

TO SHINJUKU →

⑩

⑧ **⑨** **⑫**

Koenji
卍 Temple

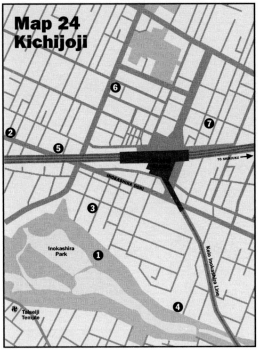

Map 24
Kichijoji

⑥

⑦

②

⑤

TO SHINJUKU →

INOKASHIRA DORI

③

Inokashira
Park

①

Keio Inokashira Line

④

卍 Taiseiji
Temple

Index

Index

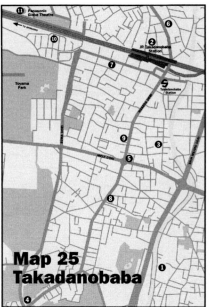

Index

Accommodation
1. Four Seasons at Chinzan-so, p114
2. Japan Minshuku Association, p124
Restaurants
3. La Dinette, p132
4. Rera Chise, p142
Bars
5. The Fiddler, p154
6. Footnik, p154
Coffee Shops
7. Ben's Café, p165
Film
8. ACT, p198
9. Waseda Shochiku, p199
Sport
10. Shinjuku-ku Sports Centre, p217
Theatre
11. Panasonic Globe-za, p222

Map 25
Takadanobaba

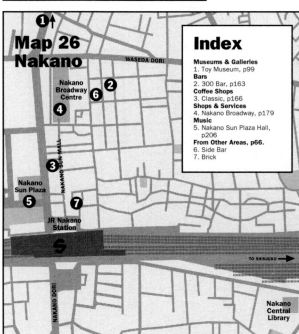

Map 26
Nakano

Index

Museums & Galleries
1. Toy Museum, p99
Bars
2. 300 Bar, p163
Coffee Shops
3. Classic, p166
Shops & Services
4. Nakano Broadway, p179
Music
5. Nakano Sun Plaza Hall, p206
From Other Areas, p66.
6. Side Bar
7. Brick

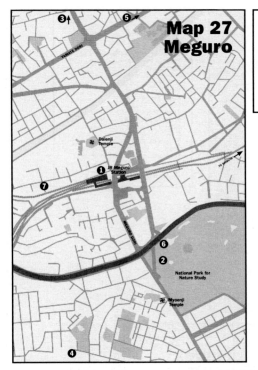

Map 27
Meguro

Index

Index

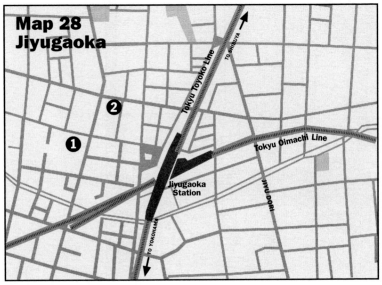

Map 28
Jiyugaoka

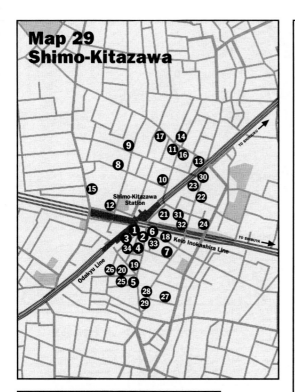

Map 29
Shimo-Kitazawa

TO SHIBUYA

Shimo-Kitazawa Station

Keio Inokashira Line

TO SHIBUYA

Odakyu Line

Map 30
Sangenjaya

Nishi-Taishido Station

Tokyu Setagaya Line
Sangenjaya Station

Shin-Tamagawa Line
Sangenjaya Station

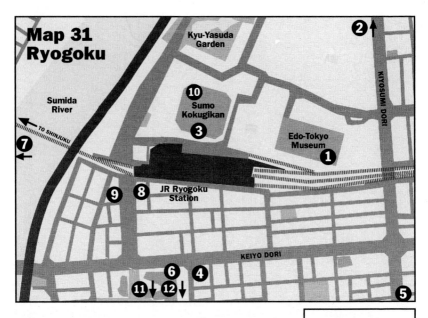

Map 31
Ryogoku

Kyu-Yasuda Garden

Sumida River

TO SHINJUKU

Sumo Kokugikan

Edo-Tokyo Museum

KIYOSUMI DORI

JR Ryogoku Station

KEIYO DORI

❷ **❼** **❿** **❸** **❶** **❾** **❽** **❻** **❹** **⓫** **⓬** **❺**

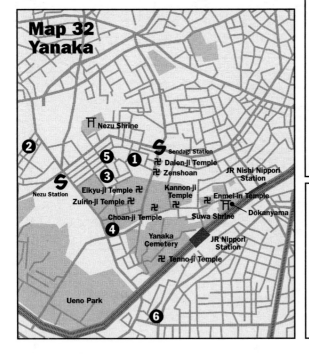

Map 32
Yanaka

Nezu Shrine

Sendagi Station

Dalen-ji Temple

Zenshoan

JR Nishi Nippori Station

Nezu Station

Elkyu-ji Temple

Zuirin-ji Temple

Kannon-ji Temple

Enmei-in Temple

Choan-ji Temple

Suwa Shrine

Dokanyama

Yanaka Cemetery

JR Nippori Station

Tenno-ji Temple

Ueno Park

❷ **❺** **❶** **❸** **❹** **❻**

▲ Index

Museums & Galleries
1. Edo-Tokyo Museum, p91
2. Tokyo Metropolitan Memorial & Tokyo Reconstruction Memorial Museum, p94
3. Sumo Museum, p97
4. Sumo Photograph Museum, p97
5. Tabi Museum, p97
6. Fireworks Museum, p97
7. Japan Stationery Museum, p98
Accommodation
8. Hotel Bellegrande, p121
9. River Hotel, p121
Sport
10. Kokugikan, p216
11. Izutsu Beya, p216
12. Oshima Beya, p216

◄ Index

Museums & Galleries
1. Asakura Sculpture Museum, p87
2. Yayoi & Takehisa Yumeji Museum & Tachihara Michizo Memorial Museum, p88
3. Daimyo Clock Museum, p91
4. Scai – The Bath-house, p108
Accommodation
5. Ryokan Sawanoya, p122
Restaurants
6. Sasanoyuki, p142

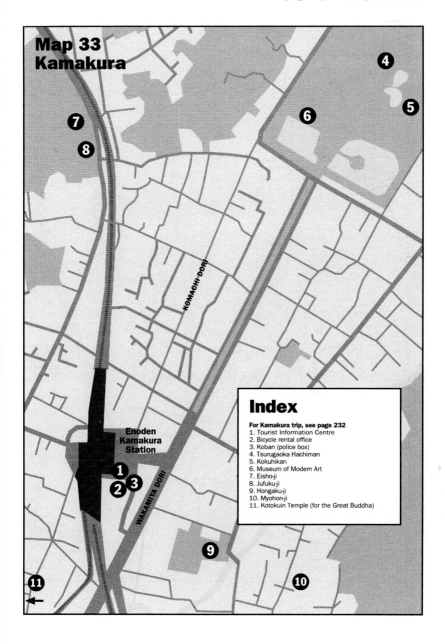

**Map 33
Kamakura**

KOMACHI DORI

Enoden
Kamakura
Station

WAKAMIYA DORI

Index

For Kamakura trip, see page 232
1. Tourist Information Centre
2. Bicycle rental office
3. Koban (police box)
4. Tsurugaoka Hachiman
5. Kokuhikan
6. Museum of Modern Art
7. Eisho-ji
8. Jufuku-ji
9. Hongaku-ji
10. Myohon-ji
11. Kotokuin Temple (for the Great Buddha)

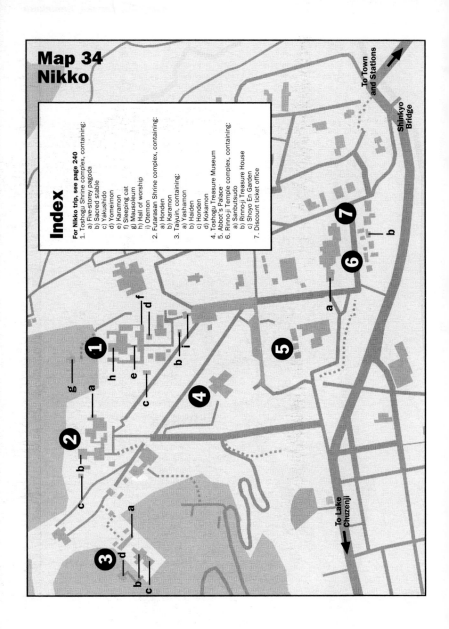

Map 34
Nikko

To Town
and Stations

Shinkyo
Bridge

To Lake
Chuzenji